Facing Up to the American Dream

———————————————

PRINCETON STUDIES IN AMERICAN POLITICS:
HISTORICAL, INTERNATIONAL, AND
COMPARATIVE PERSPECTIVES

SERIES EDITORS
IRA KATZNELSON, MARTIN SHEFTER, THEDA SKOCPOL

Facing Up to the American Dream

RACE, CLASS, AND THE SOUL
OF THE NATION

Jennifer L. Hochschild

PRINCETON UNIVERSITY PRESS

PRINCETON, NEW JERSEY

Copyright © 1995 by Princeton University Press
Published by Princeton University Press, 41 William Street,
Princeton, New Jersey 08540
In the United Kingdom: Princeton University Press, Chichester, West Sussex

Library of Congress Cataloging-in-Publication Data

Hochschild, Jennifer L., 1950–
Facing up to the American dream: race, class, and the soul of
the nation / Jennifer L. Hochschild.
p. cm.
Includes bibliographical references and index.
ISBN 0-691-02957-1
ISBN 0-691-02920-2 (pbk.)
1. United States—Race relations.   2. Afro-Americans—Social
conditions—1975–   3. Afro-Americans—Economic conditions.
4. Social classes—United States.   I. Title.
E185.615.H55   1995
305.8'00973—dc20   95-13061

The epigraph on p. 93 is excerpted from "The Eighties Re-examined,"
Copyright © 1992 by Calvin Trillin. Originally appeared in *The Nation*

This book has been composed in Galliard

Princeton University Press books are printed on acid-free paper and meet the
guidelines for permanence and durability of the Committee of Production
Guidelines for Book Longevity of the Council on Library Resources

Printed in the United States of America by Princeton Academic Press

Fifth printing, and first paperback printing,
with corrections and a new preface, 1996

5   7   9   10   8   6

For Eleanor, Raphael, and the others

What I want to see above all is that this country remains a country where someone can always get rich. That's the one thing we have and that must be preserved.

—President Ronald Reagan, 1983

I ran for president because I believed the American Dream was at risk for millions of our fellow citizens.

—President Bill Clinton, 1995

Yes, we is all the same under God so we has the same problems, but colored folk has special ones, too. It's the same being colored as white but it's different being colored, too. . . . It's the same, but it's different.

—elderly woman interviewed by Robert Coles, 1966

There is no surer way of misunderstanding the Negro or of being misunderstood by him than by ignoring manifest differences of condition and power.

—W. E. B. Du Bois, 1899

CONTENTS

PART FOUR: *Under the Spell of the Great
National Suggestion*

PART FIVE: *Race and the American Dream*

TABLES AND FIGURE

TABLES

FIGURE

PREFACE TO THE PAPERBACK EDITION

EVENTS SINCE this book appeared in August 1995 have confirmed my arguments and deepened my concern about the need to address the United States' vexatious racial dilemmas. Most importantly and obviously, issues revolving around race—the trial of O. J. Simpson, the Million Man March, the possible presidential candidacy of Colin Powell—dominated political discourse for a season. Whether one man murdered his former wife and her friend mattered more to Americans than did genocide in Bosnia (or Somalia or Rwanda . . .), and more than how the federal government would spend billions and trillions of dollars, all because the man was black and celebrated, and the wife white and beautiful. Race matters, as Cornel West has famously punned.

Not only does race matter, but it matters in ways that conform to the paradoxes and puzzles I describe in this book. Consider the first paradox, "what's all the fuss about?" (See chapter three.) Many whites could not understand why many African Americans were so delighted by the acquittal of O. J. Simpson. He had not, after all, been a black hero (in fact, quite the reverse—he had made his fortune and reputation within the white world), he had allegedly beaten his wife, and the scientific evidence connecting him to the murders seemed unassailable to many. Whites who were surprised radically underestimated blacks' proclivity to rally around one of their own in trouble with white society (see chapter six on this point), they did not share blacks' view that the racist Mark Fuhrman was a symptom of a systemic disease rampant within police forces, and they disagreed with blacks' presumption that the criminal justice system is fundamentally biased against African Americans (see chapter three). (African Americans, perhaps because they are perforce more attuned to the mores of the other race, were less surprised that whites found it easy to believe that a black man had committed murder, that whites saw Mark Fuhrman in individual rather than systemic terms, and that whites saw the defense lawyers' invocation of race to be inappropriately incendiary rather than fundamental to the case.) At any rate, the races split over the verdict. Fully 85 percent of blacks, compared with only 34 percent of whites, "agree[d] with the decision of the . . . jury," according to a *Washington Post* poll. Almost nine in ten whites disagreed that "the white establishment is always trying to bring down successful black people," although only four in ten blacks shared that disagreement (see chapter five). Whites could not understand what all the fuss about O. J. was in the black community, and two-thirds of them concluded simply—and poisonously—that "blacks often use race as an excuse to justify wrongdoing."[1]

The O. J. Simpson case illustrates the first paradox through a sensational incident. More sober data from the fall of 1995 reinforce the depth and breadth of the paradox. In another *Washington Post* survey, 55 percent of whites (compared with 29 percent of blacks) mistakenly agreed that "the average African American" is as well off as or better off than "the average white person" in their enjoyment of jobs and education. Over 40 percent of whites (and about 20 percent of blacks) held the same wrong view with regard to housing and income.[2] No wonder that people who hold these false perceptions are unsympathetic to the "whining" of civil rights leaders who keep asserting the fact of persistent racial discrimination and inequality (see chapter five).

Presidential politics in the fall of 1995 similarly demonstrated the depth of the disparity between white and black Americans' views. In early October 1995, over twice as many whites as blacks (54 percent to 25 percent) endorsed Colin Powell for president, whereas close to twice as many blacks as whites (68 percent to 37 percent) endorsed Bill Clinton. Citizens had not suddenly abjured racial identification in favor of its converse. Rather, it was that just what whites liked about Powell was what African Americans mistrusted. More whites thought Powell "understands special issues . . . facing blacks" than thought he understood issues facing whites, although a majority supported him even on the latter point. But more blacks thought Powell understood issues facing *whites* than thought he understood blacks' concerns. And he did not receive majority support among blacks for either question.[3] Thus, whites saw him as a black leader who understood them almost as well as he understood his apparently natural constituency; blacks saw him as an African American who was on the verge of leaving his own community for the other.

The Million Man March illustrates, and reinforced, the pattern created by combining the second and third paradoxes, "succeeding more and enjoying it less" and "remaining under the spell of the great national suggestion." (Together, these paradoxes combine into the fact that poor blacks now have more faith in American society and in whites than do well-off blacks, which is a reversal from the 1960s; see chapter four.) No matter how one evaluates the importance of Minister Farrakhan as a motivating factor, one must agree that the March demonstrated and helped to deepen black nationalism (see chapter six). This nationalism is compounded of abandonment of hope in the good will of whites, fear about the deterioration of black neighborhoods, and conviction that African Americans themselves have the resources—material and otherwise—to confront their own problems. Thus the astounding finding in a *Wall Street Journal* survey soon after the March that more whites than blacks (63 percent to 56 percent) think racial integration has been good for society. It is hard to know who would be more surprised by that result—Reverend Martin Luther King Jr. or Sheriff Bull Connor. And the participants in the Million Man March were disproportionately from the middle class. That can be explained partly by the simple fact that it takes money to get to Washington, D.C., as well as a job in which one has some discretion over the use of one's time. But the March illustrated clearly that many African Americans are close to giving up on white society in favor of turning inward to others like themselves—and "others like themselves" are relatively well educated, affluent, and politically efficacious.[4]

People pondering the findings in this book during the past few months have asked about its implications for partisan politics and public policy-making. I do not think my argument has many implications for partisan politics. After all, Colin Powell—the epitome of the American dream—could not decide if he was a Democrat or a Republican for quite a while, and he eventually chose the party that one would not have predicted had one focused only on the racial composition of the parties. More generally, candidates of both parties evoke the trope of the American dream about equally, as one would expect if my arguments in chapter one are correct. Both parties would like to have the allegiance of black voters, neither party knows how to foster that allegiance without alienating its majority of white voters, and both parties fall back on exhortations about opportunity for all, self-reliance, and the need for the United States to remain Abraham Lincoln's "last, best hope of earth." I am not saying that the Democratic and Republican parties are identical; there are great differences, which disproportionately affect African Americans. But the differences lie at the level of policy proposals to enable people to achieve the American dream, not in commitment to the dream or interpretation of what it means.

My argument does, however, have deep implications for public policy-making, and clarifying those implications was my main purpose in writing this preface. The polity is responsible for carrying out the tasks implied by the first two tenets of the American dream (see chapter one). That is, only governmental policies can ensure that "everyone, regardless of ascriptive traits, family background, or personal history" can pursue their dreams. Similarly, only governmental policies can ensure that all Americans have "the reasonable anticipation . . . of success." The first tenet requires policies that ensure strict and complete nondiscrimination against people of color, women, religious minorities, the poor, and other groups and individuals whose characteristics are disfavored in society. The second tenet requires policies that ensure more than a formal chance to get ahead. That means a good education through high school, enough shelter and sustenance that one can focus on how to define success rather than how to eat or stay warm, and neighborhoods that are safe and decent enough that one can focus on how to pursue success rather than how to make it home alive. It might imply the availability of jobs for all who seek them, and it might imply a political process and structure that allow all citizens to share in making decisions that affect their communities.

These are large responsibilities, and just how to achieve them is the subject of many (other) books. But they are balanced by responsibilities held by citizens, which are encapsulated by the third and fourth tenets of the American dream. That is, if the government fulfills its mandate in accord with the dream, then individuals must pursue success "through actions and traits under their own control" and "in association with virtue." There can no longer be publicly legitimate excuses for illiteracy if schools are good, for unemployment if jobs are available, for abandoning one's children if social networks are in place, for claiming victimhood or an irresistable temptation to do evil.

These too are large responsibilities, and just how to achieve them is the subject of even more (other) books. But my basic point should be clear. The genius of the ideology of the American dream is the balance it creates—between, on the one hand, what the polity must do because individuals cannot and, on the other hand, what individuals must do because the polity cannot. The polity must provide the means to success for all; individuals must pursue that success as best they can. This combination cuts across disputes between "bleeding-heart liberals" who stereotypically place all of the responsibility on the polity and "hard-hearted conservatives" who stereotypically place all of the responsibility on individuals. Neither side is right, both sides have a piece of the truth, and the tenets of the American dream provide the recipe for an equilibrium between too much and too little responsibility.

Even if we could figure out the right policies to achieve this balance— which we will never do—the United States would not become John Winthrop's city upon a hill. The American dream has inherent flaws (see chapters one and fourteen) which make me at best ambivalent about it. But for better or for worse, it is *our* ideology, and we are stuck with it. We had better make the best of our situation, and strive to use the strictures of the American dream to enable more Americans to achieve the fantasies lurking within it.

NOTES

1. One-third of blacks concurred with this sentiment (Richard Morin, "Poll Reflects Division over Simpson Case," *Washington Post*, Oct. 8, 1995, pp. A31, A34). Similar reactions to the Simpson verdict appear in "Whites and Blacks Agree: Verdict Hurt Race Relations," *USA Today*, Oct. 9, 1995, p. 5A.

2. Richard Morin, "A Distorted Image of Minorities," *Washington Post*, October 8, 1995, pp. A1, A26, A27. The survey included a black oversample.

3. "More Blacks Back Clinton than Powell," *USA Today*, Oct. 10, 1995. For similar results, see Newsweek Communications, "After the March: A *Newsweek* Poll," Oct. 18–20, 1995; and Yankelovich Partners, "Black Leadership," Oct. 18–19, 1995. All three surveys included a black oversample.

4. Thus in the same survey, more whites than blacks agreed that emphasizing "integration and opportunity" is the best means for "improving the situation for blacks in America." More blacks than whites opted for the strategy of "building strong institutions within the black community." Malcolm X would have been delighted, Reverend King would have been perplexed, and Governors George Wallace and Orville Faubus would have been dumbfounded by these results (Hart/Teeter, *Wall Street Journal*/NBC News Poll, Oct. 27–31, 1995). For an analysis of the March, see Lorenzo Morris, "The Million Man March and Presidential Politics" (unpublished paper, Howard University, 1996).

PREFACE

THIS BOOK makes two claims about the American dream. Both will be controversial. The first I believe to be true, and the second I hope is false (although I believe it also to be true). The first claim is that the American dream is and has been, for decades if not centuries, a central ideology of Americans. By the American dream, I mean not merely the right to get rich, but rather the promise that all Americans have a reasonable chance to achieve success as they define it—material or otherwise—through their own efforts, and to attain virtue and fulfillment through success. As an ideology it is a brilliant construction; as a guide for practice, its defects may match or even outweigh its virtues. Not all Americans share it. Certain categories of Americans have always shared it less than others; at certain periods of our history its preeminence has waxed or waned; its definition has varied, as have its competitors. But since the era of Andrew Jackson (and perhaps before), the American dream has been a defining characteristic of American culture, aspirations, and—ostensibly, at least—institutions, against which all competitors must contend.

The second claim is that the ideology of the American dream faces a severe challenge. The challenge is intricately entwined with race in two ways. First, too often whites and blacks see a barrier, if not an enemy, when they look at each other. Many middle-class African Americans see white placeholders denying them their earned and deserved success, or granting it only on uncomfortable, even humiliating, terms. A few poor African Americans see white bodies and purses to be exploited, if not killed, and other poor blacks are finding it harder and harder to dispute this view. Many whites see middle-class blacks making excessive demands and blaming their personal failures on a convenient but nonexistent enemy. Even more whites see poor blacks as menacing, degraded strangers.

These views are not new. What *has* changed over the last three decades is that there are now enough middle-class African Americans to make a political difference and enough poor African Americans with the technological means to wreak havoc on themselves and their near neighbors. Under those conditions, if blacks and whites continue to hold these views of each other, a society based on belief in the American dream is in jeopardy.

Race is implicated in yet another challenge to the American dream. In many arenas of life, ranging from demands that the ideals of the Declaration of Independence be incorporated into the Constitution to a rise in unmarried teenage parenthood, African Americans have taken actions that later were imitated by whites. Once again they may be bellwethers—in this case of a general disaffection with the dominant ideology. Many of the flaws that wealthy or poor blacks see in the American dream—the hollowness of materialism, the denigration of community, the hypocrisy of claims to equal opportunity, the selfishness of the lucky—are not unique to their race. Similarly, many of the structural conditions that lead to unemployment among high school dropouts and insecurity among college graduates affect whites as well as blacks. If whites come to view the dream for themselves as blacks are increasingly coming to view the dream for *them*selves, the ideology and the society based on it will be threatened.

Either a hardening of racial lines or a shared disaffection with the dream is enough to jeopardize it. Both in combination could capsize it. Whether one welcomes such a shipwreck or shrinks from it depends on how one evaluates the ideology of the American dream and what one projects as an alternative. My own reaction to the prospect of a wholesale rejection of the ideology is ambivalence tending toward distress. After all, the ideology of the dream is capable of inspiring great deeds and noble values, and it has done so on occasion throughout our history. Furthermore, I see no alternative for the United States that is both plausible and preferable. Racial and class enclaves, with an implicit triage system that writes off the poorest and most despised, are plausible but not preferable. Redistribution of wealth downward and the development of a sense of community beyond ascriptive lines are, in my view, preferable but not plausible. My particular combination of values and pessimism leads me to argue that Americans' best chance for a future that we want our children to inherit is to insist that the practice of the American dream be made to live up to its ideology. That is, Americans must face up to their dream and decide whether they really mean it to be a reality.

This book makes the case for these two claims in quite different ways. The first claim, of the centrality of the American dream, is made largely by assertion in the first chapter. I am bolstered in this assertion by three things. First, in seminars based on this book in manuscript, Americans have been full of caveats and alternatives, but non-American auditors have concurred that the United States has a coherent, widely recognized, mostly shared, ideology captured by my definition. They were only surprised that Americans could not see it clearly.

My second reassurance appears in the illustrations reproduced here. Advertisers and cartoonists are not authorized interpreters of American culture, but their expertise lies in capturing concisely what the rest of us

EXPORTING THE AMERICAN DREAM

On November 29th, Hungarians came one step closer to something they've been fighting for since 1956. Freedom.

Not just political freedom but freedom of the press. And the first American consumer magazine published in Hungarian was PLAYBOY. No surprise, since we're the magazine that led a social revolution in America by standing for personal, political and economic freedom.

That's the power of PLAYBOY. A power that reaches 15,000,000 readers worldwide. And it's continuing to grow.

15,000,000 readers are devoted to us because we're devoted to them. That's why more Americans buy PLAYBOY each month than *Esquire, GQ, Rolling Stone* and *Business Week* combined. Making us the largest-selling men's magazine—not just in the country—but in the world.

So here's to freedom. Or, as they say in Hungary, *Eljen a Szabadsag.*

THE POWER OF PLAYBOY

Reprinted by special permission of *Money*, copyright 1991, Time Inc.

"Wake up, Tom. You're having the American dream again."

Drawing by P. Steiner; © 1992 The New Yorker Magazine, Inc.

THE AMERICAN DREAM

THE PEOPLE, THE HOPE, THE GLORY

1 4 9 2 &ea; 1 9 9 2

INTRODUCTION

by

Gerald R. Ford,

President, United States of America

1974 - 1977

As President, I had a rare opportunity to discover the American Dream in a way that might never have been open to me otherwise. People wrote and openly voiced their feelings about their hardships, joys and hopes. It was a privilege to be allowed to look into the hearts of individuals from all walks of life. Along the way, this experience moved me to ask myself, "What makes an American?"

That is why I've accepted this invitation to introduce *The American Dream Collection.* Authorized by the U.S. Postal Service and revealingly subtitled *The People, the Hope, the Glory,* it answers my question in a most unusual way. *The American Dream* consists of images from twenty-five postage stamps engraved on solid sterling silver ingots. These images have been chosen because they typify what we as a nation are about. The Collection will be issued to coincide with the 500th Anniversary of Columbus's landing.

Since 1847, American stamps have been commemorating *us* — the giants of our history as well as ordinary folks — and what makes this country unique. Minting in precious metals makes these images more permanent, so that you, your children and their children can know the pleasures of owning them.

I invite you to celebrate with me both Columbus's dream of a new world and your and my American Dream as well. The connection, I believe, is most appropriate. In a real sense, Columbus was one of the first dreamers of a new world. He had vision, determination, and a willingness to make mistakes — qualities that have always been part of the American character. &ea;

Gerald R. Ford

United States Postal Brochure.

strive to articulate. Thus it is telling that the fiercely competitive markets of *New Yorker* cartoons and *New York Times* ads constantly evoke the American dream. I, at any rate, am more puzzled by why so few political scientists have examined the ideology of the American dream than by whether the phrase really does capture a central element of American political and social life.

Third, some historians and students of American studies are returning to the once-discredited claim that Americans really do participate, willingly or not, in a shared worldview. Some describe that worldview as liberalism, which is closely allied with but not identical to my "American dream"; others describe it as a "democratic wish" or a jumbled accretion of commitments. But despite powerful claims that Americans have developed several distinct political cultures, I am in good company in asserting that they all must deal with, even if they do not all accede to, a dominant ideology in which the American dream is a central component.

My other claim, that the American dream is threatened by Americans' racial antagonisms and blacks' increasing disillusionment, grows almost implicitly through most of the rest of the book. My chief explicit focus is how and why middle-class and poor African Americans have changed their beliefs in the American dream over the past three decades. To see what is distinctive about those beliefs, I compare them with the beliefs of middle-class and poor whites, and with the beliefs of ethnic white immigrants a century ago. In the course of these comparisons—over time, across class and race, between racially specific views and views about the American dream more generally—I demonstrate that race is entwined with the future of the American dream and of the society it represents. I offer this argument in the hope that by the end we will all be persuaded to do what is needed to nudge our nation closer to its own best instincts.

ACKNOWLEDGMENTS

IN WRITING this book I, like all authors, had several invisible but vocal kibitzers peering over my shoulder. Four people in particular perched behind me: W. E. B. Du Bois, Louis Hartz, William J. Wilson, and Christopher Jencks. Du Bois was simply one of the most versatile and talented social scientists America has ever produced. A scholar who can publish poetry, a wrenching depiction of his child's death, and careful empirical analysis in the same book deserves our emulation. And of course his examinations of "the problem of the color-line" and the "two warring ideals in one dark body" established the framework for anyone studying race in the United States in the twentieth century. Louis Hartz established the other framework within which I operate—the analysis of the values and visions that distinguish residents of the United States and pull them together into a single nationality. Hartz's arguments are controversial and subject to severe distortion if not actually wrong, but anyone studying American political identity must grapple with his insistence on the fundamentally liberal core of American society.

These two figures may know of their role in this book, but I cannot thank them directly. The other two I can. Bill Wilson taught me how to think about the relationship between race and class, gave me confidence that I could write a book on the subject, and provides me and many others with a model of how to express the courage of one's convictions with dignity, evidence, and toughness. Sandy Jencks showed me the importance of getting the data right and of following where they lead without fear or favor. His example of iconoclasm about the right answer, combined with passion for finding the right answer, drove me much harder than I sometimes wanted to be driven.

Others gave invaluable help in more concrete ways. Dana Ansel, Deborah Baumgold, Lawrence Bobo, Lawrence Jacobs, David Kirp, Richard Merelman, Kristen Monroe (twice!), Douglas Rae, Lillian Rubin, Theda Skocpol, Earl Smith, Raphael Sonenshein, Clarence Stone, Hanes Walton, Sean Wilentz, and an anonymous reader for Cambridge University Press commented on the whole manuscript with just the right mix of criticism and encouragement. Derrick Bell, Michael Burns, Michael Dawson, Paul DiMaggio, Stephen Elkin, Roxanne Euben, Gary Gerstle, Albert Hirschman, Byron Jackson, Glenn Loury, Christopher Mackie-Lewis, Jacqueline Mitchell, Rupert Barnes Nacoste, Russell Nieli, David Perlmutter, Noah Pickus, James Scott, Edward Tufte, Susan Welch, and Roger Wilkins provided insights that pushed wayward arguments onto the straight and narrow path of narrative coherence and (I hope) more intellectual depth. The skepticism of Carlton Long and Mary Summers was more helpful than it was painful. Seminar participants at the Center for Advanced Study in the Behavioral Sciences, the Institute for Advanced Study, the Commissariat Général du Plan of the French government, Columbia University, Rutgers University, Princeton University, Stanford University, SUNY at Binghamton, Texas Christian University, the University of California at Berkeley, the University of Chicago, the University of Michigan, the University of North Carolina at Greensboro, the University of Pittsburgh, and Yale University all showed me how to communicate my ideas better and even how to make them better. Herbert Abelson, Lisa Cziffra, William Drew, Louis Harris, John Hutcheson, James Jackson, Michael Kagay, Marc Maynard, and David Sheaves gave invaluable aid in finding and analyzing survey data. I hope at least a few cellars are cleaner as a result of searches for old punch cards.

I could not have completed the book without the help of several research assistants. Chief among equals were Deborah (Cricket) Cohen and Dana Ansel, whose respective expertises in analyzing ancient data and ferreting out unpublished reports are matched only by their cheerfulness, energy, and acute insights. I also relied on Lynda Bazarian, Daniel David, Marissa Donalds, Elana Hahn, Kathryn Larin, Michelle Mulder, Jonathan Newman, Kristina Palmer, and Noah Pickus. The Spencer Foundation, the Center for Advanced Study in the Behavioral Sciences, the Institute for Advanced Study, the Woodrow Wilson School of Public and International Affairs of Princeton University, and the Princeton University Committee on Research in the Humanities and Social Sciences gave the different but equally valuable help of funding and wonderful places to work. Walter Lippincott, Malcolm DeBevoise, Sterling Bland, and Anita O'Brien have my gratitude for nudging and pulling a bulky manuscript (and sometimes balky author) into an elegant product.

My husband, Tony Broh, and our children, Eleanor and Raphael Broh, contributed to this venture in different ways. The latter two made sure that I took so long to write this book that I could be certain that I really meant what I was saying; the former did his best to offset the latter. He did a lot of other things, too, for which I thank him from the bottom of my heart.

Facing Up to the American Dream

INTRODUCTION

TWO EXPERIENCES impelled me to write this book. The first was hearing students of color in my university assert over and over that nothing has changed, that American society is as racist now as it has always been. I had two reactions. On the one hand, they are wrong. Thirty years ago they (and I) would not have been sitting in a university seminar room discussing racism in America or anything else; seventy five years ago they might have been lynched for talking about racism in public. On the other hand, their vehemence, intelligence, and sheer repetition convinced me that there was something to their views that I did not understand or share but that mattered a lot.

The second experience was a series of conversations with Isaac Fulwood, at that time the assistant chief of police of Washington, D.C., and residents of public housing projects in the District. As Fulwood huddled with Mayor Marion Barry, gave instructions on what to do if the police car we were riding in was shot at ("Duck below the seatback. And don't get out!"), and consulted with his staff on routine matters, I watched a wise and experienced man become overwhelmed by what was happening to his city. He did not give up, he never lost sight of the larger picture, and he insisted that we meet community members who were fighting to preserve safety, decency, and hope for their children. But he was frustrated and frightened, and he looked to us academics for help. I remain embarrassed at how little I had to offer.

These incidents, as incidents always are, were filtered through idiosyncratic perceptions and knowledge. I share the common belief that issues revolving around race reveal both the practices of Americans at their worst and the ideals of (some) Americans at their best. But the experiences with my students and Chief Fulwood convinced me that "issues revolving around race" are changing rapidly and that talking about "race" without also talking about class now illuminates little more about blacks than it does about whites. I also teach American political thought and write about conflicts among Americans' ideals and between their ideals and practices. In seeking to make sense of these incidents, therefore, I instinctively sought to place them in the larger frame of American political thought. From that starting point I moved eventually to the two claims described in the preface—that the American dream is a central although contentious ideology of Americans, and that it is threatened for all Americans in ways that the disaffection of most middle-class blacks and the fury of a few poor blacks most clearly reveal.

Thus, as the book's title and the epigraphs indicate, I have three sub-jects—the American dream, race in America, and class differences within races—and my goal is to use each subject to illuminate the others. Whether African Americans achieve their versions of the dream, and the effort they undergo to do so, tells us much about America's deepest and most bitter social divide. Conversely, the degree to which African Americans embrace, reject, redefine, or ignore the American dream tells us much about the meaning and value of the ideology for all Americans. How poor and rich blacks, as well as poor and rich whites, vary in their views of the American dream tells us much about how immobile the racial divide in America really is. The ideology provides a context for understanding the relationship among the races and between race and class, and those relationships in turn largely determine the meaning of the ideology.

OUTLINE OF THE CHAPTERS

My agenda is best illuminated through a brief outline of the book. Chapter 1 examines the meaning, history, and appeal of the American dream. The ideology promises that everyone, regardless of ascription or background, may reasonably seek success through actions and traits under their own control. True success, however, must be associated with virtue. The ideology so defined is both capable of inspiring great acts and responsible for creating deep despair, and the first chapter begins my analysis of those effects.

Chapter 2 sets the empirical context for examining African Americans' changing beliefs in the dream. It establishes three sets of facts: first, by some measures the status of blacks has improved since the 1960s, but by other measures it has not. Second, disparities within the black population are now vastly greater than they used to be and are arguably so great that well-off and poor blacks live in distinctly different worlds. Third, disparities between the best-off and worst-off thirds of blacks are growing more than are comparable disparities among whites.

Part 2 uses public opinion surveys to connect the data of chapter 2 to the philosophy of chapter 1. The two chapters in this part organize survey questions according to the four tenets of the American dream and compare responses by race and class over time. Chapter 3 shows that blacks and whites believe equally in the dream as a prescription for society and almost equally as a description of their own lives. But when they consider racial issues, the first of three paradoxes emerges. I call it "what's all the fuss about?" It refers to the fact that as blacks have become more discouraged about whether the American dream applies to their race, whites have become considerably more convinced of the in-clusion of blacks in the dream.

Chapter 4 disaggregates the categories of "black" and "white" to consider class differences within races. Doing so reveals two additional paradoxes. One is "succeeding more and enjoying it less": As the objec-tive circumstances of the best-off third of blacks have improved dramati-cally over the past thirty years, their belief in the American dream has *declined* sharply. The other is "[remaining] under the spell of the great national suggestion": As the objective circumstances of the worst-off third of blacks have remained dismal or worsened, their belief in the American dream has *not* declined very much.

Parts 3 and 4 (chapters 5 through 12) examine possible explanations for the latter two paradoxes. They rely on more focused surveys as well as on qualitative evidence such as memoirs, essays, and ethnographies. Explanations for succeeding more and enjoying it less include the pro-pensity to make excuses, frustrations attendant on racial and gendered barriers to success, a sense of collective responsibility and despair, and ideological alternatives to the American dream. I conclude that how one measures success in achieving the American dream is the key to unravel-ing the paradox.

Exploration of why so many poor African Americans remain under the spell of the great national suggestion begins with the psychological, historical, and institutional supports for continued belief in the Ameri-can dream. It then considers poor blacks whose belief in the dream is not matched by actions to achieve it or whose belief distorts the dream as conventionally understood. Finally, it examines those who reject the American dream in favor of an alternative ideology or sheer unbounded egotism. I conclude that the fluidity of poor blacks' beliefs poses a deep challenge to the American dream, even as its persistence gives other Americans a little more time to face up to the demands of the dream.

Part 5 (chapters 13 and 14) examines the implications of the chang-ing beliefs of African Americans for the stability and allure of the Ameri-can dream. Chapter 13 finds that the beliefs of white ethnic immigrants around the turn of the century resemble the beliefs of poor African Americans more than of well-off African Americans. I explain immi-grants' and their descendants' continued support for the American dream, and I conclude by weighing the likelihood of greater conver-gence in beliefs between blacks and whites.

The final chapter returns to the meaning and value of the ideology of the American dream. It posits that the paradoxes I have been tracing apply not only to questions of race but also to questions of class, gender, culture, and international inclusiveness. It then discusses tensions within the ideology revolving around the meaning of equality, the indeterminacy of success and virtue, and the self-referential character of the dream. It ends by arguing that the ideology contains within itself the seeds of both its salvation and its destruction.

CLARIFYING TERMS

Several words on terminology are essential for a book on such sensitive issues. I use "black," "black American," and "African American" interchangeably; the choice of one or another term in a given sentence is aesthetic rather than substantive.[1] On occasion I distinguish between "whites" and the more inclusive "nonblacks"; where appropriate, I distinguish among "whites" by ethnicity.

More generally, the book uses "black" and "white" as though they are clear, distinct, real categories. They are none of those things. But one needs to keep some issues simple in order to address the complexities of others, and analyzing the social construction of race is mostly a different concern from mine in this book. I do address this issue briefly in chapter 13, in examining whether "race" is fundamentally different from "ethnicity" in the United States.

Other terms also carry political baggage. Some of that baggage I do not want either to accept or to jettison; thus "riot," "rebellion," "uprising," and "explosion" are used interchangeably in discussing the events in Los Angeles in early May 1992. My purpose is not false neutrality; I am selectively drawing from episodes in these events to make points about some other issue, so I do not want to be sidetracked into an argument about just what happened in Los Angeles. In other cases, it *is* important for my purposes to take a stand on the political baggage carried by certain terms. Thus I reject the word "underclass" in favor of "estranged poor," for reasons explained in chapter 10.

Finally, "ideology" is used analytically rather than judgmentally. That is, unless I say so explicitly, I never imply that an ideology is a false belief, a Procrustean bed, or an imposed worldview that seeks to control through the creation of false consciousness. Rather, an ideology is "the dominant, more or less culturally universal scheme by which the social order is understood and explained. Through ideological formulation, members of the society account for and understand the social order of which they are a part. It is the public's best effort—at any given time—to make sense of, comprehend, and explain the problematic world of everyday life."[2] I usually talk of an ideology, such as the American dream or Afrocentrism, as though it is a coherent set of beliefs rationally joined; I know that it is not, at least in usual practice, and I sometimes talk of the American dream as an inchoate fantasy. But I need to impose structure—even a slightly artificial one—in order to explicate its many facets.

CLARIFYING METHODS

Readers will quickly see that my sources range from census data to opinion polls to ethnographies to letters to the editor. They will appropriately ask about criteria for choosing or excluding material, or for judging the worth of one claim over another. I have several answers.

One way to conduct research is to develop a hypothesis and select the best available data to test it. That is how chapters 2, 3, and 4 proceed. Chapter 2 relies mainly on the most extensive, carefully conducted, and widely used collections of national data available. Thus census reports, findings from the Federal Reserve Board, and test results from the National Assessment of Educational Progress predominate. The chapter also relies on analyses by social scientists known to be scrupulous about their interpretation of evidence—Walter Allen, Reynolds Farley, Robert Hauser, Christopher Jencks, Douglas Massey, William J. Wilson, and the like. Of course one can (and I do) dispute their and others' particular findings, but the scholars I have relied on are the best we have, and they set a high standard.

Chapters 3 and 4 also rely mainly on the most extensive, carefully conducted, and widely used national surveys. But here I added the criterion of comprehensiveness to that of quality, especially for the more scarce and questionable surveys of the 1960s. The surveys had to meet the highest contemporary standards of sample selection, sample size, question wording, interview technique, and so on to be included in those chapters. If surveys were of questionable quality but contained intriguing arguments or evidence, I noted a caveat. In these chapters, too, I relied on the best scholars—Lawrence Bobo, Michael Dawson, James Jackson, Donald Kinder, Howard Schuman, Katherine Tate, Susan Welch, and others—of racial attitudes and racially distinctive opinions.

Another way to conduct research is to seek insight by drawing inferences from particularly telling incidents or pieces of evidence. Chapters 1 and 5 through 13 partly use that technique. The writings of Leanita McClain before she killed herself, the survey conducted by the hapless executives of the Merck Corporation, Robby Wideman's efforts to make his brother understand how he ended up in prison, immigrant children's letters home—these illuminate to me, and I hope to readers, aspects of the lives of Americans that ring true. If readers disagree or are left cold by them, so be it. I hope in that case that the more systematic data in these chapters, and the overall cumulation of small pieces of evidence into large and comprehensible patterns, substitute for the "ah-ha" experience.

A third way to conduct research is to seek inclusiveness, so that material that seems to contradict an argument is incorporated into a revised explanation rather than dismissed as aberrant or of poor quality. That is the other technique of chapters 5 through 13. In developing an argument, I sought to read virtually everything available on the point and to figure out how to accommodate all plausible points of view. That is why the book is so complex and the list of works cited so extensive (and also why it took so long to write). I dismissed some claims as shallow or empirically unfounded, but not many—and then reintroduced many of those dismissed in order to portray a point of view even if it was in my judgment wrong. (In the interest of maintaining the flow of the narrative, I have submerged many examples, details, or caveats into the endnotes; I urge readers to peruse the notes carefully.)

Finally, this project is a beginning, not a final word. Much more can be done with the surveys—comparisons by gender, age, urbanicity, or region as well as multivariate analyses. And I could not keep up with the flood of research reports, books, and essays on the beliefs and actions of wealthy and poor African Americans and of white ethnic immigrants, so there are still more points of view and pieces of evidence available to bolster or modify my claims. But one must stop at some point.

Clarifying the Logic of the Argument

The book is structured around explicating, explaining, and then drawing the political implications of the three paradoxes—what's all the fuss about, succeeding more and enjoying it less, and remaining under the spell of the great national suggestion. What I mean by those paradoxes will become clear in the next few chapters, but here I need to explain what I mean by a paradox. It is simply a result that, given at least my preconceptions, is surprising on its face. The first paradox, for example, revolves around the fact that blacks and whites live in the same society, have experienced the same history, are affected by the same political and economic events, and yet see the world in sharply *and increasingly* different ways. The second paradox revolves around the fact that as people become richer they do not in any simple way become happier or more gratified with their lives.[3] The third starts from the fact that as people become poorer they do not in any simple way become more embittered or despairing. From a naive starting point, those phenomena are puzzling.

I start at that point not because I think readers are naive or because I imagine myself to be the first person to notice discrepancies among beliefs or between circumstances and beliefs. Instead, I start naively in order to underline what needs to be explained and to justify spending the rest of the book explaining it. People normally presume that if we see the same thing we will agree on what we saw, and that if we have more money we will enjoy our lives more; in the case I am studying, those presumptions are mostly false, and it is important to explain why.

The explanations themselves proceed according to the same logic. I start from a simple presumption and then complicate it in the process of analyzing it. For example, chapters 3 and 4 presume that people mean what they say when they respond to public opinion polls. If we believe survey data, whites really do believe in more integration and hold fewer racial stereotypes than they used to; poor blacks really do continue to believe in the American dream. Successive chapters explore and in some cases explode these simple starting points by examining white racism, black weakness of will, universal hypocrisy or self-delusion, and the discrepancy between beliefs and behaviors. In the end, I hope my naive paradoxes will dissolve into a set of claims about the connections among ideology, beliefs, attitudes, and behaviors that both captures the complexity of the real world and reduces it to mentally if not politically manageable proportions.

The Role of the Outsider

A final introductory comment: How can (and why does) a white woman write a book focusing on the beliefs of African Americans?[4] I have been told that I either cannot or should not write this book. I see several reasons for that view: white scholars studying black problems are parasitic or engaging in intellectual imperialism, white scholars' voices will drown out black scholars' voices in what remains a racially biased intellectual world, and whites cannot ever really understand and convey what it means to be black in America. Ralph Ellison put the sentiment most elegantly:

> There is an argument in progress between black men and white men [sic] as to the true nature of American reality. Following their own interests, whites impose interpretations upon Negro experience that are not only false but, in effect, a denial of Negro humanity. Too weak to shout down these interpretations, Negroes live nevertheless as they have to live, and the concrete conditions of their lives are more real than white men's arguments.[5]

In the face of that outrage, why persist? Partly because it is no longer the case, if it ever was, that African Americans are "too weak to shout down" false or offensive interpretations of their lives; in discussing this book in manuscript form I learned that lesson frequently. Partly because I felt emboldened by the plethora of material written by African Americans explaining what they felt and why. Partly because outsiders may have insights that are missed by insiders, or have insights that are rejected by insiders but are still important, possibly even right.[6]

But my main response to Ellison's outrage is the conviction that the distinction between insiders and outsiders does not and should not always hold up. For one thing, as a woman working in a man's world, I felt it not presumptuous to claim some empathy with the situation of middle-class blacks. I too have felt invisible in professional meetings, have wondered if a failure was due to my actions or to my ascriptive traits (and have realized that it was impossible to know), have needed to deal with people who operated according to rules and assumptions that I neither understood nor respected. Being a black man or woman is not in any simple way analogous to being a white woman; the several kinds of ascription may even be more different than similar. But a little empathy combined with a lot of data gives courage and, I hope, credibility. (The reverse side of this coin was my comparative discomfort analyzing the beliefs of poor African Americans. I would feel almost as distant analyzing the lives of poor whites—a hint that in crucial ways class is at least as significant as race.)

My other ground for rejecting the distinction between insiders and outsiders is that any study of black Americans' beliefs is also a study of white Americans' beliefs, and vice versa. Those studying African Americans have been quicker to realize this point than those studying whites have been (just as students of women and politics realized long before students of "politics" that gender is implicated in most political choices and structures). Much of this book explicitly compares blacks with whites, or blacks of one class with whites of the same class. But even where comparisons are not explicit, they are always there. More importantly, it is the interaction between blacks' and whites' beliefs that is and must be the real subject of any book about race in America and—if my central thesis is correct—about the ideology of the American dream. We have shaped each other too much and too long to imagine that we can make a pristine distinction between subjects that African Americans are best able to write about and subjects that European Americans are suited for. In short, a white partakes of race as much as does a black, and is no more or less privileged an interpreter of the meaning of race in America.

In the end, I wrote this book because I had to. I started to write a different book, and I thought I was writing several others along the way. But this book kept imposing itself, just as Pudd'nhead Wilson kept insisting on turning Mark Twain's farce about Siamese twins into a serious book about race and class. The book you are reading is where the material, my political convictions and anxieties, and my intellectual background took me. I wrote it in order to respond to my students and Chief Fulwood—and to contribute my share to averting the threat of Americans' losing faith in the American dream with nothing better to put in its place.

PART ONE

The Philosophical and Empirical Context

Chapter One

WHAT IS THE AMERICAN DREAM?

"IN THE BEGINNING," wrote John Locke, "all the world was *America*."[1] Locke was referring specifically to the absence of a cash nexus in primitive society. But the sentence evokes the unsullied newness, infinite possibility, limitless resources that are commonly understood to be the essence of the "American dream." The idea of the American dream has been attached to everything from religious freedom to a home in the suburbs, and it has inspired emotions ranging from deep satisfaction to disillusioned fury. Nevertheless, the phrase elicits for most Americans some variant of Locke's fantasy—a new world where anything can happen and good things might.

Millions of immigrants and internal migrants have moved to America, and around within it, to fulfill their version of the American dream. By objective measures and their own accounts, many have achieved success. Probably just as many have been defeated and disillusioned. Millions of other immigrants—predominantly but not exclusively from Africa—were moved to America despite their preferences and have been forced to come to terms with a dream that was not originally theirs. How they have done so, and how their experiences compare with those who came to America to seek their dream, is the chief subject of this book.

But one cannot address that subject, nor eventually move beyond it to evaluate the future of the American dream and its society, without knowing what the dream is and how it operates. That knowledge is the goal of this chapter.

The Meaning of Success

The American dream consists of tenets about achieving success. Let us first explore the meaning of "success" and then consider the rules for achieving it.

People most often define success as the attainment of a high income, a prestigious job, economic security. My treatment is no exception. But, *pace* President Reagan, material well-being is only one form of accomplishment. People seek success from the pulpit to the stage of the Metropolitan Opera, from membership in the newest dance club to membership in the Senate. Success can be as amorphous and encompassing as "a right to say what they wanta say, do what they wanta do, and fashion a world into something that can be great for everyone."[2]

Different kinds of success need not, but often do, conflict. A classic plot of American family sagas is the children's rejection of the parents' hard-won wealth and social standing in favor of some "deeper," more meaningful form of accomplishment.[3] The rejection may be reversed, as Cotton Mather sadly reported:

> There have been very fine settlements in the north-east regions; but what is become of them? . . . One of our ministers once preaching to a congregation there, urged them to approve themselves a religious people from this consideration, "that otherwise they would contradict the main end of planting this wilderness"; whereupon a well-known person, then in the assembly, cryed out, "Sir, you are mistaken: you think you are preaching to the people at the [Plymouth] Bay; our main end was to catch fish."[4]

Mather "wished that something more excellent had been the main end of the settlements in that brave country," but the ideology of the American dream itself remains agnostic as to the meaning of "something more excellent."[5]

A definition of success involves measurement as well as content. Success can be measured in at least three ways, with important normative and behavioral consequences. First, it can be *absolute*. In this case, achieving the American dream implies reaching some threshold of well-being, higher than where one began but not necessarily dazzling. As Bruce Springsteen puts it, "I don't think the American dream was that everybody was going to make . . . a billion dollars, but it was that everybody was going to have an opportunity and the chance to live a life with some decency and some dignity and a chance for some self-respect."[6]

Second, success can be *relative*. Here achieving the American dream consists in becoming better off than some comparison point, whether one's childhood, people in the old country, one's neighbors, a character from a book, another race or gender—anything or anyone that one measures oneself against. Relative success implies no threshold of well-being, and it may or may not entail continually changing the comparison group as one achieves a given level of accomplishment. A benign version of relative success is captured by James Comer's "kind of competition . . . we had . . . going on" with "the closest friends that we had":

> When we first met them, we had a dining room and they didn't. They went back and they turned one of their bedrooms into a dining room. . . . After that we bought this big Buick car. And we came to their house and they had bought another car. She bought a fur coat one

Like it or not, success often means stepping over others.

Harold Smelcer, *U.S. News & World Report*

year and your dad bought me one the next. But it was a friendly thing, the way we raced. It gave you something to work for, to look forward to. Every year we tried to have something different to show them what we had done, and they would have something to show us.

William Byrd II articulated a more malign version in 1736: slaves "blow up the pride, and ruin the industry of our white people, who seeing a rank of poor creatures below them, detest work for fear it should make them look like slaves."[7]

Success can, alternatively, be *competitive*—achieving victory over someone else. My success implies your failure. Competitors are usually people, whether known and concrete (opponents in a tennis match) or unknown and abstract (all other applicants for a job). *U.S. News and*

World Report, in an article celebrating "SUCCESS! The Chase Is Back in Style Again," graphically illustrates the relationship among competitors in the business world. An opponent may, however, be entirely impersonal. John Henry, "the steel-drivin' man," is famed for beating a machine, and Paul Bunyan for taming the primeval forest.

TENETS OF SUCCESS

> The American dream that we were all raised on is a simple but powerful one—if you work hard and play by the rules you should be given a chance to go as far as your God-given ability will take you.
>
> —President Bill Clinton, speech to Democratic Leadership Council, 1993

In one sentence, President Clinton has captured the bundle of shared, even unconsciously presumed, tenets about achieving success that make up the ideology of the American dream. Those tenets answer the questions: *Who* may pursue the American dream? In *what* does the pursuit consist? *How* does one successfully pursue the dream? *Why* is the pursuit worthy of our deepest commitment?

The answer to "who" in the standard ideology is "everyone, regardless of ascriptive traits, family background, or personal history." The answer to "what" is "the reasonable anticipation, though not the promise, of success, however it is defined." The answer to "how" is "through actions and traits under one's own control." The answer to "why" is "true success is associated with virtue." Let us consider each rule in turn.

Who May Pursue Success?

The first tenet, that everyone may always pursue their dream, is the most direct connotation of Locke's "in the beginning . . . ." But the idea extends beyond the image of a pristine state of nature waiting for whoever "discovers" it. Even in the distinctly nonpristine, nonnatural world of Harlem or Harlan County, anyone can pursue a dream. A century ago, one moved to the frontier to hide a spotted past and begin afresh; Montana frontierswomen "never ask[ed] women where they come from or what they did before they came to live in our neck of the woods. If they wore a wedding band and were good wives, mothers, and neighbors that was enough for us to know."[8] Today one finds new frontiers, as Gary Trudeau demonstrates.[9]

But seldom, say Americans, does one need to take such dramatic

Doonesbury

BY GARRY TRUDEAU

Doonesbury © 1988 G. B. Trudeau. Reprinted with permission of Universal Press Syndicate.
All rights reserved.

steps; fewer than one-fifth see race, gender, religion, or class as very important for "getting ahead in life." Even two-thirds of the poor are certain that Americans like themselves "have a good chance of improving our standard of living," and up to three times as many Americans as Europeans make that claim.[10] In effect, Americans believe that they can create a personal mini-state of nature that will allow them to slough off the past and invent a better future.

What Does One Pursue?

The second tenet, that one may reasonably anticipate success, is less straightforward. "Reasonable anticipation" is far from a guarantee, as all children on the morning of their birthday know. But "reasonable anticipation" is also much more than simply longing; most children are fairly sure of getting at least some of what they wish for on their birthday. On a larger scale, from its inception America has been seen by many as an extravagant birthday party:

> Seagull: A whole countrie of English is there, man, . . . and . . . the Indians are so in love with 'hem that all the treasure they have they lay at their feete. . . . Golde is more plentiful there than copper is with us. . . . Why, man, all their dripping pans and their chamberpots are pure golde; and all the chaines with which they chaine up their streets are massie golde; all the prisoners they take are fettered in golde; and for rubies and diamonds they goe forthe on holy dayes and gather 'hem by the sea shore to hang on their childrens coats.[11]

Presumably few Britons even in 1605 took this message literally, but the hope of abundant riches—whether material, spiritual, or otherwise—persists.

"GO FOR IT."

Marc Rankin
Marketing Representative

Callie Mitchell
Senior Supply Representative

Ron Richards
Manager, Environment Affairs

Bill Studzinski
Chemist

Carol Trisket
Superintendent, Planning and Shipping

Kelly Moyo
Systems Analyst

Thus Americans are exhorted to "go for it" in their advertisements as well as their commencement addresses. And they do; three-quarters of Americans, compared with only one-third of Britons, West Germans, and Hungarians (and fewer Dutch), agree that they have a good chance of improving their standard of living. Twice as many Americans as Canadians or Japanese think future generations of their nationality will live better than the present generation.[12]

How Does One Pursue Success?

The third premise, for those who do not take Seagull literally, explains how one is to achieve the success that one anticipates. Ralph Waldo Emerson is uncharacteristically succinct on the point: "There is always a reason, *in the man*, for his good or bad fortune, and so in making money."[13] Other nineteenth-century orators exhorted young men to

> Behold him [a statue of Benjamin Franklin], . . . holding out to you an example of diligence, economy and virtue, and personifying the triumphant success which may await those who follow it! Behold him, ye that are humblest and poorest . . . —lift up your heads and look at the image of a man who rose from nothing, who owed nothing to parentage or patronage, who enjoyed no advantages of early education, which are not open,—a hundredfold open,—to yourselves, who performed the most menial services in the business in which his early life was employed, but who lived to stand before Kings, and died to leave a name which the world will never forget.[14]

Lest we smile at the quaint optimism (or crude propaganda) of our ancestors, consider the recent advertisement from Citicorp Bank reproduced here. This carefully balanced group of shining faces—young and old, male and female, black, Latino, Nordic, and Asian—all gazing starry-eyed at the middle distance over the words "THE WILL TO SUCCEED IS PART OF THE AMERICAN SPIRIT" conveys the message of the third tenet in no uncertain terms.

This advertisement is well aimed; surveys unanimously show Americans' strong support for rewarding people in the marketplace according to their talents and accomplishments rather than their needs, efforts, or simple existence.[15] And Americans mostly believe that people are in fact rewarded for their acts. In 1952 fully 88 percent of Americans agreed that "there is plenty of opportunity and anyone who works hard can go as far as he wants"; in 1980, 70 percent concurred.[16]

Comparisons across space yield the same results as comparisons across time. In a 1973 survey of youth in ten nations, only Swedes and British disagreed more than did Americans that a man's [*sic*] future is "virtually

FROM SEA TO SHINING SEA, THE WILL TO SUCCEED IS PART OF THE AMERICAN SPIRIT.

The instant you become an American, whether by birth or by choice, you are guaranteed a particular freedom that is nowhere mentioned in the Constitution, but in fact flows from it.

You are guaranteed the freedom to succeed.

You are free to dream your own dream of success, to study, to work, to create and discover and build, for yourself and your children, the success you want.

Our deep belief in that idea is one reason that our company—Citicorp and Citibank—has grown to become by far the nation's largest financial services organization.

For over 175 years, our freedom to innovate, to create new financial ideas and services, has led to an unbroken line of initiatives allowing us to help countless millions of individuals.

Today, more Americans are pursuing college education and graduate degrees with help from us than from any other private lender.

More are getting what they want with the help of MasterCard* and Visa cards from Citibank than from any other company.

And more Americans who once dreamed of "some day" owning their own homes now own them, or are buying them, with help from Citicorp and Citibank.

Meanwhile, here at home and in 90 other countries around the world, we offer the full range of financial services, from new automated machines for personal banking to corporate funding in the billions.

Over 90,000 people of Citicorp and Citibank serve over 25,000,000 customers, thousands of companies and many governments, in every major world marketplace.

We can help you, or your company, achieve success, here and abroad.

Whether you get to know us as Citicorp or Citibank, we'd like you to get to know us better.

CITICORP⦿
BECAUSE AMERICANS WANT TO SUCCEED, NOT JUST SURVIVE.™

Citicorp / Citibank New York.

determined" by his family background. A decade later only 31 percent of Americans agreed that in their nation "what you achieve in life depends largely on your family background," compared with over 50 percent of Austrians and Britons, and over 60 percent of Italians.[17] Most pointedly, half of American adolescents compared with one-fourth of British adolescents agreed in 1972 that "people get to be poor . . . [because] they don't work hard enough."[18]

Americans also believe more than do Europeans that people ought not to be buffered from the consequences of their actions, so long as they have a fair start in life. Thus up to four times as many more Americans think college opportunities should be increased, but roughly half as many think the government should reduce the income disparity between high- and low-income citizens, or provide jobs or income support for the poor.[19]

Why Is Success Worth Pursuing?

Implicit in the flows of oratory and survey responses is the fourth tenet of the American dream, that the pursuit of success warrants so much fervor because it is associated with virtue. "Associated with" means at least four things: virtue leads to success, success makes a person virtuous, success indicates virtue, or apparent success is not real success unless one is also virtuous.

That quintessential American, Benjamin Franklin, illustrates three of these associations: the *Autobiography* instructs us that "no Qualities were so likely to make a poor Man's Fortune as those of Probity & Integrity." Conversely, "Proverbial Sentences, chiefly such as inculcated Industry and Frugality," are included in *Poor Richard's Almanack* as "the Means of procuring Wealth and thereby securing Virtue, it being more difficult for a Man in Want to act always honestly, as . . . *it is hard for an empty Sack to stand upright.*" Finally, mere wealth may actually impede true success, the attainment of which requires a long list of virtues: "Fond *Pride of Dress*, is sure a very Curse;/ E'er *Fancy* you consult, consult your Purse"; "A Ploughman on his Legs is higher than a Gentleman on his Knees"; and "Pride that dines on Vanity sups on Contempt."[20]

Americans have learned Franklin's lessons well: they distinguish between the worthy and unworthy rich, as well as the deserving and undeserving poor. For example, most Americans characterize "yuppies" as people who "play fashionable games" and "eat in trendy restaurants," and on the whole they enjoy watching such forms of conspicuous consumption. But they also characterize yuppies as selfish, greedy, inclined to flaunt their wealth, and imbued with a false sense of superiority.

These traits they mostly find unacceptable. Overall, Americans over-whelmingly deplore the 1980s sentiment of "making it fast while you can regardless of what happened to others."[21] This is not simply a reaction against the Reagan years. In surveys throughout the 1970s, four in ten Americans deemed honesty to be the most important quality for a child to learn, compared with 2 percent proclaiming that a child should try hard to succeed. Virtually all Americans require that their friends be "honest" and "responsible"—core components of the third and fourth tenets.[22]

Americans also focus more on virtue than do citizens of other nations, at least in their self-descriptions. A survey of youth in ten nations found that more Americans than people in any other country described their chief goal in life as "sincerity and love between myself and others," and in only one other nation (the Philippines) did more youth seek "salvation through faith." Conversely, only in Sweden did fewer youths seek "money and position," and only in three other countries did fewer seek "freedom from restrictions." More Americans than Europeans gain strength from religion, report prayer to be an important part of their daily life, and agree that there are universally applicable "clear guidelines about what is good or evil."[23] In short, "this country succeeds in living a very sinful life without being deeply cynical. That is the difference between Europe and America, and it signifies that ethics *means* something here."[24]

The American Dream as Fantasy

Throughout this book, I will use the four tenets just described to analyze Americans' changing beliefs about the American dream. But we must beware reducing the dream to its components; as a whole it has an evocative resonance greater than the sum of its parts. The theme of most Walt Disney movies boils down to the lyric in *Pinocchio*: "When you wish upon a star, makes no difference who you are, your dreams come true." It is no coincidence that Disney movies are so durable; they simply update Locke's fantasy. And the global, amorphous vision of establishing a city upon the hill, killing the great white whale, striking a vein of gold, making the world safe for democracy—or simply living a life of decency and dignity—underlies all analyses of what success means or what practices will attain it.

VIRTUES OF THE AMERICAN DREAM

Combining the amorphous fantasy or the more precise tenets of the American dream with the various meanings of success shows the full richness—and seductiveness—of the ideology. If one measures success absolutely and accepts a wide array of indicators of success, the ideology portrays America as a land of plenty, and Americans as "people of plenty."[25] This is the great theme of one of the most powerful children's sagas ever written in America, the *Little House in the Big Woods* series. Decades (and nine volumes) of grasshopper plagues, ferocious blizzards, cheating and cowardly railroad bosses, even hostile Indians cannot prevent Pa and his girls from eventually "winning their bet with Uncle Sam" and becoming prosperous homesteaders. In the words of one of Pa's songs:

> I am sure in this world there are plenty
> of good things enough for us all. . . .
> It's cowards alone that are crying
> And foolishly saying, "I can't."
> It is only by plodding and striving
> And laboring up the steep hill
> Of life, that you'll ever be thriving,
> Which you'll do if you've only the will.[26]

If success is measured competitively and defined narrowly, however, the ideology portrays a different America. Hard work and virtue combined with scarce resources produce a few spectacular winners and many dismissible losers. This is the theme of John Rockefeller's turn-of-the-century Sunday school address:

> The growth of a large business is merely a survival of the fittest. . . . The American Beauty rose can be produced in the splendor and fragrance which bring cheer to its beholder only by sacrificing the early buds which grow up around it. This is not an evil tendency in business. It is merely the working out of a law of nature and a law of God.[27]

The *Little House* series has sold well over four million copies; Americans prefer the self-image of universal achievement to that of a few stalwarts triumphing over weaker contenders.[28] What matters most, however, is not any single image but rather the elasticity and range of the ideology of the American dream. People can encourage themselves with soft versions, congratulate themselves with harder ones, and exult with the hardest, as their circumstances and characters warrant.

Thus the American dream is an impressive ideology. It has for centuries lured people to America and moved them around within it, and it has kept them striving in horrible conditions against impossible odds. Most Americans celebrate it unthinkingly, along with apple pie and motherhood; criticism typically is limited to imperfections in its application. But like apple pie and motherhood, the American dream turns out upon closer examination to be less than perfect. Let us look, then, at flaws intrinsic to the dream.

FLAWS IN THE TENETS OF THE AMERICAN DREAM

The First Tenet

The first tenet, that everyone can participate equally and can always start over, is troubling to the degree that it is not true. It is, of course, never true in the strongest sense; people cannot shed their existing selves as snakes do their skin. So the myth of the individual mini-state of nature is just that—a fantasy to be sought but never achieved.

Fantasies are fine so long as people understand that that is what they are. For that reason, a weaker formulation of the first tenet—people start the pursuit of success with varying advantages, but no one is barred from the pursuit—is more troubling because the gap between ideological claim and actual fact is harder to recognize. As a factual claim, the first tenet is largely false; for most of American history, women of any race and men who were Native American, Asian, black, or poor were barred from all but a narrow range of "electable futures."[29] Ascriptive constraints have arguably been weakened over time,[30] but until recently no more than about a third of the population was able to take seriously the first premise of the American dream.

This flaw has implications beyond the evident ones of racism and sexism. The emotional potency of the American dream has made people who *were* able to identify with it the norm for everyone else. White men, especially European immigrants able to ride the wave of the Industrial Revolution (and to benefit from the absence of competition from the rest of the population) to comfort or even prosperity, are the epitomizing demonstration of America as the bountiful state of nature. Those who do not fit the model disappear from the collective self-portrait. Thus the irony is doubled: not only has the ideal of universal participation been denied to most Americans, but also the very fact of its denial has itself been denied in our national self-image.

This double irony creates deep misunderstandings and correspondingly deep political tensions. Much of this book examines one such tension—the fact that whites increasingly believe that racial discrimination is slight and declining, and blacks increasingly believe the opposite. But this form of racial conflict is not unique. For example, surveys show that more women than men believe that women are discriminated against in employment and wages, in "being able to combine family and work," and in their overall chance to pursue their dreams. Similarly, regardless of when the survey was conducted, more men than women believe that women are better off now than a decade earlier with regard to these issues. Not surprisingly, bitter disagreements about the need for affirmative action, policies to stem sexual harassment, family leave policies, and the like ensue.[31]

The Second Tenet

The flaws of the second tenet of the American dream, the reasonable anticipation of success, stem from the close link between anticipation and expectation. That link presents little problem so long as there are enough resources and opportunities that everyone has a reasonable chance of having some expectations met. Indeed, panegyrics to the American dream always expound on the bounty and openness of the American continent. Governor James Glen typified eighteenth-century entrepreneurs of colonization by promising that

> Adventurers will be pleased to find a Change from Poverty and Distress to Ease and Plenty; they are invited to a Country not yet half settled, where the Rivers are crouded with Fish, and the Forests with Game; and no Game-Act to restrain them from enjoying those Bounties of Providence, no heavy Taxes to impoverish them, nor oppressive Landlords to snatch the hard-earned Morsel from the Mouth of Indigence, and where Industry will certainly inrich them.[32]

Three centuries later, the message was unchanged:

> All my life I am thinking to come to this country. For what I read in the magazines, and the movies. . . . I would have a beautiful castle in the United States. I will have a thousand servant. I will have five Rolls-Royces in my door. . . . We thinking everybody has this kind of life. . . . I have this kind of dream.[33]

These fantasies are innocuous so long as resources roughly balance dreams for enough people enough of the time. But if they do not—worse yet, if they used to but do no longer—then the dream rapidly loses its appeal. The circumstances that cause resources no longer to balance dreams vary, from an economic downturn to a rapid increase in the number of dreamers to a narrowing of the grounds on which success is publicly recognized. The general point, however, always holds: no one promises that dreams will be fulfilled, but the distinction between the right to dream and the right to succeed is psychologically hard to maintain and politically always blurred. It is especially hard to maintain because the dream sustains Americans against daily nightmares only if they believe that they have a significant likelihood, not just a formal chance, of reaching their goals.

In short, the right to aspire to success works as an ideological substitute for a guarantee of success only if it begins to approach it. When people recognize that chances for success are slim or getting slimmer, the whole tenor of the American dream changes dramatically for the worse.

The general problem of scarcity varies depending on how people measure success and how broadly they define possible goals. It is most obvious and acute for those focused on competitive success in only a few arenas; by definition resources and opportunities are insufficient to satisfy all dreamers in such a case. But it may be more problematic for those who measure success relatively or who admit a wide array of outcomes into their picture of success. After all, there are more such people and they have no a priori reason to assume that many will fail.

The problem of scarcity may be most devastating, however, for people anticipating absolute success or for people willing to see success almost anywhere. They, after all, have the least reason to expect failure. Losers of this type have an unmatched poignancy: "I don't dream any more like I used to. I believed that in this country, we would have all we needed for the decent life. I don't see that any more."[34]

Conversely, the availability of resources and opportunities may shape the kind of success that Americans dream of. If resources are profoundly scarce (as in a famine) or inherently limited (as in election to the presidency), people almost certainly envision competitive success in that arena. If resources are moderately scarce, people will be concerned about their position relative to that of others, but will not necessarily see another's gain as their loss. When resources and opportunities seem wide open and broadly defined—anyone can achieve salvation, get an "A" on the exam, claim 160 acres of western prairie—people are most free to pursue their idiosyncratic dreams and to measure their achievement by their own absolute standard.

This logic suggests a dynamic: as resources become tighter or success is more narrowly defined, Americans are likely to shift their understanding of success from absolute to relative to competitive. Before the 1980s, claims one journalist, "there was always enough to go around, plenty of places in the sun. It didn't even matter much about the rich—so long as everyone was living better, it seemed the rich couldn't be denied their chance to get richer." But "today [in 1988] that wave [of prosperity] has crested. . . . Now when the rich get richer, the middle class stagnates—and the poor get decidedly poorer. If left unchecked, a polarization of income . . . is likely to provoke consequences that will affect America's politics and power, to say nothing of its psyche."[35]

The risks of anticipating success do not stop with anticipation. Attaining one's dreams can be surprisingly problematic. From William Shakespeare to William Faulkner, writers have limned the loneliness of being at the top, the spiritual costs of cutthroat competition, the shallowness of a society that rewards achievement above all else. Alexis de Tocqueville characteristically provides one of the most eloquent of such admonitions:

> Every American is eaten up with longing to rise. . . . In America I have
> seen the freest and best educated of men in circumstances the happiest

in the world; yet it seemed to me that a cloud habitually hung on their brow, and they seemed serious and almost sad even in their pleasures. The chief reason for this is that . . . [they] never stop thinking of the good things they have not got. . . . They clutch everything but hold nothing fast, and so lose grip as they hurry after some new delight.[36]

The obsession with ever more material success threatens the body politic as well as the individual soul:

When the taste for physical pleasures has grown more rapidly than either education or experience of free institutions, the time comes when men are carried away and lose control of themselves at sight of the new good things they are ready to snatch. . . . There is no need to drag their rights away from citizens of this type; they themselves voluntarily let them go. . . . The role of government is left unfilled. If, at this critical moment, an able and ambitious man once gets power, he finds the way open for usurpations of every sort.[37]

Not only nineteenth-century romantics cautioned against the failures of success. Today psychotherapists specialize in helping "troubled winners" or the "working wounded," for whom "a life too much devoted to pursuing money, power, position, and control over others ends up being emotionally impoverished."[38] In short, material—and perhaps other forms of—success is not all it's cracked up to be, even (or especially) in a nation where it is the centerpiece of the pervasive ideology.

The problems of success, however, pale beside the problems of failure. Because success is so central to Americans' self-image,[39] and because they expect as well as hope to achieve, Americans are not gracious about failure. Others' failure reminds them that the dream may be just that—a dream, to be distinguished from waking reality. Their own failure confirms that fear. As Zora Neale Hurston puts it, "there is something about poverty that smells like death."[40]

Furthermore, the better the dream works for other people, the more devastating is failure for the smaller and smaller proportion of people left behind. In World War II, members of military units with a high probability of promotion were less satisfied with advancement opportunities than members of units with a much lower probability of promotion, because failure to be promoted in the former case was both more salient and more demonstrably a personal rather than a systemic flaw. The "tunnel effect" is a more nuanced depiction of this phenomenon of relative deprivation. The first stage is one of relative gratification, in which others' success enhances one's own well-being. After all, drivers in a traffic jam in a tunnel are initially pleased when cars in the adjacent lane begin to move "because advances of others supply information about a more benign external environment; receipt of this information produces gratification; and this gratification overcomes, or at least suspends, *envy*." At some point, however, those left behind come to believe that their heightened expectations will not be met; not only are their hopes now dashed, but they are also worse off than when the upward mobility began. "Nonrealization of the expectation ['that my turn to move will soon come'] will at some point result in my 'becoming furious.'"[41] And one is still stuck in the tunnel. In short, the ideology of the American dream includes no provision for failure; a failed dream denies the loser not only success but even a safe harbor within which to hide the loss.

The Third Tenet

Failure is made more harsh by the third premise of the American dream—the belief that success results from actions and traits under one's own control. Logically, it does not follow that if success results from individual volition, then failure results from lack of volition. All one needs in order to see the logical flaw here is the distinction between necessary and sufficient. But that distinction is not obvious or intuitive, and in any case the psychologic of the American dream differs from strict logic. In the psychologic, if one may claim responsibility for success, one must accept responsibility for failure.

Americans who do everything they can and still fail may come to understand that effort and talent alone do not guarantee success. But they have a hard time persuading others. After all, they are losers—why listen to them? Will we not benefit more by listening to winners (who seldom challenge the premise that effort and talent breed success)?

The Fourth Tenet

Failure, then, is unseemly for two reasons: it challenges the blurring between anticipation and promise that is the emotional heart of the American dream, and people who fail are presumed to lack talent or will. The coup de grace comes from the fourth tenet of the dream, the association of success with virtue. By the psychologic just described, if success implies virtue, failure implies sin.

American history and popular culture are replete with demonstrations of the connection between failure and sin. In the 1600s, indentured servants—kidnapped children, convicts, and struggling families alike—were described by earlier immigrants as "strong and idle beggars, vagabonds, egyptians, common and notorious whoores, theeves, and other dissolute and lousy persons."[42] Nineteenth-century reformers concurred: fallen women are typically "the daughters of the ignorant, depraved, and vicious part of our population, trained up without culture of any kind, amidst the contagion of evil example, and enter upon a life of prostitution for the ratification of their unbridled passions, and become harlots altogether by choice."[43]

Small wonder that in the late twentieth century even the poor blame the poor for their condition. Despite her vivid awareness of exploitation by the rich, an aging cleaning woman insists that many people are poor because they "make the money and drink it all up. They don't care about the kids or the clothes. Just have a bottle on that table all the time." Losers even blame themselves: an unemployed factory worker, handicapped by a childhood accident, "wish[es] to hell I could do it [save money for his children]. I always said for years, 'I wanna get rich, I wanna get rich.' But then, phew! My mind doesn't have the strong will. I say, 'Well, I'm *gonna* do it.' Only the next day's different." These people are typical. In 1985, over 60 percent of poor people but only 45 percent of the nonpoor agreed that "poor young women often have babies so they can collect welfare." Seven years later, the same proportions of poor and well-off agreed that welfare recipients "are taking advantage of the system."[44]

The equation of failure with evil and success with virtue cannot be attributed to poor education or low status. College students "who learned that a fellow student had been awarded a cash prize as a result of a random drawing were likely to conclude that he had in fact worked especially hard." In another experiment, subjects rated a presumed victim of electric shocks who was randomly selected to receive compensation for her pain more favorably than a victim who would not be compensated. "The sight of an innocent person suffering without possibility of reward or compensation motivated people to devalue the attractiveness of the victim in order to bring about a more appropriate fit between her fate and her character."[45] Devaluing losers allows people to maintain their belief that the world is fundamentally just, even when it patently is not.

Losers are obviously harmed by the association of success with virtue. But the association creates equally important, if less obvious, problems for winners. Fitzwilliam Darcy, in Jane Austen's *Pride and Prejudice*, epitomizes the defect of pride: if I believe that virtue produced my success, or that success has made me even more virtuous, I am likely to become insufferably smug. That may not bother me much, but the fact that people around me feel the same way will.[46] In addition, this equation raises the stakes very high for further rounds of endeavor. If I continue to win, all is well; if I falter, I lose my *amour propre* as well as my wealth or power. Alternatively, if I recognize that I partly owe my success to lying to a few clients, evading a few taxes, cheating a few employees, then I am likely to feel considerable guilt. This guilt might induce reform and recompense, but it may instead induce drinking to assuage the unease, persecuting other nonvirtuous winners, striving to show that losers are even more sinful, or simple hypocrisy.[47]

These problems intensify when patterns of group success rather than the idiosyncrasies of individual success are at issue. When members of one group seem disproportionately successful, that group acquires a halo of ascribed virtue. Consider a 1907 article by Burton J. Hendrick on "The Great Jewish Invasion" in *McClure's Magazine*. The author's name, the publication, the date, and the title all lead one to expect an (at best, thinly veiled) anti-Semitic diatribe. The first few pages seem to confirm that expectation, with their claims that "the real modern Zion, greater in numbers and wealth and power than the old, steadily gathers on Manhattan Island," and that "the Jews are active, and invariably with success, in practically every business, professional, and intellectual field. The New Yorker constantly rubs shoulders with Israel." These feats are all the more "remarkable" because "the great mass of its [New York's] Jews are not what are commonly regarded as the most enlightened of their race" since they come from eastern Europe. After all, "no people have had a more inadequate preparation, educational and economic, for American citizenship."[48]

Yet the article goes on to describe in careful and admiring detail how these dirt-poor, ignorant, orthodoxly non-Christian immigrants work, save, cooperate, sacrifice for their children—and end up wealthy beyond anyone's wildest imaginings. Nor are they merely money-grubbers; Russian Jews are "individualist[s]," the "city's largest productive force and the greatest contributor to its manufacturing wealth," demonstrating "intense ambition," abstinence, and foresight. In his highest accolade, Mr. Hendrick even insists that the Russian Jew's

> enthusiasm for America knows no bounds. He eagerly looks forward to the time when he can be naturalized. . . . The rapidity with which the New York Jew adopts the manners and trappings of Americans almost disproves his ancient heritage as a peculiar people. . . . Better than any other element, even the native stock, do they meet the two supreme tests of citizenship: they actually go to the polls, and when once there, vote independently.[49]

In short, in one generation the east European Jewish immigrant has gone from an unassimilable, bovine drag on the American spirit to the epitome of all the American virtues. Nothing succeeds like success.

The contemporary equivalent of Mr. Hendrick's amazing Jews are Southeast Asians. A century ago, Chinese and Japanese immigrants could hardly be derogated enough.[50] Now newspapers have a seemingly endless supply of rags-to-riches stories about destitute boat people whose daughter became the high school valedictorian a scant five years

FIGURE 2.   *Thistleton's Jolly Giant*, II (February 21, 1874), 1.

"The *Jolly Giant's* artist, George F. Keller, is a believer in Darwinism; he has made a careful study of this subject and in proof of the theory of which Darwin is the originator, he has produced the first of a series of that class in the *Jolly Giant* of this week showing conclusively that John Chinaman has had his origin in a Monkey; from thence to a Chinaman, and eventually into a pig; any further comment would be useless."

Reproduced in Caldwell 1971: 124.

later and is now a pre-med student at Stanford. Such success is inevitably attributed to hard work, self-discipline, family support, and refusal to follow the bad example set by American-born peers.[51] This portrayal is so ubiquitous that spokespeople for Asian immigrants feel impelled to insist publicly that not *all* Asians escape poverty, crime, and discrimination, and that even the successful pay a heavy emotional cost.[52]

It would be churlish to argue that excessive praise is as bad as racism or ethnic slurs. But newly anointed groups are too often used to cast aspersions on some despised group that has not managed to fulfill the American dream. In Burton Hendrick's case, the main negative reference group is the Irish, who drink and gamble, yield their productive jobs to Jews, and—worst of all—band together in labor unions, in the "Irish vote," and in political party machines. In the case of immigrant Asians, the usual (if slightly more subtle) message is "Why can't African Americans do the same thing? At least they speak English when they start school." This dynamic adds yet another component to the nightmare of a failed American dream. Members of a denigrated group are disproportionately likely to fail to achieve their goals; they are blamed as individuals (and perhaps blame themselves) for their failure; and they carry a further stigma as members of a nonvirtuous (thus appropriately denigrated) group.

This effect of the fourth tenet can be taken a further, and most dangerous, step. For some Americans always, and for many Americans in some periods of our history, virtuous success has been defined as the dominance of some groups over others. This phenomenon extends the idea of competitive success from individual victories to collective hierarchies. If women are weak and emotional, it is *right* for men to control their bodies and wealth; if blacks are childlike pagans, it is *right* for whites to ensure their physical and spiritual survival through enslavement and conversion; if citizens of other nations refuse to recognize the value of capitalism and free elections, it is *right* for Americans to install a more enlightened government in their capitol. I find it hard to present these sentiments with a straight face, but they have arguably done almost as much as the American dream to shape Americans' beliefs, practices, and institutions.[53]

FLAWS IN THE AMERICAN DREAM TAKEN AS A WHOLE

Atomistic Individualism

Not only each tenet, but also the ideology of the American dream as a whole, is flawed. One problem stems from the radical individualism often associated with the dream (although the ideology entails nothing that prohibits groups from pursuing collective success). Achievers mark their success by moving away from the tenement, ghetto, or holler of their impoverished and impotent youth, thus speeding the breakup of their ethnic community. This is a bittersweet phenomenon. The freedom to move up and out is desirable, or at least desired. But certainly those left behind, probably those who leave, and arguably the nation as a whole lose when groups of people with close cultural and personal ties break those ties in pursuit of or after attaining "the bitch-goddess, success."[54] The line between autonomy and atomism is hard to draw.

American culture is full of stories about the mixed effects of success on communities and their residents. A Polish-American folk song tells of a man who emigrated to America, worked for three years in a foundry, returned home with "gold and silver," but found that "my children did not know me, for they fled from me, a stranger." The emancipated children may be as pained as the abandoned parents, as illustrated by the five brothers who complained to the *Jewish Daily Forward* in 1933:

> Imagine, even when we go with our father to buy something in a store on Fifth Avenue, New York, he insists on speaking Yiddish. We are not ashamed of our parents, God forbid, but they ought to know where it's proper and where it's not. If they talk Yiddish among themselves at home, or to us, it's bad enough, but among strangers and Christians? Is that nice?[55]

Only irresponsible romanticism permits the wish that peasants and villagers would opt for tradition rather than opportunity. It is surely significant that across the world and throughout centuries, they almost never do.[56] But one can still regret what is lost. And Thomas Hooker's warning cannot be shrugged off: "For if each man may do what is good in his owne eyes, proceed according to his own pleasure, so that none may crosse him or controll him by any power, there must of necessity follow the distraction and desolation of the whole."[57]

Narrowing "Success"

William James followed his comment on "the moral flabbiness born of the exclusive worship of the bitch-goddess, success" with the less well-known observation that "that—with the squalid cash interpretation put on the word success—is our national disease."[58] It was at best indecorous for a man as wealthy and prestigious as William James to castigate others' pursuit of wealth or inattentiveness to philosophy. But his concern is warranted. The American dream is susceptible to having the open-ended definition of success, which can equally include salvation or writing the great American novel, narrowed to wealth, job status, or power. Well-educated women (not to speak of men) are embarrassed to admit that they would rather raise happy children than practice corporate law; environmentalists worry that the value of a beautiful forest cannot be monetized and therefore will not be considered in regulatory decisions. Even high school seniors, for whom "having lots of money" has become increasingly important over the past two decades, overwhelmingly and increasingly agree that "people are too much concerned with material things these days."[59]

Sometimes market values colonize, rather than submerge, other values.[60] Economists designing environmental regulations assign monetary value to a stand of redwood trees, thereby cheapening (note the metaphor) the meaning of the primeval forest in the eyes of environmentalists.[61] Some feminists seek to enhance the status of women by calculating the wages due to housework and including them in the gross national product; other feminists see this move as turning loving wives and mothers into calculating *homo economici*. The problem in these and similar cases is not that the assignment of monetary worth is too high or low, but that the very process of assigning monetary worth reduces an array of values to a single thin one.

Only sentimentalism allows one to value the purity of artistic poverty over the sordidness of corporate wealth unless one made the choice after experiencing both states. But it is a serious flaw in the American dream if those who envision success in artistic or religious or altruistic terms must defend their vision as well as fight to achieve their chosen goals. Nothing in the ideology requires reducing success to money and power, but the ideology is so vulnerable to the reduction that that point must count as an internal flaw, not merely as grounds for an external attack.

The Ideology as Deception

I have argued that the American dream need not be individualistic in the narrow sense, given that one can under its rubric pursue success for one's family or community as well as for oneself. But it is highly *individual*, in that it leads one to focus on people's behaviors rather than on economic processes, environmental constraints, or political structures as the causal explanation for social orderings. That focus is not itself a flaw; it is simply an epistemological choice with methodological implications for the study of American politics. But to the degree that the focus carries a moral message, it points to a weakness at the very heart of the dream.

The idea of the blank slate in the first tenet, the almost-promise of success of the second, the reliance on personal attributes in the third, the association of failure with sin in the fourth—all these elements of the dream make it extremely difficult for Americans to see that everyone cannot simultaneously attain more than absolute success. Capitalist markets require some firms to fail; elections require some candidates and policy preferences to lose; status hierarchies must have a bottom in order to have a top. But the optimistic language of and methodological individualism built into the American dream *necessarily* deceive people about these societal operations. We need not invoke hypocrites out of Mark Twain or "blue-eyed white devils" in order to understand why some people never attain success; hypocrisy or bias only enter the picture in determining *who* fails. But our basic institutions are designed to ensure that some fail, at least relatively, and the dream does nothing to help Americans cope with or even to recognize that fact.

Few Alternative Visions

All ideologies are designed to put the best possible face on the social structure within which they operate, and all privilege some values over others. So all of the flaws I have described, damning though they may seem, must themselves be judged in light of the comparable flaws of other ideological formations. That point is intended to soften slightly the critique of the American dream, but it also raises a final problem with it.

Americans have few alternative ideologies against which to measure the distinctive virtues and flaws of the American dream. Alternatives are not completely absent: Thoreau's *Walden* has long been recognized as a sharp political challenge couched in a literary classic. "Country-party" or labor republicanism, Protestant fundamentalism, and ascriptive Americanism similarly have deep roots and on occasion strong adherents and powerful institutional manifestations.[62] But most Americans honor these alternative visions more in the breach than in the observance, if then. *Walden* is read by more students majoring in English than in political science. "Small is beautiful" and "social limits to growth" are slogans for a few, but warnings to many more.[63] And many possible visions—within-class solidarity and cross-class warfare, a military or theocratic polity pursuing collective glory, small cooperative enterprises living lightly on the land—are barely visible in the American political spectrum. In short, the political culture of the United States is largely shaped by a set of views in which the American dream is prominent, and by a set of institutions that make it even more prominent than views alone could do.[64]

THE DREAM AS A FRAMEWORK FOR SUCCESS

Tocqueville assured his readers that "up to now the Americans have happily avoided all the reefs I have just charted."[65] Some Americans continue, 150 years later, to sail free, and perhaps they always will. But some have wrecked, and some have never gotten anywhere near the boat. For those afloat, the ideology of the American dream is a vindication, a goad to further efforts, a cause for celebration—and also grounds for anxiety, guilt, and disillusionment. For the shipwrecked and drifters, the dream is a taunt, a condemnation, an object of fury—and also grounds for hope, renewed striving, and dreams for one's children.

African Americans have only recently clambered aboard Tocqueville's ship in large numbers. Equally large numbers are drowning. The rest of this book examines their views of the American dream, and whites' views of blacks' views, with the goal of evaluating the worth, actuality, and trajectory of the American dream. Only after that evaluation can we face up to what the dream really requires of us.

Chapter Two

RICH AND POOR AFRICAN AMERICANS

> The impression arose that the Negro community might be dividing. A middle class was clearly consolidating and growing, and yet the overall indicators continued to worsen, not precipitously but steadily. These two things could not be true unless a third fact—that things were falling apart at the bottom—was also true. And that meant trouble in the Northern slums.
>
> —Daniel P. Moynihan, 1967

As DANIEL MOYNIHAN pointed out almost three decades ago, understanding the African American class structure requires us to attend to four phenomena: the "overall indicators" of relative positions held by blacks and whites; the "consolidating and growing" middle class; the "falling apart at the bottom"; and the fact that "the Negro community . . . [is] dividing." In conjunction, these phenomena "mean . . . trouble in the Northern slums"—but not only there, and not only trouble.

THE OVERALL INDICATORS

African Americans are in many, but not all, ways better off than their forebears were. Whether they are also better off in comparison to white Americans depends on what is measured and how it is measured. Let us consider, respectively, arenas of unambiguous improvement, ambiguous improvement, and deterioration.

Unambiguous Improvements

African Americans' average occupational status has improved over the last few decades no matter how it is measured. Table 2.1 shows changes in blacks' and whites' "socioeconomic index score," which ranges from 7 for domestic servants and day laborers to 74 for professionals. All four race and gender groups enjoyed higher job statuses in 1980 than in 1940. In addition, blacks' job status improved relative to whites' status among both men and (especially) women.[1] The ratio of black to white men's occupational status rose from .53 to .72; the corresponding rise for women was from .36 to .84.

TABLE 2.1
Average Job Status for Employed Adults, by Race and
Gender, 1940–1980

	1940	1960	1980
Socioeconomic Index			
Black men	16	21	31
Black women	13	21	36
White men	30	36	40
White women	36	39	43

Source: Farley and Allen (1987: 264–265).

For years of schooling, too, the results are unambiguous. In 1940 whites averaged about nine years of education and blacks about six. In the succeeding fifty years, whites gained over three years and African Americans about five. Thus African Americans' absolute gain in years of formal education is large, and the relative gap between the races has declined from three years to one year.[2] Fewer students of either race drop out of high school now than did twenty years ago, and the decline in dropping out is steeper among blacks than among whites.[3]

What children learn in school matters more than how many years they sit in a classroom. Here too improvement in the "overall indicators" is clear. Blacks always score lower than whites on nationwide standardized tests, regardless of the subject, students' age, or test year. But the racial gap is getting smaller. Whereas, for example, white students' reading and mathematics scores improved somewhat between 1971 and 1990, African American students of all ages showed significant improvements. A weaker version of the same pattern obtains for science and civics. Thus the gap between whites' and blacks' proficiency in all four fields diminished.[4]

Finally, blacks are more involved in the formal political system than they were four decades ago. Barely one-tenth of southern blacks could vote for the president in 1952, but by 1984 about 55 percent did. The proportion of all voters who are black increased from 8 percent in 1964 to 10 percent in 1992.[5] Largely as a consequence, the number of black elected officials has risen from the ludicrous number of thirty-three in 1941 to over eight thousand in 1993, changing the proportion of elected officials who are black from a minute fraction to almost 2 percent.[6]

Mixed Results

Despite occupational, educational, and political gains, African Americans are not unambiguously better off than they used to be. Consider incomes: in 1967 black per capita income was about $5,400 (in 1992 dollars); the corresponding figure for whites was about $10,100. In

TABLE 2.2
Life Expectancies at Birth, by Race and Gender,
1940–1990 (in years)

	1940	1970	1990
Black men	51	61	65
Black women	69	77	78
White men	62	68	72
White women	82	81	83

Source: Farley (1992: chap. 1, fig. 1).

1992 blacks received $9,300 and whites $16,000.[7] Thus African Americans clearly have more money than their parents had. But are their incomes now more equal to whites'? In relative terms, yes, since the ratio of black incomes to white incomes increased from .53 in 1967 to .58 in 1992. In absolute terms, no, since the discrepancy in income rose from $4,700 to $6,700.[8]

Measures of wealth give similarly mixed results. The mean net worth for white households in 1991 was $112,000, compared with a paltry $27,900 for black households. But black households held only 4 to 21 percent of the net worth of white households in the 1960s and 1970s, compared with 25 to 33 percent as much at present.[9] African Americans remain dramatically less wealthy than whites, but the gap is slowly closing.

African Americans, like whites, are healthier than they used to be and live longer, as table 2.2. shows. Black women can expect to live longer than white men; thus several decades ago "the gender gap in the life span became larger than the racial gap." However, "the racial gap in mortality, after declining between [the] 1940s and the 1960s, has not gotten much smaller. . . . An extrapolation of current trends implies that the death rates of blacks will continue to be higher than those of whites into the future."[10]

Mobility across generations is yet another overall indicator that cuts both ways. Among white men, those born during the 1920s were upwardly mobile compared with their fathers; those born during the Great Depression have moved down as well as up the mobility ladder; and those born after 1936 are on balance downwardly mobile. In contrast, "successive cohorts of black men have had higher levels of occupational status relative to their fathers." Furthermore, young white men are not reaching the job levels that their background and education would lead them to expect; older white men and black men of all ages are. However—and herein lies the ambiguity—"intergenerational gains in status among blacks have been consistently lower than those enjoyed by any cohorts of white men at any age."[11]

Persistent Racial Disparities

African Americans are unambiguously gaining on white Americans in job status, education, and political involvement; they are or are not gaining economically and demographically, depending on how one interprets the data. But by some measures they are unambiguously losing ground.

Many people (some of whom are not real estate agents) consider owning one's home to be a central component of the American dream. Fewer blacks than whites own their own homes, and the disparity is growing. In 1950, 35 percent of nonwhite and 57 percent of white heads of households were homeowners; forty years later, only 9 percent more nonwhites and 11 percent more whites were. A smaller fraction of African Americans owned houses in 1990 than did whites in 1920. Houses owned by blacks are worth on average barely more than half of houses owned by whites, and the value of the former, but not of the latter, may be declining.[12]

Blacks also remain about half as likely as Latinos or Asians to live in suburbs. And despite their consistent preference for residential integration, blacks in almost all central cities remain highly segregated from non-Hispanic whites.[13] They are more racially isolated from whites than are Latinos and Asians, and high incomes or levels of education make it no easier for African Americans to move into white neighborhoods.[14]

Finally, African Americans are much more likely to become and remain unemployed than are white Americans, and the disparity is growing. Through the 1940s and early 1950s, the ratio of nonwhite to white unemployment was below 2; in the twenty years after 1955, it hovered around 2.2. But since 1977 the black/white unemployment ratio has risen as high as 2.4. Even if the earliest ratio partly reflects hidden unemployment among farm laborers, we have no grounds for supposing that the ratios are moving or will move toward equality. Jobless blacks also stay unemployed longer than jobless whites do.[15]

Thus one can tell almost any story one chooses about whether African Americans are moving toward parity with whites in their ability to pursue their dreams. They are gaining in nonmaterial resources, perhaps holding their own with regard to money, and losing in living conditions. Is that an improvement? Probably, compared with even more consistent deterioration during the previous half-century, but not certainly.

What that equivocal conclusion implies is the need to disaggregate. African Americans can pursue their dreams in some arenas of life better than in others. Similarly, some African Americans can pursue any dream more readily than can others. Let us turn, then, to the other trends that Moynihan identified in 1967 in order to make sense of the "overall indicators."

THE MIDDLE CLASS—CONSOLIDATING AND GROWING

Ebony magazine recently celebrated the "new Black middle class" as "young, vibrant, on the go, with new interests and orientations, and a bumper crop of MBA's and high-tech managers." It distinguished these "salaried workers in high-level occupations that serve the society at large" from "the old Black middle class" of "ministers, educators, doctors and small businessmen who served primarily the Black community."[16] It is this new middle class, firmly if uneasily planted in what whites consider to be the mainstream of society, that comprises most of the best-off third of blacks.[17]

Improving Status

The growth of the black middle class is most simply described in terms of income. Table 2.3 shows the changes over the past three decades. The first and second lines of the table show that the proportion of blacks who are poor or almost poor has declined by almost 10 percent, but the third and fourth lines are of most interest here. The third line shows a slightly larger percentage of African Americans now enjoying middle-class incomes than was the case in 1967; the opposite is the case for whites. The fourth line shows over twice as many well-off blacks now as twenty-five years ago, a proportionally greater rise among blacks than among whites. In all, one in four black households, compared with just under half of white households, now receives an income that provides comforts or luxuries.

African Americans who earn enough to acquire comforts or luxuries also hold more wealth than other African Americans, not only absolutely but also in comparison with whites. The median black household owns just over one-tenth as much as the median white household, but households in the top two quintiles of black income own up to 40 percent as much as white households earning a comparable amount.[18]

Measures of job status show the same pattern: the black middle class has grown considerably and is slowly gaining on the white middle class, even though it remains far smaller. In 1950, 5 percent of employed blacks were professionals or managers; by 1990, about 20 percent were. Another 20 percent held clerical or sales positions in 1990, also up from 5 percent in 1950. Thus up to two-fifths of black workers, depending on how stringently one defines a middle-class occupation, are in the middle class.[19]

An increasing number of African Americans also have middle-class educations, although here too the proportions lag behind those of whites. In 1960, 3 percent of black and 8 percent of white adults had completed college; by 1992, the comparable figures were 12 and 22 per-

TABLE 2.3
Household Income, by Race, 1967–1992 (in constant 1992 dollars;
percent making each amount)

	1967		1977		1987		1992	
	Black	White	Black	White	Black	White	Black	White
0–$15,000	45.6	23.4	41.9	22.0	41.8	20.5	42.7	21.6
$15,000–35,000	38.3	39.5	35.3	33.3	32.4	31.0	31.5	31.8
$35,000–50,000	10.2	19.8	13.0	20.1	12.4	18.5	12.8	17.7
Over $50,000	5.8	16.8	9.9	24.4	13.5	30.0	13.0	28.9
Total	100.0	100.0	100.0	100.0	100.0	100.0	100.0	100.0

Source: U.S. Bureau of the Census (1993a: B–3, B–4).

Note: Income is measured before taxes; it includes cash transfers but not in-kind benefits. These are the earliest and latest years, respectively, for which these data are available.

cent. In the lower grades, black students from "advantaged" communities are gaining on "advantaged" whites in their reading ability. The proportion of students taking the Scholastic Assessment Test (SAT) who are black is rising, and the disparity in SAT scores between whites and blacks has dropped since 1972.[20]

Mobility across Generations

One has not really succeeded in America unless one can pass the chance for success on to one's children. Until the 1960s even those few African Americans who comprised the old black middle class had great difficulty in doing so. A massive survey in 1962 found race to be "such a powerful variable that even the more modest of the class effects that stratified whites were cancelled by the skin color of blacks." Blacks, in other words, "experienced a perverse sort of egalitarianism"—neither the disadvantages of poverty nor the advantages of wealth made much difference in what they could achieve or pass on to their children.[21] Discrimination swamped everything else.

Between 1962 and 1973, however, class position began to affect mobility for blacks as it had always done for whites. "Upward mobility . . . was greatest among [black] men from the most advantaged socioeconomic backgrounds"; well-off black men thus could begin for the first time in American history to expect their success to persist and cumulate.[22] Since 1973 these trends have continued, although less dramatically.[23]

Thus the black middle class is growing, is narrowing the gap between itself and the white middle class, and is increasingly stable across generations. Roughly one-third of black families can reasonably be called middle class, compared with well below one-tenth a few decades ago and about half of white families now. The best-off third of blacks, in short, is vastly better off than the best-off third of blacks has ever been before in American history.[24]

The Poor—Falling Apart at the Bottom

Unchanging or Deteriorating Status

No sentient being can doubt the existence of a group of deeply impoverished African Americans. In 1959, 55 percent of blacks and 18 percent of whites had incomes below the poverty line; in 1992, the figures were, respectively, 33 and 12 percent. The ratio of black to white poverty has remained at 3—hardly a victory in the war on racially disproportionate poverty. Absolute numbers tell the same story: there are now about four million fewer poor whites than thirty years ago, but 686,000 *more* poor blacks.[25]

It is bad enough to be poor, but it is worse to be deeply poor or poor for a long time. One-quarter of black children, compared with 6 percent of white children, lived below half of the poverty line in 1988. (The number of destitute children declined from 1960 to 1980 but has risen since then.)[26] Black children's poverty is long as well as deep: during the past twenty years about one-third of black children remained poor for six or more years, and the number is slowly rising.[27]

Poor African Americans lack wealth as well as incomes. Although even the poorest fifth of whites have a median net worth of $10,300, the net worth of the poorest fifth of blacks is 0.[28] Furthermore, blacks with little wealth are even less likely to attain any than poor whites. Seventy-seven percent of black men in the poorest quintile of wealth holders in 1966, compared with 57 percent of comparable white men, were still in the poorest quintile in 1981.[29]

Measures of occupation, or lack thereof, tell an equally dismal story. An increasing number of men, especially black men, have no job at all. In 1960, 17 percent of civilian men of both races were unemployed or looking for jobs; by 1993, an additional 7 percent of white men and 14 percent of black men were out of the labor force. In 1968 four-fifths of poorly educated central-city black male residents held jobs; by 1992 fewer than half worked. Barely a third held full-time jobs. In the poorest neighborhoods of large cities, four-fifths of young male high school dropouts have no work.[30] As a consequence, between 1967 and 1992 an increasing proportion of black men, compared with a decreasing proportion of white men, reported receiving no income.[31]

Even holding a job does not ensure an escape from poverty. In 1992, 15 percent of African American and 6 percent of white job holders did not earn enough to get above the poverty line. To be a single mother of preschool children is itself a full-time job. But of those single mothers with young children who also worked full-time outside the home, one-fifth of blacks and one-tenth of whites were rewarded for their extraordinary efforts with incomes below the poverty line.[32]

As those figures suggest, even when they work blacks still hold a disproportionate share of the least desirable jobs. In 1950, 61 percent of black men and 72 percent of black women workers were service workers, domestics, laborers, or farm laborers, whereas 25 percent or fewer of white men and women workers were similarly employed. In 1990, about one-third of both male and female black workers were service workers or laborers, compared with two-tenths of white workers.[33]

Poor blacks come no closer to achieving their dreams of a nice place to live than of a decent income or job. Television has shown all of us the filthy, burned-out blocks of northern cities and the sewerless, tarpaper shacks of southern countrysides, and the cold data of government surveys confirm the hot images of television stories. One-third of poor black households, compared with one-seventh of poor white households, lived in substandard housing in 1985.[34] To be deemed substandard, housing must, among other criteria, show "evidence of rats" (57 percent of such units were occupied by Latinos and blacks in 1985), have "holes in the floor" (51 percent were occupied by Latinos and blacks), or have "exposed wiring" (33 percent were occupied by Latinos and blacks).[35]

Poor African Americans are increasingly likely to live among other people with such dismal housing conditions. In the 100 largest central cities, the proportion of poor non-Hispanic blacks living in neighborhoods where more than 40 percent of their neighbors were also poor rose from 28 percent in 1970 to 42 percent in 1990.[36] A likely consequence of being poor in a poor neighborhood is attending a low-quality school, with predictable consequences. In 1988 about 30 percent of poor black eighth graders were "below basic" in their reading proficiency, and about 37 percent had less than basic math proficiency. (Seven percent fewer poor whites were "below basic" readers, and 4 percent fewer were "below basic" in math.)[37] Fully half of the non-Hispanic black (and white) adults living in extreme poverty areas of large cities have not completed high school.[38]

Another likely consequence of being poor in a poor neighborhood is being a victim of crime. On average, Americans are safer now than they were twenty years ago. But suburban and rural dwellers are becoming safer from theft and household crime (although not from violence) at a faster rate than are urban residents, who over the same period were increasingly likely to be people of color. The ratio of urban to suburban theft increased from 1.0 to 1.3 between 1973 and 1992, and the ratio of urban to suburban household crime increased from 1.2 to 1.6. City dwellers have became even more likely than rural residents to suffer from crime; the victimization ratios rose from 1.4 to 1.6 for theft, and from 1.6 to 1.9 for household crimes.[39]

Mobility across Generations

For the well-off, being able to pass on one's status to one's children is a critical element of the American dream. For the poor, *not* passing on one's status is equally critical. But it is an element of the dream that eludes many poor African Americans. In 1962, 43 percent of the grown sons of white men who had held "lower manual" jobs held similar jobs; by 1973, that figure had declined by 3 percent. Among blacks, the decline was steeper but the absolute level remained much higher: 71 percent of laborers' sons in 1962 and 61 percent in 1973 were also laborers. One-third of a 1978 sample of young adults were black, but almost half of the bottom quintile were.[40] Finally, parents who are poor enough to need welfare are disproportionately likely to have dependent children; the probability that the daughter of a black recipient of aid to families with dependent children (AFDC) has a child and receives welfare herself is .486, compared with a probability of .136 for the daughter of a nonrecipient.[41]

THE DIVIDING COMMUNITY

> The gap between haves and have-nots widened strikingly; and the most rapid widening was among Negroes—between those outside the slums who were rising, beginning finally to cash in on the American dream, and those still in the hard-core ghetto, on limited rations of income and hope. . . . Not only distance is building up between the two poles, but tension as well—as with electrodes approaching a sparking point.
>
> —Walter Williams, 1967

Although these words depict Cleveland from 1960 to 1965, they could, slightly modernized, be my own. Growing inequality is not the problem. After all, only a fanatical egalitarian would oppose the move from equally shared poverty to inequality caused by the fact that some have gained wealth. But polarization—improving conditions for some ac-

TABLE 2.4

Share of Families' Aggregate Income Held by Richest and Poorest Fifths,
by Race, 1947–1992

	1947		1967		1987		1992	
	Nonwhite	*White*	*Black*	*White*	*Black*	*White*	*Black*	*White*
Poorest fifth	4.3	5.5	4.7	5.8	3.3	5.1	3.0	4.9
Richest fifth	45.3	42.5	44.6	40.9	47.7	43.1	48.8	43.8
Gini index	.406	.366	.400	.349	.447	.380	.462	.389

Sources: 1947: U.S. Bureau of the Census (1989: 42–43); 1967–1991: U.S. Bureau of the Census (1993a: B–13, B–14).

companied by or at the expense of deteriorating conditions for others—
is the problem, and not only in Cleveland.

We can begin to examine this point by comparing the share of aggregate income held by various fractions of the population at different
times (table 2.4). Three points are important with regard to the table:
first, rich blacks have always held a larger share of their race's income
than have rich whites, and poor blacks have always held a smaller share
of their race's income than have poor whites. Second, the disparities
within both races are increasing. Third, and most important here, the
income disparity among blacks is increasing at a faster rate. The Gini
indices summarize that phenomenon, and the rest of the table demonstrates it more precisely: the richest fifth of whites lost, then gained income and have ended up 3 percent better off than they were forty years
ago. The poorest fifth of whites gained, then lost income and are now 10
percent worse off. Africans Americans followed the same trajectories,
but at a faster rate. By 1992 the poorest quintile had lost 30 percent of
its meager 1947 income, and the richest quintile had gained 8 percent
over its comparatively high 1947 income.[42]

Table 2.5 translates abstract shares of aggregate income into actual
dollar amounts. In the first period the richest and poorest quintiles
gained equally as a proportion of their previous income, although the
wealthy gained much more in absolute dollars. Blacks gained proportionally almost as much as whites, but their actual incomes grew much
less. Thus this period can be interpreted as moving either toward equal
overall improvement or away from racial and class equality, depending
on which set of figures one looks at.

The second period allows for no ambiguity of interpretation. The
poor, especially among African Americans, lost substantial ground,
while the wealthy barely held their own. This was a period of unambiguous growth in inequality.

TABLE 2.5
Income Gains of Top and Bottom Quintiles of Families, by Race,
1967–1992 (in 1992 dollars)

	Black		White	
	Income Gained	% Increase over Period	Income Gained	% Increase over Period
1967–1972				
Bottom fifth	$711	13%	$1,619	16%
Top fifth	7,064	14	10,797	15
1973–1982				
Bottom fifth	−1,426	−23	−1,402	−11
Top fifth	1,098	2	2,953	3
1983–1992				
Bottom fifth	−558	−12	570	5
Top fifth	8,950	15	12,966	15

Note: 1967 is the first year for which these data are available.
Source: U.S. Bureau of the Census (1993a: B–13, B–14).

The third period, from 1983 to 1992, saw yet another step away from equality, into polarization. The poorest fifth of African Americans *lost* almost as large a share of their income as the richest fifth *gained* of theirs. The wealthiest fifth gained a large amount in absolute terms as well. Well-off blacks did as well proportionally, although not absolutely, as well-off whites. Poor whites gained a little, whereas well-off whites surged ahead. In short, whites became more unequal; blacks polarized.[43]

Other indicators of well-being show the same pattern of growing polarization between well-off and poor African Americans. Consider housing, for example: in 1980 the index of residential dissimilarity between classes was higher among blacks (.50) than among whites (.39). Residential separation by class had increased slightly among African Americans during the 1970s, even though it decreased slightly among whites, Asians, and Latinos.[44] Or jobs: white employers penalize black applicants for low-skill jobs for being black even after all of their specific traits are taken into consideration, but they reward black applicants for high-skill jobs for being black. Furthermore, African American men in the top fourth of the occupational status distribution have seen a consistent improvement in the prestige of and rewards accruing to their jobs over the past two decades. But the job quality of those in the bottom quartile has fallen from their already very low starting points.[45] Even controlling for experience, the wage gap between black and white women with twelve or fewer years of education grew between 1973 and 1989, whereas it declined between black and white women with a college education.[46]

TABLE 2.6
Crime Victimization, by Race and Class, 1976–1992
(per 1,000 people)

	Violence				Theft			
	1976	1981	1986	1992	1976	1981	1986	1992
Total	32.6	35.3	28.1	32.1	96.1	85.1	67.5	59.2
Blacks								
Poor	50.5	57.3	44.4	60.1	64.5	71.4	55.3	59.2
Well-off	40.5	34.2	19.6	35.0	137.6	116.4	82.8	70.2
Whites								
Poor	39.1	45.2	46.0	44.7	81.5	74.7	69.1	60.3
Well-off	26.6	28.2	19.9	20.7	117.8	104.1	75.9	70.0

Source: U.S. Department of Justice (1994c: 247, 267), and earlier years of the same volume.

Note: "Violence" includes rape, robbery, and assault (but not homicide, which represents about 1% of all violent crime). "Theft" includes personal larceny. No comparable data are available for "household crimes," which include burglary, larceny, and motor vehicle theft. These are the earliest and latest years, respectively, for which these data are available.

Polarization is also occurring in the likelihood of being a victim of crime, as table 2.6 shows. The number of well-off Americans who are victims of violence is steadily *decreasing*, while the number of poor Americans who are victimized by violence is steadily *increasing*. The pattern holds for both blacks and whites, although the former are always more likely to be victims of violence than are the latter. Poor blacks not only began the period with the highest rates of victimization from violence, but they are also suffering from the greatest increase. (The pattern is different for theft. The well-off used to be dramatically more likely than the poor to suffer from theft; they are now only slightly more likely to be victimized, and all groups suffer from less theft now than they did two decades ago. Here is a pattern to celebrate.)

African Americans are becoming more disparate politically and demographically as well as economically and socially. Through the 1960s and 1970s, poorly educated blacks outvoted poorly educated whites (mainly because black women voted at very high rates). But by the late 1980s that disparity was reversed. Furthermore, although overall participation rates dropped from the 1960s to the 1980s, the decline in voting among the poorly educated was greater than the corresponding decline among the well-educated. Well-educated blacks vote, campaign, organize, and petition at the same rates as well-educated whites. Thus the worst-off in general are losing political influence, and the worst-off blacks in particular are losing the most.[47]

Even birth and death are increasingly affected by the interaction of race and class. "The effects of age, family structure, and socioeconomic variables on age at first childbirth are stronger among blacks than among whites. . . . An increased internal stratification of the black population [with regard to child-bearing] may be taking place." At the other end of life, in the two decades after 1960, the disparity in mortality rates between well-educated and poorly educated black men doubled. It rose by 30 percent between well-educated and poorly educated black women. (The growth in disparity was the same for white as for black men but lower for white than for black women.)[48]

Improvement at the top combined with worsening at the bottom is a disaster for the American dream. It radically undermines the first and second tenets and raises the stakes for the third and fourth. It adds class conflict within races to racial conflict across and within classes. Polarization is especially disastrous for the dream if it is concentrated in the race that is already most tenuously attached to the dominant ideology. And that is what is occurring.

CONCLUSION

Moynihan worried about "trouble in the Northern slums." Williams worried about "tension . . . building up . . . as with electrodes approaching a sparking point." The explosions in Miami in 1980 and in Los Angeles in 1992 suggest that these worries were well-founded. Yet we know that participants in the riots of the 1960s were not disproportionately poor blacks who saw other blacks getting ahead of them and were therefore playing out the last scene of Hirschman's tunnel effect. Indeed, the rioters were not especially likely to be poor or jobless.[49] So we must beware any easy assumption that being on the losing end of increasing polarization translates into anger or rebellion. The move from social condition to purposive action is mediated by beliefs and perceptions, to which we now turn.

PART TWO

The Three Paradoxes

"WHAT'S ALL THE FUSS ABOUT?": BLACKS' AND WHITES' BELIEFS ABOUT THE AMERICAN DREAM

THE PREFACE claimed that America's racial situation threatened the future of the ideology of the American dream in two distinct ways. This chapter focuses on the first challenge—blacks' and whites' increasing divergence in their descriptions of and explanations for America's racial situation. The two races share an overwhelming support for the American dream as a prescription for their own and other Americans' lives. The races disagree only slightly when people consider the American dream as a description of their own lives, but they disagree considerably when people consider the dream as a description of others' lives. African Americans increasingly believe that racial discrimination is worsening and that it inhibits their race's ability to participate in the American dream; whites increasingly believe that discrimination is lessening and that blacks have the same chance to participate in the dream as whites. I call that finding the paradox of "what's all the fuss about?"

THE AMERICAN DREAM AS PRESCRIPTION

Americans are close to unanimous in endorsing the idea of the American dream. Virtually all agree that all citizens should have political equality and that everyone in America warrants equal educational opportunities and equal opportunities in general. Three-fourths or more of both races agree that all people warrant equal respect, that skill rather than need should determine wages, that "America should promote equal opportunity for all" rather than "equal outcomes," that "everyone should try to amount to more than his parents did," and that they are ambitious themselves. Seventy percent of black, and 80 percent of white, Californians agree that "trying to get ahead" is very important in "making someone a true American." An even more overwhelming majority of black than white Americans endorse self-sufficiency as one of their primary goals. These views are, if possible, even more strongly and uniformly expressed now than four decades ago.[1]

Sophisticated elites as well as the gullible public hold these views. At least 85 percent of leaders of all groups—including blacks and feminists, labor leaders and businessmen, Democrats and Republicans—endorse equality of opportunity over equality of results. And at least seven of ten black leaders (and almost all leaders of some other groups) think earnings should depend on ability rather than being distributed equally.[2] Even purportedly rebellious or cynical youth concur. Three-quarters of white youths, and even more black youths, see "fair treatment for all" (tenet 1) and "self-reliance" (tenet 3) as extremely important values; half of the former and two-thirds of the latter similarly rank "helping the less fortunate" (tenet 4); one-fourth of whites and over half of blacks rank "economic success" (tenet 2) equally highly.[3]

Most Americans not only endorse the American dream in general, but also increasingly endorse its appropriateness for both blacks and whites. Although a majority did not do so in the 1950s, by the 1980s almost all whites agreed that blacks should be able to attend the same schools as whites, have the same chances for jobs, live where they choose, and otherwise have the same freedom of movement and personal choice. Blacks, of course, agreed in even larger proportions, as they have done for decades.[4]

"Is" is a more stringent test than "ought." Nevertheless, eight-tenths of blacks and nine-tenths of whites agree that "the American dream [is] alive today." The more pointed and difficult question, whether "the American dream has real meaning to you personally," is still answered affirmatively by six-tenths of blacks and seven-tenths of whites. And slightly *more* blacks than whites agree that "there are more opportunities for Americans today than in the past." Thus it may, upon reflection, not be so surprising that *more* blacks than whites (89 to 70 percent) deem it very important for public schools to teach "the common heritage and values that we share as Americans."[5]

BELIEFS ABOUT ONE'S OWN CHANCES TO ACHIEVE A DREAM

Whites and blacks resemble each other almost as much when the topic shifts from general endorsement of the American dream to interpretations of one's own particular life course.

The Second Tenet

Consider, for example, the conviction that one can reasonably anticipate success. In the mid-1960s a study of "values . . . most likely to facilitate achievement and social mobility" found, to the author's astonishment, that blacks scored higher than Italians and French Canadians and similar to Protestants and Greeks. Only Jews in this sample scored higher.[6] And, as table 3.1. shows,[7] this hapless researcher's findings are not anomalous; blacks have always been at least as determined as whites that they or their children will succeed.[8]

As the table shows, from the 1940s forward, majorities of both races have anticipated success for themselves and their families, just as the second tenet of the American dream prescribes. Members of both races are as sanguine now as they were four decades ago. Furthermore, the two races have been generally close to one another even on surveys that show unusually high or low levels of optimism. And when the races do diverge substantially, blacks are always the more confident.

In fact, African Americans' optimism persists even when they recognize their comparatively worse circumstances. Comparing panels 1 and 2 of table 3.1 shows that African Americans are more disproportionately optimistic for their children than they are for themselves. More precise queries elicit the same unwarranted optimism: fewer black than white Chicagoans think their neighborhood has improved over the past five years, and about three times as many complain of high crime and gang activity. Yet more blacks than whites expect their neighborhood to improve. Similarly, fewer than half as many black as white Chicagoans own or have ever owned a business, but more are "very likely" to start one in the next five years.[9]

The Third Tenet

Blacks and whites also come close to agreement on the third tenet—that the key to success lies in one's own hands—when they consider their own lives. In the mid-1960s almost six in ten members of both races endorsed "plan[ning] your life a good way ahead" rather than relying on luck, and over eight in ten blacks (compared with slightly fewer whites) insisted that "no weakness or difficulty can hold us back if we have enough willpower." By the mid-1980s more African Americans were prepared to admit a partial role for fate, but still half (compared with two-thirds of whites) insisted that their life course reflected solely their own abilities.[10]

The First Tenet

These findings are especially surprising in light of divergence between the races in their beliefs about the existence and effects of discrimination. The point is easily made: whites see little and lessening discrimination, and blacks feel themselves to be the objects of a lot, even increasing amounts, of discrimination. A majority of blacks always report discrimination in their lives, and in 1970 a quarter experienced it "almost every day of my life." A 1980 survey of workers provides illustrative detail: For

TABLE 3.1

How Good Are Your Chances to Pursue the American Dream? by Race
(percent agreeing; sample N in appendix A)

	Black	White	Difference

1. Your Own Prospects

1947: "Your opportunities to succeed are better than . . . those your father had."*

| | 68 | 70 | −2 |

1954: "Life will be better for you . . . in the next few years than it is now." (percent agreeing of those with opinion)

| | 64 | 61 | 3 |

1968: "[Over] the next few years, . . . you expect your family's financial situation to get better."

| | 79 | 54 | 25 |

1970: "Ambitious" is among those adjectives which "best describe yourself."

| | 29 | 25 | 4 |

1976: Your own opportunities to succeed are better than your parents' were.

| | 74 | 61 | 13 |

1986a: "As far as the future is concerned, . . . you feel . . . very optimistic" about:

your own quality of life	41	44	−3
your family's financial outlook	29	26	−3
opportunities for you to get ahead	38	30	8

1986a: "How far along the road to your American Dream do you think you will ultimately get?" (9 or 10 on 10-point scale)

| | 51 | 47 | 4 |

1987: "The way things are in America, people like me and my family have a good chance of improving our standard of living."

| | 63 | 71 | −8 |

1989: "My opportunities for advancement [in my main job] are high."

| | 34 | 35 | −1 |

1990: "How likely is it that you will ever be rich?" (very and fairly likely)

| | 39 | 25 | 14 |

1991: "In the next five years, how likely are you to be promoted?" (very likely or likely)

| | 43 | 40 | 3 |

2. Your Children's Prospects

1947: "Your son's opportunities to succeed will be better than those you have had."*

| | 75 | 62 | 13 |

TABLE 3.1 (*cont.*)

	Black	White	Difference
1976: Your children's opportunities to succeed will be better than your own.			
	79	56	23
1986a: "A generation from now . . . the American Dream will be easier to attain than today . . . or about the same."			
	48	43	5
1986a: "As far as the future is concerned, . . . you feel . . . very optimistic" about:			
quality of life for the next generation	23	16	7
opportunities for the next generation to get ahead	32	23	9
1986b: "Are you very optimistic . . . about your children's future?" (yes)			
	62	50	12

* "National total" instead of "White"; men only.

Source: 1947: Erskine (1969a: 148); 1954: Pettigrew (1964: 184–85); 1968: Campbell and Schuman (1968: var. 160); 1970: Harris (1970a: var. 22.6; 1970b: var. 20F); 1976: Schlozman and Verba (1979: 172); 1986a: Roper (1986: vars. 10–14, 61, 64); 1986b: Harris (1986b: 152); 1987: GSS (1987: var. 508); 1989: GSS (1989: var 556C); 1990: ABC News/*Washington Post* (1990: var. 10); 1991: GSS (1990–91: var. 420).

two-fifths, being black kept them from "the really good jobs"; one-fifth claimed that because of their race they had not been hired for a particular job, had been treated "unfairly" or "badly" at work, got worse jobs than whites in their current workplace, and had been given worse jobs than whites in their previous workplace. One-seventh had been denied a promotion.[11]

It is possible, of course, that some of these insults and denials either did not take place or did so for reasons having nothing to do with race. Nevertheless, blacks see themselves as engaged in a constant battle against racial discrimination; whites simply have no corresponding experience.[12]

The Fourth Tenet

What gives the American dream its moral power is the fourth tenet, that success is justified because (and only when) it is associated with virtue. When they think about their own lives, both races, especially African Americans, are committed to this claim. In 1986 over two-thirds of whites and three-fourths of blacks agreed that good relationships with family and friends, commitment to religious beliefs, and social utility are all "very important element[s] of success." At most only half of both races defined success as fame, power, or wealth.[13] Two decades earlier, more members of both races were proud to be Americans because of the virtues of our nation—its helpfulness, love of peace, and religious character—than because of its wealth or power.[14]

In short, black and white Americans occupy the same moral domain when they think about the American dream as an ethical imperative, and they occupy almost the same perceptual domain when they think about the validity of the American dream in their own lives. Up to now we have only one hint of serious disagreement—beliefs about how much discrimination blacks face in their daily lives.

BELIEFS ABOUT OTHERS' CHANCES TO ACHIEVE THEIR DREAMS

Probing that hint, however, opens a floodgate. When Americans look at the prospects of others or at the overall pattern of racial interaction, African Americans are increasingly dismayed at the height of racial barriers to the American dream while whites are increasingly gratified by the decline of those barriers.[15]

The First Tenet

Let us begin with beliefs about the first tenet's claim of equal opportunity to pursue one's dream. African Americans are a little more skeptical of the claim in general, since about 10 percent fewer blacks than whites agree that "a worker's child has . . . some chance to get ahead" or that "chances for success are distributed fairly."[16] But blacks and whites diverge more sharply when they consider racial discrimination.

Blacks see more racial discrimination than do whites. Whites' perceptions of racial discrimination varied widely in the 1960s, and seldom do more than a third now believe that blacks continue to experience racist treatment in jobs, housing, the media, or the criminal justice system. Blacks saw it then and continue to see it now.[17] For example, only a handful of whites think that more than half of whites share the attitudes of the Ku Klux Klan; a quarter of blacks see more than half of whites as Klan sympathizers. In that context it is not surprising that over half of blacks but only a quarter to a third of whites think our nation is moving toward two separate and unequal societies.[18]

Whites, in fact, are increasingly convinced that racial equality is growing in the United States. In the mid-1960s, 30 to 45 percent (depending on the year and the wording of the question) felt that the nation was making progress in solving its racial problems; by the 1970s, 50 to 70 percent concurred, and by 1988, fully 87 percent of whites believed that "in the past 25 years, the country has moved closer to equal opportunity among the races."[19] African Americans, meanwhile, are becoming increasingly discouraged on the same point. The proportion of blacks who see increasing racial equality *declined* from between 50 and 80 percent in the mid-1960s to between 20 and 45 percent in the 1980s. In some surveys up to half claim that the situation of blacks has *worsened* since some referent point in the past.[20]

One example will demonstrate this striking divergence. From 1988 to 1993 the proportion of African American New Yorkers who said race relations in their city were good increased from 19 percent to 34 percent. The corresponding proportion of white New Yorkers declined from 28 percent to 22 percent. In 1994, however, a majority of whites who perceived any recent change thought New York's race relations had *improved* recently; a majority of blacks who perceived change thought relations had *worsened*. Thus no matter what direction opinion is moving, blacks and whites are following opposite trajectories. Racial divergence, not merely growing black pessimism, is the underlying phenomenon.[21]

Divergence that follows the pattern of "what's all the fuss about?" remains, however, much more common. Thus in the late 1950s and 1960s, roughly half of whites expected racial integration to occur in the near future. Since the late 1970s, as many as two-thirds or more expect further racial progress or complete racial equality soon.[22] But as whites see an ever-more-equal future, blacks become more pessimistic. In the mid-1960s up to three-fourths of blacks anticipated racial integration and full racial equality sometime in the future; since the late 1970s, that proportion has dropped to two-fifths or fewer.[23]

Most importantly, the races differ on the specific question, crucial to the first tenet of the American dream, of whether racial discrimination affects Americans' life chances. Table 3.2 shows the survey responses.

In the 1960s a majority, or at least a plurality, of blacks were optimistic about blacks' chances to succeed. Their conviction was exceeded only by whites' (if we can rely on one survey item). By the 1980s most blacks were *not* optimistic about blacks' chances to succeed. Whites remained much more convinced of blacks' equal chances, and throughout the three decades generally a majority of whites agreed that race did not impede blacks' attainment of their dreams.

These results are critical for the viability of the American dream. The first tenet is the foundation of our nation's faith in liberty and equality for all. Absent disparate views on this tenet, disputes over the rest of the American dream lose much of their racial edge. But given the disparate views evident in table 3.2, one cannot talk about the meaning or future of the ideology of the American dream without also talking about race.

TABLE 3.2

Does Racial Discrimination Inhibit Blacks' Participation in the American Dream? by Race (percent agreeing; sample N in appendix A)

	Black	White	Difference (Black–White)
1. 1960s			
"Compared to five years ago, . . . white people have changed their attitude about Negro rights for the better."			
1963	52	—	—
1966	58	—	—
1969	54	—	—
"In the next five years, . . . the attitude of white people about Negro rights will get better."			
1963	73	—	—
1966	69	—	—
1969	61	—	—
1964: "Negroes who want to work hard can get ahead just as easily as anyone else."			
a:	48	66	–18
b:	64	—	—
1966: "A Negro high school student with good grades has as good a chance . . . or a better chance of getting into a top college than a white student with the same grades."			
	44	—	—
1966: "A Negro college graduate with good grades has as good a chance . . . or a better chance of getting into a top . . ."			
law school	43	—	—
medical school	43	—	—
engineering school	40	—	—
scientific school	37	—	—
1968: "If a young Negro works hard enough, . . . he or she can usually get ahead in this country in spite of prejudice and discrimination. . . ."			
	78	—	—
2. 1980s–1990s			
Compared with whites, blacks have equal or greater opportunity to get ahead generally.			
1986	39	59	–20
1987	46	59	–13
1988b	50	70	–20
1988c*	28	58	–30
1988c*	30	39	–9
1991c	55	67	–12

TABLE 3.2 (*cont.*)

	Black	White	Difference (Black–White)
2. 1980s–1990s (*cont.*)			
Compared with whites, blacks have equal or greater educational opportunity.			
1988a	47	73	−26
1989**	32	59	−27
1989**	40	67	−27
1991b	56	83	−27
Compared with whites, blacks have equal or greater job opportunity.			
1988a	28	64	−36
1988b	15	46	−31
1989	12	44	−32
1991a	10	46	−36
1991b	40	69	−29
1991d†	33	60	−27
Compared with whites, blacks have equal or greater opportunity for promotion to supervisory or managerial jobs.			
1988a††	14	43	−29
1988a††	13	36	−23
1988b	35	54	−19
1991a	20	37	−17
1991b	44	71	−27
1989: Compared with whites, blacks have equal or greater opportunity to hold elective political office.			
	22	45	−23

* The first question refers to current opportunities; the second to achieving equal opportunity in your lifetime.
** The first question refers to "a good education"; the second to "college admission."
† The question asks about "good jobs and education."
†† The first question refers to managerial, and the second to supervisory, positions.

Sources: 1963: Brink and Harris (1964: 130, 234); 1964a: Survey Research Center, Berkeley (1964: var. 13R); 1964b: Marx (1964: var. 10h); 1966: Harris (1966a: vars. 21b, 21c, 27c, 27e); 1968: Campbell and Schuman (1968: var. 273); 1969: Goldman (1969: 252); 1986: Roper (1986: var. 38); 1987: GSS (1987: var. 507I); 1988a: derived from Harris (1989b: 104, 106, 159, 160, 198, 200, 256, 257); 1988b: derived from Harris (1988: ques. A, D, F); 1988c: Media General/AP (1988: vars. RC01, RC03); 1989: NBC News (1989: vars. 14, 27, 71, 80); 1991a: ABC News/*Washington Post* (1991: vars. 42, 44); 1991b: Gallup (1991b: vars. 8, 10, 25); 1991c: Sniderman et al. (1991: vars. skin, sk2); 1991d: *Los Angeles Times* (1991b: Q50).

The Second Tenet

It follows logically that those who think discrimination is slight, declining, and unimportant in its consequences would anticipate more success for the less favored race than those who think discrimination is great, increasing, and potent in its consequences. And data support logic, for a change; whites have always been convinced of rapid black economic progress. In 1966 over two-thirds of whites declared blacks to be "moving too fast" or "asking for more than they are ready for."[24] By the 1990s whites' main response to black aspirations had shifted from denigration to satisfaction, but their conviction that these aspirations were likely to be fulfilled had not changed.[25]

Blacks, however, have traditionally felt and continue to feel frustrated with the past and pessimistic about the future prospects of their race. For example, in 1989 only 45 percent of blacks (compared with over 70 percent of whites) thought opportunities for blacks had improved during the 1980s; a fifth of blacks but only a handful of whites thought opportunities had worsened. Roughly the same proportions were optimistic or pessimistic about prospects in the decade to come.[26]

The political arena resembles the economic arena: most whites but few blacks believe that blacks can reasonably anticipate political success. In the 1960s no more than 6 percent of whites thought progress in promoting civil rights was too slow, compared with over half of blacks. By 1988 the proportion of impatient whites had risen to just over 20 percent, whereas a majority of blacks remained frustrated at the pace of civil rights progress.[27] More generally, whites have more faith than blacks that political officials can be brought to attend to the needs and wants of ordinary citizens.[28]

The Third Tenet

Blacks and whites differ as much over the third tenet—that the key to success lies in one's own hands—as over the first two when they focus on people other than themselves. We saw above that blacks are almost as likely as whites to attribute their own success (or lack thereof) to their own abilities. Nevertheless, they are less likely than whites to attribute the success or failure of other Americans to ability rather than to fate or birth. For example, from 1972 through 1991, up to 70 percent of whites compared with 50 to 60 percent of blacks agreed that people get ahead through hard work rather than through luck or help.[29] Conversely, blacks are at least twice as likely as whites to claim that having wealthy or well-educated parents, having political and personal connections, or being of the right religion, region, political conviction, or sex are crucial for getting ahead in life. Blacks are almost three times as likely as whites to agree that "society gives some people a head start and holds others back" (although a majority of both races also agree that hard work is the chief determinant of success).[30]

As table 3.3 shows, however, the two races disagree most sharply over the explanation for blacks' success or lack thereof.[31] This table is not hard to interpret; whites have always been more likely than African Americans to attribute racial inequality to flaws within individual blacks or in the black community. This is hardly surprising, if only because everyone is more likely to attribute others' failings to the others' rather than to their own flaws. (If surveyors ever asked parallel questions about the problems of whites, we would presumably see the opposite pattern in the responses.) Perhaps the only surprise in this table is that the racial gap is not larger. In some surveys up to half of blacks were willing to accept responsibility for their race's lack of success—perhaps the most persuasive indicator yet of the strength of the ideology of the American dream.

The Fourth Tenet

Just as blacks are slightly more likely than whites to associate virtue with success in their own lives, they are a little more inclined to judge others' lives in moral terms. Blacks worry a bit more even than whites do that drugs and crime threaten the future of the American dream.[32] They are, however, a little more likely to absolve the poor from and accuse the rich of sinfulness.[33] And when they focus on the virtue of their own race, blacks are ambivalent. The most pointed set of survey questions addresses the moral standing of what Harold Cruse calls "an *empty class* that has flowered into social prominence *without a clearly defined social mission*."[34] That is, are successful blacks also virtuous, if virtue is defined as concern for others of their race? Table 3.4 gives the relevant results.

African Americans, and whites for that matter, agree that blacks *should* share responsibility for others of their race, but both groups are split on whether they actually do. We have too few questions, never mind data over time or comparable questions about whites' collective racial responsibility, to say more about beliefs in the fourth tenet. Nevertheless, survey data on the first three tenets give us enough material to articulate the first racially based threat to the American dream.

IMPLICATIONS OF BLACKS' AND WHITES' BELIEFS FOR THE AMERICAN DREAM

The fact that more whites than blacks see blacks' failure as their own fault reinforces whites' belief that discrimination is slight and unimportant and that blacks can reasonably anticipate success. Conversely,

TABLE 3.3
Are African Americans Responsible for Their Low Status? by Race
(percent agreeing; sample N in appendix A)

	Black	White	Difference (Black–White)
1. 1940s–1960s			
1948: Disparagement of fellow blacks			
	11	—	—
1961: "On the whole, . . . white people try to get ahead more than Negroes."			
	60	83	–23
1964: "Generally speaking, Negroes are lazy and don't like to work hard."			
a:	8	40	–32
b:	17	—	—
2. 1980s–1990s			
On average, blacks have worse jobs, income, and housing than whites. . . . The differences are due to . . . lack of motivation.			
1981	47	58	–11
1983	45	56	–11
1985–86	34	59	–25
1988a	14	26	–12
1989a	43	44	–1
1989b	42	49	–7
1988–89	33	58	–25
1990–91	40	59	–19
1991c	43	51	–8
1991d*	16	28	–12
1992c**	19	10	9
Many of the problems which blacks in this country have today are brought on by blacks themselves.			
1978	20	42	–22
1981	50	73	–23
1986a	47	—	—
1988b	30	29	1
1989a	52	56	–4
1991d*	9	18	–9
1992c**	45	55	–10
Black people are not achieving equality as fast as they could because many whites don't want them to get ahead. (disagree)			
1981	20	47	–27
1986a	18	—	—
1989a	20	52	–32
1992a	20	46	–26
"If blacks would try harder, they could be just as well off as whites."			
1989a	60	60	0
1992a	51	38	13

TABLE 3.3 (*cont.*)

	Black	White	Difference (Black–White)
Blacks are more to blame than whites for blacks' problems.			
1991a	9	18	–9
1991b	25	53	–26
1992b	32	54	–22

1991a: "Most black parents don't teach their children the self-discipline and skills it takes to get ahead in America."

	Black	White	Difference
	24	21	3

* Coded from open-ended responses. ** Youth, aged 15–24.

Sources: 1948: derived from Noel (1964: 81); 1961: Matthews and Prothro (1961: var. 391); 1964a: Survey Research Center, Berkeley (1964: var. 13P); 1964b: Marx (1964: var. 10K); 1978: CBS News/*NYT* Poll (1978: var. 18); 1981, 1986a: Sigelman and Welch (1991: 91); 1983: Lewis and Schneider (1983: 13); 1985–86, 1988–89, 1990–91: GSS (1985–86, 1988–89, 1990–91: var. 266D); 1988a: Harris (1989b: 162; 1989c: 234); 1988b: Gallup (1988: var. 10); 1989a: ABC News/*Washington Post* (1989: vars. 21.4, 22.2, 22.3, 22.7); 1989b: NBC News (1989: var. 81.4); 1991a: Sniderman et al. (1991: vars. blam, kid2); 1991b: Gallup (1991b: var. 7); 1991c: *Los Angeles Times* (1991b: var. 63); 1991d: Knight (1992: tables 2, 3b); 1992a: *Washington Post* (1992: vars. 3a, 3b); 1992b: Gallup (1992: var. 14); 1992c: People for the American Way (1992: 76–77).

TABLE 3.4
Are Successful Blacks Virtuous? by Race (percent agreeing; sample N in appendix A)

	Black	White	Difference (Black–White)
1988b: "Middle-class blacks have an obligation to help poorer blacks."			
	76	54	22

"Black people who have 'made it' are doing a lot to improve the social and economic position of poor blacks."

	Black	White	Difference
1984	49	—	—
1988a*	66	—	—

1988b: "Most middle-class blacks . . . do as much as they should to help improve conditions for poorer blacks."**

	Black	White	Difference
	22	22	0

1988c: "Blacks who have achieved middle-class status have . . . tended to be less understanding about the lot of less privileged blacks." (disagree)

	Black	White	Difference
	43	48	–5

* Reinterview of 1984 respondents. ** Classes measured by education.

Sources: 1984: Brown et al. (1994: table 15.1, 1984); 1988a: ibid. (table 15.1, 1988); 1988b: Gallup (1988: var. 9); 1988c: Harris (1989b: 142; 1989c: 171).

the fact that more blacks see blacks' failure as due to forces beyond their control—or due to whites in particular—reinforces blacks' belief that discrimination is powerful and pervasive and that blacks cannot anticipate success. More analytically, the beliefs of each race about the first, second, and third tenets are internally consistent, but externally contradictory.

That finding implies a powerful challenge to the ideology of the American dream. Whites believe it works for everyone; blacks believe it works only for those not of their race. Whites are angry that blacks refuse to see the fairness and openness of the system; blacks are angry that whites refuse to see the biases and blockages of the system. If that disparity persists or worsens, as it has every appearance of doing, the American dream cannot maintain its role as a central organizing belief of all Americans.[35]

Whites' Quandary

But this is only the first challenge to the American dream. Adding the findings about how the dream applies to one's own life produces a curious inconsistency within each race that generates yet more challenges to it. Consider whites' quandary first: although whites are *more* sure than blacks that discrimination is not a problem (tenet 1), *more* sure that blacks are increasingly able to succeed (tenet 2), *more* sure that people's future lies within their own control (tenet 3), and *more* sure that they control their own fate (tenet 3), they are *less* optimistic about their own future (tenet 2).[36] These reasons combine to make blacks' continued complaints about glass ceilings or hiring biases ring false to whites. It is only a short step from here to the view, held by one-tenth to one-third of whites, that compared with whites blacks have more opportunities, are less vulnerable to economic upheaval, receive better health care, are treated better in the courts and the media, and are more likely to obtain good jobs and be admitted to good colleges.[37] It is only another short step, for a few, to global racial hostility.

And the quandary itself is deeply puzzling and destabilizing. If whites believe that they control their own future as blacks control theirs, why do whites not anticipate as much success for themselves as blacks do? Perhaps because they know that they are less talented or hardworking. But prejudice and self-esteem militate against that answer. So does the fact that blacks on average are poorer and less well employed, therefore presumably *less* talented or hardworking by the logic of the third tenet. Then could something other than talent and hard work—bad luck or externally imposed barriers—determine the degree to which people achieve their dreams? That answer is equally unacceptable to most whites because it contradicts both the claim that motivation determines outcomes and the claim that discrimination does not inhibit blacks' chances to succeed.

Whites are left at an impasse, which possibly explains the emotional charge of some whites' racial views. *Something* is wrong with the American dream, and the problem is associated with blacks in some way. But identifying what is wrong and how blacks are implicated in it is a difficult and thankless task for which they receive almost no institutional support.[38] It is far easier to cling to the dream, insist that it really works, and find someone to blame for the lacunae.

Blacks' Quandary

African Americans face the opposite quandary. They are *more* sure than whites that racial discrimination inhibits black Americans (tenet 1), *more* pessimistic about how much success blacks can anticipate (tenet 2), *more* convinced that blacks' life chances are not within their control (tenet 3), and slightly *less* confident that they control their own life chances (tenet 3). Nevertheless, African Americans remain *more* confident than whites about their own prospects (tenet 2). That quandary could be resolved simply by assuming that each optimistic black believes that "I am so special, talented, determined, or whatever that I will beat the odds even though other blacks cannot." That sentiment is initially plausible, since everyone sees themselves and their children as special. But in that case why are not whites equally optimistic for themselves? Alternatively, African Americans could believe that they personally are only reasonably talented and so forth, but that other blacks are for some reason especially unable to cope with the demands of American society. Thus "*I* can handle the challenge of the dream but others like me are too handicapped by racism, poverty, or whatever to do so." This sentiment is also plausible but unappealing to anyone with a sense of collective identity. And African Americans have a strong sense of collective identity.[39]

Blacks are left at as much of an impasse as are whites. For them, too, *something* is wrong with the American dream that is vaguely but certainly the fault of the other race. Identifying what is wrong and how whites are implicated in it seems easy at first but more difficult as one probes further. Far easier for African Americans, too, to cling to the dream personally, doubt it collectively, and find someone to blame for the lacunae.

THE NEXT STEP

The paradox of "what's all the fuss about?" has several nuances. Most centrally, whites either do not understand or understand but reject blacks' claims that opportunities are racially biased and that blacks cannot control their own life chances. As whites become more and more satisfied with the trajectory of racial change in the United States, African Americans become less and less satisfied with it; on the few occasions when black gratification increases, so does white disapprobation. Within that central perceptual divide lie several other quandaries that complicate each race's beliefs about the dream and evaluations of each other. These external contradictions and internal puzzles would threaten any dominant ideology, but they are especially threatening to one as predicated on equality and on faith as is the American dream.

But this is only the beginning of the story. Chapter 2 showed that disaggregation of "blacks" enabled a much clearer analysis than did simple interracial comparisons. Racial comparisons yielded a confused and contradictory picture; comparisons within the black race showed a clear, albeit disheartening, pattern. If we apply the methodological lesson about disaggregation and the substantive lesson about the growth of a black class structure to the survey data of this chapter, we see the need for comparisons across classes within each race as well as across races. It is to those more complex comparisons that we now turn.

POSTSCRIPT: EVALUATING SURVEY RESPONSES

Even if one accepts my definition of the American dream and the operationalization of its four tenets in extant survey questions, interpreting the American public's views of the dream is inexact at best. Comparing across years, surveys, races, classes, and aspects of the dream compounds the difficulties inherent in any secondary analysis.

Consider, for example, the effect of subtle differences in question wording. More people (with little difference between the races) are more gratified by or optimistic about their own and other Americans' past and future "opportunities to get ahead" than about parallel aspects of "the American dream." Yet in the same survey most define the American dream largely in terms of getting ahead.[40]

The problems multiply when we compare different surveys, even in the same year with the same question wording. Table 3.5 gives two examples. To sort out which set of results is more "correct" is probably impossible, given the lack of detailed records of how the surveys were conducted and sampling problems in both.

The variations multiply when we compare responses simultaneously across surveys, question wordings, and years. As table 3.2 shows, the proportion of blacks convinced that the first tenet of the American dream obtains for their race ranges from 10 to 78 percent, and the number of whites who believe the same thing ranges from 36 to 83 percent.

What are we to make of this enormous range? I see several ways of

TABLE 3.5
Responses Vary Across Surveys Even in the Same Year (percent agreeing)

	Black	White
1964: "Generally speaking, Negroes are lazy and don't like to work hard."		
a:	8	40
b:	17	—
1964: "Most people on welfare could take care of themselves if they really wanted to."		
a:	38	53
b:	55	—

Sources: 1964a: Survey Research Center, Berkeley (1964: vars. 13C, 13P); 1964b: Marx (1964: vars. 10K. 50D).

dealing with it. First, one can do some rough averaging by decade (if enough data from the 1960s are available for a given tenet). One generally finds in doing so that most Americans claimed to believe in the American dream in the 1960s and that fewer, but still a plurality or majority, do so in the 1980s or 1990s. That makes intuitive sense, but is hardly a distinctive or definitive finding.

Comparisons across races (or, in the next chapter, across classes and races) within each survey are more valuable. They are less common and thus more distinctive. They also control for variations among survey techniques that produce results like those in table 3.5.[41]

Finally, one can compare differences within surveys across races (or across races and classes) over time. That is how we can reach claims about the three paradoxes, and how the results are generally described in chapters 3 and 4.

To put the point more analytically: one cannot trust variation in responses across surveys to anywhere near the same degree that one can trust variation in responses within one survey. Thus my emphases on changes over time in intrasurvey racial differences (or in intrasurvey class differences within a race or racial differences within a class). These intrasurvey differences are not only important substantively but also preferable methodologically.

Chapters 3 and 4 therefore present difference scores in addition to (in chapter 3) or instead of (in chapter 4) actual responses. Appendix A specifies where I got the survey data and how I derived the categories for analysis. Appendix B provides the actual survey results for the tables in chapter 4.

"SUCCEEDING MORE" AND "UNDER THE SPELL": AFFLUENT AND POOR BLACKS' BELIEFS ABOUT THE AMERICAN DREAM

ADDING COMPARISONS within each race to comparisons across races reveals two additional paradoxes beyond that of what's all the fuss about? They are:

> Succeeding more and enjoying it less: As the African American middle class has become larger, more powerful, and more stable, its members have grown disillusioned with and even embittered about the American dream.[1]
>
> Under the spell of the great national suggestion: As black poverty has deepened and become concentrated, poor African Americans have continued to believe in the American dream almost as much as poor blacks did thirty years ago. But that support is tenuous and under great pressure.[2]

In combination these paradoxes produce the surprising pattern that poor blacks now believe more in the American dream than rich blacks do, which is a reversal from the 1960s. But these paradoxes are more than merely surprising; together they point to the second threat posed by American race relations to the future of the American dream. If poor blacks and all whites follow middle-class blacks in their deepening disillusionment with the American dream, then the dream faces an even greater problem than the comparatively simple racial hostility depicted in the last chapter. Whether that threat is to be deplored as a danger to "the last, best hope on Earth" or welcomed as the puncturing of a hypocritical hegemony is a subject I shall defer till later.

THE FIRST TENET

> The Negro has more ambition than the whites. He's got farther to go. "The man" is already there. But we're on your trail, daddy. You still have smoke in our eyes, but we're catching up.
> —"a hustler," 1966

> I have the desire to do all kinds of things, but I got to have
> the opportunity to do them. I can't just jump out there and
> say, "I'm going to do it." Because there's somebody out there
> to stop me. There's always hindrance; regardless what you
> started there's a hindrance. Because if I could jump right out
> there and say I'm going to do this and that, I wouldn't be
> living in this neighborhood. . . . These higher persons, if they
> had any mercy, we wouldn't be here in this neighborhood.
>
> —Jacqueline Rahlins, a homemaker in South
> Philadelphia, 1970

For African Americans to believe with the hustler that everyone, even they, can participate in the search for success, they must believe that the barriers of race, class, and (for half the population) gender have all been knocked down low enough for people like themselves to climb over them. That is a lot to believe, and it is not surprising that many, like Jacqueline Rahlins, do not.

But many do. Although many if not most poor blacks[3] believe that African Americans continue to experience racist treatment,[4] relatively few report suffering from discrimination in their own lives[5] or see it as a dominant problem. In 1988, for example, fewer than one in five deeply poor African Americans chose "not being discriminated against" as their most important hope for their children. That is less than a third of the number choosing school, college, or a good job, considerably fewer than those focusing on good housing, family planning, Head Start, or general respect, and about as many as hoped their children would have a car.[6]

Well-off African Americans see *more* racial discrimination than do poor blacks, see less decline in discrimination, expect less improvement in the future, and claim to have experienced more in their own lives.[7] For example, in 1988 three-fourths of affluent, compared with three-fifths of poor, African Americans agreed that "American society is racist."[8] When asked what is important for getting ahead in life, poor blacks are almost as likely to choose being of the right sex and more likely to choose religious conviction and political connections than to choose being of the right race. Well-off blacks, however, think race matters more than any of those characteristics.[9] Affluent blacks are also more likely to see blacks as economically worse off than whites, and to see discrimination as blacks' most important problem.[10]

Comparing perceptions of discrimination over time yields the most surprising results: in the 1950s and 1960s, well-off African Americans frequently saw *less* racial discrimination, both generally and in their own lives, than did badly-off African Americans. In 1961 three in five poorly-educated but only one in five well-educated blacks agreed that "all white

TABLE 4.1
Do Whites Want to Keep Blacks Down? (percent saying yes; blacks only)

	Less than High School	More than High School	Difference*	Poor	Middle Class	Difference*
1. 1960s						
1964	71	59	−12	68	69	1
1966	44	23	−21	43	29	−14
1968	28	23	−5	26	27	1
1969(north)	—	—	—	26	48	22
1969(south)	—	—	—	43	38	−5
2. 1970s–1990s						
1978	14	24	10	12	21	9
1980	37	43	6	36	42	6
1984	35	39	4	34	38	4
1988	24	29	5	—	—	—
1991a**	55	53	−2	58	63	5
1991b	18	27	9	22	33	11
1992	28	18	−10	29	21	−8

Question: "On the whole, do you think most white people want to see blacks get a better break, or do they want to keep blacks down, or don't you think they care either way?"

* High status minus low status.

** Question asks only about whites who are "to blame" for the fact that "blacks are worse off than whites."

Sources: 1964: Marx (1964: var. Q10c); 1966: Harris (1966a: var. 26A); 1968: Cambell and Schuman (1968: var. 316); 1969: Goldman (1969: 250); 1978: CBS News/NYT (1978: var. 33); 1980: NSBA (1980: var. 1229); 1984: Brown et al. (1994: table 7.7); 1988: Gallup (1988: var. Q5); 1991a: Sniderman et al. (1991: var. bw2); 1991b: Los Angeles Times (1991b: var. 67); 1992: Gallup (1992: var. 11).

people in the south are prejudiced against Negroes." Two years later almost twice as many affluent as poor blacks saw no wage discrimination in their jobs.[11] Throughout the 1950s and 1960s, more high- than low-income African Americans agreed that whites' racial attitudes were acceptable or were changing for the better, would continue to improve, and would improve out of conviction rather than through coercion.[12]

The same pattern of reversal in the most disaffected obtains in the more confrontational question about whether "most white people want to see blacks get a better break or . . . keep blacks down." Table 4.1 shows the trend in distrusting responses.

The absolute level of African Americans' bitterness about white intentions varies across time and surveys, and probably any given set of numbers is not to be trusted. What matters here is that the relative degree of mistrust switched between the 1960s and 1980s, as shown by the columns labeled "Difference."[13] Panel 1 shows that up until 1969, whenever the classes varied, lower-status blacks perceived *more* white hostility than did their higher-status counterparts. Panel 2 shows that, with the exception of a single year, that discrepancy was reversed by the end of the 1970s.[14]

Perceptions of discrimination, however, do not necessarily translate into rejection of the first tenet of the American dream. To make that translation, African Americans must see racial discrimination as not merely an annoyance but a serious impediment to their pursuit of success.

As chapter 3 showed, blacks do not always assume that discrimination keeps them from pursuing their dream. It is true that in 1980, 65 percent of low-status and 45 percent of high-status blacks believed that something had "held them back" in their efforts to "make the most of [them]selves." But they were not alone; 40 percent of low-status and even 15 percent of high-status whites agreed.[15] Nor do even discouraged blacks always define the something that has held them back in racial terms. In 1989 two-fifths of deeply poor blacks saw "racial discrimination by employers" as having "a major effect" on their (in)ability to get a job—but racial discrimination was the *least* popular of six proffered explanations for being jobless.[16]

Nevertheless, Americans' beliefs about the first tenet of the American dream are unquestionably colored by their perceptions of discrimination. Table 4.2 shows these effects.

Our focus is on column 1; the others are there for comparison. In many of the 1960s surveys, middle-class blacks were at least as optimistic, or even more so, for their race as were poor blacks (the difference scores are positive).[17] In virtually none of the 1980s and 1990s surveys do the same results obtain; poor blacks were almost always more optimistic for their race than were affluent blacks (the difference scores are negative). Although the actual responses fluctuate considerably across surveys and are therefore not trustworthy, one can discern a general pattern from them that explains this reversal: both classes of African Americans were more optimistic for their race in the 1960s than in the 1980s, but affluent blacks' optimism has plummeted while poor blacks' optimism has declined more gently.[18] Thus the combination of the two paradoxes—succeeding more and enjoying it less and remaining under the spell of the great national suggestion—produces the results seen here.

Column 2 shows the results for whites. We lack sufficient survey data for the 1960s to make comparisons across decades. But in the 1980s whites have the same pattern of responses as blacks; poor whites are always more confident of blacks' chances than are middle-class whites (the difference scores are negative). The substantive meaning of this formally similar pattern is, of course, very different across the races. To blacks, these questions ask about their race's chances *despite* discrimination; to whites, these questions ask whether discrimination still exists.

TABLE 4.2

Does Racial Discrimination Inhibit Blacks' Participation in the American Dream? by Race and Class (difference scores; sample N in appendix A, percent agreeing in appendix B)

	Middle Class–Poor		Black–White	
	Black	White	Middle Class	Poor

1. 1960s

A. "Compared to five years ago, . . . white people have changed their attitude about Negro rights for the better."

1966	12	—	—	—
1969 (north)	1	—	—	—
1969 (south)	–8	—	—	—

B. "In the next five years, . . . the attitude of white people about Negro rights will get better."

1963 (north)	26	—	—	—
1966	4	—	—	—
1969 (north)	3	—	—	—
1969 (south)	0	—	—	—

C. 1964: "Negroes who want to work hard can get ahead just as easily as anyone else."

a:	–16	—	—	—
b:	–30	—	—	—

D. 1966: "A Negro high school student with good grades has as good a chance . . . or a better chance of getting into a top college than a white student with the same grades."

	–1	—	—	—

E. 1966: "A Negro college graduate with good grades has as good a chance . . . or a better chance of getting into a top. . ."

law school	4	—	—	—
medical school	–5	—	—	—
engineering school	5	—	—	—
scientific school	2	—	—	—

F. 1968: "If a young Negro works hard enough, . . . he or she can usually get ahead in this country in spite of prejudice and discrimination."

	8	—	—	—

2. 1980s–1990s

A. Compared with whites, blacks have equal or greater opportunity to get ahead generally.

1986	–4	–9	–13	–18
1987*	–3	–1	–12	–8
1988b**	–13	–17	–17	–21
1988c†	–33	–11	–42	–20
1988c†	–29	–1	–16	12
1991c	–18	0	–21	–3

TABLE 4.2 (*cont.*)

	Middle Class–Poor		Black–White	
	Black	White	Middle Class	Poor

2. 1980s–1990s (*cont.*)

B. Compared with whites, blacks have equal or greater educational opportunity.

1988a	−7	−6	−27	−26
1989a	−10	—	—	—
1989b††	−1	−4	−25	−28
1989b††	−3	15	−36	−18
1991b	−6	1	−34	−27

C. Compared with whites, blacks have equal or greater job opportunity.

1982	−9	—	—	—
1988a	−7	−9	−39	−41
1988b	−4	−1	−37	−32
1989a	−27	—	—	—
1989b	0	−1	−32	−33
1991a	−8	4	−37	−25
1991b	7	−2	−26	−35
1991d	−14	−12	−26	−24

D. Compared with whites, blacks have equal or greater opportunity for promotion to supervisory and/or managerial positions.

1988a@	−10	−7	−33	−30
1988a@	−10	−6	−27	−23
1988b	−11	−15	−17	−21
1991a	−33	1	−26	8
1991b	−3	11	−34	−20

E. 1989b: Compared with whites, blacks have equal or greater opportunity to hold elective political office.

	−5	3	−24	−16

* The question asks about blacks' "opportunities to live a middle-class life."

** The question asks if one needs to be "of the right race" to get ahead.

† The first question refers to current opportunities; the second to achieving equal opportunity in your lifetime.

†† The first question refers to "good education"; the second to "college admissions."

@ The first question refers to supervisory and the second to managerial positions.

Sources: see note 25, chapter 3, and 1963: Brink and Harris (1966: 258); 1982: GSS (1982: var. 146); 1988a: Harris (1989c: 47, 53, 224, 227); 1989a: Gordon Black (1989a: vars. 2, 3).

Column 3 shows that, even if affluent whites see more discrimination than do poor whites, they see vastly fewer effects of it than do affluent blacks (the difference scores are negative). And column 4 shows that poor whites see vastly less discrimination than do poor blacks (again, negative difference scores). In short, table 4.2 shows both a class difference within each race and a racial difference within each class. Middle-class blacks have become much more pessimistic; poor blacks have become slightly more pessimistic; middle-class whites are fairly confident of blacks' chances to succeed; and poor whites are very confident of blacks' chances. All three paradoxes obtain[19] for the first tenet of the American dream.[20]

THE SECOND TENET

> I worked hard to serve God and to see that my three girls didn't have to serve nobody else like I did except God. . . . I'm satisfied to know I came a long way. . . . Look at me, with more than I ever dreamed I'd have. And my three, with houses and jobs. My girls in an office, and the baby—my son—over twenty years in the Army.
>
>   I get full thinking about it. I had it bad, but look at them.
>
> —Orra Fisher, a domestic worker
>
> I have a hard way to go along so far as my living affairs. If I could get me a job that was worthwhile to where I could live, where I could school my children, then I could overlook some other few things that's happened. I would love to be able to get my kids clothes, keep 'em in school to where they could get a fair learning. And I would love to live inside my house, too, well, decent. . . . We have a heap of unfair things to go through with.
>
> —a tenant farmer in Louise, Mississippi, 1968

The ideology of the American dream specifies not only who may participate but also what they participate in—the search for success, which one can reasonably expect to attain. African Americans, like other Americans, do not always translate a clear-eyed view of the past into a hard-nosed evaluation of the future. Some such as Orra Fisher are gratified by painfully achieved gains for their children; others such as the tenant farmer are in despair at the hopelessness of it all. How typical are these views? Who holds which view, and how has the relative frequency of each view changed over the past few decades?

Table 4.3 begins to answer these questions.[21] Several features of this

TABLE 4.3
Who Is Making Progress, 1984?
(blacks only; percent agreeing; sample N in appendix A)

	Household Income		
	Less than $10,000	$30,000 and More	Difference
Your family is better off financially than 1 year ago	36	62	26
Blacks are better off economically than 1 year ago	32	22	−10
The nation is better off economically than 1 year ago	15	28	13

Source: Brown et al. (1994: tables 8.2, 8.4, 8.5 [1984 only]).

table are noteworthy. First, that almost two-thirds of well-off respondents are gratified seems appropriate, since in the aggregate their class is thriving. That over one-third of the poor are pleased is astonishing. Second, consistent with chapter 3, everyone, especially members of the middle class, attributes more success to themselves than to others. Third, well-off blacks are *less* sanguine about the success of African Americans in general than are poor blacks, despite being more encouraged in both of the other two comparisons. Poor blacks, in contrast, are about as gratified for their race as for themselves and are *more* gratified about both than about the nation as a whole. Well-off blacks are, once again, disproportionately discouraged in general in the face of their own well-being, and poor blacks are disproportionately encouraged in general in the face of their own poverty and poor prospects.

Other surveys confirm these findings. From the 1950s into the 1990s, poor blacks almost always felt less pleased with their own progress from the recent or distant past than did well-off blacks. The discrepancies were sometimes as great as two to one.[22] Poor blacks have also been less optimistic than well-off blacks about their own future ever since the 1950s. Here, too, there are sometimes huge discrepancies between the levels of optimism of rich and poor (among whites almost as much as among blacks).[23] But when the next generation is invoked, poor blacks—defying logic and history—are much more hopeful than their well-off fellows.[24] This phenomenon is the first suggestion of the operation of the paradoxes "succeeding more" and "remaining under the spell" with regard to the second tenet of the American dream.

Poor African Americans are similarly more discouraged than are well-off blacks about the United States as a whole and various groups within it. On the nation: in 1991, 30 percent of middle-class but only 6 percent of poor blacks thought the nation was in better shape than it had been a year earlier.[25] On women: in 1970, almost half of middle-class but only 40 percent of poor blacks thought women received more respect than a decade earlier.[26] On the poor: more affluent than poor blacks think poor Americans are doing well now, were doing well a decade earlier, or will do well a decade hence.[27] On "the average man": in three of four surveys in the 1970s, more poor than well-off blacks agreed that "the lot of the average man is getting worse."[28]

But despite this broad and deep pessimism, poor blacks are at present *more* cheerful about the past and future progress of their race than are their well-off counterparts. Table 4.4 depicts this surprising reversal. As before, column 1 is our chief concern. It shows the consequence of the operation of the two paradoxes, succeeding more and remaining under the spell. That is, in the 1960s middle-class African Americans were *more* confident than poor African Americans that members of their race could reasonably anticipate success (difference scores are positive).[29] By the 1980s well-off blacks had lost so much gratification with the past and confidence about the future that they were uniformly *less* sure than poor blacks that members of their race could reasonably anticipate success (difference scores are negative).

We have no data on whites' views in the 1960s about blacks' ability to anticipate achieving their dreams. By the 1980s middle-class whites were generally less sure than poor whites of blacks' prospects (difference scores in column 2 are mostly negative). What is striking is the huge disparities in gratification about the past and confidence about the future in columns 3 and 4; affluent blacks see much less chance for blacks to achieve their dreams than do affluent whites, as do poor blacks compared with poor whites (difference scores are negative and large). These findings provide a more refined view of the paradox of "what's all the fuss about?" described in chapter 3.

In short, the paradoxes of succeeding more and enjoying it less and remaining under the spell of the great national suggestion hold with regard to the second tenet of the American dream in two ways. First, although the best-off third of blacks became dramatically better off during the past three decades, they simultaneously became much more cautious about anticipating success for their race. As the worst-off third of blacks became relatively or even absolutely worse off, they simultaneously became only a little more cautious about the likelihood that members of their race would achieve their dreams. Thus the two classes reversed positions.

Second, the paradoxes hold for comparisons across substantive topics as well as across time. During the 1980s and 1990s, well-off African Americans were relatively gratified and optimistic for themselves, the na-

TABLE 4.4

Can African Americans Reasonably Anticipate Achieving Their Dream?
by Race and Class (difference scores; sample N in appendix A,
percent agreeing in appendix B)

	Middle Class–Poor		Black–White	
	Black	White	Middle Class	Poor

1. 1960s

A. 1961: "The Southern Negro does have a chance to make something of himself."

	10	—	—	—

B. 1964: "In general things are getting better . . . for Negroes in this country."

	8	—	—	—

C. 1966: "Opportunities for Negroes to get ahead in the professions have improved a lot in the past three years."

	3	—	—	—

2. 1980s–1990s

A. "Opportunities for blacks to get ahead [or blacks' situation] have improved in the last five [or ten] years."

1982	−3	—	—	—
1988a*	−7	2	−15	−6
1989a	−11	8*	—	—
1989b	−4	−6	−23	−25
1992	−5	−4	−19	−18

B. 1984: "Blacks as a group are getting along economically" very well and fairly well.

	−13	—	—	—

C. 1991: "Opportunities for black people in this country . . . today are" excellent and good.

	1	0	−34	−35

D. In the next five [or ten] years, opportunities for blacks to get ahead [or conditions for blacks] will improve.

1982	−10	—	—	—
1989a	−15	−6*	—	—
1991**	−9	−12	−22	−25

E. 1988b: "Blacks who have achieved middle-class status have . . . to be aware at all times that their . . . status could be quickly undermined." (disagree)

	−1	16	−39	−24

F. 1988b: "The present public education system is doing the job of educating . . . poor and minority . . . children to be part of the new labor force this country will need."

	−4	−8	−17	−21

* Classes measured by education.

** Response categories are "will be excellent" and ". . . good."

Sources: 1961: Matthews and Prothro (1961: var. 437); 1964: Marx (1964: var. 1); 1966: Harris (1966a: var. 21d); 1982: GSS (1982: vars. 148A, 148B); 1984: Brown et al. (1994: table 8.7); 1988a: Gallup (1988: var. 4); 1988b: Harris (1989b: 143, 153; 1989c: 44, 174); 1989a: Gordon Black (1989a: vars. 18, 19; 1989b: vars. 1, 2); 1989b: ABC/ *Washington Post* (1989: var. 25); 1991: *Los Angeles Times* (1991b: vars. 57, 59); 1992: Gallup (1992: var. 10).

tion, and other groups of Americans—but were worried for their race. Conversely, poor African Americans were less gratified and optimistic for themselves, the nation, and other Americans—but were more sanguine for their race.[30]

THE THIRD TENET

> Each day we must work to break down the barriers of racism by showing that we can be the best whether we are making deals on Wall Street or delivering goods on Main Street. . . . We must acknowledge and confront the obstacles and put forward our maximum effort. We must not run or hide if we want to ultimately achieve our goals.
>
> —Earl Graves, publisher of *Black Enterprise*, 1988

> The man had boxed them [blacks] in; you see how he's fixed everything so he can't lose; whitey is smart, nobody's fool. He gets the brothers to fight each other, when all the time he's out there behind it.
>
> —"a brother" in Los Angeles c. 1968

Chapter 1 showed that most Americans agree with Earl Graves that even in the face of unfair barriers people are responsible for their own success. Thus it is hardly surprising that most white Americans believe that the best way to overcome discrimination is "for each individual black to be even better trained and more qualified than the most qualified white person" rather than to use "pressure and social action."[31] African Americans, also not surprisingly, have rather more varied views on this point, as we saw in chapter 3. However, disaggregating blacks by class shows a more complex pattern even than the one described in that chapter: middle-class African Americans agree with Earl Graves when they think about their own fate, but with the Los Angeleno when they think about blacks in general. Poor African Americans are inclined in just the opposite direction.

On the first point, the data are unanimous: within each race, the higher one's status, the more one feels in control of one's own life. In 1962 almost half of low-status urban blacks, compared with only one-fourth of high-status urban blacks, demonstrated high "anomia."[32] Six times between 1961 and 1976, up to twice as many poor as well-off blacks agreed that "a person has to live pretty much for today and let tomorrow take care of itself."[33] In 1968 poorly educated blacks rated themselves less personally competent than did blacks in general, whereas highly educated blacks deemed themselves much more competent.[34] Twenty years later, fewer badly-off blacks than well-off blacks or whites of any class claimed that their situation was within their control rather than a result of luck or fate.[35]

However, poor African Americans are more inclined, and well-off African Americans less inclined, to hold *other* people responsible for their circumstances. Fully 90 percent of the former agreed in 1964 that "no weakness or difficulty can hold us back if we have enough will power," and almost as many agreed that if one tries hard enough, one will succeed.[36] In repeated questions since 1970, poor blacks usually agree more than do rich blacks that people get ahead mainly through hard work rather than luck.[37]

That reversal is even clearer when African Americans focus on explanations for racial disparities. On this topic, the higher one's status, the *less* likely one is to attribute blacks' situation to their own actions. Consider table 4.5, which is distressingly easy to interpret.[38]

Column 1, in which we are mainly interested, shows that poor blacks are always more likely than affluent blacks to blame African Americans for their unhappy circumstances (the difference scores are negative). Even in the 1980s up to three-fifths of poor blacks blame their race for its poverty (see appendix B).

Column 2 shows that poor whites rely on the third tenet almost as disproportionately as do poor blacks in explaining racial inequality (difference scores are negative). Column 3 shows a lot of volatility in the disparity between middle-class blacks' and whites' agreement with the third tenet as it applies to African Americans, but never do middle-class blacks blame other blacks more than do middle-class whites (difference scores are always negative). Finally, column 4 shows that, on a few occasions, poor blacks actually blame their own race for its poverty more than do poor whites (a few positive difference scores). Again we see racial differences within each class and class differences within each race.

Two features of table 4.5 in particular are striking. First, well-off blacks are least likely to hold African Americans directly responsible for their unequal status.[39] Thus the very group that seems to exemplify the success of the American dream believes less than any other racial/class group that the key to black success lies in black hands.[40] That view has not changed since the 1960s, so the fullest version of the paradox of "succeeding more" does not obtain. Nevertheless it remains psychologically and politically very important that well-off African Americans use the third tenet to explain their own lives but not those of other blacks.

The other striking feature of table 4.5 is that poor African Americans do precisely the reverse—they use the third tenet to explain the lives of

TABLE 4.5
Are African Americans Responsible for Their Low Status?
by Race and Class (difference scores; sample N in
appendix A, percent agreeing in appendix B)

	Middle Class–Poor		Black–White	
	Black	*White*	*Middle Class*	*Poor*
1. 1940s–1960s				
A. 1948: Disparagement of fellow blacks*				
	−19	—	—	—
B. 1961: "On the whole, . . . white people try to get ahead more than Negroes."				
	−9	−7	−32	−16
C. 1964: "Generally speaking, Negroes are lazy and don't like to work hard."				
a:	−6	−7	−30	−31
b:	−4	—	—	—
2. 1980s–1990s				
A. On average, blacks have worse jobs, income, and housing than whites. . . . The differences are due to . . . lack of motivation.				
1983	−20	−10	−19	−9
1985–86	−5	−5	−24	−24
1988a	−5	−2	−14	−11
1989a	−23	−22	4	−5
1989b	−19	−11	−6	−2
1988–89	−17	−8	−31	−22
1990–91	−12	−11	−11	−10
1991c	−5	−15	−4	−14
B. Many of the problems which blacks in this country have today are brought on by blacks themselves.				
1978	2	−6	−8	−26
1986b	−11	—	—	—
1988b**	−2	−8	−4	−2
1989a	−12	−7	−2	3
C. Black people are not achieving equality as fast as they could because many whites don't want them to get ahead. (disagree)				
1989a	−1	2	−31	−28
1992a	4	9	−29	−24
D. "If blacks would try harder, they could be just as well off as whites."				
1986b	24	—	—	—
1989a	−29	−19	−4	6
1992a	−7	−9	8	6
E. Blacks are more to blame than whites for blacks' problems.				
1991a	0	3	−10	−7
1991b	−8	5	−31	−18
1992b	9	2	−21	−28
F. 1991a: "Most black parents don't teach their children the self-discipline and skills it takes to get ahead in America."				
	−8	−6	−3	−5

* Classes measured by occupational status.
** Classes measured by education.
Sources. See notes to table 3.3 and 1986b: "Predicting Behavior" (1987: A9).

fellow blacks, even though they recognize how little control they exercise over their own lives. Their faith in the American dream is as extraordinary, and in as much need of explanation, as is the lack of faith of the best-off in their race.

THE FOURTH TENET

> In the long run, it is only to the man of morality that wealth comes. We believe in the harmony of God's Universe. . . . Only by working along the lines of right thinking and right living can the secrets and wealth of Nature be revealed. . . . Godliness is in league with riches.
>
> —Bishop William Lawrence, 1901

This tenet changes the ideology of the American dream from a mere formula for getting ahead into an ideal that Americans have found to be worth dying for. But startlingly few survey questions probe it. The previous chapter showed that African Americans are arguably more committed to the pursuit of virtue (as well as to the pursuit of material goods) in their own lives than are white Americans, and that they are perhaps less likely to equate material and spiritual success. But given the indistinctness of these patterns, it is not surprising that class-based patterns within each race are even less distinct.

For example, within their own lives, poor blacks initially appear to be more morally inclined than middle-class blacks. More poor than rich define success as a happy marriage, a life lived according to religious beliefs, or excellence in one's job. But badly-off blacks (as well as badly-off whites) *also* claim to care more about achieving material success— fame, wealth, or power—than do those who have in fact attained it.[41] Thus it remains unclear whether poor blacks really place more importance on morality or whether they simply have more expansive notions of success.[42]

Variations in concern about national virtue are similarly indeterminate. On the one hand, in 1964 badly-off blacks were more likely than any other group to base their patriotism on our nation's virtues—its helpfulness, peacefulness, and religiosity—rather than on its power or wealth. On the other hand, twenty years later they were less worried than well-off African Americans that vices such as laziness, irreligiousness, familial irresponsibility, or crime might threaten the future of the American dream.[43] With only two questions, not themselves close to identical, I cannot venture a conclusion about class disparities or change over time.

TABLE 4.6

Are Successful Blacks Virtuous? by Race and Class (difference scores; sample N in appendix A, percent agreeing in appendix B)

	Middle Class–Poor		Black–White	
	Black	White	Middle Class	Poor
A. 1988b: "Middle-class blacks have an obligation to help poorer blacks."				
	5	−3	27	19
B. "Black people who have 'made it' are doing a lot to improve the social and economic position of poor blacks."				
1984	−19	—	—	—
1988a*	4	—	—	—
C. 1988b: "Most middle-class blacks . . . do as much as they should to help improve conditions for poorer blacks."**				
	−10	6	−5	11
D. 1988c: "Blacks who have achieved middle-class status have . . . tended to be less understanding about the lot of less privileged blacks." (disagree)				
	25	9	3	−13

* Reinterview of 1984 respondents.   ** Classes measured by education.
Sources: See notes to table 3.4.

Finally, poor blacks are probably more satisfied with the morality of at least some members of their own race than are well-off blacks. Table 4.6 gives the relevant results.

Column 1 of the first question shows that slightly more affluent than poor blacks accept a collective interpretation of the fourth tenet. Two (or perhaps three) of the next four questions, however, suggest that more poor than well-off blacks credit the latter with actually living up to those moral standards. Absent more evidence or reason to discount any of these surveys, we must regard these data as suggestive but not definitive in their portrayal of middle-class African Americans as more alert to the association of virtue with success in the American dream, but less convinced of its actual practice.[44]

IMPLICATIONS OF AFFLUENT AND POOR BLACKS' BELIEFS FOR THE AMERICAN DREAM

We see now the outlines of the second threat to the future of the ideology of the American dream. Blacks and whites increasingly diverge in their evaluations of whether the American dream encompasses African Americans—that was the message of chapter 3. In addition, middle-class blacks are increasingly disillusioned with the very ideology of the dream itself, and poor blacks may not be far behind—that is the message of this chapter. By the 1990s well-off blacks have come to doubt the reality of the dream for African Americans. They have also become increasingly pessimistic about the future of the dream in general, and more embittered about American society than white Americans expect, given their class's improved standing. Poor African Americans are relatively less skeptical about blacks' chances to achieve their dreams, are only a little more pessimistic about the dream than they used to be, and are much less embittered about American society than white (and well-off black) Americans expect, given the deterioration of their circumstances. Still, they show hints of increasing despair.

The ideology of the American dream has always relied on previously poor Americans not only achieving upward mobility, but also recognizing that they had done so, feeling gratified, and consequently deepening their commitment to the dream and the nation behind it. That, very roughly speaking, has been the experience of most immigrants. But middle-class blacks are not following the prescribed pattern. They recognize their own mobility, they are pleased by it, but their commitment to the American dream is declining, not rising. That is an unprecedented risk to an ideology that depends so heavily on faith in its ultimate fairness and benevolence.[45]

It is a risk both because middle-class African Americans are themselves increasingly important in the political, social, and economic life of the nation and because blacks have always led the way for other Americans in beliefs as in behaviors. The convictions of (mostly middle-class) blacks and their white allies led to the incorporation of the ideal of equality into the Constitution in the mid-nineteenth century.[46] One hundred years later, the determination of (mostly middle-class) blacks and their white allies to make that ideal a reality led to an expansion of the political influence and legal rights of all women, children, and other previously excluded groups. But we cannot assume that African Americans lead other Americans only along paths that reinforce the American dream; they could as well show the way to suspicion and bitterness.

The relative lack of disillusionment of poor African Americans comprises the other threat to the American dream revealed by disaggregation. The ideology has historically relied not only on the gratification of the upwardly mobile but also on the pacification of the deeply poor. That is, for the American dream's vision of success for all to stabilize rather than destabilize American society, the poor must be enticed to believe in the same process of upward mobility, with the same consequent commitment to the nation at large, as the no longer poor. That, again very roughly speaking, has been the experience of most immigrants not favored enough to join the middle class. So far, that remains the experience of most deeply poor African Americans. But any nightly newscast suggests how fragile that continued commitment is for those subject to drive-by shootings and schools innocent of plumbing, let alone textbooks. Thus if middle-class African Americans may lead other Americans into disillusionment with the ideology despite their success, so a few poor African Americans may, with even greater reason, lead other poor Americans into a rejection of the dream that will make affluent alienation seem trivial.

Let me repeat: whether one sees these threats to the American dream as a revelation of hypocritical class and racial domination or as an attack on "the last, best hope on Earth" (or as something in between) depends on one's judgment about Americans' potential to make their ideology live up to its own best values. It also depends on one's judgment about its likely replacement. But that subject comes later. Let us first explore in more detail the challenges to the American dream revealed in the last two chapters.

PART THREE

Succeeding More and Enjoying It Less

Chapter Five

BELIEFS ABOUT ONE'S OWN LIFE

> I have had some success. I was well-trained, . . . prepared . . . for the *real world*. I know how to get along with my white and black subordinates as well as my superiors. I work hard. I get results. I make my boss look good. I get promotions when my turn comes.
>
> —a "highly paid vice president of a large corporation," 1985

> The racial situation is going to get worse. There're more white people beginning to hate us now than ever before. And there's a couple of reasons for it. One is that the whites are afraid to let the blacks live on the same level with them. It's all right if we can just be a little below him. . . . The other reason they are afraid is because they cannot assimilate us. You marry freely into every race but us.
>
> —Howard Spence, alderman in Verian, Mississippi, 1976

THE RISE of the new black middle class seems to confirm all the promises of the American dream, for three reasons. Its rapid growth appears to show that white Americans have abjured racial discrimination and thus finally accepted the first tenet. African Americans' strenuous efforts to join the middle class show, in general, the appeal of the dream as a guide for life choices and, in particular, the validity of the second tenet. That many have been rewarded for those efforts shows the effectiveness of the third tenet. Thus the new presence of blacks in mayors' offices, Big Ten universities, and Wall Street law firms is typically taken to show that the American dream is universal, alluring, and efficacious.

This benign picture is not wrong in any simple sense. After all, if it were wrong, there would be neither a highly paid black vice president of a large corporation to express his gratification nor even the possibility of a paradox of succeeding more and enjoying it less. But the picture is not simply right either. At a minimum, a complacent interpretation of black success fails to recognize that African Americans have entered the mainstream middle class only at costs ranging from heartache to death. At a maximum, Howard Spence may be right—whites never intended the American ideology of success to include blacks, and they will not allow it to extend to more than an unthreatening handful of African Americans.

Affluent blacks themselves are increasingly convinced that the benign picture *is* simply wrong—hence the paradox of succeeding more and enjoying it less. Why? Are they hanging on unwarrantedly to outmoded fears and resentments? Or are they, like the canaries in mine shafts, especially sensitive to dangers in the environment that can harm all Americans unless we correct the problems we have created? Answering those questions will help us to decide whether the new black middle class exemplifies the difficult but ultimately triumphant march of the American dream or its limits and hypocrisy.

Measuring the Costs of Success

Leanita McClain rose from poverty to a position on the editorial staff of the *Chicago Tribune* and at age thirty-two committed suicide. Four years earlier, she had written:

> I am a member of the black middle class who has had it with being patted on the head by white hands and slapped in the face by black hands for my success. . . . We have forsaken the revolution, we are told, we have sold out. . . . The truth is, we have not forgotten; we would not dare. We are simply fighting on different fronts and are no less war weary, and possibly more heartbroken, for we know the black and white worlds can meld. . . .
>
> My life abounds in incongruities. . . . Sometimes when I wait at the bus stop with my attaché case, I meet my aunt getting off the bus with other cleaning ladies on their way to do my neighbors' floors. . . . But I am not ashamed. Black progress has surpassed our greatest expectations. . . .
>
> I have made it, but where? Racism still dogs my people. . . . I run a gauntlet between two worlds, and I am cursed and blessed by both. I travel, observe, and take part in both; I can also be used by both. I am a rope in a tug of war. If I am a token in my downtown office, so am I at my cousin's church tea. . . . I have a foot in each world, but I cannot fool myself about either. . . . I know how tenuous my grip on one way of life is, and how strangling the grip of the other way of life can be.[1]

Most successful blacks do not kill themselves, nor did Ms. McClain's suicidal despair have only to do with her dual identity.[2] Nevertheless, her story dashes any remaining illusions that success comes easy to the new black middle class.

One could save the unblemished image of the American dream if Ms.

McClain were alone in her anguished response to success. She was not. We have already seen that over time African Americans have become more skeptical about the American dream as they have become more successful. Comparisons at one point in time also suggest how much company Ms. McClain has. Unlike whites, for whom socioeconomic status is closely associated with subjective quality of life, blacks do not express greater happiness or more satisfaction with their life as their economic position improves. (Sometimes, in fact, well-off blacks are less happy or satisfied than poor blacks.) Well-off and well-educated African Americans are also slightly more likely to experience depression at some point during their life than are poor African Americans.[3]

Most researchers interpret these results to suggest that religion, family, and friends matter more or differently for blacks than for whites, or that poor blacks lower their expectations to fit their possibilities more than poor whites do. Without denying these hypotheses, let me suggest another: middle-class blacks find their lives much more problematic than do middle-class whites, so the comfort that a broader education, better job, and more money usually bring to whites is denied to similarly situated blacks. Thus the paradox of succeeding more and enjoying it less.

Why is this the case? Let us begin to answer that question by focusing on the most common understanding of the American dream—achieving economic success.

ECONOMIC INSECURITY

> Statistics now show where the boom dough went.
> The middle classes hardly gained a nickel.
> Two-thirds went to the richest one percent.
> A breakthrough: We produced an upward trickle.
>
> —Calvin Trillin, 1992

Following the logic laid out in the introduction, I begin with the simple proposition that middle-class African Americans' declining faith in the American dream accurately reflects the declining efficacy of the dream. After all, if the economy slows, individuals' chances to succeed also slow, and it would not be surprising if their faith in progress declined as well. In my terms, the simple logic would argue that well-off blacks no longer believe in the second tenet of the dream because it no longer is true.

At first glance, this seems a powerful if not sufficient explanation for growing middle-class disillusionment. From 1949 to 1969 median family income grew by more than 40 percent per decade, the proportion of people in poverty declined by 10 percent per decade, the income share of the poorest quintile of families grew by 20 percent, and productivity grew well over 3 percent per year. Household wealth increased 2.7 percent a year in the 1950s and 1.3 percent a year in the 1960s.

Then came 1973 and the ensuing "quiet depression." In the next two decades, household incomes declined then rose then declined again to their 1973 levels, the fraction of people in poverty rose then declined only to the levels of the mid-1960s, the income share of the poorest fifth fell below the level of the mid-1960s, productivity grew at 1 percent or less a year, and household wealth grew only 0.4 percent annually.[4]

Nothing here suggests much grounds for optimism in the 1980s about achieving success. Nor do more immediately visible patterns of mobility over a lifetime. Men passing from age twenty-five to thirty-five in the 1950s and 1960s saw their incomes more than double, but the corresponding cohort passing through the 1970s enjoyed income gains of only 16 percent. Men aged forty to fifty experienced small rises in the 1950s and 1960s (36 percent and 25 percent, respectively), but a decline (of 14 percent) in the 1970s.[5]

Patterns of economic change across generations gave similarly scant grounds for faith in the American dream in the 1980s. "The upward mobility of men decreased between 1972–75 and 1982–85, while their downward mobility increased. Men's upward mobility is still 78 percent higher than downward mobility in 1982–85, but the margin is shrinking. In 1962, it was 237 percent higher."[6]

Thus Americans can no longer assume that they will do better than their parents did or than they did in their wayward youth. That is a big change economically, and an even bigger one psychologically.[7] But the bad news does not end there: many people are actually losing ground compared with their own past. "America's vast middle class . . . is shrinking right before the worried eyes of economists." The proportion of households with a middle-class ratio of income to needs rose from two-thirds in the late 1960s to a peak of three-quarters in the 1970s and fell back to two-thirds by the late 1980s.[8] That fall is precipitous by historical standards of change in the distribution of income.

A closer look, however, yields a more complex portrait: "middle-class change" occurred at both ends of the range. It is true that more middle-class Americans fell into poverty and fewer poor people rose after 1980 than before—but it is also the case that more middle-class Americans became rich and fewer rich fell into the middle class after 1980 than before.[9] Measures of wealth similarly show the rich getting richer, the poor getting poorer, and the great middle moving toward both extremes during the 1980s.[10]

Mobility data are also more complex than they initially appear. Upward mobility for children compared with their parents declined in the

1980s not only because high-status jobs grew more slowly but also because managers' and professionals' children are themselves becoming managers and professionals, leaving little room for lower-status children to move up.[11] Here too the well-off are becoming better off, but the less-well-off are not.

How have middle-class blacks fared in comparison with middle-class whites? Not as well, but with the same pattern of bifurcation. During the 1980s African Americans experienced the same middle-class meltdown in income as whites, and they were even less likely to rise in status. Wealthy blacks were not, however, more likely than wealthy whites to fall in rank.[12] Blacks similarly suffered more downward than upward change in their wealth holdings, but proportionally more blacks than whites rose from well-off to rich in the fifteen years after 1966.[13]

The pattern of recent changes in the distribution of well-being, then, is fairly clear. Those of both races able to grab the brass ring in the booming 1960s hung on and even improved their position in the sagging 1970s and 1980s. Those who missed the ring or got only a piece of it are in trouble.[14] Calvin Trillin's epigraph got it right.

If well-off blacks, like well-off whites, were largely insulated from the general downward trend of the economy in the 1980s, we return to the paradox of succeeding more and enjoying it less. If any part of its explanation lies in individuals' declining belief in the second tenet of the dream, that part must turn on interpretations of the facts, not the facts themselves.

Let us turn, then, to interpretations of changing economic status. Middle-class blacks may be operating—mostly incorrectly—under a reverse tunnel effect. The tunnel effect, one can recall from chapter 1, is the feeling of gratification one receives when, in the midst of a traffic jam in a tunnel, cars in the adjacent lane begin to move. Even though I can't see why they are moving and I am still stuck, the bettering of their lot implies that mine will soon improve. A reverse tunnel effect occurs when the adjacent line of traffic, but not one's own, slows to a halt. "Once again I shall take what is happening to my neighbor as an indication of what the future might have in store for me, and hence I will be apprehensive and worried—less well off than before, just as he."[15]

Why might we suspect the operation of a reverse tunnel effect among affluent African Americans? First, it is easy for them to see their peers "falling from grace."[16] After all, over twice as many black as white male college graduates (23 percent to 11 percent) earned poverty-level wages in 1986, and that frightening number has steadily risen since 1969 among blacks but not among whites.[17] One out of four is a lot of people; little wonder that the other three worry that their turn for such ignominy is coming soon.

Second, affluent blacks' economic well-being is especially sensitive to political choices. In 1989 the Supreme Court narrowed the grounds on which minority business set-asides could be deemed constitutional. As a consequence, many believe, "thousands of such [minority] companies have closed or are foundering in the aftermath of [district] court rulings that the racial preferences are unconstitutional."[18] Furthermore, middle-class African Americans continue to hold a disproportionate share of jobs in the public sector, especially in its "soft" side. In 1992, for example, although blacks occupied 6.5 percent of all professional and managerial jobs, they held 12 percent of public administrators' jobs, 11 percent of school counselors' jobs, and 20 percent of social workers' jobs. During the recent era of antigovernment fiscal austerity, public employees, particularly social service workers, could hardly rest easy.[19]

Even in the private sector, African Americans are concentrated in staff positions such as public relations, personnel, and labor relations. These jobs are especially vulnerable to recessions, corporate downsizing, and release from federal affirmative action pressure. Thus, even controlling for age, education, industry, and occupation, African Americans were more likely than whites to be laid off in the 1990–91 recession.[20]

Finally, the reverse tunnel effect is amplified by everybody's favorite scapegoat, media hyperbole. Consider the following headlines or article titles in the popular press:

"The Declining Middle"

"Those Vanishing High-Tech Jobs"

"New Punishment for the Middle Class"

"This Time, the Downturn Is Dressed in Pinstripes"

"White Collars and Mortarboards Are No Shield in This Recession"[21]

Authors of these and similar articles often point out that the middle class is polarizing, not sliding downward en masse. But since most affluent Americans see themselves as members of the vast middle rather than as (what they actually are) unusually well off,[22] they tend to believe that they are among those for whom the bell is or soon will be tolling.

The media are not shy about feeding the special anxieties of middle-class African Americans about the prospects for success, as the following headlines and article titles suggest:

"U.S. Finds Black Economic Improvement Halted"

"Good Jobs Keep Receding Beyond Black Workers' Grasp"

"Will Black Managers Survive Corporate Downsizing?"

"Race and Money: . . . How Racial Discrimination is Eroding Black Middle Class . . ."

"Blacks See Bias Trend in Job Cuts"[23]

It is not hard to see why successful African Americans might worry about doing as well in the future as they have done in the recent past.

And some do worry. After all, the promise of the first tenet of the American dream—that everyone may always participate in the search for success—has a flip side: if one may always begin afresh, one must always face the possibility of having to do so. This is the feeling of being "one paycheck away from poverty." A black couple whose two professions and real estate investments yield an annual income over $70,000 (in early 1980s dollars) worry that "send one kid to school, and you might as well be on welfare. . . . A guy could have a good job and after an affirmative action cut, could have nothing." The term "middle class" is to them divisive and misleading: "We need to eradicate the boxes people tend to put us in. We're all in the same boat. There's really no difference."[24]

They are in good company. In 1977 the higher the authority among black managers, the greater their job insecurity and alienation from peers and subordinates. The reverse obtained among white managers.[25] In 1983 a third of middle-class black respondents felt "economically vulnerable," and even more "belong[ed] to the 'have-nots.'"[26] In 1988 fully 80 percent of college-educated African Americans agreed that middle-class blacks "have to be aware at all times that their middle-class status could be quickly undermined,"[27] and half of high-income blacks (in a different survey) found blacks "more vulnerable than whites to changes in individual companies, industries, or the economy."[28] Although the income of *Black Enterprise* readers is much above the black median, a majority see their current income as inadequate, and almost half do not expect financial security in ten years.[29] Up to a fifth of high-status blacks anticipate losing their job, and many do not expect to find another as good.[30] It is hardly surprising, in light of these views, that up to a third of high-status blacks consistently rank job security as one of the most desirable features of a job.[31]

Economic insecurity among recent escapees from poverty is common. Most recent descendants of poor immigrants can tell cherished (or despised) family stories about parents who saved string and would never take a vacation. And chapter 2 showed that even African Americans with high incomes lack the wealth, housing stock, prestigious degrees, and social networks held by apparently similar whites. Thus newly wealthy blacks' lack of faith in the second tenet of the dream should not be surprising, even if it is not fully warranted.

Yet a puzzle remains. Table 3.1 showed that African Americans rate their own prospects, and especially those of their children, at least as high as whites do. They are also almost as convinced that their future is under their own control rather than hostage to luck or external conditions. Chapter 4 showed further that well-off blacks are more optimistic about their own lives than are poor blacks. Compared with well-off whites, they are just as optimistic for themselves and more hopeful for their children. Middle-class blacks are also more like affluent whites than like poor blacks in their belief that their future lies in their own hands. This is not a portrait of despair or insecurity.

The evidence on changes in economic status, journalists' accounts,[32] and the most broadly based survey data, in short, suggest that well-off blacks in the 1980s and 1990s are not and should not be disproportionately driven by anxiety for their economic future. Focused survey data and anecdotal evidence show just the opposite. What is one to infer from this?

I come down on the side of skepticism. One cannot discount personal economic insecurity, whether warranted or not, as a partial explanation for the paradox of succeeding more and enjoying it less. But it is not a persuasive explanation on its own.

AFFIRMATIVE ACTION

> It will take till eternity for the number of second-rate blacks in the university to match the number of second-rate whites.
>
> —Professor Isaac Kramnick, 1990

Economic insecurity is a poor explanation for the paradox of succeeding more and enjoying it less. But insecurity may flow not from the size of one's paycheck but from anxiety about whether one deserves it at all. This concern shifts our focus from the second to the third tenets of the American dream; more conventionally, it is the "rumor of inferiority," the "disbelieving antiself," or the undermining of self-respect.[33] These phrases suggest that African Americans appointed to high-level positions through affirmative action criteria not only receive little respect from whites[34] but also doubt their own capacities. After all, black recipients as well as white observers are presumed to think, if blacks were talented enough to deserve their impressive positions, they would have attained them without the boost of racial compensation.[35] Garry Trudeau captures this irony as well as anyone can.

The justice of a strong form of affirmative action (roughly speaking, a policy with clear requirements, rather than simply targets) is deeply

controversial. To critics, it bestows unmerited rewards on one ascriptive group—thus violating the first and third tenets of the American dream. To supporters, it overrides the ability of a different ascriptive group to use its historical advantage to attain unmerited rewards—thus redeeming the promise of the first and third tenets. The normative stakes are clear and have been exhaustively debated.[36]

But the debate over the empirical consequences of affirmative action—that is, how long it will take to even out the proportions of second-rate blacks and whites—is most striking for its high ratio of claims to evidence. We have little systematic knowledge of whether highly placed blacks feel more insecure about their capabilities than do highly placed whites or whether they interpret what insecurity they feel in racial terms. Evidence is just as scarce on whether whites denigrate highly placed blacks presumably aided by affirmative action, or whether such appointees overcome initial skepticism by demonstrated accomplishments or mere habituation.[37]

Anecdotes pull in equal but opposite directions. On the one hand is the Detroit Symphony Orchestra, which responded to pressure for more racial diversity by hiring a substitute black bass player rather than holding the usual blind auditions. The bassist took the job but "would have rather auditioned like everybody else. Somehow this devalues the audition and worth of every other player." A black assistant conductor was equally torn: "Now even when a black player is hired on the merits of his playing, he [*sic*] will always have the stigma that it was to appease some state legislator."[38] On the other hand is a businessman who found a simple resolution to the envy of a coworker:

> I was promoted into my present job over some people who thought they deserved the shot. One . . . said to me, "You got this job because you're black!" I said that might have contributed to the selection; it was probably a factor, although its weight was not nearly as great as my record and my objective capacities to do the job. He said, "This affirmative action shit has gone too far. I think this stinks."
>
> Well, it turns out that in the midst of a lot of reorganization, and some people shuffled out, this guy needs me for a job. He doesn't like it, he thinks it's unfair, but he needs a job. So I say, "Well, watch your mouth. I worked for you last year, and now you work for me this year." It's working out O.K.[39]

The few extant laboratory experiments also pull in opposite directions. People told that they have received a reward or a test score solely or mainly on the basis of their gender devalued the reward or their own performance, especially if they believed affirmative action to be unfair.[40] However, African Americans who could be seen by a (bogus) white evaluator dismissed both negative and positive evaluations of themselves as due to prejudice. Their self-esteem was affected by whites' judgments only if the judges could not see them.[41] Thus people either do or do not devalue their position when it is linked to their race or sex. Whether they do or not apparently depends on (among other things) the credibility of the evaluator, the views they bring to the process, and the procedures by which they attained their position.

Experiments are more consistent on the eventual results of prophesies about another's performance. Coworkers who initially believe a new black manager to be incompetent are most likely to change their minds when the perceivers want to help the new employee succeed, when they believe the new employee can easily change his or her behavior, when the new employee works hard to correct misimpressions, and when the new employee has great self-confidence.[42] The self-evident nature of these research findings should suffice to make us skeptical about any pronouncements on the inevitable consequences of an affirmative action appointment.

Surveys show the clearest pattern. On balance they refute the claim that affirmative action makes black recipients uncertain about whether they are following the third tenet of the dream. That claim occasionally receives support: over half of a small sample of black college students thought white matriculants were more qualified than black matriculants. The more the black students believed affirmative action to have played too great a role in college admissions, the greater the discrepancy they perceived between blacks and whites.[43] But more typical is the finding that only one-tenth of black faculty think that affirmative action "perpetuates the myth of minority and female inferiority," "robs women and minorities of a clear sense of deserved accomplishments,"[44] or causes "serious strains among the faculty in my department."[45] Fewer than 15 percent of black managers think affirmative action lowers standards, half as many think it has harmed their careers, and three to four times as many think it has enhanced their career opportunities.[46] Half of well-educated blacks, but only a quarter to a third of well-educated whites, believe that the success of their organization depends a lot on their work, that they work harder than their peers, and that they do their job much better than their peers.[47] Overall, 55 percent of well-off blacks think affirmative action programs help recipients, and only 4 percent think such programs hurt recipients.[48]

The *Black Enterprise* surveys provide the richest data. Roughly two-thirds of the respondents believe that their qualifications, not the exigencies of a quota system, led to their job. Over 80 percent see affirmative action as "effective" and over half have been positively affected by it. Nevertheless, almost three-fifths see (unspecified) "negative effects."

One might be frustration: 86 percent of the 1982 respondents claimed to make "meaningful and useful contributions to my organization," but 32 percent felt treated as the "token black." At least half of the purported tokens must be among the "contributors" and therefore very frustrated.[49]

Thus it is clearly false that "when appointments are being made partly on a racial or sexual basis, the inevitable result is to weaken the extent to which the recipients can confidently assert, if only to themselves, that they are as good as their achievements would seem to suggest."[50] A clumsy or grudging program of affirmative action will probably have this effect—as would (or should) a clumsy program to admit alumni children to elite universities or to put the boss's new son-in-law in charge of the front office.[51] But doubts about whether one deserves what one has received as a result of affirmative action policies contribute little, on balance, to the paradox of succeeding more and enjoying it less.

RELATIVE DEPRIVATION

> Considering their background as sharecroppers, my parents were very successful with their children—they sent all of us to college. If my daughters aren't given the opportunity to own a Fortune 500 company, I don't know if I will have considered myself truly successful.
>
> —*Black Enterprise* respondent, 1986

Affluent blacks are not disproportionately insecure about the second or third tenets of the American dream. However, the insecurity discussed so far is absolute—can I pay my bills? do I deserve my job? I have not yet discussed *relative* insecurity—am I doing as well as I expected to? am I doing as well as others like me? This is the classic sociological concept of relative deprivation.

The possibility of relative deprivation rests on the infinite expansiveness of the American dream and the teasing quality of the second tenet. Once one can reasonably anticipate absolute success—in the case at hand, once the formal barriers of racial discrimination are mostly dismantled—then one is tempted to anticipate more and more success, even if less and less reasonably. As one achieves more, one seeks even more (*pace* the economists' assumption of the diminishing marginal returns to utility).[52] People may eventually reach an equilibrium, through either astonishing achievements or, more likely, scaling down their hopes. But in the meantime they run the risk of becoming more dissatisfied as they become more successful.

Evidence of rising expectations, and correspondingly rising frustrations, is abundant. Middle-class African American children consistently expect more success than poor black children or white children in tasks set by an experimenter, even after many experimentally induced failures. They feel more competent despite repeated "failures," and they are much more likely to blame failure on their own lack of effort than on inability, task difficulty, or luck.[53]

On this issue, survey data reinforce experimental data. In the mid-1960s high-status black auto workers uniquely combined low expectations for advancement and high anomia; among whites and lower-status blacks, frustration was lower and expectations were commensurate with seniority and skill. In 1977 about 30 percent of black, compared with just over 20 percent of white, managers had progressed less rapidly than they expected in their company. Black men reported a larger gap between their desire for senior executive positions and their expectations of achieving them than did white men or women of any race.[54] In 1980 over four-fifths of black professionals and managers claimed "skills and abilities for a better job than the one you have now," yet only half thought they had any chance for promotion.[55] One-third of a small group of black professionals and managers felt overqualified for their job or thought more was expected of them than of white peers; about half thought discrimination had retarded their salary or job prospects. Twice as many well-off as poor African Americans describe insufficient pay or challenge as the feature of their job that bothers them the most.[56] Over half of the *Black Enterprise* respondents feel inadequately rewarded in job status or pay given their education, experience, and seniority. Over two-thirds are dissatisfied with their opportunities for advancement; the next most severe problem —their boss—elicited only 48 percent dissatisfaction. Over 40 percent of aspirants to a "top managerial position" think it unattainable in that organization.[57] Half or fewer of the black members of the American Chemical Society rate their chances for advancement or pay raises as high as those of similar employees, compared with two-thirds or more of the white members.[58] Although a majority of professors of both races admit to "excessively high self-expectations," considerably more black than white faculty members think their "career progress is not what it should be" and claim to receive insufficient salaries and inadequate recognition.[59] Over half of graduates of black colleges think they are more qualified for their position than comparably situated whites, and about 40 percent are frustrated about the rate of past promotions or skeptical about future advancement. Among Chicagoans, many more well-educated blacks than poorly-educated blacks or whites feel underpaid.[60]

A series of questions in one survey suggests the dynamic of frustration about occupational advancement. Among high-status respondents, about half of blacks and 40 percent of whites have recently been promoted, and about a fifth of both races expect promotion within a few years. But fully half of black respondents, compared with a third or fewer whites, say that promotion is very important to them, that they are much better at their job than are their peers, and that they do much more work than their peers.[61] A sense of deprivation follows close on the heels of such views.

Political as well as economic expectations can rise, with a similar potential for frustration. Before David Dinkins was elected mayor of New York City, only 2 percent of the city's residents wanted the next mayor to focus on race relations even though a majority thought race relations were bad and getting worse. A third of blacks thought a black mayor would improve the city, and over half of both races agreed that a mayor "can do a lot about . . . race relations." Six months after his election, a fifth of New Yorkers of both races wanted Mayor Dinkins to concentrate on race relations—the only problem that jumped more than a point or two in priority. A year and a half later, however, a third of New York's black residents thought the mayor had had no impact on race relations, and an additional 10 percent thought his impact was harmful. Fully 80 percent of blacks now thought a black mayor made no difference "in the way black people are treated in the city," and a majority of both races continued to see deterioration in race relations.[62] Mayor Dinkins was subsequently defeated, partly because of a low black turnout.

If blacks are like whites, in that their standards for success rise as they begin to experience some,[63] affluent blacks' increasing frustration with the ideology of the American dream makes sense. In 1967 African Americans who sought a promotion but expected to be denied it were disproportionately militant or nationalistic. There is no reason to expect a different reaction in 1995—and there are now many more African Americans in such circumstances. After all, "it's been bottled up for so long, and now that they are beginning to get a few advantages—and a little road upward—they're impatient to have more."[64]

It is uncontroversial to assert that personal relative deprivation partly explains the paradox of succeeding more and enjoying it less. After all, "the more one gets, the more one wants" has been a stock plot of children's stories from Rumpelstiltskin to *Yertle the Turtle*. Controversy lies in the next step—judging whether middle-class African Americans are justified in their complaints of being deprived of what they deserve.

Logically that question has three answers—no, yes, and it depends on who is making comparisons with what. The answer "no"—that middle-class African Americans are not justified in complaining that they are deprived of what they deserve—can be described as whining. The answer "yes"—that middle-class African Americans *are* justified in their complaints—can be described as racism. The answer "it depends" can be illustrated, although not exhausted, by an examination of gender tensions. Let us look at each claim in turn.

WHINING

> Some of these people better thank God that their skin is black. Because if it weren't, they would have to face up to the fact that their failures are due to themselves as individuals and *not* because their skin is black.
>
> —Dick Wilson, 1968

> Whatever you think about Khallid Mohammed . . . , whatever racism you think you saw on the [Phil] Donohue show, try to remember that it was made in America by a European. Whatever we react to, no matter how negative, it was made in America by a European. Whoever we denigrate or mis-place, try to remember that it was made in America by a European.
>
> —Akua Abotare, 1994, on electronic bulletin board AFAM-L

One can easily turn the academic concept of relative deprivation into the political charge of "whining" by shifting the focus slightly from the common human desire for more to individuals' unwillingness to face their own failings. Some believe that well-off African Americans' skepticism about the American dream is primarily an excuse for not doing better. After all, the dream is infinitely expansive, and as one moves from a low threshold of absolute success to the more demanding goals of relative and competitive success, the likelihood of achieving one's dream diminishes. None of us wants to believe that our anticipated success did not materialize because of blind luck or our own flaws, so we all look for excuses. For members of the black middle class, in this view, the excuse of white racism is readily available and just often enough justified to be plausible—no wonder African Americans reach for it.[65]

The term whining is obviously contentious. The view it captures may be expressed bluntly—"I can't see where they feel like they are still repressed"—or more subtly—"The rush to identify oneself as a victim is rather a new feature of modern life. Why this should be so isn't very complicated: to position oneself as a victim is to position oneself for sympathy, special treatment, even victory."[66] However it is expressed, it is probably safe to say that many more people hold the view than will state it for the record.[67]

TABLE 5.1
Who Is Responsible for Problems in the Black Community?
by Race and Class, 1990 (percent agreeing)

	Black			White		
	Total	< High School	College	Total	< High School	College
1. "The Government deliberately singles out and investigates black elected officials in order to discredit them in a way it doesn't do with white officials."*						
True	32	25	37	6	3	5
Might be true	45	28	47	28	28	32
2. "The Government deliberately makes sure that drugs are easily available in poor black neighborhoods in order to harm black people."**						
True	25	18	29	4	3	5
Might be true	35	24	38	12	18	15
3. "The virus which causes AIDS was deliberately created in a laboratory in order to infect black people."†						
True	10	10	9	1	2	1
Might be true	19	8	31	4	7	5

* "The [Mayor Marion Barry] Inquisition is part and parcel to the plantation mentality that permeates our society's political and social structure. During the time that Barry has been investigated by . . . anybody . . . with a walkie-talkie . . . , similar allegations were made against then Senatorial candidate Chuck Robb. . . . But he [Barry] is the only one 'they' decided to pursue" (Reed 1989: 8). See also *Journal of Intergroup Relations* 1991.

** Speaking on needle exchanges to combat AIDS amoung intravenous drug users, a Congregational minister in Roxbury comments, "First they [whites] . . . cripple the community politically and economically with drugs. . . . *Then* someone hands out needles to maintain the dependency. Meanwhile, grandmothers live in fear of their own children because of what white society made them become—crack addicts, throwaways" (Kirp and Bayer 1993: 39; see also Marable 1992: 7; *NYT* 1994: ques. 34).

† "As HIV infection continues to increase among Black men, women, and children, . . . Blacks have come to fear that research scientists have exposed the race to a deadly 'Andromeda Strain'" (Black Coalition Caucus, quoted in Thomas and Quinn 1993: 328–36; see also Peterson 1988). The only evidence I could find on genocide fears in the 1960s showed low-status blacks to be more fearful of genocide than high-status blacks—just as the patterns described in chapter 4 would predict (Turner and Wilson 1976: 145; Turner and Darity 1973: 1032–33).

Sources: Questions and race totals are in de Parle 1990. My thanks to Michael Kagay of the *New York Times* for the analyses reported here, from *NYT*/WCBS TV News (1990a).

I know of no evidence comparing how much blacks and whites actually do blame others for their own failure. But one fascinating survey does allow for comparisons between well-off and poor blacks' propensity to make excuses for their race. If table 5.1 can be believed, middle-class blacks make more.

In my judgment, it is plausible that the federal government investigates black political officials more assiduously than white ones, especially when the individual officials are Democrats and the government is controlled by Republicans. Thus the first question in the table can be read as a control for the others. I see very little plausibility in the second claim and none in the third, and therefore I read them as examples of making excuses. But many African Americans, especially among the college-educated, do see considerable plausibility in them. It would be hard to find a starker indicator of the gap between the races than the results of the third question.

I am not alone in interpreting agreement with the second and third views as a dangerous form of whining. A white journalist sees the use of racism to explain ghetto drug use as "madness. . . . In the memory of oppression, oppression outlives itself. The scar does the work of the wound. That is the real tragedy: that injustice retains the power to distort long after it has ceased to be real."[68] A black essayist uses almost the same language to make the same point:

> Our memory of oppression has such power, magnitude, depth, and nuance that it constantly drains our best resources into more defense than is strictly necessary. . . . A recent and striking example of this is the claim by many blacks that the drug epidemic in black neighborhoods across the country is the result of a white conspiracy. . . . Memory and the mistrust born of it . . . make events into racial issues by recasting them as examples of black victimization.[69]

In short, middle-class blacks who are disaffected from the American dream are in this view misreading the ideology, their circumstances, and themselves. They mistakenly believe that the ideology promises success, and they mistakenly believe that their failures are due to external constraints rather than to internal shortcomings.[70]

Sometimes excuses can be recognized; after all, President Lincoln did eventually fire General McClellan. But the issue of white racism and black competence is much too raw for Americans to be able very often to make judicious assessments about the relationship between the two. And the evidence is too ambiguous to lower the emotional heat. For example, what is indicated by the fact that black students achieve lower SAT scores than whites or Asians with the same levels of family income and parental education[71]—lesser abilities, biased tests, an oppositional culture, or the fact that parents' income or education is a poor measure of social class and cultural capital? Or how shall we interpret the finding that black (and Asian, Latino, and Native American) public employees recently denied promotion see more discrimination in their place of employment than do those not so denied?[72] Are they right, or are they making excuses?

If we accept that whites sometimes blame others for their failure, we must accept that blacks sometimes do too. But whining is hardly the only possible explanation for a feeling of relative deprivation, and there is good reason to think that it is not a very important one. Another is the inherent slipperiness—the *relativity*—of relative deprivation.

GENDER RELATIONS

> It is . . . frustrating when you get the message from Black men that you took a slot another brother could have had.
>
> —student at a major university, 1979

> Equality is false, it's the devil's concept. Our concept is complementarity. Complementarity means you complete or make perfect that which is imperfect. The man has the right not to destroy the collective needs of his family; the woman has the two rights of consultation and separation if she isn't getting what she should be getting.
>
> —M. Ron Karenga

Relative deprivation is such a slippery, and useful, concept because of its relativism. Most of the work in using the concept is done once one has specified who is comparing what to whom. A good illustration of that general point, and possibly a good explanation of the paradox of succeeding more and enjoying it less, lies in relations among black and white men and women.

Much of what makes affluent black women feel deprived compared with others has more to do with gender than with race. Women of all races are nudged into "pink collar" positions and away from many professional, managerial, craft, and operative jobs. Within any job category, women of all races enjoy lower pay, lesser authority, and diminished chances for promotion compared with men of all races. Women of all races are typically more responsible for children and other dependents, and face the same problems in meeting those responsibilities while working in unaccommodating institutions. Women of all races face sexual harassment.[73]

Well-off African American women recognize this point. Three-fourths see sex discrimination as a serious problem, claim "a common fate" with other women, and endorse collective action among all women.[74] Black and white female legislators agree that, although women "bring unique assets into the policy-making arena" and are "better suited emotionally" for political activity, they must "work harder to prove themselves" in politics.[75] Almost three times as many black women managers as craftspersons perceive rampant sexism in their company.[76] And they are even more attuned than white women to gender discrimination.[77]

Ambitious black women, however, have further reasons for a sense of deprivation that white women can ignore. (White women also face distinct obstacles to success, but they are not the subject of my analysis.) One barrier is the "paradox of 'underattention' and 'overattention'"; visible black women are called on to articulate "the woman's view" *and* "the minority view" before decisions are made, but they are ignored at the actual point of decision making. Thus black women faculty report more stress than the other three race/gender groups over both "frequent requests for community service" (overattention) and "inadequate recognition for community service" (underattention). Or they are simply an unwelcome surprise: "a woman [seeking a lawyer] obtained my name from the American Bar Association and sent her husband to me. . . . When . . . I introduced myself, and he saw that I am Black, he said, 'I knew you were a woman, but this is too much,' and he turned and left."[78]

Black women also fall through the cracks of the legal system. Corporations insist, perhaps correctly, that they have hired the requisite number of blacks *and* of women—but if all the blacks are men and all the women are white, obedience to the dictates of affirmative action still leaves black women out in the cold.[79]

Other grounds for a sense of deprivation arise from relations with apparently similar white women. Feminist journals are full of angry questions and agonized responses about "how . . . Black females react to a call for unification with a group which heretofore has been a source of subjugation and humiliation for them."[80] African American women accuse white women of using the egalitarian ideology of feminism to hide the facts of dominance and subordination: "it is only possible for a woman who does not feel highly vulnerable with respect to other parts of her identity, e.g., race, class, ethnicity . . . etc., to conceive of her voice simply or essentially as a 'woman's voice.'"[81] Thus although more black than white women endorse feminist goals,[82] black feminists see white feminists as, at best, untrustworthy allies and, at worst, even more oppressive than men.

As the epigraphs to this section suggest, however, one of the most troubling gender barriers for black women is black men. Sometimes interpreting subtle signals is not the problem: when a Peace Corps volunteer resisted Representative Gus Savage's attack in the back seat of a car "he told me I was a traitor to the black movement if I didn't go along." The congressman dismissed, but did not deny, the charge.[83] More typically, black women professionals report pressure to be less successful, or at least less aggressive, on the grounds that their accomplishments exacerbate white society's continued emasculation of black men.[84] Only one-third of 6,200 female respondents to a 1980 mail-back survey by *Essence* magazine thought black men support black women. Half agreed that "sex discrimination will persist long after race discrimination is eliminated"; almost three-quarters saw black men and women as competitors; and eight-tenths agreed that black women encounter sexist attitudes and behaviors from black men as much as from white men.[85] A decade later, little had changed: "asked whether men are trying to take away the gains made by women over the past 20 years, fewer than one-quarter of white women—but more than half of black women—said yes." Almost one-fourth of black, but only 15 percent of white, women thought that "men's attitudes toward women have changed for the worse in the past 20 years."[86]

Examples of this conflict are easy to find. Shirley Chisholm retired from the House of Representatives in 1983 because, despite "lov[ing] a good fight, . . . what hurts me more than anything is the brothers in politics. . . . If the brothers would stop attacking me so much and stop giving out wrong statements about me, I'd continue. . . . But they won't get off my back. . . . How much can I take of this constant pressure and lies?" Black men at one university "go to the white man when they need something in my area of responsibility, even though I'm in charge. I get more respect from white males and females."[87] African Americans (of both genders) supported Clarence Thomas more than Anita Hill in the Senate hearings on sexual harassment partly because of "the myth of the greatly advantaged, black super-female versus the greatly disadvantaged and besieged black male."[88]

At least some well-off black men do feel disadvantaged just as black women fear. As the second epigraph suggests, they perceive demands by black women for equality with black men as undermining the solidarity and distinctiveness of the black community. More personally, almost three-fifths of a small sample agreed that "Black women seem to have more opportunities today than Black men"; two-fifths agreed that "many Black women, without realizing it, have helped to keep the Black man down because of their low regard for him"; and three-tenths saw "a growing distrust, even hatred, between Black men and Black women." These men presumably agree with James Baldwin that tension between successful black women and men "is one of the symptoms of black middle-classdom. . . . The anti-male thing which is now beginning seems to me to be one of the offshoots of the American dream as ingested by blacks."[89]

African American men sometimes respond to these anxieties by clinging to traditional gender roles. In 1970 well-off black men were less likely than similarly situated white men or women of both races to agree that "a woman can be both successful in a career and feminine."[90] From

1974 onward, among affluent respondents fewer than one-fourth of women (of both races) and white men agreed that women should run the home and leave running the country to men; only among black men did agreement rise above one-third. Agreement rates reach 40 percent among first-year black male college students.[91] Until recently more black than white men or women of either race believed that women should stay out of the paid work force if they had a husband to support them.[92] (None of these surveys asked about appropriate activities for married men.)[93]

Some middle-class black men see even white men's sexism as enabling the unfair ascendance of black (and white) women.[94] In this view, affirmative action policies merely set up further barriers to black men's progress, since black women count as "two-fers" on the balance sheet of equality. In addition, white male managers are believed to see black men as "arrogant, impatient, unwilling to conform to business standards, and lacking in basic job skills," whereas black women are presumably less assertive, more malleable, less threatening to clients, even more fun to have around because of the sexual possibilities. In short, "the black male has always been castrated by white America. Black women have always been used to keep black men in their place."[95]

Successful black men see yet other barriers to success distinctive to their race and sex. They are "the phantom of American family studies": twenty-seven "popular family texts and readers" contain "*no* articles, chapters, sections, or index references to the 'present' black father."[96] Or they are altogether too visible, but mute: "being a black man in America is like being a spectator at your own lynching. Everybody gets to make a speech about you but you."[97] Or they are visible and vocal, but only selectively: a famous Bill Moyers television show on "The Vanishing Family: Crisis in Black America" had the effect of "reinforcing, with 'liberal' authority, the most archetypal of racist myths, fears and stereotypes—a picture of 'jungle' immorality and degeneracy, inarticulateness and sloth."[98]

Thus African Americans of both sexes believe that their gender interacts with their race to inhibit their climb up the ladder of success. The ratio of assertion to fact is high, however, because very few studies directly compare black men and women in similar situations. And those that do show mixed results. For example, among black college faculty, accountants, executives, and middle-class magazine readers, more men report racial discrimination in hiring but more women report racial discrimination in advancement.[99] At least three times as many black women as men report gender discrimination in advancement.[100]

Studies of actual treatment, as distinguished from perceptions, are just as sparse. The only study to compare black managers' rates of in-

trafirm promotion by gender found no difference, although black men
had more company seniority and black women had higher performance
ratings.[101] In 1977 black male and female corporate managers rated
their own performance equally highly (exactly in between white men
and women's self-ratings), but supervisors rated black men the lowest of
all ethnic/gender groups and black women about in the middle.[102] This
discrepancy might demonstrate bias against black men, if one assumes
that self-ratings are more accurate than supervisors' ratings. Nevertheless, carefully focused studies usually show more discrimination against
black women than against black men. Black female chemists and bankers
still exercise less authority and receive lower pay than black men with
comparable education and experience.[103] Minority women on law
school faculties begin teaching at lower ranks, teach in less prestigious
schools, and teach more low-status courses. These disparities cannot be
explained by lesser credentials or more personal constraints; they are
simply a function of sex.[104]

The results for specific professions are bolstered by national-level
data. At least as many black women as men hold professional or other
white-collar jobs. However, well-educated black men have always
earned more than well-educated black women, and at the end of the
1980s they still earned at least 15 percent more.[105] In fact, black men
earn considerably more than black women across all job categories.
Some of the earnings gap is due to differences in labor market skills or
experience, but most results from gender discrimination.[106] Black men
earn more for each additional year of education or seniority than do
black women, and that disparity changed little between 1960 and
1980.[107] On balance, successful black men *feel* relatively deprived,
whereas successful black women not only feel but *are* relatively deprived.

RACIAL BIAS

Is This Your Pro-Family Team for 1988?

By now you have heard of the Dukakis/Bentsen team. But
have you heard of the Dukakis/Willie Horton team? You,
your spouse, your children, your parents, and your friends can
have the opportunity to receive a visit from someone like Willie Horton if Mike Dukakis becomes president.

—fund-raising letter from the Maryland Republican party,
1988

The final possible answer to the question raised earlier, of whether middle-class African Americans' sense of relative deprivation is warranted, is

"yes." Yes here means that well-off blacks are correct in believing that, despite their economic standing, because of their race they are not permitted to achieve the varied forms of success they deserve. As chapter 4 indicated, this is the answer that affluent blacks themselves now favor; they see more racial discrimination than do poor blacks or all whites, more often claim to have suffered from it, and more often think it inhibits blacks' chances to succeed.[108] Relative deprivation, in short, is in this view a euphemism for the stultifying and enraging reaction to racism.

Raw Racism

Are they right? Examples of raw, unmitigated racism are trivially easy to find. A quotation from Robert Kennedy calling for compensation for blacks for slavery evoked these comments from blue-collar workers in 1985:

> That's bullshit.
> No wonder they killed him.
> There was white slavery long before there was black slavery.
> What do I owe you? I owe you because you were a slave for 400 years?
> . . . I don't care if you were a slave for 500 years.

Public officials are on occasion no less explicit. After pointing out (at a civil rights training conference, no less) that male monkeys are "hyperaggressive" and "hypersexual," the nation's former chief mental health officer opined in 1992 that "high impact inner-city areas . . . may have gone back to what might be more natural, without all of the social controls that we have imposed upon ourselves over thousands of years in our own evolution. . . . Maybe it isn't just the careless use of the word when people call certain areas of certain cities, jungles." A few years earlier, a United States attorney could not understand why people were upset that he "may have said something about the NAACP being un-American or Communist." After all, "I meant no harm by it."[109]

Surveys reinforce colorful but selective quotations. In 1993, 21 percent of whites agreed that African Americans enjoyed living on welfare; 12 percent agreed that African Americans cannot get ahead on their own; and another 12 percent agreed that African Americans have less native intelligence than other groups. In 1987 three times more whites thought an (unspecified) white candidate would exemplify a string of virtues than thought a black candidate would. (Blacks returned the compliment in roughly equal proportions.)[110]

More subtle survey techniques elicit even more racial stereotyping, as figure 5.1 shows. Whites rank whites most positively on all six traits.

Figure 5.1: Whites' Ratings of Dispositional Traits of Whites, Blacks, Hispanics, and Asians, 1990

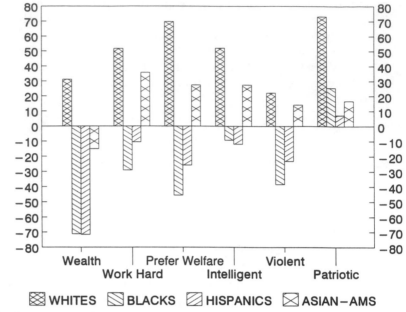

Note: The figure measures the balance of positive to negative trait ratings of all four ethnicities, as judged by whites. The more positive the score, the more whites deem that group to rate favorably on that trait.
Source: Bobo and Kluegel (1991: 14).

Whites rank blacks lower than all other groups on three of the six dimensions, equally low on two more, and higher than Latinos and Asians only on their patriotism.[111]

Elusive Bias

Racial stereotypes are not new, however, and are declining if we can believe surveys.[112] So they cannot explain middle-class blacks' growing sense of relative deprivation. What *is* largely new is elusive racial bias—subtle actions with the foreseeable effect but not necessarily the overt intention of fostering racial subordination. To fight it, one must demand new perspectives on old phenomena, such as the euphemism of "cultural disadvantage":

> The central dilemma of my professional training . . . [was]: I am a black child—one of the subjects whose behavior needed an alternative explanation [from the "deficit theory" she had been taught]. By enrolling in

graduate school, I was embedding myself in an environment that denied the complexity of my experience. . . . I expected to develop new
methods through activity that was based on the premises and methods
of the very system I questioned. If I were successful, I might have to
regard myself as a failure.

Or one must combat barriers manifested not in bulldogs and fire hoses
but in the absence of invitations to meetings:

> [I felt] a lack of closeness, support, and protection. . . . No matter how
> much I achieved, how hard I worked, or how many personal adjust-
> ments I made, this system was trying to reject me. . . . "What do they
> expect?" I thought. They know that I am bound to run into prejudice;
> yet no one lifts a finger when I am treated unfairly. Do they expect a
> person to be stupid enough to come right out and say, "Get out,
> blackie; we don't want your type here"? This surely wouldn't happen—
> such overt behavior would endanger the offending person's career.[113]

Elusive racial bias is elusive. It is thus not surprising that black managers,
much more than their white counterparts, see minorities contending
with inhospitable personnel officers, informal social ostracism, excessive
penalties for mistakes, exclusion from communication networks, resistance from subordinates, assumptions about cultural and personal inferiority, lower ratings from white bosses, and "ghettoized" assignments.
Conversely, they are much less likely than whites to explain minorities'
slow rate of promotion through defects in education, training, skills, or
confidence.[114] They are, finally, much more likely than white managers
to see racially specific characterizations as invidious stereotypes rather
than neutral, more or less true, descriptions.[115]

For the nation to move from outright racism to elusive racial bias is
progress; after all, a high-tech lynching is preferable to a real lynching.
But its subtlety should not be mistaken for triviality. Jim Crow laws applied to all blacks and were indifferent to anything literally more than
skin deep. One could hope to learn the rules, obey overtly while scorn-
ing them covertly, and keep one's psyche intact. Elusive racial bias applies to concrete, identifiable individuals; thus "I have no objection to a
black boss, but *you* are not qualified to give me orders," or "We are
eager for black students to attend our school, but *your* daughter lacks
the ability to keep up." The new rules deny the significance of skin-deep
characteristics and attack the ones that really matter, and they are therefore much harder to defend against.[116]

To make it worse, African Americans argue, as soon as we learn to
follow the rules, they are changed so that once again we are found want-

ing. If the opposing team gets to set the rules, rewrite them at will, choose the players, referee the game, claim ownership of the ball and playing field—and then call for a fair competition and blame the losers for losing—the home team is likely not only to lose but also to find the game bitterly unfair.[117]

The new, elusive racial subordination is politically as well as professionally and personally dangerous. One Louisianan was "not just worried about David Duke. I know where he's coming from." What worried him more were the "local Dukes, the smiling-in-your-face Dukes, the Dukes in the plant, the Dukes in the courthouse, the Dukes holding a dagger, waiting for you to turn your back." Despite Republican protestations that the Willie Horton advertisements in the 1988 presidential campaign were about crime, not race, the ads had a racial impact lost on no one. An experiment to isolate their effects found that "exposure to the Horton coverage increase[d] the effect of prejudice" among white television viewers who scored high on a measure of modern (nonexplicit) racism. Exposure had no effects on the salience of or attitudes toward crime per se.[118] A stand in the schoolhouse door at least tells everyone where you are; subtle, indirect racial animosity could be nowhere—or everywhere.

In a given case, African Americans who protest elusive discrimination may be oversensitive, incompetent, or on the losing side of a political contest. But their general claims are bolstered by an array of experiments. Whites interpret a videotaped shove as violence when the shover is black, but as playing around when the shover is white. Whites consistently sit farther away from, make more speech errors when talking to, have less eye contact with, and conduct shorter interviews with blacks than with whites. On occasion, white "subjects who claimed verbally to be the most friendly were actually rated as being the least friendly in their tone of voice and in their other behavioral responses."[119] Whites evaluate the performance of highly accomplished black workers significantly lower than that of similar whites. White subjects disproportionately assign a résumé with poor qualifications to a black man rather than to the white alternatives. Whites "attributed significantly less ability, more effort, and more luck to a white female, a black male, or a black female than to an identically successful white male" in explaining banking careers.[120] When white subjects anticipate retaliation from apparent victims, they become more aggressive toward black, but not white, victims. Whites favor a gubernatorial candidate whose résumé shows a white face over an identical black candidate. Finally, "whites respond more favorably to blacks in stereotypically subordinate or nonassertive roles than to blacks in equal roles."[121]

These experiments illuminate the minute, day-to-day interactions within which racial dynamics are played out in individual lives. Experiments do not show animosity or discrimination by all whites against all blacks, and they do show some equivalent racial animosity on the part of blacks. Nevertheless, they demonstrate that many whites act more hostilely or distantly toward blacks than toward other whites, even absent intent or awareness, and that racial subordination is especially likely when the black person is in some way a threat.

Racial Discrimination

I introduced experiments to persuade skeptics that racial subordination is pervasive even among people who endorse equality in surveys or in their daily lives. But experiments—artificial, short-term interactions among a few psychology majors—are themselves vulnerable to criticisms of superficiality. To answer that new skeptic, we need "real world" evidence of acts of racial subordination. They too are easy to find.

Federal judges are still ruling school systems and public housing authorities guilty of intentional segregation. Even the Reagan-appointed Office of Federal Contract Compliance Programs (OFCCP) required Harris Bank of Chicago to pay female and nonwhite workers $14 million to compensate for "present effects of past disparate treatment." The same administration's Department of Labor found that "attitudinal and organizational barriers . . . are an indication that the progress of minorities and women in corporate America is affected by more than qualifications and career choices"—a glass ceiling, in plain English. This glass ceiling "exist[s] . . . at a much lower level than first thought," and "minorities have plateaued at lower levels of the workforce than women."[122] Still in the same administration, the Federal Reserve Bank found that, controlling for income and other factors, banks redline black neighborhoods and give fewer loans to black would-be homeowners than to whites. Controlling for risk, black business owners of both genders are much less able than nonblack men to obtain commercial bank credit.[123]

Given this array of institutional discrimination, it should not surprise us that individuals are treated differently according to their race. When potential home-buyers are matched on all family and economic characteristics except race, African Americans "experience . . . discrimination in at least half of their encounters with sales and rental agents." Among similarly matched job applicants, "blacks receive unfavorable differential treatment 20 percent of the time they compete against comparable whites for entry level positions." Whites are treated unfavorably 7 percent of the time.[124] Blacks have a harder time hailing taxis, obtaining kidney transplants or coronary bypass operations, and buying cars or hamburgers than do whites.[125]

African Americans usually see public employment as more congenial than private jobs. However, the advantage is only relative. In the early 1980s over 40 percent of one group of black state employees perceived discrimination in their jobs, and black public employees disproportionately quit in another state, citing racism at work as the reason. Government employee organizations with many minority members are less effective in wage negotiations than those with few minorities because community interest groups are more hostile toward them and more active against them. Black FBI agents have experienced "disparities" in pay and chances for promotion, and harassment from coworkers ranging from death threats to apes' heads taped over family photos— "healthy" pranks, according to one agent's supervisor. A commission appointed by the chief judge of New York State was "constrained to draw the basic conclusion that there are two justice systems at work in the courts of New York State, one for Whites, and a very different one for minorities and the poor." Holding measures of job performance equal, African American postal workers are more than twice as likely to be fired as white coworkers.[126] The public sector may be more hospitable to African Americans than the private sector, but that hardly implies racial equity.

Manipulation of Race

Besides sharing discriminatory practices with private employers, public officials enjoy a mode unique to their office—the manipulation of race to foster their political career or agenda. Candidate Ronald Reagan went to Philadelphia, Mississippi, to endorse states' rights; those who remembered the murder of three civil rights workers there could not see such a move as an innocent coincidence. President Ronald Reagan supported federal tax exemptions for segregated Bob Jones University, opposed the extension of and ignored violations of the Voting Rights Act, almost abolished the Civil Rights Commission, opposed extant affirmative action plans for public employees, opposed a consent decree to desegregate the university system of Tennessee, opposed a new national holiday to honor Martin Luther King, Jr., cut the budgets and regulatory powers of the Equal Employment Opportunity Commission (EEOC) and OFCC, and urged the Supreme Court to allow institutions receiving federal funds to discriminate in areas not directly affected by the funding.[127]

President Reagan was not unusual. Candidate George Bush permitted the Willie Horton ad campaign; President Bush pursued policies to slow civil rights activism more aggressively than did President Reagan.[128] In 1983 a white mayoral candidate campaigned against Harold Washington in Chicago under the slogan of "Epton. Before It's Too Late." He was perhaps inspired by a white campaigner facing a black opponent a year earlier, who had proposed that voters "Elect Webb Franklin to Congress. He's One of Us." In 1978 Newt Gingrich won election to the House of Representatives on his third try, after an advertisement picturing his opponent (a white woman) with Julian Bond, graced by the caption, "If you like welfare, you'll love Virginia Shapard."

In each case, spokespeople argued that the candidate's slogan was misinterpreted or that the official's stance would benefit all Americans, including those of African descent.[129] From this perspective, the real problem of racial policy during the 1980s was the entrenched power of a self-serving or misguided "civil rights elite" and the inability or unwillingness of the president and his advisers to take them on. But to many blacks and not a few whites, politics and policies of the 1980s "legitimized a depthless egoism and cruelty of perspective and meanness of spirit that is unprecedented in our lifetime. . . . People feel encouraged now to be racist— . . . to be big and bad and base out loud."[130]

I am not arguing, as some do, that "the [former] President of the United States is a racist."[131] I have no evidence on the point (never mind a precise definition of racism). I *am* arguing that Presidents Reagan and Bush, along with other white politicians, choose words and take policy positions that at best continue racial tensions and at worse inflame whites' hostility to blacks and harm blacks' interests. They do so for political gain.

There is nothing new here. "Throughout American history major conflicts between opposing white groups have been resolved through compromises that victimized blacks [such as] the colonial decision to legitimate slavery, the Founding Fathers' agreement to . . . protect slavery in the Constitution, and the Hayes-Tilden Compromise of 1877)." Add to this list the extension of suffrage to all white men and the simultaneous withdrawal of suffrage from free black men in the early nineteenth century, the Missouri Compromise of 1820, the Compromise of 1850, the resolution of Populist unrest through Progressive reforms, the resolution of national party conflict through racial disenfranchisement, and Republican party politics since 1964.[132] In these cases and others, we see the precursors of Bob Jones University and Willie Horton.

Explaining Change with an Unchanging Variable

> We, the children of the dream, often feel as if we are holding
> 30-year bonds that have matured and are suddenly worthless.
> There is a feeling . . . of having been suckered. This distaste is
> festering into bitterness. . . . I see that I am often treated the
> same as a thug, that no amount of conformity, willing or un-
> willing, will make me the fabled American individual.
>
> —Anthony Walton, 1989

Even if middle-class African Americans are largely right about the perva-
siveness of racial bias, an analytic (not to speak of a political) problem
remains. Raw racism is not new and is arguably declining; elusive racial
subordination is debatable as a concept and in any case is elusive; institutional discrimination continues but is probably abating; and the political
use of racial animosity is an old trick. So how can the unchanging facts
of racism explain well-off blacks' *growing* sense of relative deprivation?
Only if relative deprivation is growing, after all, can it contribute to an
explanation of the paradox of succeeding more and enjoying it less.

I see two, interacting, answers. The first focuses on expectations for
the trajectory of racial animus. Affluent blacks could reasonably believe
in the early and mid-1960s that prejudice and discrimination were declining. Some hoped that whites were learning that racism was immoral;
others relied on the expanding economy, international tensions, or
whites' need to undermine increasing black militancy. Whatever the reason, it was not naive for blacks to think that the practice of the American
dream was at last moving toward its promise. And they were right—
opportunities really did become more equal than they had ever been in
American history, and blacks who were advantageously positioned took
them. Thus the new black middle class.

Then came the 1970s and 1980s, with oil cartels, "stagflation," new
white female and young workers, the flight of multinational corporations. Political and psychological changes accompanied these demographic and economic shocks. Politicians and academics cautioned
against too much democracy and too high expectations. Books about
rip-offs of the welfare system became best-sellers. The nightly news fea-
tured drug-induced mayhem in inner cities. The number of whites who
preferred "something in between" to either "desegregation" or "strict
segregation" rose from 48 to 61 percent between 1964 and 1978. After
dropping considerably during the 1970s, racial segregation in public
schools increased in the 1980s, "reaching the level [in 1991] that had
existed before the Supreme Court's first busing decision in 1971."[133]

Michael Griffiths and Yusef Hawkins were killed for the crime of walking into white neighborhoods; Rodney King was viciously beaten for the crime of trying to escape further blows.

In short, the 1960s' drive to realize the first tenet of the American dream ran out of steam before it fully succeeded. By the 1980s the rhetoric and vision of the 1960s, but little of the political commitment, remained. Into this context came the children of the 1960s generation. Their grandparents expected little from the larger society so were not surprised to receive almost nothing. Their parents expected and demanded more, especially for their children, and for some the dreams came true. Those children inherited convictions of their rights and aspirations for their future along with apparently narrowing chances to fulfill them. The consequence was the sentiment expressed in the epigraph to this section.

Unchanging racial bias also changed well-off African Americans' beliefs in the American dream because of changes in the nature of that class. Working among whites, members of the new black middle class now constantly encounter instances of either real or presumed racial differentiation from which the more segregated old black middle class was partly insulated. More aspire to mortgages, corporate boardrooms, or tenure—and therefore more bump their heads against skeptical bankers, unhelpful bosses, and narrow definitions of scholarly merit. Racism is, in short, less brutal but just as salient as in the Jim Crow era.[134]

Thus relative deprivation—caused by a mix of unfulfilled (and occasionally unwarranted) rising expectations, gender competition, and the frustrations of living with white racial bias—partly explains the paradox of succeeding more and enjoying it less. But all of these explanations tell only half of the story, since they focus on individuals' experience of their own lives. Let us turn to the other half of the story—individuals' interpretations of others' lives—before drawing conclusions about the encounter between the new black middle class and the American dream.

Chapter Six

BELIEFS ABOUT OTHERS

Stories about how difficult it had been years ago for blacks to obtain education of any sort made me strive even harder toward my goals. I knew that my grandmother, as brilliant as she was, . . . did not have the same opportunities that I had. . . . I never wanted to let opportunities pass me by; so many people had sacrificed so much so I could have them.

—a pre-med college student, c. 1990

It was a conversation I had had many times with white people who had grown up poor. They had known deprivation. They had been outsiders. They knew. It was all the same. . . .

It is not the same. Being poor and white in my generation was not the same as being black and middle class. And, it was surely not the same as being black and poor. . . . I don't believe in the perfectibility of white people anymore.

—Roger Wilkins, 1982

EXCEPT FOR hermits and sociopaths, people allow their own sense of well-being to be affected by what happens to people around them. Mere convention, then, would suggest that well-off African Americans' feelings about changes in other blacks' lives must contribute to the paradox of succeeding more and enjoying it less. But in this case, convention has more bite than usual, since affluent blacks arguably feel a strong collective identity. Well-off African Americans feel closer and warmer toward their race than toward their class, and they feel much closer to their own race than does any other race/class group.[1] Up to two-thirds of blacks believe that "what happens generally to black people in this country will have something to do with what happens in your life," and slightly more high- than low-status blacks see their fate to be linked to that of others of their race.[2] Since 1952, well-educated blacks have consistently expressed more group consciousness than have poorly-educated blacks.[3]

The fact of strong attachments, however, says nothing about the effect of those attachments on beliefs about the American dream. The quotations that begin this chapter suggest two opposite effects—a passion for success in order to honor one's family and race, and a rejection of whites and possibly of white standards of success, in reaction to mistreatment of one's family and race. Both occur; which is more common, and with what impact, are the questions we turn to now.

ECONOMIC INSECURITY

Consider first the issue of economic insecurity. Americans' votes, and perhaps their broader political allegiances and evaluations, rest less on their own success or their expectations thereof than on how well they think the nation or an important reference group is doing. This point is known as the theory of sociotropic voting.[4] Chapter 4 showed that most middle-class African Americans think (correctly) that the nation and their race are worse off than they themselves are and are likely to do even worse in the future. More pointedly, over half of the black respondents in a 1985 survey—and a greater fraction of nonpoor than of poor blacks—overestimated the proportion of the poor who are black.[5] The higher one's status, the more one agrees that "the economic position of blacks is . . . worse than whites."[6] Applying the general point about sociotropic voting to those specific findings leads to the suggestion that affluent blacks are losing faith in the American dream not because they expect to do badly in the future but because they know other blacks or other Americans of any race are doing and will continue to do badly.

RELATIVE DEPRIVATION

One can add to a concern about collective economic insecurity a sense of collective racial relative deprivation: just as middle-class African Americans think they do not receive the (noneconomic) rewards they deserve, they also think their race does not have the standing it deserves.[7]

For example, affluent blacks are less satisfied with the pace of civil rights progress than are poor blacks, are much less satisfied than whites, and are increasingly dissatisfied. (These results obtain despite the fact that well-off blacks are much more likely than poor blacks to agree that the civil rights movement affected their lives.)[8] In 1980 a quarter of the *Black Enterprise* respondents thought opportunities for blacks had decreased between 1970 and 1980; over 40 percent agreed for the 1975–1985 and 1980–1990 decades. In 1982 over 70 percent disagreed that "blacks have the same opportunities as whites for advancement in my organization."[9] Although the absolute level of black unemployment affects African Americans' presidential approval ratings, the relative gap between levels of black and white unemployment has more substantive and statistical significance.[10] Most generally, 7 percent of well-educated African Americans believe that blacks have "more opportunities than other Americans"—compared with 70 percent who think they have fewer.[11]

Elites agree. Seventy percent of black leaders deny that young black women professionals "expect to get too much power in too little time," and most believe it harder to become an executive now (1985) than a decade earlier.[12] Most African American (and white) executives think blacks have achieved high status more slowly than they anticipated. A quarter are similarly pessimistic about progress over the next fifteen years.[13] Eight of ten black bankers deny that "minority Americans" have the same opportunities in the banking industry as whites. Whites mostly disagree.[14]

Switching from an individualist to a collective framework, therefore, makes the claim of economic insecurity plausible, and the claim of relative deprivation even more plausible, as contributors to the paradox of succeeding more and enjoying it less. Both explanations gain further force from the fact that the collective framework itself is the locus of emotions and beliefs as intense as they are ambivalent. Well-off African Americans are entwined with other blacks, both because they choose to be and because they cannot escape.

CONNECTIONS WITH POOR BLACKS

> The salvation of the Negro middle class is ultimately dependent upon the salvation of the Negro masses.
> —Reverend Martin Luther King, Jr., 1967

The fourth tenet of the American dream tells us that mere wealth and power are not enough; one must also be virtuous to be successful. If virtue is defined as concern for the well-being of others, African Americans are quintessentially American, since the black community is especially receptive to its needy claimants.

Affluent African Americans vigorously monitor each other's commitment to the poor.[15] Cornel West decries the "flagrant self-loathing among black middle class professionals" that "tends to yield a navel-gazing posture that conflates the identity crisis of the black middle class with the state of siege raging in black working-poor and very poor communities." Reverend Martin Luther King, Jr., was gentler but no less pointed: "It is time for the Negro middle class to rise up from its stool of indifference, to retreat from its flight into unreality and to bring its full resources—its heart, its mind and its checkbook—to the aid of the less fortunate brother."[16] Half of the graduates of traditionally black colleges think members of the black middle class need to do more to help poor blacks, and another third charge middle class blacks with negligence or even exploitation of those worse off than themselves.[17]

Some reject the equation of virtue with concern for other African Americans: "Guilt about the ghetto is passé. A lot of blacks won't admit that. But most of us have a lot of other things on our minds."[18] Others mourn rather than celebrate the weakening links; an ex-urbanite finds it "difficult to maintain close ties to two communities, as much as I want to. We've got to participate in . . . [the new suburban neighborhood] as a matter of survival and so as not to be isolated. . . . [But] I miss my old ties. It's painful, damned painful."[19] Still others flee links that will not break. "Many of today's middle class women have deep fears of sliding back into poverty—fears that . . . [keep the] 'haves' running fast and hard from the 'have nots.' "[20] It is all too easy to see how similar one is to friends, cousins, siblings who did not make it; and the urge to justify "Why me? Why not him?" can propel one far from those rejected origins.[21]

But many well-off African Americans affirm deep connections among all blacks and recognize their special responsibilities. Former mayor Maynard Jackson insists that "just because I wear a white handkerchief in my breast pocket doesn't mean that's all I care about. Material possessions only give you the freedom to help others, not to escape from the issues. We can't ever forget where we came from."[22] Unlike comparable whites, middle-class blacks "prefer . . . the poor and the working class *over their own class.*" That attachment perhaps explains why roughly 80 percent of blacks of all classes agree that well-off blacks should do more to help the poor, and why 90 percent of the *Black Enterprise* respondents accept such a moral obligation.[23]

Whether they welcome or resist the connection, affluent blacks must wrestle with the expectation, much greater than for comparable whites, that they will take special responsibility for the poor of their race. Most recognize that the gap in living standards between rich and poor African Americans is increasing; many think successful blacks do too little for the poor; many fear, perhaps as a consequence, that the values of middle-class and poor blacks are also diverging.[24] It is increasingly difficult for them to retain belief in the ideology of the American dream in the face of these felt obligations and perceived trajectories.

CONNECTIONS WITH THE PAST

Felt or imposed obligations to poor blacks stem partly from the extraordinary history of the last four decades. African Americans' almost unprecedented efforts to smash the walls blocking their pursuit of the American dream had at least two negative effects along with their many positive ones. First is a bittersweet nostalgia for the bad old days of Jim Crow: "Many who attended Douglass [a black high school in Oklahoma City] during those years . . . breathe a sigh of gratitude and say, 'Thank God' for segregation! The nurturing and support received from those teachers was something not many African-American students . . . were blessed with—and it's even worse today."[25] Middle-class blacks mourn the loss of their culture as well as of their formerly simpler lives:

> All that I believed then, all that molded me into the person that I am, it's gone. Or going. The whole black culture. . . . We're losing that because of integration. . . . Every little town in the South had one little area that all the blacks hung out in. Man, that area is dead now in my hometown. Because they can go into the white . . . bars or nightclub. So who the hell is going to go there now? God, that hurts me. My whole damn culture's gone. . . . Another damn California.[26]

Second, successful African Americans contrast the self-centered, apolitical present with the moral and political fervor of the 1960s. Julius Lester's students were no more surprised than he was at his tears during a lecture on the civil rights movement: "I cried . . . for then and now and for me, like darkness, in the chasm between the two." Lester insists that his students learn details of the lives of martyred civil rights workers, out of fear that "the values the civil rights movement embodied would not be transmitted to the generation coming after us."[27]

Not only the old, who always think their generation was more heroic than today's youth, denigrate the present in comparison with the past. The young do too, as evidenced by a poem entitled "Epitaphs," which contrasts a student who died thirty years ago of "gunshot wounds inflicted by police at demonstration" while shouting "freedom now" with a student who died recently of "cultural deficiency and historical amnesia" while averring "I got into this school all by myself."[28] The poetry is flawed, the emotion raw and painful. Thus the very passion once invested in African Americans' struggle to participate in the dream now leads some to question the efforts to achieve it that shape blacks' lives in this more mundane era.

RESPONSIBILITY FOR THE RACE

> Whites may well be conspiring against us, but when we are
> able to win and hold public office—after much struggle— . . .
> we have to commit ourselves to operate under certain rules.
> Those rules mean that we . . . do indeed have to walk a
> straighter and narrower path. Maybe we ought to have the
> constitutional right to walk the same path, but we have to
> hold to a higher standard. That's just the reality today and for
> the future.
>
> —John Hope Franklin, reflecting on the indictment of Mayor
> Marion Barry, 1990

The fourth tenet's association of virtue with success runs deeper even
than feeling responsible for poor blacks and to heroic forebears. Some
middle-class African Americans feel responsible for their entire race in a
way that whites almost never do. The classic case is Jackie Robinson's
first interview with Branch Rickey:

> "You get into the World Series. . . . It's no holds barred." The older
> man's face wrinkled into an evil frown. "I hate niggers. I also want to
> win in the worst possible way. . . . [You tag me out.] 'You tar baby son
> of a bitch,' I scream, 'You can't do this to me, you coon.' I punch you
> in the face." Rickey . . . swung his clenched fist under Robinson's
> chin. . . . "What do you do now, Jackie? . . ."
>   "I get it, Mr. Rickey. I've got another cheek. I turn the other cheek."
>   "Wonderful!" Mr. Rickey was finally satisfied. . . . "I merely was test-
> ing you and I apologize for it. But you are a pioneer, and this whole
> experiment depends on you. You can never forget that for a moment."

Jackie Robinson's other cheek almost seems embarrassingly anachronis-
tic until one listens to a student at Princeton University:

> I can't begin to describe the tension I sense in a classroom when I—the
> only black student in the class—speak. Before I open my mouth, I have
> to carefully edit in my mind everything I want to say. If I fumble with
> my words or say something that isn't exactly right, I see some turn away
> in embarrassment. . . . When this happens, I leave the room feeling as
> though I've further damaged young white America's perception of
> black students.
>   On the other hand, if what I say is well-orchestrated and sounds plau-
> sible, I see two reactions: one of surprise on the face of the other stu-

dents that I could articulate and relate to such a mainstream topic, and another of relief, from those students who were hoping that I wasn't as one-dimensional as they had thought. When this sort of thing happens, I get a warm feeling inside, the feeling that comes from knowing you have represented your people adequately in the eyes of the disillusioned majority.[29]

This student may be overly sensitive, if only because few students pay such careful attention to the words of others. But regardless of how fully it is warranted, the feeling remains.[30]

Jackie Robinson's success would not be deemed real, and would not even be permitted, unless accompanied by virtue; the Princeton student's success *is* virtuous and creates virtue. It is easy to see why affluent blacks could feel vastly more burdened by the demands of the American dream than do whites or their poorer, less symbolically freighted, fellows.

To this burden of virtue we can add another weight—the feeling that one must defend all blacks in trouble with white society no matter what they have done to call down this trouble. African Americans sometimes argue that convicted criminals are political prisoners,[31] that unwed teen-aged mothers on welfare are no less rational or moral than single professional adoptive mothers in their forties, that drug sellers are no different from hat salesmen, that Tawana Brawley "was telling the truth. . . . Something bad happened to her. . . . She is afraid. I think she is being threatened by law officials."[32]

Reactions to the arrest of Mayor Marion Barry of Washington, D.C., for drug use are a good illustration. Almost 20 percent of black but only 6 percent of white Washingtonians agreed that "law enforcement officials were out to get Marion Barry any way they could." Forty-two percent of the former, compared with 14 percent of the latter, thought federal investigators "would not have tried as hard to arrest the mayor if he were white." Few black professionals would speak on the record about him—"You want me to talk after what white folks did to Barry? Shoot, they might spend 35, 40 million to catch *me*!"—but at least some shared the common D.C. view that whites "want a white man in that chair. They really think the drugs will end, things will calm down if they get a white man in there." More sophisticated commentators argued that Mayor Barry was indeed at fault for smoking crack, but that his downfall was the consequence of "bearing the burden of being the black mayor of the white man's plantation," as one newspaper headline put it. "Racism was truly eating away at Barry, as he frequently made known. That he dealt with it poorly by allegedly using cocaine proved his point, because racism does nothing if not make the victim destroy himself."[33]

What matters here is not whether Mayor Barry or Ms. Brawley deserve condemnation, support, both, or neither. It is simply that to take on the defense of every member of one's race who gets into trouble is a terrific strain, and is unequally distributed across the population.[34] Little wonder that the glittering promise of the American dream tarnishes as more blacks become prominent enough to warrant white scrutiny or to feel compelled to exonerate those so honored.

THE AMERICAN DREAM AS SELFISH INDIVIDUALISM

> I'm aware of my condition because of what's been missing—
> Human rights for people of color.
> The white man's disease is the same across the seas.
> He's full of greed—stab his own mother.
>
> —"Battle for My Life," Evelyn Harris, Sweet Honey in the
> Rock, 1983

But even this discussion of virtue as responsibility to the race, the fallen, the past, and the poor only partly explains how middle-class blacks' sense of collective identity undermines their belief in the American dream. Some have such a strong sense of distinctive collective identity that they reject not only the failure of the American dream to encompass others of their race, but also the ideology itself. If well-off African Americans increasingly reject the very values embodied by the dream, that rejection could contribute considerably to the paradox of succeeding more and enjoying it less.

I argued in chapter 1 that the American dream need not celebrate individualism. But many Americans see it as inherently individualistic, and some even believe that one individual's success comes only at the expense of others. Holding that view could lead African Americans to reject the American dream as the epitome of selfishness.

Do middle-class African Americans increasingly perceive atomistic individualism to be at the heart of the American dream? Consider first the grueling extent to which blacks pursue both individual and collective betterment: "I know that when I get paid on the first of the month, I'm going to get a call. . . . It's expected that I have it and that I'm going to give it. I feel I'm working for the whole extended family." This first-generation professional with an insecure job (as an assistant professor) goes to extraordinary lengths for down-and-out relatives and friends but worries about his own huge bills and empty bank account. "When I think about it, it really kind of frightens me. Sometimes I find myself frustrated and depressed. I'm called on by my children, my wife, family members, students, colleagues, friends, needing, asking, wanting. The cycle never ends."[35]

Systematic data reinforce anecdotes. Black (male) executives devote more hours a week to community service than (white) chief executive officers of the largest companies and much more than (mostly white) women executives.[36] Black business and public leaders have served as mentors for twice as many people during their careers as have white leaders. African American business owners consider the well-being of employees and of blue-collar workers in general to be highly important for their own success. White business owners, in contrast, see employee well-being as desirable but not essential to their success and are indifferent to blue-collar workers.[37] Black college faculty are expected (and expect themselves) both to produce excellent scholarship and to be deeply invested in the social, cultural, and political life of black students and the surrounding black community.[38] Black Chicagoans participate more than whites in school and community groups, meet more often with neighbors to solve problems, and give more help to neighbors and other "nonrelatives."[39] Over 90 percent of well-off blacks who perceive gender discrimination think black women should fight it by working together rather than seeking to make it on their own.[40] Asked if they "owe a lot for the help given to you by your family and relatives," many white professional women were "perplexed and asked what the question meant." Black respondents, in contrast, "immediately [said] that they felt a sense of obligation to family and friends in return for the support they had received." Although black college faculty on average hold lower rank than white faculty, they are more committed to their department, university, students, and discipline.[41]

Thus well-off African Americans help, and are philosophically committed to helping, others of their race—perhaps more than are comparable whites.[42] But that phenomenon would contribute to the paradox of "succeeding more" only if, in addition, collective engagement seems to come at the expense of one's own success, more middle-class blacks endorsed collective engagement in the 1980s than in the 1960s, and collective engagement is seen as a rejection rather than a component of the American dream.

On the first point, African Americans—especially those who see fellow blacks as a bulwark against a racist white society—often see communal support and individual striving as mutually reinforcing rather than contradictory. Thus the more hours black business executives spend in their job, the more hours they contribute to community service. Black leaders are more likely than white leaders to see networking and involvement in civic groups as very important elements of acquiring power. A thriving association of entrepreneurs begins its meetings with the prayer, "Bless our president and his family and help us bring up our skills to compete with others. Oh Lord, help us support our young people." The "career goal" of an ambitious university student is "redevelop[ing] black America based on real-estate acquisition."[43] The higher their family income, the more often blacks receive help from relatives, and the more help they receive.[44] Almost three times as many well-off black as white women think women should improve their position both by joining women's rights groups and by becoming individually better trained. Although more affluent than poor blacks strongly endorse racial collective action, both classes endorse individual striving as well.[45] Among both adults and (especially) college students, blacks are more likely than whites to see both collective betterment and individual success as "essential" or "very important" objectives for their lives. In short, many black professionals concur that "because I have more opportunities, I've got an obligation to give more back and to set a positive example for Black people."[46]

On the second point, we do not know if middle-class African Americans have engaged in more collective involvement recently than in the 1960s. One survey suggests just the opposite: in 1958 more white than black Protestant parents in Detroit ranked "help[ing] others when they need help" high on the list of qualities they wanted to teach their children. In the succeeding twenty-five years, white Protestant parents strengthened that commitment, whereas black Protestant parents lessened it. Thus what started as a small disparity ended as rather a large one.[47]

On the final point, some middle-class blacks do see opposition between individual and collective success.[48] But even they contribute little to the paradox of succeeding more and enjoying it less, for two reasons. First, they are a minority, and probably a small one. Second, I see no grounds for arguing that more well-off blacks now believe communal and individual betterment to be antithetical than did thirty years ago. If anything, fewer now see such an antithesis: in the 1960s, "progressive" blacks often opposed affirmative action programs as evidence that "the power structure was seeking to . . . co-opt the best minds in the black community . . . , who would . . . [otherwise] lead black America toward equality."[49] By the 1980s, however, most blacks endorsed affirmative action as both individually and collectively beneficial. For all of these reasons, then, I doubt that the paradox of succeeding more is explained by growing rejection of the supposed atomism of the American dream.

The American Dream as "Acting White"

> You could say it is a failure of the American dream. But the
> American dream has never attempted to deal with us.
>
> —Robert S. Browne, economist, 1992

How about a more global rejection of the American dream—spurning
the whole idea of striving for success through hard work and virtue,
whether individually or collectively? Does the growth of this view help
to explain the paradox of succeeding more and enjoying it less?

Probably—but we cannot say how much. Since the 1960s some African Americans have come to define black identity in opposition not
merely to some amorphous white identity, but specifically to white middle-class values. Working hard, saving money, acceding to authority,
doing well in school, maintaining a stable two-parent family—all those
mainstream, Protestant, bourgeois values that are precisely what the ideology of the American dream is about became for some blacks associated
with illegitimate white dominance and intolerable black submission. For
them, achieving the American dream means becoming white—something no self-respecting African American would choose to do. Conversely, honoring one's blackness means rejecting conventional success.[50] After all, if "those virtues preached but not practiced by the white
world were merely another means of holding Negroes in subjection,"
then "for a black to embrace the Horatio Alger myth, to assert as a guide
to *personal* action that 'there is opportunity in America,' becomes a *politically* repugnant act."[51]

But well-off African Americans have, by definition, succeeded in the
terms of the white world. Wrestling with this "polarity of images" is
painful: "Middle-class blacks . . . are caught in a very specific double
bind that keeps two equally powerful elements of our identity at odds
with each other. . . . There is no forward movement on either plane that
does not constitute backward movement on the other. . . . As I spoke
about class, . . . I was betraying race. Clearly, the two indispensable
parts of my identity were a threat to one another." It is also destructive:
"School learning is . . . perceived *as a subtractive process*: a minority person who learns successfully in school or who follows the standard practices of the school is perceived as becoming acculturated into the white
American cultural frame of reference at the expense of the minorities'
cultural frame of reference and collective welfare."[52] Thus black high
school students with high grades refuse to come forward in a student
assembly for recognition even after an order from the principal.[53] Successful black women are "penalized" if they do not "continually dem-

onstrate that they haven't lost their roots, their commitment to ethnic issues and causes."[54] Black students are more comfortable striving for good grades in all-black than in predominantly white colleges because they can avoid the equation of success with treason.[55]

Political ideology affects how one explains the "polarity of images." Shelby Steele claims that once blacks revived the old ideology of black pride and separatism during the 1960s, the twin drives to repudiate the punishing white society and to join the embracing black society were so powerful that even well-socialized middle-class children like himself were swept up. Those former children, and their own children, are now paying the price for their earlier self-indulgence.

John Ogbu, conversely, blames the polarity on white society, which appears to promise success if one makes the right moves but which actually will not allow more than a few blacks to win or even enter the game. Everything from the pictures on the covers of their textbooks[56] to teachers' treatment of their parents shows black students that "discrimination against them . . . [is] more or less permanent and institutionalized. Although they 'wish' they could get ahead like white Americans, they know they 'can't.' They respond by equat[ing] school rules and practices that enhance academic achievement with the norms and cultural practices of . . . their 'oppressors' or 'enemy.' "[57]

We do not know if affluent African Americans' global rejection of white culture and its (white) American dream has increased since the 1960s, but three reasons suggest that it has. First, anyone with a radio or television set now has easy access to the oppositional vision of black nationalists. Thus the more that African Americans watch black-oriented television, the more they identify with their race, identify with members of their race "who hold a problematic or contentious position within American society," and endorse black separatism.[58]

Second, desegregation itself may have inadvertently strengthened the equation of success and whiteness. "When schools were all black there was pressure in the home and the black community to make something of yourself and education was seen as the way. . . . We were told that we had to be 'twice as good' to make it but we never thought learning was a special province of whites." Now, in supposedly integrated schools, blacks are disproportionately steered into lower tracks, so the few "success stories" appear to be exceptions and teacher's pets—anathema for most American teenagers.[59] School desegregation may also have inadvertently increased young blacks' hostility to whites and white culture. Middle-class African American college students "are wholly neither inside nor outside of the American mainstream. . . . But, like Malcolm, they wish to rid themselves of their feelings of ambiguity, their sense of the precariousness of their belonging. For many, . . . integration is the badge of degradation and dishonor, of shame and inferiority, that segregation was for my generation."[60]

Nevertheless, ambivalence about adhering to white standards is venerable. William Wells Brown wrote in 1865 of being "scraped, scrubbed, soaked, washed" as he moved from field slave to house slave, and James Weldon Johnson wrote in 1912, after marrying a white woman, "I cannot repress the thought that I have sold my birthright for a mess of potage." In 1955 James Baldwin mockingly explained that "Aunt Jemima and Uncle Tom are dead, their place taken by a group of amazingly well-adjusted young men and women, almost as dark, but ferociously literate, well-dressed, and scrubbed, who are never laughed at, who are not likely ever to set foot in a cotton or tobacco field or in any but the most modern of kitchens." In the early 1960s black students threatened to beat up black cheerleaders.[61] So the horror of becoming an Oreo (black on the outside, white on the inside) is not new.

Surveys have asked too few relevant questions to help us decide whether middle-class African Americans increasingly reject the American dream. Blacks have, however, repeatedly been asked their opinion of whites and white society. Throughout the 1960s, from 5 to 25 percent of well-off blacks were "suspicious of whites who try to help Negroes," agreed that "Negroes should give up working together with whites and just depend on their own people," or trusted no whites.[62] Between 10 and 25 percent did not think the United States was worth fighting for in a hypothetical future war.[63] In 1968, 3 percent of seniors in black colleges and universities preferred a separate black society to integration, and 6 percent did not want to work with whites in their jobs. The greatest support for a separate black nation came in 1969, when 15 percent of well-off (and poor) blacks liked the idea.[64]

The proportion of well-off blacks willing to espouse antiwhite statements remained equally small two decades later. In the early 1980s, 10 percent or fewer preferred to shun whites, were taught "fear and distrust of whites" as children, taught those values to their own children, or trusted no white people.[65] Only 5 percent of black feminists were unwilling to ally with like-minded white women.[66] In most surveys since 1980, support for autonomous black institutions is lower among African Americans with a college education and high incomes than among their low-status counterparts.[67] In 1988 a fifth of well-educated blacks saw racial separatism as "the most effective way for black people to improve their situation," but by 1993 only 7 percent of blacks endorsed the separation of the races, and only 13 percent reported themselves becoming "less favorable toward race integration in recent years."[68] Fewer than 10 percent of well-off blacks (sometimes 1 or 2 percent) prefer to live in a mostly black neighborhood or work in a mostly black workplace.[69]

If (a big question) problems of sampling and response set are small enough that these data can be trusted, we can draw two inferences: a few African Americans do indeed spurn whites, but that proportion is small and has changed little in the past few decades. So I see no grounds for claiming that rejection of the American dream as too white plays much role in the paradox of succeeding more and enjoying it less.[70]

THE AMERICAN DREAM AS A HOLLOW PROMISE

> It is not the destiny of black America to repeat white America's mistakes. But we will, if we mistake the trappings of success in a sick society for the signs of a meaningful life.
>
> —Audre Lorde, 1979

Concluding that only a few middle-class African Americans reject the American dream as too white is not quite the end of this line of argument. One can reject the American dream for reasons that are not racially specific. American literature is full of laments of the prosperous who discover that despite their millions they are still bald, their children still do not respect them, Daisy is still impregnable in her West Egg mansion. Emily Dickinson put it best: "Success is counted sweetest / By those who ne'er succeed." Newly thriving African Americans may simply be the most recent group to discover that the implicit promise of the American dream—that success will yield not only power and wealth but also happiness, fulfillment, peace of mind—is met much less often than its explicit promise.

Little systematic evidence bears directly on this possibility. In 1986, 12 percent of well-off blacks claimed that "the American Dream is . . . not really alive today," and twice as many claimed that the American dream is "just a phrase which doesn't really have meaning to anyone."[71] Perhaps they are expressing bitterness about the hollowness of their achievements, but the survey does not tell us that. In any case, I know of no similar questions asked in earlier years, so I can say nothing about trends even for a question whose meaning remains ambiguous.

Indirect evidence is suggestive but equally insufficient. Almost half of black teens watch over four hours of television a day, and half "learn a lot from it." On both points, they exceed all other ethnic groups. Well-off blacks watch more than do well-off whites.[72] African Americans of all ages are "among the heaviest consumers of television." Black viewers rely on television for political information and for information on other blacks. They "believe in the reality of television" (including advertisements) and "learn behaviors from televised models" and ads more than do whites. Well-off blacks may watch more prime-time television, and well-educated blacks hold more favorable attitudes toward television, than their less favored counterparts. African Americans with low self-esteem watch more entertainment television than do those with high self-esteem.[73]

Television is the medium most devoted to portraying the attractions and ignoring the dark side of the American dream. Shows with black male leads in particular "emphasize . . . individualism, racial invisibility, professional competence, success, upward social mobility, and the routinization of racial issues. Absent . . . are representations of black collectivity . . . , racial conflict and struggle . . . [and] competing alternatives to the dominant assimilation model." It is plausible that members of the *new* black middle class would acquire more beliefs about middle-class life from television than would people who have grown up immersed in the joys and frustrations of that life. It is also plausible that people who watch a lot of television and rely on it for knowledge—and they are disproportionately black—would try to model their lives on it more than do people who watch less and believe less. And to grow up half-believing that joining the middle class will enable one to look and act like Claire and Cliff Huxtable is to be vulnerable to a rude awakening.[74]

Thus it is possible that more blacks now perceive success to be hollow since a growing middle class makes more blacks available for disillusionment. But a growing middle class eventually inures children to disillusionment since more and more of them are raised with the knowledge that success may not produce happiness. When these two paths will cross (or have crossed), and how many people (of any race) are on either, remains a matter of speculation.

In short, I see no dispositive reason, although several plausible ones, for ascribing the paradox of succeeding more to global rejection of the American dream. Middle-class African Americans are indeed increasingly disillusioned by the dream—that is the point I am seeking to explain—but their alienation has more in common with the spurned suitor than with the rejecting object of desire.

AFROCENTRICITY

Some affluent African Americans who have rejected the American dream have moved to an alternative vision. Making such a move is not racially specific: Americans from Henry David Thoreau to Edward Bellamy have rejected the dream not for its failures but for its ugliness, and have substituted for it a new vision. But compared with other groups, African Americans have developed alternative ideologies more fully and sustained them more consistently. Marcus Garvey offered a distinctive ideal in the 1920s (albeit without much appeal to middle-class blacks), as did W. E. B. Du Bois in the 1930s and the American Society of African Culture in the 1950s (with about as much appeal). Currently some proponents of Afrocentric education pit their vision of traditional African values against the American dream.

Afrocentricity is variously described, but two common formulations speak directly to the ideology of the dream. The first specifies the seven values of Nguza Saba, the cultural system that provides "the matrix and minimum set of values by which Black people must order their relations and live their lives, if they are to liberate themselves and begin to build a new world and a new people to inhabit it." The three most important for my purposes are Umoja (Unity), Ujima (Collective Work and Responsibility), and Nia (Purpose). The first emphasizes "commitment to family, community, nation, and Black unity." The second strengthens this commitment by "elevating the interests of the community above those of the individual. . . . Individualistic behavior is defined as a sign of immaturity and boyhood." The third specifies the commitment by proposing "to make our collective vocation the building and developing of our community in order to restore our people to their traditional greatness." The other four goals suggest ways to achieve unity, including self-determination ("to define ourselves, . . . create for ourselves, and speak for ourselves"), cooperative economic enterprises, creativity ("to leave our community more beautiful and beneficial than we inherited it"), and faith ("in our people, our parents, . . . our leaders, and the righteousness and victory of our struggle").[75]

Most proponents see Afrocentricity as antithetical to a Eurocentric worldview. But the Nguza Saba and the American dream are not necessarily in contradiction, especially if one defines success in nonmaterial terms and allows for collective pursuit of the dream.[76] Another common depiction of Afrocentricity, however, is more intrinsically opposed to the underlying presumptions and explicit values of the American dream. Its principles include "the interconnectedness of all things; oneness of mind, body, and spirit; collective identity; consanguineal family structure; consequential morality; analogue thinking; phenomenological time; and spirituality."[77]

This formulation is less programmatic and more evocative than the seven goals of Nguza Saba. It seeks unity among all people who have been, are now, or will be living, as well as unity among people, animate and inanimate nature, and God. It also seeks unity within the person, so that spiritual, emotional, and physical illness (or well-being) are indistinguishable. A frequently quoted Ashanti proverb suggests the intensity of collective sentiment: "I am because we are, without we I am not. I am because we are; and since we are, therefore I am." Thus collective survival dominates individual achievement, wealth is to be shared rather than saved or consumed within the family, and "aggression directed toward another person is also aggression against oneself."[78]

The abhorrence of boundaries extends to morality, temporality, and the very meaning of reality. Afrocentrists with these convictions reject European binary thinking, which "divides concepts into mutually exclusive polar opposites such as good/bad" in favor of African analogue thinking or "personalism," which permits a much more modulated morality. Moral boundaries are abhorrent because other boundaries are also: "We do not have to make absolute distinctions between mind and matter, form and substance, ourselves and the world."[79] Similarly, Afrocentrists reject the European conception of time as future-oriented and mathematical; they favor instead the traditional African conception of time as present-oriented and associated with specific events. To Europeans, time is a commodity; to Africans, time simply *is*, and can be produced or created but not used or wasted. Finally, Afrocentrists argue, phenomena that Westerners decry as supernatural or even superstitious (such as seeing the dead enter a room or being made ill by spirits) are just as "real" as microbes or the force of gravity.

It is immaterial here how much some or all Africans (or Westerners) actually believe and act as the Afrocentrists describe. What matters is the "paradigm shift . . . [intended] not simply to 'get our piece of the pie'— the same pie that we now know. No! . . . There is one kind of change in particular that . . . [we seek]: *A change in the way we think, and teach students to think; a change in thinking itself.*" Afrocentricity can have a hard edge: "Political, social, and cultural activities must be scrutinized constantly. *Deviations are intentional or unintentional misapplications of symbols and images which subvert the collective consciousness of our people.*"[80] But whether patrolling boundaries or wooing the young, those who promote this form of Afrocentricity see their worldview as a direct challenge to the dominant American ideology.

How much does Afrocentrism explain the paradox of succeeding more and enjoying it less? Strictly speaking, not much, because it has existed as a self-conscious movement for roughly a decade. Less strictly, of course, something like Afrocentrism (in the form of Garveyism, Negritude, black power, or pan-Africanism) has long had adherents among black Americans. Surveys give hints, although little solid evidence, on the content, extent, and trajectory of this cluster of alternatives to the American dream.

Anywhere from a minuscule fraction to a commanding majority of high-status blacks endorsed "black power" in the 1960s, depending on what they thought it meant. In 1968 over two-thirds approved of "black power" defined as starting more businesses, buying black, and taking pride in black history. But only 40 percent approved when black power was defined as teaching black children an African language, and only 3 percent approved of black power defined as a separate black nation.[81] Those results were typical; in most surveys almost half of high-status African Americans approved of black power so long as it meant that "Negroes should have their say in things" or that blacks should have "political and economic equality." Fewer than two in ten (and in one case, only 1 percent) endorsed black nationalism or defined black power as control of black communities.[82]

Similar results obtain for opinions about the Nation of Islam, the main alternative to dominant white values in the 1960s. In 1963, 10 percent or fewer of both well-off and poor blacks approved the aims of the Black Muslims [sic]. In 1964, 3 percent of black urbanites thought the Muslims were "doing the most . . . to help Negroes" and 57 percent "disapprove[d]" of them. In 1968 about one in ten students in black colleges thought Elijah Mohammed or the Black Muslims were doing an "excellent" job "in the fight for Negro rights."[83]

Now consider the decade of the 1980s. In 1980 fully 56 percent of African Americans felt closer to blacks in Africa than to whites in America, but only 1 percent chose the "black cultural heritage" as the "thing about black people that make[s] you feel the most proud." Low-status blacks identified more with Africans than did high-status blacks, and fewer than 15 percent of any status identified more with being black than with being an American.[84] About 20 percent of high-status blacks deny that their values are similar to those of the organization in which they work—but so do 20 percent of high-status whites. Over 20 percent of black members of college faculties deny that academics "share a common set of professional values"—but so do over a third of white faculty members.[85]

Views of particular actors reinforce the findings on movements or values. As blacks in New York City became more familiar with the Reverend Al Sharpton, Alton Maddox, and Vernon Mason during the Tawana Brawley, Bensonhurst, and Howard Beach incidents, favorable ratings of the three activists dropped by half and unfavorable ones rose by a factor of three. By 1990 a substantial majority of black New Yorkers gave them unfavorable ratings.[86] Also by the early 1990s, about 20 percent of blacks approved of Louis Farrakhan or described Black Muslim [sic] leaders as very effective in "representing black people like you"; only 12 percent of high-income, compared with 19 percent of low-income, blacks rated "leaders of black militant groups" similarly.[87]

If these disparate questions allow for a common interpretation, and if the responses can be trusted, we can draw three conclusions. Most African Americans abjure strong versions of black nationalism, especially when the survey question implies rejecting mainstream values rather than adding a distinctive black component to them. Only a few blacks, mainly among the poor, endorse clear alternatives to the dominant culture or ideology.[88] Finally, there are no grounds for concluding that support for African-centered positions *instead of* the American dream has increased, or decreased, since the 1960s.

We are left with two sets of views based on collective identity as candidates for explaining the paradox of succeeding more and enjoying it less. One contributes a lot, the other little. Many middle-class blacks feel an acute responsibility to their history, their poorer fellows, their race, and each other. That sense of responsibility may not be growing, but the sense that American society will not allow them to fulfill their responsibility despite new-found wealth and power clearly *is* growing. The new frustration leads to bitterness against other Americans, and eventually against the American dream.

A few middle-class blacks extend their anger at the failures of the dream into a rejection of its precepts and underlying values. They have always been a small, though highly vocal and visible, minority and there is no evidence that their numbers are growing. They certainly reinforce other African Americans' disillusionment with the American dream and deepen African Americans' political threat to the dream. But they do not in themselves contribute much to the paradox of succeeding more and enjoying it less.

We have at this point two sets of explanations for the paradox. One centers around individual feelings of relative deprivation, based minimally on whining, somewhat on gender competition, and mostly on a perception of white hostility. The other centers around the frustrations attendant on a collective identity that seems constantly to be under attack. Let us connect the two sets of explanations and locate them more firmly in the context of the American dream, before drawing implications for the future of the ideology and the nation.

Chapter Seven

COMPETITIVE SUCCESS AND COLLECTIVE WELL-BEING

> Nothing could be more satisfying to the biased hearts of today's Bull Connors and Sheriff Raineys than to see African Americans caught in the web of their own sense of powerlessness. . . . We have to rethink the extraordinary emphasis put on racism in this country. When we assert that racism creates all of society's ills, we are really saying that the way some people think holds some magical power that prevents African Americans from relying upon their own personal powers.

—Evan Kemp, then chair of the EEOC, 1990

> The tragedy of race relations in the United States is that there is no American dilemma. White Americans are not torn and tortured by the conflict between their devotion to the American creed and their actual behavior. They are upset by the current state of race relations, to be sure. But what troubles them is not that justice is being denied but that their peace is being shattered and their business interrupted.

—Charles Silberman, 1964

WHO IS RIGHT? Are middle-class African Americans mainly wrestling with monsters that are, if not of their own making, exacerbated by their sensitivities, insecurities, paranoia? Or are they confronting what white Americans refuse to face—that whites' main concern about race relations is that there is altogether too much of it? Are well-off blacks new participants in the American dream who do not (yet?) trust their own good fortune, or will they never be allowed fully to share the dream?

These questions can never be answered definitively because they are inherently contestable. The politics of next year are as likely to be a reaction against as a continuation of the politics of last year. Nevertheless, the paradox explored in chapter 3—what's all the fuss about?—opens the door to at least an interim answer.

WHITES' VIEWS OF BLACKS' COMPETITIVE SUCCESS

Over the past thirty years, as blacks have become more skeptical about their race's chance to participate in the American dream, whites have become more sanguine about the same point. Whites impatiently point to all the progress in racial equality since the bad old days of Jim Crow; blacks even more impatiently point to all the inequality that remains. The races talk past each other, with increasing intensity and disgust.

More precisely, whites see dramatic progress because blacks are now able, as they mostly were not thirty years ago, to pursue absolute and relative success.[1] Blacks see blockage because they still feel that they are generally not able to pursue competitive success.

Let me recapitulate those terms from the first chapter. If success is defined in absolute terms, achieving the American dream implies reaching some threshold of well-being, probably higher than where one began but not dazzling. If success is defined relatively, achieving the American dream consists in becoming better off than some point of comparison. Finally, competitive success consists in victory over someone else—my success implies at least your lack of success, at most your failure.

In brief, middle-class blacks sense and react with fury to what is trivialized as the "glass ceiling" but is really a fear of losing control in a competitive situation. As they see it, just enough whites cannot unlearn 350 years of racial domination, so that whites will permit a certain number of blacks to rise to a certain level of wealth, power, and prestige—but never so many or so high as to threaten dominion. Compared with the blanket "no" of three decades ago, "two out of three ain't bad."[2] But compared with the promise of the dream, it is insufferable—especially to the most successful African Americans, those precisely poised to pursue competitive success.[3]

Well-off African Americans make the point in various ways.[4] When the University of Massachusetts proclaimed Civility Week in response to a white-instigated racial brawl, black students renamed it Servility Week. A business executive "was the good nigger coming up, I wasn't a threat and my white peers helped me out, until now when I have moved up. Now those just above me who used to help me out are beginning to question my ability because I am a threat. As long as we're down in the company, they're secure, and we're alright." And a professor contrasts her experience with that of her students:

> I was not a threat at Yale [in the 1940s]. Young women mention the antagonism that they feel from their colleagues, but I worked and studied with other students. They knew that when I completed my studies,

I would leave their world. We were not in the same job market, we were not competitors. I was there to get an education and to take it back [to the black community]. And that was clearly understood by all.

In short, over three-quarters of blacks agree that whites "control power and wealth in America and do not want to share it with nonwhites."[5]

Whites make the same point, albeit often with a very different emotional valence. Sometimes they are explicit about their fear of black domination:

[Whites move from desegregating neighborhoods because] they're afraid the colored people are gonna get the upper hand; they're gonna move in and *take over*. So many of them will come that there'll be a majority of colored people instead of a majority of the whites.

And there should always be a majority of the whites? Yes. Because they *are* white. A majority rules, you know.

I'm not on welfare and I don't draw food stamps, and if I had to, I'd probably have to stand at the end of the line because there'd probably be a black person up there telling me I couldn't get them.

Nothing against the black folks from around here. They're a genteel people on the whole. But when you bring some folks up, when you try to equalize them, you've got to bring other folks down. And we're tired of being brought down.

They stole my pay, they stole my promotion.[6]

Surveys confirm comments. Even in 1961 a quarter of whites agreed that "Negroes . . . have more power than they should really have"; thirty years later, one-sixth agreed.[7] In 1966 about a quarter of whites agreed that if blacks got "better job opportunities" or a desegregated education, whites would lose.[8] In 1967, 40 percent of white Detroiters defined "black power" as a design for black domination of whites, although only 7 of 461 blacks concurred.[9] Although only half as many whites as blacks said their neighborhoods were damaged in the 1992 Los Angeles disturbances, more whites felt physically threatened. More generally, although African Americans are more likely to perceive a rise in overt racial violence, whites are more likely to claim that they have been victims of it.[10] And given that 15 percent of whites agree with the very strong statement that "almost all of the gains made by blacks in recent years have come at the expense of whites," it is especially striking that the "average American" estimates one-third of Americans to be black and one-fifth to be Latino (the real figures are 12 percent and 9 percent).[11]

The most prominent institutions in people's daily lives are their home, their children's school, and their job. In all three locations, some whites feel threatened by black encroachment and act accordingly. In 1992, 30 percent of white residents of Detroit claimed discomfort and 15 percent would try to move away if blacks comprised 20 percent of the neighborhood's residents. Over 40 percent disliked the idea of living in a one-third black neighborhood, and 30 percent would try to escape. Two-thirds would have disliked a half-black area, and over half would seek to move.[12] The effects of these views can be plainly seen in the persistence of residential segregation between blacks and whites, even while it is declining between whites and Asians or Latinos.[13]

The same phenomenon occurs with schools. As late as 1990–91, 3 percent of whites objected to sending their children to school with a few blacks; an additional 17 percent objected to a half-black school, and an additional 41 percent—over three-fifths in all—objected to a school where more than half of the students were black.[14] The effects of these views can be seen in white flight from cities and from public schools in racially mixed school districts, and in whites' resistance to mandatory desegregation plans.[15]

Ditto for jobs. Although only 7 percent of whites claim to have lost a job or promotion due to affirmative action, up to two-thirds believe it likely that a white person will suffer such a loss.[16] One-third of whites think affirmative action programs frequently "deprive someone . . . of their rights," and two-tenths think "blacks have more of a chance to get good jobs and education than whites." Half of white youth (compared with one-fifth of black youth) think that more whites lose out to blacks due to "special preference" than blacks lose to whites due to prejudice.[17] White men in firms with affirmative action programs suffer no significant loss in salary or authority compared with white men in firms without such programs, but the former anticipate more "reverse discrimination" than the latter do.[18]

A few whites move beyond avoidance or complaint into active aggression when they feel threatened by blacks. Most "hate crimes" against African Americans committed by white Chicagoans occur in neighborhoods with few black residents, low rates of homicide, and low rates of public assistance—but with high levels of perceived threat. That is, neighborhoods with few black residents but a large percentage increase in black immigrants suffer the most hate crimes, as do working-class neighborhoods whose residents fear an influx of low-income blacks or increasing crime.[19]

White politicians have traditionally fanned whites' exaggerated fears of losses to blacks. In his 1990 candidacy for the United States Senate, the former Klansman David Duke complained of welfare recipients "having children faster than they can raise your taxes to pay for them." Although both parties rejected him and his opponent outspent him three to one, Duke was supported by almost 60 percent of the white voters in Louisiana. Other things being equal, the more blacks living in a parish, the higher the proportion of whites in that parish who voted for him.[20] In the same year, Jesse Helms won a close senatorial race against a black Democratic candidate, Harvey Gantt, partly on the strength of an advertisement that showed a white fist crumpling a piece of paper with the voice-over of "You needed that job, and you were the most qualified. But they had to give it to a minority because of a racial quota. Is that fair?"[21]

Whites seek to maintain control of public, as well as of private, institutions. White Detroiters became more race-conscious in their votes for city council members as their status changed from that of the majority to that of a minority of voters. In Alabama, county commissioners revoked the authority of individual commissioners to allocate jobs and tax money in their districts, giving spending authority to the council as a whole in one case and to a county engineer in another. The former decision came just after a black was elected as a commissioner, the latter (perhaps) in anticipation of such an election. One stymied black commissioner commented, "You have influence, but power? None. . . . You're voted down on almost everything you try to do if it concerns black representation." A white townsman concurred: "White people run this county and that's the way it is."[22]

BLACKS' VIEWS OF WHITES' COMPETITIVE SUCCESS

Now, to some whites' expansive notion of competitive success add some middle-class blacks' equally expansive, although substantively different, understanding of competitive success. The issue here is often less one of numbers, position, or clout than of what counts as success. Where whites see racial neutrality in words, symbols, customs, or even actions, African Americans (increasingly?) see white domination.[23]

The phenomenon is best described through examples. In a complicated tangle at George Mason University, a white fraternity and sorority were penalized for dressing one contestant in blackface during an "ugliest girl" contest. After apologizing for its unintended insult to blacks, the fraternity sued the university for paying insufficient attention to the sexism in the incident. "A number of leading African American scholars say that legal arguments used against George Mason are consistent with attempts by an increasingly recalcitrant white society to redefine and muddle the issues of race and gender in an effort to maintain the status quo. . . . The issue [i]s a 'question of *power* . . . the ability to redefine reality,'" claims one psychologist.[24]

Afrocentrists similarly attend to the power of language:

"What kind of salad dressing do you prefer?" This question . . . elicits replies like "French," "Russian," or "Italian." We are asked to participate subconsciously in the drama of Europe. . . . We now have sauces and dressings with names like Ghanaian, Nigerian, Senegalese, and Tanzanian. The idea is that the Afrocentrist refuses to be inundated by a symbolic reality which denies her existence.[25]

Speech, as the Supreme Court tells us, extends beyond words. Black students at the University of Massachusetts want no more Minuteman mascot ("to have a white male represent a student body that is not exclusively white or male . . . promotes racism"); white students bemoan the "politically correct wasteland." Black aldermen and Mayor Harold Washington sought to replace the high-masted sailing ship on the seal of the city of Chicago because it looked like a slave ship and thus "represent[s] institutionalized racism in this country"; "ridiculous" and "preposterous" responded white aldermen. Black residents of Memphis were furious over a McDonald's promotional calendar that had "National Nothing Day" printed on the birthday of Martin Luther King, Jr.; the calendar's originators were horrified but called it an "innocent mistake." Students demand that schools named for the slave-owners George Washington and Thomas Jefferson be renamed; the school board refuses.[26] In all these cases blacks see unacceptable domination where whites see, at most, a faux pas.

Even institutional changes seen only a few decades ago as the means to eliminate white supremacy now seem to many African Americans to reinforce it, albeit a little more subtly. School desegregation is the epitomizing case. For decades black activists fought to desegregate schools, whether to attain more resources, eliminate the stigma of exclusion, or foster a truly liberal society. But a few African Americans in the 1960s, and many more by the 1980s, saw desegregated schools as yet another ploy by whites to retain political, social, and psychological control. Their reasoning is partly pragmatic—desegregation turned out to destroy the cohort of black teachers and administrators in the south, burden black more than white children with transportation and adjustment, and substitute classroom tracking for school-level segregation. But it is also ideological—it is insulting to imply that "black kids can learn only by chasing after white kids," and the distinctive qualities of black nationhood are destroyed by the bland amalgam of mainstream (read white) society. Thus where liberal whites (and blacks) see school deseg-

TABLE 7.1
Who Gets Special Treatment? by Race and Gender
(percent saying yes)

	Respondent		
Response Category	Men	Women	Blacks
Men	4	33	—
Women	24	4	12
Minorities	42	45	2
Whites	—	—	47

Source: Strohmer (1988: 290).

regation as opening opportunities, nationalist blacks see it as shutting the doors against collective pride and national self-determination.

Affirmative action and its descendant, the management of diversity, often have the same effect: an institutional reform designed to benefit first African Americans and eventually all Americans produces a situation in which all four race/gender groups think they are losing to the others. A stunning demonstration of this point was a survey of all 16,000 employees of Merck Corporation (table 7.1).[27] Men think women and minorities benefit unfairly; women think men and minorities benefit unfairly; blacks think whites and perhaps women benefit unfairly. Here is a Condorcet cycle with a vengeance.

Some whites resist losing to blacks. They define losses very broadly, so broadly that sometimes they feel as though they have lost when blacks see neither win nor loss on the part of anyone.[28] Most blacks resist losing to whites. They also define losses very broadly, so broadly that sometimes *they* feel as though they have lost when whites see neither win nor loss. The dimension on which whites define winning and losing is often different from the dimension on which blacks define winning and losing. The more successful the African Americans, the more they challenge positions and statuses that whites cherish, and the more attuned they are, in turn, to symbolic slights. We have here plenty of reason for the paradox of succeeding more and enjoying it less.

SUBMERGING THE INDIVIDUAL INTO
THE COLLECTIVE

But even this complicated mess does not complete the story. After all, the surveys show that only a minority of whites resist black competitive success.[29] Some are indifferent. Many vote for black gubernatorial or mayoral candidates; a few live in predominantly black neighborhoods. Whites pay huge sums of money to applaud and enrich black entertainers and athletes. And resistance to blacks' competitive success is not necessarily racist in origin or intent; white politicians fight incursions by white outsiders as much as and for many of the same reasons as they fight black challengers.

Furthermore, not all blacks lose competitions; some are as gratified as the corporate vice president quoted at the beginning of chapter 5. Black frustration about white domination is sometimes unfounded, itself racially tinged, or simply a cover for a power move.

If we shift our focus from individual actors to institutions and processes, another set of caveats emerges. After all, it is "doubtful that whites have a capacity to act in unison to determine what is an acceptable level of success by African Americans and then to ration black opportunity accordingly. . . . Everyone, white and non-white, has difficulty acting in unison."[30] And to the degree that there *has* been unified, systematic change in white-dominated institutions and processes over the past three decades, that change has most frequently opened up opportunities to African Americans—hence the growth of the new black middle class and the possibility of the paradox of succeeding more and enjoying it less.

Nevertheless, well-off African Americans increasingly believe that as they achieve absolute and relative success, they run headlong into barricades erected by whites against competitive success. To explain the intensity and breadth of that belief in the face of a complicated social reality, we must add beliefs about the collectivity to beliefs about individual chances.

One concern is as simple to state as it is hard to solve: middle-class African Americans see what is happening to other blacks, and it disheartens and frightens them. It frightens them because they fear being sucked back into a life where even absolute success is barely imaginable. It disheartens them because they are close enough in time and in personal ties to remember how it feels to be poor as well as stigmatized. It is one thing to be passed over for CEO or to lose an election for mayor; it is another to see black children refused food, education, or police protection. Whites may not actually be doing any such thing, at least intentionally. But their apparent denial of competitive success to blacks at the top of the social scale makes it plausible to believe that they deny even absolute success at the bottom.

Middle-class African Americans not only see poor blacks being prohibited from pursuing their dream; they also see the race as a whole excluded from whites' vision of who the dream could even possibly encompass. Whites seem incapable of imagining black people without "distortions":

In newspapers, on television, in movies, and in the scholarly literature
. . . [w]e are routinely presented visions of Black males as raging, roar-
ing beasts set loose among the populace to prey on them as lion-on-
sheep. . . . Black children are presented and painted as inevitable failures, doomed from the womb as certain candidates for welfare, prison,
and school dropout. . . . Black women [are portrayed] as loud-talking,
loose-hipped bitches held to blame for the demise/deterioration of
Black men, Black children, and Black communities.[31]

Even worse, perhaps, is the feeling that whites do not see blacks at all in
the ways that really matter. White contributors to the literary canon depict universal human concerns; black candidates for a revised canon
bring "diversity" or even "fragmentation." White feminists seek what is
good for women; black feminists seek what is good for their race. Poll-
sters—predominantly well-off, white men—ask endless questions about
poor people, women, and African Americans; it seldom occurs to them
to probe views about their own kind. Santa Claus and Jesus Christ are
white; so are the gowns of debutantes and confirmation classes. The
South lost the Civil War. Enough of this may make one feel even more
like an outsider than does deliberate racism—which at least focuses on
its object.[32]

In this context, the 1992 verdict in the trial over the beating of Rodney King in Los Angeles hit like a thunderclap. Survey questions show
the breadth of the damage: although the level of "ethnic alienation from
American society" did not change among white and Latino residents of
Los Angeles interviewed before and after the verdict and subsequent
riot, it rose sharply among African Americans. The best-off respondents
demonstrated the strongest rise in alienation.[33] Comments show the
depth of the damage. A middle-class mother three thousand miles away
from Los Angeles who has "inculcated" her children with her "color
blindness and beliefs in the fairness of democracy" watched television in
despair: "How could I tell my children that in spite of our economic
status and their privilege that they shared more with the hopeless black
lives they witnessed on television than with the friends (all white) that
they've had all their lives?" A resident of Los Angeles was less rumina-
tive: "I was filled with rage. Every time I heard a Simi Valley juror I
wanted to shoot the radio. It feels so awful to feel I have no value in this
society. . . . And if I'm feeling this level of rage, what must they be feeling in South Central?"[34]

The worst off of the race live atrocious lives; the race is seen as an
indistinguishable dangerous blur or not seen at all. The best off, no matter how much they succeed personally, cannot escape either *feeling* at-

tached to their race or *being* attached by others to their race.[35] Where is there room for the American dream's promise of equality for all in the pursuit of one's chosen goals?

Some well-off African Americans respond to the fact that whites attach them, willy nilly, to their race by struggling to escape: "I am black, but blackness is not the totality of my identity. It is not even the core of my identity. . . . I have the freedom to define myself as I think best (and after all, who's living my life?) *and* if I have to fight white *and* black America to retain that freedom, so be it."[36] To one holding this view, to be defined mainly as black is to be diminished, not because blackness is intrinsically diminishing but because any ascribed identity is:

> The most important challenges and opportunities that confront me derive not from my racial condition, but rather from my human condition. I am a husband, a father, a son, a teacher, an intellectual, a Christian, a citizen. In none of these roles is my race irrelevant, but neither can racial identity alone provide much guidance for my quest to adequately discharge these responsibilities.[37]

Other well-off African Americans view this struggle to separate oneself from the race as treason: "Our leaders should be proactive cultural personifiers of our people and not individual humans."[38] Still others view it as simply impossible, whether desirable or not: "the possibility of honor for an individual is integrally tied to the possibility of his or her community having, or potentially having, honorable status. . . . The moral community of America is most often conceived in ways that exclude the African-American community."[39] Still others wish the deviants luck, perhaps hoping against hope that they will finally be the ones to break the mold that white society has poured African Americans into.

Like so many phenomena that I have discussed, the sense that one can neither escape one's race nor combat the unremitting hostility or blindness to which it is subject is not new. So how can it help explain the change in attitudes captured by the paradox of succeeding more? Because what is new is the success of middle-class blacks, who believed (or whose parents believed) what the American dream told them, that this conundrum should not exist and could be solved. Individual achievement is supposed to enable one to escape collective identity if one wishes to—yet it does not. Achievement by many individuals is supposed to dissolve collective denigration—and yet it has not. The dream is supposed to allow each person or group to define success for itself—yet it will not.

This is the context in which many affluent African Americans view those few whites who can be identified as resisting black competitive success. In such a context, overtly hostile whites seem to be merely the tip of the iceberg of white resistance to any black's achievement. In such a context, white-dominated institutions and processes that purportedly enable and encourage black success appear to be mere covers for—or at best anomalous exceptions to—those institutions and processes that function to keep blacks as a race stigmatized, nonindividuated, and mostly poor. Individuals cannot fully succeed because the group is not allowed to succeed; the group is not allowed to succeed despite the fact that an increasing number of individuals are to some degree successful. One is left only with Kenneth Clark's elegy, so moving because so restrained:

> Reluctantly, I am forced to face the likely possibility that the United States will never rid itself of racism and reach true integration. I look back and I shudder at how naive we all were in our belief in the steady progress racial minorities would make through programs of litigation and education, and while I very much hope for the emergence of a revived civil rights movement . . . , I am forced to recognize that my life has, in fact, been a series of glorious defeats.[40]

SUCCEEDING MORE AND THE AMERICAN DREAM

These emotional and political clashes affect the viability of the American dream itself. If whites are pushed into recognizing that they are still defending racially discriminatory barricades, they must then face up to their own, their ideology's, and their society's imperfections. Perhaps such a realization will lead to personal and societal reformation in the service of the cherished dream; that hope fueled the strategy of Martin Luther King, Jr., for most of his career. And he did, to a degree unimaginable ahead of time, succeed. But the danger is that "the psychic price of confronting . . . the basic questions that black people have raised is too high for white Americans to pay."[41] If middle-class African Americans insist on their proportionate share of the pie, whites must either give up a lot or admit that the dream is exclusionary and hypocritical.[42] If middle-class African Americans insist that blackness means no more— or less—than whiteness, middle-class whites must address the possibility that "they have practiced dehumanizing repression and engaged in self-destructive conformity—and all this in a society that values . . . freedom and individual worth." If whites refuse to face up to these issues, they risk reifying the dream and their own behavior, pushing "theory and practice . . . farther apart," and substituting blame and wishful thinking for the egalitarian optimism implied by the dream at its best.

Threats to the American dream come also from the other side of the racial divide. If middle-class African Americans insist that every time they are passed over for a promotion it is due to racism, or that every white who denies resistance to blacks' competitive success is either a liar or an oddity, then the dream is in trouble. If enough well-off African Americans are so blindly nationalistic that they will, for example, permit parentless black children to remain in the limbo of foster care rather than be adopted by whites, then efforts to extend the dream across the color line may be doomed. Most seriously, if more than a small proportion of the best-off African Americans come to equate the American dream with white oppression or selfish shallowness, they will as a matter of self-respect give up even trying to succeed or helping others to succeed by its tenets. And, for better or worse, a nation in which a substantial minority (of any race) believes that it is honor-bound to fail by the precepts that the majority (of any race) holds dear is a nation that cannot sustain itself for long, at least as it has always been.

Thus two possibilities emerge at this point. A benign "tipping point" could occur, when enough blacks occupy prominent positions that whites no longer resist their presence and blacks feel that American society sometimes accommodates them instead of always the reverse.[43] That point is closer than it has ever been in our history.[44] After all, half of black corporate managers surveyed in 1979 feel that they have a lot of power in their job, and 44 percent perceive a "high degree of fit" in their corporation. (An additional 40 percent have "moderate" power and feel moderately well integrated.) At least eight in ten African-American state legislators are satisfied with their careers, feel that black legislators have considerable influence and their issues receive a fair hearing, and agree that legislation important to blacks sometimes or frequently is approved. The youngest are the most satisfied. Almost 80 percent of blacks claim "a good friend" who is white, and high-status blacks are especially likely to make such claims.[45] Conversely, when whites are clearly outnumbered by blacks, they frequently settle down and get along fairly well. White voters sometimes elect black candidates and participate in interracial coalitions.[46] Whereas a decade ago problems of "equal employment opportunity" came in almost last (just above sexual harassment) on a list of executives' "human-resource management issues," by 1992 "cultural diversity" led corporate executives' list of "workforce concerns."[47]

Alternatively, the closer blacks come to *really* breaking down three and a half centuries of racial walls, the more whites might resist and the greater the degree of interracial conflict and intrapsychic strain that will ensue. In this scenario, the "homeostatic . . . principle of the . . . system of racial domination" will persist. Slavery was followed by debt peonage; debt peonage was followed by Jim Crow laws; Jim Crow was followed by resegregation within purportedly desegregated schools; desegregation and affirmative action were followed by "an upsurge of direct racism, reflected most crudely in . . . overt racist attacks . . . but . . . far more dangerously, in the powerful cultural signals given by the Reagan presidency that racist intolerance is once again acceptable."[48]

The benign tipping point was not possible before the growth of the new black middle class in the 1970s and 1980s; the homeostatic principle of racial domination has always been available. Which alternative white Americans choose over the next few decades, and whether well-off black Americans regain their faith, will largely determine whether the promise of the American dream can become our practice.

Under the Spell of the Great National Suggestion

Chapter Eight

REMAINING UNDER THE SPELL

> In America, it's your duty and responsibility to try to get up there, at least up into the middle class, so when your kids grow up they will have a better living. Someday you could have some millionaires in your family if everyone works hard enough.

> Ain' nothin' happ'nin' down here. Watts riot didn't really change nothin'. All dat poverty money what got spent, never got to d' people. Still cain't get a job, polices ever'time on yo' case. People just don't have no hope. Next time d' riot ain' gon' just stay down here. It's a whole bunch o' white folks gon' know 'bout what's happ'nin' up dere in Hollywood and Beverly Hills.

THE FIRST COMMENT is from Patrick François, a born-again Christian teen who is the son of a Haitian farmworker now living in Florida. Patrick's mother picks crops six days a week, fifteen hours a day, earning $45 to $125 a day during the season, to support her six children. Patrick shares a three bedroom trailer with eight other people. But "we have everything we need. When it comes to money, if my mamma don't have it, we understand and we do without it."

The second comment is from a prescient resident of Watts of about the same age and social status, in the early 1970s.[1] What distinguishes these men from each other? Which better represents the sentiments of most poor black Americans? What does each envision when he thinks of the American dream? Which will pay a higher cost for his beliefs and actions as he moves into and through adulthood?

The central paradox to be understood about poor African Americans is the reverse of that for wealthy blacks: why are so many poor blacks like Patrick and not like the Watts resident? That is, why do most poor blacks remain under the spell of the great national suggestion despite the fact that they have no realistic chance to succeed in conventional terms? That poor blacks are in many ways falling behind other blacks and most whites is common knowledge. That most poor blacks have no real chance to catch up is just as well known, though often carefully ignored. That most poor blacks nevertheless subscribe to the American dream, or

at least do not reject it, is often obscured behind widespread concern
about the urban "underclass." Why their support continues, and how
long it will continue, are unclear. The purpose of this part of the book
is to remind readers of the first two points, elucidate the third, and speculate about the fourth.

I will explore the paradox of remaining under the spell of the great
national suggestion in the spirit of a joke told by a black playwright to a
white journalist:

> We come in four types—Afro-Americans, blacks, colored folks, and nig-
> gers. . . . Take vacations. An Afro-American goes to the Bahamas. A
> black goes to Harlem. Colored folks load their kids in the car and go
> down south to visit their kinfolks. . . . [And] niggers don't go on vaca-
> tion—they wait for you to go on vacation.[2]

The four types of poor blacks to be analyzed here are distinguished not
by their vacation plans but by their responses to the ideology of the
American dream. Many poor African Americans believe in it, strive for
success according to its precepts, and hope for their children when they
give up hope for themselves. Some respond to surveyors and other ques-
tioners as though they believe in the dream, but do little to pursue their
apparent goals and may really not believe in much at all. Others believe
in the ideology of the American dream, but their beliefs become distorted and their behaviors troublesome as they respond to constraints in
seeking success. A few, finally, reject either the ideology of the dream, its
precepts about how to succeed, or both.[3]

BELIEF IN THE DREAM

Poor African Americans experience plenty of discrimination, whether
working or merely standing on the sidewalk:

> My boss'll watch me like a hawk, thinking I'm gon' steal something.
> And it's the whites that be stealing him blind. Like, anytime somebody
> black comes in and I wait on 'em, th' Man gon' check me out. Now this
> been goin' on for two years, the cat still don't trust me. He don't do the
> whites that way; they come in, stay for two or three weeks and they got
> the run of the place. They can walk away with the whole place, but he'll
> blame it on me.

> Most of the time, you know, in dem white cars, they look at you like
> you got somethin'—like some disease or we animals. I's cold man! Dem
> honkies righteously prejudice!"

They are similarly aware of their poverty, whether it affects where they
live—"It's an MF . . . living in this kind of neighborhood. . . . People

don't want to live like this, but there ain't nothing else they can do. They ain't making no money. So what are you going to do? You don't have no choice"—or what they can give their children—"It's easier in the summertime. The kids eat less in the summer. We can kind of make it. In the winter, you got the heating bill and the light bill and the phone bill. In the winter, some peoples can't make it."[4]

Yet the majority still believe that everyone in America can be successful, that achievement lies within one's own hands, and that success is associated with virtue. Some attend to the hard edges of the American dream: "Our people is got to learn this: responsibility and privilege goes together. If a man don't accept his family and be responsible for his family, he's got no business having any privileges." Others revel in softer fantasies: "It's easy to do anything, as long as you set your mind to it, . . . if you really want to be something. . . . I wanna be somethin'. I don't wanna be living in the projects the rest of my life." Some give the American dream a racial spin:

> I'm tired of begging. . . . Until we find out that we have the power ourselves to do some of the things we're waiting for the Man to do, . . . we're going to be sort of stuck. . . . We have a responsibility to produce, and I don't think we can hold the white man responsible at this time.

Others focus on class differences within their race:

> What I can't stand is these *siddity* folks who move out of town, them little bourgeois-ass niggers. They go out there and just tear up. They don't know anything about lawns, anyway. The only thing a black person wants to do with something green is put it in a pot and boil it with some ham hocks.[5]

But the central theme remains the same; one can achieve one's dreams by dint of hard work, virtue, and perhaps some racial or class solidarity.

EDUCATION AND WORK

Most poor blacks who remain under the spell of the great national suggestion see two paths to achieving their dreams: education and work.

Education

Despite being "teased at school when roaches used to crawl out of my lunch sack," one boy "told my little brother we were going to make it ourself and go to school like we should." He was in crowded company. Over 90 percent of youth in public job training programs see education as very important in "getting ahead." This response receives 30 percentage points more support than the next most important criterion, "hard work," which comes in ahead of "money in the family" and "knowing the right people." Although almost all of this sample was black, fewer than one-third deemed race very important in determining success.[6] More poor black than white, Latino, or Asian students agree on the need to learn core subjects. More poorly educated blacks than any other racial/class group express "a great deal" of confidence in schools, even though they are not notably more confident about other American institutions (except, inexplicably, banks).[7] It is thus not surprising that more poor black than Latino, Asian, or white parents discuss their children's school experiences and plans, restrict television on school nights, set rules about grades, help with homework, and join the parents' association.[8]

Furthermore, poor African Americans act in accord with their belief in education. Controlling for sex and socioeconomic status, African Americans are no more likely to drop out of school than whites, are more likely to choose an academic than a vocational curriculum, and are more likely to choose a four-year than a two-year college.[9] Blacks are more sanguine than whites in their views of whether schools provide children with skills, interest in and ability to think for themselves, citizenship training, and even discipline. Controlling for socioeconomic status, more black than white parents engage in "supportive activities" in the newly decentralized Chicago public schools.[10] In light of the horrible conditions in some high schools,[11] and in light of the number of black students thought to be at risk of poor school performance,[12] those results are almost heartbreaking in the degree of faith that they reveal.[13]

Work

Jobs are even more important than education[14] (which itself may be valued mainly as a credential for getting a job).[15] A minister begins his service by reading want ads, then exhorting his congregation: "Now, you can get that job, church. There are jobs out there. . . . Out of 85,000 pilots in this country, only 200 are black. You can be a pilot. . . . Say amen. Now say amen again."[16] Many more black than white or Latina poor jobless mothers want a regular job and are willing to work more than five days a week. The level of wages below which poor blacks will not accept a job is almost as low as immigrants' and much lower than comparably poor whites'. Jobless young black men are much more willing than comparable white men to accept unskilled jobs at low wages, despite their higher aspirations to skilled or white-collar jobs.[17] Although many fewer poorly educated blacks than whites have been pro-

moted or expect a promotion soon, just as many value highly the opportunity to be promoted. Almost twice as many poor blacks (24 percent)
as poor whites (14 percent) agree that learning "to work hard" is the
most important thing a child can do to "prepare him or her for life."[18]
Many more low-status blacks than any other racial/class group describe
themselves as "hard-working";[19] conversely, three times as many well-
off as poor blacks admit that "not trying hard enough" has kept them
from getting good jobs. More poor African Americans than any other
race/class group claim that the most important quality of a friend is
being "responsible."[20]

When they can do so, poor African Americans act on their claims
about wanting to work. A program to guarantee poor youths jobs if they
completed high school enrolled 73 percent of eligible blacks, compared
with 48 percent of eligible Latinos and only 30 percent of eligible
whites. Black youths participated longer, were more gratified by the program, and showed better results. Black men obtained 72 percent, and
black women 128 percent, more jobs than they would have had absent
the program. (Gains for whites and Latinos were under 25 percent.) As
the evaluators cautiously noted, "these findings suggest that racial discrimination may be operating in the labor market in the absence of [the
school/jobs program]."[21] Another demonstration project found that
two years after completing a program to move AFDC recipients into
jobs, black, but not white or Latina, mothers were working significantly
more hours and earning significantly more money than otherwise similar
nonparticipants.[22]

Even absent demonstration projects, poor African Americans are
often determined to work. Welfare recipients supplement their grants
through work off the books, sometimes in illegal activities. This activity
may cheat taxpayers, but it also shows determination to be productive
and to earn enough to live decently. Poor blacks who obtain subsidized
housing in the suburbs work more than otherwise similar recipients who
stay in the city. The reasons are simple: jobs are available, earnings and
children are safe, and coworkers "ma[ke] me feel that I'm worth something." Even among AFDC recipients who receive support from family
and friends, blacks are more likely to work than are whites or Latinos.[23]
Despite the authoritarian and sometimes dangerous working conditions
of the United States armed forces, black youths disproportionately volunteer to serve, and "vastly more blacks attempt to join the military than
are accepted." Black central-city residents cope with a longer commut-
ing time to their work than do similarly located whites.[24] The main
cause of young white men moving from school or work into "idleness"
is having poor or poorly educated parents; young black men, in contrast,
move into idleness mainly when the local labor market is poor.[25] Perhaps most tellingly, one-third of black service workers, operatives, and

unskilled laborers claim that "nothing" bothers them about their job—fully twice as many as black professionals and managers.[26]

Thus the question "How do you know that what poor blacks say on surveys is valid?" has a simple answer: many work now, and most would given the chance.

THE IMPORTANCE OF BEING IN CONTROL

> Nothing I can think of [will keep me from finding a job]. I'm able bodied, willing, and able. I do go and check on jobs. . . . It's just a matter of time.
>
> —AFDC recipient in Chicago, 1987

Why do so many poor blacks remain under the spell of the great national suggestion, despite the obvious reasons they have to reject it? Consider first psychologically based explanations for persistent faith that education and work will lead to success. The Supreme Court based its decision in *Brown* v. *Board of Education* on the assertion that racial segregation of children "generates a feeling of inferiority as to their status in the community that may affect their hearts and minds in a way unlikely ever to be undone."[27] But that assertion is arguably wrong. The most thorough reviews of "minority self-evaluation" find "no need to assume that blacks suffer from low self-esteem or low aspirations" and conclude that "personal self-esteem among black populations [is] either equal to or greater than that among whites."[28] Studies focusing on the combination of race *and* class are more mixed. Some find that even after controlling for a wide range of variables, high-status African Americans have significantly higher self-esteem or greater hopes than lower-status African Americans.[29] Most recent studies, however, find broad concurrence with Ruby Lee Daniels' proud claim that "I know I don't have what other people have—money, cars—but I never felt lower than other people. My grandfather always taught me to feel equal to other people—the big-shot people who went to this and that college and have degrees. I can talk just as good as them. I know the words."[30]

If poor African Americans are as confident as other Americans that they know the words, it follows that they would be just as eager for success. And they are: aspirations of poor blacks are usually as high as those of whites or well-off blacks.[31] For example, in 1980 half of a sample of poor young black men in inner cities aspired to white-collar positions by age 30, and a fifth thought their chances of achieving such a position were excellent. A decade later, almost twice as many poor black as white parents anticipated that their children would complete college or attain advanced degrees, and the children concurred.[32] In 1988 more poor black than white urban eighth graders thought their mother expected them to graduate from college, and many more held the same expectations for themselves.[33]

As chapter 4 showed, however, poor blacks are usually less sure than well-off blacks or whites that they actually control the means of achieving their aspirations. It is at this point that the American dream as a rational set of rules for success recedes into the American dream as a fantasy or dream of success despite realistic expectations.[34] The nonrational props underlying poor blacks' belief in the American dream take several forms.

One is "the denial of personal disadvantage." Most community college students in one study saw themselves as suffering from more discrimination than either "men as a group" or "women as a group." Nevertheless, most thought their "chance for a successful life" was at least as good as others'.[35] If these data can be generalized as chapter 3 suggests that they can, the ideology of the American dream is unbelievably powerful: even self-described victims of discrimination believe that they are more likely to succeed than are those who need not fight discrimination.

Reinforcing the denial of personal disadvantage is the denial of collective disadvantage when the collectivity is closely linked to oneself. Most Americans think Congress is doing a bad job but their own representative is fine.[36] Nine-tenths think crime is rising in the nation, but only half think it is rising in their community. Teachers in *all* Chicago schools see students in their own school as "basically good kids" or "the quiet, sweet ones" but fear the gangs and students at the "really tough schools" elsewhere in the city.[37]

Racial issues follow the same pattern. Only 20 percent of blacks think race relations are "generally good" across the United States, but three times as many are satisfied with their own community. A slight majority of both races predict "a lot of racial prejudice and discrimination in America," but only one-fourth of whites and one-third of blacks say the same for their community. Although two-thirds of African Americans think the police in most big cities are unfair to blacks, a plurality (45 percent) think their local police are racially fair.[38] Although everyone outside large public housing projects, and many inside them, deplore their filth, crime, and disrepair, a surprising number of residents resist moving even to presumably better surroundings.[39]

Psychologists explain these anomalous views by the need to believe that one controls one's own life. After all, "crime can't be seen as being too bad in respondents' neighborhoods; the schools must be good and the health care fine. If not, people might be forced to ask themselves why they haven't moved."[40]

That comment reflects the perspective of a person who could afford to move if he chose to; many poor people cannot. Nevertheless, the sentiment may be universal among Americans. The urge to assert control, even when the assertion is manifestly false, is extremely powerful. One of psychology's most arresting sets of results appears in a small study of victims of accidents that left them partially or fully paralyzed. Almost two-fifths attributed no blame to themselves; over two-fifths percent attributed half or more of the blame to themselves. Self-blame was functional: "the more victims blamed another, or . . . believed they could have avoided the accident, the worse they coped. The more victims blamed themselves, however, the better they coped." Those who had been the only person involved in the accident—and who thus could not blame anyone else for it—were happier than those who could blame an adversary. The authors' subtle analysis of why victims blamed themselves and why self-blamers coped better leads not to the conclusion that these people are crazy, but to two intriguing speculations. First, "people may have an exaggerated notion of their own causal powers. . . . If the immediate cause of an accident is not avoidable or controllable, the victim may look for a prior cause that is." Second, "the data may be . . . indicative of a need for an orderly and meaningful world."[41]

We cannot safely leap from a single study of a few quadriplegics or community college students to conclusions about the third of African Americans who remain desperately poor. But the findings are suggestive: the urge to feel in control of one's own life and to believe that the world is orderly and meaningful is very strong, at least among those imbued with the ideology of the American dream.[42] Even people who are constantly confronted with evidence that, because of their race and class, they lack any say in where they live or what their children can do persist in asserting the authorship of their own lives.

Thus these apparently irrational survey results: in 1968 fewer than a third of poor black respondents "usually" succeeded in carrying out their plans, and only a quarter had found their life to "work out the way you want it to." Nevertheless, almost half affirmed that "it's better to plan your life a good way ahead" than to leave things to chance, and over half insisted that "they can run their lives pretty much the way they want to."[43] Twenty years later, three-fifths of a group of long-term unemployed African Americans, most of whom thought it almost impossible to find any job, nevertheless insisted that they could run their lives as they wished rather than finding the problems of life too big for them.[44]

It is probably the case that poor African Americans with high motivation and self-confidence do better than those without.[45] But the actual relationship between a sense of efficacy and success is murky, and sometimes greater motivation and higher expectations are "the *result* of past changes in economic status and not the cause of subsequent better-ment."[46] It seems clearer that poor African Americans cling to their be-lief in the American dream despite their circumstances than that they have any grounds for doing so or that their belief will make much mate-rial difference in their lives.

HISTORICAL COMPARISONS

History as well as psychology explains why so many poor African Ameri-cans remain under the spell of the great national suggestion. People old enough to remember Jim Crow appreciate that, however bad things still are, they can now walk down the center of the sidewalk without antici-pating a lynching. Some focus on the changes in their own lives:

> Now there may be some hostility when you go up and try to get this job that the guy is trying to apply for. . . . But there's a law to make that all go even . . . [Racism] is still going on, but they set out laws which like say: hey, you got to have a certain amount of blacks in this job, you know. So that eased the pressure, you know—the race thing, a little bit. It's easier now for the black man 'cause he got a little more ground, a little more opportunity, so he goes forward. It's a little slack now.

Others focus on broader structural and political changes:

> When I was young, the Ku Klux Klan hung a boy 'cause a white girl say he looked at her. Driving down to Florida one time, a man refused to sell me gas. Just 'cause I was black. But Dr. King, he changed a lot of things. He said there'll come a time when white chillun and black chil-lun will play together. That happened. And all the folks down at city hall, they all black folks. I'm sure glad I lived long enough to see things turn out the way they did. All those bad old days, they gone with the wind.

Those old enough to remember "all those bad old days" attest to their lasting damage: "I still feel uncomfortable shaking the white man's hand," confessed one elderly participant in the 1983 March on Washing-ton. But for him the lesson of that damage is determination, not bitter-ness: "that's why the younger people have to keep the struggle going."[47]

Some young people accept that lesson. Thus black residents of public housing projects may express more optimism than white residents pre-cisely *because* they are black. For poor white youths to accept the achievement ideology "is to admit that their parents are lazy or stupid or both. . . . [But] acceptance of the ideology on the part of the [black] Brothers does not necessarily involve such harsh implications, for they can point to racial prejudice to explain their parents' defeats." Further-more, "the Brothers believe [in] the achievement ideology . . . because they perceive the racial situation to be substantially different for them than it was for their parents."[48]

Finally, a few poor blacks who fought beside whites during the civil rights movement retain, almost despite themselves, a residual hope in the goodness of white Americans and the openness of white institutions: "We thought it was really important to let white people know what was happening. It sounds silly now, but then I believed that if people really knew what conditions were like, they wouldn't let them continue. I guess I still haven't completely gotten away from believing that white people will respond to black problems."[49]

To be able plausibly to interpret the past in terms of clearly etched evil and clearly triumphant good feeds directly into the mythical quality of the American dream. The fact that what happened in that past really did make a difference for many African Americans, and was framed in language that promised a difference for all, reinforces the myth with concrete success and a recipe for extending it. We can thus begin to understand how an attractive fantasy bolstered by evidence and endorsed by the broader society can override the gritty reality of daily existence.

FINDING SOMEONE TO BE BETTER THAN

Poor blacks are among the poorest Americans. Yet like most others, they strive to find someone that they are doing better than in order to persuade themselves that they can do still better.[50] Those just above the poverty line condemn welfare recipients; welfare recipients condemn long-term recipients; long-term recipients condemn those who have abandoned their children and thus cannot claim AFDC, and so on.[51]

Thus despite considerable variation across years and survey questions, up to two-thirds of poor African Americans agree that "most people on welfare could take care of themselves if they really wanted to," that "poor young women often have babies so they can collect welfare," or that "welfare benefits make poor people dependent and encourage them to stay poor."[52] More poor than well-off blacks are deeply angered by welfare recipients too lazy to get a job; seven times as many poor as well-off blacks think most poor people prefer government assistance to hard work.[53]

Qualitative studies show what motivates this drive to distance oneself from those worse off. Although Pearl is "on public aid now, I've been on and off for eleven years with [her daughter]," she criticizes General Assistance (GA) recipients (usually men without dependent children) who "should be able to get up and do something." Too many "feel that you should support them . . . and all that they talk about is aid. . . . That burns me up." In contrast to GA recipients, she "learned I had to stand on my own two feet and I had to try not to depend on nobody. . . . I keep busy all the time. You have to teach kids that they have to have something to do."

Michael is equally scornful, although his gendered critique cuts in the opposite direction: "For a girl to get on public aid who has one child and wind up and get another child because she wants more money from public aid, she has cut off her chances of really doing anything. . . . That is wrong. . . . They just lazy." After all, "if I can get out here, tired as I am, goin' to school, tryin' to work, tryin' to bring some money home, why can't you? . . . There are jobs, you just got to know how to get 'em."[54] Given those sentiments, it is not surprising that when welfare recipients do attain a job, they proclaim proudly that "the way I do things now is totally different" because "I always like to feel I'm doing something to help somebody. A lot of people really don't care. I do."[55]

In short, poor African Americans spend a lot of time persuading themselves and others that they are better than someone else because their discipline, energy, or virtue has raised them above their circumstances. And if they have done it before, they will do it again. The phenomenon is by no means unique to the poor, but it is especially important here because it plays a large role in creating the paradox of remaining under the spell of the great national suggestion. On the one hand, one *must* be able "to feel I'm doing something"[56] to have any pride at all; on the other hand, the permission given by the American dream to define success absolutely—and thus very minimally—means that almost everyone *can* "feel I'm doing something." Self-congratulatory comparisons are essential for self-esteem, but they are also available; that point links the hard and soft edges of the American dream. And poor African Americans, no less than other Americans, are both disciplined by the hard edge and reassured by the soft one.

CHURCH, COMMUNITY, TELEVISION, SCHOOL, AND FAMILY

> I believe God is going to help me get into a better position so I get a job and get off welfare.
>
> —Mary Taylor, an AFDC recipient studying for her high school diploma

Religion

Institutions contribute crucially to maintenance of faith in the American dream. The church is one of the most important. Mothers pray, "Help me get a high-paying job. Give me health. And help me control my son," and are comforted by purchasing cards inscribed with inspirational messages such as "I am, I am in perfect harmony with the law of prosperity." Following the tenets of the American dream was possible only once "I got saved. . . . Before that I was just into drinking and drugs and that whole life. . . . I can tell you, this works better than any drug program."[57] Thus poor black teens in Washington, D.C., who neither use nor sell drugs are more religious than users or sellers. Poor young black men who attend church spend less time in illegal activities and drug or alcohol use than nonchurchgoing peers. They attend school more, work more, and have higher incomes, less of which comes from crime.[58]

Religion works in at least three ways to enable poor African Americans to remain under the spell: Individuals find strength to carry on through their beliefs. Church officials use their position to help poor blacks obtain whatever education, resources, and jobs are available. Christian theology can be interpreted to reinforce the tenets of the dream.

Strength to carry on is best demonstrated by the testimony already cited, or by a hundred similar examples. More generally, at least one-fourth of blacks (of all classes) describe their church's capacity to sustain them or to help them overcome despair as the most important thing it does.[59]

A recent survey of black clergy illustrates the second connection between black churches and the American dream. Internally, the many official roles within the church "help to spread the available quantums of status, dignity, and recognition among lay members." Externally, over two-thirds of black churches have "cooperated with social agencies . . . in dealing with community problems," through programs whose focus ranges from civil rights to employment to tutoring. A few reach as far as government-funded social or educational projects, or their own commercial businesses. Some ministers also engage in electoral politics, and their congregations are correspondingly more active politically than are most.[60]

Christian theology can reinforce the American dream in two very different ways. On the one hand, conservative interpretations of the Bible emphasize personal virtue, hard work and humility, and the deferral of gratification—all teachings clearly within the purview of the ideology. On the other hand, radical interpretations of the Bible emphasize the fundamental equality of all God's children, the joyous strength associated with righteous rebellion, and the virtue of pursuing collective well-being—all teachings equally, if less commonly recognized, within the purview of the ideology.[61]

Like some Christian churches,[62] the Nation of Islam encourages adherence to the American dream even as it helps poor blacks affirm an identity in opposition to the dominant white society.[63] The epitomizing example is, of course, Malcolm X, who was diverted from a life of drug dealing and hustling by the words of Elijah Mohammed. His *Autobiography* is the classic stuff of the ideology of the American dream. His prison conversion shows that anyone can participate in the dream, and one can always start over. His work to expand membership in and institutions of the Nation of Islam shows that participation in the dream consists of pursuing a goal with the reasonable expectation of success. By teaching himself to read and write, Malcolm shows that the route to success is through hard work and initiative. By admitting guilt about his past life, finally, Malcolm shows that worldly success must be associated with virtue to be truly successful. The elements are all here, even though Malcolm used them through most of his life to resist the blue-eyed devil, his institutions, and his racial ideology.[64]

Community Groups

Secular organizations join the church in reinforcing poor African Americans' faith in the American dream. Community groups tear down crack houses, tutor school children, campaign for aldermen, and endeavor to find or create jobs. More generally, the more politically organized the community, the more do its black residents adhere to the dominant ideology. In cities with "exemplary programs for involving residents in the political process at the neighborhood level," four-fifths of blacks of all classes have an active sense of community.[65] Up to a third of poor blacks in these communities, even those living in poor neighborhoods, have engaged in direct political action.[66] A majority of poor blacks in poor neighborhoods in these communities trust the government of their city, think that city government is run in the interests of all and that city officials attend to citizens, and think their city is very well run. As many poor blacks in poor neighborhoods as nonpoor whites in nonpoor neighborhoods think city officials would pay serious attention to their problems if asked to do so (about 40 percent in each case).[67] This is not the portrait of an alienated and passive population, at least in locations where community groups and political organizations make a serious effort to mobilize the poor.

Schools

Schools are a third institution that reinforces the spell of the great national suggestion. Surrounded by the hideous conditions of the Henry Horner Homes of Chicago, teachers organize spelling bees to encourage the pursuit of competitive excellence through hard work and determination. In case the students somehow miss the message, assembly recitations provide even more explicit injunctions:

Try, try, try, try, that's what special effort means.
And when you put your best foot forward, it really isn't hard as it seems.
Success comes to those who when given the chance
Do their very best and work hard to advance.
The special effort award is what they've earned.
Though it can't begin to match the things they've learned.[68]

As poetry, it does not bear discussion; as ideological training, it cannot be beat.[69]

And poor blacks respond to the schools' efforts. Although poor black Chicagoans are less likely than any other race or class group to perceive their children's school as safe, they are more likely to proclaim that their child enjoys school and works hard.[70]

Television

The schools' major rival for influencing youth may be the mass media. Students of television programming typically decry its shallowness, violence, materialism, and sexism. But they note less often its main characteristic, celebrating values as close to the center of the mainstream as it can get.[71] Networks and most cable companies are, after all, seeking the largest audience possible, and like American political parties they calculate that most people cluster in the middle.

Two facts make it plausible that poor African Americans are especially influenced by television. First, compared with other Americans, they watch more television and it forms a larger share of their entertainment. Poor black children are less likely than well-off black children or all white children to go to parks, beaches, cultural facilities, or entertainment centers with their parents. Their parents are able to spend less time in activities with them than parents of wealthier or white children, and they spend less time in nonschool lessons. Conversely, poor black children live in a more "permissive television environment." The television is on six or more hours a day in the homes of almost two-fifths of poor black Chicagoans; it is on fewer than half as many hours in the homes of all other race/class groups.[72]

Second, low-status blacks disproportionately cite "learning" as a motive for watching television and disproportionately express "a great deal" of confidence in the institution of television. Coupling those facts with the finding that "television appeared to provide knowledge about occupations with which the children had no firsthand experience" suggests how important the medium is in modeling the upper reaches of conventionally defined success.[73]

Television teaches our dominant ideology well. Heavy watchers overestimate the number of professionals and managers in the United States more than do light watchers, and low-status blacks (who on average watch the most television) feel closer to black elites than do high-status blacks. It is therefore sad but not surprising that three-quarters of inner-city black children (compared with about half of middle-class white children) describe families in television commercials as happier than their own.[74]

Cultural institutions beyond television similarly reinforce poor African Americans' desire to succeed. Although he is failing high school and has been arrested for selling drugs, Terry Jackson wants to emulate Eddie Murphy by becoming an actor. A Detroit teen plans to be a rapper in order to earn enough money for law school. Another praises a performing arts program modeled after Motown because "it shows . . . that people can accomplish something, not just go out in the street and act the fool. Smokey Robinson lived on my grandmother's street. We know him real well."[75] And the number of black boys who spend hours perfecting their jump shots is legendary. The likelihood of becoming the next Diana Ross or Michael Jordan is slim, of course—but so is the likelihood of becoming president, the possibility of which has been used to encourage every little white (Christian) boy for the past two centuries.

Families

Finally, families help poor African Americans remain under the spell of the great national suggestion. The presence of children motivates some to follow the injunctions of the third tenet:

> All I want to do is get out there and make an honest living. To bring my kids, to keep them from growing up like I was in the ghetto, you know, in the ghetto with a bunch of hoodlums out there, begging, stealing, robbing. I don't want my kids to do that. . . . I want it, . . . to get a *decent honest job.* You understand? So they can go out in the world and their kids can keep going.[76]

The absence of parents similarly motivates others:

> By him [my father] not being there, you know, that made me think I'm not going to let my son grow up without me being there. . . . I'll make sure that he get everything that I didn't have when I was growing up. . . . I think because he [my father] missed a lot of my birthdays and

stuff like that—you know, he missed my graduation—I don't give my father as much respect. . . . [But] I'm going to make sure he get all the way through school and make him go to college even though I didn't have no money and stuff.[77]

Systematic data reinforce eloquent comments. Parents' encouragement and expectations, direct involvement, level of education, and marital stability significantly affect poor black students' years of schooling, educational and occupational expectations, and grades.[78] How parents approach schooling probably matters more than how much schooling they had: poor black children who succeed in school are likely to be blessed with parents who invoke enough but not too much discipline, interact respectfully with their children, and provide emotional support as well as many opportunities for learning.[79]

Families affect jobs and life-styles as well as education. Inner-city black men who are married, live in a household with adults who work, or have children use their time more productively (that is, work or look for work, attend school, or care for children), are less often unemployed, obtain jobs more quickly, spend more time working, and earn less from crime than unmarried or familyless youths. Among inner-city black families, religious adults are more likely to have religious children, and families with no member who has gone to jail or succumbed to drug or alcohol problems are more likely to have children who also avoid these problems.[80]

Demonstration projects show the clearest effects of families. Parents (mostly women) with dependents benefited disproportionately from projects to enable high-school dropouts, ex-addicts, and ex-offenders to obtain and keep jobs. With some exceptions, parents completed more schooling, got more jobs, kept their jobs longer, earned more money, used fewer drugs, and were arrested less often than similar but childless adults.[81] The most successful demonstration project involved AFDC recipients, who by definition have dependent children.[82]

SHEER STUBBORN DETERMINATION

What do poor African Americans do if they cannot persuade themselves that they control their own destiny, if they are not sufficiently motivated by their historical heritage or their scorn for the even less fortunate, and if the institutions of family, community, school, television, or church do not sustain them? Some nevertheless remain under the spell of the great national suggestion. Others simply carry on as though they believe in the American dream because they see no alternative:

It's still the same old thing: whites get ahead much quicker than blacks. . . . On this job right now, I can see that. But there's nothing you can do about [it] if you want [to] keep your job, you gotta just lay dead and try to make it. . . . I can say this much: a man gotta do what he gotta do. If he gotta work, he gotta work: it's as simple as that. *You got to work.* If you don't do that, you gonna rob, and steal, and I can't do that, 'cause what would I do in jail with 5 kids and a wife, you know? So I *have to work.*[83]

Still others are either not so determined or more imaginative. It is to them that we now turn.

Chapter Nine

WITH ONE PART OF THEMSELVES THEY ACTUALLY BELIEVE

> Well, you know all over the state of Mississippi we have had a hard time and it doesn't seem to be getting any better, but, if you all say so, through the Lord, we may conquer later. I am praying to the Lord that it will be better in the future because it seem just like we haven't done any good yet.
>
> —letter from "B.E.F." to a friend of Alice Walker, c. 1970

MANY POOR African Americans cannot maintain the shields of determination or optimism against despair. They "believe" in the American dream—but only sort of. Gunnar Myrdal followed his observation about remaining under the spell of the great national suggestion with a crucial caveat: "*with one part of themselves they actually believe*, as do the Whites, that the [American] Creed is ruling America."[1] Some poor blacks believe in the American dream—but they do not believe in it very much, or they do not believe in anything very much, or they are incapable of mounting the effort it takes to maintain faith in the face of overwhelming obstacles. So they believe with one part of themselves, but do not act as those fully under the spell do.[2]

This point is methodological as well as substantive. The previous chapter explained the central tendency among poor African Americans—the paradox of remaining under the spell of the great national suggestion despite most of the evidence of their lives. This chapter queries the validity of that central tendency and shows that for some poor African Americans, belief in the American dream is little more than acquiescence. Let us consider reasons for that half-hearted endorsement.[3]

LACK OF KNOWLEDGE AND WEAKNESS OF WILL

> I always wanted to be a bookkeeper, but you have to know how to read, filing, math. Now I think about a porter job in a hospital. Nothing I have to use reading for. I would like to think of nice things: nice clothes, . . . nice jobs. I see ladies all

dressed up, legs crossed . . . , bubble baths, but I can't be thinking too many dreams 'cause I got five kids. I hope I can make it when I go home.

—inmate in Bedford Hills Correctional Facility, c. 1990

Some poor African Americans sincerely believe in the American dream but do not translate that belief into action. Unlike the boy with the roaches in his lunch sack or the man who insists that "*you got to work*," they do not try very hard to achieve their dreams.

They do not try for many reasons. One is cognitive: some poor blacks simply do not know how to start climbing the ladder of success. The missing information may be as simple as not knowing how to find the employment office if the bus routes are altered,[4] or as complex as having "little awareness of job or career alternatives and even less knowledge about the education or training necessary to achieve them."[5]

The reasons for these cognitive gaps are themselves various. Some people lack ability or energy to ferret out even simple information. Others are subjected to abysmal schooling or even deliberate misinformation. A guidance counselor in New York City responsible for 700 students cannot provide detailed career advice;[6] a student who graduates from high school despite being unable to read or add bears only part of the responsibility for her plight.[7] Little wonder that when confronted with an employer or the Armed Forces Qualifying Test, these students are surprised, intimidated, and stymied by the gap between what they thought they knew and what they actually know.[8]

But a lack of information only partly explains why some poor African Americans appear to believe in the American dream but do little to pursue it. After all, some people get a map to deal with a changed bus route or get tutoring to compensate for deficient schooling, thereby joining those fully under the spell of the great national suggestion. Others remain blocked—some by a lack of confidence. Despite high aspirations and willingness to work, black welfare recipients and their sons in 1970 were significantly less confident of their ability to succeed than were well-off whites or blacks in the Work Incentive Program (WIN). Perhaps as a result, they found living on welfare more acceptable than did equally poor but more self-assured recipients, and they were less likely to work outside the home. The link between attitudes and behaviors was circular: poor black welfare recipients "who failed to obtain jobs after termination from WIN . . . felt greater dependence on welfare and even less confidence in themselves than they did at the start of their training . . . [although] adherence to the work ethic . . . [was] essentially unchanged."[9]

Two decades later the pattern persisted. In 1990 welfare recipients who felt inefficacious also felt more dependent, were less likely to see work as an alternative to AFDC, and were much less likely to envision any alternative at all than those with greater confidence. They were also, not surprisingly, less optimistic about their ability to escape AFDC recipiency.[10]

Like welfare recipiency, unemployment can combine with loss of confidence to make one less active in pursuing success:

> It comes down to just frustration and disappointment when people will go and look and they get turned down or just not anybody hiring, and then you start putting yourself down and feel that . . . "maybe I should have went further in school," . . . or "I don't have enough skills or the skills that they need." . . . And start feeling that what's the use? . . . And then you start watching the news and they talking about unemployment and that and then they say what things are so bad, you know, and what's the use, why should I keep looking? You know, it's just all these negative thoughts start coming into your head.[11]

In 1980 over half of black workers who were jobless and discouraged agreed that "the problems of life are sometimes too big to handle," that their lives were "not very useful," and that they were not "a person of worth"; over two-thirds felt that "life is too much a matter of luck to plan ahead." Only a third of jobless black workers who were not discouraged felt worthless, useless, or overwhelmed, and under half thought life was mostly a matter of luck. Jobless workers who attributed their situation to their lack of ability or effort rather than to racial bias, poverty, or family responsibilities—that is, those who most firmly ascribed to the ideology of the American dream—were the most likely to feel overwhelmed and among the least likely to be actively searching for a job.[12]

Joining insufficient information or lack of confidence is weakness of will. It is *hard* to get up early in the morning in an ugly and dangerous apartment, to feed, dress, and dispose of several young children, to take several loud and dirty buses through the rain to a boring and demeaning job that pays too little—and to do it all again the next day. Absent the supports of church and family, and absent motivation strong enough to border on the irrational, many people will eventually give up.[13]

Poor blacks are often more critical of their own and others' weakness of will than most whites would dare to be out loud. One Watts resident reflected, "I haven't put forward all my effort. When I was younger, I had ambition. Now that I'm older, I have less, though I may get a chance." A resident of Chicago echoed him in a reflection on his friends:

> You can give a guy a job, but it's up to the individual to . . . be there on time and do what's required to keep that job. . . . That's something

that the state can't impose on him. . . . I think the majority of 'em, man, if they did work it, they'd work it for the longest, a couple of months—get fired for tardiness, bad attendance, neglect, stealing, all that kind of stuff, some would quit. . . . The thing is, is what lengths are you willing to go through to keep and maintain a job, you know? . . . They try to find easier routes.[14]

These reasons for inaction in the pursuit of what one wants are linked. Lack of relevant knowledge diminishes one's confidence; lack of confidence makes one less able to demand of teachers and case workers the information needed to negotiate a complex and dangerous world.[15] Weakness of will affects how much one learns and how confident one is in being able to follow through on a commitment. Thus for some poor African Americans, the paradox of remaining under the spell of the great national suggestion simply dissolves because the belief in the American dream captured in survey data is hollow. The belief is sincerely held but has little to do with the way the apparent believers live their lives.

TOO MUCH KNOWLEDGE

Some poor blacks believe in but do not act on the American dream because they have too much, rather than too little, knowledge. Faith in the dream requires just that—faith that the future will be better than the past. Those whom experience or observation has taught to expect the future to resemble the dreary past are unlikely to take the leap of faith required by the great national suggestion. And poor African Americans are more vulnerable to unpredictable disasters than almost any other group of Americans. They are therefore prone to be risk-averse, "preferring to insure against likely kinds of material hardship" rather than risk-seeking, as one must be fully to engage in the dream.[16]

Thus blacks with capital to spare invest less than do comparable whites and Latinos in dividend-bearing stocks or interest-bearing bonds, and more in apparently safe and solid things like houses and cars.[17] Poor blacks stay on AFDC rather than risk pursuing more education or taking a job that might disappear, leaving them empty-handed.[18] They reinforce ties with equally poor family members rather than venture into social and physical realms that might enable success—or produce disaster.[19] They choose low-risk, "adaptive" acts whose consequences they understand, such as dropping out of school to join a gang or have a baby, rather than high-risk and unpredictable acts like staying in school and pursuing a professional job in the alien white world.[20] Black students who know that schooling will not enhance their social status or job prospects engage in "manipulative . . . skills, attitudes, and behaviors," ascribe to a "reverse work ethic, which . . . insists that one

should 'make it' by not working," and reject "effort optimism" by refusing to persevere in school work.[21]

Parents are especially likely to know too much to be able to believe
wholeheartedly in the American dream. Poor blacks disproportionately
claim that children get into trouble if their parents work, that parents
spend too little time with their children, and that too many parents do
not know where their children are.[22] Given that knowledge, amply supported in many inner-city neighborhoods, single mothers sometimes
choose to forgo the possible long-term benefits of employment in favor
of the certain short-term benefits of keeping an eye on their children.
That judgment is reinforced by their dismal experience with the labor
market, which has already taught them to reduce their commitment to
jobs, if not to the work ethic. If "when you go out and get those jobs you
don't make enough to pay rent, then medical coverage and bills," then
"it's really not worth it to go out working when you think about it."[23]

In short, if too little knowledge can lead people not to act on their
belief in the American dream, so can too much. After all, the dream is
constructed around some combination of the fantasy of a windfall and
the discipline of striving; it takes only a little knowledge for a poor African American either to dissipate the fantasy or to calculate the odds attendant on striving.

FANTASY

> Felipe Lopez is certainly a born athlete. But he may also be
> one of those rarer cases—a person who is just born lucky,
> whose whole life seems an effortless conveyance of dreams,
> and to whom other people's dreams adhere.
>
> —Susan Orlean, on a New York City high school
> basketball player, 1993

Another reason for believing with only one part of oneself has as much
to do with the nature of the American dream as with the psychology or
circumstances of the dreamers. The ideology not only prescribes rules
for pursuing success but also allows a softer, dreamier wish for success.
It is considerably easier to believe that I am the one who is just born
lucky, that my life will be an effortless conveyance of dreams, than to
seek an unattractive job from a potentially hostile outsider. Thus Rita,
who dresses like "a spectacle," has trouble finding work "because of her
unconventional looks. [But] she does not worry, she says, because . . .
'when everythin' is everythin' I'm gonna have two cars, a big house and
a garage and private school for my children. Get out of this dump.'" In
one survey, African American students are distinguished from other stu-

dents, not by doubt that getting a good education will pay off for them, as John Ogbu suggests, but by the absence of fear that *not* getting a good education will harm their prospects. Thus "unwarranted optimism, rather than excessive pessimism, may be limiting [some] African-American . . . students' school performance."[24]

Sports is an especially fertile, though hardly effortless, field of dreams. Three-fifths of black teenage athletes, compared with two-fifths of their white counterparts, expect to play on a college team; three times as many blacks as whites (43 percent to 16 percent) expect to be professional athletes. Those ambitions are largely futile in a context in which the National Basketball Association recruits forty to fifty new basketball players a year from a pool starting with 500,000 male high school basketball players.[25] Nevertheless, "the possibility of transcendence through basketball is an article of faith."[26]

Rearing a young child is equally amenable to fantasy (as well as equally effortful). It has long been a cliché to point out that Americans hope for their children what they have given up hoping for themselves; poor people are especially vulnerable to unfounded hope while their children are very young. Thus a high school dropout confesses that "I wasn't never good at nothing. In school I felt stupid and older than the rest. But I'm a great mother to Chita. Catholic schools for my baby, and maybe a house in New Jersey." Although many poor black unmarried mothers do manage to make a life for their children better than the one they grew up in, for others the dream remains a fantasy.[27] It is, however, a fantasy that keeps them clinging to the margins of the American dream.

The poorer one is, and the more horrendous one's surroundings, the more the American dream slides from a set of prescriptive rules into an elusive vision. That slide from rules to vision is, paradoxically, perfectly rational; some neighborhoods are so devastated and dangerous, and some people so poor and cut off from mainstream society, that living according to the tenets of the dream would simply drive them crazy or get them killed:

> Somewhere inside, he [Rickey] realizes confusedly the unreality that enshrouds the hope of an athletic career suddenly brought back from oblivion and of a school career miraculously rejuvenated. . . . Under such conditions of relentless and all-pervading social and economic insecurity, where existence becomes reduced to the craft of day-to-day survival . . . , the present becomes so uncertain that it devours the future and forbids that one conceive of it but in the form of fantasy.[28]

Rickey dreams of a job "with the Post Office, or bus driver, somethin' with *benefits*, . . . able to take care of fam'ly, pay my bills an' a home, two-car garage." But in his youth he "didn't really know the *value* of an education" so he left school, and he is still *"hyper. . . .* I cannot stay behin' no counter for no eight hours." Thus he concludes that "you gonna en' up with the short en' of the stick, ev'ry time."[29] The saga of this "professional hustler" is deeply revealing; even in his fantasy he stays within the boundaries of his dream: It is his fault that he could never get ahead, and he must live as best he can with the consequences.

AMBIVALENCE

> What kind of future does he have, actually? He could prob-
> ably finish school, he can go to college, but then, actually,
> what does he have then, actually, after that? . . . He going to
> have shit. He's just going to be another colored guy that fin-
> ished college.
>
> —Carl Foreman, on his girlfriend's eighteen-year-old son,
> Michael, c. 1970

Some poor blacks literally believe in the American dream with only one part of themselves. That is, they partly believe in the dream and partly do not. Most commonly, they accept it as a general depiction of their own and others' guiding principles, but they discount it heavily in explaining and organizing their daily lives. This form of ambivalence is widely recognized by surveyors and intensive interviewers,[30] not to speak of any dieter who succumbs to a chocolate sundae.

Thus poor black adolescents hold general career aspirations as high as those of wealthier or whiter teens, but their specific job expectations are much lower.[31] African American migrant farm workers desire a better life as much as Jamaican farm workers do, but they are much more discouraged about their actual prospects and pick many fewer crops. Most black AFDC recipients agree that in general Americans can succeed "if they work hard enough"; most also agree that the poor or unlucky have an especially hard time achieving success. There is no relationship in the latter survey between responses to the general question and to the two specific ones.[32] Black students in (pre-riot) Los Angeles high schools believed more in the generic American dream than did whites, but they were much less convinced that education and hard work would improve their own lives. Middle-class whites were most confident that the general principles would have concrete application, followed by working-class whites, middle-class blacks, and finally working-class blacks. Beliefs about the specific impact of education on one's life, but not beliefs about the general value of education for mobility, significantly affected students' grades.[33]

Gangs perhaps epitomize the ambivalence between general beliefs and concrete choices. In gangs of "serious delinquents" or gangs "at risk for becoming a more formal criminal organization," at least two-fifths of the members recently engaged at least "a few times" in robbery, felony theft, the use of weapons, or extortion. Yet most members describe school and work as "important to me" or to the gang, and 90 percent "want to work." Two-fifths have in fact worked during the previous six months.[34] Do they or do they not believe in the American dream? It all depends on how you define "believe."

Institutional contexts affect whether poor blacks remain completely under the spell of the great national suggestion or only believe with one part of themselves. If model schools or heroic teachers enhance poor students' outlooks and prospects, indifferent or venal schools reinforce despair and illiteracy.[35] If an inspirational minister and supportive fellow worshipers keep some exhausted mothers going, hypocritical preachers and superficial religiosity tip others into hopelessness.[36] If moving into subsidized housing in the suburbs enables some people to "feel that I'm worth something, [that] I can do anything I want to do if I get up and try it," remaining in inner city public housing projects "deteriorates you. You don't want to do anything."[37] If good parenting enables some children to overcome severe handicaps, bad parenting can inhibit the most promising child.[38] If neighborhood organizations keep poor blacks politically engaged, neighborhood violence and poverty can leave community members isolated, fearful, and bereft of any voice at all.[39] In short, although some people fail in the best of circumstances and others succeed in the worst,[40] on balance, context makes a difference.

ACQUIESCENCE

> We really had a hard time in school, . . . like if I go home and do my homework and really learn something and really get into it, we go back to school the next day. Then the teacher start asking about the lesson, getting us to go to the board and asking questions. We sitting and raising our hands and they would just look over the top of us. And I got, [pause] I had went so far I just got tired. I had got to the place where I didn't care if I learned anything or not.
>
> —Lilly, a housekeeper in North Carolina, c. 1986

Finally, some poor blacks endorse the American dream simply as the path of least resistance. More formally, they acquiesce; pressed by a friendly gray-haired lady with a clipboard to say something, they agree with the common currency of belief in the American dream even though what they really mean is that they do not believe in much of anything at all.[41]

Surveys can at most dimly discern the number and composition of acquiescers. The extent of the phenomenon is best inferred through the disparity between expressed belief and lack of appropriate action once other explanations are eliminated. Ethnographies, however, can at least give us a sense of how acquiescence feels and why it occurs. Lilly slid reluctantly into acquiescence as a defense against brutal indifference.[42] Wigfall, a "regular who is just barely hanging onto his regular affiliations," explains the acquiescence of "wineheads" as a defense against economic blockage:

> People are depressed. They can't live like they want to live, . . . without workin'. But he don't want to work for this little bit of money he gon' get. 'Cause the little bit of money still won't put him where he want to be. . . . This hurts a man, when he see a friend of his can drive a El Dorado and got a nice clean apartment and a beautiful lady and two or three kids. And he can't do it! . . . Don't care how he work and how he save. He can't handle it, and so he give up.[43]

A community organizer explains poor blacks' acquiescence in political terms:

> Black people are in worse—way worse—condition now than then [the 1960s]. The people are too passive. They've been literally *beat* into [passivity] because any black man that tries to lead anything is killed. Martin Luther King, who believe in peace. They shot and killed him. Malcolm X, he's dead. People that even stuck up for black people gets killed. In the sixties, people kept you conscious. . . . Now a few dudes might sit back and kick about what we gonna do here, but as far as getting out to really generate the people, everyone's afraid. Because you don't want to go to jail. You don't wanna be killed.[44]

Judging by other ethnographies, his is not a common view. But acquiescence based on fear is surely more common than most whites (and many middle-class blacks) want to admit.[45]

Ralph Ellison, finally, locates the grounds for acquiescence most broadly. In 1961 he predicted that after the civil rights movement succeeded, blacks would for a while be "wandering around because, you see, we have had this thing [i.e., racial inferiority] thrown at us for so long that we haven't had a chance to discover what in our own background is really worth preserving. For the first time, we are given a choice. And this is where the real trouble is going to start."[46] Perhaps acquiescers are those still wandering around thirty years later, unable to choose between the promise and discipline of the dominant ideology, on the one hand, and either the despair of nihilism or the exhilaration of rebellion, on the other.

Most poor African Americans, however, have made a choice. The bulk have chosen to pursue the conventionally defined dream; a few of the rest either redefine the dream or reject it altogether—and "this is where the real trouble . . . start[s]." Let us turn, then, to those latter two choices.

Chapter Ten

DISTORTING THE DREAM

> 1988 changed us. We can never go back to being what we were. . . . It's not just the volume of murders, it is the viciousness—the kinds of wounds that you see, . . . where young people have had their kneecaps shot off, had their testicles shot off. . . . Today's kids are cocky. We . . . charge them with taking another person's life, and there's no remorse. For them, it's just a matter of fact. . . . This is not the city that I grew up in. . . . Something has changed to produce the kids that I see.
>
> —Isaac Fulwood, former chief of police for Washington, D.C., 1989

ISAAC FULWOOD, himself a product of a poor black District family, goes on to describe a recently arrested eighteen-year-old with "a hard-working mother who is doing her best to provide him with what he needs in life—not a wealthy family, but a working family. Yet this kid has 30, 40, 50 pairs of tennis shoes, all kinds of jogging suits, and he is defining himself in terms of these material things. . . . His world is not next year, not next week. His world is today. Instant gratification, right now." Asked how this man thinks, Chief Fulwood speculates:

> This kid doesn't see the same world that I saw when I was growing up, a world that was expanding, where there was hope, where I had the possibility to achieve. He's got to have it all, right now. . . . Because that's what he is, those material things, . . . and he doesn't care about the impact of his behavior on other people. [Students say to me] "Chief Fulwood, you're full of bullshit. Why should I go and make $3.50, $4.25 an hour at a regular job? I can make that in one minute on the street. . . . I can make all the money I want to make."

He concludes, in rather an understatement, "There's something insidious about what is happening."[1]

We do not know just how the lack of legitimate opportunity and the desire for status and wealth spiral downward into solipsism, disdain, and killing. We do know that most poor blacks do not follow this spiral and that some rich whites do.[2] Nevertheless, something is happening in the inner cities, enough to bring a police chief who has seen it all to despair.

Actually two distinct things are happening to the subjects of Chief Fulwood's ruminations. Some share other Americans' belief in the American dream but believe in ways that distort the dream and ultimately harm the dreamers; they are the concern of this chapter. Others simply reject the American dream, either because they reject all moral codes or because they live by an alternative moral vision; the next chapter considers them.

WHO ARE THE ESTRANGED POOR?

The first step in understanding why some poor blacks distort or reject the American dream is to clarify who the estranged poor are.[3] One widely used measure of estrangement among the poor combines four indicators of "distress" in a neighborhood: residents below the poverty line, adult men not in the labor force, households headed by a woman with children, and households receiving welfare. A census tract is defined as a "distressed neighborhood" if the proportion of the population exhibiting all four features is at least one standard deviation above the mean value of that indicator for the nation in 1980.[4]

By this measure, the population of distressed areas of the nation's 100 largest central cities grew from 1,022,000 people in 1970 to 5,704,000 in 1990, an increase from 1.7 to 11.1 of the cities' population. The number of distressed census tracts grew from 296 to 1,850, a 625 percent increase. The African American proportion of the residents of distressed neighborhoods dropped from 77 percent in 1970 to 68 percent in 1990, although that change represented a growth from 6.6 percent to fully 29.7 percent of all non-Hispanic blacks.[5]

These calculations are better than most. They are not, however, dispositive. What appear to be small changes in what is measured (e.g., not including the indicator of high school dropouts), how the indicators are measured (using values for metropolitan regions rather than the nation, or measuring change relatively rather than absolutely), where the measures are applied (to cities, census tracts, or the nation), or how the term "distress" is defined make big differences in claims about the size, racial composition, and trajectory of the estranged poor. Estimates of the number of estranged poor residents in the United States in 1980 range from fewer than 1 million to 11.6 million; estimates of the proportion of the estranged poor who are black or Hispanic range from 59 percent to 90 percent.[6]

These technical disputes matter here because their results affect the plausibility of my claim that most poor African Americans believe in and try to act in accord with the precepts of the American dream. I cannot resolve them, but two points seem conclusive. First, as of 1990 under 30 percent of blacks were part of the estranged poor, since not all residents of distressed neighborhoods themselves share the problems that lead the neighborhood to be defined as distressed.[7] Second, the number of estranged poor is growing, although the growth has slowed since 1980.[8] In short, the magnitude of the problem represented by the estranged poor is tractable, but not trivial.

THE ESTRANGED NONPOOR

We cannot understand the circumstances and beliefs of the estranged poor, or their implications for the viability of the American dream, without placing them in the context of the rest of American society. Consider, for example, the three behavioral indicators of distressed neighborhoods just described (being out of the labor force, living in a mother-only household, and receiving welfare). From 1970 to 1980 not only did the number of distressed areas and individuals increase dramatically, but so did the mean levels for all three indicators across each of eight metropolitan areas. However, the coefficients of variation decreased. In other words, the "'worst' neighborhoods of these metropolitan areas have gotten worse, *but so have the 'average' neighborhoods; and, if anything, the 'average' neighborhoods have worsened to a greater extent.*" The claim of a growing underclass incorrectly "associates a local, identifiable subpopulation with problems more accurately associated with the general population. If female headship and irregular employment are 'underclass' characteristics, then we are an 'underclass' society, not a society with an 'underclass.'"[9]

If we disaggregate the behavioral components of the standard definition of neighborhood distress, we see that blacks—even among the estranged poor—differ less from whites than discussions of the "urban underclass" typically imply. The similarity takes three forms. First, on two of the three standard measures, blacks and whites are following a similar trajectory. Although the proportion of black men not in the civilian labor force rose from 15 percent in 1954 to 30 percent in 1992, the analogous proportion of white men rose almost as much, from 14 to 24 percent. The proportion of children born to unmarried mothers has also increased in both races, albeit with a higher starting point and greater absolute growth among blacks.[10]

Second, the two races are converging on some measures of socially undesirable behavior. The proportion of AFDC recipients who are black declined from 45 percent in 1969 to 40 percent in 1990—which means that the proportion of AFDC recipients who are white is simultaneously rising.[11] Acts of direct violence also show convergence. Murder is the most reliably reported crime, and the one for which concerns about ra-

cial bias in the criminal justice system (up to the point of capital sentenc-
ing) are least severe. In 1976, 4.1 per 100,000 white men committed
murder, whereas in 1992, 4.0 did so. Among black men the corresponding figures are 35.3 and 31.5. The absolute disparities remain huge, but
the ratio of black to white murderers has dropped slightly. A much
higher proportion of blacks than whites also continue to commit robberies and assaults, but the ratio of black to white assailants has dropped
since the late 1970s.[12] Acts of indirect violence through white-collar
crime, however, remain largely the province of whites, and the amount
and magnitude of fraud is rising.[13]

Finally, in contrast to common understanding, whites engage in *more*
drug use than blacks if abuse of alcohol is included in the definition of
drug use. Whites drink more alcohol than blacks (or Latinos), drink
more frequently, start drinking at a younger age, and (among those
under age twenty-five) drink more on any given occasion.[14] They also
use illicit drugs at least as much as do blacks.[15] Up to twice as many
white as black high school students report drug use, and the racial discrepancy increases with the potency of the drug.[16] Among prison inmates or arrestees surveyed in 1986, 1989, and 1991, fewer blacks than
whites had ever used a major drug, used drugs before their first arrest or
incarceration, shared needles or engaged in multiple drug use, and reported drug dependency.[17]

Wealth as well as whiteness may be associated with drug and alcohol
use.[18] In some surveys the college-educated report at least as much use
as those without high school educations.[19] In 1990 slightly more residents of the best-off two-thirds of neighborhoods in the Washington,
D.C., metropolitan area reported ever having used illicit drugs than did
residents of the poorest third of neighborhoods.[20] Among pregnant
women in Florida, those in private obstetrics practices used drugs just as
often as those receiving prenatal care in public health clinics.[21] The more
money available to adolescents and young adults, the more marijuana or
cocaine they ingest. Well-off black and white men and well-off white
women are all more likely to be diagnosed as drug abusers than are their
poor counterparts.[22]

Thus poor African Americans who distort or reject the American
dream are in many ways similar, and perhaps are increasingly similar, to
other Americans. On some measures of "deviance," the two races follow
similar paths; on others they are converging; on still others whites are
the more "deviant" race. That point is partially reassuring since it means
that most of the estranged poor are not unintelligible aliens. It is also
disturbing since it suggests that the damage done by the estranged poor
to themselves and their neighbors could easily be adopted by many
other Americans.

The First Tenet

> I was just stupid, immature about a lot of things. When you
> are young, you don't really think about the future. You say,
> "If I have another baby, then I have another child." . . .
> [Children] lock you into something that, when you are
> young, you don't have the wisdom to think about.
>
> —Dorothy Sands, AFDC recipient in Chicago, 1986

The first tenet of the dream proclaims that anyone, regardless of ascriptive traits, family background, or personal history, may pursue success. It implies therefore that one may always start over. The hopeful, egalitarian thrust of this vision can, however, be twisted into the claim that what happened in the past does not matter and that one can ignore the consequences of past acts.

The rejection of responsibility is most poignant when children are involved. A few men resist acknowledging paternity:

> [If his girlfriend said she was pregnant,] only thing I can do is either I
> try to deny, which I can do 'cause I know that some of the chicks I'm
> messing with ain't just really messing with me. . . . See, that's the way
> a lot of brothers mess up. . . . They willing to just up and "OK, it's
> mine," you know, agree to it.

Others resist caring for even their acknowledged children:

> What-you-call-it, when the court subpoena you an' make you give her
> child support . . . I'm like, "hold it." . . . The way I feel I quit my job
> first, I'll go back to work doing contracting work as a subcontractor
> who get paid in cash. Or deal drugs or something, 'cause I'm not going
> to give her no money, period.[23]

A few women seek to detach children from their fathers—"Sometime when I think about it, I don't want her to know [who her father is]. Just because of the type of person he is. . . . The guy I'm with now makes Lionnel look real small"—or reject the constraints of marriage: "Marry? Nothin' but problems. I ain't ready to settle down. . . . I got at least ten more years left of fresh air. [Will you marry the father of your daughters?] You kidding? What I need him for? He bad news."[24]

This distortion of the first tenet is growing. Poor black men on average have a child several months or even several years before marrying, if they marry at all, and the period between child's birth and father's marriage is lengthening.[25] Fewer than one-fifth of AFDC mothers receive any formal child support from the legally recognized father(s) of their children, and what support they receive is almost never enough to allow them to leave the welfare rolls.[26] And those data say nothing about what matters most to children—the simple matter of having parents present as a matter of course.

Rejection of all forms of hierarchy is another way to distort the first tenet of the American dream. The tenet spurns social orders based on inherited class or caste, but it does not proscribe all structure. Indeed, the whole point of the ideology is to substitute legitimate for illegitimate orderings. Thus rejecting all hierarchy exaggerates to the point of falsifying the American dream's first precept.

Such a distortion is clearest in jobs. Employers complain that African American workers, especially young men, "have an attitude, pride," or have a "chip on their shoulder, resent being told what to do," or are "very intimidating to the supervisors because they know everything by the time they get to be a sophomore in high school."[27] Some African American workers, especially young men, confirm this view:

> I try to be always outthinking this man. He's honky. First I look at him, I know he didn't dig me. He wanted to fire me. I wasn't laughing or tee-heeing or mingling with them [whites] or adjusting to their set. Because I'm real. If you notice me on the job, brother, I am myself. . . . So I keep him off my back, I don't talk too much. And do my job. He's scared of me, and I know he's trying to figure me out, but I've got him psyched. When a person figure you out, they know you, then you just hung up, you been conquered. But long as you stay obvious, they don't know you. You got them.[28]

Having a honky employer is not necessary for rejecting authority: "Ain't nothin' worse than having a black cat over you for a boss. I got this cat over me who's always on me. He worse than the white man. . . . He always askin' me questions, checkin' on me, you know. He done already fired four studs off my job. . . . I don't know how long I'm goin' last with him."[29] But racial antagonisms add an edge to prickliness about hierarchy.[30] "Self-consciously aspiring toward personal independence and self-respect [as the American dream teaches them to do], many young blacks see themselves and are seen by others as not taking 'the stuff' that traditionally has been dished out to black Americans."[31]

Rejection of authority takes many forms. About 20 percent of a group of newly employed welfare recipients resisted requests or quarreled with supervisors; almost all lost their jobs within six months. Another 20 percent defined their tasks narrowly and felt demeaned when asked to do something outside their specific job description; all who responded to requests with "I don't do that kind of labor" lost their jobs. Others were unwilling or unable to be as warm and polite to customers as their supervisors required; one waitress "set herself as enemies to" the restaurant's diners, and she too lost her job.[32] Yet other poor blacks "rejected these invidious distinctions [of speech and dress styles], espousing a strong egalitarianism, and were bitter or scornful about those who thought they were too good to associate with others." They too quickly become targets for dismissal.[33]

Resistance to hierarchy extends beyond the workplace. Inner city teens role-playing a hostile encounter with a mall security guard reject the choice of simply leaving the scene. After all, "you might feel like you got *beat*. And then you might go home and take it out on other people." Released from jail after a drug arrest, Terry Jackson immediately returned to selling because "I had taken a downfall. I had to get back on *top*."[34]

Most poor African Americans accept hierarchy, perhaps more than they should. After all, only 4 percent of low-income blacks (compared with 3 percent of low-income whites and 5 percent of high-income blacks) reported "trouble" with their boss in 1990–91.[35] But those who do resist authority, whether legitimately or not, may be especially harmed by their actions because they lack other resources to fall back on and because more favored Americans find in their behavior justification to separate themselves further from the "underclass."

THE SECOND TENET

> Broke with no money and knowing that all these other people had all these things that I wanted so bad. I want to make a living and this is just survival, you know, making your ends meet. I don't want to do that anymore. I want to make enough money where I can relax and buy the things I want.
>
> —a young man about to embark on a career in drug dealing, c. 1990

The American dream's second tenet, that participants can reasonably anticipate some success, is subject to several distortions. At their core is the slide from "reasonable anticipation" to a guarantee. People who believe that they are promised success may become angry, petulant, or disoriented if it is not forthcoming—and may take destructive actions in order to get what they think is due them.

Examples are easily found. Anger: "We want your goods. We want a fine home and a car; what they got up in Piedmont. We don't want to take your stuff away from you, but if you come down here and mess with us, we'll give you one up side the head." Or sulking: "I don't have a ride right now. Don't like American-made cars. I always wants a foreign model car—so I can't have d' car I want, I don' want a car. I wanna

Jag—Jag 70 XKE, Benz 70. They cost some dough. My money ain' long enough—maybe sometime. So I be takin' the extra car [public bus]." Or lack of direction: "Our youth today often desire a $200,000 life-style but possess only five-dollar skills. Youths say 'I'm going to *be* Magic Johnson or Whitney Houston' without an appreciation of what it requires to *become* anything. . . . Somehow youth feel they can skate from kindergarten to twelfth grade then accelerate, bloom, and blossom in college."[36]

People who know that they might not get what they want are usually able to withhold some of themselves from investing in that desire.[37] But expecting that at any moment a desire will turn into a reality can make a person a little crazy:

> I wanted to be a star. I wanted to make it big. My way. I wanted the glamour. I wanted to sit high up. . . . See, in my mind I was Superfly. I'd drive up slow to the curb. My hog be half a block long and these fine foxes in the back. Everybody looking when I ease out the door clean and mean. Got a check in my pocket to give to Mom. Buy her a new house with everything in it new. Pay her back for the hard times. I could see that happening as real as I can see your face right now. *Wasn't no way it wasn't gon happen.* Rob was gon make it big.[38]

These are the words of Robby Wideman, serving a life sentence for armed robbery and being an accessory to murder. He goes on to point out that the gap between wanting and getting becomes even more frustrating when one is constantly confronted with those who do have: "Them little white kids had everything. . . . Nice houses, nice clothes. They could buy pop and comic books and candy when they wanted to. We wasn't that bad off, but compared to what them little white kids had I always felt like I din't have nothing. . . . I wanted what they had. Wanted it bad."[39] The ubiquitous television is one source of dispiriting comparison; so is, ironically, residential or school desegregation by class. Thus poor young men in Chicago who live in middle- or high-status communities are much more delinquent than poor youths living in poor communities.[40]

In the face of frustration when the presumed promise of success is not redeemed, some poor blacks turn to illegitimate channels to achieve their desires. In 1988, 27 of 346 "underclass" respondents to a national survey admitted to involvement "in an illegal activity [mostly drug sales or theft] in which you made money." All but two "earn[ed]" good money." Up to one-half of all the respondents thought lawbreakers "enjoy the good life," and one-fifth would be tempted to engage in illegal acts if they "could get away with it."[41] A year later, two-thirds of poor young black men in Boston thought they could earn "more on the street doing something illegal than on a straight job." That figure had increased from 44 percent in 1980. This was not just idle talk; poor blacks' illegal earnings "rose by 100 percent between 1980 and 1989 compared to a much smaller increase in pay from work" even though Boston enjoyed an economic boom during the decade.[42]

Convicted criminals confirm these motives and the rewards of illegal activity. Twice as many (40 percent) young black felons in Ohio commit crimes because "I need the money" as for the next most common reason. Young black (and Latino) lawbreakers in New York are more motivated by economic gain than are their better-off white counterparts, who are seeking "thrills."[43] Three times as many prison inmates (about 18 percent) in California agreed that crime pays as agreed that going straight pays. They were right; that sample earned in legal wages only three-quarters of their illegal gains in the year preceding arrest. Black prisoners were slightly more likely than white prisoners to see economic returns to crime. For both races, the lower the ratio of legal to illegal expected earnings, the greater the likelihood of selling drugs; had black convicts earned the wages of their white peers, their drug dealing would have declined by nearly 90 percent.[44] Finally, twice as many black male residents of inner cities who had committed a crime (almost 50 percent) as those who had not believed that they could make more on the street than in a legitimate job. They too were correct; criminals had incomes of about $4,000 in the previous year, compared with about $3,000 for the full sample.[45]

The route to illegitimate success through the drug trade warrants special attention. Although some crack dealers sell to support their addiction, many sell because they see a lucrative business and a chance to succeed at something.[46] After all, "coke is just a way for me to make some money and do some of the things I would otherwise not have the chance of doing in the real world. Coke ain't real."[47] Once again, they may be right; in some neighborhoods "the crack industry . . . is the only expanding and dynamic equal opportunity employer for black and Puerto Rican kids. . . . Most don't make it, but there are BMW's being washed on my street corner, and there are people with gold, so that the American dream is a touchable reality, even if statistically it is not a reality." Fully 84 percent of black, and 67 percent of white, urban young men agree that "dealing in drugs is a good way to make money." Half or more of poor black youth in Washington, D.C., believe that adult dealers make at least $1,000 a week, and a third believe that high school dealers make that much. Selling drugs is especially attractive to poor blacks because "one does not have to talk white or dress white or act white to get ahead"—thus adding the resistance to hierarchy of the first tenet to the promise of success of the second.[48]

One must not reify the line between legitimate striving and illegitimate criminality. The line is blurred in American society, and poor blacks, like other Americans, find it easy to straddle it in pursuit of their dreams. To make money, Joe says, "you can fix some people's car, . . . paint houses, cut grasses. . . . That's what I be trying to do—anything to make a little money. . . . When I be wanting some money in the middle of that, so, well, some friend, where they be going stealing cars and stripping the tires off and selling those."[49] Ten percent of Washington youth expect to sell drugs to supplement their regular job after graduating from high school.[50] AFDC recipients of both races are slightly more tolerant of "quasi-illegal activities" than are better-off blacks or whites, and most AFDC recipients have unreported earnings (itself illegal). A few make money through drug sales or prostitution.[51] Black inner city youths who broke the law in 1980 were almost as likely to be employed as those who did not. Up to three-quarters of drug dealers in Washington, D.C., hold legitimate jobs; most sell only part-time in "an underground version of 'moonlighting.'" The most assiduous sellers also earn the most from regular jobs, thus demonstrating the energy and initiative vital to success in accord with the ideology of the American dream.[52] Almost half of a group of career criminals were employed, and a few had held their current job for five or more years. Most generally, white gang members or convicted criminals maintain a sharper distinction between being a criminal and being "straight" than do similarly situated blacks.[53]

Poor African Americans, in short, may become frustrated by the gap in the American dream between the probability and promise of success. Some respond by tolerating or engaging in illegal activity. Their motives, abilities, and activity all accord with the ideology of the dream; all that is distorted is the slide from reasonable anticipation to guarantee, and their willingness to cross the line of conventional morality in order to cash in that guarantee. A small deviation from the ideal, with large consequences for themselves and their other victims.

THE THIRD TENET

The third precept of the American dream prescribes the pursuit of success through actions and traits under one's own control. Those actions typically include attaining an education, developing a talent, working hard, and saving money. Some poor African Americans distort the third tenet by using this prescription in the service of socially illegitimate goals.

The point is clearest and most poignant in the drug trade. Dealers bear an uncanny resemblance to American captains of industry. They work their way up the ladder: "Nobody trusted me with any material at first. I had to convince people I could do it. I didn't have my hand out for no charity. I worked hard to get established." They exhibit self-discipline and a strong work ethic: "Selling coke is just like any other business—you gotta work hard, stay on your toes, protect what's yours, and not fuck up with silly matters." They are patriotic: a graffito in a New York City copping zone reads, "God bless America and the Yankee dollar." They defer gratification: "You can't sell drugs and use dope at the same time, 'cause you won't get nowhere. You're not going to make no money. So, basically, I try to keep myself away from people who sell and use drugs, 'cause otherwise you come up short for money." They attend to their reputation: a successful hustler needs "diplomacy: be trustworthy, consistent. You and I make a deal. We're both happy. Let's keep it that way. Do it the same way next time." They build corporate morale through pep talks: a notice on the wall of a Detroit crack house promises that with "hard work and dedication we will all be rich within 12 months."[54] They develop detailed job descriptions, write technical operations manuals, use computerized spreadsheets to track cash flows, polish salespeople's manners, create distinctive brand names and packaging, give free samples and credit to good customers, offer drugs on consignment, scout out new markets to undersell established firms, provide discount coupons, hold two-for-one sales, give paid vacations and medical benefits, and organize contests and profit-sharing plans for employees.[55]

In fact, it is drug sellers' resemblance to junior members of the Chamber of Commerce that makes them and their trade so frightening to other Americans. Were their actions less in accord with the precepts of the American dream, they could be dismissed as merely crazy or evil. But the combination of a product as tempting as it is destructive and behavior as praiseworthy as it is injurious is extraordinarily hard to cope with psychologically and politically.[56]

Drug dealing is only one forum in which socially valued behaviors serve criminal ends. A Puerto Rican teen is a "meticulous and manually skilled burglar." He "always plan[s] everything" and closely researches the schedules of the workers and layout of the buildings he robs. To prepare for the technical aspects of his work, "his sister takes out books on alarms from the library and reads them to him because he can't read very well." Black former drug dealers learn business skills to enter the more lucrative trade of fencing stolen jewelry:

> They buy and sell gold. They stand in front of the jewelry store and catch people on the way in and say, "I'll give you top dollar." They have a kit with acid, a pennyweight scale, just like a jeweler. They check the

prices everyday. Of course you got to have money to make money. . . .
But the other day he bought a bracelet for seven hundred and resold it
for fifteen hundred. That's all profit.[57]

Mr. Tiffany himself could do no better.

Instead of using means sanctioned by the American dream to pursue
criminal goals, one may do the reverse—use illegitimate means to pursue
socially approved forms of success. This distortion takes seriously the
third tenet's focus on "actions under one's own control," but leaves
open the question of what those actions may be.[58]

A simple example is the "black 17-year-old honor student with a 3.8
grade point average at a prestigious Catholic high school. His mother is
a single, unemployed alcoholic. . . . The boy told the counselor that he
was selling drugs to save money for college because he expected that his
mother could not afford to send him."[59] The few women who succeed
as drug dealers "described these times as . . . those of which they were
most proud: they were working independently, often took care of their
own children, [and] made a reasonable amount of money." More sophisticated examples are dealers who "have left to set up legitimate businesses. Video and record stores are popping up. . . . A lot of drug boys
essentially have turned into banks. Not only for the lower class, but also
for the black middle class who cannot normally get SBA loans."[60] Beyond the drug trade, hustling enables "young men . . . to pursue life
aspirations, adopting those strategies that will permit them to . . . ex-
ploit . . . their limited environment to the maximum."[61]

With this tenet, as with the first two, one can subscribe to most aspects of the American dream and to its overall gestalt while radically undermining it through distortion of one feature. And here as before, poor
African Americans, while not unique in these distortions, are peculiarly
vulnerable to harm and to be harmed by them.

THE FOURTH TENET

The fourth tenet of the American dream justifies allegiance to, even worship of, the dominant ideology by distinguishing mere accomplishment
from true success, which is in some way associated with virtue. To accept
the association but to redefine virtue in destructive ways is to distort the
ideology.

In the flush of wealth and power, Benjamin Franklin defined virtue as
humility, self-discipline, and pragmatism. Young African Americans
mired in poverty and powerlessness sometimes define virtue as pride,
coolness, and toughness. Jobs and school are fertile arenas for illusory
displays of pride. A destitute alcoholic "want[s] to be communicating.

I don't want to be standing under no machine metal pressing some bullshit all day." A young mother will not return to high school because "I don't have anything to wear. I'm not going to go up there looking like a bum. No way."[62] With few resources or prospects, the temptation to salvage self-respect through false pride is hard to resist.

Another plausible substitute for real power is a show of power through acting "cool." "Black men learned long ago that the classic American virtues of thrift, perseverance and hard work did not give them the same tangible rewards that accrued to most whites." In reaction, some "have channeled their creative energies into the construction of a symbolic universe. . . . The 'cool pose' belies the rage held in check. . . . [It] is a way to say, 'you might break my back but not my spirit.' "[63]

Coolness has clear merits. Cool blacks refuse not only minimum-wage jobs but also drugs because they make the imbiber lose control. The urge to demonstrate coolness leads to musical, athletic, and verbal inventions, occasionally of a very high order.[64] The cool pose also, however, leads African Americans to deny problems, suppress affection, and commit crimes.[65] Being cool makes young black men quick to believe that they are being "dissed," or disrespected—leading to everything from even more hurt feelings to murder. And the cool pose may "thwart the enrichment and growth of a black youth because he avoids exposure to experiences that could help expand his personal, social, and political consciousness."[66] Thus this distortion of the American dream inhibits the already small chance of poor African Americans to achieve success according to its other precepts.

Coolness is a distinctly individualistic (as well as gendered) virtue. A cool dude is proud, autonomous, self-directed—an exaggerated epitome of the liberal's ideal man. Americans, however, are communitarians as well as liberals and sometimes define virtue as collective rather than individual enhancement. The simplest distortion of collective virtue is communality in illicit activity. Drug dealers in positions of authority do not "even call them workers. We just say 'They's down with us.' It was more like a big family. Everybody watch each other's back."[67] When his older brother Hector lost his nerve and stopped "taking care of business," fourteen-year-old Max sent him out of the country and sold most of his own possessions to pay "the connect" to whom Hector owed $20,000.[68]

Sometimes communality receives an extra measure of virtue through a racial comparison: "It's like an unwritten law. I know people who would kill for me. I would do the same for them. . . . When your brother needs you . . . you got to be there. . . . White people are always counting every penny, but it's not about that. It's about taking care of your brother, your woman, whoever, and you know they're going to take care of you when you need it."[69] This statement has at least three interesting elements. It celebrates collective rather than individualistic virtue, which is a variant but not a distortion of the classic American dream. It celebrates collectivism to the point of endorsing murder, which pushes the American dream past its limits. And it contrasts warm, generous blacks to cold, calculating whites—a sentiment more common among middle-class than among poor African Americans.

A more lethal distortion occurs when criminal acts are performed to maintain the collectivity. In cultural gangs, which "hold respect, fraternity, trust, and loyalty to gang and neighborhood as bedrock values," participants help their relatives join the gang, give each other expensive gifts and loans, and ensure that imprisoned members are treated well and have a place to return to. They also engage in internal policing—"If you was my homeboy and I asked you for [some money] and he says 'no I can't,' but you know he got it, . . . he got to go. Either somebody's going to rob him, kill him, or kick him off the set"—as well as external aggression—"Like if someone come shooting up our neighborhood, we go back and shoot up theirs. If we kill somebody, we kill somebody. . . . The only thing you have to do is protect the 'hood.'" This is not just tough talk. Of ninety-six homicides investigated by the Los Angeles Sheriff's Department in 1988, only seven were "drug-related." The remainder were "gang-related," apparently over "matters of honor" between the Bloods and the Crips.[70]

Virtue can be distorted in yet other ways. Poor African Americans occasionally find their worth in protecting some people against the ravages that they are committing against others. A Los Angeles gang member assures the interviewer that "like if you is my homeboy and you start to smokin' dope and . . . I see you going down the hill, every time I see you puffin' on something I'm going to beat you down until you stop." When an incarcerated black youth confessed a theft from his mother, others scorned him. "One group member even went to the extent of moving his chair away, stating that to steal from one's mother is 'the worst crime in the world. . . . That's cold!'" A veteran dealer distinguishes between types of drugs in drawing his limits: "Dope [heroin] kills, and I ain't about that. I provide a service. . . . I sell coke and smoke, and I wouldn't sell anything I wouldn't take myself."[71] Robby Wideman sold drugs, engaged in armed robberies, and participated (more or less accidentally) in murder. But the act that made him sorry enough to attempt suicide was stealing his brother's television set. Before allowing guests to relax with a drink, the "hoodlum" Calvin enunciates "rules of the apartment":

I don't 'low no bad language in my apartment. I'm the only one to use bad language in my house. . . . When peoples come to my apartment they got to act decent. Ain't gon' be no humbuggin' [fighting] up in here, less'n I'm doin' it myself. When you come over you can relax, 'cause it ain't gon' be no mess. Not in my house. I pay the rent here. I bought all this here furniture you see 'round here.

Most generally, "socialized delinquents" are distinguished from unsocialized delinquents by their "ties of affection and loyalty to family and friends. They may be hostile, intolerant, and unfair toward those they regard as the enemy, but they are willing to make some sacrifices for the feelings and welfare of those they believe and feel to be of their own group."[72]

Many more men than women sell drugs and commit acts of violence. But women too distort classic definitions of virtue. One young mother of two rejects the idea that virtue requires marriage before children, but insists that "if you want babies, you get pregnant by one man. It don't seem right to have all these fathers all over the place! If I had an urge for sex today, I would go to Sherita and Jeremiah's father" even though she no longer loves him.[73] Others take great pride in caring for their children regardless of the method: "I had a son to support, you know. I had to make money even quicker. . . . Then the job they was offerin' me, oh, 'I can't work for this less money. You got to be crazy,' I said. There's a faster way out there"—in this case, hustling.[74]

Some (formerly) poor African Americans make their success virtuous by putting illicitly gained wealth to socially approved ends.[75] As so often, drug dealing provides the most vivid examples. A murdered gang leader left an essay explaining that he sold drugs so that poor black children could become doctors and lawyers. Jimmie Lee, head of Chicago's Conservative Vice Lords, bought food and shoes for destitute families and lectured children about the excesses of drugs and gangs. Felix Mitchell, head of Oakland's 69 Mob, "would buy a large portable swimming pool and install it in a lot next to the housing project. . . . He would ride through in his car and toss basketballs out the window. He would pay the Good Humor man to drive into the project and give away all his ice cream."[76]

Beyond specific acts of largess, these men conveyed broader virtues even to those they most exploited. Jimmie Lee was personally abstemious, protective of children, long and contentedly married—and thus used as a model by some mothers. The flamboyant Felix Mitchell taught Oakland's poor that one could "manage the impossible dream. . . . 'There's no jobs, no money, no places to go for teenagers here. At least he did it, he made a living.'" Here too a racial comparison heightens the virtue: "Felix was the man who said, 'Hey, brother, if you can't do it their way, look at how I'm doing it.' . . . [Joseph] Kennedy was white and did it [through bootlegging] in a white society. Felix was black, and did it in black society. That's the only difference."[77]

Finally—and at this point distortion of the American dream blurs into rejection of it—some poor blacks invert conventional definitions of virtue and vice. The New Haven public defender observes that "in the newspaper, what they used to call the police-blotter page, that's my clients' Social Register." Cocaine sellers in Washington, D.C., renamed their product "Len Bias" after the great athlete's death from an overdose, and they did a thriving business. The number of hospital admissions for PCP intoxication is "a status symbol among their [Washington, D.C., adolescents'] crowd, much as getting a driver's license was for me."[78] So is going to jail—as well as "a rite of passage, a definition of adulthood," "an alternative kind of 'homeboy' status," and a great opportunity for networking. To those with more sophistication or intelligence, just going to jail is not good enough. One must go in style:

> Got me in the police station and I'm thinking, What the fuck is happening? This ain't spozed to be happening. Shooting for the big time and they got me for them nine half-spoons in my back pocket. Ain't no way, I'm thinking. . . . Like, my feelings was hurt. Like, shit. Ima big-time gangster and they jamming me over this little jive-time shit.[79]

There are, then, many ways for poor African Americans to distort the American dream. There are not many poor African Americans doing so; most, like most other Americans, remain under the spell of the great national suggestion. But some do, and the very richness and complexity of the dominant American ideology allow for an array of distortions.

But at least the distorters are in some fashion participating. We turn now to those who have completely broken the spell by rejecting the American dream.

Chapter Eleven

BREAKING THE SPELL

Where every man is enemy to every man . . . there is no place for industry . . . ; no arts; no letters; no society; and which is worst of all, continual fear, and danger of violent death; and the life of man, solitary, poor, nasty, brutish, and short.

—Thomas Hobbes, *Leviathan*

Do I really *want* to be integrated into a burning house? . . . How can one respect, let alone adopt, the values of a people who do not, on any level whatever, live the way they say they do, or the way they say they should? . . . The only thing white people have that black people need, or should want, is power—and no one holds power forever.

—James Baldwin, 1963

A FEW POOR African Americans reject the dominant ideology altogether. Some live in a Hobbesian world, resisting all social constraints on their preferred actions. Others, with Baldwin, do not believe that whites and the white-dominated ideology of the American dream are worthy of allegiance. They subscribe instead to a competing ideology.

Let us first consider the Hobbesians. Thirty percent of African Americans live in distressed neighborhoods of large cities, and many of them are not themselves among the estranged poor.[1] Furthermore, I judge that a majority of those who *are* estranged are distorters rather than rejectors.[2] Even if half of the estranged poor are rejectors, that is still at most only 5 percent of all blacks, less than 1 percent of all Americans.[3] Nevertheless, a few people can do great damage to themselves, their families, and their community. They warrant careful attention.[4]

INDIVIDUAL VIOLENCE

Nostalgia is rampant. . . . Even the junkies in New Haven are nostalgic. They recall a camaraderie, . . . when there was little violence. . . . The rise of violent posses and the devolution of street dealing onto younger and younger boys have made the addict's world a far colder, more frightening place. . . . These new, young dealers are heartless, the addicts say.

—William Finnegan, 1990

Journalists and their subjects capture the flavor of violent rejectors better than academics do—whether because journalists are more or less romantic, I am not sure. Pete Hamill, citing his long-term liberal credentials and "bone-poor" ethnic origins, bemoans the "Underclass . . . living in anarchic and murderous isolation. . . . In the last decade, I've watched this group of American citizens harden and condense, moving even further away from the basic requirements of a human life: work, family, safety, the law. . . . This ferocious subculture . . . [is] the single most dangerous fact of ordinary life in the United States." A black minister with a Ph.D., who was born in the projects and has spent his life as a teacher there, describes "children who only feel secure with a big wad of money in their pockets, who don't care how they get it. Children who have a complete depletion of moral values. This is not white phobia. This is real."[5]

Nowhere is the slippery slope from distortion to rejection of the American dream more slick than in the possession of a gun. Young black men acquire guns for all kinds of reasons—to protect a bicycle, to impress a girlfriend, as a gift from their brother, simply because "I found [it] on the block." Many carry their new possession in order to "look bad" and to keep others from "mess[ing] with me." But eventually, just carrying it does not protect the bicycle or impress the girl if others know that one will not use it. Besides, "the gun want to get blood on itself. It want to get a body on it." So does its owner: "You get it to seem bad, then start thinking you *are* bad. It's simple: Have it, use it." And some who succumb have a hard time looking back: "Shooting the gun, it made me feel the whole madness comin' out. I didn't want to stop shooting. I never thought about getting shot myself." At the bottom of the slope is sociopathy. Pressed, one crack dealer guesses that he and his posse have shot "maybe a dozen." Does he feel bad? "Bad? Not in the sense of remorse. I mean, these wasn't citizens in midtown—these was niggers would have inflicted pain on us if we hadn't inflicted pain on them. I'm sorry they [are] shot, but glad it ain't me."[6]

Carrying and using weapons is not common—except in a few places. Over 40 percent of one sample of inner city children claim to have witnessed a homicide; so do a quarter of the students in Chicago and 40 percent of the black children in a public housing project in "a large

TABLE 11.1
Causes of Death among Young Men, by Race and Age, 1960–1990
(number of deaths per 100,000 persons in each group)

	1960	1970	1980	1990
15–24 year olds				
Whites				
All causes*	143.7	170.8	167.0	131.3
Infections, malignancies,				
cardiovascular disease**	17.6	18.8	12.6	11.5
Accidents, suicide	100.8	122.8	123.2	91.9
Homicide	4.4	7.9	15.5	15.4
Proportion of deaths due				
to homicide	3.1%	4.6%	9.2%	11.7%
Blacks†				
All causes	213.8	304.6	209.1	252.2
Infections, malignancies,				
cardiovascular disease	27.6	24.7	20.5	20.8
Accidents, suicide	104.1	132.3	77.7	69.6
Homicide	43.7	92.0	84.3	138.3
Proportion of deaths due				
to homicide	20.4%	30.2%	40.3%	54.8%
25–34 year olds				
Whites				
All causes	163.2	176.6	171.3	176.1
Infections, malignancies,				
cardiovascular disease	44.1	34.6	26.4	54.4
Accidents, suicide	82.6	97.8	99.5	82.3
Homicide	6.2	13.0	18.9	15.1
Proportion of deaths due				
to homicide	3.8%	7.3%	11.0%	8.6%
Blacks				
All causes	386.4	504.1	407.3	430.8
Infections, malignancies,				
cardiovascular disease	92.5	80.0	59.0	141.6
Accidents, suicide	119.0	153.2	111.8	92.8
Homicide	84.7	137.3	145.1	125.4
Proportion of deaths due				
to homicide	21.9%	27.2%	35.6%	29.1%

* Includes many not detailed here.
** The three most common medical reasons for death.
† Nonwhites in 1960 and 1970.
Sources: U.S. Department of Health, Education, and Welfare (1963: 26–33; 1974: 26–43); U.S. Department of Health and Human Services (1985: 36–48; 1994a: 40–52). 1990 is the most recent year for which data are available.

southern central city." (Many more have witnessed equally frightening, if not quite so lethal, violence.) In New York City, 15 percent of public schools reported no incidents of violence in the 1993–94 school year, but 30 percent of the schools reported an average of forty-four incidents each, accounting for 90 percent of the total.[7] Overall, black (but not white) men aged fifteen to thirty-five are now much more likely to die from homicide than from any other cause, a considerable change from the 1960s and 1970s.

Table 11.1 shows the ultimate results of substantial social and political changes over the past three decades. The number of young men who died rose, then fell. Deaths from physical ailments declined in the younger group, and declined and then soared among the older men, presumably as a result of better medical care and AIDS, respectively. Deaths from accidents and suicide rose, then fell, as a result of the combination of better medical care, safer vehicles, and rising suicide rates.

It is the last row in each panel that matters here. Both white and black rates of death by homicide rose in the twenty years after 1960. But among whites and older blacks they then held steady or declined, whereas among young blacks they continued to climb. Thus, given the decrease in most other causes of death, over half of young African American men who die, compared with three-tenths of older African American men and about one-tenth of white men, now die from violence at the hands of others (almost always of their own race).

Why do people hurt or kill others?[8] Sometimes for political reasons, which I will consider later. Sometimes because "the gun want to get blood on itself." But two reasons are directly connected to the ideology of the American dream and therefore of special concern here. First, violence may be part of the business of getting ahead. All employers want loyal workers, especially if the workers have become experts in their employ; most, however, stop well short of one drug dealer's method for keeping his staff. If his sellers buy from another source, "they get fucked up. They ain't going to get killed, but they'll get beat up. Take their car, take their jewelry, slap their bitch in the face, spit on them. 'Get on fool, why don't you get with another group. You can be as dead as they are.' They like, 'That's okay man.' They be scared to leave." Similarly, all salesmen try to keep competitors away from their turf, but most stop short of "driving by and shooting. . . . That started because . . . Hunter's Point is fightin' for control of the drug game in San Francisco. Fillmore . . . wasn't goin' for it . . . because, if it was to happen Fillmore wouldn't be making that much money. That's why it's still pretty much the same as far as the drive-by shooting and all the killings."[9] The impulses accord perfectly with the American dream's encouragement to strive for success; it is only the move from talking about violence to engaging in it that puts these men outside the bounds of the dream.

To put the point more analytically, it is comments like those just quoted that lend urgency to the claim that violence is simply an extension of the American drive for accumulation. In this view, capitalism run amok is destroying black communities and will ultimately destroy the United States. The older practice of hustling—itself a response to discrimination in the capitalist job market—did not crowd out the decencies of life in black neighborhoods. But recently an "outlaw culture" has taken over "that has rejected African-American communal norms in favor of the predatory individualism of the capitalist marketplace. These youngsters . . . have embraced a doctrine of 'might makes right' that converts everyone into a potential victim."

This argument continues by blaming three phenomena for the devastation of black communities: the economy, particularly the decline of manufacturing jobs and the lack of alternatives in cities; middle-class blacks' desire for social and economic mobility, which lured them out to the suburbs; and "mainstream popular culture," which teaches jobless blacks to want things they cannot afford and which "present[s] us with heroes . . . who pursue . . . wealth and power without conscience or compassion."[10]

This analysis is overdrawn.[11] Overall, black homicide has declined since its peak in the 1970s; popular culture has always glorified outlaws; many well-off blacks have always kept their distance from the poor; and perhaps the "black ghetto" never did have a "golden age."[12] But the basic point is right. Actions that embody the American dream and actions that deform it beyond legitimacy are not as far apart as proponents of the dream claim.[13] And a few poor African Americans are now more willing or able to shoot anyone who gets in the way of their success than their counterparts were a generation ago.[14]

The other reason for direct personal violence that is relevant here is important precisely because it is so *un*related to the ideology of the American dream. One-fifth of incarcerated youth in Ohio committed crimes because "it is fun."[15] Among black youth in Washington, D.C., heavy drug users, frequent sellers, and recent lawbreakers were, compared with nonsellers and noncriminals, dramatically more inclined to break rules, less interested in socially approved goals, and more alienated and isolated. They did not, however, have lower self-esteem, evince emotional instability, or feel much stress. They also had plenty of trusted and supportive friends. In short, "these youth appear to have, by and large, successfully segmented themselves off from mainstream society to immerse themselves in the drug [or crime] subculture."[16]

Others are even further removed from mainstream norms. Asked for an alternative to killing another drug dealer, young murderers in Washington, D.C., speculate only that they could have shot their rival once rather than six times, or could have stabbed instead of shot him. Their sole regret is that incarceration "took a lot of my life"; one went to his victims' funerals to assure himself that they were indeed dead. Most chillingly, some seem incapable of seeing the future as potentially different from the past; "when asked, 'what are your thoughts about the future?' several youth asked for an explanation of the question." One cannot be further removed from the ideology of the American dream than to be unable to imagine a future.[17]

Debates about the existence and causes of a "criminal subculture" have a long and venerable history.[18] Without getting into them, it seems safe to say that some lawbreakers hold different values than most other Americans. And the interaction of race and poverty may play a role in determining who that subset of lawbreakers are. Unlike imprisoned whites, imprisoned young blacks' self-esteem is significantly related to their perceptions of likely success in a criminal career (but not in a straight career) and to the amount of money they have made from crime.[19] Poor young urban blacks who break laws reject conventional beliefs in the legitimacy of law and the illegitimacy of violence much more than do similar, law-abiding youth.[20] Black ex-offenders and ex-addicts rank both conventional and (especially) criminal occupations higher than do their white counterparts, and those (of both races) who rate criminal activity highly make more money from crime.[21]

At least these youths hold standards and set goals. Beyond them lie "unsocialized delinquents" who "care only about themselves, . . . are egocentric and narcissistic . . . , and react . . . to frustration with . . . *behavior without a goal*." Their "ethos of brutal bravado . . . signal[s] the end of politics, a retreat into a world of despair, a world without culture, obligation, or larger meaning of any kind."[22] I know of no study that systematically examines the racial or class composition of unsocialized delinquents, or analyzes whether their number has changed over time. But a few such people, now armed with Uzis, are at the core of what Cornel West calls the "nihilistic threat to . . . [the] very existence" of black America—the "monumental eclipse of hope, the unprecedented collapse of meaning, the incredible disregard for human (especially black) life and property."[23]

Thus one can reject the American dream through the use of violence for several reasons. Some believe so strongly in its promise of success that they overcome its demands for virtue (or any other restraint on the pursuit of one's goals). Others set goals without a passing thought to virtue; a few cannot conceive what a goal is. In all of these cases, the rejector not only harms himself and his neighbors, but also reduces the very possibility that Americans can be persuaded to face up to the dangers of the American dream in order to recast it so that it can fulfill its promises to all.

HARM TO CHILDREN

I say "himself and his neighbors" advisedly; boys and men engage in most of the gun-toting, beating, and murder.[24] But women too contribute to the "nihilistic threat to the existence of black America," most typically and wrenchingly by violating norms of family protection and love. Thus they implicitly abjure the second and third tenets of the American dream because their actions make it extremely difficult for their children to anticipate, and later to pursue, success.

Here too reporters' anecdotes are a provocative starting point. Mothers prostitute their daughters to obtain crack or "use their children in front of crack houses because they knew the police would hesitate." After being told that he could call his adoptive father's mother "Grandma," a four-year-old asked, "If I call you Grandma, does that mean you can burn me?" Another grandmother drove across the country to find that her addicted daughter weighed eighty-five pounds, "and her one-and-a-half-year-old granddaughter [was] taking old McDonald hamburger buns out of the garbage and feeding them to her eight-month-old brother." Six-year-old Dooney Waters begs his teacher, "I'll sleep on the floor. Please don't make me go home. I don't want to go back there," because "my mother don't take care of me. All she want is drugs."[25]

More sober analyses reinforce these sensational anecdotes.[26] Young black women are more likely than young white or Latina women to be introduced to lawbreaking by family members and are more likely to commit crimes as part of their family relationships: "the only time they so nice to me is when I'm turning them on. . . . Other than that we fuss and damn near kill each other." More generally, as black city neighborhoods have deteriorated, "the community 'mother'—once an omnipresent figure on the neighborhood porches and in local beauty shops and corner groceries—has also undergone a serious decline in numbers, prestige, and authority. . . . The few such women who remain active in the community are overwhelmed by a virtual proliferation of 'street kids'—children almost totally without parental supervision, left to their own devices—and they lament the decline of the local community."[27]

Children at all stages of life are harmed by parents who cannot or will not show concern for their future. The number of babies born to women who use drugs in pregnancy rose dramatically during the 1980s. To cite only one instance, from 1978 to 1986, just over 2 percent of black babies and just under 2 percent of white babies born in New York City were affected by illicit drugs; at the peak of the "crack epidemic" in 1989, just over 3 percent of white babies, but fully 7.5 percent of black babies, were affected.[28] The number of "boarder babies"—children who remain hospitalized because they have no home—rose at the same time; New York City was confronted with almost 13,000 boarder babies in the thirty-one months after February 1987.[29] And when they do go home, some babies face devastating conditions. Substantiated reports of child abuse have risen from 500,000 in 1980 to over one million in 1993, and child abuse is higher among the poor and African Americans than among the rest of the population.[30] (It apparently is not, however, higher among African Americans once social class is controlled for.)[31] The foster care caseload in New York State doubled between 1987 and 1989 and grew by 44 percent in California from 1985 to 1988; "the rapid pace of change and corroborative data from other sources leave little doubt about the effect of substance abuse on family well-being."[32] Foster children too are disproportionately poor and African American.[33]

As in the case of pubescent gunslingers, the proportion of all children who suffer these traumas is tiny. But as in that case, the numbers need not be large for the abandonment of ordinary standards of parental care to have a calamitous ripple effect on the children, on other poor African Americans, and on the nation as a whole. Parents with no ability or commitment to give their children the foundation they need for even an *un*reasonable anticipation of success, or for the substitution of some other faith, have implicitly rejected the American dream and have drastically reduced their children's chances for even imagining, let alone achieving, success and virtue.

REFUSAL TO WORK

> Man, you go two, three years not working and hanging around and smoking reefer or drinking and then you get a job—you can't handle it. . . . After the first two, three weeks of working, you . . . say, "I don't want to get up in the morning, get pushed and shoved. I'm gonna get on welfare."
>
> —participant in a Supported Work demonstration project

Rejection of the American dream does not always produce the dramas of murder and child abuse. It can take the much quieter form of renouncing Americans' cherished work ethic, thereby challenging the third rather than the second and fourth tenets of the dream. Refusal to work is no more the unique property of poor African Americans than are the other forms of rejection I have discussed. Nor is it new.[34] But some poor blacks' increasing willingness to express their refusal blatantly suggests a deterioration in even verbal commitment to the American dream. Three times as many poor as well-off African Americans answer "nothing" when asked what bothers them most about not working.[35] More analytically,

> the relationship between "old heads" ["a man of stable means who was strongly committed to family life, to church, and . . . to passing on his philosophy, developed through his own rewarding experience with work"] and young boys represents an important institution of the traditional black community. . . . But . . . when gainful employment and its rewards are not forthcoming, boys easily conclude that the moral lessons of the old head concerning the work ethic, punctuality, and honesty do not fit their own circumstances.[36]

People refuse to work for several reasons. One is passivity: some welfare recipients "ask, 'Who do I got to ask for this or that?' Not 'What do I do?' but 'Who should I ask?' They don't know how to think for themselves."[37] Another is acquisitiveness: "[I am] just possessed. . . . It would be very hard for me to live a straight life. . . . Temptation is always out there waiting. . . . I'm a money fanatic." A few find work to be literally too straight, that is, linear: hustling provides "excitement. It's dangerous, I guess, but you meet different people. . . . Like a square girl, what do they talk about? Nothin'! 'Oh, my boyfriend's this and that.' I think it's boring. I like to talk about somethin' excitin', . . . like money and how she went about getting the money."[38] Others see work as a futile effort to assert control of an unmanageable world:

> Whas gonna happen tomorrow is gonna happen. . . . Ain't no use sittin here sayin, "Tomorrow I'm gonna go out there, I'm gonna make this an this." Thas just . . . a whole lot of bullshit. . . . My grandmother tole me when I was a boy, like as knocked ma shoes off, she said, "You can plan an plan an wish and wish, but shit in one hand and plan an wish in the other an see what you feel first." Thas it right there. Thas the whole thing.[39]

Others draw inferences beyond ambivalence from their recognition that the American dream promises only a chance for success, not the thing itself:

> What really gets me is when I see guys that's been there all this time, man. . . . And here's a guy sweeping the floor, . . . an old man now. . . . One night I asked the guy, I said, "Man, you've been here thirty years. . . . And you got a *broom* with a pair of *yellow coveralls* on. That's all you got to show for thirty years. . . . You ain't got shit, man." . . .

I'll probably work until I get finished with this court thing, . . . and then I'll probably devise me some kind of means to get *me* something, you see.[40]

Despite years of research and pronouncements (not always in that order), one can reach no settled conclusion about the number of poor African Americans, or other Americans, who refuse to work.[41] It is smaller than the number of unemployed or labor force dropouts, but probably larger than the number of people who tell surveyors that they do not want a job.[42] Perhaps the most interesting feature of dissensus on the amount of and reasons for nonwork is the very fluidity of the concept of "the work ethic." Refusal to work is at the end of a long continuum of beliefs about the third tenet of the American dream, ranging from ambitious excitement through dogged determination, wishful thinking, and immoral practices. One's location on the continuum itself is surely deeply influenced by context: the more jobs are available and rewarding, the more people will respond to the call of the work ethic. Most poor African Americans want to work and see employment as the means to achieve their dreams; a few have no dreams or refuse to work for them; others move frequently from one point on the continuum to another nearby as their circumstances and prospects change. How much they move, where they stop, and what external forces affect their movements will have a great deal of influence on the future of the American dream.

POLITICAL REJECTION OF THE AMERICAN DREAM

Ain't nobody going to vote no more. You can get a gun.

—resident of the Corner, Detroit, 1968

Just as some middle-class blacks do, some poor blacks reject the American dream because it is politically unpersuasive. Most simply, "there ain't going to be no voting now! You just have to make your way now. . . . You don't need no president no more! You just need a world to live in. *Live for yourself!* . . . Whatever come, you take it, and do whatever you can do about it to solve your problems."[43] Electoral politics as a route to success seems so remote to poor people of color that, although 1.4 million people live in the Los Angeles city council districts at the center of the May 1992 riots, only 37,000 of them bother to elect the representatives of those districts.[44] State and federal politics have even less appeal. Most black Los Angelenos have little confidence in any government,[45] and the main reaction to President Bush's trip to Los Angeles after the disturbances was "a show of wearied shrugs." After all, "him and Reagan are the ones that caused this. Then they come— they're going to come down here and see and tell you guys how he's going to make it better. . . . What he's going to do—he's going to do what he's been doing for the last four years, nothing, but making it worse."[46]

Rioters disgusted with downtown politicos are only the tip of the nonvoting iceberg. "The percentage of blacks who actually cast ballots was greater in the Goldwater-Johnson election of 1964 before the Voting Rights Act than in the Dukakis-Bush contest of 1988." A smaller proportion of southern blacks were registered to vote in 1988 than in 1970.[47] The data are mixed on whether low-status blacks do or do not vote more than comparable whites;[48] it is clear, however, that the proportion of poorly educated adults of both races who vote has declined steadily over the past three decades.[49]

These data are too broad and thin to tell us much about views of the American dream. After all, one may abjure voting because one is too busy making money, singing an aria, or otherwise fulfilling one's dream. But it is plausible that, on balance, nonvoters believe less in the dream's promises than voters do. In addition, one-fourth of African Americans (of all classes) claim that the election of blacks to "important political offices" has made no difference to "the cause of blacks" (and a few more argue that it has hurt the cause), and almost 40 percent of poorly educated African Americans expect that their local government would ignore any complaint they made to it.[50]

These findings support two conclusions. On the one hand, many badly off blacks (and whites) retain faith in the political system despite the paucity of evidence that the political system cares about them. On the other hand, badly off African Americans (among others) are losing faith in electoral politics.[51] If we consider political equality to be an integral part of the first tenet of the American dream, that downhill slide is deeply troubling.

IDEOLOGICAL REJECTION AND VIOLENCE

> No way Ima be like the rest of them niggers scuffling and kissing ass to get by. . . . The shame is they ain't even getting by. They crawling. They stepped on. Mize well be roaches or some goddamn waterbugs. White man got em backed up in Homewood and he's sprinkling roach powder on em. He's steady shaking and they steady dying. . . . The shit's still coming down. . . . Falls till it knocks you down. So you better believe Ima go for it [an armed robbery]. I'm scared and I know something ain't right, . . . but I got to go."
> —Robby Wideman, c. 1980

A step beyond political withdrawal from the American dream is ideolog-ical scorn. It is sometimes connected with the violence discussed earlier when political claims are used to justify otherwise unacceptable behav-ior: "We have the right to get up every morning and go shoot some white cats. . . . I mean we're asking for our damn rights, man. And they keeping them from you. There's no way in the world a Negro can be raised up in this society and think otherwise."[52]

Slightly more subtle is Robby Wideman's claim quoted above, that white oppression causes (and therefore excuses?) black violence: "There is a war in Detroit, and young black men are the targets. Our sons are at risk—to suicide, murder, jail, and hopelessness. Really it's genocide; the enemy is the society that has forced the situation on them." Even if most young black men are killed by other blacks, "it's misleading. The real enemy is hopelessness."[53]

The changing nature of race riots indicates most clearly African Americans' increasing willingness to use violence as a political state-ment. In most twentieth-century racial conflagrations, whites attacked blacks; "White people [themselves] got hurt because they got in the way or because they provoked a confrontation." But the 1980 riot in Lib-erty City, Miami, was "different. . . . The purpose was to kill white peo-ple. That's a whole new ballgame to deal with."[54] Black youths fought over an ax with which to beat a white passerby; one white victim had his ears and tongue cut off; rioters prevented an ambulance from reaching three dying white teenagers. For a few days, the racial savagery almost reached the level of the daily lynchings of the first several Jim Crow decades.

The 1992 explosion in Los Angeles was even more innovative: "In '65 we didn't have assault rifles, Uzis, hand grenades, bulletproof vests. We got 'em now. There's a whole new generation out here right now. . . . Not a generation of asskicker takers, but is giving out asskick-ers now."[55] Many nonwhite residents of Los Angeles saw violence as a legitimate retaliation for the unpunished brutality against Rodney King (and others) by members of the Los Angeles Police Department. Thus firefighters and journalists as well as police were attacked with automatic weapons and bricks. A truck driver staggering away after a beating was greeted with "no pity for the white man. That's how Rodney King felt, white boy." Fidel Lopéz was beaten, his genitals were painted black, and "his body was doused with gasoline, apparently for the purpose of set-ting him afire."[56] Over and over reporters were told that looting "is the only way black people know how to take back their community. I'm not condoning it, but how else are we going to do it? The politicians, they can't get anybody who's in there who's not in it for the money, the power." Over two-thirds of black Los Angelenos, compared with roughly two-fifths of whites, Asians, and Latinos, saw the uprising as "mainly a protest by blacks against unfair conditions" rather than "a way of engaging in looting and street crime."[57]

IDEOLOGICAL ALTERNATIVES

Some let abhorrence of the American dream's hypocrisy justify attacking whites; others use that abhorrence to fuel efforts at remaking their community. That line is neither clear nor easy to toe. But poor black rejectors' choice makes a considerable difference, to other poor blacks most of all.

Grass-roots social and political organizations in many cities are powered by ideological rejectors.[58] "The young black activists in New Haven are all cultural nationalists, intent on replacing 'Eurocentric' models with 'Afrocentric' ones." Organizers assure parents that "'If you educate your children correctly in the seven principles [of Nguza Saba], they won't turn on you when they become teenagers, the way they do today.'" Community organizers arrange festivals and protests, provide workshops and classes, supervise athletic facilities, field trips, and rites of passage to manhood—all in the service of "offer[ing] them [adolescent boys] another model for black manhood" than the one they see on the streets.[59] The Louis Armstrong Manhood Development Project in New Orleans is based on the premise that "instilling Black youth with the cultural values of their ancestors is one promising way to . . . increase their capacity to survive and flourish in an often hostile world." Young men are assigned to an African nation—each a "self-contained teaching and learning module"—within which they learn everything from geography to "proper male social demeanor" and "respect, responsibility, reciprocity, and restraint." This program serves two hundred teens a year, reports considerable success, and hopes to expand.[60] Among the most energetic reformers of inner city education are proponents of all black, usually all male, schools distinguished by high standards, hard work, and an Afrocentric curriculum.[61] Community groups in Boston, Milwaukee, Philadelphia, and elsewhere "not only seek 'redistribution' but a fundamental change in the social position of black vis-à-vis white power structures."[62] Programs to eliminate violence among young black men claim that "the high rate of African American interpersonal violence is a product of cultural misorientation and disorganization," which can be combated only by an "Afrocentric Community Development Agenda."[63] To the degree that rejection of the white-created dominant ideology moves beyond posturing into activities to improve housing, jobs, political accountability, and self-respect, poor blacks who reject the dream may enhance their lives as well as protect themselves against the harsh lessons of the third and fourth tenets.

One can also reject the American dream by abjuring from consumerism and middle-class values, whether held by whites or blacks. Ideological rejection of whites and of materialism can be closely linked: "I used to have a theory that black people were born rich, just naturally rich in nature, you know, and white people weren't. That white people created false riches, like money and things, and created a society where everybody had to strive to achieve these false riches and in doing so, they never feel their true riches."[64]

But renouncing the search for wealth is conceptually, and sometimes politically, distinct from rejecting white society. After all, some poor African Americans express allegiance to their class at the expense of racial ties. Almost one-fifth of poor blacks feel warmer or closer to their self-identified class than to their race; that is half the rate of poor whites' class affiliation, but four times the rate of affluent blacks' class affiliation.[65] Fully a quarter of poorly-educated African Americans perceive "very strong" conflict between the rich and poor in America.[66] Some of that class identification develops into full-scale resistance to putatively middle-class selfishness and atomism· "I don't believe they should climb up individually. They should pull each other up. . . . Get together and help everybody make it, man. . . . Once somebody get on his way, he ain't thinking about all those black people. He is with the white man. Middle-class Negroes. I don't like them. They look down on people like me."[67]

Thus poor blacks reject the American dream for reasons ranging from nihilistic solipsism to communal commitment. But the wide range of reasons for rejection and the intense media focus on the most florid rejectors should not make us lose sight of the fact that most poor African Americans remain more or less under the spell of the great national suggestion. Given the conditions of inner cities and rural villages, and the lack of any persuasive reason to believe that they have a real chance to achieve their dreams, the many poor blacks' continued commitment to the American dream needs more explanation than the few poor blacks' rejection of it. Let us turn, then, to an explanation of the patterns I have delineated in this part.

Chapter Twelve

THE PERVERSITY OF RACE AND THE
FLUIDITY OF VALUES

> You asked a question about Martin Luther King. . . . All that
> stuff about "the dream" means nothing to the kids I
> know. . . . He died in vain. He was famous and he lived and
> gave his speeches and he died and now he's gone. But we're
> still here. Don't tell students in this school about "the
> dream." Go and look into a toilet here if you would like to
> know what life is like for students in this city.
>
> —a student at East St. Louis High School, 1990

MOST TOILETS in this student's school do not work or have been ripped
out; school closes when sewage flows into the kitchen. How is it possible
for people who live in these circumstances to retain faith in the American
dream? What will happen if more come to feel as this teen and his friends
do, that the dream means nothing?

My discussion of poor blacks has been structurally different from that
of well-off blacks, so the nature of the conclusions to be drawn also differs. I judged that most readers would believe, but not understand the
reasons for, the paradox of succeeding more and enjoying it less. Therefore the part of the book on well-off African Americans focused on examining an array of possible explanations and eliminating the weakest
until only a few remained. I then concluded by pulling those few together into a single, though complicated, perspective. I also judged that
most readers would be skeptical of the very truth of the paradox of remaining under the spell of the great national suggestion. Therefore the
part on poor African Americans has focused more on examining evidence that variously supports it, qualifies it, and denies it. My task now
is to draw together all of these strands of the paradox by judging their
relative weight and linking them across the possibly artificial boundaries
that I have heretofore set up.

Despite these different analytic strategies, however, I can begin to
draw the pieces together here as I did in the discussion of affluent
blacks—with the third paradox of "what's all the fuss about?" That paradox signals the fact that over the past thirty years blacks have become

more skeptical about their race's chance to participate in the American dream while whites have become more convinced on the same point. Whites note racial change; blacks remain dissatisfied and add to that dissatisfaction frustration over whites' inability or unwillingness to share it.

CLASS DIFFERENCES IN ATTENTIVENESS TO RACE

Whites' conviction of increasing racial equality points to a crucial but ambiguous change in the lives of poor blacks. Until the mid-1960s poor blacks were directly controlled by whites, whether individually or collectively through laws, institutions, and custom. It was easy to see who the oppressors were—white mayors, city council members, police, sheriffs, social workers, teachers, judges and jailers, housing project supervisors, and downtown bureaucrats. Pressure from African Americans, changes in whites' moral views and political calculations, and transformations of urban political and economic structures combined to replace many of those white officials with black ones. Norms of public interracial exchange changed concomitantly and dramatically. Thus poor blacks probably have less contact now with whites than their counterparts did three decades ago, and what contact they have is often ostensibly neutral or intended to help, not oppress, them.

Whites mostly see these changes as evidence of clear and significant progress in blacks' lives. They now explain blacks' continued disproportionate poverty, not by racism but by residues from past racism (72 percent), character flaws (69 percent), God's will (55 percent), dysfunctional black culture (52 percent), oppression by a few wealthy whites (39 percent), and racially determined genetic defects (31 percent). More globally, six in ten whites explain racial inequality in individualistic terms: "Blacks have less of the good things in life because they do not try hard enough, not because rich whites keep them down."[1] Thus whites' most common interpretations of racial change over the past three decades reinforce their belief in the efficacy of the American dream.

The modal poor black's explanation for continued poverty in the face of apparent racial equality lies somewhere between concurrence with whites' individualism and confusion.[2] A few reject the claim of progress, seeing domination that is all the more powerful because it is covert. Why do not more poor African Americans rise up in fury over the injustice of an ideology that almost promises success in the abstract but almost guarantees their particular failure?

The evidence in this book suggests at least proximate answers to that question. First, at the level of beliefs and values, the "declining significance of race" operates exactly in reverse of the way it operates at the level of structures and practices. Between 1945 and 1980, overt racism and legal discrimination declined and the American economic system moved fully into a modern industrial (or even postindustrial) mode. In consequence, "class has become more important than race in determining black life-chances." More precisely,

> poorly trained and educationally limited blacks of the inner city . . . see their job prospects increasingly restricted to the low-wage sector, their unemployment rates soaring to record levels . . . , their labor-force participation rates declining, their movement out of poverty slowing, and their welfare roles increasing. . . . [But] talented and educated blacks are experiencing unprecedented job opportunities in the growing government and corporate sectors, opportunities that are at least comparable to those of whites with equivalent qualifications.[3]

Little in this book disputes that claim, and much confirms it. It is, in fact, the basis for the paradoxes I have identified and explored: middle-class blacks, structurally most freed from the constraints of race, are often obsessed by it; poor blacks, whose lives are largely shaped by the mistake of being born the wrong color, generally do not think about race very much.[4] The *economic* significance of race is declining among well-off but not poor blacks, whereas the *interpretive* significance of race is declining among poor but not well-off African Americans. Thus

> to the people living in the Robert Taylor Homes [a public housing project in Chicago], its conditions were a miserable fact of life for which there was no good explanation. Anger, at least articulated anger at whoever was to blame, was relatively rare. The traditional ghetto animus against white exploiters was far below the level it had reached in earlier decades. . . . "People didn't talk about white people [says one resident]. . . . White people weren't an issue."[5]

THE BEST AVAILABLE ALTERNATIVE

The relative invisibility of white domination compared with the constant pressure of poverty, danger, and degrading surroundings works in an odd way to reinforce poor African Americans' belief in the American dream. The United States has never had a robust socialist tradition that teaches people to understand poverty as a structural phenomenon in which they happen to be caught.[6] Nor has a republican tradition that would encourage attentiveness to the common good had much more appeal, at least to poor African Americans in the past few decades. Black nationalism has been more visible, more widely ascribed to, and more salient—but still, fewer than a fifth of poor African Americans are vehemently nationalist, except for brief periods or in unusual circumstances. (The best recent chance for widespread nationalist allegiance—the Black Panther party—was quickly destroyed by a combination of internal demoralization and external repression.)[7]

Thus someone for whom poverty feels like a more severe day-to-day problem than racism has almost no ideological choices beyond the American dream that plausibly offer a way out of immediate grinding necessity. And the paucity of extant ideological alternatives is reinforced by the lack of enough money, organizational connections, and emotional space to develop an alternative on one's own. "Groups with such negative autonomy [autonomy from . . . power structures in the sense of exclusion] usually do not have sufficient resources to develop a great deal of ideological independence; even if they do, . . . such independence is a very risky venture sure to elicit negative sanctions"—as in the Panthers. Such excluded groups "hold a formulation of that [dominant] ideology that is distinct in emphases (because some of the dominant views are simply irrelevant to their situation) but may be a bit vague and thus lacking in real oppositional potential."[8]

In such a context, faith in the American dream is intelligible, even wise. After all, the dream does have some real virtues. Its commitment to individual autonomy, equality, and rights has pushed our nation far from the slavery and serfdom of a century ago, and its emphasis on hope has deep psychological resonance. Furthermore, many African Americans *have* succeeded according to its precepts—certainly more than have succeeded by the precepts of nationalism, republicanism, or socialism. Most poor blacks are related to or know or at least know of someone who started out poor and, apparently by dint of courage and sweat, achieved some level of absolute success.[9] Thus poor African Americans may plausibly if not correctly calculate that their odds of living a happy life are improved more by following the tenets of the dream than by making any other available choice. (Put less rationalistically, the fantasy of success through the American dream has a more powerful magnetic field than the fantasies of power through nationalism, pursuit of the common good through republicanism, or class solidarity through socialism.)[10]

This belief-by-default is reinforced by the ideology's enormous flexibility as to what counts as success. We saw in the discussion of well-off African Americans how that flexibility opens the door to the corrosive phenomena of blacks' relative deprivation and whites' fear of competitive losses. But the flexibility also permits relative *gratification* over small increments of absolute success. Thus the elusive racism that middle-class African Americans find so infuriating seems a mere annoyance to a recent escapee from the inner city: "[I] only have to deal with people who don't like me, right? They're not doing anything to hurt me as far as I can see. They're not trying to break into my house. They're not trying to bust my child up the side of his head. They're not trying to lure him into [gangs and drugs]."[11] More generally, affluent blacks (and whites) are more likely than poor blacks (and whites) to include starting one's own business or rising to become president of a company in their understanding of what the American dream means; low-status blacks usually rest content with a college education for themselves and their children.[12] Over six-tenths of poor blacks (and whites) think their family could live "in reasonable comfort" on less than $30,000 a year (in 1986 dollars); barely one-tenth of well-off blacks (and whites) concur.[13] If the ideology can teach people that trading attacks for prejudice is a vast gain—as indeed it is—or that a family income not far above the poverty line suffices for comfort, then its continuance is not so hard to understand.

Even the internal contradictions of the American dream can make it easier rather than harder for poor African Americans to believe in it. By submerging structural reasons for failure—racial or gender discrimination, the unequal division of economic and social capital, the simple lack of jobs—under individual explanations for failure, the dream contributes to ensuring that some cannot succeed. But that very submerging makes it appear that the reasons for failure really *are* individual, and thus subject to conquest by any one individual, or even all individuals. Poor African Americans are usually badly educated and not widely traveled, so they are unlikely to see structural patterns underlying individual actions and situations. Thus even if (or because) the American dream fails as a description of American society, it is a highly seductive prescription for succeeding in that society to those who cannot see the underlying flaw.

UNSTABLE AND FLUID BELIEFS

Belief-by-default may be surprisingly deep, but it is not stable. Conceptually, a belief in the American dream that rests on the false premise of the lack of relationship between individual poverty and structural constraints has a shaky base. Empirically, alternative ideologies do exist, and adherents to Afrocentrism or the Nation of Islam could further develop their organizational bases in ways that would change poor blacks' perceptions of their array of choices. In any case, much apparent belief in the American dream is weak, ambivalent, or distorted.[14]

The instability of poor African Americans' faith in the American dream may be better described as fluidity. Although the ends of the continuum—from remaining under the spell of the great national suggestion to nihilistic rejection—are worlds apart, the points in between are not sharply differentiated. That is true by definition in any continuum. It is also demonstrable in fact, as individuals move from selling drugs to selling drug paraphernalia to selling sneakers (and back again). Even the verb "move" may be too rigid; many participants in the 1992 explosion in Los Angeles seemed almost randomly and simultaneously to make political attacks on whites and white institutions, to make ethnic attacks on foreign "invaders," to loot furniture and liquor stores, to help those attacked by someone else, and to participate in cleaning up the mess afterward. Judgments of the uprising were equally fluid: across the country, three-fourths of poor African Americans "blame[d]" the "riots" *both* on "years of frustration on the part of black people living with poverty and discrimination" *and* on "irresponsible people just taking advantage of the situation."[15]

This point has several implications. In scholarly terms, we cannot determine precisely how many poor African Americans fall at any point along the continuum of beliefs about the American dream. I am sure that most poor blacks continue to believe in some sense in the dream, and that only a tiny minority abjure it completely. Those proportions are critical but hardly definitive—not, as we so often say, because our research is incomplete but because an effort at precision would be misguided.[16]

But it is in political terms that the point about fluidity really matters. Herbert Croly first and best articulated its dangers for American society:

> A considerable proportion of the American people is beginning to exhibit economic and political . . . discontent. A generation ago the implication was that if a man remained poor and needy, his poverty was his own fault, because the American system was giving all its citizens a fair chance. Now, however, the discontented poor are beginning to charge their poverty to an unjust political and economic organization, and reforming agitators do not hesitate to support them in this contention. Manifestly a threatened obstacle has been raised against the anticipated realization of our national Promise. Unless the great majority of Americans not only have, but believe they have, a fair chance, the better American future will be dangerously compromised.[17]

A half-century later, another great political analyst gave the same warning, this time including racial as well as economic cleavages. David Truman cautioned that if "only a particular class interpretation" is politically influential, groups such as Negroes who are "inadequately activated" or suffer "recurrent and prolonged frustration" may reject "the rules of the game." Thus Americans must attend to the "great task" of ensuring the conditions of a viable system. "These conditions are not threatened . . .

so long as the 'rules of the game' remain a meaningful guide to action, meaningful in the sense that acceptance of them is associated with some minimal recognition of group claims. In the loss of such meanings lie the seeds of the whirlwind."[18]

WHITHER THE FUTURE?

If "our national Promise" is not more than occasionally fulfilled, if blacks cannot see any "recognition of [their] group claims," then the very strength of poor blacks' belief in the dominant ideology can back-fire. Disillusionment is much more powerful when it follows deep belief, or belief that has been clung to in the face of constant disappointment, than when it follows casual or contested acquiescence. Thus the more powerfully the ideology of the American dream restrains protest or crim-inality by poor African Americans, the more disrupted the social system becomes when those restraints are broken.

Increasing drug and gun use, and parents' increasing unwillingness or inability to care for their children, may be chronic harbingers of social breakdown. The uprising in Los Angeles may be an acute indicator of social breakdown. Three out of five poor blacks—twice as many as poor whites and well-off blacks—now agree that "it's pretty hard to keep up hope of amounting to anything." Up to a quarter—again, twice as many as poor whites and well-off blacks—agree that "human nature is funda-mentally perverse and corrupt."[19]

But along with signs of growing despair and fury come signs of new attention to the problems that create despair and fury. The growth of "distressed" neighborhoods almost stopped between 1980 and 1990.[20] In the early 1990s, the federal government seemed to be lurching to-ward a commitment to attack at least some social problems; whether that commitment will continue beyond 1994 is unclear as of this writ-ing. Most hearteningly, the efforts of some blacks and a few whites to combat the breakdown of communities and lives through imaginative local organizations, community mobilization, and sheer determina-tion[21] could possibly lead to a reorganization of the social order in ways that give real chances for success to more than a lucky few.

What happens to poor African Americans in destitute communities will determine what happens to all other Americans. That point is easy to see literally; if people fear to walk down city streets or compel them-selves to pay more and more taxes to hire police and build prisons, their security about their own chance to achieve their dream is undermined. The connection is harder to see but more important normatively. White Americans want to believe that they live in a meritocratic society and therefore deserve the positions they occupy. Affluent black Americans also want to believe that they live in a meritocratic society and therefore deserve the positions for which they are striving. Neither group can really hold that belief as long as so many African American children are living in circumstances that they cannot in any sense be said to deserve. The United States is lucky well beyond its deserts that poor blacks cling as tightly as they do to the American dream. It is in the interests of all—morally as well as materially—to face up to the misery of their situation and to give them more reasons to continue to believe than they have at present.

Race and the American Dream

Chapter Thirteen

COMPARING BLACKS AND WHITE IMMIGRANTS

> I am the poor white, fooled and pushed apart,
> I am the Negro bearing slavery's scars. . . .
> I am the immigrant clutching the hope I seek—
> And finding only the same old stupid plan
> Of dog eat dog, of mighty crush the weak.
>
> O, let America be America again—
> The land that never has been yet—
> And yet must be—The land where *every* man is free.
>
> —Langston Hughes, 1938
>
> The [white] immigrant advanced in an expanding economy
> while the Negro remained in a permanent subproletariat. . . .
> Beyond the significant and often visible differences of skin
> color and social caste position, American Negroes and immi-
> grants are set apart by their cultural memories. . . . In short,
> the story of Negro and immigrant experience in this country
> contains few significant analogies and many significant differ-
> ences.
>
> —John Appel, 1970

LANGSTON HUGHES, a black poet, depicted black Americans and white immigrants as occupying the same structural location and holding the same ideological convictions. John Appel, a white historian, thought the condition of black Americans and white immigrants so different as to invalidate comparisons between the two groups.[1] Who was right? The answer to that question is crucial to my concern about the consequences of changing beliefs in the ideology of the American dream. If blacks and whites who are similarly situated react similarly to the gap between promise and practice of the American dream, then our concern about the ideology should focus on the dream itself. If blacks and whites who are similarly situated react very differently to the gap, then our concern must also include a focus on the interaction between race and ideology.

Up to now, I have considered white Americans only insofar as they help to illuminate or explain African Americans' views. That is the reverse of the usual treatment, which is partly why I did it. This chapter considers the views of whites directly. Not, however, whites as a group, since I argued in chapter 3 that one must disaggregate the flat-footed categories "black" and "white" in order to understand changing beliefs about the American dream. Up to now I have disaggregated by comparing people of different races in roughly the same class at the same historical moment. But a more subtle understanding of what it means to be "similarly situated" requires comparing people in roughly the same class at the same psychological or structural, rather than chronological, time. That is, it is important to compare people at the same stage of engagement with the promise of the American dream.

To do so requires a choice. Africans were among the first immigrants to the so-called New World, so they could perhaps be compared to Anglo-Saxon Protestants with the oldest pedigrees. But almost no African Americans were able to pursue the American dream until the Fourteenth Amendment was passed, so they should perhaps be compared to immigrants who trace their American pedigree to the mid-nineteenth century. But most African Americans were precluded by law, culture, and murder from pursuing the American dream until the 1960s. That implies that they should be compared either to other Americans who began the pursuit thirty years ago or to other Americans about one generation after the point at which *their* group was first able to overcome the barriers to the pursuit of their dream.

The problem with the first of the two latter comparisons is that most of those who also began to pursue the dream thirty years ago are also not "white" in the conventional sense. Thus a temporal comparison would be confounded with a racial one. That comparison also does not allow us to say anything about how several generations after the first spurt of upward mobility dealt with the American dream. The problem with the second comparison is that it is hard to find a point analogous for white Americans to the black civil rights movement and its aftermath. No historical period is very similar to any other, and the 1960s in particular may be unique in American history.

This chapter cuts through this Gordian knot as follows: I will compare the views of African Americans over the last thirty years to the views of Irish immigrants and the "new immigrants" from eastern and southern Europe during the decades of peak migration to the United States, roughly 1880 to 1920. I choose that comparison because the rapid entry into American life of huge numbers of people from a group characterized by poverty, very low status, and political powerlessness is similar to the explosive entry of equally poor, stigmatized, and powerless blacks into the mainstream of American life in the 1960s.

Thus I am comparing people at the same point in their psychological or ideological lives—when they first confront and wrestle with the relationship between the promise and the practice of the American dream.[2] This comparison, combined with earlier ones between the races or between classes of blacks and whites at the same historical moment, will enable us to draw conclusions about whether African Americans' beliefs about the American dream are racially distinctive.

"THE NEW IMMIGRANTS"

> [Suburban] householders view with fear and jealousy the erection of any dwelling of less than a stated cost, . . . and when the calamitous race actually appears, a mortal pang strikes to the bottom of every pocket.
>
> —William Dean Howells on the Irish, 1898

In the late nineteenth century, "whites"—that is, earlier immigrants—were as vicious toward members of the Irish, southern Italian, and eastern European "races" as toward blacks, Chinese, and Japanese.[3] An enterprising merchant advertised John's Restaurant as "Pure American. No Rats. No Greeks." Editorialists blamed the Haymarket Riot of 1896 on "long-haired, wild-eyed, bad-smelling, atheistic, reckless foreign wretches, who never did an honest hour's work in their lives." Ever alert to its responsibility as the newspaper of record, the *New York Times* was a bit more analytic. It reminded readers of "a powerful 'dangerous class,' who care nothing for our liberty or civilization, . . . who burrow at the roots of society, and only come forth in the darkness and in times of disturbance, to plunder and prey on the good things which surround them, but which they never reach." Some members are homeless young men, who are "ignorant, dissolute, passionate, living partly on the spoils of crime and partly by chance jobs or political services"—to Democrats only. These "'gangs' . . . murder on the slightest provocation," as do "the regular and professional criminals . . . [who] com[e] . . . forth like wild beasts at night." The real danger, however, lies not with any of these but with "the poorest and lowest laboring class . . . [who] drudge year after year in fruitless labor . . . [and] never rise above their position. . . . They hate the rich. . . . They are densely ignorant, and easily aroused by prejudice or passion." These criminally envious paupers "are mainly Irish Catholics."[4]

The *Times* contented itself with warning readers to beware Irish Catholics' propensity to attack "the property of the rich and the well-to-do." But some people took more active steps to control the dangerous classes. Even controlling for alcohol consumption and the number of police, the more foreign-born residents there were in the fifty largest cities at the turn of the century, the more arrests police made for "public drunkenness." A 1 percent increase in foreigners produced up to a 3 percent increase in arrests.[5] Of the 1,713 lynchings in the decade after 1882 (the first year for which accurate records exist), half of the victims were white. In the succeeding decade, 23 percent of the 1,367 victims were white.[6]

Less horrific but more widely destructive was residential, wage, and employment discrimination. "Hunkies," Italians, and Russian Jews could live and socialize only in a "foreign colony" in an undesirable area of town.[7] Men from southern and eastern Europe received at least 10 percent less pay than did workers from northern and western Europe, even after controlling for skill and the industry in which they worked.[8] Furthermore, unless the new immigrants were lucky enough to live in a city with a large and growing number of blacks, they were segregated into low-skilled and low-paying jobs.[9]

Instances of native-born whites' discrimination against white immigrants of other "races" could be multiplied, exponentially if we examined whites' responses to Asians and Native Americans.[10] How did the new immigrants respond to this treatment? Did many, like middle-class African Americans, slowly lose faith in the American dream as they became more familiar with its workings? Or did most, like poor African Americans, retain faith despite their own experience with the dream?

The New Immigrants and Work

On balance, white ethnic immigrants seem to have retained beliefs more like those of poor than of well-off African Americans, even as they or their descendants followed the social and economic trajectory of contemporary middle-class blacks. That is, they succeeded more *and* remained under the spell of the great national suggestion. Let us look at the evidence, then suggest some reasons.

Judging by letters home, memoirs, and scholars' reconstructions, the dominant theme of immigrants' lives was hard work.[11] In a collection of 176 letters from Polish immigrants written in 1890 and 1891 all "mentioned hard work." The work was "'slave-like'; 'everybody had to work very hard, as hard as a horse belonging to a Jew who burdened it excessively without giving it enough to eat'; 'in America one has to sweat more during a day than during a whole week in Poland.'" A peculiarly difficult job is characterized as "'hard American work.'" Seventy-five years later a former millworker remembers, "I went to work very young. We used to work very hard. . . . I couldn't keep up." Another remembers her father "working in the mill, seven days a week without a day off, without a vacation. He did that for seven years, without loafing one day. . . . He died at the age of fifty-eight." In short, "if you worked twice as hard as the next man you would soon transform yourself into a normal American immigrant."[12]

Many abhorred the work. "There is no freedom here at all" from the eye of the foreman and the demands of the time clock. "God only knows how many tears I shed in the evenings" because of an inability to understand instructions barked out in an unknown language. "It is [on occasion] necessary to run away, as the walls could fall down" in a mine or factory.[13] Even in a factory touted as the most modern and attentive to its workers in the world, "spinning was a terrible job; . . . except for the card room, it was the dirtiest job. . . . I went into a mill myself for just fifteen minutes. . . . I got a headache in those fifteen minutes. I then went to the shoe shop. . . . I couldn't stand it—I got sick from the smell. . . . In the weave room, where my mother worked, there the noise was terrible. It would shake and everything. . . . It was very hot and humid." More typical was work not in model factories:

> My job was my *via crucia*, my misery, my hatred, and yet I lived in continuous fear of losing the bloody thing. THE JOB that damnable affair, THE JOB. Nightmare of the hunted, THE JOB, this misery, this anxiety, this kind of neurasthenia, this ungrateful, this bloodsucking thing. THE JOB, this piecemeal death, this fear that grips you in the stomach, this sovereign lady who leaks terror, who eats the very heart out of man.[14]

The New Immigrants and the American Dream

But throughout most letters and reminiscences runs a theme of acceptance, even attachment, to hard and dangerous work because of what it might bring. For some, hope barely reached a minimal level of absolute success: "[my mother's] one dream in coming to America had been to earn her daily bread, a wild dream in itself." Or "so long as one is healthy and may work hard—everything is all right." Others dared a little more fantasy, if only in their lullabies:

> Your daddy's in America, little son of mine.
> But you are just a child now so hush and go to sleep.
> America is for everyone, they say, it's the greatest piece of luck.
> For Jews, it's a garden of Eden, a rare and precious place.
> People there eat challah in the middle of the week.

And a few threw their arms wide and embraced the whole vision:

> America may be a fascistic, warmongering, racially prejudiced country today. It may deserve the hatred of its revolutionary young. But what

a miracle it once was! What has happened here has never happened in any other country in any other time. The poor who had been poor for centuries—hell, since the beginning of Christ—whose children had inherited their poverty, their illiteracy, their hopelessness, achieved some economic dignity and freedom. You didn't get it for nothing, you had to pay a price in tears, in suffering, but why not?[15]

Looking at immigrants' dreams more systematically shows strong and persistent adherents to each tenet of the American dream, as well as to the global ideology. Consider the first tenet—everyone may participate. Immigrants expressed this conviction in at least four ways. Although not without ambivalence, they "tended to identify not with a downtrodden class but with exemplars of success among their own people." Thus they were, as Werner Sombart sadly pointed out, poor candidates for class consciousness and class-based revolution.[16] Second, European immigrants appropriated the symbolism of the Statue of Liberty. It was designed to be, and understood by native-born Americans as, a symbol of the United States' republican virtue, a celebration of international peace and friendship with France, and a beacon and warning to less enlightened nations. But the millions of steerage passengers who passed it on the way to Hell's Kitchen insisted on seeing it "as a redemptive salutation to themselves, . . . big with promise." They probably would have chosen other words to describe themselves than "wretched refuse." But in the main they agreed with Emma Lazarus' sentiments, written a half century before the rest of the nation came around to the view, that the Statue of Liberty was the gateway for Europe's "huddled masses yearning to breathe free."[17]

Third, immigrants reported over and over that they came to America because people like them had at least the possibility of making something of their lives. A young man from German-occupied Poland left because "I applied to . . . a technical school. Well, they wouldn't take me because my name was Polish." A Ukrainian immigrant found that the oppressed made good oppressors: "That was a bad place to live for the Ukrainians. . . . The Polish people would persecute them, wouldn't let them talk their language." Again: "All Jews had one overwhelming motive: to get out of the tyrannical regime of Czarist Russia, where there was no hope for advancement, to come to the free world, the land of promise." A labor organizer summarized neatly the millions of similar claims: immigrants "acquired the *right to a personality* which they had not ever possessed in the old country."[18]

Finally, some immigrants interpreted the first tenet to include political rights and democratic control, even over such traditional hierarchies as the Catholic church and the family and over such new ones as corporations. Striking Polish miners carried American flags and demanded, "Why this war [World War I]? For why we buy Liberty Bonds? For mills? No, for freedom and America—for everybody. . . . For eight-hour day." More sophisticated, or more English-language fluent, workers sought to induce immigrants of all nationalities to join a union precisely on the grounds that everyone may equally participate in America: "While there will be varied differences in our physical makeup and thoughts, there is one thing which we all hold in common, and that is our right to a living wage, and our rights in the pursuit of happiness as American citizens."[19]

Political contestation in the family and church was (usually) less violent, but no less intense than in the workplace. Chicago's Polish Women's Alliance proclaimed in its newspaper, *Voice of Polish Women*, that "in the area of rights, everything must be taken and one must never wait to be given [them] for they will never be given. And so with Woman when she struggles for a right she must win it and take it."[20] Women sometimes acted on these new ideas. In Detroit in 1885, for example, 800 Polish parishioners (mostly women) jeered priests, pelted them with gravel and mud, swarmed into the sanctuary to disrupt mass, and forcibly ejected a priest from the church of Saint Albertus. Their immediate grievance was the dismissal of an adored, but possibly financially and sexually corrupt, priest. The underlying tension lay between a clerical vision of the clergy's total authority on all church-related matters and a more democratic vision of parishioners' rights to insist on due process, to make decisions about church finances, and to hold contractual relationships with the parish priest and local bishop. Irish immigrants had earlier challenged their bishops on just the same issues. These challenges were distinctively if not uniquely American: "it does not appear that either the Poles or the Irish were accustomed in their homelands to challenge episcopal authority as they did in the United States."[21]

Immigrants were just as emphatic about the second tenet, the reasonable anticipation of success. "My mother had a passion about success, American style. It was in the streets, easy to find. . . . It was for the sons of immigrants who were willing to apply themselves to stuff the American dream with the dollars of success . . . and with my mother as a suddenly inspired banker, my two older brothers by the time they were, respectively, eighteen and sixteen, already had a future." A Polish girl did a month of brutal field work in anticipation of pay "like in America, fifty cents and a handkerchief on the head." Denied her wages by a cruel sister-in-law, she retaliated with, "Listen, I'm going to dress beautiful when I get to America. I'll wear hats! You can have your . . . babushka. And maybe you'll ask me to send you a hat."[22]

For some, these visions turned out not to be chimeras:

> We had said that when we saved $1,000 each we would go back to Italy
> and buy a farm, but now that the time is coming we are so busy and
> making so much money that we think we will stay. We have opened
> another [bootblacking] parlor. . . . The business is very good. . . .
> There are plenty of rich Italians here, men who a few years ago had
> nothing and now have so much money that they could not count all
> their dollars in a week.[23]

How did immigrants expect to get the money to buy hats rather than
babushkas? Just as the third tenet prescribes—mostly through hard
work, with a little help on the side from luck, petty theft, or political
patronage.[24] Hard work defined immigrants' lives not only by necessity
but also, for some, by choice: "You never felt you'd done enough. When
you think you don't have enough money, you want to work to make
more." Or "smarts was what one needed. Those who were more aggressive and operated fast, tried and established themselves."[25] Community
leaders exhorted their fellows that "the time had come to shake off our
lethargy and . . . to act as examples for the rest of the Rumanians in this
country." The hearers, after all, "belonged to the hard-working middle
class of the community—men who will work with great zeal and sacrifice
to create a national culture in America." The upwardly mobile were
especially wedded to "strong notions of Protestantism—hard work, so-
briety, thrift." They sought through these values to control their
employees, inspire less-successful fellow immigrants, and "insure that
their own children would retain the fragile middle-class status they had
attained."[26]

Immigrants admired and emulated achievers. But not blindly; as the
fourth tenet would predict, many made moral judgments about how
achievers attained their status and what they did with it. Among Slavs,
"a person of acknowledged wealth or an old-timer who did not participate in the immigrant communal network, did not attend social gather-
ings and national celebrations and was not seen at public group meetings, did not enjoy a high status in the community." Formal schooling
meant little, but literacy combined with "life experience and a certain
wisdom of judgment" merited deep respect.[27] Others defined virtue so
as directly to legitimate the desire for the good life that motivated so
many immigrants. A leading newspaper for former eastern Europeans
exhorted its readers that "he who can enjoy and does not enjoy commits
a sin." A Jewish clothing manufacturer from Galicia concurred: "There
is nothing sinful about spreading material goods around to the greatest
number." He aspired "to see everybody have all the gadgets in the

world." Only then—and this was written in 1942—could people devote themselves to "human and not jungle-beast activities."[28] Virtue need not always be its own reward.

The New Immigrants and Rejection of the American Dream

> Discovered by an Italian—named from Italian—But oh, that I may leave this land of disillusion!
>
> —Pietro di Donato, 1939

Not all immigrants celebrated the American dream, Americans, or the institutions purportedly designed to foster pursuit of the dream. Many, for example, recognized that public schools often sought to beat foreigners' children into Protestant docility rather than to liberate their imaginations through education. And they resisted, demanding schools in their own languages that would teach their own religions and values.[29] Others recognized that "hard American work" was intended more to wring the last ounce of strength from expendable foreign bodies than to liberate them through economic independence. They too resisted, demanding unions, decent working conditions, and a living wage.[30] Nevertheless, most of these actions, like the uprisings in urban ghettos in the 1960s, are better interpreted as a furious insistence on *inclusion* in the (perhaps redefined) American dream than as rejection of it.[31]

Some immigrants did in fact reject America and its residents. Immigrants killed themselves or others at rates higher than those of native-born whites. During the period of peak migration more immigrants than native-born Americans were hospitalized for mental illness.[32] Violent gangs of Italian, Irish, or Jewish young male immigrants roamed city streets, making life even more miserable than usual for sweatshop workers and women managing tenements crammed with boarders and children. Italian padrones, corrupt Irish politicians, and Jewish bootleggers engaged in similar amoral rejection with more sophistication and greater rewards.

Others directly rejected the American dream, seeking consciously *not* to become like the Americans. Immigrants of different nationalities resisted different aspects of the dream. Southern Italians "considered American cultural priorities to be perverted. Italian culture emphasized simplicity, beauty, temperance, love of family, a spirit of economy. . . . Americans . . . looked toward work as the Great American Savior. . . . Cold and heartless, emotion had no place in their lives, but money did." Slavs were dismayed by the monetarization of life: "I lay down on the floor with three other men and the air was rotten. I did not go to sleep for a long time. I knew then that money was everything I needed. My money was almost gone and I thought that I would soon die unless I got a job, for this was not like home. Here money was everything and a man without money must die." Mexicans felt that "it would be better 'not to try to reach a goal barred by serious obstacles than to pursue a goal at the risk of failure. Not to try does not reflect negatively on their manliness and honor but to try and fail does.'" Poles "shared an antimobility work ethos. Catholic to the core, they valued humility, prayer, and otherworldly rewards. Peasant to the bone, they treasured security, stability, and steady work. Such people yearned neither for money, status, nor power in the 'land of opportunity.' What they sought was contentment in the things they prized: family, faith, and fatherland." Irish Catholics rejected the atomistic individualism, belief in the inevitability of progress, and fear of big government that dominated American social reform movements of the late nineteenth century. They, conversely, "believe[d] in the dark side of human nature, the existence of objective evil, and the influence of irrational forces on the human personality and the historical process."[33]

And so on. Each ethnic group could point to an aspect of its heritage against which America and its dream appeared, to some, distasteful if not despicable. We cannot reconstruct anything like a public opinion survey to determine the content, intensity, and demographic correlates of rejection of the American dream among the vast majority of immigrants who did not write memoirs or live to be interviewed by oral historians. But we know enough to claim confidently that, despite the widespread celebration of America and its opportunities, a nontrivial minority of ethnic white immigrants did not remain, or never were, under the spell of the great national suggestion.

Immigrants' Children and the American Dream

So far I have analyzed the immigrants themselves, finding a central tendency as well as considerable variation. But the paradoxes of remaining under the spell of the great national suggestion and of succeeding more and enjoying it less address change over an individual's lifetime and across generations. Thus the beliefs of immigrants' children are crucial in comparing the reaction of African Americans since 1960 to the American dream with the analogous beliefs of ethnic white immigrants around the turn of the century.

The discussion of changes in belief across generations can be short. Virtually every memoirist, interview subject, and scholarly analyst agrees that the second generation of ethnic white immigrants embraced America and its dream more wholeheartedly and knowledgeably than did their parents. Surveys show second-generation ethnics to be happier than their parents, and to ascribe more fully to the values associated with the dream.[34] Mothers lamented that

> during the few years she [her daughter] was here without us, she became a regular Yankee and forgot how to talk Yiddish. . . . She says it is not nice to talk Yiddish and that I am a greenhorn. . . . Once I saw her standing on the stoop with a boy so I went up to her and asked her when she would come up. . . . Later . . . she screamed at me because I had called her by her Jewish name.[35]

Young men patiently explained to their parents that "this generation, of which I am a part, never had to face the problem of pulling away from Polonia. We had never properly belonged to it. To us it was a slowly decaying world of aged folks living largely in a dream. One day it would pass and then there would remain only Americans whose forebears had once been Poles."[36] Most dramatically:

> I did not yet understand why these [older] men and women were willing to settle for less than they deserved in life and think that 'less' quite a bargain. I did not understand that they simply could not afford to dream. I myself had a hundred dreams from which to choose. For I was already sure that I would make my escape, that I was one of the chosen. I would be rich, famous, happy. I would master my destiny.
>
> And so it was perhaps natural that as a child, with my father gone, my mother the family chief, I, like all the children in all the ghettos of America, became locked in a bitter struggle with the adults responsible for me. It was inevitable that my mother and I became enemies.[37]

In short, "the new immigrants"—perceived to be of a different race from northern Europeans, received with the prejudice and discrimination previously reserved for blacks, Native Americans, and Asians—responded to the gap between promise and practice of the American dream more like poor than like well-off African Americans. Some distorted it; a few rejected it for a different vision or no moral restraints at all. But despite poverty, exploitation, and exclusion, most southern and eastern European immigrants remained under the spell of the great national suggestion and struggled to act in accord with its precepts. And if they did not, their children did.

EXPLANATIONS FOR THE NEW IMMIGRANTS' FAITH

How are we to explain this phenomenon? In fact, two phenomena need explanation. The first is analogous to the puzzle explored in the previous part of the book—why did white immigrants, like poor blacks, retain faith in the American dream despite their initial circumstances? The second throws into sharp relief the puzzle explored earlier—why did white ethnic immigrants and their children, unlike well-off African Americans, *not* lose faith in the American dream as their circumstances improved?

Self-Selection

Central to both phenomena is self-selection. It is a standard explanation, but its importance cannot be overemphasized. Self-selection operates in at least four ways.[38]

First was the self-selection involved in emigrating to the United States. Without getting involved in the myriad explanations of who came and why, I want to make the simple but crucial point that a few people—for whatever religious, political, economic, or familial reason—*chose* to come to the United States, whereas most people like them chose not to.[39] Choosing to come has both direct and indirect implications for belief in the American dream. The direct effect is obvious; immigrants were presumably more likely than those who stayed at home or emigrated to another country to believe that the United States was the land of opportunity and that they wanted opportunities.[40] The indirect effect may be just as strong: even if immigrants were initially ambivalent, the theory of cognitive dissonance reduction suggests that they would convince themselves after arrival that they had made the right decision.[41] That is, if they willingly chose (willingly in the sense that others like them took other options) to endure the horrendous passage by steerage and to cope with the miserable circumstances of work and housing when they arrived in the United States, they must have done so for a good reason.[42] Otherwise they were foolish or deluded, which no one wants to be. So even—or especially—the worst-off immigrants had a strong motivation to remain under the spell of the great national suggestion.[43]

Not all white ethnic immigrants did choose, in even this attenuated sense of choice, to come to the United States. Although some women and children fought desperately to emigrate,[44] others were brought against their will by husbands, fathers, uncles. One child's family was almost denied permission to leave Rotterdam because her eyes were so bloodshot. She did not have trachoma; instead "I was crying night and day. I was scared. I didn't want to leave Poland, as much as I loved my father [already in the United States], I didn't want to leave. I heard so many stories that once you come you don't see nobody no more that you love and leave behind." As a boy Leonard Covello watched his mother's reaction to the "towering buildings, . . . screeching elevated train and . . . long, unending streets of the metropolis. . . . She accepted it with mute resignation as *la volonta di Dio* [the will of God], while her heart longed for the familiar scenes and faces of loved ones and the security of a life she had forever left behind."[45]

But even these mothers and daughters could often be won over by love, hope, or goods. One woman who devastated her husband by crying, "So, we have crossed half the world for this?" upon her arrival at his tenement was ecstatic when he bought her a sewing machine (which it took eighteen years to pay for).[46] Children who wept on leaving relatives went to work to earn passage fare for them—and to buy the ice cream and oranges they had never seen at home.

The self-selection of emigrants, and the effects of dissonance reduction and acclimation on their views of emigration, were reinforced by a second form of self-selection. Many immigrants did not stay in America. In the decade before World War I, more than half of Hungarians, Italians, Croatians, and Slovenes repatriated, as did about a third of Poles, Danes, Germans, and Greeks.[47] Return migrants left for many reasons. Some never intended to stay; they came to America to earn enough money to go home and buy a farm or store. Others had few clear intentions and drifted back home when their hopes for fame and fortune dissipated. Others came to stay but were defeated by the brutal conditions of work and ghetto life and went home embittered and destitute. Still others rejected the norms they found in America—the prejudice, monetarization of all values, atomistic individualism.[48] They too went home, at which point they, like all returnees, dropped out of the portrait of "immigrants to America."

Removal of transient immigrants eliminates many who would otherwise have expanded the population of dissenters from the American dream. Furthermore, those who came only to make money quickly and leave, or who lacked a clear vision of what they wanted and how to pursue it, were much less concerned about finding opportunities to advance than those who came to stay. The former wanted to earn money quickly, in "dead end" jobs if necessary; the latter by definition wanted nothing very clearly. Conversely, "permanence . . . add[s] an edge to the settler's quest for opportunity: If one does not succeed, there is no going back. It is for these reasons that permanent immigrants have a reputation for being more self-assertive than temporary migrant groups."[49] The stayers, in short, are the immigrants committed to making their vision of the American dream a reality.

They are also the people who leave records. Scholars frequently point out how little we know of repatriates, so our knowledge of immigrants rests almost entirely on those who stayed in the United States. And here lie the other two forms of self-selection. They are methodological rather than substantive, and they magnify the impact of the first two forms. At issue here is who left records, and what records they left.

It is reasonable to infer, although I know of no systematic study on the point, that the more success one met as an immigrant, the more likely one was to write letters home, compose memoirs and stories, or live long enough to be the subject of oral histories. Illiterate immigrants could not write and could ill afford to spend their few pennies hiring someone to write letters to equally illiterate relatives back home. Illiterate immigrants were also the most likely to hold the terrible jobs with no future and high accident rates. Conversely, literate immigrants could both write letters themselves and attain jobs offering a little free time and more rewards than drudgery and penury. Thus the written records left by immigrants are probably biased in the direction of those with resources and leisure to write, living in situations that gave them something positive to write about.[50]

Finally, immigrants were surely selective in what they wrote at the time and what they remembered fifty or seventy years later. They had every incentive to emphasize their achievements and prospects, and deemphasize the dead ends and frustration, in letters to fiancées, parents, and *paesani*. Some of course wrote fully of their experiences, and journalists and litterateurs probably had the opposite incentives—to emphasize problems and deemphasize contentment. Nevertheless, people who knew that their letters and diaries would form the chief topic of conversation for their village for weeks could hardly be expected to detail the humiliations, filth, and discouragement they so frequently contended with.

Retrospective descriptions probably follow the same pattern as contemporary letters. Immigrants now in their eighties and nineties by definition did not die of malnutrition or in industrial accidents. And faced with eager young men and women with tape recorders, they can be expected to remember their families' courage, hope, and determination better than their despair, squabbling, and weakness. It is also, and crucially, the case that most of these interview subjects *do* live better now than they did as children or than their parents did. Thus the American dream has come true for them to some considerable degree, and one cannot be surprised that they remember better what confirms their current circumstances than what would have disconfirmed them.

Self-selection in what one chooses to write home or recall later is not only a methodological problem for scholars. It is also substantively important, since how people choose to present themselves to loved ones or posterity itself contributes to their own self-image. By emphasizing to others the more successful features of one's life, one becomes more convinced that one's life really is, at least partly, a success story.

We thus have reasons ranging from the nature of immigration to the psychology of immigrants and the bias of the historical record to explain why even destitute immigrants mostly remained (or eventually fell) under the spell of the great national suggestion. A final explanation is the hardest to pin down, but perhaps the most important.[51]

Transformation

That explanation revolves around the concept of transformation or transcendence. Analysts of immigrants' experience use those terms frequently: "The ability to buy goods in the American marketplace was not simply an act of consumption; it was also an act of transcendence, the realization of a new social status." Or "the new suit of clothes gave physical form to the essentially spiritual undertaking of aliens striving for membership in a new society. . . . Only the concept of *transformation* adequately conveys the impact of new material standards on these eastern Europeans." Immigrants gave up culture, comforts, and familiarity in favor of nature, *fortuna*, and independence. This contrast between immediate hardship and possible future benefits intensified the quality of choosing a life path that is inevitably involved in emigration. "Settlers described their migration as an irrevocable transformation in their personal and physical condition. . . . Consequently the decision to migrate was momentous, personal and irreversible. . . . The sense of reformation is both communal (in that the process is simultaneously happening to others . . .) and individual (in that it is motivated by personal election and conviction)."[52]

The intensity and extensiveness of such a rebirth spawned a genre of "transformation stories that often carry the 'from . . . to' formula openly in their titles." Examples include Mary Antin's *From Plotzk to Boston* (1899), Edward Steiner's *From Alien to Citizen* (1914), Michal Pupin's *From Immigrant to Inventor* (1923), and Richard Bartholdt's *From Steerage to Congress* (1930).[53] Their theme is consistent across idiosyncrasies of situation and personality: "Even at his wealthiest, my father lived in very much the same fashion as his tenth-generation grandfather. I have shifted my mode of living more in fifty years than my ancestors [had] in a thousand." Or "I was born, I have lived, and I have been made over. Is it not time to write my life's story? I am just as much out of the way as if I were dead, for I am absolutely other than the person whose story I have to tell."[54]

This sense of transformation was central to the belief system of white ethnic immigrants. As reborn Christians, reformed alcoholics, and other converts attest, to be able to identify the moment at which your whole life changes is extraordinarily powerful. Such an experience provides a deep and lasting (though not always victorious) motivation to perceive and behave differently. If a "transformed" person lives in a community that reinforces his or her rebirth, especially if other members of the community have experienced the same transcendence, that person is much more likely to be able to sustain the new self than if he or she is alone or unique.

Thus immigrants who chose to abandon their past by taking a long and horrible trip across the sea, passing through the ritual of Castle Garden or Ellis Island, joining compatriots and family members undergoing the same experiences, and entering into a new society through the simple medium of new clothes and new habits—such people could be expected to develop and retain a vivid new view of the world. That new view, given the array of institutional and cultural reinforcements and the paucity of alternatives, was likely to be some variant of the American dream. And the dream, with its combination of airy promise and precise rules for achieving success, is perfectly suited to be the object of transformative hope.

We have, then, ample explanation for why even desperately poor white ethnic immigrants mostly remained under the spell of the great national suggestion. Only some potential immigrants chose to come; only some of those who came chose to stay; only some of those who stayed recorded their views; and only some of those views were recorded. All of this group were subject to the tidal wave of transformation, which schools, media, clubs, jobs, and political leaders all channeled into belief in the ideology of the American dream. It would have been surprising indeed if immigrants had resisted these forces.

Persisting Beliefs among Immigrants' Children

Consider now the second phenomenon to emerge from immigrants' testimony—the fact that their children, although they succeeded more than their parents, did not enjoy it less. Much of the answer has already been discussed: children too came, stayed, wrote, and remembered selectively, and they were even more transformed than their parents. The rest of the answer lies in differences between the way members of the dominant society treated children of the new immigrants and the way they treated upwardly mobile African Americans.

Most simply, earlier white immigrants have not prohibited later white immigrants from competitive success, or categorized them by their ascriptive traits, to the same extent that they have blacks. An Irish Catholic has been president; a Greek and a Pole have been presidential nominees; Italians and Jews have been chosen by Anglo-Saxons to lead Ivy League universities and Fortune 100 corporations.

Surveys suggest a similar, comparatively rapid acceptance of new immigrants by old at less exalted levels. As early as 1926, college students ranked the Irish very high (above the French and Scandinavians) on the Bogardus social distance scale and rated even Slavs and Russians above the mean of the scale. (They placed Jews and Greeks below the mean, and Negroes below all groups except Turks, Indians, Chinese, and Koreans.) Twenty years later, all of the new immigrant groups except Italians had become more acceptable, and the range from most to least favored had narrowed. (Negroes, however, had been moved dramatically down and were now ranked well below Turks, Chinese, and Koreans.)[55] Also in the 1940s only 16 percent of high school students reported that they would refuse to marry a Catholic, and only 5 percent would reject the once-despised Irish. (Ninety-two percent would not marry a Negro.) By 1948 fewer than one-seventh of Americans would not work with Italians and did not want them in their neighborhood or homes. A fifth or fewer felt equal distaste for Jews, and only 3 percent said the same about the Catholics their grandparents had hated and feared. (Between two- and three-fifths did not want Negroes as work partners, neighbors, or dinner guests.)[56]

Experience accorded roughly with the sentiments expressed in these surveys. In 1910 the sons of Irish immigrants in New York City held jobs with an average occupational status 87 percent as high as that of the sons of native-born white New Yorkers. By 1940 their job status was 96 percent as high. The job status of sons of Russian (predominantly Jewish) immigrants rose fifteen points over the same period to 116 percent of that of native-born whites. Italian sons did not do as well; their job status declined marginally, from 74 percent to 71 percent as high as that of sons of native-born whites. But even Italians did well compared with blacks. Blacks living in New York City in 1910 had jobs enjoying only 70 percent of the status of native-born whites' jobs, and their job status *declined* over the next thirty years by either 24 or 11 percentage points, for blacks born in the South or North, respectively.[57] Across the country, despite the educational, linguistic, and occupational advantages of the old immigrant groups at the turn of the century, by 1980 a higher proportion of the new immigrant groups held professional jobs.[58] The same reversal, needless to say, did not occur among African Americans.

Incomes show the same general upward trend for children of the new immigrants. By the 1950s Irish Catholics born between 1901 and 1910 earned on average $300 more than all members of their age cohort; by the 1960s they earned $2,300 more. Jews and Italian Catholics in the same age range did as well, earning from $600 to $2,500 a year more than their agemates depending on the group and the decade. (African Americans of the same age received incomes almost $3,000 lower than those of their agemates in both the 1950s and 1960s.)[59] Averaging across all ages and many ethnicities, we find that by 1980 "the old-new [immigrant] distinction does not operate with respect to distinguishing between the incomes earned by the groups." If anything, southern-central-eastern European descendants earned slightly more than north-ern-western European descendants.[60]

In the early 1900s new immigrants almost never married outside their own nationality. But as early as 1910 intermarriages were more common if one spouse was the child of immigrants and were even more likely if both were. By 1980 almost half of Poles, over half of Irish, and 40 per-cent of Italians born before 1920 had married people outside their eth-nic group. Among those born after 1950, over 80 percent of Poles, 60 percent of Irish, and 75 percent of Italians married outsiders. In no arena of life are differences between African and other Americans more stark: the percent of blacks married to whites rose from 1.6 percent in 1960 to 3.4 percent in 1980, to 6.2 percent in 1990.[61]

Just as white ethnic immigrants came increasingly to work in the same jobs and marry each other, they came increasingly to live in ethnically mixed neighborhoods. That was not originally the case; on an index measuring residential segregation of ethnic groups, the new immigrants ranked at least 70, and in some cases 90 (out of a possible 100) in the ten largest cities in 1910. In all ten cities studied, new immigrants from at least some nations were more segregated than were blacks. Even after controlling for socioeconomic status and ability to speak English, new immigrants were much less likely to live near second- or later-generation whites than were African Americans.[62] Within a few decades, ethnic in-sulation declined dramatically, and by 1980 descendants of Poles were almost as widely disseminated in city neighborhoods as were descen-dants of the French or even English.[63] Blacks, of course, have remained residentially insulated at very high levels in our system of "American apartheid."[64]

Political activity and institutions similarly show the declining signifi-cance of white ethnic identity. Around the turn of the century, ethnic identity almost determined one's choice of party, ability to participate politically, and mode of participation. It also shaped the nature of polit-ical organizations and the processes of political mobilization. By the 1960s ethnic identification and ethnic prestige rankings had a steadily declining and eventually trivial effect on party identification. Political or-ganizations sought to nominate tickets balanced across ethnicities. In any case, slate-making mattered less, since reforms stemming from the Progressive era gave increasing control over city politics to managers and comptrollers rather than to elected officials. For these reasons among others, ethnically based machines mostly ground to a halt and were replaced largely by pan-ethnic, candidate-centered politicking driven by media displays.[65]

Finally, children of the new immigrants were able, if they chose, to shed their ethnicity and become merely "American" more readily and with greater rewards than blacks, even of the middle class, have yet been able to do. As late as the 1920s descendants of old-stock immigrants thought of southern and eastern European immigrants as a different race. But that language disappeared over the next few decades, in favor of an increasingly general category of "white" or "American." The sheer magnitude and variety of the new immigrants helped the process; it is simply too difficult cognitively to keep ten or twenty or thirty distinctions straight when members of all groups increasingly intermarry and do not, in any case, look all that different from other (white) Americans. Historical circumstances also sped up the process of conceptual Americanization; World War II especially blurred ethnic divisions into Americanness as children of the new immigrants worked and fought beside great-grandchildren of the old against the racist scourge of Nazism.[66] African Americans, however, also fought in that war, so patriotism and soldierly bonding do not fully explain the move from race to ethnicity to nationality. Indeed, the move arguably required the existence of a race that could *not* traverse the same path, since becoming American was in many ways intricately tied up with becoming white, in contradistinction to nonwhites as well as to anti-Americans. Tensions between newly identified "whites" and blacks, as well as between "whites" and Asians, heightened during World War II, and rose (or sunk) to the level of white-induced race riots and concentration camps.[67] Those tensions are partly explained by the anxiety and shortages attendant on a terrible war. But they also can be seen as a way of solidifying the new category of "us" against a category of "them" who by comparison are even more different from whites than Slavs are from Italians or Anglo-Saxons.

In sum, despite local variations across years, classes, arenas of life, and ethnicity, children of the new immigrants began to attain better jobs, more power and wealth, higher prestige, and an "American" identity within a few decades of their or their parents' arrival in the United States. They furthermore broke through almost all institutional and cultural glass ceilings within a few more decades. They have achieved, in my terms, some competitive as well as considerable absolute and relative success. Thus the children of new immigrants were able to avoid enjoying it less while succeeding more because their success came relatively more easily and completely, and because their material and political gains were accompanied by the ability to exercise their "ethnic options."[68]

Middle-class African Americans too have achieved considerable absolute and relative success, but they have not yet attained much competitive success and they still lack any leeway with regard to their ethnic identity. Hence the paradox of enjoying it less. The critical issue for the future is whether at least some African Americans will continue to gain ground as children of the new immigrants did over the twentieth century. Affluent blacks themselves are more dubious on that point, and on the general validity of the American dream, than were white ethnics at a comparable stage of mobility.[69] And it is to that prognostication and its implications that we now turn.

Conclusion: Langston Hughes or John Appel?

Is "the Negro today . . . like the immigrant yesterday," as Irving Kristol asserted in 1966?[70] Is Langston Hughes right in insisting on the material and ideological similarities between the "poor white" and the "Negro"? Or is John Appel more correct in arguing that blacks and whites are in such different—even contradictory—positions that any analogy between them is false?

In crucial ways Kristol and Hughes are right. Whites and blacks equally share a fervent belief that the American dream *ought* to obtain, and they almost equally share the conviction that it does obtain for most Americans most of the time. First-generation white ethnic immigrants and their children disproportionately remained under the spell of the great national suggestion despite poverty and exploitation—and so have most poor blacks and their children.

In equally crucial ways Appel is right. The descendants of white ethnic immigrants differed deeply from well-off blacks in the path of their integration into American society and in the trajectory of their beliefs about the American dream. The former remain committed to it; the latter are increasingly skeptical and bitter. Poor blacks may be moving in the direction of well-off blacks, thus shifting the balance sharply from Hughes' universality to Appel's division. What can we infer from all of this about the future?

Lessons from the Immigrant Comparison

If correct, the arguments of this chapter will deepen the worries of proponents of the American dream. That is, self-selection, transformation, and the diminution of barriers, which explain white immigrants' strong and continued allegiance to the ideology, have precisely the opposite effects for African Americans.

Consider first self-selection. Most white immigrants chose to come and stay; those unwillingly brought to America were mostly persuaded by love, hope, goods, and dissonance reduction that immigration had been the right choice. Those not so persuaded could leave, and many did. African Americans, of course, were as far from choosing to come to America as one could be, and they received neither love, hope, nor material inducements to make them change their minds about coming once they were here. Furthermore, their incentives for interpreting the manner of their coming and their life once here were precisely the reverse of dissonance reduction: They were forced to come and forced to stay; they had every reason to think that America was not the land of opportunity; and they had every reason to harbor their fury and foreignness as long as they could. From that perspective, the fact that a majority of blacks fell, and that most poor blacks remain, under the spell of the great national suggestion is the real puzzle.

Consider next transformation. To be able to mark the point at which one begins a new life is to obtain a benchmark against which to measure every success (and, in combination with the incentives of self-selection, to discount every failure). But African Americans have no indisputable moment of transcendence, no memory of having at a given point chosen shimmering possibility over dull certainty. Were they (by choice or not) transformed in 1619, when the first "Negers" were brought to Virginia? Were they transformed in the 1680s, when laws of slavery were codified and made more harsh? Were they transformed in 1863, or 1954, or 1964? Or were they transformed when their own direct ancestors were brought to the United States, or when their ancestors or they themselves left southern serfdom for the hope of northern freedom? And so on. The very difficulty I described of choosing an appropriate comparison group to African Americans over the past thirty years is itself an indication of the lack of a moment of transformation against which everything before and after can be measured.

For many African Americans, the late 1950s and early 1960s came close to being such a transformative moment. But the sense of rebirth into a new world has diminished, and even curdled, for many, for all the reasons that this book has been exploring. Thus the idea of transformation more often heightens the disparities than draws a link between white immigrants and black Americans. From this perspective, too, the continuing loyalty of poor African Americans to the American dream is more surprising than the current disillusionment of many other blacks.

Consider finally the diminution of material and cultural barriers. I can be brief here, because chapters 2, 5, and 7 discussed the issue extensively. After much time and pain, the descendants of the new immigrants were able to engage in the battle for competitive success on almost the same terms as the descendants of the old immigrants. They are equally American, and equally raceless in their own eyes.[71] The new black middle class, in contrast, has overcome neither the barrier against competitive success nor the barrier against racial anonymity. Arguably both barriers are even rising, as whites and blacks frame the battle for competitive success in "lose-lose" terms and as oppositional racial identities solidify.

Thus the very reasons that led immigrants and their children to embrace the American dream are reasons that lead increasing numbers of African Americans not to do so. Those reasons are psychological, ideological, institutional, and material; together they provide a more negative than positive answer to the question of whether "the Negro today is like the immigrant yesterday."

The Melting Pot, Pluralism, and Separatism

In the end, the comparison between African Americans and white immigrants suggests two opposite possibilities.[72] One is that "in America a black man, wherever he is and whatever he is, cannot escape racial considerations, an experience untrue with other immigrants."[73] Perhaps, to an extent not true for any other group, "Western understandings of the African, [including] intellectual inferiority, hypersexuality, promiscuity, and aggressiveness . . . represent a check-list of those impulses which Europeans were vigorously attempting to repress in themselves."[74] Perhaps in order "to permit them [ethnic immigrants] to be 'white,' to liberate themselves from what they regard as the shackles of ethnicity, there has to be 'blackness.' . . . The American dream is one that grants whiteness to those who wouldn't be considered white in Europe."[75] In that case, "it is the difference between blackness and whiteness that defines . . . American cultural self-understanding,"[76] and we are a society marked by "the permanence of racism" in which, despite recurrent waves of immigration, African Americans will always be "the faces at the bottom of the well."[77]

I have used quotations so extensively to make this point to demonstrate the range of analysts holding this view. Those quoted are white as well as black, activists as well as scholars. More importantly, Americans far from academia or politics hold the same dualistic view. Some African Americans interpret succeeding in accord with the tenets of the American dream as going over to the enemy; much of the history of the twentieth century suggests that some immigrants define success as demonstrating that they are not like blacks.[78] If "some" is an understatement on both sides, the very incorporation of immigrants into the ideological terrain bounded by the American dream means the failure of blacks ever to be able to join.

But the history of the new immigrants can teach another lesson. Not only can the status of a given "race" change, but also the very definition of a race has changed throughout American history. It continues to do so.[79] Furthermore, the movement of Asians from despised (they scored even lower than blacks on the Bogardus social distance scale through much of the twentieth century) to "eligibil[ity] for the honorific of 'white'"[80] shows that the sheer physical inability to "escape racial considerations" is not what distinguishes blacks from other immigrants. Thus, in the abstract, there is no reason that African Americans cannot follow the trajectory that other Americans have followed.

And what if we conceive of the transformation so central to the immigrant experience not as giving up the old life for a new one but as "active work on existing traditions and activities" so that "they articulate with different practices and positions, and take on a new meaning and relevance, a new cultural resonance or accent"?[81] When that kind of transformation occurs, immigrants share their traditional cultures with other immigrants, both share with "native" Americans, and all participate in a new culture that is neither the sum of the old ones nor a melted down amalgam but is instead a hodgepodge that everyone and no one owns. There is no reason why African Americans cannot join that kind of transformative process.

Such a pluralistic transformation sometimes occurs. White jazz, blues, and folk musicians learned from black mentors but added their own distinctive stamp to "black" music, which in turn was influenced by the new "white" styles.[82] Students at Hutchins Jr. High School in Detroit in the early 1950s "invent[ed] an inclusive common identity, language, and codes, while simultaneously acknowledging and valorizing the important differences between them." The rate of black-white interracial marriage tripled between 1960 and 1980, and doubled again between 1980 and 1990. Students in a tiny southern town protested, and one apparently burned down the school building, when a principal objected to interracial dating at the school prom.[83] A nationwide organization of parents of interracial children is pressing the federal and state governments for a new category on all government forms, including the census, to accommodate multiracial identifiers. "This movement will certainly pick up steam in the coming years with the growing numbers of interracial marriages and children of such unions."[84] Multiculturalism of some sort has come to dominate public school curricula; although one may find plenty to criticize in most implementations of the ideal, that fact in itself is a dramatic change from a decade ago.

Most generally, the message of the survey data I have analyzed throughout this book is that on balance blacks and whites do *not* occupy two distinct and warring ideological worlds. They occupy the same

one—whites more confidently and less ambivalently than, but not separately from, blacks. After all, members of both races overwhelmingly endorse the American dream, and most members of both races even believe that it describes most lives in America, sometimes including their
own.

The class divide in America needs as much attention as the racial divide; it is just as crucial to determining the future of the American dream
and just as malleable in either of two directions. Wealthy whites (and,
more slowly, wealthy blacks) may continue to move to the suburbs, buy
private schools and security guards, vote only for politicians who promise no new taxes, and otherwise withdraw from any shared commitment
and identification. Poor blacks (and, more slowly, poor whites) may
continue to resist efforts to make them live according to society's rules
of work and behavior so long as they are denied all of society's goods
and status. In that case, the American dream will be shattered, no matter
how much transformative cultural pluralism occurs in jazz clubs or on
census forms.

Alternatively, wealthy whites and blacks may develop or retain their
sense of personal connection; political and economic institutions may be
shaped in ways that open opportunities to all (or at least more) Americans. Given the scale of the federal budget and the reach of policy instruments, it would not be difficult to provide the resources and structures
needed for decent schools, homes, and jobs in distressed neighborhoods
if Americans chose to do so. Then poor blacks and whites might see
enough reason to abjure the glamour of drug-dealing and the ease of
idleness in favor of acceding to the tenets of the dream—and if they did
not, the rest of society could legitimately hold them responsible for the
consequences. In that case, the American dream could persist as a worthy vision even absent transformative cultural pluralism.

Here is the ultimate puzzle about race in America. In my view, the
description of white separatism and the hardening of class lines described above is in important ways correct. Individual whites gain standing in their own eyes and those of others by not being black, and
wealthy people gain status from simply not being poor. Institutions and
practices ranging from democratic governance to corporate capitalism
would not have developed as they did absent a strict racial hierarchy and
a hidden but vital class structure.[85] And yet most blacks and many whites
resist separatism or class conflict and hold the same values; some of both
races practice transformative pluralism.[86] Most American institutions
depend on and reinforce racial separatism (although perhaps not class
boundaries) less than they did several decades ago.[87]

I cannot predict the outcome over the next few decades of the battle
between separatism and pluralism or between more and less porous class

lines. The outcome is subject to political choice, influenced partly I hope by this book. If we look at the trajectory of the survey data I have reported, separatism and rigidity seem to be gaining ground. If we look at the absolute numbers, we can hope that pluralism and fluidity in a context of underlying unity of broad belief and practice are plausible. More precisely, if white insiders allow blacks to participate in the American dream in ways that do not violate blacks' preferences and traditions (and perhaps even in ways that incorporate some of them), *and* if blacks are willing to participate in the dream in ways that do not violate mainstream members' preferences and traditions (and that perhaps incorporate some of *them*)—then African Americans will become more similar to than different from other immigrants both in their beliefs and in their life chances.

This is the point at which the ideology of the American dream once again becomes central. If it can be construed as an *ideal*, a broad, generous, inclusive vision that encourages people to be the best they can be however they define that best, then transformative pluralism and open channels of mobility are direct and plausible extensions of Americans' core tradition. But if it is only an *ideology* in the narrow sense, a self-righteous club that winners use to justify their own actions and to push away, blame, or brainwash losers, then white separatism will continue to flourish, black separatism to grow, and class barriers to harden.[88] That is not what Langston Hughes had in mind when he concluded his poem:

> America never was America to me,
> And yet I swear this oath—
> America will be!

The dream itself, therefore, is the focus of the concluding chapter.

Chapter Fourteen

THE FUTURE OF THE AMERICAN DREAM

> "The Negro in American Literature" [is] a magnificent theme
> . . . not because there is any sharp emergence of character or
> incidents, but because of the immense paradox of racial life
> which came up thunderingly against the principles and doc-
> trines of democracy, and put them to the severest test that
> they had known.
>
> —William Stanley Braithwaite, 1925

> I propose that we view the whole of American life as a drama
> acted out upon the body of a Negro giant, who, lying trussed
> up like Gulliver, forms the stage and the scene upon which
> and within which the action unfolds.
>
> —Ralph Ellison, 1946

PERHAPS like all dreams, the American dream is open to more interpretations than there are interpreters. In lectures as I was writing this book,
audiences responded to my use of the phrase by denying it distinctive
meaning beyond general human yearnings for a better life, by affirming
that it is what distinguishes Americans from Europeans, by celebrating
it as the essence of our ideals, and by denouncing it as a hypocritical
sham.

The American dream is all of those things and yet is more than a
shapeless muddle. As an ideology, it performs brilliantly. It has distinctive boundaries but capacious content. It provides a unifying vision but
allows infinite variations within that vision. It can be used to club the
poor into accepting their lot, but it can also be used to make the rich
squirm about their luxuries. It encourages people not even to see those
aspects of society that make the dream impossible to fulfill for all Americans. It can turn "foreigners" into "Americans" whether they wish such
a transformation or not.

As a guide to practice, its performance is not so easily measured. Most
of this book has been devoted to analyzing how and how well the dream
works in practice among African Americans, and I still have no simple
conclusion.

A simple conclusion eludes me for two reasons. One involves "the
immense paradox of racial life which . . . [comes] up thunderingly

against the principles and doctrines of democracy." I disaggregated that "immense paradox" into three large paradoxes and a host of smaller puzzles. A true paradox can only be understood, not resolved. So it is perhaps fitting that for each paradox I could neither confidently predict how it would develop nor clearly allocate praise and blame to the people caught in its meshes.

The second reason that a simple conclusion remains elusive moves beyond even the "immense paradox of racial life" to "the whole of American life [which can be seen] as a drama acted out upon the body of a Negro." I remain fundamentally ambivalent about "the whole of American life," or at least that portion that revolves around the American dream, for reasons now to be explored

THE LESSONS OF RACE AND CLASS

Succeeding More and the American Dream

The dilemma posed by middle-class African Americans' growing alienation from the American dream as they come closer to achieving its promise illustrates a profound tension at its heart. Affluent blacks have, for the first time in American history, sufficient resources to challenge affluent whites for positions that only one person can hold. Some whites resist allowing blacks to achieve such competitive success; others (or perhaps the same ones) resist allowing blacks the individuation, on their own terms, necessary even to imagine competitive success. The more successful the African American, the more he or she is frustrated by this denial of the first three tenets of the American dream—hence the paradox of succeeding more and enjoying it less.

This conflict may be only the sharpest version of a contest extending across all of American society. Many successful and ambitious women (of whatever race) feel that they are denied the positions and rewards they have earned because men (of whatever race) cannot bear to be defeated by a mere female. Americans are increasingly hostile to the newest wave of immigrants partly out of fear that they will take jobs, resources, and cultural certitude away from those of us smart enough to have descended from earlier immigrants.[1] Most generally, Americans have for several decades felt encroached upon by people from other nations who demand that we control our consumption of natural resources or political might in the interests of enhancing their living conditions or political autonomy.

Thus the racial paradox of succeeding more and enjoying it less may be a window into the larger question of whether Americans are willing to allow previously subordinated others to succeed at Americans' expense. There is no a priori reason why they should; after all, non-Americans are no more inclined to relinquish their place after losing to denigrated others. But here is where the American dream places distinctive burdens on Americans. It, more than most other ideological frameworks, teaches its adherents to believe in a society in which people are able to break through old patterns of discrimination and to achieve what they deserve. But it offers no solace for new losers to allow them gracefully to accept defeat at the hands of former losers. Thus the American dream encourages everyone to win, but helps no one to lose. And the paradox of succeeding more demonstrates what happens when that discrepancy is played out in people's lives.

Remaining under the Spell and the American Dream

The dilemma posed by poor African Americans' shaky adherence to the dream illustrates another tension at the heart of the ideology. Poor blacks, for perhaps the first time in American history, are burdened by a group so alienated and so technologically well supported that they threaten the very existence of stable communities. So far, most poor blacks resist the temptations of climbing the capitalist ladder through drug sales, releasing fury through violence, or simply withdrawing from all effort. But there is no reason to expect our nation's extraordinary luck in that regard to continue.

Like the first, this conflict may be only the sharpest version of a contest extending throughout American society. Poor whites too mostly cling unreasonably to the hope and discipline embodied by the American dream. But since there are over twice as many poor whites as poor blacks, the black "underclass" is only a fraction of those eligible to be recruited into the ranks of the estranged poor. And looking beyond American borders shows a whole world full of desperately poor people. So far they too mostly behave in ways that do not deeply threaten wealthier nations, but here too there is no reason to expect our extraordinary luck to persist forever.

Aside from its obvious dangers to political stability and individual security, the paradox of remaining under the spell thus illuminates another broad flaw in the ideology of the American dream. The dream is not narrowly individualistic—it permits one to pursue success for one's family or group as readily as for oneself—but it is broadly *individual* in its focus on persons rather than on structures, processes, or historical patterns. Indeed, it not only focuses on individual agency, it insists that agency is all that matters in the end. Thus the American dream is joyously liberating in its message that people may aspire to control their own destiny rather than merely acquiesce in the vagaries of fate or an overlord. But it deceives as well as liberates when it teaches that people *do* control their own destiny rather than helping them to recognize limits that have nothing to do with their own abilities or desires. Thus for the poor as for the rich, the American dream encourages everyone to succeed but helps no one to fail. And the paradox of remaining under the spell, like the paradox of succeeding more, demonstrates what happens when that discrepancy is played out in people's lives.

EQUALITY AND DIFFERENTIATION

The tensions within the American dream illuminated by the two central paradoxes may be the most severe, but they are not the only ones. Other aspects of "the paradox of racial life" similarly exemplify ambiguities in "the whole of American life." For example, is the American dream egalitarian or differentiating? It is both.

Consider the implications of defining success absolutely, relatively, or competitively. Absolute success is in principle equally available to everyone. As Bruce Springsteen concluded, "I dreamed something and I was lucky. A large part of it came true. But it's not just for one; it's gotta be for everyone, and you've gotta fight for it every day."[2] To the degree that the American dream permits everyone to achieve some goal and provides tenets that all can use to pursue their goal, it promotes equality of results without any hint of identity of results.[3]

Relative success implies a different form of equality. The whole point of relative success is doing better than—that is, becoming unequally superior to—some standard. Thus achieving relative success requires not only that results not be identical but also that they not be equal even in the eyes of the succeeders. However, the first tenet of the American dream promises everyone an equal chance to do better than some standard. Interpreting the tenets of the American dream in terms of relative rather than absolute success, in short, shifts the meaning of equality from results to a "soft" form of equal opportunity.

Competitive success implies a "hard" form of equal opportunity. The American dream interpreted through the lens of competitive success is, in fact, better understood as a formula for legitimate differentiation. William Graham Sumner laid out the harsh glory of a world in which success and failure are equally available to all and equally absolute in their differentiating consequences:

> Competition . . . is a law of nature. Nature is entirely neutral; she submits to him who most energetically and resolutely assails her. She grants her rewards to the fittest, therefore, without regard to other considerations of any kind. If, then, there be liberty, men get from her just in proportion to their works. . . . [W]e cannot go outside of this alter-

native; liberty, inequality, survival of the fittest; not-liberty, equality, survival of the unfittest. The former carries society forward and favors all its best members; the latter carries society downwards and favors all its worst members.[4]

Nature is indifferent among strivers, all of whom have an equal right and responsibility to use her to achieve their goals. Beyond that starting point, efforts to equalize the processes or outcomes of competition cannot be justified.

Thus different specifications of success lead to opposite judgments about whether the American dream is designed to legitimate or to obliterate distinctions. Its four defining tenets similarly lead in opposite directions. They are in some ways egalitarian. The first tenet offers hope to all individuals at every point in their lives. The third tenet posits that all have the means at hand to realize their hopes. The fourth tenet dignifies all dreamers who deserve it by allying their hopes with virtue. But the same tenets also distinguish among people: the third prescribes that each individual bears sole responsibility for success or failure, and the fourth separates winners who deserve praise from those who deserve censure.

Thus one can only understand the profoundly ambiguous nature of the American dream by keeping its egalitarian and differentiating facets simultaneously in view. We have seen the effects of this ambiguity throughout the discussion of race and class in this book. Everyone may achieve absolute success? That egalitarian conviction keeps poor blacks engaged in struggle, as well as persuading whites that the status of African Americans has dramatically improved over the past thirty years. Only the best achieve competitive success? That differentiating claim underlies middle-class blacks' pride in their achievements, as well as whites' opposition to affirmative action. Everyone may participate? That egalitarian promise gave a revolutionary edge to the religious convictions of Martin Luther King, Jr., as well as giving whites grounds to believe that discrimination has disappeared. Losers have only themselves to blame? That differentiating belief keeps the not-yet-estranged poor quiescent, as well as keeping middle-class whites uneasy about their children's future.

As these paired examples demonstrate, the ambiguity of the American dream's commitment to equality is in fact doubly ambiguous. That very commitment, either to equal outcomes or to legitimately unequal ones, can galvanize people against injustice or lull them into quietude depending on whether they see what they are committed to as a goal to be fought for or an accomplishment to be celebrated. Thus to the divisions between races and classes already discussed, we must add normative distinctions about the meaning of equality within the dream and evaluative distinctions about the level of equality achieved by various dreamers.

THE MEANING OF SUCCESS

African Americans' experiences over the past three decades illuminate another ambiguity embedded in the ideology of the American dream. The issue here is the elusive nature of success. Some may always be available, and more may always be possible, but the end is never reached. When, then, can one say that one has achieved "the dream"? Alexis de Tocqueville is a penetrating analyst of this phenomenon:

> In America I have seen the freest and best educated of men in circumstances the happiest to be found in the world; yet it seemed to me that a cloud habitually hung on their brow, and they seemed serious and almost sad even in their pleasures.
>
> The chief reason for this is that . . . [they] never stop thinking of the good things they have not got.
>
> It is odd to watch with what feverish ardor the Americans pursue prosperity and how they are ever tormented by the shadowy suspicion that they may not have chosen the shortest route to get it.[5]

De Tocqueville's lyrical prose is echoed in everything from clichés about keeping up with the Joneses to well-off African Americans' conviction that they are denied what they really deserve. The point is so commonplace that we risk overlooking its importance: the comfort that the ideology provides by almost assuring everyone that they can attain something is matched by the simultaneous unease it ensures by its silence on how much is enough or how to apportion rewards to merit.

The dream is ambiguous not only on how much achievement counts as success but also on what kind of achievement ought to be pursued. Here too African Americans' experience permits insight into a problem that all Americans face. Complaints that middle-class blacks have turned away from their community in search of personal gain, or that desegregation has tempted professionals into pursuit of Eurocentric rather than Afrocentric goals, reflect a broader fear that the "right" standards are losing out. Again the dream is inherently ambiguous; the freedom granted by its liberal neutrality on the worth of individuals' goals is undermined by the constriction of real choices that accompanies a social structure in which material wealth has so much power and prestige associated with it.[6]

Finally, the dream is ambiguous on just how success is to be associated with virtue and on what counts as virtue. To an Afrocentrist, virtue consists partly in rejection of temporal, spatial, and bodily dualisms in favor of oneness with nature and the community of other Africans, past and present. To a "streetwise" inner city resident, it involves rejection of white bourgeois niceties of deference to authority and deferred gratification in favor of respect and toughness.[7] To Rayful Edmond, head of "the largest cocaine operation in Washington [D.C.]'s history," virtue is entirely relative: "I'm not saying drugs is good neither. And I'm not saying that it's bad. But it's a way of life and it's a part of our life. So it's something we have to deal with. . . . So I'm a good guy, and just something bad happened to me, you know, and I'll overcome sooner or later."[8]

To other Americans, white and black, these views are distortions, even mockeries, of virtue. Commentators have pointed out for centuries how much Americans, even descendants of white ethnic immigrants, are Puritans; we judge ourselves and others by high and narrow standards of morality. As with everything connected to the American dream, the insistence on virtue has two inseparable but opposing facets. Americans' belief that mere wealth and power are not enough to warrant respect pushes people toward worthy goals and softens the hard edges of the third tenet of the dream. But the same belief generates the willful blindness of a Rayful Edmond or the insecure narrowness of melting pot assimilationism.[9]

THE SELF-REFERENTIAL NATURE OF THE DREAM

Ambiguities in the American dream matter to more than philosophers debating its logic or individuals seeking to live by its precepts. They matter to its ability to function as the dominant ideology of a large and complex society. Like paper money, the American dream will succeed only so long as people believe in it. If the gap between praise for winners and blindness to losers, or the contradictory messages about equality and success, become worrisome to all or incapacitating to some, then the dream will lose its power to order social relations.

Its internal ambiguities are one Achilles heel of the American dream. A more simple loss of faith in either its global vision or each tenet is another. Let us consider the faith necessary to accept each tenet first before turning, in final summary, to the global vision.

Americans' proudest rallying cry, embodied in the first tenet of the American dream, is that "all men [*sic*] are created equal." They seek to reconcile that belief with obvious disparities of life circumstances in several ways: some inequalities are temporary but correctable anomalies in an otherwise well-functioning system; some are chosen by or the fault of the less fortunate themselves; some are mere differences. However they explain away inequalities, no American believer in the dream can any longer query as a point of pride, "How much would it be *worth* to a young man entering upon the practice of law, to be regarded as a *white* man rather than a colored one? . . . Indeed, is it [recognition as white] not the most valuable sort of property, being the master-key that unlocks the golden door of opportunity?"[10] Americans must not believe that the United States has immutable caste or class barriers; otherwise, the rest of the American dream is incoherent.

Americans must believe equally in the second tenet for the dream to bear its ideological weight. I discussed this issue in the first chapter, so I will merely summarize here: Americans must blur the distinction between a reasonable anticipation of success and the expectation of it. If they do not, if they engage in too much rational calculation, then too many will reject the ideology as a bad bet.

Third, Americans must believe that talent and effort will eventually yield their due recompense in order to continue to work hard in the face of little reward. They must also believe that *they* have enough talent for their efforts to be rewarded; thus early manuals for success assured readers that "the most completely provable fact in business [is] that brilliance is more likely to be a curse than an asset, and a hard-hitting mediocrity is almost certain to score over genius."[11] Conversely, they must believe that losers deserve to be at the bottom, lest those who later prove to be losers rebel.

Finally, Americans must believe that success without virtue is not really success—otherwise the restraints required by virtue will seem worthwhile only to suckers or saints. This was the great danger so feared, correctly, by Puritan divines. Increase Mather warned that "Land! Land! hath been the Idol of many in *New-England*: . . . and they that profess themselves Christians have forsaken Churches and Ordinances, and all for land and elbow-room enough in the World." With the benefit of hindsight, his son Cotton Mather confirmed his father's fears: "Religion brought forth prosperity, and the daughter destroyed the mother."[12] Americans have struggled ever since to atone for that matricide.

Thus most Americans must have faith in each component of the dream for the whole dream to bear the vast emotional and political weight that it now carries. With all elements in place, it is a well-functioning balance of inclusiveness, optimism, stern discipline, and high-mindedness. Absent any element, it permits too many demands on society and sets too few constraints on individuals to be viable across classes, ethnicities, vagaries of luck, and centuries.

Looking at African Americans' various forms of disaffection shows what happens when people start doubting one or several tenets of the dream. Rejection of the whole as hypocritical, impossible, or unappeal-

ing leads either to isolated alienation or to an alternative ideology, depending on the person's character and circumstances. The latter is probably a better choice for both person and society (depending on what the
alternative is), but from the perspective of the ideology both forms of
rejection are equally dangerous. Disbelief in the fact of the first tenet
leads people to recognize discrimination; disbelief in the *possibility* of
the first tenet leads them to depict the United States as irremediably
racist. Disbelief in the second and third tenets leads poor African Americans to remain under the spell of the great national suggestion *with
[only] one part of themselves.* Similar disbelief leads well-off African
Americans to the conviction that they (and others) can succeed only
through taking advantage of personal connections, white liberal guilt, or
belligerent black solidarity. Abjuring the restraints of the last tenet leads
to violence, destruction of children's futures, or crime.

Whites' racial experiences can similarly threaten the American
dream's character as a self-sustaining bubble. Those who despair of the
first tenet ever being realized may conclude with blacks that the American dream is a racist sham. Those who interpret the second tenet in
terms of competitive success may find their faith crumbling when too
many competitors of the "wrong" race succeed at the expense of people
like themselves. Both those who think the third tenet is violated by
granting rewards to undeserving blacks and those who think it is violated by denying rewards to deserving blacks may equally despair. And
the availability for exploitation of politically and economically weak
inner city residents may tempt some into rejecting the fourth tenet.

Thus the "drama acted out upon the body of a Negro" can come to
epitomize "the whole of American life." The genius of the American
dream is the mutual reinforcement of all tenets; its vulnerability is the
same. If a substantial number of Americans lose faith in any foundational
precept or the whole gestalt, as racial and class antagonism or white
modeling of black disillusionment make possible, the American dream
can collapse in upon itself as thoroughly as any savings and loan bank.

THE FUTURE OF THE AMERICAN DREAM

Should we be sorry if this happens? Let me pose the question more formally, since its answer is the ultimate point of this book. As I argued in
the preface, the racial experience in the United States poses two kinds of
threats to the American dream. The first comes from direct conflict between blacks and whites over jobs, political power, respect, and interpretations of meaning. Middle-class blacks and whites contend most
overtly, with the most visible effects on belief in the American dream.

But the growing number of estranged poor shows that the poor too can lose faith in the dream, partly because of racial conflict.

The other threat to the American dream from America's racial experience is indirect but just as strong. Whites may learn disaffection with the ideology or its effects by observing blacks' earlier and stronger disaffection. This chapter has discussed a variety of ways in which the experiences of African Americans "illuminate" or "illustrate" "the whole of American life." But that language is not quite right. The experiences of blacks do not just illustrate the whole of American life; they are a central part of that life and thus help to shape the possibilities for belief and practice of all Americans. So whites' options are partly shaped by blacks' choices, as whites' beliefs are partly shaped by blacks' reactions to the American dream.

Those points, then, lead to a more precise reformulation of the question asked above. Should we be sorry if direct racial conflict and indirect racial modeling and influence together make the flaws and ambiguities of the American dream so intolerable that people lose their faith in it? (Precision has its rhetorical costs!)

Certainly the ideology can be used in defense of atomism, materialism, self-righteousness, and priggishness. More fundamentally, it is flawed at the core: in a capitalist economic system, a majoritarian political system, and a status-driven social system, not all Americans can achieve their dreams no matter how hard they try. But the American dream obscures those structural facts under a cloak of individual agency, thus giving people unjustified hopes and unwarranted feelings of failure.

But debased interpretations can be contested, and it is that very insistence on hope and agency that is the glory as well as the shame of the American dream. No matter who they are, people can make a real difference, as *they* define it, in their own lives and the lives of those they love— I, along with millions of others, find that simple and powerful assertion hard to reject *as a matter of belief, not of fact.*

And anyway, I do not see an alternative that is both plausible and preferable. On plausibility: the American dream is deeply embedded in most Americans' images of themselves and their society, even—or especially—among those most critical of its practice.[13] It has outlasted powerful contenders for ideological domination; it has been embodied in institutions ranging from western land grants to the Civil Rights Act; its protagonists have honed its internal symmetries of optimism and discipline, self-aggrandizement and self-control, morality and hypocrisy into a brilliant balance.[14]

I see only two plausible alternatives to the dominance of the American dream, and neither in my view is preferable. One is ascriptive Americanism, defined as racial, class, and gender hierarchy rationalized by a claim that those on top have "an identity that has inherent and transcendent worth, thanks to nature, history, and God."[15] This whole book is devoted to the eradication of that alternative (although my refusal to make predictions indicates my fear that ascriptive Americanism will prove stronger than the American dream, at least in the arena of race).

The second plausible alternative to the American dream, at least in the arena of race, is black nationalism, whether in the guise of Afrocentrism, the Nation of Islam, or something else. It is not a plausible alternative for more than a tiny fraction of whites, and so far it has not persistently attracted more than a small minority of blacks. But it could, if the American dream yields to ascriptive Americanism among many white Americans.

Those moves—to symmetrical black nationalism and white ascriptivism—would be unfortunate, for two reasons. First, I still hold out the hope that the American dream itself will solve many of the problems of the dream. If Americans faced up to their situation, they could use the optimistic, inclusive, generous elements of their dominant ideology to override the harsh, exclusionary, hypocritical elements of it. Ideally, all Americans will fight their own worst instincts by mobilizing their best; that was Gunnar Myrdal's vision, and Martin Luther King, Jr.,'s after him. Alternatively, some Americans will use the dream's best features to contest other Americans taking advantage of its worst.

My other reason for preferring that African Americans not turn to nationalism or whites to ascriptive Americanism was best articulated by James Baldwin. Let me allow him the last word:

> Each of us, helplessly and forever, contains the other—male in female, female in male, white in black, and black in white. We are part of each other. Many of my countrymen appear to find this fact exceedingly inconvenient and even unfair, and so, very often, do I. But none of us can do anything about it.[16]

Appendix A

SURVEYS USED FOR UNPUBLISHED TABULATIONS

The list below summarizes the survey sources and analytic groupings used in this study. The surveys mainly represent two time periods: the 1960s/early 1970s and the 1980s/early 1990s. Whether changes in attitudes or values are due to time trends, generational replacement, or other phenomena is difficult to determine. It suffices here that these data produce "snapshots" of the attitudes and values held by black and white publics when the surveys were taken, and that together they depict the direction and composition of the moving process of opinion formation.

Analytic groupings were selected in order to divide blacks and whites separately into parallel, balanced categories on income, and into the exact same categories on education. This scheme called for rough division of the sample within each race into thirds based on questions about total family or household income (typically total income before taxes)—yielding a top, middle, and bottom income group for each race in that survey in that year. Education was grouped into conventional social categories—less than high school graduate, high school graduate, formal education beyond high school (occasionally including technical school, but most often not). This scheme allows for both subjective relative comparison by race on economic grounds and more objective determination of social standing based on educational achievement.

Given that these are secondary analyses of existing survey data using categories predetermined in various ways by different survey organizations over time, some groupings are less than ideal in proportion or composition. On the whole, however, the decision to compare only the top and bottom segments for both income and education groupings tends to adjust for differences in the structure of questions that inevitably create a mushy middle category. Where applicable, I include a descriptive or technical note to detail the survey's scope or limitations, and to call attention to specific aspects of the data or analytic groupings that deserve mention.

In general, the surveys represent national samples of adults living in the continental United States. Early surveys tend to be cross-section or quota samples conducted in person. Later surveys are largely probability samples (often supplemented by special efforts to oversample the black population) conducted by telephone. Sample distributions on education reflect the differences between blacks and whites noted in census figures. Income distributions by race are subject to the specific categories used in particular surveys. Nevertheless, a pattern emerges: comparing the boundaries of the top and bottom income segments, the income levels of blacks and whites persistently produce a ratio of approximately three to five. That is, if the upper limit of the lower-income range for blacks is around $9,000, then the corresponding figure for whites tends to be around $15,000. The same ratio holds for the lower limit of the upper-income range.

Compendium of Surveys

The sample sizes given below may reflect rounding or approximation based on the tabulations used. Unweighted numbers are designated (u); weighted numbers are (w). Particular circumstances are noted.

ABC News/*Washington Post* (1989) "ABC News/*Washington Post* 9/89 Poll."
National sample with a black oversample yielding: black, 376 (u); white, 1,313 (u). Hispanics allocated by race. Technical school specified as high school only. Tabulations by Roper Center, Storrs, CT.

——— (1990) "ABC News/*Washington Post* Poll: Omnibus-September 1990."
National sample yielding: black, 58 (u); white, 661 (u). Hispanics allocated by race. Technical school specified as high school only. Tabulations by Roper Center.

——— (1991) "ABC News/*Washington Post* Poll: Omnibus-June 1991."
National sample yielding: black, 156 (u); white, 1,274 (u). Hispanics allocated by race. Technical school specified as high school only. Tabulations by Roper Center.

Campbell, Angus, and Howard Schuman (1968) "Racial Attitudes in Fifteen American Cities," for National Advisory Commission on Civil Disorders. University of Michigan, Institute for Social Research.
Urban and metropolitan areas of fifteen cities in the United States yielding: black, 2,809 (u); white, 2,584 (u). ICPSR Osiris datafile. Tabulations by Princeton University.

CBS News/*NYT* Poll (1978) "The Kerner Commission—Ten Years Later."
Residents of large northern industrial cities yielding: black, 374 (u); white, 489 (u). Tabulations by Roper Center.

——— (1992) "May National Poll."
National sample yielding: black, 318 (u); white, 878 (u). Tabulations by Roper Center.

Gallup Organization (1961) "The Gallup Poll."
National sample yielding: black, 332 (w); white, 2,483 (w). Tabulations by Roper Center.

——— (1963) "The Gallup Poll."
National sample yielding: black, 484 (w); white, 3,591 (w). Tabulations by Roper Center.

——— (1964) "Hopes and Fears," for Potomac Associates.
National sample yielding: black, 138 (u); white, 1,410 (u). Data unweighted. Tabulations by Roper Center.

——— (1966) "The Gallup Poll."
National sample yielding: black, 302 (w); white, 3,172 (w). Tabulations by Roper Center.

——— (1971) "The Gallup Poll."

National sample yielding: black, 128 (u); white sample not used. Tabulations by Roper Center.

—— (1972) "State of the Nation 1972," for Potomac Associates.
National sample yielding: black, 119 (u); white, 400 (u). Data unweighted. Tabulations by Roper Center.

—— (1988) "Gallup/Newsweek Poll: Race Relations," for Newsweek.
National sample yielding: black, 305 (u); white, 605 (u). Tabulations by Princeton University.

—— (1991a) "Gallup/Newsweek Poll: Race Relations," for Newsweek.
National sample yielding: black, 54 (w); white, 429 (w). No income variable in dataset. Tabulations by Roper Center.

—— (1991b) "Gallup News Service Survey: June Omnibus, Wave 2."
National sample with black oversample yielding: black, 55 (w); white, 369 (w). Tabulations by Roper Center.

—— (1991c) "Gallup/Newsweek Poll: Sexual Harassment," for Newsweek.
National sample yielding: black, 50 (u); white, 619 (u). No income variable in dataset. Tabulations by Roper Center.

—— (1992) "Gallup News Service Survey: May Omnibus, Wave 1."
National sample yielding: black, 302 (u); white, 677 (u). Tabulations by Roper Center.

—— (1994) "CNN/USA Today—Report Card #5," for CNN/USA Today.
National sample yielding: black, 322 (u); white sample not used. Tabulations provided by Gallup Organization.

General Social Survey (1972–1993) James Davis and Tom Smith, principal investigators. U. of Chicago: National Opinion Research Center.
National samples with black oversamples in 1982 and 1987. Sample sizes vary substantially by question. Two-year groupings were used where possible to increase sample size. Questions in 1982 and 1987 tabulated separately. Roper Center datafile. Tabulations by Princeton University.

Gordon S. Black Corporation (1989a) "USA Today Poll: Racism," for USA Today.
National sample of black population yielding: black, 601 (w). Tabulations by Roper Center.

—— (1989b) "USA Today Poll: Racial Attitudes," for USA Today.
National sample of white population yielding: white, 809 (w). Tabulations by Roper Center.

Harris, Louis, and Associates (1966a) "Racial Survey: Black Sample," for Newsweek.
National sample of black population yielding: black, 1,037 (u). Income measured as weekly income. Tabulations by Institute for Research in Social Science, Chapel Hill, N.C..

—— (1966b) "Racial Survey: Random Sample," for Newsweek.

National sample yielding: black sample not used; white, 978 (u). Tabulations by Institute for Research in Social Science.

———— (1968) "College Student Peace Corps Survey: Black Sample."
Sample of black college students age 18 and over yielding: black students, 860 (u). Tabulations by Institute for Research in Social Science.

———— (1969) "Survey of College Seniors."
Sample of college seniors age 18 and over yielding: black, 70 (u); white, 920 (u). Tabulations by Institute for Research in Social Science.

———— (1970a) "American Women's Opinion Survey [Women]," for the Virginia Slim Division of Liggett and Meyers, Inc.
National sample tabulated separately for women yielding: black, 338 (u); white, 2,571 (u). Black and white income segments based on total sample for each race. Tabulations by Institute for Research in Social Science.

———— (1970b) "American Women's Opinion Survey [Men]," for the Virginia Slim Division of Liggett and Meyers, Inc.
National sample tabulated separately for men yielding: black, 126 (u); white, 864 (u). Black and white income segments based on total sample for each race. Tabulations by Institute for Research in Social Science.

———— (1970c) untitled.
National sample yielding: black, 191 (u); white, 1,258 (u). Tabulations by Institute for Research in Social Science.

———— (1988) "A Nation Divided on Black Progress," for *Business Week*/Harris Poll.
National sample with black oversample yielding: black, 531 (u); white, 1,061 (u). Tabulations by Institute for Research in Social Science.

———— (1989) *The Unfinished Agenda on Race in America*, for NAACP Legal Defense and Educational Fund.
National sample with black oversample yielding: black, 1,005 (u); white, 2,008 (u). Tabulations provided by Louis Harris and Associates.

———— (1991) "How Blacks View Thomas and Their Leaders," for *Business Week*/Harris Poll.
National sample of black population yielding: black, 500 (u). Data unweighted. Tabulations by Institute for Research in Social Science.

Los Angeles Times (1991a) Poll #253, untitled.
National sample yielding: black, 125 (u); white, 1,250 (u). Tabulations by Roper Center.

———— (1991b) Poll #259, "Judge Thomas, Race Relations and Ronald Reagan."
National sample with black oversample yielding: black, 510 (u); white, 1,029 (u). Technical school treated as more than high school. Tabulations by Roper Center.

Marx, Gary (1964) "Negro Political Attitudes" (also titled "Anti-Semitism—Negro Oversample"). Survey Research Center, U. of California, Berkeley.
Urban and metropolitan area sample of black population based on black over-sample combined with black sample in "Anti-Semitism in the United States" survey yielding: black, 1,119 (u). Tabulations by Princeton University.

Matthews, Donald, and James Prothro (1961) "The Negro Political Participation Study." U. of North Carolina.
National sample of black population yielding: black, 620 (u). Tabulations by Princeton University.

Media General/Associated Press (1988) "National Poll #21."
National sample yielding: black, 104 (u); white, 1,059 (u). Tabulations by Roper Center.

Metropolitan Chicago Information Center (1991–94) "Metro Surveys."
Chicago six-county metropolitan area sample yielding at least 3,000 interviews per year: blacks about 600 (u); whites about 2,000 (u). Random telephone sample supplemented by personal interviews with nontelephone households. Interviews conducted in English and Spanish. Sample sizes vary substantially by question. Annual samples were combined where possible to increase sample size. Tabulations by Metropolitan Chicago Information Center.

National Survey of Black Americans, 1979–1980 (1980) James Jackson and Gerald Gurin, principal investigators. U. of Michigan, Institute for Social Research.
National sample of black population yielding: black, 2,107 (u). Black interviewers used for all interviews. Self-weighting dataset. ICPSR datafile. Tabulations by Princeton University.

NBC News (1989) "Social Issues Poll."
National sample with black oversample yielding: black, 501 (u); white, 1,260 (u). Data unweighted. Tabulations by Roper Center.

National Opinion Research Center (1944) "Attitudes Toward Negroes."
National sample of white population: whites, 2,521 (u). Income segments based on interviewer estimate of social class (poor, average, average+/wealthy). Tabulations by Roper Center.

——— (1950) "Attitudes Toward Jews and Communism."
National sample yielding: black, 116 (u); white, 1,156 (u). Tabulations by Roper Center.

——— (1963) "Survey Research Service Amalgam Survey."
National sample yielding: black, 163 (u); white sample not used. Tabulations by Roper Center.

——— (1968) "SRS Amalgam Survey."
National sample yielding: black, 219 (u); white, 1,251 (u). Tabulations by Roper Center.

NYT/WCBS News (1985) "New York City Race Relations Survey."
New York City sample yielding: black, 369; white, 888. Scale used combining income and education variables (ranging from low education/income to high education/income). Tabulations by University of California, Berkeley.

NYT/WCBS TV News (1990) "Race Relations—New York City."
New York City sample yielding: black 408 (u); white, 484 (u). Tabulations provided by New York Times.

Roper Organization (1986) "The American Dream Survey," for the *Wall Street J.*
National sample yielding: black, 106 (w); white, 1,183 (w). Tabulations by Princeton University.

Sniderman, Paul, Philip Tetlock, and Thomas Piazza (1991) "Race and Politics Survey." Survey Research Center, U. of California, Berkeley.
National sample (English-speaking) yielding: black, 201 (u); white, 1,841 (u). Data unweighted. Tabulations by University of Pittsburgh.

Survey Research Center, U. of California, Berkeley (1964) "Anti-Semitism in the United States," for Anti-Defamation League of B'nai B'rith, data collection by NORC.
Urban and metropolitan area sample yielding: black, 244 (u); white, 1,717 (u). Tabulations by Princeton University.

Washington Post (1992) "*Washington Post* Poll: Race Relations."
National sample with black oversample yielding: black, 421 (u); white, 874 (u). Hispanics allocated by race. Technical school treated as more than high school. Tabulations by Roper Center.

Yankelovich Clancy Shulman (1992) "Rodney King Verdict and the Los Angeles Riots," for *Time* and Cable News Network.
National sample yielding: black, 200 (u); white, 798 (u). Tabulations by Roper Center.

SUPPLEMENTAL TABLES

APPENDIX TABLE 4.1
Does Racial Discrimination Inhibit Blacks' Participation in the
American Dream? by Race and Class (percent agreeing)

	Black		White	
	Poor	*Middle Class*	*Poor*	*Middle Class*
1. 1960s				
A. 1966	57	69	—	—
1969 (north)	49	50	—	—
1969 (south)	68	60	—	—
B. 1963 (north)	44	70	—	—
1966	72	76	—	—
1969 (north)	53	56	—	—
1969 (south)	71	71	—	—
C. 1964a	74	58	—	—
1964b	59	29	—	—
D. 1966	47	46	—	—
E. 1966				
law school	42	46	—	—
medical school	44	39	—	—
engineering school	37	42	—	—
scientific school	36	38	—	—
F. 1968	74	82	—	—
2. 1980s–1990s				
A. 1986	42	38	60	51
1987	50	47	58	59
1988b	56	43	77	60
1988c	42	9	62	51
1988c	49	20	37	36
1991c	63	45	66	66
B. 1988a	49	42	75	69
1989a	51	61	—	—
1989b	32	31	60	56
1989b	40	37	58	73
1991b	54	48	81	82

APPENDIX TABLE 4.1 (*cont.*)

	Black		White	
	Poor	*Middle Class*	*Poor*	*Middle Class*
2. 1980s–1990s (*cont.*)				
C. 1982	16	7	—	—
1988a	26	19	67	58
1988b	14	10	46	47
1989a	54	81	—	—
1989b	12	12	45	44
1991a	16	8	41	45
1991b	34	41	69	67
1991d	40	26	64	52
D. 1988a	17	7	47	40
1988a	17	7	40	34
1988b	39	28	60	45
1991a	42	9	34	35
1991b	45	42	65	76
E. 1989b	26	21	42	45

Note: See text table 4.2 for question content and notes.

APPENDIX TABLE 4.2

Can African Americans Reasonably Anticipate Achieving Their Dream?
by Race and Class (percent agreeing)

	Black			White		
	Total	*Poor*	*Middle Class*	*Total*	*Poor*	*Middle Class*
1. 1960s						
A. 1961	71	67	77	—	—	—
B. 1964	80	75	83	—	—	—
1966	68	67	70	—	—	—
2. 1980s–1990s						
A. 1982	47	49	46	—	—	—
1988a	34	38	31	50	44	46
1989a	45	48	37	72[*]	65[*]	73[*]
1989b	47	46	42	70	71	65
1992	15	19	14	37	37	33
B. 1984	55	59	46	—	—	—
C. 1991	25	23	24	58	58	58
D. 1982	35	43	33	—	—	—
1989a	40	46	31	64[*]	67[*]	61[*]
1991	55	57	48	78	82	70
E. 1988b	23	23	24	56	47	63
F. 1988b	22	21	17	41	42	34

[*] Classes measured by education.
Note: See text table 4.4 for question content and notes.

APPENDIX TABLE 4.3
Are African Americans Responsible for Their Low Status?
by Race and Class (percent agreeing)

	Black		White	
	Poor	Middle Class	Poor	Middle Class
1. 1940s–1960s				
A. 1948	23	4	—	—
B. 1961	60	51	76	83
C. 1964				
a	12	6	43	36
b	18	14	—	—
2. 1980s–1990s				
A. 1983	56	36	65	55
1985–86	38	33	62	57
1988a	17	12	28	26
1989a	60	37	55	33
1989b	55	36	53	42
1988–89	41	24	63	55
1990–91	52	40	62	51
1991c	46	41	60	45
B. 1978	19	21	45	39
1986b	65	54	—	—
1988b	29	27	31	23
1989a	63	51	60	53
C. 1989a	23	22	51	53
1992a	20	24	44	53
D. 1986b	69	45	—	—
1989a	75	46	69	50
1992a	50	43	44	35
E. 1991a	9	9	16	19
1991b	32	24	50	55
1992b	25	34	53	55
F. 1991a	29	21	24	18

Note: See text table 4.5 for question content and notes.

APPENDIX TABLE 4.4
Are Successful Blacks Virtuous? by Race and Class (percent agreeing)

		Black		White	
		Poor	Middle Class	Poor	Middle Class
A.	1988b	74	79	55	52
B.	1984	55	36	—	—
	1988a	61	65	—	—
C.	1988b	27	17	16	22
D.	1988c	31	56	44	53

Note: See text table 4.6 for question content and notes.

NOTES

INTRODUCTION

1. In 1993 about one-sixth of black respondents preferred the designation "black," one-sixth preferred "African American," and two-thirds did not care (*NYT*/CBS News 1993a: 12). In a forced choice question a year later, three in ten preferred African American, and four in ten preferred black (Morin 1994; see also Bowman 1994).

2. Prager (1982: 102).

3. Lane (1991: part 7).

4. Kennedy (1991: 121–23), Meier (1992), Mayberry (1994), and the essays in Stanfield (1993) and Stanfield and Dennis (1993) discuss whites' ability to write about what it feels like to be black.

5. Ellison (1993: 52).

6. Merton (1972).

CHAPTER ONE
WHAT IS THE AMERICAN DREAM?

1. Locke (1980: sec. 49, p. 29).

2. Ed Sadlowski, in Terkel (1980: 236). The proportion of first-year college students seeking to "be very well off financially" grew from 44% to 74% between 1967 and 1994; the proportion seeking to "develop a meaningful philosophy of life" sank from 83% to 43% over the same period (Cooperative Institutional Research Program 1987: 97; 1994: 26; see also People for the American Way 1989: 152; Warden 1994).

3. Adam Hochschild (1986); Chandler and Chandler (1987).

4. Mather (1970: 27).

5. Mather's dilemma continues: college freshmen who seek financial success overlap little with those who seek a meaningful philosophy of life or to improve the nation's social and political life (Easterlin and Crimmins 1991: 505).

6. Marsh (1987: 264).

7. Comer (1988: 83–85); Letter to Lord Egmont, July 12, 1736, quoted in Greenberg (1977: 454).

8. Jeffrey (1979: 141). The lyrics of a Burl Ives song from the nineteenth-century western frontier include, "Did you murder your wife and fly for your life? Say, what was your name in the States?"

9. Hirschman (1970: 106–12) offers the classic analysis of Americans' proclivity to "exit" in response to a political or personal problem.

10. Ladd (1993: 21; 1994: 67, 76; see also 53–56, 66).

11. Ben Jonson, George Chapman, and John Marston, *Eastward Ho!*

(1605), quoted in Beeman (1971: 618–19).

12. Tom Smith (1988: 14); "Public Opinion and Demographic Report" (1993b: 89); see also "Public Opinion and Demographic Report" (1993a: 85, 87).

13. Emerson (1863: 86).

14. Robert Winthrop, "Oration at the Inauguration of the Statue of Benjamin Franklin," Boston, 1856, quoted in Wyllie (1954: 14–15). Franklin himself was more succinct: "In America, . . . people do not inquire concerning a Stranger, What is he?, but, What can he do?" (Franklin 1987: 175). See Shklar (1991: 19–22, 63–101) on the importance of working to earn one's own way in defining American citizenship.

15. Miller (1992: 564–70); Ladd (1994: 55–58).

16. Kluegel and Smith (1986: 44). See also Lynd and Lynd (1930: 65); Huber and Form (1973); Caplow and Bahr (1979: table 1); Ladd (1994: 53–56, 68–69). In 1993 fully 94% of Americans agreed that hard work was crucial to success; the next most popular choice was God's will, with 53% agreement (Marsden and Swingle 1994: 277).

17. *Gallup Opinion Index* (1973: 28); Tom Smith (1987a: 411). See also Tom Smith (1987b); Miller (1992: 586–88); Ladd (1994: 79). Working-class respondents in all Western countries are slightly less committed to the third tenet than are members of the middle class. But the most striking feature of comparisons by class is the degree to which the poor, especially in the United States, support norms that benefit the rich more than themselves (Miller 1992: 582–86; see also Ladd 1994: 80; Hochschild 1981).

18. Stern and Searing (1976: 198). Perhaps the equation of poverty with laziness makes fewer American youths than youths of ten other countries (except for India) agree that "it is important . . . to take it easy and not to work too hard" (*Gallup Opinion Index* 1973: 36).

19. Ladd (1994: 75, 79, 80).

20. Franklin (1987: 1298–1302, 1386, 1391, 1392, 1397). Diggins (1984) gives probably the best analysis of the role of virtue in American political culture.

21. Louis Harris (1986; 1990: 2).

22. Davis and Smith (1982: vars. 127–29); Marsden and Swingle (1994: 279). Other desirable features of friends, such as being fun-loving or intelligent, received considerably less than unanimous support.

23. *Gallup Opinion Index* (1973: 34); Ladd (1994: 72–73).

24. Gunnar Myrdal, in Baldwin et al. (1964: 33). Lamont (1992; forthcoming) analyzes the greater weight placed by Americans than by the French on including morality in their definition of success. Nackenoff (1993) shows the interactions of virtue and material success in modern American history.

25. Potter (1954).

26. Wilder (1940: 334).

27. Quoted in Ghent (1902: 29).

28. My thanks to Walter Lippincott and Hugh Van Dusen for providing me with these figures.

29. The phrase is from Rae (1988).

30. Although not without backsliding, as a survivor of Japanese internment camps points out: "The American Dream? I think: for whites only. I didn't feel that way before World War Two" (Terkel 1980: 161–71; more generally, see Rogers Smith 1993).

31. Louis Harris (1978: 59–67); Kluegel and Smith (1986: 62–72, 222–35); Verba and Orren (1985: 83–88); Simon and Landis (1989); "Public Opinion and Demographic Report" (1993c: 88–95).

32. Message from Governor James Glen of South Carolina in 1749, quoted in Warren Smith (1961: 51).

33. Miguel Cortéz, in Terkel (1980: 131).

34. Florence Scala, in Terkel (1980: 116).

35. Goldstein (1988: 77).

36. de Tocqueville (1969: 627, 536). Once again, Studs Terkel's respondents parallel learned discourse. To a wealthy professional, "the American Dream always has a greater force when you don't already have it. People who grew up without it are told if you can only work long enough and hard enough, you can get that pot of gold at the end of the rainbow. When you already have the pot of gold, the dream loses its force." A struggling ex-convict is more rueful: "It was always competition. I went from competing in sports to competing in crime. . . . I always wanted to be at the top of something. So I became the first dope fiend in the neighborhood" (Leon Duncan and Ken Jackson, in Terkel 1980: 123, 218).

37. de Tocqueville (1969: 540).

38. Quotations from Douglas LaBier, in Skrzycki (1989: H1, H4). See also LaBier (1986) and Berglas (1986).

39. Consider the effects of the 1971 draft lottery on self-esteem. In one experiment, young men completed paper-and-pencil measures of self-esteem, then listened to the lottery, then retook the self-esteem index. "Subjects whose numbers put them in the fortunate half of their group tended to experience increased self-esteem, while those whose numbers put them in the unfortunate half of their group tended to experience decreased self-esteem" (Rubin and Peplau 1973: 81).

40. Hurston (1942: 116).

41. Stouffer et al. (1949: 250–57); Hirschman (1981: 41, 47). In the Latin American context that he was studying, Hirschman equated "becoming furious" with "turning into an enemy of the established order." That sometimes happens in the United States, as will be seen in succeeding chapters. But "becoming furious" may also result in spouse-battering, a lawsuit, or "the embrace of victimhood" (Sykes 1992; John Taylor 1991; Hughes 1992).

42. From a 1669 warrant of the Scottish Privy Council to local authorities, quoted in Nash (1982: 217).

43. Readers are, however, assured that such prostitutes "have a short career, generally dying of the effects of intemperance and pollution soon after entering upon this road to ruin." *Magdalen Report: First Annual Report of the Executive Committee of the N. Y. Magdalen Society* (New York, 1831), quoted in Hugins (1972: 42).

44. Hochschild (1981: 113, 116); Lewis and Schneider (1985: 7); "Public Opinion and Demographic Report" (1993c: 86).

45. Rubin and Peplau (1975: 67, 68); Lerner (1980); see also Rubin and Peplau (1973); Lerner and Lerner (1981).

46. Young (1958) gives the classic depiction of the costs to society as a whole of smugness among the successful.

47. Huntington (1981: 30–41, 61–70), Shklar (1984: 67–78), and McWilliams (1990: 177) examine hypocrisy in American liberal democracy. Mark Twain remains, however, its best analyst.

48. Some earlier Jewish immigrants concurred:

They are a bane to the country and a curse to the Jews. The Jews have earned an enviable reputation in the United States, but this has been undermined by the influx of thousands who are not ripe for the enjoyment of liberty and equal rights, and all who mean well for the Jewish name should prevent them as much as possible from coming there. The experience of the charity teaches that organized immigration from Russia, Roumania, and other semi-barbarous countries is a mistake and has proved a failure. It is no relief to the Jews of Russia, Poland, etc., and it jeopardizes the well-being of the American Jews.

Document of the United Jewish Charities of Rochester, New York, 1893, quoted in Szajowski (1951: 232).

49. Hendrick (1907).

50. The illustration on p. 33 is one example (reproduced in Caldwell 1971: 124).

51. An article headlined "Honor, Family, Work: Success" (Dillon 1988) says it all. A high-quality example of the genre is Butterfield (1986).

52. Ueda (1989); Hurh and Kim (1989); Kim (1993).

53. Rogers Smith (1993).

54. James (1920: 260). Here, as elsewhere, success is highly gendered. In this case, perhaps because James is challenging its desirability, it is cast as a woman; more often, perhaps because those discussing it want to achieve "mastery" or to encourage others to seek it, success is cast as a male or men are used as exemplars (and women as exemplars of failure). One could do a fascinating analysis of the gendered nature not only of who succeeds in America but also of the very terms of the ideology.

55. Folksong in Bukowczyk (1987: frontispiece); Yiddish letter quoted in Baritz (1988: 136).

56. Stack and Cromartie (n.d., c. 1990) and Cromartie and Stack (1989) describe the rarity of return migration.

57. "A True Sight of Sin," in Miller and Johnson (1963: 295).

58. James (1920: 260).

59. Warden (1994: 22).

60. Hochschild (1981: 250–54).

61. Kelman (1981).

62. A small sample includes Bailyn (1967); Pocock (1975); Wilentz (1984); Bellah et al. (1985); Rogers Smith (1988, 1993); and Orren (1991).

63. Schumacher (1989); Hirsch (1976).

64. Dahl (1977), Huntington (1981), Kramnick (1990), Morone (1990), Sinopoli (1992), Hirsch (1992), Ericson (1993), and Greenstone (1993) all seek to revive, in modified forms, the Hartzian notion of a dominant political culture in the United States. The American dream as I define it is only part of that culture. It does not, for example, prescribe political rights or governance structures, or articulate how much authority to grant to religious leaders or scientists, or delineate how to distinguish moral and social aristocrats from plebians. (On those points, see McClosky and Brill 1983; Merelman 1991; Lamont 1992.)

65. de Tocqueville (1969: 541).

CHAPTER TWO
RICH AND POOR AFRICAN AMERICANS

1. See also Wright et al. (1982).

2. Farley (1992: chap. 2, fig. 1).

3. Hauser and Phang (1993: 15–21); Harrison and Bennett (1995: 170–72).

4. US Department of Education (1990a; 1994a: 15, 19).

5. Jaynes and Williams (1989: 230); Farley (1992: chap. 7). Rosenstone and Hanson (1993: 219–24) explain the rise, and recent fall, of black voting.

6. Joint Center for Political and Economic Studies (1994).

7. U.S. Bureau of the Census (1993a: B-38).

8. See Jencks (1991: 46–47) and Rae et al. (1981: 104–29) on relative and absolute comparisons. Comparing blacks' and whites' earnings over the past few decades, Card and Krueger (1993: 85–86) and Sorensen (1991) both find convergence before the 1980s, but no change and divergence, respectively, since 1980.

9. Data for 1991 are in U.S. Bureau of the Census (1994: xiii); see also Oliver and Shapiro (1989); O'Hare (1983). Data for the 1960s and 1970s are in Terrell (1971: 364); Browne (1974: 35); Birnbaum and Weston (1974: 105); James Smith (1975: 360–61); Henretta (1979: 72); Sobol (1979: 586); Blau and Graham (1990); Soltow (1972). Jianakoplos and Menchik (1992: 16, table 15) and Steckel and Krishnan (1992) analyze changes in wealth by race over time.

An often-cited study for the Federal Reserve Board (Kennickell and Shack-Marquez 1992) contradicts the Census Bureau on changes in median net worth by race during the 1980s. But it appears to have changed its definition of "nonwhite" between 1983 and 1989 so I do not report those figures.

10. Farley (1992: chap. 1, pp. 4–5).

11. Hauser (1990: 15–16, 19–26); see also Grusky and DiPrete (1990: 624–25).

12. On homeowners, see U.S. Bureau of the Census (1993b: 724); Wachter and Megbolugbe (1992). On housing values, see Farley and Allen (1987: 291–92); Kennickell and Shack-Marquez (1992: 10–11); U.S. Bureau of the Census (1986: 14, 22; 1994: 3, 9).

13. Massey and Denton (1988: 605; 1993). On preferences for desegregated

neighborhoods, see, for example, Farley et al. (1993); CBS News/*NYT* (1978: vars. 27, 43).

14. Farley and Allen (1987: 139–50); Massey and Denton (1987; 1988); Jaynes and Williams (1989: 140–46); Alba and Logan (1993); Harrison and Bennett (1995: 157–64).

15. Data on unemployment derived from *Economic Report of the President* (1994: 314); GAO (1994: 19–20).

16. *Ebony* (1987: 27). Throughout this book, I use the term "class" to refer to points along a continuum of stratification rather than to dichotomous categories of owner and worker. My reasons are pragmatic: that is how most data are organized and how most Americans think of social divisions. I also mostly ignore, as not material for my purposes, the issue of whether blacks mean the same thing by "middle class" as do whites. See Williams (1964: 251); Jackman and Jackman (1983: 22–41, 81–86); A. Wade Smith (1985); Landry (1987); Boston (1988); Vanneman and Cannon (1987: 225–56); and Stricker (1982) on the latter point.

17. Six in ten blacks held jobs serving their own community in 1960; four in ten did a decade later (Hout 1986; see also Landry 1987).

18. U.S. Bureau of the Census (1994: xiii). See also U.S. Bureau of the Census (1986: 5); Oliver and Shapiro (1989: 12); Wolff (1993: 19).

19. In 1950 about 20% of whites were professionals or managers, and another fifth held clerical or sales jobs. In 1990 three-tenths of whites were in each category (Ferleger and Mandle 1991: 6).

20. U.S. Bureau of the Census (1993b: 153); Jones (1987: 7–8); U.S. Department of Education (1993a: 54, 244).

21. Quotations from Hout (1984: 308); and Hogan and Featherman (1978: 101). See also Siegel (1965); Blau and Duncan (1967); Duncan (1969).

22. Hout (1984: 308); see also Featherman and Hauser (1976; 1978); Hogan and Featherman (1978). Class origins of white men began to have *less* effect on their outcomes during this period than they did earlier. There are no data on women. For a less sanguine view, see Oliver and Glick (1982).

23. Chapter 5 discusses recent mobility among middle-class African Americans.

24. Smith and Welch (1989) give the most optimistic recent assessment of the growth of the black middle class.

25. U.S. Bureau of the Census (1993c: 2–3).

26. Eggebeen and Lichter (1991: 809); see also Rodgers and Rodgers (1991: 352). A mother and three children living under 50% of the poverty line have less than $7,000 a year to spend.

27. About 5% of white children are poor for six or more years (Duncan and Rodgers 1991: 543). See also Bane and Ellwood (1986: 17, 21); Ruggles (1989: 19); Ashworth et al. (1994: 673–74).

28. U.S. Bureau of the Census (1994: xiii; 1986: 5).

29. Jianakoplos and Menchik (1992: tables 6, 7).

30. *Economic Report of the President* (1994: 312). Women are moving in the opposite direction; in 1960, 48% of black women and 36% of white women were in the labor force, whereas in 1993, 58% of both races were working or seeking

work. Kasarda (1995) gives the best and most recent treatment of the structural causes of rising black unemployment. Chapters 8 and 11 of this book discuss poor African Americans' willingness to work.

31. In 1967, 11.8% of black men and 7.1% of white men reported no income. In 1992, the comparable figures were 12.7% and 4.4% (U.S. Bureau of the Census 1993a: B-28, B-29).

32. U.S. Bureau of the Census (1993c: 85, 86).

33. Ferleger and Mandle (1991: 6).

34. Lazere and Leonard (1989: 15); see also Lazere et al. (1991: 24); Leonard and Lazere (1992) for later years.

35. Lazere and Leonard (1989: 15).

36. Kasarda (1993: 266–68); see also Nathan and Dommel (1987: A-2); Jargowsky and Bane (1991: 252–53); Danziger and Gottschalk (1987: 213–14). Nathan and Adams (1989) and Ledebur and Barnes (1992) show that the disparities between central cities and their suburbs have grown steadily and sharply since 1970.

37. Virtually no well-off students of either race were below basic in math or reading proficiency (Burbridge 1991: 7, 9). In the mid-1980s poor urban black students at all ages read better than their predecessors did, but the two youngest groups (ages nine and thirteen) were no longer gaining on poor urban whites (Jones 1987: 7–8).

38. Kasarda (1993: 272–73. In 1970, however, three-quarters of black and white residents of severely poor neighborhoods were high school dropouts.

39. Data from U.S. Department of Justice (1994a: 16–18); 1973 and 1992 are the first and last years for which these data are available. DiIulio (1989) portrays the implications of these data in one representative city.

40. Data for 1962 and 1973 are from Featherman and Hauser (1978: 89, 326); 1978 data are from Cohen and Tyree (1986).

41. The corresponding probabilities for white daughters of recipients and nonrecipients are .261 and .066 (Gottschalk et al. 1994: 106; see also McLanahan 1988: 12–14; Gottschalk 1992).

42. See also Levy and Michel (1991); Karoly (1993: 45, 64–65); Villemez and Wiswell (1978).

43. See also Hochschild (1988: 177–81); Lichter and Eggebeen (1993: tables 4, 5); Morris et al. (1994: 212–15).

44. Massey and Eggers (1990: 1170–74).

45. Braddock and McPartland (1987: 16–17); Hauser (1990: 24–25).

46. Card and Lemieux (1993: table 5). Among men, both well-educated and poorly-educated blacks lost wages compared with similar white men over this period. Darity and Myers (1993: 8–12) show polarization by education in the labor force participation rate, especially among black men.

47. Olsen (1970); Greeley (1974); Farley (1992: chap. 7, 15–17); Kleppner (1982: 114–22); Nie et al. (1988: 11–14, fig. 3).

48. On births, see Hogan and Kitagawa (1985: 829); on deaths, see Pappas et al. (1993: 106). See also Menchik (1993: 435).

49. Sears and McConahay (1973); Caplan and Paige (1968); Fogelson and Hill (1968).

CHAPTER THREE
"WHAT'S ALL THE FUSS ABOUT?"

1. McClosky and Zaller (1984: 64–100, 116); Kluegel and Smith (1986: 112–13; GSS (1993: vars. 456, 464); Citrin et al. (1990: 1132).

2. Verba and Orren (1985: 72).

3. People for the American Way (1992: 57–59). Over 90% of both races agree that "get[ting] people to take responsibility for themselves rather than blaming others for their problems" would help solve America's racial problems (ibid.: 96–97).

4. Schuman et al. (1988: xii, xiv, 74–75, 144–45); NBC News (1989: vars. 20, 34); National Conference (1994: 22).

5. Roper (1986: vars. 29, 47, 59); New York State United Teachers (1991: 8). Many more blacks also agree that schools should teach "the separate histories and differences of America's racial and ethnic groups" (ibid.: 6). See also Schlozman and Verba (1979: 145, 166–69). As many blacks as whites (up to 90%) agree that a good education, ambition, and hard work are crucial to getting ahead; more blacks than whites add ability to the list (GSS 1987: vars. 507C-F). About 70% of both races agree that all Americans have equal educational opportunity (GSS 1984: var. 70).

It is intriguing, and alarming, in this context that over 60% of whites and almost 70% of blacks agree that "Americans are greatly divided when it comes to the most important values" (GSS 1993: var. 457A).

6. Rosen (1969: 143–47).

7. The postscript to this chapter explains my techniques for evaluating these surveys.

8. In addition to the survey data, see Beardwood (1968: 148); Hamilton (1982: 46–47); Aberbach and Walker (1970a: 379).

9. D. Garth Taylor (1991: ques. 2, 4, 14; 1992: ques. 341–43; 1993: 21, 37, 38; 1994: 30, 52–53). A more detailed look at the 1986 question about "the road to your American Dream" shows the same pattern: although blacks score lower than whites when estimating how far they have come toward achieving their dreams, they score higher in their expectations of how far they will ultimately get (Roper 1986: vars. 62, 64).

10. Survey Research Center (1964: vars. 50a, 50n); Marx (1964: vars. 50a, 50h, 50m); Campbell and Schuman (1968: vars. 176, 178); Roper (1986: var. 36). More blacks than whites insist that they have "a lot" of control over their children's future (Harris 1986b: var. C9). Kluegel and Smith (1986: 94) show no difference between whites and blacks in their attributions for personal circumstances.

11. "The Black Mood" (1970: 29); NSBA (1980: vars. 366–72, 512, 596–604, 736). See also Harris (1966a: vars. 2C, 3); Campbell and Schuman (1968: vars. 214–33); CBS News/*NYT* (1978: vars. 26, 42); Lewis and Schneider (1983: 13); *NYT*/WCBS News (1985: tables 26, 27, 32a, 33); Roper (1986: var. 30); *NYT* (1987: tables 26, 32, 36, 40–43); Gordon Black (1989a: vars. 1–9, 16); Marshall and Barnett (1991: 7); GSS (1990–91: vars. 422, 625H1); Gallup (1991a: vars. 16A–16D); Gallup (1991b: var. 12); *Los Angeles Times*

(1991a: var. 62); *Los Angeles Times* (1991b: var. 73); Yankelovich Clancy Shulman (1992: vars. 10, 11); People for the American Way (1992: 72); National Conference (1994: 28, 84–86, 100–102).

12. See citations in previous note. Whites are also less likely to perceive that they have been victimized by sexual harassment (Gallup 1991c: vars. 6A–6E).

13. Roper (1986: vars. 15–28). However, in all three years that they were queried, blacks agreed more than did whites that "to make money, there are no right and wrong ways any more" (GSS 1973; 1974; 1976: var. 175C).

14. Gallup (1964: vars. 28.1–28.8).

15. Hochschild (1988) formulates racial disparities in perceptions and beliefs somewhat differently.

16. Schlozman and Verba (1979: 167).

17. In 1946, 66% of whites but only 28% of blacks thought "most Negroes in the United States are being treated fairly" (Erskine 1962: 139). Four decades later, one-third as many whites as blacks thought being of the right race was crucial for getting ahead (GSS 1987: var. 507I). Whites' perceptions of women's opportunity "are more negative than are corresponding perceptions about blacks" (Kluegel and Smith 1986: 235–39; see also *NYT*/WCBS News 1985: var. 33; GSS 1987: var. 507L).

See also NORC (1944, vars. 01, 04, 05); Harris (1966a: var. 21a; 1966b: vars. 11D, 13.1–13.15, 14F, 14G, 16A, 18A); Campbell and Schuman (1968: var. 230); Harris (1978: 4–13, 26–34); CBS News/*NYT* (1978: vars. 10a, 11a, 12a, 13a, 20, 21, 25, 38, 39, 40); *NYT*/WCBS News (1985: vars. 20, 21, 32, 35b); Gallup (1987: 36; 1988: 23); Harris (1988: vars. A, D, F, G, N); Media General/AP (1988: var. RC06); Harris (1989b: 199–202, 213–20, 253–58); ABC News/*Washington Post* (1989: vars. 22.1, 24.1–24.5; 1991: var. 37); Gordon Black (1989a: vars. 11, 17; 1989b: var. 19); NBC News (1989: vars. 44, 74, 75); Sigelman and Welch (1991: 77); *Los Angeles Times* (1991b: var. 49); Gallup (1991b: vars. 9, 34A); Yankelovich Clancy Shulman (1992: var. 6); CBS News/*NYT* (1992: var. R21); People for the American Way (1992: 70–74, 154, 157, 159); *Washington Post* (1992: vars. 3k, 6, 9); D. Garth Taylor (1993: 20, 22, 23, 28; 1994: 29, 32, 39); "Thirty Years After" (1993); *NYT*/WCBS-TV Channel 2 News (1994: vars. 25, 27); Welch et al. (1994: 28–30); National Conference (1994: 16–19, 22, 84–86, 100–102).

18. ABC News/*Washington Post* (1989: var. 19); Gallup (1992: var. 16); "Thirty Years After" (1993).

19. Erskine (1962: 138; 1969a: 156); Hutcheson (1973: 56); Harris (1978: 56); CBS News/*NYT* (1978: var. 17); Converse et al. (1980: 79); *Los Angeles Times* (1983: tables 86, 94); Media General/AP (1988: vars. RC02, RC03, RC10); McLeod (1988b: A4); ABC News/*Washington Post* (1989: var. 17); *Los Angeles Times* (1991b: vars. 57, 58); Yankelovich Clancy Shulman (1992: var. 23); CBS News/*NYT* (1992: var. R29); People for the American Way (1992: 65–67, 155, 159); *Washington Post* (1992: var. 2).

20. In addition to the citations in the previous note, see Brink and Harris (1966: 222–31); Marx (1969: 5–11, 220); NSBA (1980: var. 1222); Joint Center for Political Studies (1984: table 2); Cavanagh (1985: 3); Schuman et al.

(1988: xiv, 141–43); Brown et al. (1994: table 15.9); Gallup (1988: var 4; 1994: var. 30).

21. *NYT*/WCBS-TV Channel 2 News (1993: 11; 1994: 1). Presumably the presence of David Dinkins and then Rudy Giuliani in the mayor's office had a lot to do with the changes in both sets of views. For another case in which blacks' increasing gratification is paralleled by whites' increasing dissatisfaction, see Abramowitz and Morin (1994).

22. *Los Angeles Times* (1983: table 86); Roper (1986: var. 38); Media General/AP (1988: var. RC03); *Los Angeles Times* (1991b: vars. 57, 59, 64); CBS News/*NYT* (1992: vars. R30, R31); People for the American Way (1992: 67–70).

23. In addition to the citations in the previous note, see Brink and Harris (1966: 258–59); Marx (1969: 13–15, 220); CBS News/*NYT* (1978: var. 48); Brown et al. (1994: table 7.6).

In this context, it is not surprising that the proportion of whites who agree that our nation is moving toward two racially unequal and separate societies has *decreased* since 1968 (from 36 to 33%) while the proportion of blacks who agree has *increased* (from 31 to 52%) ("Thirty Years After" 1993).

24. Harris (1966b: vars. 11B, 18I; 1970a: var. 12A; 1970b: 11A); Schuman et al. (1988: 118–19).

25. Harris (1966a: vars. 21D; 1966b: var. 14E); GSS (1982: var. 148A, 148B); *NYT*/WCBS News (1985: var. 49); Gallup (1988, var. 4); McLeod (1988b: A4); Harris (1988: vars. A, N); ABC News/*Washington Post* (1989: var. 25); GSS (1990–91: var. 621A, F, G, H); *Los Angeles Times* (1991b: tables 57, 58, 59, 64); Gallup (1992: var. 10).

26. Gordon Black (1989a: vars. 18, 19; 1989b: vars. 1, 2). See also citations in previous note.

African Americans perhaps see more polarization by class on the second tenet than do whites. On the one hand, more blacks believe that the number of rich Americans is increasing (ABC News/*Washington Post* 1990: var. 14). On the other hand, more blacks believe that "the lot of the average man [*sic*] is getting worse" (GSS 1973; 1974; 1976–77; 1983; 1984–85; 1987; 1988–89; 1990–91: var. 176B).

27. Brink and Harris (1966: 220, 258); Goldman (1969: 231); Schuman et al. (1988: xiii, xiv, 118–19, 146–47); Harris (1989b: 114, 208; 1989c: 79); NBC News (1989: var. 69); Gallup (1991b: var. 5). Over the past three decades, the modal white has shifted from concern about civil rights moving too fast to satisfaction with the pace, whereas the modal black has shifted from satisfaction with the pace to concerns about sluggishness.

The proportion of whites who agree that "civil rights groups are asking for too much" has risen since 1963 from 42 to 47%. (It also rose among blacks, but the order of magnitude is entirely different—from 3 to 7%) ("Thirty Years After" 1993).

28. Shingles (1981:84); Carr and Hudgins (n.d.); Harris (1989b: 192, 196, 275, 279); Harris (1989c: 285, 297); National Conference (1994: 68).

29. GSS (1972–73; 1974; 1976–77; 1980; 1982; 1984–85; 1987; 1988–89; 1991–92: var. 197). See also GSS (1984: vars. 69B, C, D, G); Schlozman

and Verba (1979: 167); Verba and Orren (1985: 73–77); Kluegel and Smith (1986: 90–100); People for the American Way (1992: 151).

30. GSS (1987: vars. 507A–507M; 1993: var. 458).

31. This table focuses only on what are commonly called individualist explanations for racial disparities. Individualists, however, often give structural explanations as well (Kluegel and Smith 1986: 201; Sigelman and Welch 1991: 94–107).

32. Roper (1986: vars. 75, 77); People for the American Way (1992: 50–51, 153).

33. Commonly, however, half or more of both races attribute sinfulness as well as failure to the poor, and virtue or special abilities to the rich. For evidence on tenets 3 and 4, see NORC (1950: vars. 18A, 18C); Middleton (1963: 976); Survey Research Center (1964: vars. 13C, 13D); Marx (1964: vars. 50D, 50I); Alston and Dean (1972: 20); Huber and Form (1973: 110); GSS (1972–73: var. 175C); GSS (1983: var. 68H); Lewis and Schneider (1985: 7); "Opinion Roundup" (1985: 28); Kluegel and Smith (1986: 97); GSS (1987: var. 510C); NBC News (1989: var. 2B); ABC News/*Washington Post* (1990: vars. 13A–13H); GSS (1990–91: var. 391B); People for the American Way (1992: 61, 154); "Public Opinion and Demographic Report" (1993c: 86).

34. Cruse (1987: 389).

35. African Americans may be ahead of white Americans in understanding the racially based threat to American stability. We saw earlier that many more blacks than whites think that over half of whites share the views of the Ku Klux Klan. But it is also the case that more blacks (24%) than whites (17%) think that *blacks* hold "racist attitudes toward whites" (ABC News/*Washington Post* 1989: var. 20).

36. Hochschild (1981: 241–42) demonstrates this quandary in one person's reasoning.

37. Harris (1978: 52); CBS News/*NYT* (1978: var. 21); Schlozman and Verba (1979: 169); Roper (1986: var. 38); Harris (1988: ques. 1C, 1D; 1989b: 198–202, 213, 271; 1989c: 47, 53, 56, 59, 94, 272); GSS (1990–91: var. 422); *Los Angeles Times* (1991b: vars. 49, 50); Sniderman et al. (1991: var. skin); People for the American Way (1992: 52, 72–74); *Washington Post* (1992: var. 3g); MCIC (1991–94: vars. 424, 425).

38. Thus only 55% of whites, compared with 77% of blacks, agree that it is "very urgent" that America "honestly faces the issue of race." These results are probably inflated for whites by the fact that the question comes at the end of a long interview about race in America (National Conference 1994: 36). Almost the only institution that provides an explanation of this quandary is white supremicist groups, which argue that secret cabals of Jews or African Americans (or Catholics, in an earlier era) are manipulating the system to deprive whites of their deserved rewards. With friends like this, the American dream does not need enemies.

39. Dawson (1994); Gurin et al. (1989); Tate (1993).

40. Roper (1986: vars. 13, 14, 29, 49–57, 60, 61–64).

41. Apart from substantive differences in views, surveys produce different results because of variations in question and response wording, question place-

ment, methods of sample selection, interviewer training, and survey techniques. Race complicates survey research even more, since more undesired variation is introduced in selecting a sample of a scattered and relatively small population like African Americans, in the choice of black or white interviewers, in the phrasing of sensitive questions to make them acceptable to both races, and in different rates of trust in the whole survey enterprise. Sampling *within* each individual's set of beliefs generates yet another source of variation (Zaller 1992).

In the end, I judge that more variation is explained by which survey organization conducted the poll or who sponsored it than by anything else (the phenomenon is known in the trade as "house effects"). That is why I report results from as many different survey organizations and sponsors as possible.

CHAPTER FOUR
"SUCCEEDING MORE" AND "UNDER THE SPELL"

1. I borrowed the construction from the cigarette advertisement with the tag line, "Smoking more and enjoying it less?" (via Aaron Wildavsky's description of the politics of American health care: "doing better and feeling worse").

2. The phrase comes from Myrdal (1944: 4): "The American Negroes know that they are a subordinated group experiencing, more than anybody else in the nation, the consequences of the fact that the [American] Creed is not lived up to in America. Yet their faith in the Creed is not simply a means of pleading their unfulfilled rights. They, like the whites, are *under the spell of the great national suggestion*. With one part of themselves they actually believe, as do the whites, that the Creed is ruling America" (emphasis added).

3. When referring to survey data that I have analyzed, this book has precise meanings for the terms poor (badly off), well off (affluent, middle class), well educated, poorly educated, high status, and low status. "Poor" and "well-off" whites or blacks are those whose family incomes are in the lowest or highest thirds of their race, respectively, in the sample for a given survey. Poorly educated blacks or whites are survey respondents with less than a high school education; well-educated blacks or whites are respondents with more than a high school education. When I refer to high- (or low-) status people, I am indicating that both the highly (poorly) educated subset of the sample in a given survey *and* the richest (poorest) third of that sample hold a particular view. For more detail on how the surveys were categorized and why I made those choices, see appendix A.

4. *NYT*/WCBS News (1985: vars. 20, 21, 45); CBS News/*NYT* (1978: vars. 10a, 11a, 12a, 13a, 17, 20, 21, 38, 39, 40, 48); NSBA (1980: var. 368); Denton and Sussman (1981); Parent and Stekler (1985: 533); Gilliam (1986: 56); Brown et al. (1994: tables 15.7, 15.9); Gallup (1988: vars. Q20, Q22); Media General/AP (1988: vars. RC02, RC06, RC10); Adams and Dressler (1988: 760); Harris (1988: ques. D, N); Harris (1989b: 105–61 passim); Gordon Black (1989a: vars. 11, 12, 17, 29B); NBC News (1989: vars. 44, 74, 75); ABC News/*Washington Post* (1989: var. 22.1; 1991: var. 37); GSS (1990–91: vars. 395B, 396B); *Los Angeles Times* (1991b: vars. 50, 64); *Washington Post* (1992: vars. 1, 2, 3E, 9); Yankelovich Clancy Shulman (1992: vars. 6, 23); Gallup (1992: var. 12); CBS News/*NYT* (1992: vars. 29, 30, 31); Gallup (1994: var. 30).

5. Campbell and Schuman (1968: vars. 206–21, 225–27, 259–60, 262–64, 270–72); CBS News/*NYT* (1978: vars. 10b, 11b, 12b, 42); NSBA (1980: vars. 346, 512, 598, 736); Lewis and Schneider (1983: 13); *NYT*/WCBS News (1985: vars. 26, 27); Adams and Dressler (1988: 760); Gordon Black (1989a: vars. 1, 4, 6, 7, 8, 9, 16); Marshall and Barnett (1991: 18); GSS (1990–91: var. 625H1); Gallup (1991a: vars. 16A–16D; 1991b: vars. 12, 34A); *Los Angeles Times* (1991b: var. 73); Yankelovich Clancy Shulman (1992: vars. 10, 11); CBS News/*NYT* (1992: vars. 20, 21).

6. Harris (1989b: 400–401).

7. See citations in notes 4 and 5, as well as People for the American Way (1992: 68, 71–72). For mixed results, see Schuman and Hatchett (1974: 58–59, 68–73); NSBA (1980: var. 1222); Sigelman and Welch (1991: 71–75). For counterevidence, see NSBA (1980: var. 1223); *NYT*/WCBS News (1985: vars. 26, 27).

A study of six ethnic groups (Jews, Irish, WASPs, blacks, Cubans, Dominicans, and Puerto Ricans) in New York City found that "among all groups, it is the middle-class respondents that tend to perceive ethnic bias in city government and their groups as the victims of this bias" (Robert Smith 1988: 183).

8. Media General/AP (1988: var. Q10).

9. GSS (1987: vars. 507H, I, J, L).

10. Brown et al. (1994: tables 8.3, 1984 and 1988; 16.3, 17.7); Dawson (1994b: 79, 92–93); National Conference (1994: 43–45).

Well off whites generally perceive more racial discrimination than do poor whites (NORC 1944: vars. 01, 04, 05A; Campbell and Schuman 1968: var. 230; *NYT*/WCBS News 1985: vars. 20, 35b, 45; Gallup 1988: var. Q20, Q22; Harris 1988; 1989c: vars. 2–1, 2–3, 2–5, 3–2, 6A, 12A–1, 12A–4, 5, 6, 12B, 15A; Gordon Black 1989b: var. 19; GSS 1990–91: vars. 395B, 396B). However, in a few surveys they do not (Sigelman and Welch 1991; *NYT*/WCBS News 1985: vars. 21, 32; National Conference 1994: 43–45).

11. Matthews and Prothro (1961: vars. 433, 434, 436); Brink and Harris (1964: 194); Murphy and Watson (1970: 201–12). As the authors of one survey put it, "the occupational groups [among black respondents] predictably differed. *Quite naturally*, the unemployed and the unskilled were more concerned about jobs and more condemnatory of police than the higher-income groups" (McCord et al. 1969: 94, emphasis added).

12. For example, in 1950 "feelings of hostility, insulation, and apathy tended to be higher among the older, *the less well-educated*, the less participant, and the Southern-born Negroes. . . . Articulate progressive sentiments about race relations were likely to be stated by the younger and *better-educated* community members who expressed sentiments of militancy, relative friendliness toward the outgroup, and a belief in the desirability of integration" (Williams 1964: 253, emphasis added). Low-status blacks also preferred to keep considerable social distance between themselves and whites, expressed more frustration, and were more likely to believe that the whole race was blamed when an individual black "did something wrong" (ibid.: 258–62; Westie and Howard 1954; Murphy and Watson 1970: 202–13).

These attitudes began to change by the end of the 1960s, judging from the extant survey results (Banks 1950; Cothran 1951; McDaniel and Babchuk 1960; Marx 1964: vars. Q7, Q27; Brink and Harris 1964: 54–58, 190; Noel and Pinkney 1964: 612; Harris 1966a: vars. 2C, 6F, 21C.1–21C.4, 21D, 27C, 27E, 27G; Campbell and Schuman 1968: vars. 206, 214, 265, 270; McCord et al. 1969: 99; Goldman 1969: 245–46; Huber and Form 1973: 93; Schuman and Hatchett 1974: 64–65; Carter 1990: 277).

Detailed series of questions suggest a caveat. When asked about arenas especially important to the middle class, better-off blacks saw more discrimination than worse-off blacks did even in the 1960s. For example, in 1968 highly educated blacks perceived more business tokenism, fewer chances for promotion, and more discrimination in government and educational hiring than did poorly educated blacks (Campbell and Schuman 1968: vars. 262, 266–69; see also Harris 1966a: 21A.1–21A.6).

13. Brink and Harris (1964: 126) show that in 1963 a much higher proportion of "rank and file" respondents than of black "leaders" agreed that whites want to keep blacks down. That disparity between optimistic black leaders and suspicious black laypeople was also reversed by the 1980s.

14. Similar sets of questions produce similar reversals over time. In 1968 fewer poorly-educated than well-educated blacks agreed that "few white people dislike Negroes." By 1983 more poor than well-off blacks thought that "most white people like [me]" (Campbell and Schuman 1968: var. 317; Lewis and Schneider 1983: 13). In 1968 more poorly-educated than well-educated blacks trusted no whites, but fifteen years later more poor than well-off blacks claimed to like white people (Schuman and Hatchett 1974: 64; Lewis and Schneider 1983: 13).

15. Kluegel and Smith (1986: 67). In 1963 only 9% of "rank and file" blacks, compared with 30% of black "leaders," claimed that discrimination had given them an "inferiority complex," made them "uneasy" and "resentful," or produced "no ambition to further [them]selves" (Brink and Harris 1964: 190; see also Huber and Form 1973: 87).

16. The other proffered explanations were lack of jobs, lack of help from various levels of government, and lack of concern for "people like you" (Harris 1989b: 388, 394 [no comparisons with other racial or class groups are possible]). Throughout the 1980s, fewer than 5% of black New Yorkers saw race relations as their city's worst problem (*NYT*/WCBS News 1985: var. 4; *NYT* 1987: ques. 1; *NYT*/WCBS-TV News 1989a: ques. 15; *NYT*/CBS News 1989: ques. 2). After a surge of attention to "race relations" during David Dinkins' mayoralty, black New Yorkers again were focusing on other problems by the end of 1993 (*NYT*/WCBS-TV Channel 2 News 1993: ques. 15). For similar results see Campbell and Schuman (1968: vars. 188, 189) and Schlozman and Verba (1979: 186).

17. More specialized surveys reinforce my claim of middle-class optimism during the 1960s. For example, among blacks who had experienced discrimination in 1967, those with little education mistrusted the political system more than than those with a lot (Aberbach and Walker 1970b). Three-fifths or more of seniors in traditionally black colleges agreed in 1968 that Negro college graduates were likely to get at least as good a job as whites in most professional settings (Harris 1968: records 55, 73). See also Searles and Williams (1962).

18. Academic writings about race also demonstrate plummeting optimism among the best-off. Until the 1960s, "studies by black scholars always tended to

be more positive and optimistic [than those by whites] about the possibilities for improvement [in race relations] and advancement [of blacks' condition]. . . . For most of these researchers, . . . integration of blacks and whites was inevitable, despite the objections of most whites and some blacks. Therefore progress in breaking down barriers to black advancement through greater desegregation was a constant source of optimism" (Franklin 1985: 20, 22). Starting in the 1960s, black scholars became more pessimistic and skeptical of the desirability of desegregation than the rest of the black population or than most white scholars of race.

19. Judgments of chances for political success differ slightly from judgments of chances for economic success. Poor African Americans have always been much less satisfied than better-off African Americans with their *own* chance to influence the government (Matthews and Prothro 1961: var. 428; Langton and Jennings 1972: 63; Aberbach and Walker 1970b; Wright 1976: 141, 176–81; Campbell 1980: 655; Shingles 1981: 84; Brown et al. 1994: tables 3.3, 1984 and 1988; 3.4, 1984 and 1988; 11.10, 11.11, 11.12; GSS 1987: vars. 337, 340; Colasanto 1988: 46; Gurin et al. 1989: 294; Smith and Seltzer 1992: 56). But better-off blacks have always been less satisfied with *their race*'s chance for political influence. In particular, high-status blacks are more likely than low-status blacks to think that their race has too little, and whites have too much, political influence (Gallup 1961: var. 05C; 1964: var. 14C; NSBA 1980: var. 1217; GSS 1987, var. 353, Brown et al. 1994: tables 13.10, 1984 and 1988; 6.5, 1984 and 1988; 6.7, 1984 and 1988; 18.12; GSS 1990–91: var. 394; Dawson 1994b: 95; Reese and Brown forthcoming: tables 1–3). For possible counterevidence, depending on how one interprets the questions, see Brown et al. (1994: tables 3.7, 1984 and 1988; 3.8, 1984 and 1988; 3.11, 1984 and 1988). For clear counterevidence, see ibid. (table 3.9, 1984 and 1988).

20. The two paradoxes roughly obtain when African Americans consider the effects of class discrimination. In the 1960s middle-class blacks were more convinced than were poor blacks that even the poor could succeed (if we can rely on one survey), but from the mid-1970s on, middle-class blacks were no more and sometimes less convinced of class-based equality of opportunity (Huber and Form 1973: 91; Schlozman and Verba 1979: 168, 170; Roper 1986: var. 42, 46; GSS 1987: vars. 507A, 507B; GSS 1990–91: var. 387D; Brown et al. 1994: table 6.10). One survey (Harris 1989b: 193, 276; 1989c: 288) has the opposite finding.

Whites are less predictable. In the 1960s and 1970s middle-class whites resembled middle-class blacks in their relative confidence about the chances of the poor (Huber and Form 1973: 91; Schlozman and Verba 1979: 168, 170), but surveys in the 1980s show conflicting results (Roper 1986: vars. 42, 46; GSS 1987: vars. 507A, 507B; 1990–91: var. 387D).

There are too few questions, with no clear trends, to say anything about how different race/class groups view the issue of opportunity for different genders (Roper 1986: var. 45; GSS 1987: var. 507L).

21. See also Gurin et al. (1989: 168–69, 187–90, 288–89); Dawson (1994b: 94).

22. Pettigrew (1964: 185); Brink and Harris (1966: 222–30); Harris

(1966a: vars. 1A.1–1A.8, 1C); Campbell and Schuman (1968: var. 159); Goldman (1969: 229–30); NSBA (1980: vars. 75, 1494); GSS (1972–73, 1982, 1987, 1990–91: var. 187B; 1987: var. 517); Gallup (1988: var. 3A–3E); GSS (1990–91: var. 625C5); Sniderman et al. (1991: var. finc.). The main exception is Roper (1986: var. 63) (with a small black sample).

23. Middle-class blacks are at least as personally optimistic as are middle-class whites, and poor blacks are more personally optimistic than are poor whites. For example, almost half of affluent black Chicagoans expect to own a business, compared with only a fourth or fewer of the other race/class groups. This occurs despite the fact that fewer middle-class blacks than whites have ever owned a business (MCIC 1991–94: vars. 406, 407). See notes to table 3.1 as well as Harris (1966a: var. 1B.1–1B.8); Harris Organization (1970a: var. 22.18; 1970b: var. 20R); Gallup (1971, var. 4E); NSBA (1980: var. 349).

24. Jacqueline Rahlins again speaks for many in her fierce aspirations for her children: "I accept life. . . . You might as well make the best of it, right? And hope that with the four kids that I got, to make it better for them. Don't brood back on what you have gone through. Think about your kids that you got, to go on forward. . . . My kids is my push, you know what I mean? They should live in a better neighborhood, have their own things, get educated, and get as high as they can. And I'll work my butt to try and see to that" (Ezekiel 1984: 25).

Fully three-fourths of deeply poor black urbanites "see hope" for their children "to do better in life than you" (and an additional 10% were not sure) (Harris 1989b: 399–401).

25. *Los Angeles Times* (1991a: var. 31; see also var. 30); see also Roper (1986: vars. 4, 9, 29) and table 4.3.

26. Harris (1970a: var. 1a; 1970b: var. 1a).

27. Lewis and Schneider (1985: 6, 7, 59); Roper (1986: var. 46).

28. Since then, poor African Americans have become slightly less discouraged and well-off African Americans slightly more so, so the two groups have converged (GSS 1972–73, 1974, 1976–77, 1980, 1982, 1984–85, 1987, 1988–89, and 1990–91: var. 176B). See also Austin and Stack (1988: 363–66); Austin and Dodge (1990).

29. In 1968, 70% or more of seniors in traditionally black colleges agreed that Negroes were doing better in job opportunities, pay, housing, children's schooling, and voting. As many black as white college seniors considered entering or expected to enter graduate school or careers in business, teaching, engineering, and social work (Harris 1968: records 43, 47; 1969: records 43, 48). We lack comparable data on poor blacks, but these results reinforce the finding in table 4.4 of a lot of optimism and confidence among young middle-class African Americans during the late 1960s.

30. Despite their *relative* gratification, badly-off African Americans, like well-off African Americans, are generally skeptical about the prospects of success for their race. Thus neither income group contradicts the findings of chapter 3 that blacks do not much trust the second tenet of the American dream when it does not refer to them personally. See Schlozman and Verba (1979) for a similar analysis.

Both paradoxes recur in African Americans' evaluations of their race's chances for political success. In 1961 well-off blacks scored race relations in their community over the previous five years 4.1 out of 10. They predicted a score of 8.0 five years hence. Poor blacks scored past race relations higher (4.6) but future race relations lower (7.1) (Matthews and Prothro 1961: vars. 404, 406; see also Campbell and Schuman 1968: vars. 258, 265, 271, 318). But by 1976 twice as many poor as well-off blacks thought there had been a lot of civil rights change (Parent and Stekler 1985: 530; see also Gallup 1991b: var. 5). Similarly, in the 1960s more well-off than poor blacks were hopeful about white attitudes toward "Negro rights"; by 1984 slightly more well-off than poor blacks doubted that American blacks will "ever achieve full social and economic equality" (Brink and Harris 1964: 130; 1966: 258; Brown et al. 1994: table 7.6; Sigelman and Welch 1991: 76).

31. McClosky and Zaller (1984: 92).

32. Killian and Grigg (1962: 663).

33. Matthews and Prothro (1961: var. 427); Marx (1964: var. 50L); Survey Research Center (1964: var. 50m); GSS (1972–73, 1974, 1976: var. 176A). See also Middleton (1963: 976); Campbell and Schuman (1968: vars. 176–78); Bullough (1972: 88). In all the surveys, whites showed the same class pattern but much lower levels of agreement.

34. Campbell et al. (1976: 453–54); see also Marx (1964: var. 50h); Survey Research Center (1964: var. 66b); NSBA (1980: vars. 72, 73).

35. Roper (1986: var. 36); see also NSBA (1980: vars. 78, 79, 81); Hughes and Demo (1989: 146–47); Gloria Johnson (1989: 38–41).

36. Marx (1964: vars. 50a, 50m). Poor blacks may have simply been responding to the tautalogous nature of these assertions. If so, they were more observant than high-status blacks, of whom about 10% fewer agreed with each statement. See also Survey Research Center (1964: vars. 50a, 50n).

37. Poor whites are slightly *less* inclined than well-off whites to attribute success to hard work (GSS 1972–73, 1974, 1976–77, 1980, 1982, 1984–85, 1987, 1988–89, 1990–91: var. 197; 1993: var. 458; for counterevidence see Survey Research Center 1964: var. 50I).

38. See also Parent (1985: 14); Broman (1989b: 7–8); Allen et al. (1989: 432); Hughes and Demo (1989: 145); Denton and Sussman (1981: A2); Sigelman and Welch (1991: 113–16); People for the American Way (1992: 77, 97). Brown et al. (1994: table 15.2) and Sigelman and Welch (1991: 111–13) neither confirm nor contradict it. Jackman and Jackman (1983: 56) contradict it (but note small cell sizes for blacks and self-identification as the criterion for class placement).

39. See also Richard Allen (1994).

40. Explanations of class inequality show different patterns: among whites, more well-off than poor blame the poor and praise the rich for their respective circumstances. Among blacks, in the 1960s the well-off also blamed the poor and praised the rich more than did the poor. But by the 1980s that pattern had disappeared, and none has emerged to take its place (Survey Research Center 1964: var. 13C; Marx 1964: vars. 50D, 50H; Alston and Dean 1972: 15; Huber

and Form 1973: 101, 106; GSS 1972–73: var. 197; Schlozman and Verba 1979: 168; Jackman and Jackman 1983: 56; GSS 1984: var. 68H; Lewis and Schneider 1985: 6–7; Kluegel and Smith 1986: 95–100; Harris 1986: table 5; Gallup 1988: var 16; Harris 1989b: 164, 261; 1989c: 240; GSS 1990–91: vars. 197, 443A–C).

41. Roper (1986: vars. 15–28). Poor whites care more about religious beliefs than do well-off whites; otherwise they are no more morally inclined (ibid.; GSS 1993: var. 464).

42. The first and third times that they were queried, poor blacks agreed less than well-off blacks that "there are no right and wrong ways . . . to make money, only easy and hard ways." But the second time they agreed more. Poor whites consistently agreed less than did well-off whites (GSS 1972–73, 1974, 1976: var. 175C). GSS (1993: var. 464) also suggests that poor blacks focus more on material well-being in setting their goals than do well-off blacks or all whites, but that question gives no information on moral stances.

43. Gallup (1964: vars. 28.1–28.8); Roper (1986: vars. 65–81).

44. Unlike with earlier tenets, a focus on class shows clearer patterns with regard to the fourth tenet than does a focus on race. Well-off blacks attribute more virtue to the rich and immorality to the poor (of any race) than do badly-off blacks. Well-off whites are only slightly more inclined than poor whites to see the poor as immoral or the rich as moral. These are surprising findings, and they highlight the importance of race in evaluations of the American dream. That is, well-off African Americans—who are usually the most skeptical about the dream—endorse it in this case; well-off whites—who usually endorse the dream—are skeptical in this case (NORC 1950: vars. 18A, 18C; Middleton 1963: 976; Survey Research Center 1964: var. 13C; Marx 1964: vars. 50D, 50I; Alston and Dean 1972: 20; Huber and Form 1973: 110; GSS 1972–73: var. 175C; Lewis and Schneider 1985: 7; Kluegel and Smith 1986: 97; GSS 1987: var. 510C; NBC News 1989: var. 2B; GSS 1990–91, var. 391B).

45. For a similar alarm, absent my ambivalence about the value of the American dream, see People for the American Way (1992: e.g., 52).

46. Katz (1988).

CHAPTER FIVE
BELIEFS ABOUT ONE'S OWN LIFE

1. McClain (1986: 12–14).

2. Campbell (1984); Klose (1984); Page (1986).

3. Campbell et al. (1976: 448–53, 463, 467–68); Schlozman and Verba (1979: 164); NSBA (1980: vars. 9, 994, 995); St. George and McNamara (1984); Jackson et al. (1986: 199–205); Neighbors (1986: 786–89); Broman (1989b: 57); Crohan et al. (1989: 228–31); Johnson (1989: 38–41); Pryor Brown et al. (1989: 146–47); Ellison and Gay (1990: 131–33); David Williams et al. (1992: 186–89). A. Wade Smith (1985: 48) shows mixed results; Mirowsky and Ross (1980) and Kessler and Neighbors (1986) have contradictory results.

4. Levy (1987: 47–66); Levy and Michel (1991: 46); U.S. Bureau of the Census (1993a: B-6; 1993c: ix); *Economic Report of the President* (1994: 323).

5. Levy (1987: 81). No data are provided for women.

6. Hout (1988: 1383). "Both the upward and the downward mobility of women remained unchanged in the 1970s and early 1980s. For women, upward mobility exceeds downward mobility by about 160%." No data are available for women's mobility in the 1960s.

7. Newman (1993); Rubin (1994).

8. Quotation is from Morin (1991: C1); data are from Duncan et al. (1993: 246–47). We see middle-class meltdown in wealth holdings as well as in income. Only a third of adult men whose wealth put them in the third or fourth quintile of the overall distribution of wealth in 1966 remained in the same (relative) places by 1981 (Jianakoplos and Menchik 1992: table 2).

9. Duncan et al. (1993: 248–50); see also Mishel and Bernstein (1992: 6–9).

10. Ibid.: 261–63; Jianakoplos and Menchik (1992: table 2); Wolff (1993: 5–14).

The proximate cause of middle-class meltdown lies in returns to education and jobs. College graduates earned much more compared with high school graduates at the end of the 1980s compared with the beginning (Murphy and Welch 1989: fig. 1; Juhn et al. 1991: 115–16). The earnings gap also increased between more and less skilled workers during the 1980s after declining in the 1970s (Blackburn et al. 1990. 32, Ryscavage and Henle 1990: 13). Finally, be tween 1974 and 1988 the unemployment rate for white male college graduates barely changed, but it doubled for those with twelve or fewer years of education (Blackburn et al. 1990: 38).

11. Hout (1988).

12. Duncan et al. (1993: 253–55, 261–63).

13. Jianakoplos and Menchik (1992: table 2). Blacks in the middle moved up or down the income scale for the same proximate reasons as whites—growing gaps in returns to education and jobs, and growing gaps in rates of unemployment (Meisenheimer 1990: 19–20; Acs and Danziger 1993; Cotton 1990: 8; see also chapter 2, section on "Polarization").

14. Explanations for these patterns abound. See Levy (1987); Vroman (1991); Bluestone (1990); Blackburn et al. (1990); Shelley Smith (1991); Levy and Michel (1991); Ryscavage et al. (1992); Bound and Johnson (1991); Green et al. (1991); Bound and Freeman (1992); Levy and Murnane (1992); Ruggles and Stone (1992); Katz (1992/93); Smolensky and Plotnick (1993).

15. Hirschman (1981: 42–43).

16. Newman (1988).

17. Danziger (1991: 148). Similarly, throughout the 1980s over twice as many black as white college graduates (especially men) were unemployed, although the absolute numbers were small (Wilson et al. 1993; Harrison and Bennett 1995: 185–87).

18. *City of Richmond* v. *J. A. Croson* (1989); the quotation is from Hinds (1991: A1). The effect on minority-owned businesses probably was not as drastic as the quotation suggests (Ward 1991; Goodman et al. 1993), and well-done

disparity studies can take the sting out of *Croson* (Rice 1992; Halligan 1991). What matters here, however, is the widespread perception that *Croson* devastated black businesses.

19. U.S. Bureau of the Census (1993b: 405). Despite common perceptions, the proportion of black men employed in the public sector actually rose from 1980 to 1990, even though it declined for white men and all women. But black men's wages in federal government jobs declined dramatically over the decade, both in actual dollar amounts and as a proportion of white male federal employees' wages (Zipp 1994: 368–72).

20. Collins (1983: 375; 1993); Work (1980); GAO (1994: 8–15).

21. Kuttner (1983); Brandt et al. (1985); Thurow (1986); "This Time, the Downturn" (1990: 130); Peterson (1992).

22. In 1975 only 20% of professionals and managers described themselves as upper middle or upper class—about as many as said they were poor or in the working class (Jackman and Jackman 1983: 73).

23. Pear (1983); McLeod (1988a); Dingle (1987); Updegrave (1989); Hicks (1991).

24. Riley (1986: 17–18, ellipsis in original).

25. Fernandez (1981: 172).

26. One fourth of middle-class white respondents felt economically vulnerable, and 19% identified with the "have-nots" (Lewis and Schneider 1983: 13).

27. Two-thirds of poorly educated blacks, 43% of poorly educated whites, and 35% of well-educated whites concurred (Harris 1989b: 143, 239).

28. One-third of low-income blacks and high-income whites, and 16% of low-income whites, agreed (Harris 1988: var. C).

29. These are results of responses to surveys periodically included in the magazine [hereafter cited as *BE*] (*BE* 1980: 49, 97; 1985: 95, 96; 1990: 78, 85). Mail-back surveys (see also the 1980 *Essence Magazine* survey analyzed later in this chapter) have a bad reputation among survey researchers. It is entirely deserved if one thinks of them as efforts on-the-cheap to report the views of a representative sample of some population (as the magazines themselves unfortunately often report them). They are, however, windows into the views of politically significant people. Magazine readers who return inserts are well-read, organized, comfortable with taking initiatives, interested in making their views known, politically intense. Thus mail-back surveys may tap the views of "opinion leaders," who are crucial to politics' "two-step flow of information." These concepts have been in, then out, of favor among political scientists and are now coming back into use (Weimann 1991; Carmines and Stimson 1989: 106–14; Zaller 1992).

30. Fernandez (1975: 157); Bowman (1991a: 146); GSS (1977–78, 1982, 1985–86, 1988–89, 1990–91: vars. 178, 179); MCIC (1991–94: var. 358). In virtually all of these surveys, many fewer high-income whites fear for their job or worry about replacing it.

31. About 10% of high-status whites concurred (GSS 1972–73, 1982, 1987, 1990–91: var. 182B; see also NSBA 1980: var. 361). High-status blacks are much more likely than high-status whites (but not more than low-status blacks)

to declare financial security one of their most important goals (GSS 1993: var. 464).

32. E.g., Cose (1993).

33. Howard and Hammond (1985); Steele (1990); Loury (1985).

34. Sixty percent of black students at Princeton University claim to have been "questioned on . . . [their] merit because of . . . [their] race/ethnicity." Half of Latinos, one-fourth of Asians, and 4% of whites concurred (Hall-Valdez et al. 1992: 3).

35. Furthermore, in this view, the very demand for affirmative action policies perpetuates racial subordination: "There can be no moral equality where there is a dependency relationship among men; there will always be a dependency relationship where the victim strives for equality by vainly seeking the assistance of his victimizer. No oppressor can ever respect such a victim, whatever he may do for him, including the provision of complete economic equality. In situations like these we can expect sympathy, even magnanimity from men, but never—and it is unfair to expect otherwise—the genuine respect which one equal feels for another" (Patterson 1973: 52). To Patterson this perspective implies "constructive public rebellion" in which blacks and others with "a potentially common class interest" create "a total, almost revolutionary change in American society." More typically it is a plea for renunciation of government handouts and rejection of the "outmoded" civil rights leadership (Loury 1985; Kemp 1990).

36. Glazer (1975); Eastland and Bennett (1979); Fullinwider (1980); Rosenfeld (1991); Nieli (1991); Ezorsky (1991).

37. Stephen Carter (1991: 58) makes the most forceful claim that this is precisely what blacks do: "We cannot afford, ever, to let our standards slip. There are too many doubters waiting in the wings to pop out at the worst possible moment and cry, 'See? Told you!' The only way to keep them off the stage is to make our own performances so good that there is no reasonable possibility of calling them into question. It isn't fair that so much should be demanded of us, but what has life to do with fairness?" He offers, however, no evidence. See Leonard (1984) for one of the few solid studies of the economic impact of affirmative action.

38. Wilkerson (1989b: 30).

39. America and Anderson (1979: 46). For black concurrence, see Hosea Martin (1991); for participants' thoughtful, and mixed, views on affirmative action, see Clayton and Crosby (1992: 106–25); Bron Taylor (1991: 90–112).

40. Austin et al. (1977); Chacko (1982); Heilman et al. (1987); Nacoste (1985; 1989). In Nacoste's 1985 study, even those with low estimates of their own performances did not in fact perform worse than others; the other studies did not address this issue.

41. The experimental manipulations produced different patterns of self-esteem and attributions of prejudice among whites (Crocker et al. 1991: 223–27).

42. Miller and Turnbull (1986: 234–50). As one beleaguered worker put it, "A person, no matter . . . how prejudiced they are, they see you trying, whether they like you or not, they'll help you in a roundabout way. And if you continue

to prove yourself, and you get what it takes to get you up there, and you climb and strive and work for it, believe it or not they'll help you instead of kicking you. . . . If you earn respect you'll get it" (Bron Taylor 1991: 226, ellipses in original.)

43. Nacoste (1994: 94–95).

44. Twice as many whites thought affirmative action was damaging in these ways (Smith and Witt 1990: 12).

45. Whites essentially agree (Carnegie Foundation for the Advancement of Teaching 1984: var. 28N).

46. About 85% of white managers think affirmative action has lowered standards (Fernandez 1981: 14, 25, 117–30; Bron Taylor 1991: 164–68; see also chapter 7).

47. Only a quarter of well-educated members of both races think they receive enough credit for a job well done (GSS 1990–91: vars. 438, 439, 440A, 440H). Two-thirds of high-status blacks think they have done "very well" in their jobs, "given the chances . . . [they] have had" (NSBA 1980: var. 985).

48. The rest think such programs are immaterial. Whites see fewer benefits and more harm (*Los Angeles Times* 1991b: var. 70).

49. *BE* (1980: 65, 97; 1982: 56; 1985: 100; 1990: 86). Sometimes affirmative action is simply irrelevant. Fully 95% of a convenience sample of black professionals and managers thought they had been hired because of merit rather than preferential treatment (Work 1980: 31). Only 3 of 375 high-level black executives saw race as contributing to their success, whereas 45% saw discrimination as "the single most impeding factor" to it (Heidrick and Struggles 1979a: 7).

50. Loury (1987: 269).

51. Julian Bond (1990) publicly pleaded with President Bush to sign the Civil Rights Act of 1990 (designed to strengthen practices of affirmative action) in order "to help white men overcome their feelings of inferiority" based on the awareness that their favored positions were due mainly to their race. "The knowledge that maids, porters, [and] garbage collectors . . . were suspicious of their credentials took a heavy psychic toll on white American males. . . . 'How would you feel,' one said, 'if everyone knew you had your job just because you were white?'"

52. The best recent reviews of relative deprivation are Olson et al. (1986); Clayton and Crosby (1992); Lane (1991).

53. Graham (1986: 48–53).

54. Lefton (1968); Fernandez (1981: 105–8).

55. Less skilled workers were somewhat less frustrated (but also even less optimistic about promotion); no data for whites are available (Bowman 1991a: 146; see also NSBA 1980: vars. 349, 354).

56. Work (1980: 31); NSBA (1980: var. 346).

57. *BE* (1982: 56).

58. Earl Smith (1991b); Gaston and Pearson (1986: table 4). Black bankers are similarly dissatisfied (Irons and Moore 1985: 27–31, 51–53). Half of a group of black women professionals report great stress over being "overqualified for the work I actually do" (Ford 1988: 62–64). I have found only one small

survey in which black managers have been disproportionately satisfied (ibid.: 58–62).

59. Earl Smith (1991a: 153–55).

60. Thompson (1986: 89); MCIC (1991–94: var. 354).

61. GSS (1990–91: vars. 418–20, 438, 439).

62. *NYT*/WCBS TV News (1989: 8–11; 1990: 2); *NYT* (1991: 5, 22).

63. A survey of black college athletes shows a disturbing tendency for whites to foster in (some) African Americans desires that later cannot be fulfilled. One-seventh of black football and basketball players at predominantly white universities would definitely not have attended such an institution had they not been recruited. (Half as many white players, and no black nonplayers, give the same response.) Once there, the athletes respond to their environment; 82% of both races place the "greatest importance" on obtaining a college degree, and a quarter "almost certainly" will go on to graduate school. Yet the African American athletes are much less likely to succeed in these new goals. Among those seeking a degree, 39% of black (compared with 15% of white) athletes have a grade point average of 1.99 or below. Similar results obtain among those anticipating graduate education (American Institutes for Research 1989: 26–27, 48–52). Are these athletically talented students receiving a chance to succeed that otherwise would be beyond their ken—or are they being set up to fail so that (predominantly white) spectators can cheer the home team?

64. Marx (1969: 119); Blauner (1989. 90).

65. In my terms, middle-class black whiners substitute an excuse based on the first tenet for an actual failure according to the terms of the third. In more conventional psychological terms, the process described here is one of "defensive attributions."

66. Greenberg (1985: 15); Epstein (1989: 21); see also Kemp (1990).

67. Between half and two-thirds of well-educated whites consistently describe blacks as "too sensitive about racial matters"; between one-third and one-half of high-status blacks typically agree (NBC News 1989: vars. Q79b, 79d; *Washington Post* 1992: var. 3I; *BE* 1985: 102). As usual, no comparable questions have been asked about whites.

68. Wieseltier (1989: 20).

69. Steele (1990: 150, 155–56).

70. Or they mistakenly believe that they are *not* successful. Black members of the American Chemical Society are on average paid at least as well as white chemists at their academic rank, and more are tenured. Yet blacks assert more often that they are not paid fairly compared with similar others (Gaston and Pearson 1986: tables 3 and 4). These data do not control for education, seniority within rank, or productivity; applying such controls could show that blacks' perceptions of underpayment are correct. That is the pattern that used to obtain for the best baseball players (Scully 1974; for an update, see Smith and Seff 1989).

71. Ramist and Arbeiter (1984: 46–47, 75–76); Hacker (1992: 138–46).

72. Naff (1994: table 3).

73. The best analysis of the relative positions of black and white women is Farley (1992). He finds bigger economic and demographic divides between the

genders than between the races. See also Goldin (1990); Malveaux and Wallace (1987).

74. Half of poor black women see extensive sex discrimination; about 40% recognize a common female fate; two-thirds endorse genderwide collective action (Brown et al. 1994: tables 7.4, 1984 and 1988; 15.16, 15.18, 15.20; these questions were not asked of black men or whites). See also NSBA (1980: vars. 513, 737).

75. Male legislators of both races disagree on all three points (Barrett 1994: 9–11).

76. Fernandez (1988: 93).

77. Harris (1970a: vars. 1b, 3a1, 3a12, 4a1–4a12, 18f1–18f4, 18g, 18L1, 3, 5, and 7); Fernandez (1981: 67–99; 1988: 81–83, 91–93).

78. Sandler (1986: 13); Smith and Witt (1994); Leggon (1980: 195). In 1986, 90% of black, but fewer than one-half of white, political and business leaders perceived occupational discrimination against black women (Harris 1986a: tables 21, 22).

79. Crenshaw (1990). The allusion is to Hull et al. (1982), one of the first books systematically to treat the distinctive situation of black women.

80. Hemmons (1980: 285); see also Collins (1991).

81. Lugones and Spelman (1983: 574). More analytically, "subordinate status is experienced more sharply than is dominant status" (Jackman and Jackman 1983: 81)—thus white women focus on "womanhood" and black women focus on racism or the interaction of racism and sexism.

82. For example, in 1970 many more well-off black than white women "favor[ed] efforts to stengthen and change women's status in society" and agreed that "if women don't speak up for themselves and confront men on their real problems, nothing will be done about these problems" (Harris 1970a: vars. 4e3, 4g). Twenty years later, more well-off black than white women agreed that women have too little political influence (GSS 1987: var. 355; see also Harris 1970a: vars. 3a3, 3a5, 3a7, 3a10, 4e1, 2, and 4; Tate 1992; Mansbridge 1992).

83. McGee (1989: A8). More generally, "like the early Malcolm and other sixties nationalists, contemporary Black nationalists have cast the pursuit of racial liberation in terms of a quest for masculine self-realization" (Dyson 1993: 46).

84. Dumas (1980); Minerbrook (1990); McMillan (1987); Scott (1991: 50–51, 73, 123). Scott (1991: 151) calls this the "hydraulic principle" of racial advancement, according to which "black men can rise only to the degree that black women are held down."

85. Braithwaite (1981). However, over half of both male and female *BE* respondents thought women should participate in the women's liberation movement (*BE* 1980: 86).

86. Belkin (1989). To Kimberlé Crenshaw (1992: 27), for example, then-Judge Clarence Thomas's misleading characterization of his sister's welfare dependency reflects "an ideology of put-down that is a growing phenomenon within the Black community." And the misogyny of gangsta rap is less striking only than the difficulty many black men have in rejecting it.

87. Giddings (1984: 340); quoted in Mosley (1980: 304); see also hooks (1992: 87–113).

88. Tate (1992: 77); see also Patterson and Datcher (1992: 64–77); "Round-table: Sexuality after Thomas/Hill" (1993: 27, 30); McKay (1992); Lubiano (1992); Crenshaw (1992); Giddings (1992).

Just after the Thomas-Hill hearings, 55% of blacks rejected the charges of sexual harassment (half of the rest did not venture an opinion). Twice as many blacks held favorable views of Judge Thomas as of Anita Hill. (Whites favored Judge Thomas to a slightly greater degree.) Most notably, 31% of blacks, compared with only 20% of whites, thought that even "if the charges of sexual harassment are true, . . . Clarence Thomas should be confirmed" (*NYT*/CBS News 1991b: 1–3; see also Rucinski 1993).

89. Baldwin, as quoted in Staples (1979b: 66); see also Staples (1979a); Cazenave (1983).

90. Harris (1970a: 3a2; 1970b: var. 2–2); see also Harris (1970a: vars. 3a4, 3a7, 3a8; 1970b: vars. 2–4, 2–7, 2–8).

91. GSS (1974–75, 1977–78, 1982, 1983, 1985–86, 1988–89, 1990–91: var. 198); Ransford and Miller (1983: 54); Cooperative Institutional Research Program (1973: 27, 37; 1994: 42, 58; and intervening years).

92. GSS (1972, 1974–75, 1977–78, 1982, 1983, 1985–86, 1988–89, 1990–91: var. 199). More black men than black women, although fewer white men than white women, agree that men are emotionally better suited for political action (GSS 1974–75, 1977–78, 1982, 1983, 1985–86, 1988–89, 1990–91: var. 201A). Dawson (1994c: table 4) finds that, after controlling for racially specific political views and socioeconomic status, black women are no more feminist than black men.

93. One series of questions, however (GSS 1988: vars. 521A-I), suggests that black men are just as feminist as white men or all women when asked about women's role in the home and with children. That is, black men may be sexually conservative only on issues dealing directly with relations between men and women in the public arena.

94. As do some white men (Thomas 1981; Sokoloff 1992: 19–21, 95–96).

95. The first quote is from Goldfarb (1980). The second comes from the chief negotiator of Operation PUSH's boycott of an affiliate of CBS. Boycotters demanded that two black male news anchors be hired, in addition to or instead of the black female news anchor already in place; this comment was intended to explain why (Boyer 1986: C26).

Some black women agree that "the role of the corporate man is a hard one for brothers to get the hang of. It is up to us to help them realize that they don't have to trade in their Air Jordans permanently only to wear hush puppies" (Nasir 1991: 26). Such sympathy may be more galling than antagonism.

96. Cazenave (1979: 583); Robert Taylor et al. (1990: 996).

97. Reed (1988). Black women sometimes concur. One bank vice president is "asked to participate in a lot of different kinds of things community-wide, and I wonder why my husband [an attorney] is not asked. . . . He is certainly capable as far as his professionalism, ability to communicate and relate. But I find a lot

of times it's the black women they're asking to participate" (Trescott and Gilliam 1986: A9).

98. Gresham (1989: 118).

99. Smith and Witt (1990: 12); Mitchell and Flintall (1990: 67); DiTomaso et al. (1988: 121–24); *BE* (1982: 52, 53). For inconclusive or contradictory results, see Nixon (1985a; 1985b; 1985c) and Fernandez (1981: 105–17).

100. *BE* (1982: 52); Fernandez (1981: 116; 1988: 90); GSS (1991: var. 421). White men and women do not show a consistent pattern.

101. Nkomo and Cox (1990: 48). The two most detailed studies of managers' response to black employees' gender are only slightly helpful here because they focus on low-skill, entry-level jobs. Both confirm black men's fears; employers often perceive women applicants to be harder workers, more responsible, less arrogant, or simply less scary (Moss and Tilly 1991: 23–27; Kirschenman 1991). These surveys do not, however, tell us three crucial things: whether employers hold the same view about professional or managerial employees, whether they hold the same view about workers of other races, and whether their judgments are on balance right. Thus they are not much help in weighing the relative merits of well-off black men's and women's sense of relative deprivation.

102. Fernandez (1981: 217, 281).

103. Irons and Moore (1985: 15, 109–12, 119–26); Koelewijn-Strattner (1990).

104. Merritt and Reskin (1992); see also Carter and O'Brien (1993: table 2); Tomaskovic-Devey (1993: 57).

105. Sokoloff (1992: 93–112); Farley and Allen (1987: 263–80; 303–6, 316–55); Xu and Leffler (1992); Woody (1992); Blau and Kahn (1992: 394). In addition, firms owned by black men earn more than firms owned by black women; how that fact translates into individual incomes is unclear (U.S. Bureau of the Census 1991).

106. Cotton (1988: 22); Blau and Kahn (1992: 394); Farkas et al. (1994); Tomaskovic-Devey (1993: 115–21); Kilbourne et al. (1994: 1159–63).

107. Farley and Allen (1987: 333). Kilbourne et al. (1994: 1166) find that black women have, compared with black men, higher returns to education but lower returns to experience.

108. Fewer than one quarter even of the highly efficacious *BE* readers think that they can protect themselves from racism, although they report a wide range of coping mechanisms (*BE* 1980: 102; 1985: 102; 1990: 82, 94).

109. Greenberg (1985: 15); Hilts (1992); Williams (1986).

110. National Conference (1994: 71–72); Linda Williams (1990: 47–51).

111. Blacks also rank whites higher than the other three ethnicities on all six ratings. African Americans rank their own race most prone to accept welfare, more patriotic and work-oriented than Hispanics, and more intelligent and peaceful than both Asians and Hispanics (GSS 1990–91: var. 388A-F). Lichter and Lichter (1989) analyze an unusual survey of stereotypes of various ethnicities.

112. The Harris Survey asked identical questions in 1963 and 1978, yielding the following responses (1978 in parentheses): 31% (15%) of whites saw blacks as inferior, 39% (25%) thought they were less intelligent, 41% (36%) thought they preferred handouts, and 66% (49%) thought they had less ambition. Ninety percent (80%) would be "concerned" if their child dated blacks, 51% (27%) disliked the idea of a black next-door neighbor, and 32% (14%) objected to trying on the same clothes (Harris 1978: 15, 16).

113. First quotation from Mitchell (1982: 34); see also Mitchell (1983). Second quotation from Jones (1973: 111–12); see also Jones (1986).

114. Fernandez (1981: 29–66; 1988: 86–90); Irons and Moore (1985: 23–33, 40–46, 50–55, 82–88); Ford (1988: 62–64); Davis (1988: 110–12); DiTomaso et al. (1988: 124). See also Davis and Watson (1982); Collins (1989); Greenhaus et al. (1990); Russell Reynolds Associates (1990); Cose (1993); Feagin and Sikes (1994).

115. Fernandez (1988: 78–81); a comparison with Fernandez (1981: 44–47) suggests that white managers' racial stereotyping is increasing. See also DiTomaso (1988: 124–33).

116. This may be an instance of Foucault's (1979) claim that simple, if horrific, punishment of the brute body for breaking the law was preferable to the subtle controls over the minute variations in individual souls and minds characteristic of the modern "disciplinary regime."

117. For example, critical rights theorists claim that proponents of critical legal studies are too ready to jettison "rights," as indeterminate, reified, or contradictory, just when blacks sometimes succeed in making rights-based claims against an otherwise overweening white political and legal structure (Williams 1987).

118. Terry (1991); Mendelberg (1992).

119. Crosby et al. (1980).

120. Pettigrew and Martin (1987); see also McConahay (1983); McConahay and Hardee (1989).

121. Stephen Johnson (1980); Terkildsen (1993); Crosby et al. (1980). See also Dienstbier (1972), Fajardo (1985), and especially Dovidio and Gaertner (1986).

122. *U.S.* v. *Yonkers Board of Education* (1985); U.S. Department of Labor (1990: 9; 1991: 4, 13).

123. On redlining, see Canner (1991); Bradbury et al. (1989); ACORN (1991) (but see Benston 1992 for cautions about excessive claims of redlining). On commercial bank credit, see Ando (1988). U.S. Department of Justice (1994d) and Spayd and Brenner (1993) describe other discriminatory banking policies.

124. On housing audits, see Winger (1986); Turner et al. (1991b); U.S. Department of Housing and Urban Development (1979); Reed (1991); *Housing Policy Debate* (1992). On employments audits, see Turner et al. (1991a: 31); Braddock et al. (1986).

125. On taxis, see Taxi and Limousine Commission et al. (1988). On kidneys, see Eggers (1988); Kjellstrand (1988); Held et al. (1988). On bypass op-

erations, see Wenneker and Epstein (1989). On cars, see Ayres (1991); Ayres and Siegelman (forthcoming). On hamburgers, see Labaton (1994a; 1994b); Kohn (1994).

126. On public employees, see Hopkins (1980); Bosworth (1989). On employee organizations, see Billeaux (1988). On the FBI, see Shenon (1988; 1990); Johnston (1992). On courts, see New York State Judicial Commission on Minorities (1992: 186). On postal workers, see Zwerling and Silver (1992: 651).

127. Amaker (1988); Golden (1992); C. Calvin Smith (1990).

128. Shull (1993).

129. For example, then Assistant Attorney General William Bradford Reynolds argued that the proposed consent decree to desegregate Tennessee's universities "does little to solve the racial problems in a higher education system and may . . . do more to destroy traditional black colleges than to desegregate them" (Aplin-Brownlee 1984). Some black students at Tennessee State University almost agreed: "We think the Reagan Administration is doing the right thing for the wrong reason" (Schmidt 1984). Prominent black Republicans, however, expressed dismay at the Reagan administration's civil rights policies (Pear 1984).

130. On civil rights elites, see Detlefsen (1991); quotation by June Jordan, in "Barriers" (1988: 44).

131. Powledge (1991: 446).

132. Quotation from Bell (1976: 23). See also Morgan (1975); Key (1984); Woodward (1963; 1991); Phillips (1970); Carmines and Stimson (1989); Edsall (1991); and Valelly (forthcoming).

133. Converse et al. (1980: 61); Orfield (1993: 6).

134. Thus a black student at Princeton University "cannot say for certain whether any real progress has been made since the 1960s." She asserts that the first verdict in the Rodney King beating "parallel[s] the racism in the university community" demonstrated by "subtle and not so subtle" mistreatment in stores and restaurants and by harassment of people of color by local police and university proctors. "There is," she concludes, "no such thing as a little bit of racism" (Pierce 1992: 9). Two features of this claim are noteworthy. First, it seems wrong; after all, Princeton University has admitted a considerable number of black students and has developed a world-class Afro-American Studies Program "since the 1960s." Ms. Pierce knows that, so what she means by "real progress" bears little resemblance to what whites (and many blacks) have congratulated themselves on for two decades. Second, her complaints about mistreatment in clothing stores and restaurants could be compiled only by a member of the black middle class who regularly uses white-dominated institutions and services with otherwise good reputations.

Analytically, this point instantiates the claim that people form "attitudes" by using ideas that are, for whatever reason, most immediately salient to them (Zaller 1992). I disagree, however, with the implication sometimes drawn that therefore these attitudes are ephemeral and readily subject to change—if only because middle-class blacks constantly receive the same ideas about white hostility and discrimination.

CHAPTER SIX
BELIEFS ABOUT OTHERS

1. Jackman and Jackman (1983: 46–50); Brown et al. (1994: table 18.11). The 1980 NSBA, however, found that the higher their socioeconomic status, the *less* close blacks felt to other blacks or the less they identified with other blacks (Allen et al. 1989: 432–33; Broman et al. 1988; Demo and Hughes 1990: 369–71). Other surveys have found no effect of status on black solidarity (Bledsoe et al. 1995a) or, like the NSBA, a negative effect (Allen and Hatchett 1986: 110–15). These results foreshadow the substantive ambivalence described in the text.

2. Gurin et al. (1989: 280); Brown et al. (1994: table 7.1, 1984 and 1988); Dillingham (1981: 436–39); Tate (1993: 28); Dawson (1994b: 79); Reese and Brown (forthcoming: tables 1–3). At least since 1964, blacks have been twice as likely as whites to conceptualize politics in terms of group benefits (Hagner and Pierce 1984: 222). The NSBA (1980: var. 1273) shows a fairly weak sense of common fate, however.

3. Zilber (1994); my thanks to Jeremy Zilber of Ohio State University for doing extra calculations in order to allow me to discuss this point.

4. Evaluations of nation and group are themselves closely linked. See Kinder et al. (1989: 511); Kinder and Kiewiet (1979); Brody and Sniderman (1977); Brady and Sniderman (1985); Dawson (1994b: 85–86, 94).

5. Half of the white respondents and 60% of the nonpoor black respondents made the same mistake (*Los Angeles Times* 1985: ques. 85).

6. Dawson (1994b: 79, 92). A sense of linked fate is also closely associated with a sense that blacks are doing worse than whites (ibid.: 92). So, as shown in table 4.3, middle-class blacks believe that they are doing well but that other blacks (and perhaps the nation as a whole) are doing badly, and they may expect that their own situation will eventually be affected. This is a concrete instance of the more general analytic claim that concern about others may blend into concern about one's own eventual position. Thus self-interested and sociotropic views may be distinguished more by short- versus long-term calculations than by a sharp distinction between one's own and others' well-being (Monroe 1983: 197–98).

7. Runciman (1966) first distinguished "egoistic" from "fraternal" relative deprivation; Olson et al. (1986) develop and test the distinction. The distinction does not matter much here, since middle-class blacks feel both egoistic and fraternal deprivation, as chapter 7 shows. Miller et al. (1981) do the best job of sorting out the components and consequences of politically relevant "group consciousness," which includes relative deprivation. The logic of my analysis accords closely with theirs, although I do not lay it out as they do.

8. Schuman et al. (1988: 118–19, 146–47); Dawson (1994b: 83–84, 93); Brown et al. (1994: table 7.2, 1984 and 1988).

9. *BE* (1980: 97; 1982: 56; 1985: 100; 1990: 86).

10. Whites' presidential approval ratings are not sensitive to the relative unemployment rates for blacks and whites and are barely sensitive to absolute levels of white unemployment (Dawson 1994b: 169–75).

11. Roper (1986: var. 38).

12. Harris (1986a: 10, table 20).

13. Heidrick and Struggles (1979a: 6). Most male executives also think that blacks have progressed more slowly than (presumably white) women in attaining executive positions, and most expect women to do better than blacks over the next fifteen years. Women executives (virtually all white in this survey) agree. They are also less disappointed with their group's progress and much more optimistic about their group's future success than are blacks (ibid. 1979b: 7; 1980: inside cover, 7; 1986: 8, 12).

14. Irons and Moore (1985: 21, 52).

15. They also overestimate the number of poor blacks even more than do whites or poor blacks themselves (*Los Angeles Times* 1985: ques. 85); Gallup 1991a: Q17).

16. West (1992: 121); King (1967: 132). See also Du Bois (1967: 317–18); Frazier (1957); Marable (1982).

17. Thompson (1986: 137); see also Center for Public and Urban Research (1981).

18. Brashler (1978: 140); more analytically, Lawson (1992). Middle-class blacks are becoming less liberal in their views on social welfare policy and government expenditures, especially for the poor (Bolce and Gray 1979: 68–69; Denton and Sussman 1981; Parent 1984; Lichter 1985; Parent and Stekler 1985: 529–33; Welch and Combs 1985; Tate 1986: 7; Welch and Foster 1987; GSS 1987: vars. 513B, 513D, 513F, 513G, 514B; Brown et al. 1994: tables 9.13, 9.15, 17.3, 17.4, 17.5, 17.10, 18.3, 19.7; Gilliam and Whitby 1989; Bobo and Kluegel 1993: 457; Tate 1993: 40–45; GSS 1993: var. 456; Dawson 1994b: 175–78). For mixed results, see Bolce et al. (1992: tables); for disagreement, see Seltzer and Smith (1985); Smith and Seltzer (1992); GSS (1993: var. 455B).

Well-off blacks sometimes act in accord with these views. They give less to charity than do whites with similar incomes (Carson 1989: 6–7). (I know of no data on charitable giving among people with comparable wealth.) Some oppose the siting of public housing in their neighborhoods (Bell 1992b: 775–77).

19. Delaney (1978: 1); see also Garreau (1991: 139–78).

20. Press (1984: C8). Anxieties that are analytically distinct can merge and reinforce one another in people's lives: the more insecure one's own middle-class status, the harder it is to help those worse off—but the more likely one is to have close ties with people recently left behind.

21. Kenneth Taylor (1992: 17); Monroe and Goldman (1988); Wideman (1984). The sentiment "why me?" may have an affinity with survivor guilt or post-traumatic stress syndrome (Lifton 1973: 105–7; Wolf and Mosnaim 1990).

22. Range (1974: 78). Roger Wilkins (1982) gives probably the best portrayal of the mix of idealism, sentiment, serendipity, and institutional context involved in negotiating a commitment to improving the lives of fellow blacks while refusing to sacrifice too much of one's own.

23. Jackman and Jackman (1983: 46–50); Ifill and Maraniss (1986: A10); *BE* (1980: 98; 1985: 102; 1990: 90).

24. On high expectations, see Brooks (1990: 131–44) as well as the discussion of the fourth tenet in chapter 4. On gaps in living standards and values, see Colasanto and Williams (1987: 51).

25. Dulan-Wilson (1991: 33).

26. Blauner (1989: 304).

27. Lester (1991: 30–32). He has some work to do: two-fifths of blacks have not heard of *Brown* v. *Board of Education*, and another fifth have heard "only a little" about it (Gallup 1994: var. 28).

28. Turner (1989: 5).

29. On Robinson, see Frommer (1982: 13–14); the Princeton student is Malebranche (1989: 8).

30. Among a small sample of Princeton students, 80% of African Americans and Latinos reported that someone at the university had at some point made assumptions about them because of their race or had "made sweeping generalizations about . . . [their] ethnic group based on . . . [their] individual behavior." However, 61% of Asian Americans and 45% of European Americans made the same claim (Hall-Valdez et al. 1992: 3).

31. "Blacks . . . have never signed the social contract governing this country. . . . Much of the antisocial behavior exhibited by blacks demonstrates their rejection of the American social contract. In this sense, the blacks who so heavily populate our prisons are political prisoners—persons who have rejected an imposed, alien set of rules" (Browne 1992: 95).

32. McFadden (1988: 32). More emphatically, Tawana "was brutally abused, sodomized, and raped by some racist animals appearing in the external garb of human beings. . . . This white (redundant) racist society responded primarily through its criminal/immoral system of injustice . . . to protect and cover up . . . the long-established American custom of white men raping African women" (Lucas 1988).

33. Survey data in Morin (1990); quotations from Britt (1990: F1); headline and final quotation from Milloy (1990).

34. Gilliam (1990). More than 80% of well-off African Americans (and of whites) overestimate the proportion of blacks among those arrested for crimes (Sniderman et al. 1991: var. bcrm).

35. Wilkerson (1990: B7); see also McAdoo (1988: 162). More middle-class than poor African Americans have taken in a needy relative or friend to live with their family (NSBA 1980: vars. 894, 903; MCIC 1991–94: var. 318).

36. Heidrick and Struggles (1979a: 6). The women spend much more time on "homemaking tasks" than their husbands, and presumably more than male executives of any race (ibid. 1980: 6; 1986: 9).

37. On mentors, see Harris (1986a: table 24); on business owners, see Watson and Simpson (1978: 317).

38. Herring (1989: 14–15); Tucker (1980: 316); Walter Allen (1994: 4).

39. D. Garth Taylor (1991: ques. 6, 12, 95; 1993: 39; 1994: 54). Other surveys in this series show equal charitable contributions of time and money across the races (ibid. 1993: 4–8; 1994: 5–9). Well-off black Chicagoans engage in more local political activity than do poor blacks, but not more than well-off

whites (MCIC 1991–94: vars. 265, 268, 269, 276, 631). By some measures, however, affluent black residents of Chicago do give more of their time and organizational skills to charity than do comparable whites (ibid.: vars. 293, 296).

40. Low-status blacks concur; most blacks also agree that black women should work with all women rather than only among themselves (NSBA 1980: vars. 1270, 1271).

41. On families, see Higginbotham and Weber (1992: 430); on faculty, see Carnegie Foundation for the Advancement of Teaching (1984: ques. 1, 8A–8E).

42. "Perhaps" because some studies find that "blacks are consistently less likely than whites or Mexican Americans to be involved in any sort of intergenerational assistance" (Hogan et al. 1993: 1433, 1450; see also Marks 1993: table 7; Gale et al. 1993: tables 5–7). Three-quarters of blacks, compared with three-fifths of whites, agree that "you have to take care of yourself first" and care for others only "if you have any energy left" (GSS 1993: var. 455A).

Middle-class and poor blacks are similar in their life goals: in 1980 half of both groups chose personal achievements as "the most important thing you hoped for out of life," almost one-fifth chose physical well-being, one-fourth pointed to connections with family and friends, and 7% focused on morality, religion, or virtue (derived from open-ended responses in NSBA 1980: var. 76). Three-fifths of both classes have "gotten mostly what . . . [they] hoped for" (ibid.: var. 75). Thirteen years later, the two classes were again broadly similar— focusing mostly on self-sufficiency, faith in God, and financial security. Beyond those choices, however, well-off blacks focused more on personal relationships, and poor blacks on material goods (GSS 1993: var. 464).

43. On executives, see Heidrick and Struggles (1979a: 6); on leaders, see Harris (1986a: table 12); on entrepreneurs, see Green and Pryde (1990: 157); on real-estate, see Lemann (1993: 46).

44. Hatchett et al. (1991: 72). No question was asked about *giving* help, but the authors speculate that because of "norms of reciprocity, . . . this item can be seen as an indicator of mutual aid." One may doubt that inference on the reasonable assumption that well-off blacks help their poor relatives more than vice versa, but that would make the survey results even more startling. This question has not been asked of whites to my knowledge. See also NSBA (1980: vars. 850, 851); Robert Taylor (1986: 71–73); Chatters et al. (1989).

45. GSS (1987: var. 356); Brown et al. (1994: tables 7.8, 7.9).

46. On student goals, see Cooperative Institutional Research Program (1994: 26). Adult goals are from Roper (1986: vars 15, 16, 17, 20, 21, 22, 23, 27); see also Chusmir and Ruf (1992: 50–54). Quotation from Higginbotham and Weber (1992: 433).

47. Alwin (1984: 368). Throughout the 1970s, twice as many well-off whites as blacks ranked being "considerate of others" high on their list of traits to teach their children (GSS 1972–73, 1975–76, 1978–80, 1983: var. 164K). In the late 1980s, well-off blacks and whites ranked "helping others" about equally low. Poor blacks ranked helping others higher than any other group did (GSS 1986, 1987, 1988–89, 1990–91: var. 167E).

48. Middle-class African Americans vary considerably across surveys when

asked to choose individualistic or collective strategies for the pursuit of success. Most surveys find strong support for collective action among middle-class blacks, and stronger support among them than among poor blacks or whites (NSBA 1980: var. 1265; Brown et al. 1994: tables 15.12, 15.19; GSS 1987: var. 510G; 1983–84, var. 68A). A few, however, find weak support and the opposite pattern among classes (e.g., GSS 1987: var. 354). Because these are strategic judgments about how best to succeed rather than ideological statements about the meaning of success, I will not pursue the issue further.

49. Carter (1991: 134–35).

50. I do not know why success as an athlete or entertainer is not subject to the same scorn as success as a scholar or businessman. I speculate that the lure of glamour and fame outweighs the stigma of succeeding by white standards and being judged by white audiences.

51. First quotation from Baldwin (1963: 37); second from Loury (1990: 17).

52. Steele (1990: 95–96); Fordham and Ogbu (1986: 7–8). Ogbu (1974; 1978) gives the most extended analysis of this phenomenon.

53. Knight (1987: A1). After all, it is hard "to keep proving to whites that I was really smart and to the blacks that I was really black" (Welsh 1988: C1). Perhaps for similar reasons, black students are less likely than white students to rate as "likable" tasks that are rewarded in school (Banks et al. 1977).

54. Moses (1989: 18).

55. Fleming (1984); Allen et al. (1991). As with so many issues in this book, there are complex generational issues here. One black professor's lament is illustrative: "Often students label us as 'sellouts' for no better reason than that we happen to be faculty and, therefore, part of an intellectual tradition they believe is racist. . . . Suddenly years of answering the call to be inspirational role models (to say nothing of the sacrifices incumbent in the preparation to do so) are undermined by accusations of assimilation and betrayal that are tantamount to labeling a black professor 'worthless' in the eyes of many black students" (Stevenson 1993: 16).

56. Commissioner's Task Force on Minorities (1989); Portland Public Schools (1987).

57. Ogbu (1988: 143, 156).

58. Allen and Hatchett (1986: 110–15).

59. Quote from an urban school librarian in Welsh (1988: C4). Meier et al. (1989) demonstrate second-generation discrimination in supposedly desegregated schools. Cusick (1973), Willis (1977), and MacLeod (1987) show that some poor whites resemble middle-class blacks in rejecting the norms of affluent white society.

60. Early (1992: 68).

61. Quotations from Delbanco (1989: 33); Baldwin (1955: 27); threats in Petroni (1970: 263).

62. Marx (1964: var. 64I); Brink and Harris (1966: 262); Harris (1966a: Q15a, B3A); Goldman (1969: 260–61, 266–67, 269).

63. Marx (1964: var. 8); Goldman (1969: 265). In 1969, however, half of middle-income blacks (compared with over three-fifths of poor blacks) opposed

the Vietnam War "because they have less freedom to fight for" (Goldman 1969: 230–31).

64. Harris (1968: records 33, 34, 56); Goldman (1969: 266).

Matthews and Prothro (1961–62: vars. 393, 394); Marx (1964: vars. 10E, 12); Survey Research Center (1964: Q. 15); Harris (1966a: vars. 5A, 16G, 19E, 19F); Campbell and Schuman (1968: vars. 294, 310, 320, 321, 323); Levy (1972: 233); Hutcheson (1973: 21, 24); Turner and Wilson (1976: 145); and Fredrick Harris (1993: 33) all show greater support for black separatism among low- than high-status blacks in the 1960s.

65. CBS News/*NYT* (1978: vars. 35b, 45); Jackson et al. (1991: 249–50); NSBA (1980: vars. 1232–34); GSS (1982: var. 144). A plurality of blacks (43%) who received any "racial socialization" as children were taught classic values of the American dream: the importance of "achieving and working hard, . . . good citizenship and moral virtues, . . . a positive self-image, . . . [and] the fundamental equality of blacks and whites." Almost as many (35%) were taught such values as "racial pride, . . . black heritage, . . . and accept[ance] of their racial background" (Thornton et al. 1990: 405–6; Bowman and Howard 1985: 137). They are teaching their children the same things (NSBA 1980: vars. 1232–34).

66. Brown et al. (1994: table 15.20); Wilcox (1992).

67. Allen and Hatchett (1986: 110–15); Demo and Hughes (1990: 369–71); Allen et al. (1989: 432–33; 1994a: 8); Dawson (1994a: 8; 1994b: 125–29, 194–96). See also CBS News/*NYT* (1978: ques. 36, 37); NSBA (1980: vars. 1212, 1420, 1421); NBC News (1989: ques. 50B, 56B); Gallup (1994: ques. 35); Brown et al. (1994: tables 14.8, 15.13, 15.22).

68. Gallup (1988: var. 8); *NYT*/CBS News (1993b: 11); People for the American Way (1992: 159).

69. CBS News/*NYT* (1978: var. 43); Gallup (1988: var. 7); Gordon Black (1989a: vars. 20, 21); NBC News (1989: ques. 12B, 37B); Gallup (1994: ques. 37, 38).

70. That judgment is tenuous: the surveys might overestimate the number of African Americans who reject the American dream because they identify only those who reject whites. One could certainly reject whites while embracing the ideology of the dream. However, the survey data might underestimate the political and cultural importance of some African Americans' rejection of whites and their dream because they tell us nothing about critical portions of the black middle class, such as upwardly mobile students, young professionals, or political activists. For example, over three-fourths of the *BE* respondents admit to "negative feelings toward whites," and black leaders are arguably more disaffected than other black citizens (*BE* 1980: 102; 1990: 82; Lichter 1985).

71. On the first question, more poor blacks and slightly fewer whites were similarly negative. On the second question, fewer of all other race/class groups concurred (Roper 1986: vars. 47, 59).

72. Almost two-fifths agree that television "shows how others solve problems I have," and three-tenths think it "shows what life is really like" (Lichter and Lichter 1988: 4; GSS 1993: var. 461). Over half of well-off black Chicagoans, compared with fewer than two-fifths of well-off whites, watch four or more hours a day (MCIC 1991–94: var. 118).

73. Poindexter and Stroman (1981) (but see GSS 1993: var. 460); Comstock and Cobbey (1979).

74. Quotation from Gray (1986: 227). More dramatically, "the TV commercial . . . offers up the symbols of the good life, of the benefits of the middle class. The young, black mother and her teenage sons and daughters, watching their favorite TV program, see the TV commercial and believe the message. . . . [However,] those few blacks allowed entrance to the upscale, yuppie, DINK, buppie lifestyle found it to be vastly different from the portrayals of the TV commerial" (Robinson 1990: 163, 165).

75. First quotation from Karenga (1977: 40); remaining quotations from Oliver (1989).

76. Asante's (1988: 41) list of "guidelines" for the "reconstruction" of an Afrocentric viewpoint—"to be *excellent, provocative, organized, educated, and dependable*"—would be music to Benjamin Franklin's ears. More abstractly, James Baldwin (1955: 123) points out with his inimitable sense of irony that "in this need to establish himself in relation to his [African] past he [the American Negro] is most American." Asante nevertheless sharply distinguishes Afrocentricity from Eurocentricity.

77. Roberta Turner (1991: 46). Unless otherwise noted, quotations and arguments in the next few paragraphs come from the same source, which elegantly summarizes a wider literature.

78. Mbiti (1969) analyzes the African (and by extension of the Afrocentrists, African American) religious emphasis on collective destiny and the importance of God and other external forces in determining that destiny. The latter point directly refutes the third tenet of the American dream.

79. Asante (1988: 81).

80. First quotation from Hodge-Edelin (1990: 43); second from Asante (1988: 86, 91). Fox (1992) gives a brief, very thoughtful, warning against the dangers of "hard Afrocentrism" to African Americans themselves.

81. Campbell and Schuman (1968: vars. 291–93, 295, 296).

82. Gallup (1966: ques. 12B, 13); Harris (1966a: var. 15B); Beardwood (1968: 148); NORC (1968: vars. 55, 56); Harris (1968: vars. 28–30); Goldman (1969: 162–63, 264); Fredrick Harris (1993: table 2.6).

For example, a survey that allowed respondents to define black power themselves found approval from half of the black residents of Detroit, but more than half of that group defined it as a fair share of the "traditional Negro goals of freedom, equality, and opportunity." The other supporters emphasized black unity and pride; none endorsed black power *in opposition to* dominant American values. Almost no black supporter of black power endorsed "total separation of the races" (although 5% of white supporters did) (Aberbach and Walker 1970a: 369–73, 383). Note that this survey was conducted only a few months after the 1967 riots, in areas of the city hard-hit by the events.

One survey (Harris 1970c: vars. P10A–P10C) found high support for the Black Panthers among high-status blacks, mainly because they "are doing good work among disadvantaged young people."

83. Gallup (1963: question 20); NORC (1963: vars. 28B, 28E); Marx (1969: 25–27, 120); Harris (1968: var. 30). See also Harris (1966a: vars. 15C,

23A-8, 23A-20); Beardwood (1968: 148); Goldman (1969: 236, 237, 240–41).

84. Brown et al. (1994: tables 15.3 (1984 and 1988), 15.11, 15.32); Thornton and Taylor (1988: 144–46); Jaynes and Williams (1989: 134, 136, 198); Demo and Hughes (1990: 370, 371).

85. GSS (1990–91: var 440E); Carnegie Foundation for the Advancement of Teaching (1984: ques. 29C, 30B).

86. During the height of Reverend Sharpton's activity as a protest leader, one-fourth of African Americans thought he helped blacks in New York City, compared with over one-third who thought he harmed them. (Most of the rest thought he made no difference.) However, despite their own disapproval, one-third of blacks thought he spoke for *other* blacks in the city (*NYT*/WCBS News 1988: 5; *NYT*/WCBS TV News 1990b: 5, 11).

87. On Farrakhan, see *NYT* (1994: ques. 25); on Muslims and militants, see *Business Week*/Harris (1991: 70, 82). Fifteen percent of blacks think Louis Farrakhan "represents the views of most black people" (*NYT* 1994: ques. 26; see also *BE* 1990: 82). Two other recent surveys (Gallup 1991a: var. 9D, and Gallup in *The Polling Report* 1994: 2) found up to one-third of blacks giving favorable ratings to Rev. Farrakhan or the Nation of Islam.

88. Some argue that Afrocentrism functions, whether cynically or delusionally, as a cover for a drive for success in white society that African Americans cannot admit to: "The more impure their music becomes . . . the more righteous are the rappers' declarations of racial purity. The more their lives entwine with whites—managers, producers, audiences, critics, film-makers—the more they insist they have no relation to whites at all, and speak to Blacks alone. . . . The richer they get and farther from the boyz in the 'hood . . . the more vehemently they claim to be organically united and identically oppressed" (Berman 1993: 17). The possibility that a radical stance is a cover for bourgeois behavior is not unique to militant Afrocentrists; it is at least as old as Thoreau's assumption that his mother would do his laundry while he camped out at Walden Pond.

CHAPTER SEVEN
COMPETITIVE SUCCESS AND COLLECTIVE WELL-BEING

1. Vivid illustrations of whites' earlier refusals to allow blacks even absolute or relative success are in McMillen (1989) and Litwack (1991).

2. With apologies to the song "Two Out of Three Ain't Bad" by Meatloaf.

3. Furthermore, it is plausible that many whites define "competitive success" expansively enough to limit, perhaps unintentionally, the possibility for blacks to achieve even absolute or relative success. It works as follows: Person A feels that "B, as a result of his increased wealth, will also acquire more power, a good that is generally acquired at the expense of others, and that this redistribution of power, besides being in itself objectionable to A, will have in time an adverse effect on his economic position" (Hirschman 1981: 55). In other words, whites worry that African Americans who acquire wealth or status—relative success—will try to translate that accomplishment into political power—competitive success—as whites have traditionally done. If that outcome is unacceptable, the step

leading to it also becomes unacceptable, and therefore the step leading to that, and so on—thus expanding the notion of unacceptable competitive success into the realm of otherwise acceptable relative success.

4. So do scholars. Predecessors to my claim include Schermerhorn (1956–57: 55); Blumer (1958: 4); Van den Berge (1967: 30); Blalock (1967); Bell (1987; 1992a; 1992b); and Sidanius and Pratto (1993). Giles and Evans (1986: 470–72) and Olzak (1992) give brief but comprehensive literature reviews. Olzak (1992), Olzak and Shanahan (1994), and Olzak et al. (1994) show the effects of racial competition on everything from lynching and urban newspapers around the turn of the century to race riots during the past few decades. Thomas and Alderfer (1989: 148–50) discuss the dynamics of racial competition within organizations. Novack (1987) provides a similar, but sympathetic, analysis from the perspective of poor whites.

5. Gannett News Service (1981: 7); Malveaux (1979: 106); National Conference (1994: 109). A few more agree that whites "believe they are superior and can boss other people around" (ibid.: 109). The specter of competititve success looms within as well as across races: "The further I go up the ladder, the more evident the leeriness in the eyes of my Black co-workers becomes. In the past, we've shared secrets, passed on information, made each other laugh. Now, their laughter is merely polite. The conversations are no longer easy. Why didn't Mama warn me that once some white person in an oak paneled office on the top floor had bestowed some arbitrary mark of 'acceptability' upon me, some of my own people would no longer trust me?" (Simmons 1992: 23).

6. Blauner (1989: 91–92, emphases and ellipses in original); Toner (1990); Glaser (1994: 23); Gates (1993: 52).

White Americans have, nevertheless, progressed at least rhetorically. Few now say, in print at any rate, what one young southerner wrote ninety years ago: "Take a young Negro of little more than ordinary intelligence, . . . train him thoroughly as to books, and finish him up with a good industrial education, send him out into the South with ever so good intentions both on the part of his benefactor and himself, send him to take my work away from me and I will kill him" (Franklin and Starr 1967: 25).

7. In 1961 one-fifth of blacks agreed (Gallup 1961: var. 5C); in 1990 barely 1% agreed (GSS 1990: var. 394C).

8. Harris (1966b: 14a, 14b, 14h). Two decades earlier, almost half of whites believed that more job opportunities for Negroes meant fewer for whites, and half agreed that "white people should have the first chance at any kind of job" (NORC 1944: vars. 9, 10).

9. Aberbach and Walker (1970a: 370–71).

10. Clifford and Ferrell (1992: A4); Jones and Jackson (1992: 17–18).

11. ABC News/*Washington Post* (1989: var. 22E); Gates (1993: 50).

12. At each threshold, many more whites would not move into the neighborhood than would try to move out. In 1976 these figures were all higher. In both 1976 and 1992 blacks were much more willing to move into neighborhoods in which they would be a small minority (Farley et al. 1993; see also GSS 1990–91: vars. 389A-D). Hacker (1992: 36) concludes from the (unspecified) literature that whites will start leaving a neighborhood if more than 8% of its residents are

black. Twenty percent of white residents of metropolitan Detroit report that they have moved at some point in their life partly because blacks were moving into their neighborhood (Bledsoe et al. 1994: 19).

13. Massey and Denton (1987; 1993); Farley and Frey (1994); Alba and Logan (1993); Logan and Alba (1993). Frey and Farley (1993) find the opposite trajectory in a few multi-ethnic metropolitan areas.

14. Under 5% of blacks objected to a school with a few or half whites, and 16% more—one-fourth in all—objected to a mostly white school (GSS 1990–91: vars. 133A-C). NBC News (1989: vars. 21A and B, 22A and B, 23A and B) shows similar white objections to black classmates and fewer black objections to white classmates. Schofield (1982) provides a fascinating depiction of whites' worries about "too many" blacks.

15. Olzak and Shanahan (1994b); Mickelson and Ray (1994).

16. Sixteen percent claimed such a loss for a family member or friend; 21% "saw it at work"; and 41% heard of such losses through the media (GSS 1990–91: vars. 399, 399A, 456). Lynch (1989) implicitly explains the GSS findings by showing the substantial growth in media attention to the issue since the late 1970s. In other surveys (e.g., *Los Angeles Times* 1991b: ques. 76) slightly higher proportions of whites claim to have lost jobs to affirmative action candidates (see also NBC News 1989: ques. 77, 78).

17. More high- than low-status whites worry about the deprivation of whites' rights (*Los Angeles Times* 1991b: ques. 50, 71). In addition, one-tenth claim that whites "suffer the most discrimination in America these days," and one-fifth claim to have suffered from racial discrimination (*Los Angeles Times* 1991b: ques. 49, 73). On youth, see People for the American Way (1992: 161); Bledsoe et al. (1994: 20). Bron Taylor (1991) provides the most nuanced exploration of why (a small sample of) whites object to affirmative action.

18. Herring (1992). These results are not driven by the views of the unenlightened uneducated. Almost half of white college faculty agree that "affirmative action is unfair to white males," and almost half of white male managers believe that affirmative action policies in their firm narrowed their career opportunities (Carnegie Foundation for the Advancement of Teaching 1984: ques. 28-O; Fernandez 1981: 14, 106, 116–21; see also Jackman and Muha 1984; Miller 1990).

A survey designed to get past responses driven by social desirability in exploring whites' anger at blacks' demands for "special advantages" finds that "more education is associated with greater covert hostility" (Knight 1992: 6–8, 12). Furthermore, what looks like greater racial tolerance on the part of whites in professional and managerial jobs may simply be the result of less direct job competition with blacks, compared with whites in the less-skilled secondary labor market (Cummings 1980). If that is the case, the growth of the black middle class will exacerbate high-status whites' racial hostility.

19. Other people of color and whites are attacked for roughly the same reasons, although in much smaller numbers (D. Garth Taylor 1992b). The same phenomenon occurred in 1866 (Waller 1984).

20. Giles and Buckner (1993). Key (1984) first made this observation; see also, among many others, Longshore (1988); Fossett and Kiecolt (1989);

Huckfeldt and Kohfeld (1989); Hertzog (1994); Giles and Hertz (1994); and Glaser (1994).

21. Kurtz (1992: A16).

22. On Detroit, see Herring and Forbes (1994); on Alabama, see Applebome 1992: A16; *Pressley v. Etowah County Commission* (1992). Clendinen (1986: A10) describes the same phenonemon in school boards and superintendencies.

This formulation of white resistance to blacks' competitive success has links with many of the standard explanations for whites' racial animosity without necessarily endorsing any to the exclusion of the others. The links between competitive success and personal self-interest or group conflict are straightforward. Links to old-fashioned prejudice also seem clear; as it declines, so does whites' resistance to blacks' absolute and relative success. Links to the ideologies of egalitarianism and individualism seem similarly straightforward: the more egalitarian whites are, the less they oppose black competitive success. Conversely, the more individualistic whites are, the more they oppose black competitive success, at least when it seems closely tied to affirmative action. Links to symbolic racism are a bit more complex. According to that theory, whites feel threatened when blacks seem to get something for nothing or to violate standard norms of morality. This sense of threat can be interpreted as a symbolic zero-sum loss; blacks are apparently receiving rewards that whites deserve but have not received, or have received only after arduous effort. Worse yet, by not being appropriately grateful, blacks are in this view claiming an unwarranted moral equality or even superiority. Elegant comparisons and combinations of the various explanations are in Kluegel and Smith (1983); Bobo (1988); Sears (1988); Kinder and Sanders (1987); Virtanen (1992); and Bobo and Kluegel (1993). Citrin and Green (1990) offer an expansive definition of self-interest, similar in spirit to my broad framing of "whites' resistance to blacks' competitive success."

23. Merelman (1994: 2) explores why "in contrast to the past, cultural conflict involving race is no longer *transient* or *episodic* but is likely to become *pervasive, enduring*, and *increasingly severe*." Blauner (1992) makes an argument similar to mine that focuses on blacks' and whites' different understandings of "racism."

24. Wiley (1991: 8, emphasis in original). The fraternity's suit was upheld on First Amendment grounds (*Iota Xi Chapter v. George Mason University* 1993).

25. Asante (1988: 89).

26. Shea (1993: A33); Schmidt (1987); Wilkerson (1989a); Applebome (1993).

27. For similar patterns among college faculty and youth, respectively, see Carnegie Foundation for the Advancement of Teaching (1984: ques. 52A–52D; and People for the American Way (1992: 13–15, 154).

28. Thus as the Detroit police force became increasingly black from 1970 to 1990, dissatisfaction with police service remained high, and white dissatisfaction soared (Welch et al. 1994: 30–31).

29. Presumably some whites lie on these surveys, but the results still typically show fewer than 20% expressing resistance to blacks' competitive success. Even

doubling the rate of agreement would almost always yield considerably fewer than a majority of whites being resistant. The only survey I have found that directly compares blacks' and whites' views of racial competition finds that the former see *more* racial competition, and feel *more* competitive, than the latter (Jones and Jackson 1992: 27). Similarly, more affluent blacks than whites are "uncomfortable" working for a boss of another race (Gallup 1991a: var. 19D).

30. Personal communication from Clarence Stone, University of Maryland, to Jennifer Hochschild, May 27, 1994.

31. Walter Allen (1994: 4); see also Cose (1993); Feagin and Sikes (1994). Reverends Jesse Jackson, Al Sharpton, and Herbert Daughtry all felt compelled to urge that blacks in general not be held responsible for Colin Ferguson's random shooting of twenty-five Long Island Rail Road commuters (Lena Williams 1993; Rabinovitz 1993). No white leader has ever felt the need to assure the world that Charles Manson or Jeffrey Dahmer did not represent all whites.

32. Almost six in ten blacks agree strongly that "very few if any white people really understand the problems that blacks face" (and most of the rest agree somewhat). Only 15% of whites agree strongly, and another half agree somewhat (Sniderman et al. 1991: var. M4M). Similarly, only 40% of well-off blacks, compared with 63% of poor blacks, agree that "white people generally realize how much racial prejudice there is in the U.S. today" (Gordon Black 1989a: var. Q28). Three-quarters of blacks but only half of whites see race relations as an important issue (GSS 1983–84: var. 149A).

33. Bobo et al. (1992: 7–8). Four times as many well-off blacks were more angered by the verdict than by the ensuing violence as the reverse. (The ratio was two and a half to one for poor blacks, and two to one in the opposite direction for whites.) (Gallup 1992: var. 22; CBS News/ *NYT* 1992: vars. 34, 35; Yankelovich Clancy Shulman 1992: vars. 1–18).

34. Ugwu-Ojo (1992: 12A); Wilkerson (1992: 20).

35. Prager (1982: 109–10) gives an analysis much like mine, although he emphasizes more than I have done here the damage that African Americans do to themselves by "similarly succumb[ing] to the representation of blacks as a homogenous entity with certain non-individuated characteristics."

36. Lester (1981–82: 84–85).

37. Loury (1993: 8); see also Kilson (1986).

38. In the rest of the sentence quoted here, the author focuses on the specific harms of interracial marriage (Salaam 1979: 23). Ben Martin (1991) gives a hostile but illuminating analysis of how adoption of the name "African American" is designed to foster racial solidarity at the expense of class or individual differentiation.

39. Leonard Harris (1992: 203).

40. Clark (1993: 18).

41. All quotations in this paragraph are from Zangrando and Zangrando (1970).

42. Arithmetic and timing are crucial here. If the group of outsiders demanding the chance for competitive success is small enough, or arrives in a slow trickle, or times its demands to match periods of great economic expansion, the

challenge to the ideology and practice of the American dream is greatly attenu-ated. (An elegant and persuasive demonstration of this point is Lieberson 1980.) But none of those conditions obtained in the 1980s and early 1990s.

43. "Multiculturalism concludes that no one should be forced into a false choice between conformity to putatively universal standards of personal morality and loyalty to one's own racial group. Instead, the multiple group cultures which compose the United States possess a unique and enduring claim on the allegiances of their members." This analyst is optimistic, claiming that multicul-turalism "has penetrated some major sites of dominant group cultural power and culture creation, including universities, the public schools, and the mass media" (Merelman 1994: 14, 36). See also my discussion of transformative plu-ralism in chapter 13.

44. The phenomenon of middle-class meltdown (see chapter 5) could halt it, regardless of whites' and blacks' attitudes, if the middle class continues to lose more members to poverty than to wealth.

45. On managers, see Nixon (1985b: 26; 1985c: 22). On legislators, see Hedge et al. (1992). Many more female than male black legislators are dissatis-fied with their own careers, the influence of black legislators, and the treatment of and outcomes for proposed legislation of interest to blacks. On friends, see National Conference (1994: 76).

These satisfied respondents perhaps exemplify "straddlers" who "negotiate a new system, . . . a hybrid system, . . . a new network of rules, regulations, and standards that are a shifting blend" (Reagon 1991: 115).

46. On being outnumbered, see Longshore (1988); Giles and Evans (1986); Carsey (1995); on interracial politics, see Browning et al. (1990); Gomes and Williams (1992); Sonenshein (1993); DeLorenzo et al. (1994).

47. Schein (1986); Towers Perrin (1992: 3).

48. Patterson (1989: 484).

CHAPTER EIGHT
REMAINING UNDER THE SPELL

1. Earley (1986: 40); Folb (1980: 66). In these as in all quotations, I am following the linguistic convention used by the author whom I cite. Similarly, I give both first name and surname when the author has provided both; other-wise, I use only the name given in the work cited.

2. Chafets (1990: 53–54).

3. See Paige (1971) for a roughly similar typology.

4. Quotations from, respectively, Anderson (1980: 74); Folb (1980: 58); Ezekiel (1984: 24); and *Chicago Tribune* (1986: 94). Over half of poor blacks, compared with 13% of affluent blacks, agree strongly that blacks would be better off if they protested less and worked "within the system" more (Brown et al. 1994: table 15.21).

5. Quotations from, respectively, Blauner (1989: 177); MacLeod (1987: 79); Blauner (1989: 188); and Chafets (1990: 99–100).

6. Coalition on Human Needs (1988: 107); Royster (1991: table 4); see also Sullivan (1989: 32–52); Harris (1989b: 395, 397, 400).

7. Datcher-Loury and Loury (1986: 383); GSS (1972–73, 1982, 1987, 1990–91: var. 162); see also Levy (1983: 73); Massey et al. (1975: 15).

8. U.S. Department of Education (1992b: 16, 21, 24, 27, 30); see also Stevenson et al. (1990).

9. U.S. Department of Education (1992a: 8; 1994b: 18); Campbell et al. (1986); Hauser and Phang (1993: 33–35); see also Weis et al. (1989); Murnane et al. (1991: 37); Hill and Duncan (1987: 45).

10. Harris (1986b: 89–93); Lewis and Nakagawa (1994: table 4).

11. About 15% of eighth graders see student drug and alcohol consumption to be a serious school problem (those figures vary little by race or poverty status). At least one-fifth of black eighth graders see tardiness, absenteeism, cutting class, theft, vandalism, and fights as serious problems for their school. Some 10 to 20% report that students bring weapons to school and attack or threaten teachers. (Roughly half as many white students cite each problem.) Students in schools in poor neighborhoods report up to twice as many of these problems as do students in better-off schools. Data are not reported for race and poverty status combined (U.S. Department of Education 1991b: 213, 214, 217; see also ibid. 1993a: 130; 1993b: 21; Bernstein 1990: 18–23).

12. Forty-four percent of black, compared with 14% of white, eighth graders have two or more of the six "risk factors" predicting poor school performance (U.S. Department of Education 1991b: 74).

13. Seven in ten poorly-educated blacks claim that Americans' quality of education is better than it was a decade ago. Three in ten well-educated blacks agree; whites fall between these extremes (GSS 1990–91: var. 621A).

14. Anderson (1980: 60–63, 87–91, 150, 173) shows the importance of a job in regulating status and conduct among poor black men.

15. In 1983, 50% of nonwhite (and 28% of white) parents saw "the primary purpose of education . . . [to be] to enable a person to achieve financial success." Twice as many poor as well-off respondents concurred. Data for race and income combined are not available (Research and Forecasts 1983: 60, 62).

16. Chafets (1990: 103).

17. Tienda and Stier (1991a: table 3); Holzer (1986: 32–46); Tienda and Stier (1991b: 143). See also Culp and Dunson (1986: 243–44); Osterman (1980); Borus et al. (1981); Stephenson (1976).

18. GSS (1990–91: vars. 167D, 418–20); see also Goodwin (1972); Datcher-Loury and Loury (1986: 383); Harris (1989b: 395, 397, 400). Poor blacks believe more than any other race/class group that blacks are "working the hardest to succeed these days in America"; more poor blacks make this claim about their race than poor whites do for their own race (*Los Angeles Times* 1991b: var. 48).

19. Percentages range from 40% of well-educated white women to 82% of poorly educated black men (Harris 1970a: var. 22–3; 1970b: var. 20-C). Two decades later, many more poor blacks than any other race/class group claimed that "self-reliance" and "excellence on the job" were extremely important to them (Sniderman et al. 1991: vars. va4, va11; see also GSS 1993: vars. 464G, 464H).

20. NSBA (1980: var. 514; see also vars. 516, 1210D); GSS (1993: var. 463G).

21. Farkas et al. (1982: xxxvii, 120–21; 1984: 67–77); see also William T. Grant Foundation Commission on Work, Family, and Citizenship (1988: 46). Other programs had either poor results for all groups (Maynard 1980) or positive results across both races (Cave and Doolittle 1991).

22. However, black mothers worked fewer hours and received more welfare and food stamps than did white or Latina mothers (Masters and Maynard 1981: 89, 154). For similar findings, see Friedlander and Hamilton (1993: 69–82). Outcomes are comparable, though weaker, for programs to move ex-offenders and ex-addicts away from drug use and into jobs (Piliavin and Gartner 1981: 60, 110, 127; Dickinson 1981: 72, 192).

23. On the desire to work, see Edin (1994a). On working while receiving welfare, see Jencks (1992: 205–8); Kathleen Harris (1991; 1993); Myers (1989: 99–101). On working in suburbs, see Popkin et al. (1993). On support from family, see Lundgren Gaveras (1991: 17).

24. Ellwood (1988: 207); Kasarda (1995: 254–56).

25. Powers (1994: 192–95).

26. Bowman (1991a: 143); see also MCIC (1991–94: var. 352). "Because not having a job is so common here, some people have not yet reached a point where they are deeply concerned with some of the nuances of occupations. The priority is work, and mothers are often just grateful that their loved one has a job" (Hicks-Bartlett 1991: 32).

27. *Brown v. Board of Education* (1954).

28. Rosenberg and Simmons (1972); Epps (1978); Porter and Washington (1979); Hughes and Demo (1989: 133–35); Veroff et al. (1981).

29. Erskine (1969a: 152); Martineau (1976: 35); Goodwin (1972: 35, 56, 73, 83); Turner and Wilson (1976: 146); Allen and Hatchett (1986: 111, 113).

30. Cosby (1971); Johnson (1990); Barnes and Farrier (1985: 200–202); *Research Bulletin* (1991: 10); Porter and Washington (1979: 64); Hughes and Demo (1989: 150–52); McAdoo (1985). Quotation from Lemann (1991: 33–34). The NSBA (1980: vars. 61–67, 71), the largest survey with a battery of questions probing self-esteem, gives mixed results by class.

31. Poor whites' aspirations, in contrast, tend to be lower than those of well-off whites. See Antonovsky and Lerner (1959); Bloom et al. (1965); Bell (1965); Parker and Kleiner (1966); Erskine (1969b: 276); Jencks et al. (1972); Lorenz (1972: 372); Rodman et al. (1974); Ramirez and Price-Williams (1976); DeBord et al. (1977); Kerckhoff and Campbell (1977); Spenner and Featherman (1978: 388); Dawkins (1983: 108–9); Kluegel and Smith (1986: 66–69); Cook and Curtin (1987: 230–38); Sewell and Hauser (1993: 42–43).

32. Datcher-Loury and Loury (1986: 383, 387); U.S. Department of Education (1992b: 41); Burbridge (1991: 31).

33. *Research Bulletin* (1992: 4–5).

34. Mische (1993) nicely depicts the struggle to move from despair to fantasy to realistic expectations.

35. Responses did not vary by ethnicity (Crosby et al. 1989: 88–93); see also Clayton and Crosby (1992).

36. The disparity in sentiments about Congress has held steady for twenty years ("Public Opinion and Demographic Report" 1994a: 84–85; *NYT/*CBS News 1994b: 5–9).

37. "My Town, the Nation" (1992: 95); Hess (1987: 31). Even residents of Harlem and the South Bronx, who deplore their neighborhood and almost all of the city services they encounter, claim that the rest of New York City has deteriorated more than their own neighborhood has (Harris 1979: 3–6).

38. On race relations and prejudice, see *NYT*/CBS News (1992: vars. 19, 20, 29, 30); on police, see Holmes (1991). The discrepancy between general and particular extends to comparisons between others and oneself. Over a quarter of respondents agree that "police rough up people unnecessarily . . . in your neighborhood," but only half as many report that they or someone they know has been roughed up (*NYT*/CBS News 1991a: 13). Similarly, as we saw in chapter 7, many more whites think affirmative action harms whites than can report harm to themselves or people they know.

39. Lee (1981).

40. Quoted in Holmes (1991).

41. Bulman and Wortman (1977). Similarly, among returning students who have already failed or been expelled from high school, those "who attribute failure to a lack of effort are not depressed, . . . have Positive Self-Image, . . . and have high reading scores" (Fine 1983b: 228–31).

42. Thus the more black AFDC recipients believe that America offers equal opportunity to all, the more they blame themselves for being on welfare (Goodban 1985: 411–13).

43. Campbell and Schuman (1968: vars. 175–78). Poor whites resembled poor blacks; well-off blacks and, especially, whites were the most gratified by their control over the past and most confident of their control over the future. In short, class more than race determined the degree of "irrational" commitment to the third tenet of the American dream.

44. Bowman (1991b: 170, 174).

45. Duncan and Hill (1975); Andrisani and Parnes (1983); Goodwin (1983); Furstenberg et al. (1987: 54–55, 63–74, 134–37); Plotnick (1992); Szekelyi and Tardos (1993).

46. Corcoran et al. (1985: 528, emphasis added); see also Zajonc and Brickman (1969); Duncan and Morgan (1981); Hill et al. (1985); Mboya (1986); Ellwood (1987: 46–47); Popkin (1990).

47. Quotations from, respectively, Blauner (1989: 268); Lubenow (1983); and Milloy (1983: A19).

48. MacLeod (1987: 129–30).

49. Balzer (1972: 13).

50. Wolf (1990) and Cook and Curtin (1987: 250–52) elegantly analyze the drive to eke out a sense of "relative advantage" even among the worst off.

51. "I didn't associate with too many people at Peralta [a Supported Work demonstration project] because you put yourself in a certain category. You want to be around people that have something. . . . You want to benefit yourself. If you are around a person who doesn't have anything, who wants to borrow something all the time, that's just tearing you down" (Ritter and Danziger 1983: 54; see also Briar 1966: 51–52; Kaplan and Tausky 1972).

52. Marx (1964: var. 50d); Lewis and Schneider (1985: 6–7). For comparisons with other race/class groups, see notes 40 and 44 of chapter 4.

53. Scores are identical for whites on the first question (Sniderman et al. 1991: var. ang6). On the second question, fewer poor whites and more well-off whites concurred (ibid.: var. poor; see also var. m3d).

54. Comments by Pearl and Michael are in Pedder (1991: 14–17).

55. Comments are from different people (Ritter and Danziger 1983: 1, 14).

56. Ritter and Danziger (1983: 22).

57. Chafets (1990: 109); Finnegan (1990b: 69).

58. On Washington, D.C., see Brounstein et al. (1989: 106). On church-going, see Freeman (1986: 366); Viscusi (1986: 319–20, 326, 339); Datcher-Loury and Loury (1986: 387); and Lerman (1986: 430–31).

59. NSBA (1980: vars. 34, 56, 59).

60. Lincoln and Mamiya (1990: 147–57, 255–67); Tate and Brown (1991); Brown and Wolford (1994); Verba et al. (1993: 480–94); Thomas et al. (1994); Gilkes (1985). For testimony from church members, see NSBA (1980: var. 59).

61. Debates rage over whether the black church is a conservatizing (Frazier and Lincoln 1974; Marx 1969; Reed 1986) or liberating (West 1988; Taylor and Chatters 1989; Cone 1986) force. The research evidence is mixed. Frequent churchgoers endorse social efforts to promote equality more than infrequent attenders do (Hunt and Hunt 1977; Allen 1994: 84; Fredrick Harris 1993: 30–31; 1994; Reese and Brown 1995). But they also describe themselves as more conservative or engage less in protests (Tate 1993: 33; Brown and Wolford 1994: 42). Highly religious blacks (and whites) are either *less* likely (McCord et al. 1969: 89–91; Allen 1994: 84; Fredrick Harris 1993: 30–31; 1994) or *more* likely (Nelsen et al. 1975; Allen et al. 1989; Brown and Wolford 1994: 42) than irreligious blacks to endorse equality or engage in political action (for mixed results, see Hunt and Hunt 1977; Secret et al. 1990; Reese and Brown forthcoming). The resolution of the debate seems straightforward; different black churches and denominations vary in their degree of religious and political conservatism or activism (Tate 1993: 95–103). From my perspective, this debate is largely beside the point since both conservatizing and radicalizing strands reinforce (different aspects of) the American dream.

62. Clergy who express the strongest black nationalism pastor the churches with the most involvement in community programs (Lincoln and Mamiya 1990: 168–87).

63. In 1964 Muslims were more likely than other blacks to claim both that promotion in their present job was important and that it was unlikely. They were, in short, thwarted believers in the dream (Marx 1969: 118–19). The link between belief in the dream and hatred of the mainstream dreamers is made painfully clear by one young Muslim: "As a kid . . . you always have dreams—fantasies—of yourself doing something later—being a big name singer or something that makes you outstanding. . . . [In my teens] I saw I was nowhere and had no way of getting anywhere. Race feeling is always with you. You always know about The Man but I don't think it is real, really real, until you have to deal with it in terms of what you are going to do with your own life. . . . You begin to hate him when you see him blocking you in your life" (McCord et al. 1969: 243–44).

64. Nicolas Lemann (1991: 303–4) points to a related irony in comparing

the Nation of Islam to the Catholic school system and the American military. These institutions all emphasize discipline and are unusually successful in enabling poor blacks actually to achieve the American dream. The point is not that the Nation of Islam is internally inconsistent; the point is rather that militant black consciousness is as likely to reinforce as to oppose the dream's recipe for success.

65. Many fewer whites concurred. Poor blacks living in poor neighborhoods showed the strongest sense of community, whereas poor whites in poor neighborhoods showed the weakest (Berry et al. 1991: 367–68). That finding implies either that poor whites but not poor blacks are demoralized or that poor whites but not poor blacks are individualistic and (they hope) upwardly mobile.

66. Poor whites are similarly engaged; nonpoor blacks and whites are more active (Berry et al. 1991: 367–68).

67. Berry et al. (1989: table 6). Hicks-Bartlett (1991: 27–31) portrays "block clubs" in poor neighborhoods more negatively; in her view, they mostly pressure people into proper etiquette. Even so, "club members generate a sense of empowerment and activism" and "block clubs . . . act as social support groups or extensions of family networks." Furstenberg (1993) sensitively explores the importance of neighborhood context for families' ability to nurture and encourage their children; Cohen and Dawson (1993) show the extent of political isolation in poor communities that are not mobilized.

68. Kotlowitz (1991: 113–16, 184–85, 199–202, 254). Rosenbaum et al. (1993) have perhaps the most straightforward demonstration of the positive effects of good schooling on poor black children.

69. One may look at teachers of the poor as heroic fighters against overwhelming and heartbreaking conditions (Weissbourd 1989; Kozol 1991; Kirp 1992; Freedman 1990) or as (conscious or not) instruments of structural inequality or institutional racism (Massey et al. 1975; Katz 1975; Bowles and Gintis 1976; Carnoy and Levin 1976; Bourdieu and Passeron 1977; Kerckhoff 1991; DeMott 1990). My focus here is on the effects, not the causes, of schools' efforts to inculcate allegiance to the American dream, so I take no position in this debate.

70. MCIC (1991–94: vars. 630, 633–35). The poor of both races are, however, less convinced than the wealthy that their local school emphasizes learning.

71. Jhally and Lewis (1992) do discuss television's promotion of an individualist, materialist version of the American dream.

72. MCIC (1991–94: var. 118); GSS (1993: var. 461A). Children's afternoon television watching is strongly associated with employed black mothers' concern about their children's safety (Medrich et al. 1982: 118–29, 172–73, 213, 216–18). On adult watchers, see Survey Research Center (1964: var. 47); Poindexter and Stroman (1981: 109); HDM/Dawson Johns and Black (1988); Allen and Hatchett (1986: 113).

73. On learning, see Comstock and Cobbey (1979: 106, 110); Poindexter and Stroman (1981: 112, 113–14). On confidence, see GSS (1972–73, 1982, 1987, 1990–91: var. 162I).

74. On heavy watchers, see Gerbner and Gross (1976); on closeness, see Allen et al. (1992: 177, 181); on happy families, see Donohue et al. (1978: 39).

75. On Terry Jackson, see Finnegan (1990b: 76); on the rapper and Motown, see Chafets (1990: 81, 90).

76. Ezekiel (1984: 181). Half of black low- or unskilled laborers (compared with only 17% of those in white-collar jobs) will be dissatisfied if their children have the same job as themselves (Bowman 1991a: 142).

77. Laseter (1991: 20–21).

78. Hout and Morgan (1975: 375); Tucker et al. (1979); Rosenbaum et al. (1993); Case and Katz (1991: table 6); U.S. Department of Education (1992a: 22); Bolger et al. (forthcoming). These links may be new since the 1960s, when the structural constraints were so great that factors explaining variation in white students' success had less impact on blacks' educational outcomes (Portes and Wilson 1976; Porter 1974).

One study offers a cautionary note: peers' influence has more effect on non-whites' than on whites' high school achievement, and among blacks it depresses their level of academic success (Steinberg et al. 1992: 727–28).

79. Clark (1983); Scheinfeld (1983); Dornbusch et al. (1991: 556–57).

80. On use of time, see Freeman (1986: 363–68); on job-holding, see Ballen and Freeman (1986: 88); Jackson and Montgomery (1986: 123–25); Datcher-Loury and Loury (1986: 387); Tienda and Stier (1991a: 145); on income from crime, see Viscusi (1986: 326); on life-styles, see Case and Katz (1991: table 6).

81. Cave and Doolittle (1991: 108, 120, 135 [but see 147]); Dickinson (1981: 72, 98, 127 [but see 111]); Maynard (1980: 88 [but see 140]); Piliavin and Gartner (1981: 60, 110, 127).

82. Masters and Maynard (1981).

83. Tienda and Stier (1991a: 28).

CHAPTER NINE
WITH ONE PART OF THEMSELVES THEY ACTUALLY BELIEVE

1. Myrdal (1944: 4, emphasis added).

2. For example, among unemployed African Americans in 1980, more poor than wealthy could not find a job they wanted, had "lost hope of find[ing] a decent job," and thought it "not likely at all" that they would try to find a job within the next year. They were, however, interested in working and would take a job if offered (NSBA 1980: vars. 719, 722, 725, 726, 727).

3. This section does not assume that all poor African Americans could succeed, at least in obtaining a job, if they acted in accord with their purported belief in the American dream. There would probably not be enough jobs if everyone playing the game of employment musical chairs really tried to sit down at once (Lafer 1994). My question here is a different one: given that jobs are available for some, why do some poor African Americans try harder than others to sit down when the music stops?

4. "You have to catch the bus to get down there [to the WIN office] and you get lost. . . . It takes a long time. I transfer to the 88. Since they go so funny now, I don't know where to get off" (Ritter and Danziger 1983: 62). Fifteen percent of poor blacks (and 4% of poor whites) report that they need but cannot use public transportation (GSS 1990–91: var. 625I).

5. Levy (1983: 58). For example, "I don't know, maybe I'll be a secretary. I don't know, I want to work with typewriters, where I could have my own desk." Or, "I want to be a beautician. . . . You have to go to school, some kind of beauty school, to learn the ropes and things." Working-class and middle-class teens typically do not lack this type of concrete knowledge (Farber 1989: 528). Many more poor urban black eighth graders do not take algebra than do take it, even though this gateway course is essential for the academic goals that these students set for themselves. Presumably this lacuna occurs partly because no one has told them the necessity of this course (*Research Bulletin* 1992: 8). On the importance of cultural competence, see Swidler (1986).

6. "You go in to your counselor. He's under pressure so he acts impatient: 'What do you need?' You ask for help on college credits. They don't know. You end up choosing on your own. . . . We need people who can *tell* us what we do not know, or what we need to know. We don't know everything. But they don't have the time." An elementary school in Paterson, New Jersey, boasts one counselor for 3,600 students (Kozol 1991: 112, 155, 160).

7. One-fourth of the graduates of the Chicago public high schools read at a sixth-grade level or below; one-half of the sixty-five high schools place in the bottom 1% of national ratings in their students' ACT scores. Nevertheless, 16% of Chicago's seniors rated their schools as "excellent" in 1987. "Students from schools with the lowest levels of performance [and the highest proportions of black, Latino, and low-income students] thought their schools, by and large, offered better writing and laboratory programs, provided more effective counseling and teacher support, and had parents who were more influential in [their school]" (Hartmann 1989: 10–16; see also Street 1969: 17; Brown et al. 1994: table 19.4). Thirteen percent of poor urban eighth-grade African Americans go to schools that do not offer algebra, even though it is an essential course for an academic track in high school (*Research Bulletin* 1992: 8).

8. Natriello and Dornbusch (1984: 84–92) show that black students receive more praise and responsiveness but less real challenge from teachers compared with white students. As a result they think that they are working as hard and doing as well, but their actual test scores and levels of effort are considerably lower.

9. Goodwin (1972: 35, 56, 83, 101–8).

10. Popkin (1990: 607–13z0. Ritter and Danziger (1983) show sharp differences in levels of confidence between long-term AFDC recipients who successfully moved from welfare to work and those who did not in a well-monitored demonstration project.

11. Pedder (1991: 29).

12. Bowman et al. (1982: 87); see also Bowman (1984: 80–84).

13. The policy implications of this rather mundane point are debated endlessly. The issue is roughly whether the carrots of better jobs, transportation, and child care will do more to bolster that irrational motivation than the sticks of work requirements or reduced AFDC benefits. In my terms, the dispute is over whether the government should be responsible for making the soft version of the American dream available to all Americans or for mandating its hard side for those who cannot soften it on their own.

Furstenberg (1993: 232–34, 237–43) and Ritter and Danziger (1983: 13–30) nicely illustrate "supermotivation."

14. Glasgow (1980: 84); Pedder (1991: 27).

15. "I'm scared to go out lookin' for a job. They be usin' words in the interview like in school. Words I don't know. I can't be askin' them for a dictionary. It's like in school. You ask and you feel like a dummy" (Fine 1992: 127).

16. Lynn (1990: 3). Although experimental subjects who saw themselves as victims of injustice were given an avenue of appeal, they seldom used it. "Asking for change or demanding a voice in the allocation may be risky. It may realistically engender further victimization, particularly if initiated by an individual victim, and [be] unlikely to promote change" (Fine 1983a: 28; see also Steil 1983). If this sentiment obtains among college students playing games for tokens and course credit, it seems even more likely among poor blacks for whom protest risks the loss of income or emotional support, and whose circumstances make fault unclear and remedies unlikely.

17. U.S. Bureau of the Census (1994: 8–9).

18. My friend "actually did start [college] and tried to cover it up. They found out and cut off her [food] stamps completely. Then, when they restored them, they gave back less than half of what she had been getting. . . . She's the one that scared me out of trying [to go to school]" (Popkin 1990: 609; Edin 1994a).

19. "Ida's youngest son, a child with some academic talent, was offered a scholarship at an exclusive private school in the center of the city. Ida never told the boy about the possibility. . . . Ida was unprepared to see her child so far removed from scrutiny. The task of avoiding dangers while promoting opportunities involves a . . . balancing act. . . . Parents, like Ida, who attempt to isolate their children from threats in their immediate environment run the risk of prohibiting them from taking steps to escape poverty" or their dangerous neighborhood (Furstenberg 1993: 242).

20. Lynn (1990: 9); Geronimus (1987); Farber (1989: 529). Conquergood (1992; 1994) emphasizes the need for some young men to join a gang in order to survive—which makes gang membership low-cost, compared with the alternatives.

21. Ogbu (1983: 178–81). For example, "reason I stay in school is 'cause every time I get on the subway I see this drunk and I think 'not me.' But then I think, 'bet he has a high school degree'" (Fine 1992: 129). Thus, although they predict grades for students of both races, IQ scores predict educational or occupational expectations only for whites. For black girls, in fact, the higher the IQ score, the *lower* the occupational expectation (Hout and Morgan 1975: 374–75).

22. GSS (1990–91: vars. 619D, E, G, and H). Poor blacks agree with all of these points more than any other race/class group.

23. Edin (1994a: 16); Andrisani and Parnes (1983: 112–15). In 1985 most poor blacks (and more poor blacks than poor or well-off whites) believed that "the Reagan budget cuts have left the truly needy unprotected," that poor people are hard-working and would rather work than receive welfare, but that "poor people find it very hard to get work" (*Los Angeles Times* 1985: ques. 25, 41, 50,

54). This combination of beliefs is not likely to inspire risk-taking in the labor market.

24. Hill (1973: 148); Steinberg et al. (1992: 726).

25. Orlean (1993: 77).

26. Frey (1993: 38).

27. Fine (1992: 133); Furstenberg et al. (1987).

28. Wacquant (1994b: 30). Anderson (1990) provides the best analysis of the need to adopt "street" rather than "decent" modes of behavior in order to survive.

29. Wacquant (1994b: 34, 40, 41, 48, emphases in original).

30. White Americans accept general principles of racial equality and integration but reject most particular means of implementing them (Schuman et al. 1988: 73–104; Hochschild and Herk 1990). They show similar disparities between general and concrete beliefs about distributive justice (Hochschild 1981: 238–59). Almost all high school dropouts in San Diego agreed that learning and graduation from high school are important; over 80% wanted to learn, expected to graduate, and had the ability to graduate. Yet none did, and they provide many explanations for why not (Barr and Knowles 1986: 16, C3–C14).

31. "Before I got pregnant, I wanted to go to college and run track. But now I'm starting to take some classes to prepare me for a job, like typing and word processing" (Farber 1989: 525).

Baly (1989) and Cook and Curtin (1987) review the relevant literature on expectancies (but see Miller et al. 1977 for contradictory findings). Both high- and (especially) low-status black students' expectations of future success do not decline nearly as much as those of (especially well-off) white students when they see the causes of their prior success as unstable (Graham 1986: 57–58; Graham and Long 1986: 7). Blacks' expectancies thus may be less dependent on causal attributions than are whites'.

32. Foner and Napoli (1978); Goodban (1985: 412–13).

33. Mickelson (1990: 52–56).

34. Fagan (1989: 650–51, 654, 656).

35. "I didn't really get no help. . . . They . . . make you feel ashamed to ask and stuff, so I never said anything. . . . When you're at [this] school you feel out of place, you feel . . . like you ain't no good and you feel like a lower class bum" (Danziger and Farber 1990: 37). Comer (1980); Weissbourd (1989); and Hess (1987: 23–44) insightfully compare successful and failing schools for poor students.

36. "By now I'm beginning to see the racism in the church. . . . I see how black converts living in the inner city took shit jobs to devote more of their lives to religious work, and whites had professional jobs and took vacations. . . . I began to see the connections between 'male rule,' which puts women, who do all the work, in the very lowest level in the organization. And I admit to myself that I am in a religious organization that is sexist and segregated and I have been in it for twenty years. Then the trap begins to close in on me" (Scott 1991: 54).

37. Popkin et al. (1993: 570); see also Rosenbaum et al. (1993); Kotlowitz (1991); Lemann (1991).

38. At age twelve, Charlie rushed home to tell his mother that he had passed

sixth grade, to find her consoling his sister who had not. "Charlie had to wait patiently while his mother consoled Theresa, who was in tears. Instead of praising him, though, his mother said to Theresa, 'Don't worry, Theresa. Charlie will fail too.'" A decade later "Charlie's voice shook with anger as he told the story. '[A mother] supposed to treat her children the same. Don't put your son down. Your son got emotionals just like the daughter got emotionals.'" Charlie failed the next two grades, and left school at age sixteen (Dash 1989: 129). See also Clark (1983); Finnegan (1990a; 1990b); Berg and Olson (1991: 27–28).

39. Garbarino et al. (1992).

40. Anson (1987); Wideman (1984); Monroe and Goldman (1988); McCall (1994); Staples (1994).

41. Even in classes and workshops on Afrocentricity, "people tend to provide what they think will be the right answer regardless of whether it's their answer. If I asked most people, 'What is your purpose?' they would probably answer by saying, 'To help somebody, to make the world better, to get closer to God.' But if I asked them, 'What do you spend most of your working hours doing, or what would you like to do with these hours?' I believe the responses would be 'Making money, shopping, feeling and looking good'" (Kunjufu 1986: 20).

My own earlier discussion of acquiescence emphasized a more engaged conflict among beliefs (Hochschild 1981: 265–72).

42. Luttrell (1993: 530).

43. Anderson (1978: 78, 118–19).

44. Blauner (1989: 224).

45. In 1985, for example, 93% of low-status black New Yorkers agreed that the police "often engage in brutality against blacks." Despite their generally greater sensitivity to racial discrimination, almost 10% fewer high-status blacks agreed. Just over 40% of whites concurred (*NYT*/WCBS News 1985: var. 45).

46. Ellison (1966: 40).

CHAPTER TEN
DISTORTING THE DREAM

1. Fulwood (1989). In 1960, 81 people were killed in the District of Columbia; in 1987, the total reached 225, and in 1988, Chief Fulwood's *annus horribilus*, it increased to 369. After an all-out effort the next year to stop the killings, including a daily murder count by a local television station, the murder rate in 1989 jumped to 434. It increased again in 1990 and 1991, peaking at 483, and dropped a bit in 1993 (to 465) (Office of Criminal Justice Plans and Analysis 1992: 35; "As Cities Reach Record Numbers of Killings . . . " 1994).

2. Consider, for example, Charles Stuart's murder of his seven-months-pregnant wife, apparently for insurance money (Martz et al. 1990).

3. Unless I am quoting or paraphrasing others, I do not speak of the "underclass," because the term has both political and analytic defects. Although William Wilson offered the best justification, he later abjured it (Wilson 1987: 8; 1991; see also Gans 1990; Mills 1994: 857–59). "Underclass" offends many blacks and encourages whites to distance themselves from the problems of inner cities. It evokes the image of a class structure in a society that denies that the

nonpoor are arrayed in classes. Most importantly, it elides the connection between long-term poverty and "deviance," since people use it variously to describe the poor, the badly behaved (by mainstream standards), or the badly behaved poor.

I propose instead the term "estranged poor." That phrase makes explicit the fact that the population in question is both poor and "deviant." It avoids the anomaly of invoking class on the bottom rung of American society while ignoring it further up the ladder. Finally, it disperses blame beyond the poor themselves since one is estranged *by* someone as well as *from* someone.

4. Kasarda (1993: 256). Crime was not included in this series of studies because it is not measured by census tract.

5. Kasarda (1993: 258, 263).

6. Mincy (1994); O'Hare and Curry-White (1992: 12); Kasarda (1993: 263). See also Reischauer (1987); Hughes (1989); Ricketts and Mincy (1990); Aponte (1990); Jargowsky and Bane (1991); Kasarda (1992); Jencks (1992: chap. 5); Jargowsky (1994).

7. In 1990–91 under 10% of low-status African Americans reported that their child had trouble in school, was arrested, or had a problem with drugs or drinking. Smaller fractions of the other race/class groups made the same admissions (GSS 1990–91: vars. 625A, 625F, and 625I). These results are not entirely reliable, but even if they are doubled we are left with roughly 20% of poor blacks in substantial trouble.

8. Kasarda (1993: 263).

9. Hughes (1988: 10–11, emphasis added).

10. U.S. Bureau of the Census (1975: I: table D42–48; 1993b: 393). See also Jencks (1992: 156).

11. Jencks (1992: 193); U.S. Congress (1992: 670).

12. U.S. Department of Justice (1994c: 388); Bogess and Bound (1993: 10–12). See also Jencks (1992: 182, 184); Austin (1992: 593–600); Darity et al. (1990: 23).

13. Geis and Jesilow (1993); U.S. Department of Justice (1994c: 395). As one atypical article puts it, "White males headed failed savings and loan institutions in numbers far greater than their proportion in the general population, according to a study released last week. The study also found that heading a failed thrift is linked to possessing a home and using multiple credit cards. . . . The presence of so many adults in these [two-parent] homes 'may trigger feelings of inferiority in young white boys. The results may be dangerously low self-esteem, which leads them, when they grow up, to gamble with depositors' money in a desperate—albeit ineffective—attempt to feel better about themselves'" (MacLean 1990).

14. U.S. Department of Health and Human Services (1988: 78–84; 1990a: 87–94; 1991a: 88–95; 1993a: 86–87, 122–23; 1994b: tables 12B, 13B); see also Redd (1989).

15. U.S. Department of Health and Human Services (1990a: 33; 1991a: 32; 1993a: 20–123 passim).

16. Bachman et al. (1991); U.S. Department of Health and Human Services (1991b: 182–84); Reuter et al. (1988: 23); U.S. Department of Health and

Human Services (1993b: 22–45). In this context it is not surprising that more white than black teachers in New Jersey describe students' use of alcohol and drugs as a serious problem (Center for Public Interest Polling 1986: 84–85).

17. U.S. Department of Justice (1988; 1990: 5; 1994b: 7).

18. I say "may be" because most research finds the heaviest drug and alcohol use, and the worst effects therefrom, in the poorest communities. The results reported in this paragraph suggest, however, that that finding may be due partly to where researchers look, partly to what is defined as a drug, and partly to the fact that poverty exacerbates the harms caused by drug and alcohol use.

19. U.S. Department of Health and Human Services (1990a: 33; 1991b: 32); but see ibid. (1993b: 80–90).

20. U.S. Department of Health and Human Services (1990b: 143, 144).

21. Chasnoff et al. (1990).

22. Kaestner (1991; 1994); Mills and Noyes (1984); Williams et al. (1992: 187).

23. Laseter (1991: 11, 26). Almost one-fifth of poorly educated blacks, compared with 3% of similar whites, strongly agree that personal freedom is more important than marriage. Almost one-fifth of the former, and one-tenth of the latter, deny that people who want children should marry (GSS 1988–89: vars. 526B, 526F). Fewer poor African Americans than any other race/class group include marriage as one of their most important goals (GSS 1993: var. 464B).

24. Furstenberg et al. (1992: 49); *Chicago Tribune* (1986: 96–97). Anderson (1990: 112–37) portrays poor black teenaged boys as sexual predators and their girlfriends as wistful victims; Dash (1989), conversely, presents gullible young men and determined female pursuers. Murray (1986) blames both parents equally; Furstenberg et al. (1992) sympathetically portray black fathers who fail in their obligations.

25. Well-off black men also, although less frequently, have children before they marry; both poor and well-off white men marry on average one to six years before having children. "Racial differences are largest in the lowest socioeconomic stratum" (Testa 1991: 8–10, table 2; see also Sullivan 1989).

26. Furstenberg et al. (1992: 2); Edin (1994b: 2).

27. Moss and Tilly (1991: 23); Neckerman and Kirschenman (1991: 440); Kirschenman and Neckerman (1991: 224). On the gender distinction, see Kirschenman (1991).

28. Blauner (1989: 145).

29. Anderson (1980: 72–73).

30. Indeed, the explanation of the person just quoted for his boss's behavior is that "he fraid o' the white man gettin' on him."

31. Anderson (1980: 85).

32. Berg and Olson (1991: 18–27). Taub (1991: 13) illuminatingly contrasts poor African Americans who resent extra work and Mexican immigrants who accept it as part of the job.

33. Neckerman (1991: 26).

34. Finnegan (1990b: 67, 64).

35. GSS (1990–91: var. 625B).

36. McCord et al. (1969: 241); Folb (1980: 84); Kunjufu (1986: 30).

37. "Russell, Corey, and Stephon are the natural heirs to this vaunted tradition [of local basketball stars who almost made it to the pros]. But . . . given the failures that have preceded them, the new crew is watched by the neighborhood with a certain skittishness, a growing reluctance to care too deeply" (Frey 1993: 41).

38. Wideman (1984: 85, 89–90, emphasis added).

39. Wideman (1984: 91).

40. Johnstone (1978). The locus classicus of this argument is Merton (1938); see also, among others, Cloward and Ohlin (1960); Farnworth and Leiber (1989).

41. Harris (1989b: 403–8). These figures may be too high, if people want to shock or impress the interviewer or other listeners, or too low, if people do not want to admit such activities and proclivities to a stranger. Short et al. (1965) show a strong association among race, class, and belief in the existence of legitimate opportunities, on the one hand, and gang membership, on the other.

42. Poor whites in the 1989 survey gave the same response (Freeman 1989: 18).

43. Jackson (1988: 33); Sullivan (1989: 116 and more generally 113–23).

44. Myers (1992).

45. Viscusi (1986: 307–15). Chiricos (1987) and Allan and Steffensmeier (1989) review the literature on the connection between unemployment and crime.

46. Adler (1985); Terry Williams (1989); Fagan (1989); Inciardi and Pottieger (1991); and Johnson et al. (1992) find that young drug sellers typically are heavy users. Finnegan (1990a; 1990b); Brounstein et al. (1989); Skolnick et al. (1990); and Skolnick (1989) find that they typically are not. Reuter et al. (1990) and Carl Taylor (quoted in McFate 1989: 2) find wide variation on this point.

47. Terry Williams (1989: 20).

48. Quotations from Bourgois in McFate (1989: 8); survey data from Case and Katz (1991: table 4); and Brounstein et al. (1989: 122).

Ingesting cocaine is a simpler way to achieve the American dream, albeit fleetingly: "You hit the pipe, you are whatever you fantasize you want to be. . . . You're into basketball, you are Magic Johnson. Say you're into music and you're basing. You feel like you *are* James Brown or Stevie Wonder or Michael Jackson. It makes you feel like what you really want to be" (Skolnick et al. 1990: 27).

49. Pedder (1991: 21).

50. Brounstein et al. (1989: 129).

51. Jencks (1992: 208); Edin (1994a: 7–8).

52. Viscusi (1986: 310); Reuter et al. (1990: ix, 62–69); see also Brounstein et al. (1989: 107).

53. Brown et al. (1991: 156); Short and Strodtbeck (1965); Anthony Harris 1976: 438).

54. The first three quotations are from Terry Williams (1989: 32, 89, 24); then, successively, Skolnick et al. (1990: 19); Sullivan (1989: 170); Adler (1990: 25).

55. Interview with Isaac Fulwood, February 16, 1989; Johnson et al.

(1992); Williams (1989); Adler (1985); Covino (1985); Skolnick (1989); Skolnick et al. (1990); Wilkerson (1988); Horwitz (1988); Hamid (1990); Hiss (1992). Most generally, "youth who sell but do not use drugs look much like youth who neither sell nor use drugs in terms of progress in school, family and peer support, religiosity and the way they spend their free time. These youth seem to embrace mainstream values, expressing entrepreneurial drive through both traditional/legitimate as well as unconventional/illicit means (Brounstein et al. 1989: 108).

56. Drug sellers vary in their motives and modes of operation according to ethnicity, locality, and tradition. It appears that as methods of drug dealing become less chaotic and more businesslike, blacks are moving into the forefront of the trade at least at the street level (Skolnick et al. 1990; McFate 1989: 2; Sullivan 1989: 204; Hamid 1990; Fagan and Chin 1989: 6).

57. Sullivan (1989: 126–30, 162).

58. Merton (1938) first articulated this argument, although not in the context of either race or the American dream. See Flowers (1988) for a racially focused review of various theories of criminal causation, some of which I implicitly use in this chapter.

59. Ferguson (1994: 72). Jones (1992: 274) reminds readers that structural constraints combined with the tantalizing hope of the American dream have always induced poor people to use criminal means to seek good ends; what has changed is the coming of "the twin plagues of drugs and guns."

60. Miller (1986: 136); Taylor, in McFate (1989: 5). Dealers may, however, face the opposite problem—good business skills with no legitimate outlet: "I know I could run lots of kinds of businesses but I can't go up to somebody and say, 'Listen, I know how to buy and sell. I've been buying and selling drugs for years'" (Sullivan 1989: 175). Drug selling apparently returns many fewer benefits to poor black communities than did earlier illegal markets in gambling and bootlegging (Reuter et al. 1990: 85–89).

61. Glasgow (1980: 90); see also Valentine (1978); Wacquant (1994b).

62. *Chicago Tribune* (1986: 190, 133).

63. Majors and Billson (1992: 1, 2, 8, 29); see also Glasgow (1980: 96–97).

64. On drugs, see Folb (1980: 174–75); Glasgow (1980: 95); Jackson (1988: 71–72). On artistic expression, see Majors and Billson (1992: 69–77, 91–102).

65. Ferguson (1987: 27–33); Kotlowitz (1991); Majors and Billson (1992: 37–53).

66. Majors and Billson (1992: 45). Some employers prefer to hire black women over black men "because there is not the interference with the macho imaging stuff that gets in the way. For men, is it really cool to say 'I've got to go to work tomorrow 'cause my employer needs me'?" (Kirschenman 1991: 9). Taub (1991: 14–23) discusses how a well-designed jobs policy could constructively tap poor blacks' strong sense of honor.

67. Finnegan (1990a: 83). Terry Jackson is echoed by a Chicago dealer: "The guys are not all hoggish. They take turns throwing. They watch each other's back when the other guy is throwing" (quoted in Kunjufu 1986: 7).

68. True to the fourth precept of the American dream, Max's virtue was re-

warded; he took over Hector's connect and list of customers and never looked back (Terry Williams 1994: 43–48).

69. Sullivan (1989: 173).

70. Skolnick (1989: 2–6); Skolnick et al. (1990: 8–18). See also Huff (1990); Jankowski (1991); Hagedorn (1988). Just as some historians lament that liberal individualism squelched republican virtue, gang members mourn the ascendency of instrumental over cultural gangs: "Back in the old days it was like everybody was together, like a big old family. Now ever since the drugs hit the street, everybody wants to go their own way, forget about the neighborhood" (Skolnick 1989: 7).

71. Skolnick (1989: 4–5); Jackson (1988: 76); Sullivan (1989: 169).

72. Wideman (1984: 93–106); Anderson (1978: 141); Jenkins (1991: 140).

73. Dash (1989: 127).

74. Miller (1986: 82).

75. "Sixteen years ago I came to Chicago with forty dollars in my pocket. Three years afterward I was married. My son is now twelve. I am still married and love my wife dearly. We had to make a living. . . . I didn't believe in prohibiting people from getting the things they wanted. I thought prohibition an unjust law and I still do. Somehow I just naturally drifted into the racket" (Vanderbilt 1972: 12). Excepting the last word, these comments could epitomize the association of success with virtue. But they come from Al Capone, thereby demonstrating that poor blacks are not the only distorters of the fourth tenet of the American dream, that distortion was not invented by drug dealers, and that the line between love of family and evil is fine indeed.

76. Kotlowitz (1991: 136, 35); Covino (1985: 85). Al Capone again: "This is going to be a terrible winter. Us fellas has gotta open our pocketbooks, and keep on keeping them open, if we want any of us to survive" (Vanderbilt 1972: 11).

77. Marinucci and Gibbs (1986: A10); see also Anderson (1990: 243). Chants of "hero, hero, hero" at Pablo Escobar's funeral in Colombia and Woody Guthrie's ballad of "Pretty Boy Floyd, an Outlaw" ("Some rob you with a six-gun, some with a fountain pen") remind us that adulation of successful lawbreakers is not unique to the drug trade, African Americans, the 1980s, or even the United States (Morgan 1993; Brooke 1993).

78. Finnegan (1990a: 70); Ferguson (1987: 8).

79. McFate (1989: 10); Skolnick et al. (1990: 23–24); Wideman (1984: 133).

CHAPTER ELEVEN
BREAKING THE SPELL

1. By a measure similar to Kasarda's (1993), 13% of the people living in "underclass" areas were themselves members of the underclass in 1970; the equivalent percentage in 1980 was 18 (Ricketts and Mincy 1990: 142). We have no count of the number of "distressed" people living in the "distressed" neighborhoods of the 100 largest cities in 1990, as described in chapter 10. But even if we assume that as many as 30% of the residents of the relevant tracts are them-

selves among the estranged poor, we are still talking about less than 10% of the African American population (30% of the 30% who live in distressed tracts) (Kasarda 1993).

2. The distinction between distorters and rejectors is fuzzy but important. Some people make it for themselves, choosing either to interpret the American dream idiosyncratically or to abjure it altogether. When I make the distinction, I draw the line behaviorally: people who act violently to satisfy their desires have moved outside the realm of the American dream, regardless of their views on the matter. That criterion is not entirely clear—is selling crack to a pregnant woman an act of violence? Is selling a car of the same model as others that have exploded upon impact? I answer "yes" to both, but one can argue cases endlessly. Nevertheless, the principle seems clear: those who throw off the restraints that most people impose on themselves against violence and irresponsibility, and permit their worst impulses to swamp their best, have in effect rejected the American dream. Or so I claim.

One can also reject the American dream in favor of an alternative set of ideals; in principle that is an entirely different matter from the denial of constraints, although in practice the two forms of rejection are not always separated. I discuss that issue later in this chapter.

3. See note 1 for the calculations. An outside estimate is 11% of the black male population. That is the fraction of adult black men who in 1986 were in prison or jail, on probation, or on parole. To accept that estimate, however, would require one to assume that all black convicts are criminals or that the numbers of convicts unjustly convicted exactly matches the number of black offenders not caught (either of which is possible but unlikely) and that all black offenders are rejectors rather than distorters (which is even more unlikely) (DiIulio 1989: 35).

4. Fewer than 5% of a national sample of youth in the early 1980s reported using hard drugs and engaging in serious crimes. They accounted for about 40% of all delinquencies, 60% of all index offenses, 50 to 75% of all felonies, over 80% of drug sales, and 60% of drug use other than marijuana (Johnson et al. 1986). Among inmates of California prisons in 1976, the median number of robberies per year was 3.75, but about 5% had committed over 180 robberies a year (Blumstein et al. 1986: 62). See also Carpenter et al. 1988; Fagan 1990; DiIulio 1989.

5. Hamill (1988: 91–92); Bragg (1994: A28).

6. Pooley (1991: 25, 28). Finnegan (1990a: 67–69) describes in almost identical language how "once the guns are in circulation they take on a life of their own," with identical results. Straight (1994) describes a middle-class man's similar fascination with guns and their power.

7. Morganthau (1992: 29); Shakoor and Chalmers (1991); Fitzpatrick and Boldizar (1993: 427); Richters and Martinez (1993); Osofsky (1993a; 1993b); U.S. Department of Justice (1993); New York City Board of Education (1994). In a 1993 survey by Louis Harris, 15% of all high school students claimed to carry a gun in the previous month, about 11% had been shot at in the previous year, and 9% had themselves at some point shot at another person (LH Research Inc. 1993). Data from the National Crime Victimization Survey, however, suggest figures on the order of 3% carrying a gun, and fewer than 1% shot at, threat-

ened, or shooting (Kleck 1993). Whatever the total magnitude, it is certain that carrying and using guns varies enormously between wealthy (mostly white) and poor (mostly nonwhite) communities.

8. Rose and McClain (1990) give a thorough discussion of the structural and contextual causes for high rates of black homicide.

9. Skolnick (1989: 16); see also Covino (1985).

10. Naison (1992: 128–29); William Wilson (1987) and West (1993) make essentially the same argument in less inflammatory language.

11. Jones (1992: 282–84), for example, faults "comparisons between big-time drug dealers and Wall Street inside traders" because they ignore the element of direct personal violence. "This is not to exonerate white-collar (often white) criminals, but to suggest that drug dealing attracted a few young men (of all races) for reasons other than purely 'financial.'"

12. Quotation from title of Fainstein and Nesbitt (1994); see also Frazier (1957); Clark (1965).

13. The drug trade fosters capitalism as well as the reverse. One line of Gucci shoes is sold only in a few cities, and Nike's Air Jordan sneakers are heavily promoted in inner cities. Owners of small businesses now specialize in custom trimming Mercedes Benzes; banks proliferate in Miami and southern California; suppliers sharply criticize store owners who do not welcome dealers as customers (McFate 1989: 2; Naughton 1992: 27–28; Finnegan 1990a: 82).

14. "Some of the OGs, the original gangsters as the inactive Crips and Bloods like to call themselves, are openly disgusted with the drive-by shootings in which innocent civilians are often maimed or killed. They're nostalgic for the 'old days,' when revenge killings took place face to face" (ABC News 1992a: 7).

15. Jackson (1988: 33).

16. Brounstein et al. (1989: 99–115). Consistent with the evidence in the previous chapter, fewer than 10% of this sample of inner city teenaged boys were heavy drug users or frequent sellers. About half, however, had committed a non-drug-related crime in the past year.

17. Office of Criminal Justice Plans and Analysis (1992: 27–30).

18. Wolfgang and Ferracuti (1967); Wolfgang et al. (1987); Bernard (1990).

19. Whites' self-esteem is related to their expectations for success in a straight, not a criminal, career. It is also *inversely* related to their illegal earnings (Anthony Harris 1976: 439–40; Harris and Stokes 1978: 76–80; see also Leung and Drasgow 1986).

20. Fagan (1990: 208).

21. Matsueda et al. (1992: 760–64).

22. Quotations from, respectively, Jenkins (1991: 141–42); and Jones (1992: 283).

23. West (1993: 12).

24. Jang and Krohn (c. 1994).

25. On prostitution, see Kolata (1989); on crack houses, see McFate (1989: 2); on adoptive grandmother, see Greene (1989: 23); on grandmothers, see U.S. Congress (1989: 154–72) and Gross (1989); on Dooney, see Norris (1989).

26. One of the last ethnographic taboos, apparently, is the issue of poor black mothers who mistreat their children. I found no scholarly ethnographies beyond Anderson (1990) that explored this topic except in passing.

27. Miller (1986: 100, also 72–83); Anderson (1990: 4, 73–76).

28. Mocan and Topyan (1993: 9). See also U.S. Department of Health and Human Services (1990b: 2–3); U.S. Congress (1989: 5, 55–57, 110, 257); Vega et al. (1993); Dunlop (1992).

29. U.S. Department of Health and Human Services (1990c: 2); see also U.S. Congress (1989: 120–31); Child Welfare League of America (1992). I say "apparently" because the only systematic survey of boarder babies over time that I know of is too small to permit generalizations (New Jersey Hospital Association 1993).

30. Besharov (forthcoming); National Center on Child Abuse Prevention Research (1994: 5). Besharov, like virtually all analysts of child abuse and neglect, cautions about the unreliability of these figures either across race and class or over time.

31. Ards (1989).

32. Wulczyn and Goerge (1992: 279–80).

33. Besharov (forthcoming); National Center for Children in Poverty (1990: 60); U.S. Congress (1989: 46–88); National Black Child Development Institute (1989: 23–51).

34. Most of Edward Ferrars' problems in Jane Austen's *Sense and Sensibility*, for example, would dissolve if he found a profession rather than living on his mother's wealth.

35. NSBA (1980: var. 556; see also var. 708).

36. Anderson (1990: 71–72).

37. *Chicago Tribune* (1986: 93); for an echo, see Anderson (1990: 72).

38. Both quotations from Miller (1986: 163, 162).

39. After all, this young man continues in illustration, he could plan to rob a bank today but "I go down there, I don' stick that bank up. Somethin stop me." The next day, " 'stead of goin down eleven o'clock, . . . I go down there four o'clock, and the bank's closed." Again "you [go] down there . . . git hit by a car, wind up in the hospital. Thas the future for you" (Hill 1973: 164).

40. Ezekiel (1984: 120).

41. Tienda (1991a: 143) estimates that "about 6 percent of Chicago's inner-city residents qualif[y] as potentially shiftless." Mead (1992: 148, 151), conversely, gives no figures but argues that "the [contemporary] worldview of blacks makes them uniquely prone to the attitudes contrary to work." Holzer (1994: 708–10) discusses the inconclusiveness of the evidence.

42. In addition to better data and comparable data over time, one would need a precise definition of "rejection." Jencks (1992: 127) distinguishes among those who would take any job, those who want only a good job, and those who want no job. We also need more persuasive arguments about the relationship between discouragement and refusal in order to know whether nonworkers adhere to, are ambivalent about, or reject the American dream.

43. Ezekiel (1984: 187).

44. Rutten (1992: 54).

45. Bobo et al. (1992: ques. C4, C5, C6). Fewer Anglos, Latinos, and Asians lack confidence in all three levels of government.

46. Reinhold (1992: 1); ABC News (1992b: 5).

47. Rosenstone and Hansen (1993: 244); Jaynes and Williams (1989: 233); see also Farley (1992: chap. 7, pp. 6–9). Actual discrepancies in voting are probably greater than those reported here, since blacks may overreport voting more than whites do (Highton 1991; Farley 1992: chap. 7, pp. 5–8; Rosenstone and Hansen 1993: 58–60).

48. Jaynes and Williams (1989: 234–37) provide evidence that, controlling for socioeconomic status, blacks vote more than whites. Farley (1992: chap. 7, pp. 15–17) and Rosenstone and Hansen (1993: 130–33) show the opposite.

49. Farley (1992: chap. 7, pp. 15–17).

50. NSBA (1980: vars. 1218, 1219); GSS (1987: var. 340). On the latter question, poorly-educated whites are almost as pessimistic, but well-educated blacks are only half as pessimistic.

51. And the parties are no longer seeking to mobilize their support (Rosenstone and Hansen 1993: 219–24).

52. Blauner (1989: 140–41).

53. Chafets (1990: 65).

54. Quote from black civic activist in Miami, in Lardner and Hornblower (1980: A1).

55. ABC News (1992a: 5). The uprising in Los Angeles cannot be understood without attention to its multiethnic nature; my purpose here, however, is not a general interpretation, so I am ignoring that aspect, among others, of the events.

56. On firefighters and journalists, see Marriott (1992: 7); ABC News (1992c: 6, 9, 12); on "no pity," see Rohrlich and Connell (1992: A1); on Mr. Lopez, see Gross (1993). Mr. Lopez was saved from burning by "a black preacher [who] threw his body on Mr. Lopez's"; other African Americans also rescued the wounded, helped the homeless, and cleaned up after the uprising (ABC News 1992c: 6, 10).

57. "My God, This Is It" (1992: 11); Bobo et al. (1992: fig. 12); see also Bledsoe et al. (1995b: 12). However, in a survey with a small black sample, 31% of well-educated, and only 17% of poorly-educated, blacks deemed the outbreak of violence justified by the verdict against Rodney King. The pattern was reversed among whites (Yankelovich Clancy Shulman 1992: var. R15).

58. As chapter 6 showed, poor blacks are more likely than well-off blacks to endorse nationalism or separatism, especially as either becomes more militant. Madhubuti (1993) is a good example of the use of the Los Angeles uprising to fuel ideological rejection of the American dream.

59. Finnegan (1990a: 76). The gendered language is unintentionally revealing; few Afrocentric programs directly aim at wayward girls and few Afrocentrists give them much attention.

60. Jeff (1994); see also Ferguson (1994: 68–69); McFate and Turner (1994: 18–12).

61. Frey (1992); Amos Wilson (1991). Only 4% of poorly-educated (compared with 11% of well-educated) African Americans think black children do

worse in racially mixed than in all-black schools, but most blacks of all classes would "allow" public schools for black boys (Gallup 1988: var. 6; *Los Angeles Times* 1991b: var. 78).

62. Jennings (1990: 119–26); see also Hogan (1992).

63. At least one such program is framed specifically against (a narrow definition of) the American dream: "the African American community is losing too many of its educated people to lifestyles structured around individualism and materialism. This is primarily due to the fact that middle class African Americans have not been socialized to internalize an Afrocentric or collective orientation" (Isaacs 1992: 55–64 [quotes on pp. 57, 59]). See also Amos Wilson (1990: 182–205).

64. Blauner (1989: 231).

65. Fewer poor blacks feel closer to their race than to their class (Jackman and Jackman 1983: 50; see also Williams 1992: 167–68).

66. Almost as many poorly-educated whites concur, as do one-seventh of well-educated blacks (GSS 1987: var. 516A).

67. Blauner (1989: 115). One should not overestimate this rejection of middle-class values, however; as we might expect from the evidence in chapter 8, low-status blacks are considerably more likely than high-status blacks or any class of whites to define success in terms of personal wealth, fame, or power (Roper 1986: vars. 15, 16, 21, 23, 24).

CHAPTER TWELVE
THE PERVERSITY OF RACE AND THE FLUIDITY OF VALUES

1. The remaining two-fifths split roughly evenly among "progressive," "fundamentalist," and "historicist" views (Sniderman 1985: 30, 35–39). See also Apostle et al. (1983); Sigelman and Welch (1991: 88–100).

2. Sigelman and Welch (1991: 111–13).

3. William Wilson (1980: 150–51).

4. "One cannot but be struck by the fact that *whites appear nowhere in Rickey's narrative* [a three-hour interview with a 'professional hustler' on Chicago's South Side]. . . . From Rickey's point of view, the dichotomous opposition between whites and blacks, which earlier constituted the generative matrix of all perceptions and grievances, has seemingly dissolved by itself in this ceaseless guerrilla [war] that must now be waged first of all *against one's own kind*, 'brother against brother,' poor against poorer" (Wacquant 1994b: 31–32, emphasis in original). Among African Americans, the higher one's socioeconomic status, the more one interacts with whites; among whites, status has no effect on interracial contacts (Sigelman et al. 1993: 21).

5. Lemann (1991: 266–67). The football coach at East St. Louis High School, who dreams of someday buying goalposts for his field, puts the point clearly: "In certain ways it's harder now because in those days [the 1960s] it was a clear enemy you had to face, a man in a hood and not a statistician. No one could persuade you that you were to blame. Now the choices seem like they are left to you and, if you make the wrong choice, you are made to understand you are to blame" (Kozol 1991: 26). Thus poor black residents of Detroit are more

dissatisfied with the police (who are largely black) than are other blacks. Conversely, wealthier black residents of mostly white suburbs, who deal mainly with white police, are more satisfied with police services than are other blacks. In short, class—not race—shapes perceptions of police (Welch et al. 1994: 33–34). See also Kaufman (1989: 19, 36, 37).

6. Hochschild (1981); Lipset (1977); Foner (1984).

7. Brown (1992); Pearson (1994).

8. First quotation from Burns (1992: 131); second from personal communication by Gene Burns, Princeton University, September 27, 1993.

9. Rickey describes "one guy, we goo' buddies now: we ha' tot'ly two diff'ren' lifestyles, but we was goo' frien's. Like right now, he . . . bought him a buildin', he own him a home, he work ev'ryday, never been in no trouble. . . . An' he made it on the *legit side*, jus' workin' an' workin'-workin'-workin'" (Wacquant 1994b: 44).

10. A comparison with well-off blacks sharpens the point. They, like well-off whites, can afford to experiment with their beliefs and strategies, since they have a material cushion, they are widely educated, and they are in little physical danger. Their options for belief as well as for action are greater than those of the poor.

11. Rosenbaum et al. (1993: 1541).

12. Roper (1986: vars. 52, 53, 55, 56). African Americans who already have a college education are the *least* likely of all black groups, whether defined by income or by educational level, to include a college education in their understanding of the American dream. Relative deprivation strikes again! (This pattern does not hold among whites.)

13. Roper (1986: var. 83; see also vars. 85, 87).

14. On poor people's "hidden transcript" of resistance to the dominant ideology, see Scott (1985; 1990); Genovese (1972); and Kelley (1992).

15. CBS News/*NYT* (1992: vars. R40, R41).

16. Zaller (1992).

17. Croly (1963: 20).

18. Truman (1951: 522–24). My thanks to Ira Katznelson for bringing this passage to my attention.

19. Sniderman et al. (1991: var. cpi3); GSS (1985–86, 1987, 1988–89, 1990–91: var. 121D). Wacquant (1994a) provides one of the most imaginative dystopias of the inner city that I have seen.

20. Kasarda (1993).

21. E.g., Jennings (1992); Berry et al. (1993); Mincy (1994); McFate and Turner (1994).

CHAPTER THIRTEEN
COMPARING BLACKS AND WHITE IMMIGRANTS

1. Hughes (1938: 9); Appel (1970).

2. This is a politically controversial choice, since middle-class blacks' anger at the American dream is partly driven by the insult implied in the idea that they reached "immigrant status" only in the middle of the twentieth century. After

all, if anyone other than American Indians are "old stock" Americans, African Americans are. I nevertheless make the comparison because it is analytically useful in illuminating contemporary racial politics.

3. Higham's (1963) discussion of "race feeling" toward European immigrants continues to be among the best.

4. Dinnerstein et al. (1990: 241); Altschuler (1982: 49–50); "'The Dangerous Classes'" (1871: 4). "In the antebellum South it was widely believed that Irish should be employed in dangerous, high mortality jobs rather than risking the loss of valuable Negro slaves" (Daniels 1990: 136–37). See also Lieberson (1980: 24).

5. Brown and Warner (1992: 298–99). Counties with high proportions of immigrants produced the most support (mostly by nonimmigrants) for prohibition in Missouri in 1918. The proportion of blacks had no impact on support for prohibition (Wasserman 1989). See also Gusfield (1963); Timberlake (1963); Harring (1983); Beisel (1990).

6. In the two decades after 1902, 90% of the victims were black (U.S. Bureau of the Census 1975: 412, 422).

7. Morawska (1982: 79–81); Lieberson (1980: 260–77).

8. McGouldrick and Tannen (1977); no data are reported for women. English immigrants earned about 15% more than otherwise similar Irish or West Indian immigrants in 1910 (Borjas 1994: table 3). Black men received at least 30% less pay than white men, largely because they were limited to much less skilled jobs (Meeker and Kau 1977).

9. Olzak (1992: 135–59); Lieberson (1980: 301–20).

10. For an example, see note 50, chapter 1. For detailed and systematic evidence, see Sandmeyer (1939); Higham (1963); Saxton (1971); Paul (1970); Matthews (1970); Takaki (1979); Barrera (1979); Knobel (1986); Chalmers (1987).

11. Memoirs and letters home are unreliable sources, since they are selfselective and partial in a variety of ways I describe below. They also can tell us little about the structural forces shaping the social context about which they are selectively reporting. Nevertheless, if approached with appropriate skepticism and placed by the user in the relevant context, they are highly revealing.

12. Walaszek (1988); Hareven and Langenbach (1978: 55, 161); Roskolenko 1971: 157); see also Rodgers (1978: 170–73).

13. Walaszek (1988).

14. Hareven and Langenbach (1978: 55–56); La Sorte (1985: 61); see also Pacyga (1991). The melodrama of the last quotation here reveals not only the intensity of the immigrant's relationship to work, but also the artificiality of memoirs.

15. Quotations from, respectively, Puzo (1971: 46); Walaszek (1988: 7); Ewen (1985: 54); Puzo (1971: 46).

16. Quotation in Higham (1984: 24); on ambivalence, see Morawska (1982); on belief in upward mobility, see Sombart (1976).

17. Higham (1984: 71–80). Immigrants remember being urged not to crowd the side of the ship on which the Statue appeared, lest the ship capsize (Brownstone et al. 1979: 145).

18. Brownstone et al. (1979: 26, 68, 52); Ewen (1985: 106, emphasis in original). Higham (1984: 27) neatly depicts Harry Houdini as the "symbolic re-enactment" of immigrants' desperate attempts to escape confinement and move to freedom of movement and choice. Heinze (1990) describes immigrants' enthusiastic recognition that they could equal their bosses in the realm of consumption long before they could aspire to parity at work, in language facility, or in politics.

19. Bukowczyk (1987: 29–30); Walaszek (1989: 89); Tuttle (1969: 422–23).

20. Bukowczyk (1987: 39).

21. Tentler (1983); see also Bodnar (1985: 144–68).

22. Roskolenko (1971: 171, second ellipsis in text); Brownstone et al. (1986: 38–39).

23. Underlining the bittersweet nature of success in America, this budding entrepreneur continues, "The richest ones go away from the other Italians and live with the Americans" (Katzman and Tuttle 1982: 12).

24. On petty theft: "One of our uncles . . . worked as an assistant chef. . . . Every day, six days a week, this uncle brought home, under his shirt, six eggs, a stick of butter, and a small bag of flour. By doing this for thirty years he was able to save enough money to buy a fifteen-thousand-dollar house on Long Island and two smaller houses for his son and daughter" (Puzo: 1971: 40). Erie (1988) elegantly analyzes what political patronage could, and could not, provide to immigrants.

25. Hareven and Langenbach (1978: 62); Morawska (1982: 96, also 98–99).

26. Barton (1978: 164–65); Bodnar (1985: 134, 139); see also Bukowczyk (1987: 37–38); Timothy Smith (1966: 1270–71). Even Sombart's (1976) and Stevenson's (1895) hostile or bemused portrayals of immigrants convey the same sense of determined or desperate striving.

27. Morawska (1982: 87–90).

28. Heinze (1990: 130, 190).

29. Spring (1972); Tyack (1974); Sanders (1977); Nasaw (1979); Tyack and Hansot (1982); Weiss (1982); Brumberg (1986); Perlmann (1988). As late as 1936, one newspaper lamented that "with a public school education they [children] go forth into the world, lost completely to the Slovaks. Their idea of life is a breezy and snappy novel, a blood curdling movie and lots of money. But our duty to our people commands us to save youth from the moral catastrophe that is confronting it" (quoted in Bodnar 1985: 195).

30. Bodnar (1985: 85–116); Walaszek (1989); Howe (1976); Avrich (1984); Gordon (1977); Krause (1992).

31. Gerstle (1989); Barrett (1992).

32. Lane (1979); Monkkonen (1989: 88–91); Cohler and Lieberman (1977: 21–25).

33. On Italians, see La Sorte (1985: 145, 195–97); on Slavs, see Katzman and Tuttle (1982: 108); on Mexicans, see Dinnerstein et al. (1990: 185); on Poles, see Bukowczyk (1987: 32); on Irish Catholics, see McCaffrey (1976:

150). More generally, Schooler (1976) shows that descendants of northern and western European immigrants adhere much more firmly to the values of self-direction, "personally responsible morality," internal sense of control, and self-criticism—all elements of the strictest version of the American dream—than do descendants of the "new immigrants." The greater the impact of their ethnicity on respondents' lives, the more they adhere to these values. Stein (1975) discusses more abstractly the tensions inherent in reconciling traditional European and new American values.

34. Feagin and Fujitaki (1972); Cohler and Lieberman (1977: 27–31); Constantinou and Harvey (1985); Gold (1989). Since I make no assertions about third and later generations, I am making a weaker argument than that associated with the classic "straight line assimilation model" (phrase from Waters forthcoming; model from Warner and Srole 1945).

35. Ewen (1985: 72). This daughter might have answered her mother as did another: "I didn't mean to go to work at fourteen, marry at sixteen, be a mother at eighteen, an old woman at thirty. I wanted a new thing—happiness" (ibid.: 195).

36. Dinnerstein et al. (1990: 189).

37. Puzo (1971: 36). For fascinating depictions of how children adopted the consumption patterns and mores of America, and how they then trained their parents, see Ewen (1985); Heinze (1990); Moore (1981). The novels and memoirs are endless; among my favorites are Cather (1941), Mangione (1942); Rodriguez (1981); Rivera (1982); Simon (1982, 1986).

38. To my knowledge no commentator has addressed all of them.

39. Out of the population of the homeland, at most 3% emigrated to the United States in any given year. That maximum was reached in the largest and most rapid migration of all, Ireland's potato famine (Fried 1968: 117).

40. More dramatically, "the process of self-selection turned . . . upon ambition, upon a wish and a will to believe that the future was more real than the past, and upon a readiness to accept changes and make adjustments. . . . Many an immigrant . . . inquired carefully of those he met . . . the lessons he must learn to make his venture a success. . . . His ultimate objective was the fulfillment of a dream of success that owed nothing at all to Horatio Alger" (Timothy Smith 1966: 1273–74; see also Fried 1968: 119–20).

41. Festinger (1957).

42. Stevenson (1895).

43. Many analysts in fact distinguish the United States from other nations by its history as a nation by choice rather than by geography or descent (de Tocqueville 1969; Kohn 1957; Gleason 1980; Huntington 1981: 23–30; Sollors 1986; Mann 1979).

44. A majority of Irish immigrants were young single women, and they were on balance happier and more successful than their male counterparts (Pagnini and Morgan 1990: 409; Dinar 1983). Since the 1930s, more women than men have immigrated to the United States, and their experience has been mixed (Pedraza 1991).

45. Brownstone et al. (1979: 134–35); Ewen (1985: 60).

46. Ewen (1985: 60–65).

47. Dinnerstein and Reimers (1988: 46); Bukowczyk (1987: 32). Only 5% of Jews and 8% of Irish returned to their native countries (Bodnar 1985: 53). These figures are inexact because of intermittent or seasonal reemigrations to the United States. See also Archdeacon (1983: 115–19, 137–40).

48. On those who came to earn, see La Sorte (1985: 133, 191); Bodnar (1985: 53–54); Dinnerstein et al. (1990: 140). On drifters, see Brownstone et al. (1979: 240); on embittered and moral rejectors, see La Sorte (1985: 111, 194–97).

49. Waldinger et al. (1990: 42–43).

50. Public opinion surveys often depict blacks' (and whites') views very differently, and in some ways more reliably, than do the accounts of journalists, political activists, and memoirists. It is reasonable to assume that the same would have been true a century ago.

51. I do not include the standard argument about different occupational contexts as an explanation for immigrants' allegiance to and blacks' disavowal of the American dream because it does not work. That is, many analysts have pointed out that the burgeoning economy of the early 1900s needed unskilled workers, whereas the stagnant economy of the 1970s and 1980s left them bereft of jobs. Thus, this argument goes, the difference between immigrant support for the American dream and recent black disillusionment with it is the result of structural changes rather than changes in beliefs or expectations per se. The problem with that argument is that it predicts that middle-class blacks—who faced a burgeoning economy in the 1960s eager for their skills—should have believed like immigrants did, and poor blacks—who fell out the bottom of the stagnant economy—should have rejected the American dream. In fact, however, the reverse is the case.

52. Ewen (1985: 67); Heinze (1990: 103, emphasis in original); Fender (1992: 13). Even reluctant immigrants, especially children, often underwent a transformation (that prospect may, indeed, have been what made many of them reluctant to come).

53. Sollors (1986: 32); see also Boelhower (1991).

54. Heinze (1990: 33); Mary Antin, *The Promised Land*, quoted in Sollors (1986: 32).

55. Smith and Dempsey (1983: 588). In 1964 blacks ranked above only gypsies; in 1989 blacks also ranked higher than "Wisians" (an invented group), Mexicans, and Puerto Ricans. Over that period Japanese and Chinese gained the most in the the rankings (Lewin 1992). Schaefer (1984: 66–70) analyses the scale itself.

56. Erskine (1973: 289); Smith and Dempsey (1983: 588–89).

57. Model (1993: 171–86); Barton (1975: 91–146) for specific groups, see Kessner (1977). Bodnar (1985: 170–83) paints a less sanguine portrait of immigrants' and their children's job mobility but points out the very high rate of homeownership among immigrant families. Similar findings on homeownership are in Lieberson and Waters (1988: 141).

58. Lieberson and Waters (1988: 122, and more generally 119–35); see also

Darity et al. (1994: table 1G) for ethnic groups' occupational levels in 1990. Except for Russians (largely Jews) who were overemployed, new and old immigrant groups were not distinguishable in 1980 in terms of the relationship between their educational level and their occupational achievement; African Americans, however, held jobs with much less status than their schooling would predict. Male descendents of new immigrants enjoyed a greater gain in income given their education and job than did other Europeans; black men earned much less (Lieberson and Waters 1988: 145–55; see also Neidert and Farley 1985: 847–48).

59. Among six groups of old immigrants (northern and western Europeans) in this age cohort, only English Protestants did as well as the new immigrants reported in the text (Greeley 1973). Borjas (1994: figs. 1 and 2) shows a clear association between immigrants' education and wages and those of their children. He also shows that, within that association, the second generation of some ethnic groups did exceptionally well or poorly; those variations do not depend on old or new immigrant status.

60. Lieberson and Waters (1988: 137–39); see also Borjas (1994: fig. 4). Darity et al. (1994: tables 1E, 1F) portray ethnic groups' incomes and poverty levels in 1990.

61. On 1910, see Pagnini and Morgan (1990). On 1980, see Alba (1990: 12–14) (see also Alba and Golden 1986). On black/white intermarriage, see Rolark et al. (1994: table 2); Kalmijn (1993). Lieberson and Waters (1988: 171–78) point out that inmarriage rates are lower for the old (northern and western European) immigrants than for the "new immigrants."

62. White et al. (1994); Lieberson (1980: 263–67).

63. Lieberson (1980: 270–77); White (1987: 111).

64. Massey and Denton (1993).

65. Dahl (1961); Allswang (1971); Archdeacon (1983: 189–92); Pinderhughes (1987); Erie (1988). On party identification, see Knoke and Felson (1974).

66. Gerstle (1993). Neather (forthcoming) sees the beginning of the shift to "American" at the expense of nonwhite races in the 1890s; Orsi (1992) finds such a movement in the 1920s; and Judith Smith (1992) locates its highpoint in the 1950s. The precise historical moment is immaterial, and the shift is best seen as a process rather than an event in any case.

67. Gerstle (1993: 316–19); Irons (1983); Hirsch (1983); Dower (1986); Hirsch (1983); Roediger (1991, 1994); Theodore Allen (1994).

68. Waters (1990); see also Rubin (1994: 143–216).

69. In a meeting, Attorney General Robert Kennedy once tried to temper the insistent anger of black participants' demands by proclaiming his and his brother's sympathy and understanding. But he reminded his interlocuters that "other Americans also had to endure periods of oppression. In support of this fact he noted that his grandfather was an Irish immigrant. Jim Baldwin responded . . . 'You do not understand at all. Your grandfather came as an immigrant from Ireland and your brother is President of the United States. Genera-

tions before your family came as immigrants, my ancestors came to this country in chains, as slaves. We are still required to supplicate and beg you for justice and decency'" (Clark 1985: 15). See also Baldwin et al. (1964: 32).

70. Kristol (1966).

71. Rubin (1994: part 3); Waters (1990); Alba (1990).

72. Or rather, at least two; Glazer (1983: 70–93) discusses the many political implications that can be derived from comparisons between African Americans and white ethnic immigrants.

73. Williams (1971: 145); see also Waters (1990: 155–64).

74. Prager (1982: 104); see also Jordan (1968); Norton (1986).

75. Reed et al. (1989: 228).

76. Prager (1982: 111). Shklar (1991) shows how American citizenship came to be defined as *not* being a slave; Morrison (1992) shows how much of American literature revolves around the presence or absence of blackness.

77. Bell (1992a). Some modify this view to distinguish between (white) ethnicity and race, including Asians, native Americans, and sometimes Latinos in the latter category (Takaki 1979; 1994; Omi and Winant (1986).

78. Waters (forthcoming); Loewen (1988).

79. Omi and Winant (1986); Winant (1994); Petersen (1987). In a lovely irony, the Conference of Americans of Germanic Heritage petitioned the federal Office of Management and Budget in 1994 to "eliminate the category of 'white' as a racial or ethnic designation, . . . and to include the category 'Germanic' as both a racial and ethnic identification" in federal statistics and census documents. It claimed that this change was necessary "for reasons of equity and justice." A Polish historian quibbled with the expansive definition of Germanic in the petition but reported that it "echoes what Polish and other east and south Europeans have been saying for a long time. . . . Subsuming hundreds of ethnic and cultural groups under the single term 'white' is homogenization, not diversity" (Holford 1994; Radzilowski 1994). The more things change . . .

80. Hacker (1992: 15); see also Citrin et al. (1990: 1138); Tom Smith (1990).

81. Hall (1981: 228, 236).

82. Teres (forthcoming: chap. 9). For example, Odetta's influence on white folk musicians is legendary, and one need only attend one of her concerts to see how white musical styles have affected even black singers with deep racial roots.

83. On intermarriage, see Rolark et al. (1994: table 2); Harrison and Bennett (1995: 164–69); on student culture, see Wellman (1993: 5); on prom, see Gross and Smothers (1994); Harrison (1994: 1).

84. Hirschman (1994: 21); on the movement, see Njeri (1993); Graham (1994); Douglass (1994). The multiracial movement has at least two magazines and several "umbrella organizations" or "clearinghouses."

85. Hochschild (1984) develops this argument under the rubric of the "symbiosis thesis."

86. Johnson and Warren (1994) depict what it is like to live transformative pluralism through intermarriage; Spickard (1989) speculates plausibly about its likely growth, mainly through the black middle class.

87. On schools, see Hochschild (1984); on the federal government, see Graham (1990).

88. My thanks to Ian Shapiro of Yale University for that formulation of the puzzle of the American dream.

CHAPTER FOURTEEN
THE FUTURE OF THE AMERICAN DREAM

1. In 1993 about six in ten Americans agreed that "immigrants take the jobs of U.S. workers," that "many immigrants wind up on welfare and raise taxes for Americans," and that "the increasing diversity that immigrants bring to this country mostly threatens American culture." Since 1965, the proportion of Americans who agree that immigration should be reduced has risen from 33% to 63%. However, at least as many agreed, in the same surveys, that "immigrants work hard, often taking jobs that Americans don't want" and that "immigrants help improve our country with their different cultures and talents." Just half of white Americans (and only 30% of black Americans) agree that public schools should use only the English language. Ambivalence may be a common trait of Americans ("Public Opinion and Demographic Report" 1994a: 97–98; *NYT/*WCBS News 1994a: 6; GSS 1993: var. 462D).

2. Marsh (1987: 264).

3. Rae et al. (1981: 82–103) analyze the relationship between equality and identity of results under the rubric of lot-regarding versus person-regarding equality.

4. Sumner (1914: 25).

5. de Tocqueville (1969: 536).

6. This is a variant, as is so much else in this book, on one of de Tocqueville's insights, in this case on the tyranny of majority opinion.

7. Anderson (1990).

8. Juan Williams (1990: 19–20).

9. Schlesinger (1992) and Bloom (1987) demonstrate this insecurity—the former with considerably more sophistication and grace.

10. This was the argument of Homer Plessy's attorney in 1896 in his claim that Plessy was denied due process of law when he was ejected from a train car reserved for whites (Lofgren 1987: 154).

11. Barton (1929: 78).

12. In *An Earnest Exhortation to the Inhabitants* (Boston, 1676), quoted in Hall (1988: 123–24, emphasis in original); Mather (1970: 27).

13. Student protest is not an effort "to subvert institutions or an attempt to challenge values which have been affirmed for centuries. . . . We are affirming the values which you have instilled in us and which you have taught us to respect," argued one "radical" student leader at Harvard University's 1969 graduation ceremonies (Huntington 1981: 2). Ralph Abernathy provided a somewhat harder-edged version of the same point. Asked by an exasperated white official at a civil rights demonstration, "What do you *want?*" Abernathy reportedly replied, "What have you *got?*" (Goldman 1969: 31).

14. "To make this sort of argument is to resurrect the much-maligned ghost

of 'consensus history,'" as T. J. Jackson Lears (1985: 576) comments about a similar argument of his own. However, as he goes on, "one does not have to embrace the fantastic version of a a conflict-free American past [or future] to acknowledge the power of the currents in the American mainstream" (see also Kammen 1993).

15. Rogers Smith (1993: 550).

16. Baldwin (1985: 690).

WORKS CITED

ABBREVIATIONS

AJPS   *American Journal of Political Science*
AJS   *American Journal of Sociology*
APSR   *American Political Science Review*
ASR   *American Sociological Review*
NYT   *New York Times*
APSA   American Political Science Association
ASA   American Sociological Association
IRP   Institute for Research on Poverty
MWPSA   Midwest Political Science Association
NBER   National Bureau of Economic Research
USGPO   United States Government Printing Office

ABC News (1992a) "Nightline in South Central," Transcript of *Nightline*, May 4 (American Broadcasting Company).

—— (1992b) "The L.A. Riots and a View of History," Transcript of *Nightline*, May 7 (American Broadcasting Company).

—— (1992c) "Moment of Crisis: Anatomy of a Riot," May 7 (American Broadcasting Company Inc.).

ABC News/*Washington Post* (1989) "ABC News/*Washington Post* 9/89 Poll," Sept. 28–Oct. 3.

—— (1990) "ABC News/*Washington Post* Poll: Omnibus-September 1990," Sept. 20–24.

—— (1991) "ABC News/*Washington Post* Poll: Omnibus-June 1991," May 30–June 2.

Aberbach, Joel, and Jack Walker (1970a) "The Meanings of Black Power," *APSR* 64, 2: 367–88.

—— (1970b) "Political Trust and Racial Ideology," *APSR* 64, 4: 1199–1219.

Abramowitz, Michael, and Richard Morin (1994) "Prince George's: Views in Black and White," *Washington Post*, Aug. 7: A12, A19.

ACORN (Assoc. of Community Organizations for Reform Now) (1991) *Banking on Discrimination: An Analysis of Home Mortgage Lending in 10 Cities in 1990* (Washington, D.C.: ACORN).

Acs, Gregory, and Sheldon Danziger (1993) "Educational Attainment, Industrial Structure, and Male Earnings through the 1980s," *J. of Human Resources* 28, 3: 618–48.

Adams, James, and William Dressler (1988) "Perceptions of Injustice in a Black Community," *Human Relations* 41, 10: 753–67.

Adler, Patricia (1985) *Wheeling and Dealing: An Ethnography of an Upper-Level Drug Dealing and Smuggling Community* (Columbia U. Press).

Adler, William (1990) "Nothing to Lose," *Southern Exposure* 18, 4: 22–27.

Alba, Richard (1990) *Ethnic Identity: The Transformation of White America* (Yale U. Press).

Alba, Richard, and Reid Golden (1986) "Patterns of Ethnic Marriage in the United States," *Social Forces* 65, 1: 202–23.

Alba, Richard, and John Logan (1993) "Minority Proximity to Whites in Suburbs," *AJS* 98, 6: 1388–1427.

Allan, Emilie, and Darrell Steffensmeier (1989) "Youth, Underemployment, and Property Crime," *ASR* 54, 1: 107–23.

Allen, Richard (1994) "Structural Equality in Black and White," *Howard J. of Communication* 5, 1–2: 69–91.

Allen, Richard, and Shirley Hatchett (1986) "The Media and Social Reality Effects," *Communication Research* 13, 1: 97–123.

Allen, Richard, Michael Dawson, and Ronald Brown (1989) "A Schema-Based Approach to Modeling an African-American Racial Belief System," *APSR* 83, 2: 421–41.

Allen, Richard, Michael Thornton, and Samuel Watkins (1992) "An African American Racial Belief System and Social Structural Relationships," *National J. of Sociology* 6, 2: 157–86.

Allen, Theodore (1994) *The Invention of the White Race* (Verso).

Allen, Walter (1994) "Through a Mirror Darkly: Reflections on Distortions of African Americans," *ABS* [newsletter of the Assoc. of Black Sociologists] 21, 1: 3–8.

Allen, Walter, Edgar Epps, and Nesha Haniff, eds. (1991) *College in Black and White* (SUNY Press).

Allswang, John (1971) *A House for All Peoples: Ethnic Politics in Chicago, 1890–1936* (U. of Kentucky Press).

Alston, Jon, and K. Imogene Dean (1972) "Socioeconomic Factors Associated with Attitudes toward Welfare Recipients and the Causes of Poverty," *Social Service R.* 46, 1: 13–23.

Altschuler, Glenn (1982) *Race, Ethnicity, and Class in American Social Thought, 1865–1919* (Harlan Davidson).

Alwin, Duane (1984) "Trends in Parental Socialization Values: Detroit, 1958–1983," *AJS* 90, 2: 359–82.

Amaker, Norman (1988) *Civil Rights and the Reagan Administration* (Urban Institute Press).

America, Richard, and Bernard Anderson (1979) "Must Black Executives Be Superstars?" *Wharton Magazine* (Spring): 44–48, 58.

American Institutes for Research (1989) *Report No. 3: The Experiences of Black Intercollegiate Athletes at NCAA Division I Institutions* (Washington, D.C.: American Institutes for Research).

Anderson, Elijah (1978) *A Place on the Corner* (U. of Chicago Press).

——— (1980) "Some Observations of Black Youth Employment," in Bernard Anderson and Isabel Sawhill, eds., *Youth, Employment and Public Policy* (Prentice Hall), 64–87.

——— (1990) *Streetwise: Race, Class, and Change in an Urban Community* (U. of Chicago Press).

Ando, Faith (1988) *An Analysis of Access to Bank Credit* (UCLA, Center for Afro-American Studies).

Andrisani, Paul, and Herbert Parnes (1983) "Commitment to the Work Ethic and Success in the Labor Market," in Jack Barbash et al., eds., *The Work Ethic —A Critical Analysis* (Madison: Industrial Relations Research Assoc.), 101–19.

Anson, Robert (1987) *Best Intentions: The Education and Killing of Edmund Perry* (Random House).

Antonovsky, Aaron, and Melvin Lerner (1959) "Occupational Aspirations of Lower Class Negro and White Youth," *Social Problems* 7, 2: 132–38.

Aplin-Brownlee, Vivian (1984) "Administration Objects to Plan to Integrate Tennessee's Colleges," *Washington Post*, Sept. 30: A3.

Aponte, Robert (1990) "Definitions of the Underclass," in Herbert Gans, ed., *Sociology in America* (Sage), 117–37.

Apostle, Richard, et al. (1983) *The Anatomy of Racial Attitudes* (U. of California Press).

Appel, John (1970) "American Negro and Immigrant Experience," in Leonard Dinnerstein and Frederic Jaher, eds., *The Aliens: A History of Ethnic Minorities in America* (Appleton-Century-Crofts), 339–47.

Applebome, Peter (1992) "In Alabama, Blacks Battle for the Authority to Govern," *NYT*, Jan. 31: A16.

———— (1993) "Enduring Symbols of the Confederacy Divide the South Anew," *NYT*, Jan. 27: A16.

Archdeacon, Thomas (1983) *Becoming American* (Free Press).

Ards, Sheila (1989) "Estimating Local Child Abuse," *Evaluation R.* 13, 5: 484–515.

"As Cities Reach Record Numbers of Killings, Youths Play Grim Roles" (1994) *NYT*, Jan. 1: 7.

Asante, Molefi (1988) *Afrocentricity* (Africa World Press).

Ashworth, Karl, et al. (1994) "Patterns of Childhood Poverty," *J. of Policy Analysis and Management* 13, 4: 658–80.

Auletta, Ken (1982) *The Underclass* (Random House).

Austin, Roy (1992) "Race, Female Headship, and Delinquency," *Justice Q.* 9, 4: 585–607.

Austin, Roy, and Steven Stack (1988) "Race, Class, and Opportunity: Changing Realities and Perceptions," *Sociological Q.* 29, 3: 357–69.

Austin, Roy, and Hiroko Dodge (1990) "Despair, Distrust and Dissatisfaction among Blacks and Women, 1973–1987," paper at the annual meeting of the ASA, Washington, D.C.

Austin, William, et al. (1977) "Responses to Favorable Sex Discrimination," *Law and Human Behavior* 1, 3: 283–98.

Avrich, Paul (1984) *The Haymarket Tragedy* (Princeton U. Press).

Ayres, Ian (1991) "Fair Driving: Gender and Race Discrimination in Retail Car Negotiations," *Harvard Law R.* 104, 4: 817–72.

Ayres, Ian, and Peter Siegelman (forthcoming) "Race and Gender Discrimination in Bargaining for a New Car," *Am. Economic R.*

Bachman, Jerald, et al. (1991) "Racial/Ethnic Differences in Smoking, Drinking, and Illicit Drug Use among American High School Seniors, 1976–1989," *Am. J. of Public Health* 81, 3: 372–77.

Bailyn, Bernard (1967) *The Ideological Origins of the American Revolution* (Harvard U. Press).

Baldwin, James (1955) *Notes of a Native Son* (Beacon Press).

———— (1963) *The Fire Next Time* (Dial Press).

———— (1985) *The Price of the Ticket* (St. Martins's/Marek).

Baldwin, James, et al. (1964) "Liberalism and the Negro: A Round-Table Discussion," *Commentary* 37, 3: 25–42.

Ballen, John, and Richard Freeman (1986) "Transitions between Employment and Nonemployment," in Richard Freeman and Harry Holzer, eds., *The Black Youth Employment Crisis* (U. of Chicago Press), 75–112.

Baly, Iris (1989) "Career and Vocational Development of Black Youth," in Reginald Jones, ed., *Black Adolescents* (Cobb & Henry), 249–65.

Balzer, Richard (1972) *Street Time* (Grossman).

Bane, Mary Jo, and David Ellwood (1986) "Slipping Into and Out of Poverty," *J. of Human Resources* 21, 1: 1–23.

Banks, W. Curtis, Gregory McQuater, and Janet Hubbard (1977) "Task-liking and

Intrinsic-extrinsic Achievement Orientation in Black Adolescents," *J. of Black Psychology* 3, 2: 61–71.

Banks, W. S. M. (1950) "The Rank Order of Sensitivity to Discriminations of Negroes in Columbus, Ohio," *ASR* 15, 4: 529–33.

Baritz, Loren (1988) *The Good Life: The Meaning of Success for the American Middle Class* (Knopf).

Barnes, Mary, and Shirley Farrier (1985) "A Longitudinal Study of the Self-Concept of Low-Income Youth," *Adolescence* 20, 77: 199–205.

Barr, Robert, and Gary Knowles (1986) "The 1984–85 School Leaver and High School Diploma Program Participant Attitude Study" (San Diego City Schools).

Barrera, Mario (1979) *Race and Class in the Southwest* (U. of Notre Dame Press).

Barrett, Edith (1994) "The Role of Gender and Race in the Legislative Process" (Brown U., Dept. of Political Science).

Barrett, James (1992) "Americanization from the Bottom-Up: Immigration and the Remaking of the Working Class in the United States, 1880–1930," *J. of Am. History* 79, 3: 996–1020.

"Barriers" (1988) *Life Magazine*, spring: 42–44.

Barton, Bruce (1929) "Their Strength Was to Sit Still," *Am. Magazine* 108 (Oct.): 24–25, 77–78.

Barton, Josef (1975) *Peasants and Strangers: Italians, Rumanians, and Slovaks in an American City, 1890–1950* (Harvard U. Press).

——— (1978) "Eastern and Southern Europeans," in John Higham ed., *Ethnic Leadership in America* (Johns Hopkins U. Press), 150–75.

Beardwood, Roger (1968) "The New Negro Mood," *Fortune Magazine* 127, 1: 146–51, 230–32.

Beeman, Richard (1971) "Labor Forces and Race Relations: A Comparative View of the Colonization of Brazil and Virginia," *Political Science Q.* 86, 4: 609–36.

Beisel, Nicola (1990) "Class, Culture, and Campaigns Against Vice in Three American Cities, 1872–1892," *ASR* 55, 1: 44–62.

Belkin, Lisa (1989) "Bars to Equality of Sexes Seen as Eroding, Slowly," *NYT*, Aug. 20: A1, 26.

Bell, Derrick (1976) "Racial Remediation: An Historical Perspective on Current Conditions," *Notre Dame Lawyer* 52, 1: 5–29.

——— (1987) *And We Are Not Saved* (Basic Books).

——— (1992a) *Faces at the Bottom of the Well* (Basic Books).

——— (1992b) *Race, Racism, and American Law*, 3rd ed. (Little, Brown).

Bell, Robert (1965) "Lower-Class Negro Mothers' Aspirations for Their Children," *Social Forces* 43, 4: 493–500.

Bellah, Robert, et al. (1985) *Habits of the Heart* (Harper & Row).

Benston, George (1992) "The Relationship between the Demand and Supply of Home Financing and Neighborhood Characteristics," *J. of Financial Services Research* 5, 3: 235–60.

Berg, Linnea, and Lynn Olson (1991) "Causes and Implications of Rapid Job Loss among Participants in a Welfare to Work Program," paper at the annual meeting of the Assoc. for Public Policy Analysis and Management, Bethesda MD.

Berglas, Steven (1986) *The Success Syndrome: Hitting Bottom When You Reach the Top* (Plenum).

Berman, Marshall (1993) "Close to the Edge: Reflections on Rap," *Tikkun* 8, 2: 13–18, 75–78.

Bernard, Thomas (1990) "Angry Aggression among the 'Truly Disadvantaged,'" *Criminology* 28, 1: 73–96.

Bernstein, Lawrence (1990) "Policy Changes and School Climate: An Analysis of the

NAEP Questionnaire (1987–1988)" (Princeton: Policy Information Center, Educational Testing Service, RR-90-3).

Berry, Jeffrey, Kent Portney, and Ken Thomson (1989) "The Political Behavior of Poor People," paper at Conference on the Truly Disadvantaged, Northwestern U.

—— (1991) "The Political Behavior of Poor People," in Christopher Jencks and Paul Peterson, eds., *The Urban Underclass* (Brookings Institution), 357–72.

—— (1993) *The Rebirth of Urban Democracy* (Brookings Institution).

Besharov, Douglas (forthcoming) "Child Abuse Reporting," in Irwin Garfinkel, Jennifer Hochschild, and Sara McLanahan, eds., *Social Policies for Children* (Brookings Institution).

Billeaux, David (1988) "Explaining the Impact of Racial Make-up on Government Employee Organization Effectiveness," paper at the annual meeting of the APSA, Washington, D.C.

Birnbaum, Howard, and Rafael Weston (1974) "Home Ownership and the Wealth Position of Black and White Americans," *R. of Income and Wealth*, series 20, no. 1: 103–18.

Black Enterprise (1980) "Black Americans Speak Out," 11 (Aug.): 47–102.

—— (1982) "Speaking Out About Work" 13 (Aug.): 51–56.

—— (1985) "B.E. Readers Speak Out" 16 (Aug.): 95–102.

—— (1986) "Let's Hear It for Success" 16 (March): 45–51.

—— (1990) "A View of the Past, a Look to the Future" 21, (Aug.): 77–94.

"The Black Mood: More Militant, More Hopeful, More Determined" (1970) *Time Magazine*, April 6: 28–29.

Blackburn, McKinley, David Bloom, and Richard Freeman (1990) "The Declining Economic Position of Less Skilled American Men," in Gary Burtless, ed., *A Future of Lousy Jobs?* (Brookings Institution), 31–76.

Blalock, Hubert (1967) *Toward a Theory of Minority-Group Relations* (Wiley).

Blau, Francine, and John Graham (1990) "Black-White Differences in Wealth and Asset Composition," *Q. J. of Economics* 105, 421, Issue 2: 321–39.

Blau, Francine, and Lawrence Kahn (1992) "Race and Gender Pay Differentials," in David Lewin et al., eds., *Research Frontiers in Industrial Relations and Human Resources* (U. of Wisconsin, Industrial Relations Research Assoc.), 381–416.

Blau, Peter, and Otis Dudley Duncan (1967) *The American Occupational Structure* (John Wiley).

Blauner, Bob (1989) *Black Lives, White Lives: Three Decades of Race Relations in America* (U. of California Press).

—— (1992) "Talking Past Each Other: Black and White Languages of Race," *Am. Prospect* 10: 55–64.

Bledsoe, Timothy, et al. (1994) "Race in the City and the Suburbs" (Wayne State U., Dept. of Political Science).

—— (1995a) "Residential Context and Racial Solidarity among African Americans," *Am. J. of Political Science* 39, 2: 434–58.

—— (1995b) "The Social Contract in Black and White," in Stephen Craig, ed., *Broken Contract? Changing Relationships between Citizens and Their Government in the United States* (Westview).

Bloom, Allan (1987) *The Closing of the American Mind* (Simon and Schuster).

Bloom, Richard, Martin Whiteman, and Martin Deutsch (1965) "Race and Social Class as Separate Factors Related to Social Environment," *AJS* 70, 4: 471–76.

Bluestone, Barry (1990) "The Impact of Schooling and Industrial Restructuring on Recent Trends in Wage Inequality in the United States," Am. Economic Assoc., *Papers and Proceedings of the Annual Meeting* 80, 2: 303–7.

Blumer, Herbert (1958) "Race Prejudice as a Sense of Group Position," *Pacific Sociological R.* 1, 1: 3–7.

Blumstein, Alfred, et al., eds. (1986) *Criminal Careers and "Career Criminals"* (National Academy Press).

Bobo, Lawrence (1988) "Group Conflict, Prejudice, and the Paradox of Contemporary Racial Attitudes," in Phyllis Katz and Dalmas Taylor, eds., *Eliminating Racism* (Plenum Press), 85–114.

Bobo, Lawrence, and James Kluegel (1991) "Whites' Stereotypes, Social Distance, and Perceived Discrimination Toward Blacks, Hispanics, and Asians," paper at the annual meeting of the ASA, Cincinnati.

——— (1993) "Opposition to Race-Targeting: Self-Interest, Stratification Ideology, or Racial Attitudes?" *ASR* 58, 4: 443–64.

Bobo, Lawrence, et al. (1992) *Public Opinion Before and After a Spring of Discontent: A Preliminary Report on the 1992 Los Angeles County Social Survey* (UCLA, Center for the Study of Urban Poverty).

Bodnar, John (1985) *The Transplanted: A History of Immigrants in Urban America* (Indiana U. Press).

Boelhower, William (1991) "The Making of Ethnic Autobiography in the United States," in Paul Eakin, ed., *American Autobiography* (U. of Wisconsin Press), 123–41.

Bogess, Scott, and John Bound (1993) "Did Criminal Activity Increase During the 1980s?" (NBER).

Bolce, Louis, and Susan Gray (1979) "Blacks, Whites, and 'Race Politics,'" *Public Interest* 54: 61–75.

Bolce, Louis, Gerald de Maio, and Douglas Muzzio (1992) "Blacks and the Republican Party," *Political Science Q.* 107, 1: 63–79.

Bolger, Kerry, et al. (forthcoming) "Psychosocial Adjustment among Children Experiencing Persistent and Intermittent Family Economic Hardship," *Child Development.*

Bond, Julian (1990) "The Civil Rights Act: White Men's Hope," *NYT*, June 24: E21.

Borjas, George (1994) "Long-Run Convergence of Ethnic Skill Differentials" (NBER).

Borus, Michael, et al. (1980) "Job Search Activities of Youth," in Michael Borus et al., *Pathways to the Future*, vol. 1 (Ohio State U. Center for Human Resource Research), 223–76.

Boston, Thomas (1988) *Race, Class, and Conservatism* (Unwin Hyman).

Bosworth, Kris (1989) *Study of Turnover in Racial/Ethnic Minorities in Wisconsin State Government* (U. of Wisconsin, Center for Health Systems Research and Analysis).

Bound, John, and George Johnson (1991) "Wages in the United States during the 1980s and Beyond," in Marvin Kosters, ed., *Workers and Their Wages* (American Enterprise Institute Press), 77–106.

Bound, John, and Richard Freeman (1992) "What Went Wrong? The Erosion of Relative Earnings and Employment among Young Black Men in the 1980s," *Q. J. of Economics* 107, 1: 201–32.

Bourdieu, Pierre, and Jean-Claude Passeron (1977) *Reproduction* (Sage).

Bowles, Samuel, and Herbert Gintis (1976) *Schooling in Capitalist America* (Basic Books).

Bowman, Karlyn (1994) "What We Call Ourselves," *Public Perspective* 5, 4: 29–31.

Bowman, Phillip (1984) "A Discouragement-Centered Approach to Studying Unemployment among Black Youth," *International J. of Mental Health* 13, 1–2: 68–91.

——— (1991a) "Work Life," in James Jackson, ed., *Life in Black America* (Sage), 124–55.

—— (1991b) "Joblessness," in James Jackson, ed., *Life in Black America* (Sage), 156–78.

Bowman, Phillip, et al. (1982) "Joblessness and Discouragement among Black Americans," *Economic Outlook, USA* 9, 4: 85–88.

Bowman, Phillip, and Cleopatra Howard (1985) "Race-related Socialization, Motivation, and Academic Achievement," *J. of the Am. Academy of Child Psychiatry* 24, 2: 134–41.

Boyer, Peter (1986) "Rights Group Seeks Changes at CBS Outlet," *NYT*, March 27: C26.

Bradbury, Katharine, Karl Case, and Constance Dunham (1989) "Geographic Patterns of Mortgage Lending in Boston, 1982–1987," *New England Economic R.*, Sept./Oct.: 3–30.

Braddock, Jomills II, et al. (1986) "Applicant Race and Job Placement Decisions," *International J. of Sociology and Social Policy* 6, 1: 3–24.

Braddock, Jomills II, and James McPartland (1987) "How Minorities Continue to Be Excluded from Equal Employment Opportunities," *J. of Social Issues* 43, 1: 5–39.

Brady, Henry, and Paul Sniderman (1985) "Attitude Attribution: A Group Basis for Political Reasoning," *APSR* 79, 4: 1061–78.

Bragg, Rick (1994) "Where a Child on the Stoop Can Strike Fear," *NYT*, Dec. 2: A1, A28.

Braithwaite, Ronald (1981) "Interpersonal Relations between Black Males and Black Females," in Lawrence Gary, ed., *Black Men* (Sage), 83–97.

Brandt, Richard, Aaron Berstein, and John Hoerr (1985) "Those Vanishing High-Tech Jobs," *Business Week*, July 15: 30–31.

Brashler, William (1978) "The Black Middle Class: Making It," *NYT Magazine*, Dec. 3: 34–36, 138–57.

Briar, Scott (1966) "Welfare from Below: Recipients' Views of the Public Welfare System," in Jacobus Tenbroek, ed., *The Law of the Poor* (Chandler), 46–61.

Brink, William, and Louis Harris (1964) *The Negro Revolution in America* (Simon and Schuster).

—— (1966) *Black and White* (Simon and Schuster).

Britt, Donna (1990) "Barry's Arrest: The View from Black and White," *Washington Post*, Jan. 28: F1, F6.

Brody, Richard, and Paul Sniderman (1977) "From Life Space to Polling Place," *British J. of Political Science* 7, part 3: 337–60.

Broman, Clifford (1989) "Race and Responsiveness to Life Stress," *National J. of Sociology* 3, 1: 49–64.

Broman, Clifford, Harold Neighbors, and James Jackson (1988) "Racial Group Identification among Black Adults," *Social Forces* 67, 1: 146–58.

Brooke, James (1993) "Drug Lord Is Buried as Crowd Wails," *NYT*, Dec. 4: 7.

Brooks, Roy (1990) *Rethinking the American Race Problem* (U. of California Press).

Brounstein, Paul, et al. (1989) *Patterns of Substance Use and Delinquency among Inner City Adolescents* (Urban Institute).

Brown, Elaine (1992) *A Taste of Power* (Pantheon).

Brown, M. Craig, and Barbara Warner (1992) "Immigrants, Urban Politics, and Policing in 1900," *ASR* 57, 3: 293–305.

Brown, Ronald, and Monica Wolford (1994) "Religious Resources and African-American Political Action," *National Political Science R.: The Challenge to Racial Stratification* (Transaction Publishers), 4: 30–48.

Brown, Ronald, et al. (1994) *The 1984–1988 National Black Election Panel Study [NBES]: A Sourcebook* (U. of Michigan, Institute for Social Research).

Brown v. *Board of Education of Topeka, Kansas* 347 US 484 (1954).

Brown, Waln, et al. (1991) "Guidelines from Follow-Up Surveys of Adult Subjects Who Were Adjudicated Delinquent as Juveniles," in Warren Rhodes and Waln Brown, eds., *Why Some Children Succeed Despite the Odds* (Praeger), 149–58.

Browne, Robert (1974) "Wealth Distribution and Its Impact on Minorities," *R. of Black Political Economy* 4, 4: 27–37.

———— (1992) "The Road to Rectification," *Am. Prospect* 10: 93–96.

Browning, Rufus, Dale Rogers Marshall, and David Tabb (1990) *Racial Politics in American Cities* (Longman).

Brownstone, David, Irene Franck, and Douglass Brownstone (1979) *Island of Hope, Island of Tears* (Penguin Books).

Brumberg, Stephen (1986) *Going to America, Going to School: The Jewish Immigrant Public School Encounter in Turn-of-the-Century New York City* (Praeger).

Bukowczyk, John (1987) *And My Children Did Not Know Me: A History of the Polish-Americans* (Indiana U. Press).

Bullough, Bonnie (1972) "Alienation in the Ghetto," in Charles Bullock III and Harrell Rodgers, Jr., eds., *Black Political Attitudes* (Markham), 83–96.

Bulman, Ronnie, and Camille Wortman (1977) "Attributions of Blame and Coping in the 'Real World,'" *J. of Personality and Social Psychology* 35, 5: 351–63.

Burbridge, Lynn (1991) "The Interaction of Race, Gender, and Socioeconomic Status in Education Outcomes" (Wellesley College, Center for Research on Women).

Burns, Gene (1992) *The Frontiers of Catholicism* (U. of California Press).

Butterfield, Fox (1986) "Why Asians Are Going to the Head of the Class," *NYT*, Aug. 3: sec. 12 ("Education Life"): 18–23.

CBS News/*NYT* (1978) "The Kerner Commission—Ten Years Later," Feb. 16–19.

———— (1992) "May National Poll," May 6–8.

Caldwell, Dan (1971) "The Negroization of the Chinese Stereotype in California," *Southern California Q.* 53, 2: 123–31.

Campbell, Angus, and Howard Schuman (1968) "Racial Attitudes in Fifteen American Cities," for National Advisory Commission on Civil Disorders (U. of Michigan, Institute for Social Research), Jan.–March.

Campbell, Angus, Philip Converse, and Willard Rodgers (1976) *The Quality of American Life* (Russell Sage Foundation).

Campbell, Bebe (1984) "To Be Black, Gifted, and Alone," *Savvy*, Dec.: 67–74.

Campbell, Bruce (1980) "The Interaction of Race and Socioeconomic Status in the Development of Political Attitudes," *Social Science Q.* 60, 4: 651–58.

Campbell, Paul, et al. (1986) *Outcomes of Vocational Education for Women, Minorities, the Handicapped, and the Poor* (Ohio State U., Center on Education and Training for Employment [formerly NCRVE]).

Canner, Glenn (1991) "Home Mortgage Disclosure Act," *Federal Reserve Bulletin* 77, 11: 859–81.

Caplan, Nathan, and Jeffery Paige (1968) "A Study of Ghetto Rioters," *Scientific Am.* 219, 2: 15–21.

Caplow, Theodore, and Howard Bahr (1979) "Half a Century of Change in Adolescent Attitudes: Replications of a Middletown Survey by the Lynds," *Public Opinion Q.* 43, 1: 1–17.

Card, David, and Alan Krueger (1993) "Trends in Relative Black-White Earnings Revisited," *Am. Economic R.* 83, 2: 85–91.

Card, David, and Thomas Lemieux (1993) "Wage Dispersion, Returns to Skill, and Black-White Wage Differentials" (Princeton U., Dept. of Economics).

Carmines, Edward, and James Stimson (1989) *Issue Evolution: Race and the Transformation of American Politics* (Princeton U. Press).

Carnegie Foundation for the Advancement of Teaching (1984) *1984 National Sur-*

veys of College Faculty and Undergraduates: Technical Report and Detailed Tabulations (Princeton: Carnegie Foundation for the Advancement of Teaching).

Carnoy, Martin, and Henry Levin, eds. (1976) *The Limits of Educational Reform* (Longman).

Carpenter, Cheryl, et al. (1988) *Kids, Drugs, and Crime* (Lexington Books).

Carr, Leslie and John Hudgins (c. 1989) "Race, Class, and External Political Efficacy" (Old Dominion U., Dept. of Sociology).

Carsey, Thomas (1995) "The Contextual Effects of Race on White Voter Behavior," *J. of Politics* 57, 1: 221–28.

Carson, Emmett (1989) *The Charitable Appeals Fact Book: How Black and White Americans Respond to Different Types of Fund-Raising Efforts* (Joint Center for Political Studies).

Carter, Deborah, and Eileen O'Brien (1993) "Employment and Hiring Patterns for Faculty of Color," *Research Briefs* (American Council on Education): 4, 6.

Carter, Gregg (1990) "Black Attitudes and the 1960s Black Riots," *Sociological Q.* 31, 2: 269–86.

Carter, Stephen (1991) *Reflections of an Affirmative Action Baby* (Basic Books).

Case, Anne, and Lawrence Katz (1991) "The Company You Keep: The Effects of Family and Neighborhood on Disadvantaged Youths" (NBER).

Cather, Willa (1941) *O Pioneers!* (Virago).

Cavanagh, Thomas (1985) *Inside Black America: The Message of the Black Vote in the 1984 Elections* (Joint Center for Political Studies).

Cave, George, and Fred Doolittle (1991) *Assessing Jobstart: Interim Impacts of a Program for School Dropouts* (N. Y.: Manpower Demonstration Research Corporation).

Cazenave, Noel (1979) "Middle-Income Black Fathers," *Family Coordinator* 28, 4: 583–93.

——— (1983) "Black Male-Black Female Relationships: The Perceptions of 155 Middle-Class Black Men," *Family Relations* 32, 3: 341–50.

Center for Public and Urban Research, Georgia State U. (1981) "Selected Responses to a Survey Conducted in the Five-County Metro Area in July–Aug., 1981" (ms.).

Center for Public Interest Polling (1986) *The New Jersey Public School Teacher* (Rutgers U., Eagleton Institute of Politics).

Chacko, Thomas (1982) "Women and Equal Employment Opportunity," *J. of Applied Psychology* 67, 1: 119–23.

Chafets, Ze'ev (1990) *Devil's Night* (Random House).

Chalmers, David (1987) *Hooded Americanism: The History of the Ku Klux Klan* (Duke U. Press).

Chandler, David, and Mary Chandler (1987) *The Binghams of Louisville* (Crown).

Chasnoff, Ira, Harvey Landress, and Mark Barrett (1990) "The Prevalence of Illicit-Drug or Alcohol Use During Pregnancy and Discrepancies in Mandatory Reporting in Pinellas County, Florida," *New England J. of Medicine* 322, 17: 1202–6.

Chatters, Linda, Robert Taylor, and Harold Neighbors (1989) "Size of the Informal Helper Network Mobilized in Response to Serious Personal Problems," *J. of Marriage and the Family* 51, 3: 667–76.

Chicago Tribune (1986) *The American Millstone: An Examination of the Nation's Permanent Underclass* (Contemporary Books).

Child Welfare League of America (1992) *The Youngest of the Homeless II* (Washington, D.C.: Child Welfare League of America).

Chiricos, Theodore (1987) "Rates of Crime and Unemployment," *Social Problems* 34, 2: 187–212.

Chusmir, Leonard, and Bernadette Ruf (1992) "Racial and Ethnic Differences in Importance of Success and Relationship to Job Outcomes," *J. of Social and Behavioral Sciences* 37, 1: 43–60.

Citrin, Jack, and Donald Green (1990) "The Self-Interest Motive in American Public Opinion," *Research in Micropolitics* (JAI Press), 3:1–28.

Citrin, Jack, Beth Reingold, and Donald Green (1990) "American Identity and the Politics of Ethnic Change," *J. of Politics* 52, 4: 1124–54.

City of Richmond v. *J. A. Croson* (1989) 109 S. Ct. 706.

Clark, Kenneth (1965) *Dark Ghetto* (Harper Torchbook).

——— (1985) *King, Malcolm, Baldwin: Three Interviews* (Wesleyan U. Press).

——— (1993) "Racial Progress and Retreat: A Personal Memoir," in Herbert Hill and James Jones Jr., eds., *Race in America* (U. of Wisconsin Press), 3–18.

Clark, Reginald (1983) *Family Life and School Achievement: Why Poor Black Children Succeed or Fail* (U. of Chicago Press).

Clayton, Susan, and Faye Crosby (1992) *Justice, Gender, and Affirmative Action* (U. of Michigan Press).

Clendinen, Dudley (1986) "White Grip on Southern Schools: Keeping Control," *NYT*, June 23: A10.

Clifford, Frank, and David Ferrell (1992) "L.A. Strongly Condemns King Verdicts, Riots," *Los Angeles Times*, May 6: A1, A4.

Cloward, Richard, and Lloyd Ohlin (1960) *Delinquency and Opportunity* (Free Press of Glencoe).

Coalition on Human Needs (1988) *How the Poor Would Remedy Poverty* (Washington, D.C.: Coalition on Human Needs).

Cohen, Cathy, and Michael Dawson (1993) "Neighborhood Poverty and African American Politics," *APSR* 87, 2: 286–302.

Cohen, Yinon, and Andrea Tyree (1986) "Escape from Poverty: Determinants of Intergenerational Mobility of Sons and Daughters of the Poor," *Social Science Q.* 67, 4: 803–13.

Cohler, Bertram, and Morton Lieberman (1977) "Ethnicity and Personal Adaptation," *International J. of Group Tensions* 7, 3 and 4: 20–41.

Colasanto, Diane (1988) "Black Attitudes," *Public Opinion* 10, 5: 45–49.

Colasanto, Diane, and Linda Williams (1987) "The Changing Dynamics of Race and Class," *Public Opinion* 9, 5: 50–53.

Collins, Patricia (1991) *Black Feminist Thought* (Routledge).

Collins, Sharon (1983) "The Making of the Black Middle Class," *Social Problems* 30, 4: 369–82.

——— (1989) "The Marginalization of Black Executives," *Social Problems* 36, 4: 317–31.

——— (1993) "Blacks on the Bubble: The Vulnerability of Black Executives in White Corporations," *Sociological Q.* 34, 3: 429–47.

Comer, James (1980) *School Power: Implications of an Intervention Project* (Free Press).

——— (1988) *Maggie's American Dream* (New Am. Library).

Commissioner's Task Force on Minorities: Equity and Excellency (1989) *A Curriculum of Inclusion* (Albany: U. of the State of New York).

Comstock, George, and Robin Cobbey (1979) "Television and the Children of Ethnic Minorities," *J. of Communication* 29, 1: 104–15.

Cone, David (1986) *Speaking the Truth: Ecumenism, Liberation, and Black Theology* (Eerdsman).

Conquergood, Dwight (1992) "Street Sense as Cultural Communication" (Northwestern U., Center for Urban Affairs and Policy Research).

——— (1994) "Homeboys and Hoods: Gang Communication and Cultural Space," in Lawrence Frey, ed., *Group Communiation in Context* (Erlbaum), 23–55.

Constantinou, Stavros, and Milton Harvey (1985) "Dimensional Structure and Intergenerational Differences in Ethnicity: The Greek Americans," *Sociology and Social Research* 69, 2: 235–55.

Converse, Philip et al. (1980) *American Social Attitudes Data Sourcebook, 1947–1978* (Harvard U. Press).

Cook, Thomas, and Thomas Curtin (1987) "The Mainstream and the Underclass," in John Masters and William Smith, eds., *Social Comparison, Social Justice, and Relative Deprivation* (Erlbaum), 217–64.

Cooper, James Fenimore (1838) *The American Democrat* (H & E Phinney).

Cooperative Institutional Research Program (1973) *The American Freshman: National Norms for Fall 1973* (UCLA, Graduate School of Education, Higher Education Research Institute).

——— (1987) *The American Freshman: Twenty Year Trends* (UCLA, Graduate School of Education, Higher Education Research Institute).

——— (1994) *The American Freshman: National Norms for Fall 1994* (UCLA, Graduate School of Education, Higher Education Research Institute).

Corcoran, Mary, et al. (1985) "Myth and Reality: The Causes and Persistence of Poverty," *J. of Policy Analysis and Management* 4, 4: 516–36.

Cosby, Arthur (1971) "Black-White Differences in Aspirations among Deep South High School Students," *J. of Negro Education* 40, 1: 17–21.

Cose, Ellis (1993) *The Rage of a Privileged Class* (HarperCollins).

Cothran, Tilman (1951) "Negro Conceptions of White People," *AJS* 56, 5: 458–67.

Cotton, Jeremiah (1988) "Discrimination and Favoritism in the US Labor Market," *Am. J. of Economics and Sociology* 47, 1: 15–28.

——— (1990) "Recent Changes in the Structure and Value of African-American Male Occupations," *Trotter Institute R.* 4, 3: 6–1.

Covino, Michael (1985) "How the 69th Mob Maximized Earnings in East Oakland," *California Magazine* Nov.: 83–90, 124–27.

Crenshaw, Kimberlé (1990) "A Black Feminist Critique of Antidiscrimination Law and Politics," in David Kairys, ed., *The Politics of Law*, 2d ed. (Pantheon), 195–218.

——— (1992) "Whose Story Is It Anyway? Feminist and Antiracist Appropriations of Anita Hill," in Toni Morrison, ed., *Race-ing Justice, En-gendering Power* (Pantheon), 402–40.

Crocker, Jennifer, et al. (1991) "Social Stigma: The Affective Consequences of Attributional Ambiguity," *J. of Personality and Social Psychology* 60, 2: 218–28.

Crohan, Susan, et al. (1989) "Job Characteristics and Well-being at Midlife," *Psychology of Women Q.* 13, 2: 223–35.

Croly, Herbert (1963 [1909]) *The Promise of American Life* (E. P. Dutton).

Cromartie, John, and Carol Stack (1989) "Reinterpretation of Black Return and Nonreturn Migration to the South, 1975–1990," *Geographic Perspectives* 79, 3: 297–310.

Crosby, Faye, Stephanie Bromley, and Leonard Saxe (1980) "Recent Unobtrusive Studies of Black and White Discrimination and Prejudice," *Psychological Bulletin* 87, 3: 546–63.

Crosby, Faye, et al. (1989) "The Denial of Personal Disadvantage among You, Me, and All the Other Ostriches," in Mary Crawford and Margaret Gentry, eds., *Gender and Thought* (Springer-Verlag), 79–99.

Cruse, Harold (1987) *Plural but Equal* (William Morrow).

Culp, Jerome, and Bruce Dunson (1986) "Brothers of a Different Color: A Preliminary Look at Employer Treatment of White and Black Youth," in Richard Freeman and Harry Holzer, eds., *The Black Youth Employment Crisis* (U. of Chicago Press), 233–59.

Cummings, Scott (1980) "White Ethnics, Prejudice, and Labor Market Segmentation," *AJS* 85, 4: 938–50.

Cusick, Philip (1973) *Inside High School* (Holt, Rinehart and Winston).

Dahl, Robert (1961) *Who Governs?* (Yale U. Press).

——— (1977) "On Removing Certain Impediments to Democracy in the United States," *Political Science Q.* 92, 1: 1–20.

"'The Dangerous Classes'" (1871) *NYT*, July 16: 4.

Daniels, Roger (1990) *Coming to America* (HarperCollins Publishers).

Danziger, Sandra, and Naomi Farber (1990) "Keeping Inner-City Youths in School," *Social Work Research Abstracts* 26, 4: 32–39.

Danziger, Sheldon (1991) "Education, Earnings, and Poverty," in David Hornbeck and Lester Salamon, eds., *Human Capital and America's Future* (Johns Hopkins U. Press), 139–67.

Danziger, Sheldon, and Peter Gottschalk (1987) "Earnings Inequality, the Spatial Concentration of Poverty, and the Underclass," *Am. Economic R.* 77, 2: 211–15.

Darity, William, et al. (1990) "Microeconomic vs. Structural Models of the Underclass," paper at the Joint Center for Political Studies/HHS Forum on Models of the Underclass, Washington, D.C.

Darity, William, and Samuel Myers (1993) "Racial Earnings Inequality and Family Structure," paper at annual meeting of Western Economics Asso., Lake Tahoe, NV.

Darity, William, David Guilkey, and William Winfrey (1994) "Dressing for Success? Explaining Differences in Economic Performance among Racial and Ethnic Groups in the USA" (U. of North Carolina, Dept. of Economics).

Dash, Leon (1989) *When Children Want Children* (William Morrow).

Datcher-Loury, Linda, and Glenn Loury (1986) "The Effects of Attitudes and Aspirations on the Labor Supply of Young Men," in Richard Freeman and Harry Holzer, eds., *The Black Youth Employment Crisis* (U. of Chicago Press), 377–99.

Davis, George (1988) "The Changing Agenda," in Donna Thompson and Nancy DiTomaso, eds., *Ensuring Minority Success in Corporate Management* (Plenum Press), 101–13.

Davis, George, and Glegg Watson (1982) *Black Life in Corporate America* (Anchor Press/Doubleday).

Davis, James, and Tom Smith (1982) *General Social Surveys, 1972–1982: Cumulative Codebook* (U. of Chicago, National Opinion Research Center).

——— (1991) *General Social Surveys, 1972–1991: Cumulative Codebook* (U. of Chicago, National Opinion Research Center).

Dawkins, Marvin (1983) "Black Students' Occupational Expectations," *Urban Education* 18, 1: 98–113.

Dawson, Michael (1994a) "African American Political Discontent," *Polling Report* 10, 8: 1, 6.

——— (1994b) *Behind the Mule: Race and Class in African American Politics* (Princeton U. Press).

——— (1994c) "Black Feminism and Black Nationalism: Ideological Tendencies in the Black Mass Public," paper at the annual meeting of the APSA, New York.

de Tocqueville, Alexis (1969 [1848]) *Democracy in America*, trans. George Lawrence, ed. J. P. Mayer (Doubleday).

DeBord, Larry, Larry Griffin, and Melissa Clark (1977) "Race and Sex Influences in the Schooling Processes of Rural and Small Town Youth," *Sociology of Education* 42, 2: 85–102.

Delaney, Paul (1978) "Middle-Class Gains Create Tension in Black Community," *NYT*, Feb. 28: 1.

Delbanco, Andrew (1989) "Talking Texts," *New Republic*, Feb. 9 and 16: 28–34.

DeLorenzo, Lisa, Carol Kohfeld, and Lana Stein (1994) "Cross-Racial Voting and the Organization of Politics," paper at the annual meeting of the MWPSA, Chicago.

Demo, David, and Michael Hughes (1990) "Socialization and Racial Identity among Black Americans," *Social Psychology Q.* 53, 4: 364–74.

DeMott, Benjamin (1990) *Why Americans Can't Think Straight about Class* (William Morrow).

Denton, Herbert, and Barry Sussman (1981) " 'Crossover Generation' of Blacks Expresses Most Distrust of Whites," *Washington Post*, Mar. 25: A1, A2.

deParle, Jason (1990) "Talk of Government Being Out to Get Blacks Falls on More Attentive Ears," *NYT*, Oct. 29: B7.

Detlefsen, Robert (1991) *Civil Rights Under Reagan* (Institute for Contemporary Studies Press).

Dickinson, Katherine (1981) *The Impact of Supported Work on Ex-Addicts* (N. Y.: Manpower Demonstration Research Corporation).

Dienstbier, Richard (1972) "A Modified Belief Theory of Prejudice Emphasizing the Mutual Causality of Racial Prejudice and Anticipated Belief Differences," *Psychological R.* 79, 2: 146–60.

Diggins, John (1984) *The Lost Soul of American Politics* (U. of Chicago Press).

DiIulio, John Jr. (1989) "The Impact of Inner-City Crime," *Public Interest* 96: 28–46.

Dillingham, Gerald (1981) "The Emerging Black Middle Class: Class Conscious or Race Conscious?" *Ethnic and Racial Studies* 4, 4: 432–51.

Dillon, Pat (1988) "Honor, Family, Work: Success," *San Jose Mercury News*, Mar. 29: B1.

Dinar, Hasia (1983) *Erin's Daughters in America: Irish Immigrant Women in the Nineteenth Century* (Johns Hopkins U. Press).

Dingle, Derek (1987) "Will Black Managers Survive Corporate Downsizing?" *Black Enterprise* 17, 8: 49–55.

Dinnerstein, Leonard, and David Reimers (1988) *Ethnic Americans: A History of Immigration*, 3d ed. (Harper & Row).

Dinnerstein, Leonard, Roger Nichols, and David Reimers (1990) *Natives and Strangers: Blacks, Indians, and Immigrants in America* (Oxford U. Press).

DiTomaso, Nancy, Donna Thompson, and David Blake (1988) "Corporate Perspectives on the Advancement of Minority Managers," in Donna Thompson and Nancy DiTomaso, eds., *Ensuring Minority Success in Corporate Management* (Plenum Press), 119–36.

Donohue, Thomas, Timothy Meyer, and Lucy Henke (1978) "Black and White Children: Perceptions of TV Commercials," *J. of Marketing* 42, 4: 34–40.

Dornbusch, Sanford, Philip Ritter, and Laurence Steinberg (1991) "Community Influences on the Relation of Family Statuses to Adolescent School Performance," *Am. J. of Education* 99, 4: 543–67.

Douglass, Ramona (1994) Testimony before House Subcommittee on the Census, in *Interracial/Intercultural Connection* (newsletter for Biracial Family Network), Chicago.

Dovidio, John, and Samuel Gaertner (1986) *Prejudice, Discrimination, and Racism* (Academic Press).

Dower, John (1986) *War Without Mercy: Race and Power in the Pacific War* (Pantheon).

Du Bois, W. E. B. (1967 [1899]) *The Philadelphia Negro: A Social Study* (Schocken Books).

Dulan-Wilson, Gloria (1991) "Douglass High School of Oklahoma City: A Century of Excellence," *Crisis* 98, 8: 33–34.

Dumas, Rhetaugh (1980) "Dilemmas of Black Females in Leadership," in La Frances Rodgers-Rose, ed., *The Black Woman* (Sage), 203–15.

Duncan, Greg, and Daniel Hill (1975) "Attitudes, Behavior, and Economic Outcomes," in Greg Duncan and James Morgan, eds., *Five Thousand American Families—Patterns of Economic Progress* (U. of Michigan, Institute for Social Research), 3: 61–113.

Duncan, Greg, and James Morgan (1981) "Sense of Efficacy and Subsequent Change in Earnings—A Replication," *J. of Human Resources* 16, 4: 649–55.

Duncan, Greg, Timothy Smeeding, and Willard Rodgers (1993) "W(h)ither the Middle Class? A Dynamic View," in Dmitri Papadimitriou and Edward Wolff, eds., *Poverty and Prosperity in the USA in the Late Twentieth Century* (Macmillan), 240–74.

Duncan, Greg, and Willard Rodgers (1991) "Has Children's Poverty Become More Persistent?" *ASR* 56, 4: 538–50.

Duncan, Otis (1969) "Inheritance of Poverty or Inheritance of Race?" in Daniel Moynihan, ed., *On Understanding Poverty* (Basic Books), 85–110.

Dunlop, Eloise (1992) "Impact of Drugs on Family Life and Kin Networks in the Inner-City African-American Single-Parent Household," in Adele Harrell and George Peterson, eds., *Drugs, Crime, and Social Isolation* (Urban Institute Press), 181–207.

Dyson, Michael (1993) "Malcolm X and the Revival of Black Nationalism," *Tikkun* 8, 2: 45–48.

Earley, Pete (1986) "Rich Town Poor Town," *Washington Post Magazine*, Mar. 16: 10–17, 29–41.

Early, Gerald (1992) "Their Malcolm, My Problem," *Harper's Magazine*, Dec.: 62–74.

Easterlin, Richard, and Eileen Crimmins (1991) "Private Materialism, Personal Self-fulfillment, Family Life, and Public Interest," *Public Opinion Q.* 55, 4: 499–533.

Eastland, Terry, and William Bennett (1979) *Counting by Race* (Basic Books).

Ebony (1987) Special Issue on "The New Black Middle Class" 42, 10.

Economic Report of the President (1994) (USGPO).

Edin, Kathryn (1994a) "The Myths of Dependence and Self-Sufficiency" (Rutgers U., Center for Urban Policy Research).

—— (1994b) "Single Mothers and Absent Fathers: The Possibilities and Limits of Child Support Policy" (Rutgers U., Center for Urban Policy Research).

Edsall, Thomas (1991) *Chain Reaction: The Impact of Race, Rights, and Taxes on American Politics* (Norton).

Eggebeen, David, and Daniel Lichter (1991) "Race, Family Structure, and Changing Poverty among American Children," *ASR* 56, 6: 801–17.

Eggers, Paul (1988) "Effect of Transplantation on the Medicare End-Stage Renal Disease Program," *New England J. of Medicine* 318, 4: 223–29.

Ellison, Christopher, and David Gay (1990) "Region, Religious Commitment, and Life Satisfaction among Black Americans," *Sociological Q.* 31, 1: 123–47.

Ellison, Ralph (1966) *Shadow and Act* (Signet).

—— (1993) "Harlem is Nowhere," in Katharine Whittemore and Gerald Marzorati, eds., *Voices in Black and White* (Franklin Square Press), 47–52.

Ellwood, David (1987) *Understanding Dependency: Choices, Confidence, or Culture?* Report prepared for U.S. Dept. of Health and Human Services, Assistant Secretary for Policy Evaluation, Washington, D.C.

—— (1988) *Poor Support: Poverty in the American Family* (Basic Books).

Emerson, Ralph Waldo (1863) "Wealth," in *The Conduct of Life* (Ticknor and Fields), 71–110.

Epps, Edgar (1978) "The Impact of School Desegregation on the Self-Evaluation and Achievement Orientation of Minority Children," *Law and Contemporary Problems* 42, 3: 57–76.

Epstein, Joseph (1989) "The Joys of Victimhood," *NYT Magazine*, July 2: 20–21, 39–41.

Ericson, David (1993) *The Shaping of American Liberalism* (U. of Chicago Press).

Erie, Steven (1988) *Rainbow's End: Irish-Americans and the Dilemmas of Urban Machine Politics, 1840–1985* (U. of California Press).

Erskine, Hazel (1962) "The Polls: Race Relations," *Public Opinion Q.* 26, 1: 137–48.

——— (1969a) "The Polls: Negro Philosophies of Life," *Public Opinion Q.* 33, 1: 147–58.

——— (1969b) "The Polls: Negro Finances," *Public Opinion Q.* 33, 2: 272–82.

——— (1973) "The Polls: Interracial Socializing," *Public Opinion Q.* 37, 2: 283–94.

Ewen, Elizabeth (1985) *Immigrant Women in the Land of Dollars: Life and Culture on the Lower East Side, 1890–1925* (Monthly R. Press).

Ezekiel, Raphael (1984) *Voices from the Corner: Poverty and Racism in the Inner City* (Temple U. Press).

Ezorsky, Gertrude (1991) *Racism and Justice: The Case for Affirmative Action* (Cornell U. Press).

Fagan, Jeffrey (1989) "The Social Organization of Drug Use and Drug Dealing among Urban Gangs," *Criminology* 27, 4: 633–69.

——— (1990) "Social Processes of Delinquency and Drug Use among Urban Gangs," in C. Ronald Huff, ed., *Gangs in America* (Sage), 183–219.

Fagan, Jeffrey, and Ko-lin Chin (1989) "Initiation into Crack and Cocaine," *Contemporary Drug Problems* 16, 4: 579–617.

Fainstein, Norman, and Susan Nesbitt (1994) "Did the Black Ghetto Have a Golden Age?" paper at the annual meeting of the Organization of American Historians, Atlanta.

Fajardo, Daniel (1985) "Author Race, Essay Quality, and Reverse Discrimination," *J. of Applied Social Psychology* 15, 3: 255–68.

Farber, Naomi (1989) "The Significance of Aspirations among Unmarried Adolescent Mothers," *Social Service R.* 63, 4: 518–32.

Farkas, George, et al. (1982) *Impacts from the Youth Incentive Entitlement Pilot Projects: Participation, Work, and Schooling Over the Full Program Period* (N. Y.: Manpower Demonstration Research Corporation).

——— (1984) *Post-Program Impacts of the Youth Incentive Entitlement Pilot Projects* (N. Y.: Manpower Demonstration Research Corporation).

——— (1994) "Skill, Skill Demands of Jobs, and Earnings among Euro-American, African-American, and Mexican-American Workers" (U. of Texas-Dallas, Dept. of Sociology).

Farley, Reynolds (1992) "The Changing Status of Blacks and Whites, Men and Women" (U. of Michigan, Population Studies Center).

Farley, Reynolds, et al. (1993) "Continued Racial Residential Segregation in Detroit: 'Chocolate City, Vanilla Suburbs' Revisited," *J. of Housing Research* 4, 1: 1–38.

Farley, Reynolds, and Walter Allen (1987) *The Color Line and the Quality of Life in America* (Russell Sage Foundation).

Farley, Reynolds, and William Frey (1994) "Changes in the Segregation of Whites from Blacks during the 1980s," *ASR* 59, 1: 23–45.

Farnworth, Margaret, and Michael Leiber (1989) "Strain Theory Revisited: Economic Goals, Educational Means, and Delinquency," *ASR* 54, 2: 263–74.

Feagin, Joe, and Nancy Fujitaki (1972) "On the Assimilation of Japanese Americans," *Amerasia J.* 1, 4: 13–30.

Feagin, Joe, and Melvin Sikes (1994) *Living with Racism: The Black Middle-Class Experience* (Beacon Press).

Featherman, David, and Robert Hauser (1976) "Changes in the Socioeconomic Stratification of the Races, 1962–1973," *AJS* 82, 3: 621–51.

——— (1978) *Opportunity and Change* (Academic Press).

Fender, Stephen (1992) *Sea Changes: British Emigration and American Literature* (Cambridge U. Press).

Ferguson, Ronald (1987) "The Drug Problem in Black Communities," Report to the Ford Foundation.

——— (1994) "How Professionals in Community-Based Programs Perceive and Respond to the Needs of Black Male Youth," in Ronald Mincy, ed., *Nurturing Young Black Males* (Urban Institute Press), 59–98.

Ferleger, Lou, and Jay Mandle (1991) "African Americans and the Future of the U.S. Economy," *Trotter Institute R.* 5, 1: 3–7.

Fernandez, John (1975) *Black Managers in White Corporations* (Wiley).

——— (1981) *Racism and Sexism in Corporate Life* (Lexington Books).

——— (1988) "Racism and Sexism in Corporate America," in Donna Thompson and Nancy DiTomaso, eds., *Ensuring Minority Success in Corporate Management* (Plenum Press), 71–99.

Festinger, Leon (1957) *A Theory of Cognitive Dissonance* (Stanford U. Press).

Fine, Michelle (1983a) "The Social Context and a Sense of Injustice," *Representative Research in Social Psychology* 13: 15–33.

——— (1983b) "Perspectives on Inequity: Voices from Urban Schools," in Leonard Bickman, ed., *Applied Social Psychology Annual* (Sage), 4: 217–46.

——— (1992) *Disruptive Voices* (U. of Michigan Press).

Finnegan, William (1990a) "Out There—I," *New Yorker*, Sept. 10: 51–86.

——— (1990b) "Out There—II," *New Yorker*, Sept. 17: 60–90.

Fitzpatrick, Kevin, and Janet Boldizar (1993) "The Prevalence and Consequences of Exposure to Violence among African-American Youth," *J. of the Am. Academy of Child and Adolescent Psychiatry* 32, 2: 424–30.

Fleming, Jacqueline (1984) *Blacks in College* (Jossey-Bass).

Flowers, Ronald (1988) *Minorities and Criminality* (Greenwood Press).

Fogelson, Robert, and Robert Hill (1968) "Who Riots? A Study of Participation in the 1967 Riots," in *Supplemental Studies for the National Advisory Commission on Civil Disorders* (USGPO), 217–48.

Folb, Edith (1980) *Runnin' Down Some Lines: The Language and Culture of Black Teenagers* (Harvard U. Press).

Foner, Eric (1984) "Why Is There No Socialism in the United States?" *History Workshop* 17: 57–80.

Foner, Nancy, and Richard Napoli (1978) "Jamaican and Black-American Migrant Farm Workers," *Social Problems* 25, 5: 491–503.

Ford, David, Jr. (1988) "Minority and Nonminority MBA Progress in Business," in Donna Thompson and Nancy DiTomaso, eds., *Ensuring Minority Success in Corporate Management* (Plenum Press), 57–69 .

Fordham, Signithia, and John Ogbu (1986) "Black Students' School Success: Coping with the Burden of 'Acting White,'" *Urban R.* 18, 3: 1–31.

Fossett, Mark, and K. Jill Kiecolt (1989) "The Relative Size of Minority Populations and White Racial Attitudes," *Social Science Q.* 70, 4: 820–35.

Foucault, Michel (1979) *Discipline and Punish*, trans. Alan Sheridan (Vintage Books).

Fox, Robert (1992) "Afrocentrism and the X-Factor," *Transition*, 57: 17–25.

Franklin, Benjamin (1987) *Writings*, ed. J. A. Lemay (Library of America).

Franklin, John, and Isidore Starr, eds. (1967) *The Negro in 20th Century America* (Vintage).

Franklin, V. P. (1985) "From Integration to Black Self-Determination," in Margaret Spencer, Geraldine Brookins, and Walter Allen, eds., *Beginnings: The Social and Affective Development of Black Children* (Erlbaum), 19–28.

Frazier, E. Franklin (1957) *Black Bourgeoisie* (Free Press).

Frazier, E. Franklin, and C. Eric Lincoln (1974) *The Negro Church in America* (Schocken Books).

Freedman, Samuel (1990) *Small Victories: The Real World of a Teacher, Her Students, and Their High School* (Harper & Row).

Freeman, Richard (1986) "Who Escapes? The Relation of Churchgoing and Other Background Factors to the Socioeconomic Performance of Black Male Youths from Inner-City Poverty Tracts," in Richard Freeman and Harry Holzer, eds., *The Black Youth Employment Crisis* (U. of Chicago Press), 353–76.

—— (1989) "Help Wanted: Disadvantaged Youths in a Labor Shortage Economy" (Harvard U., Dept. of Economics).

Frey, Daniel (1992) "Miracle or Mirage? Social Science and Educational Reforms for African-American Males" (Princeton U., Woodrow Wilson School of Public and International Affairs, senior thesis).

Frey, Darcy (1993) "The Last Shot," *Harper's Magazine*, April: 37–60.

Frey, William, and Reynolds Farley (1993) "Latino, Asian and Black Segregation in Multi-Ethnic Metropolitan Areas," paper at the annual meeting of the Population Assoc. of America, Cincinnati.

Fried, Marc (1968) "Deprivation and Migration: Dilemmas of Causal Interpretation," in Daniel Moynihan, ed., *On Understanding Poverty* (Basic Books), 111–59.

Friedlander, Daniel, and Gayle Hamilton (1993) *The Saturation Work Initiative Model in San Diego: A Five-Year Follow-up Study* (N. Y.: Manpower Demonstration Research Corporation).

Frommer, Harvey (1982) *Rickey and Robinson: The Men Who Broke Baseball's Color Barrier* (Macmillan).

Fullinwider, Robert (1980) *The Reverse Discrimination Controversy* (Rowman and Littlefield).

Fulwood, Isaac, Jr. (1989) "Washington's Year of Shame," *Washington Post*, Jan. 1: B1, B4.

Furstenberg, Frank, Jr. (1993) "How Families Manage Risk and Opportunity in Dangerous Neighborhoods," in William Wilson, ed., *Sociology and the Public Agenda* (Sage), 231–58.

Furstenberg, Frank, Jr., Jeanne Brooks-Gunn, and S. Philip Morgan (1987) *Adolescent Mothers in Later Life* (Cambridge U. Press).

Furstenberg, Frank, Jr., Kay Sherwood, and Mercer Sullivan (1992) *Caring and Paying: What Fathers and Mothers Say about Child Support* (N. Y.: Manpower Demonstration Research Corporation).

Gale, William, Nancy Maritato, and John Scholz (1993) "Effects of Public and Private Transfers on Income Variability and the Poverty Rate" (U. of Wisconsin, IRP).

Gallup, George, ed. (1987) *Gallup Poll: Public Opinion, 1987* (Wilmington: Scholarly Resources).

Gallup Opinion Index (1973) Report no. 100, Oct.

Gallup Organization (1961) "The Gallup Poll," June 23–28.

Gallup Organization (1963) "The Gallup Poll," May 23–28.

―――― (1964) "Hopes and Fears," for Potomac Associates, Oct.

―――― (1966) "The Gallup Poll," Sept. 8–13.

―――― (1971) "The Gallup Poll," Aug. 27–30.

―――― (1972) "State of the Nation 1972," for Potomac Associates, May.

―――― (1988) "Gallup/Newsweek Poll: Race Relations," for Newsweek, Feb. 19–22.

―――― (1991a) "Gallup/Newsweek Poll: Race Relations,' for Newsweek, April 23–25.

―――― (1991b) "Gallup News Service Survey: June Omnibus, Wave 2," June 13–16.

―――― (1991c) "Gallup/Newsweek Poll: Sexual Harrassmen," for Newsweek, Oct. 10–11.

―――― (1992) "Gallup News Service Survey: May Omnibus, Wave 1," May 7–10.

―――― (1994) "CNN/USA Today—Report Card #5," for CNN/USA Today, April.

Gannett News Service (1981) Equality: America's Unfinished Business (Washington, D.C.: Gannett News Service) .

Gans, Herbert (1990) "Deconstructing the Underclass," J. of the Am. Planning Assoc. 56, 3: 271–77.

Garbarino, James, et al. (1992) Children in Danger: Coping with the Consequences of Community Violence (Jossey-Bass).

Garreau, Joel (1991) Edge City (Doubleday).

Gaston, Jerry, and Willie Pearson (1986) "The Social Status of Contemporary Black Chemists," paper at the annual meeting of the Am. Chemical Society, New York.

Gates, David (1993) "White Male Paranoia," Newsweek, Mar. 29: 48–53.

Geis, Gilbert, and Paul Jesilow, eds. (1993) "White Collar Crime," special issue of Annals of the Am. Academy of Political and Social Science v. 525 (Jan.).

General Social Survey (GSS) (1972–73) James David and Tom Smith, principal investigators (U. of Chicago: National Opinion Research Center).

Genovese, Eugene (1972) Roll, Jordan, Roll (Pantheon).

Gerbner, George, and Larry Gross (1976) "The Scary World of TV's Heavy Viewer," Psychology Today 9, 11: 41–45, 89.

Geronimus, Arline (1987) "On Teenage Childbearing and Neonatal Mortality in the United States," Population and Development R. 13, 2: 245–79.

Gerstle, Gary (1989) Working-Class Americanism: The Politics of Labor in a Textile City, 1914–1960 (Cambridge U. Press).

―――― (1993) "The Working Class Goes to War," Mid-America 75, 3: 303–22.

Ghent, W. J. (1902) Our Benevolent Feudalism (Macmillan).

Giddings, Paula (1984) When and Where I Enter: The Impact of Black Women on Race and Sex in America (Morrow).

―――― (1992) "The Last Taboo," in Toni Morrison, ed., Race-ing Justice, En-gendering Power (Pantheon), 441–65.

Giles, Micheal, and Arthur Evans (1986) "The Power Approach to Intergroup Hostility," J. of Conflict Resolution 30, 3: 469–86.

Giles, Micheal, and Melanie Buckner (1993) "David Duke and Black Threat," J. of Politics 55, 3: 702–13.

Giles, Micheal, and Kaenan Hertz (1994) "Racial Threat and Partisan Identification," APSR 88, 2: 317–26.

Gilkes, Cheryl (1985) " 'Together and in Harness': Women's Traditions in the Sanctified Church," Signs 10, 4: 678–99.

Gilliam, Dorothy (1990) "Breaking the Chains of Collective Black Guilt," Washington Post, July 9: E3.

Gilliam, Franklin Jr. (1986) "Black America: Divided by Class?" *Public Opinion* 9, 1: 53–57.

Gilliam, Franklin Jr., and Kenny Whitby (1989) "Race, Class, and Attitudes toward Social Welfare Spending," *Social Science Q.* 70, 1: 88–100.

Glaser, James (1994) "Back to the Black Belt: Racial Environment and White Racial Attitudes in the South," *J. of Politics* 56, 1: 21–41.

Glasgow, Douglas (1980) *The Black Underclass* (Jossey-Bass).

Glazer, Nathan (1975) *Affirmative Discrimination* (Basic Books).

―――― (1983) *Ethnic Dilemmas, 1964–1982* (Harvard U. Press).

Gleason, Philip (1980) "American Identity and Americanization," in Stephan Thernstrom, ed., *Harvard Encyclopedia of Am. Ethnic Groups* (Harvard U. Press), 31–58.

Gold, Steven (1989) "Differential Adjustment among New Immigrant Family Members," *J. of Contemporary Ethnography* 17, 4: 408–34.

Golden, Marissa (1992) "Exit, Voice, Loyalty, and Neglect: Bureaucratic Responses to Presidential Control during the Reagan Administration," *J. of Public Administration Research and Theory* 2, 1: 29–62.

Goldfarb, Robert (1980) "Black Men Are Last," *NYT*, Mar. 14: A27.

Goldin, Claudia (1990) *Understanding the Gender Gap* (Oxford U. Press).

Goldman, Peter (1969) *Report from Black America* (Simon and Schuster).

Goldstein, Mark (1988) "The End of the American Dream?" *Industry Week*, April 4: 77–80.

Gomes, Ralph, and Linda Williams (1992) "Coalition Politics," in Ralph Gomes and Linda Williams, eds., *From Exclusion to Inclusion: The Long Struggle for African American Political Power* (Greenwood Press), 129–60.

Goodban, Nancy (1985) "The Psychological Impact of Being on Welfare," *Social Service R.* 59, 3: 403–22.

Goodman, Marshall, Alfred Tuchfarber, and Andrew Smith (1993) "Minority Rights and Majority Interests," paper at the annual meeting of the APSA, Washington, D.C.

Goodwin, Leonard (1972) *Do the Poor Want to Work?* (Brookings Institution).

―――― (1983) *Causes and Cures of Welfare* (Lexington Books).

Gordon, Michael (1977) "Irish Immigrant Culture and the Labor Boycott in New York City, 1880–1886," in Richard Ehrlich, ed., *Immigrants in Industrial America 1850–1920* (U. Press of Virginia), 111–22.

Gordon S. Black Corporation (1989a) "*USA Today* Poll: Racism," for *USA Today*, Aug. 30–31.

―――― (1989b) "*USA Today* Poll: Racial Attitudes," for *USA Today*, Sept. 12–14.

Gottschalk, Peter (1992) "Is the Correlation in Welfare Participation across Generations Spurious?" (Boston College, Dept. of Economics).

Gottschalk, Peter, Sara McLanahan, and Gary Sandefur (1994) "The Dynamics and Intergenerational Transmission of Poverty and Welfare Participation," in Sheldon Danziger, Gary Sandefur, and Daniel Weinberg, eds., *Confronting Poverty* (Harvard U. Press), 85–108.

Graham, Hugh (1990) *The Civil Rights Era* (Oxford U. Press).

Graham, Sandra (1986) "An Attributional Perspective on Achievement Motivation and Black Children," in Robert Feldman, ed., *The Social Psychology of Education* (Cambridge U. Press), 39–65.

Graham, Sandra, and Anna Long (1986) "Race, Class, and the Attributional Process," *J. of Educational Psychology* 78, 1: 4–13.

Graham, Susan (1994) "An Assessment of the Federal Standard for Race and Ethnicity Classification," statement at the Workshop on Race and Ethnicity Classification, National Academy of Sciences, Committee on National Statistics, Feb.

Gray, Herman (1986) "Television and the New Black Man," in Richard Collins, ed., *Media, Culture and Society* (Sage), 8: 223–42.

Greeley, Andrew (1973) "Making It in America: Ethnic Groups and Social Status," *Social Policy* 4, 2: 21–29.

––––––– (1974) "Political Participation among Ethnic Groups in the United States," *AJS* 80, 1: 170–204.

Green, Gordon, et al. (1992) "Factors Affecting Black-White Income Differentials," *Studies in the Distribution of Income*, P60-183 (U.S. Dept. of Commerce, Bureau of the Census), 31–50.

Green, Shelley, and Paul Pryde (1990) *Black Entrepreneurship in America* (Transaction).

Greenberg, Michael (1977) "William Byrd II and the World of the Market," *Southern Studies* 16, 4: 429–56.

Greenberg, Stanley (1985) "Report on Democratic Defection" (New Haven: Analysis Group).

Greene, Marcia (1989) "Abuse, Neglect Rising in D.C.," *Washington Post*, Sept. 10: 1, 22, 23.

Greenhaus, Jeffrey, Sarjoj Parasuraman, and Wayne Wormley (1990) "Effects of Race on Organizational Experiences, Job Performance Evaluations, and Career Outcomes," *Academy of Management J.* 33, 1: 64–86.

Greenstone, J. David (1993) *The Lincoln Persuasion* (Princeton U. Press).

Gresham, Jewel (1989) "The Politics of Family in America," *Nation*, July 24: 116–20.

Gross, Jane (1989) "Grandmothers Bear a Burden Sired by Drugs," *NYT*, April 9: 1, 26.

––––––– (1993) "Body and Dreams Trampled, a Riot Victim Fights On," *NYT*, Oct. 22: A18.

Gross, Jane, and Ronald Smothers (1994) "In Prom Dispute, a Town's Race Divisions Emerge," *NYT*, Aug. 15: A10.

Grusky, David, and Thomas DiPrete (1990) "Recent Trends in the Process of Stratification," *Demography* 27, 4: 617–37.

Gurin, Patricia, Shirley Hatchett, and James Jackson (1989) *Hope and Independence: Blacks' Response to Electoral and Party Politics* (Russell Sage Foundation).

Gusfield, Joseph (1963) *Symbolic Crusade: Status Politics and the American Temperance Movement* (U. of Illinois Press).

Hacker, Andrew (1992) *Two Nations: Black and White, Separate, Hostile, Unequal* (Scribner's).

Hagedorn, John (1988) *People and Folks: Gangs, Crime, and the Underclass in a Rustbelt City* (Lake View Press).

Hagner, Paul, and John Pierce (1984) "Racial Differences in Political Conceptualization," *Western Political Q.* 37, 2: 212–35.

Haley, Alex, ed. (1965) *Autobiography of Malcolm X* (Ballantine Books).

Hall, Michael (1988) *The Last American Puritan: The Life of Increase Mather, 1639–1723* (Wesleyan U. Press).

Hall, Stuart (1981) "Notes on Deconstructing 'the Popular,'" in Raphael Samuel, ed., *People's History and Socialist Theory* (Routledge and Kegan Paul), 227–40.

Halligan, Patrick (1991) "Minority Business Enterprises and *Ad Hoc* Hypotheses," *Urban Lawyer* 23, 2: 249–79.

Hall-Valdez, Jessica, Maria Cordero, and Eduardo Pagan (1992) "Racial Harassment at Princeton" (Princeton U.).

Hamid, Ansley (1990) "The Political Economy of Crack-Related Violence," *Contemporary Drug Problems* 17, 1: 31–78.

Hamill, Pete (1988) "Breaking the Silence: A Letter to a Black Friend," *Esquire* 109, 3 (March): 91–102.

Hamilton, Charles (1982) "Integrating the American Dream," *Public Opinion* 5, 3: 45–47.

Hareven, Tamara, and Randolph Langenbach (1978) *Amoskeag: Life and Work in an American Factory-City* (Pantheon).

Harring, Sidney (1983) *Policing a Class Society: The Experience of American Cities, 1865–1915* (Rutgers U. Press).

Harris, Anthony (1976) "Race, Commitment to Deviance, and Spoiled Identity," *ASR* 41, 3: 432–41.

Harris, Anthony, and Randall Stokes (1978) "Race, Self-Evaluation and the Protestant Ethic," *Social Problems* 26, 1: 71–85.

Harris, Fredrick (1993) "Religion Reconsidered: Black Protest and Electoral Activism in an Age of Transformation," paper at the Workshop on Race, Ethnicity, Representation, and Governance, Harvard U.

——— (1994) "Something Within: Religion as a Mobilizer of African-American Political Activism," *J. of Politics* 56, 1: 42–68.

Harris, Kathleen (1991) "Teenage Mothers and Welfare Dependency," *J. of Family Issues* 12, 4: 492–518.

——— (1993) "Work and Welfare among Single Mothers in Poverty," *AJS* 99, 2: 317–52.

Harris, Leonard (1992) "Honor: Emasculation and Empowerment," in Larry May and Robert Strikwerda, eds., *Rethinking Masculinity* (Rowman and Littlefield), 191–208.

Harris, Louis (1986) "Yupppie Lifestyle Felt To Be Unattractive to Americans" (N. Y.: Harris Survey), Feb. 3.

——— (1990) "Public Looks Back on 1980s with Growing Sense of Criticism" (N. Y.: Harris Poll), July 29.

Harris, Louis, and Associates (1966a) "Racial Survey: Black Sample," for *Newsweek*, June.

——— (1966b) "Racial Survey: Random Sample," for *Newsweek*, June.

——— (1968) "College Student Peace Corps Survey: Black Sample."

——— (1969) "Survey of College Seniors."

——— (1970a) "American Women's Opinion Survey [Women]," for the Virginia Slim Division of Liggett and Meyers, Aug.

——— (1970b) "American Women's Opinion Survey [Men]," for the Virginia Slim Division of Liggett and Meyers, Aug.

——— (1970c) untitled, April.

——— (1978) *A Study of Attitudes toward Racial and Religious Minorities and Toward Women*, for National Conference of Christians and Jews, Nov.

——— (1979) *A Survey of Residents' Perceptions of Neighborhood Services in the Southeast Bronx and Central Harlem*, for Community Service Society of New York, May.

——— (1986a) "A Survey of Leaders on Leadership Development and Empowerment for Black Women," for National Coalition of 100 Black Women, Aug.

——— (1986b) "Children's Needs and Public Responsibilities," for Group W— Westinghouse Broadcasting Co., Sept.

——— (1988) "A Nation Divided on Black Progress," for *Business Week*/Harris Poll, Jan. 20–26.

Harris, Louis, and Associates (1989a) *The Unfinished Agenda on Race in America*, vol. 1, for NAACP Legal Defense and Educational Fund, June–Sept. 1988.

—— (1989b) *The Unfinished Agenda on Race in America*, vol. 2, for NAACP Legal Defense and Educational Fund, June–Sept. 1988.

—— (1989c) *The Unfinished Agenda on Race in America* (unpublished tables).

—— (1990) "The View from the Trenches," June.

—— (1991) "How Blacks View Thomas and Their Leaders," for *Business Week/ Harris Poll*, Aug. 29–Sept. 2.

Harrison, Eric (1994) "Dating Changes, Discord Rock a Tiny Alabama Town," *Los Angeles Times*, Aug. 12: A1ff.

Harrison, Roderick, and Claudette Bennett (1995) "Racial and Ethnic Diversity," in Reynolds Farley, ed., *State of the Union: America in the 1990s, Vol. 2: Social Trends* (Russell Sage Foundation), 141–210.

Hartmann, Douglas (1989) "The Chicago Public School Senior Survey: Student Perceptions and High School Reality" (U. of Chicago, Metropolitan Opportunity Project).

Hatchett, Shirley, Donna Cochran, and James Jackson (1991) "Family Life," in James Jackson, ed., *Life in Black America* (Sage), 46–83.

Hauser, Robert (1990) "Changes in Occupational Status among U.S. Men from the 1970s to the 1980s" (U. of Wisconsin, Center for Demography and Ecology).

Hauser, Robert, and Hanam Phang (1993) "Trends in High School Dropout among White, Black, and Hispanic Youth, 1973 to 1989" (U. of Wisconsin, IRP).

HDM/Dawson Johns and Black (1988) *Media Consumption Habits of Blacks* (Chicago: HDM).

Hedge, David, James Button, and Mary Spear (1992) "Black Leadership in the 1990s: A View from the States," paper at the annual meeting of the APSA, Chicago.

Heidrick and Struggles (1979a) "Profile of a Black Executive" (Chicago: Heidrick and Struggles Inc.).

—— (1979b) "Chief Personnel Executives Look at Blacks in Business" (Chicago: Heidrick and Struggles Inc.).

—— (1980) "Profile of a Woman Officer" (Chicago: Heidrick and Struggles Inc.).

—— (1986) "The Corporate Woman Officer" (Chicago: Heidrick and Struggles Inc.).

Heilman, Madeline, Michael Simon, and David Repper (1987) "Intentionally Favored, Unintentionally Harmed? Impact of Sex-Based Preferential Selection on Self-Perceptions and Self-Evaluations," *J. of Applied Psychology* 72, 1: 62–68.

Heinze, Andrew (1990) *Adapting to Abundance: Jewish Immigrants, Mass Consumption, and the Search for American Identity* (Columbia U. Press).

Held, Philip, et al. (1988) "Access to Kidney Transplantation," *Archives of Internal Medicine* 148 (Dec.), 2594–99.

Hemmons, Willa Mae (1980) "The Women's Liberation Movement: Understanding Black Women's Attitudes," in La Frances Rodgers-Rose, ed., *The Black Woman* (Sage), 285–99.

Hendrick, Burton (1907) "The Great Jewish Invasion," *McClure's Magazine* 28, 3: 307–21.

Henretta, John (1979) "Race Differences in Middle Class Lifestyle: The Role of Home Ownership," *Social Science Research* 8, 1: 63–78.

Herring, Cedric (1989) "Identifying Who Represents Black America," (U. of Illinois at Chicago, Dept. of Sociology).

—— (1992) "Affirmative Action in America" (U. of Illinois at Chicago, Dept. of Sociology).

Herring, Mary, and John Forbes (1994) "The Overrepresentation of Whites on an

At-Large City Council: Racial Voting Patterns in Detroit, 1961–1989," *Social Science Q.* 75, 2: 431–45.

Hertzog, Mark (1994) "White Flight in the Voting Booth: The Racial Composition of Localities and Partisan Voting in Virginia in the 1980s," *National Political Science R.: The Challenge to Racial Stratification* (Transaction), 4: 163–83.

Hess, Fred (1987) "A Comprehensive Analysis of the Dropout Phenomenon in an Urban School System," paper at the annual meeting of the Am. Educational Research Assoc., Washington, D.C.

Hicks, Jonathan (1991) "Blacks See Bias Trend in Job Cuts," *NYT*, Sept. 23: D1, D2.

Hicks-Bartlett, Sharon (1991) "A Suburb in Name Only: The Case of Meadow View," paper at the Urban Poverty and Family Life Conference, U. of Chicago.

Higginbotham, Elizabeth, and Lynn Weber (1992) "Moving Up with Kin and Community: Upward Social Mobility for Black and White Women," *Gender and Society* 6, 3: 416–40.

Higham, John (1963) *Strangers in the Land: Patterns of American Nativism, 1860–1925* (Atheneum).

——— (1984) *Send These to Me: Immigrants in Urban America* (Johns Hopkins U. Press).

Highton, Benjamin (1991) "New Findings on Racial Differences in Turnout and Misreporting" (U. of California, Berkeley, Dept. of Political Science).

Hill, Carol (1973) *Subsistence USA.* (Holt, Rinehart, and Winston).

Hill, Martha, et al. (1985) *Motivation and Economic Mobility* (U. of Michigan, Institute for Social Research).

Hill, Martha, and Greg Duncan (1987) "Parental Family Income and the Socioeconomic Attainment of Children," *Social Science Research* 16, 1: 39–73.

Hilts, Philip (1992) "Federal Official Apologizes for Remarks on Inner Cities," *NYT*, Feb. 22: 6.

Hinds, Michael (1991) "Minority Business Set Back Sharply by Courts' Rulings," *NYT*, Dec. 23: A1, A15.

Hirsch, Arnold (1983) *Making the Second Ghetto: Race and Housing in Chicago, 1940–1960* (Cambridge U. Press).

Hirsch, Fred (1976) *Social Limits to Growth* (Harvard U. Press).

Hirsch, H. N. (1992) *A Theory of Liberty: The Constitution and Minorities* (Routledge).

Hirschman, Albert (1970) *Exit, Voice, and Loyalty* (Harvard U. Press).

——— (1981) *Essays in Trespassing* (Cambridge U. Press).

Hirschman, Charles (1994) "The Meaning of Race and Ethnic Population Projections," paper at conference on American Diversity: A Demographic Challenge for the Twenty-First Century, SUNY at Albany, April.

Hiss, Tony (1992) "Breaking Ground," *New Yorker*, Oct. 26: 101–2.

Hochschild, Adam (1986) *Half the Way Home: A Memoir of Father and Son* (Viking).

Hochschild, Jennifer (1981) *What's Fair? American Beliefs about Distributive Justice* (Harvard U. Press).

——— (1984) *The New American Dilemma: Liberal Democracy and School Desegregation* (Yale U. Press).

——— (1988) "The Double-Edged Sword of Equal Opportunity," in Ian Shapiro and Grant Reeher, eds., *Power, Inequality, and Democratic Politics* (Westview Press), 168–200.

——— (1991) "The Politics of the Estranged Poor," *Ethics* 101, 3: 560–78.

——— (1993) "Middle-class Blacks and the Ambiguities of Success," in Paul Sniderman, Philip Tetlock, and Edward Carmines, eds., *Prejudice, Politics, and the American Dilemma* (Stanford U. Press), 148–72.

Hochschild, Jennifer, and Monica Herk (1990) "'Yes, but . . .': Principles and Caveats in American Racial Attitudes," in John Chapman and Alan Wertheimer, eds., *Nomos XXXII: Majorities and Minorities* (New York U. Press), 308–35.

Hodge-Edelin, Ramona (1990) "Curriculum and Cultural Identity," in Asa Hilliard III, Lucretia Payton-Stewart, and Larry Williams, eds., *Infusion of African and African American Content in the School Curriculum* (Aaron Press), 37–45.

Hogan, Dennis, and David Featherman (1978) "Racial Stratification and Socioeconomic Change in the American North and South," *AJS* 83, 1: 100–126.

Hogan, Dennis, and Evelyn Kitagawa (1985) "The Impact of Social Status, Family Structure, and Neighborhood on the Fertility of Black Adolescents," *AJS* 90, 4: 825–55.

Hogan, Dennis, David Eggebeen and Clifford Clogg (1993) "The Structure of Intergenerational Exchanges in American Families," *AJS* 98, 6: 1428–58.

Hogan, Lloyd (1992) "The Role of Land and African-Centered Values in Black Economic Development," in James Jennings, ed., *Race, Politics, and Economic Development* (Verso), 165–74.

Holford, Tom (1994) "Re: German-Americans: Don't Call Us 'White,'" message to bulletin board h-ethnic@uicvm.uic.edu, July 18.

Holmes, Steven (1991) "When Grass Looks Greener on This Side of the Fence," *NYT*, April 21: E6.

Holzer, Harry (1986) "Black Youth Nonemployment," in Richard Freeman and Harry Holzer, eds., *The Black Youth Employment Crisis* (U. of Chicago Press), 23–70.

—— (1994) "Black Employment Problems," *J. of Policy Analysis and Management* 13, 4: 699–722.

hooks, bell (1992) *Black Looks: Race and Representation* (South End Press).

Hopkins, Anne (1980) "Perceptions of Employment Discrimination in the Public Sector," *Public Administration R.* 40, 2: 131–37.

Horton, John (1967) "Time and Cool People," *Transaction* 4, 5: 5–12.

Horwitz, Sari (1988) "A Drug-Selling Machine That Was All Business," *Washington Post*, April 24: A1, A16.

Housing Policy Debate (1992) special issue on Discrimination in the Housing and Mortgage Markets 3, 2.

Hout, Michael (1984) "Occupational Mobility of Black Men: 1962 to 1973," *ASR* 49, 3: 308–22.

—— (1986) "Opportunity and the Minority Middle Class," *ASR* 51, 2: 214–23.

—— (1988) "More Universalism, Less Structural Mobility: The American Occupational Structure in the 1980s," *AJS* 93, 6: 1358–1400.

Hout, Michael, and William Morgan (1975) "Race and Sex Variations in the Causes of the Expected Attainments of High School Seniors," *AJS* 81, 2: 364–94.

Howard, Jeff, and Ray Hammond (1985) "Rumors of Inferiority," *New Republic*, Sept. 9: 17–21.

Howe, Irving (1976) *World of Our Fathers* (Harcourt Brace Jovanovich).

Huber, Joan, and William Form (1973) *Income and Ideology* (Free Press).

Huckfeldt, R. Robert and Carol Kohfeld (1989) *Race and the Decline of Class in American Politics* (U. of Illinois Press).

Huff, C. Ronald, ed. (1990) *Gangs in America* (Sage).

Hughes, Langston (1938) "Let America Be America Again," in *A New Song* (International Workers Order), 9–11.

Hughes, Mark (1988) "Concentrated Deviance and the 'Underclass' Hypothesis" (Princeton U., Woodrow Wilson School of Public and International Affairs).

—— (1989) "Concentrated Deviance and the 'Underclass' Hypothesis," *J. of Policy Analysis and Management* 8, 2: 274–82.

Hughes, Michael, and David Demo (1989) "Self-Perceptions of Black Americans," *AJS* 95, 1: 132–59.

Hughes, Robert (1992) *The Culture of Complaint* (Oxford U. Press).

Hugins, Walter, ed. (1972) *The Reform Impulse, 1825–1850* (U. of South Carolina Press).

Hull, Gloria, Patricia Scott, and Barbara Smith, eds. (1982) *All the Women Are White, All the Blacks Are Men, But Some of Us Are Brave* (Feminist Press).

Hunt, Larry, and Janet Hunt (1977) "Black Religion as Both Opiate and Inspiration of Civil Rights Militancy," *Social Forces* 86, 1: 1–14.

Huntington, Samuel (1981) *American Politics: The Promise of Disharmony* (Harvard U. Press).

Hurh, Won Moo, and Kwang Chung Kim (1989) "The 'Success' Image of Asian Americans," *Ethnic and Racial Studies* 12, 4: 512–38.

Hurston, Zora Neale (1942) *Dust Tracks on a Road*, 2d. ed. (U. of Illinois Press).

Hutcheson, John (1973) *Racial Attitudes in Atlanta* (Emory U., Center for Research in Social Change).

Ifill, Gwen, and David Maraniss (1986) "In Atlanta, Struggling with Success," *Washington Post*, Jan. 20: A1, A10.

Inciardi, James, and Anne Pottieger (1991) "Kids, Crack, and Crime," *J. of Drug Issues* 21, 2: 257–70.

Iota Xi Chapter of Sigma Chi v. George Mason University (1993) 773 F. Supp. 792 (E.D. VA 1991).

Irons, Edward, and Gilbert Moore (1985) *Black Managers* (Praeger).

Irons, Peter (1983) *Justice at War: The Story of the Japanese American Internment Cases* (Oxford U. Press).

Isaacs, Mareasa (1992) *Violence: The Impact of Community Violence on African American Children and Families* (Arlington, VA: National Center for Education in Maternal and Child Health).

Jackman, Mary, and Robert Jackman (1983) *Class Awareness in the United States* (U. of California Press).

Jackman, Mary, and Michael Muha (1984) "Education and Intergroup Attitudes," *ASR* 49, 6: 751–69.

Jackson, James, Linda Chatters, and Harold Neighbors (1986) "The Subjective Life Quality of Black Americans," in Frank Andrews, ed., *Research on the Quality of Life* (U. of Michigan, Institute for Social Research), 193–213.

Jackson, James, et al. (1991) "Race Identity," in James Jackson, ed., *Life in Black America* (Sage), 238–53.

Jackson, Mary (1988) "Drug Use and Delinquency in the Black Male Adolescent" (Case Western Reserve U., Ph.D. diss.).

Jackson, Peter, and Edward Montgomery (1986) "Layoffs, Discharges, and Youth Unemployment," in Richard Freeman and Harry Holzer, eds., *The Black Youth Employment Crisis* (U. of Chicago Press), 115–41.

James, William (1920) Letter to H. G. Wells, in *The Letters of William James*, ed. Henry James (Atlantic Monthly Press), 2: 260.

Jang, Sung, and Marvin Krohn (c. 1994) "A Relational Approach to the Explanation of Sex Differences in Delinquency" (Ohio State U., Dept. of Sociology).

Jankowski, Martín (1991) *Islands in the Street: Gangs and American Urban Society* (U. of California Press).

Jargowsky, Paul (1994) "Ghetto Poverty among Blacks in the 1980s," *J. of Policy Analysis and Management* 13, 2: 288–310.

Jargowsky, Paul, and Mary Jo Bane (1991) "Ghetto Poverty in the United States,

1970–1980," in Christopher Jencks and Paul Peterson, eds., *The Urban Underclass* (Brookings Institution), 235–73.

Jaynes, Gerald, and Robin Williams, eds. (1989) *A Common Destiny: Blacks and American Society* (National Academy Press).

Jeff, Morris, Jr. (1994) "Afrocentrism and African-American Male Youths," in Ronald Mincy, ed., *Nurturing Young Black Males* (Urban Institute Press), 99–118.

Jeffrey, Julie (1979) *Frontier Women: The Trans-Mississippi West 1840–1880* (Hill and Wang).

Jencks, Christopher (1991) "Is The American Underclass Growing?" in Christopher Jencks and Paul Peterson, eds., *The Urban Underclass* (Brookings Institution), 28–100.

———— (1992) *Rethinking Social Policy* (Harvard U. Press).

Jencks, Christopher, et al. (1972) *Inequality* (Basic Books).

Jenkins, Richard (1991) "Socializing the Unsocialized Delinquent," in Warren Rhodes and Waln Brown, eds., *Why Some Children Succeed Despite the Odds* (Praeger), 141–48.

Jennings, James (1990) "The Politics of Black Empowerment in Urban America," in Joseph Kling and Prudence Posner, eds., *Dilemmas of Activism* (Temple U. Press), 113–36.

————, ed. (1992) *Race, Politics, and Economic Development* (Verso).

Jhally, Sut, and Justin Lewis (1992) *Enlightened Racism: The Cosby Show, Audiences, and the Myth of the American Dream* (Westview Press).

Jianakoplos, Nancy, and Paul Menchik (1992) "Wealth Mobility" (Michigan State U., Dept. of Economics).

Johnson, Bruce, et al. (1986) "The Concentration of Delinquent Offending," in Bruce Johnson and E. Wish, eds., *Crime Rates among Drug Abusing Offenders* (N. Y.: Narcotic and Drug Research), 106–43.

Johnson, Bruce, Ansley Hamid, and Harry Sanabria (1992) "Emerging Models of Crack Distribution," in Thomas Mieczkowski, ed., *Drugs, Crime, and Social Policy* (Allyn and Bacon), 56–78.

Johnson, Gloria (1989) "Estimated Reference Group Effects of Underemployment and Underpayment on Psychosocial Functioning among Working Men," *National J. of Sociology* 3, 1: 25–50.

———— (1990) "Underemployment, Underpayment, Attributions, and Self-Esteem among Working Black Men," *J. of Black Psychology* 16, 2: 23–43.

Johnson, Stephen (1980) "Reverse Discrimination and Aggressive Behavior," *J. of Psychology* 104: 11–19.

Johnson, Walton, and D. Michael Warren (1994) *Inside the Mixed Marriage* (U. Press of America).

Johnston, David (1992) "F.B.I. Promises Gains to Blacks in a Settlement," *NYT*, April 22: 1, 22.

Johnstone, John (1978) "Social Class, Social Areas, and Delinquency," *Sociology and Social Research* 63, 1: 49–72.

Joint Center for Political Studies (1984) "JCPS Releases In-Depth Survey of Black Political Attitudes," press release, August 30.

Joint Center for Political and Economic Studies (1994) *Black Elected Officials, 1993* (U. Press of America).

Jones, Dionne, and Monica Jackson (1992) *Interracial Violence and Community Conflict* (Washington, D.C.: National Urban League).

Jones, Edward (1973) "What It's Like To Be a Black Manager," *Harvard Business R.* 51, 4: 108–16.

——— (1986) "Black Managers: The Dream Deferred," *Harvard Business R.* 64, 3: 84–93.

Jones, Jacqueline (1992) *The Dispossessed: America's Underclasses from the Civil War to the Present* (Basic Books).

Jones, Lyle (1987) "Trends in School Achievement of Black Children" (U. of North Carolina, Institute for Research in Social Science).

Jordan, Winthrop (1968) *White Over Black: American Attitudes Toward the Negro, 1550–1812* (U. of North Carolina Press).

J. of Intergroup Relations (1991) special issue on Harassment of African American Elected Officials 18, 3.

Juhn, Chinhui, Kevin Murphy, and Brooks Pierce (1991) "Accounting for the Slowdown in Black-White Wage Convergence," in Marvin Kosters, ed., *Workers and Their Wages* (American Enterprise Institute Press), 107–45.

Kaestner, Robert (1991) "The Effect of Illicit Drug Use on the Wages of Young Adults," *J. of Labor Economics* 9, 4: 381–412.

——— (1994) "New Estimates of the Effect of Marijuana and Cocaine Use on Wages," *Industrial and Labor Relations R.* 47, 3: 454–70.

Kalmijn, Matthijs (1993) "Trends in Black/White Intermarriage," *Social Forces* 72, 1: 119–46.

Kammen, Michael (1993) "The Problem of American Exceptionalism," *Am. Q,* 45, 1: 1–43.

Kaplan, H. Roy, and Curt Tausky (1972) "Work and the Welfare Cadillac," *Social Problems* 19, 4: 469–83.

Karenga, M. Ron (1977) *Kwanzaa: Origin, Concepts, Practice* (Kawaida Publications).

Karoly, Lynn (1993) "The Trend in Inequality among Families, Individuals, and Workers in the United States," in Sheldon Danziger and Peter Gottschalk, eds., *Uneven Tides: Rising Inequality in America* (Russell Sage Foundation), 19–97.

Kasarda, John (1992) "The Severely Distressed in Economically Transforming Cities," in Adele Harrell and George Peterson, eds., *Drugs, Crime, and Social Isolation* (Urban Institute Press), 45–97.

——— (1993) "Inner-City Concentrated Poverty and Neighborhood Distress: 1970 to 1990," *Housing Policy Debate* 4, 3: 253–302.

——— (1995) "Industrial Restructuring and the Changing Location of Jobs," in Reynolds Farley, ed., *State of the Union: America in the 1990s, Vol. 1: Economic Trends* (Russell Sage Foundation), 215–67.

Katz, Lawrence (1992/93) "Understanding Recent Changes in the Wage Structure," *NBER Reporter,* winter: 10–15.

Katz, Michael (1975) *Class, Bureaucracy, and Schools* (Praeger).

Katz, Stanley (1988) "The Strange Birth and Unlikely History of Constitutional Equality," *J. of Am. History* 75, 3: 747–62.

Katzman, David, and William Tuttle, Jr., eds. (1982) *Plain Folk: The Life Stories of Undistinguished Americans* (U. of Illinois Press).

Kaufman, Jonathan (1989) "The Color Line," *Boston Globe Magazine,* June 25: 19–20, 35–42, 49–55.

Kelley, Robin (1992) "An Archeology of Resistance," *Am. Q.* 44, 2: 292–98.

Kelman, Steven (1981) "Economists and the Environmental Muddle," *Public Interest* 64: 106–23.

Kemp, Evan Jr. (1990) Statement of Chairman, Equal Employment Opportunity Commission, before the National Research Council Commission on Behavioral and Social Science and Education, Washington, D.C., March 15.

Kennedy, Randall (1991) "'Keep the Nigger Down!' Mississippi in the Age of Segregation," *Reconstruction* 1, 3: 115–23.

Kennickell, Arthur, and Janice Shack-Marquez (1992) "Changes in Family Finances from 1983 to 1989," *Federal Reserve Bulletin*, Jan.: 1–18.

Kerckhoff, Alan (1991) "Creating Inequality in the Schools," in Joan Huber, ed., *Macro-Micro Linkages in Sociology* (Sage), 153–69.

Kerckhoff, Alan, and Richard Campbell (1977) "Race and Social Status Differences in the Explanation of Educational Ambition," *Social Forces* 55, 3: 701–14.

Kessler, Ronald, and Harold Neighbors (1986) "A New Perspective on the Relationships among Race, Social Class, and Psychological Distress," *J. of Health and Social Behavior* 27, 2: 107–15.

Kessner, Thomas (1977) *The Golden Door: Italian and Jewish Immigrant Mobility in New York City, 1880–1915* (Oxford U. Press).

Key, V. O. (1984 [1949]) *Southern Politics in State and Nation*, 2d ed. (U. of Tennessee Press).

Kilbourne, Barbara, et al. (1994) "Effects of Individual, Occupational, and Industrial Characteristics on Earnings: Intersections of Race and Gender," *Social Forces* 72, 4: 1149–76.

Killian, Lewis, and Charles Grigg (1962) "Urbanism, Race, and Anomia," *AJS* 67, 6: 661–65.

Kilson, Martin (1986) "Paradoxes of Blackness," *Dissent*, winter: 70–78.

Kim, Claire (1993) "A Model Minority Compared to Whom? Myths, Hierarchy, and the New Convergence on Race" (Yale U., Dept. of Political Science).

Kinder, Donald, and D. Roderick Kiewiet (1979) "Economic Discontent and Political Behavior," *AJPS* 23, 3: 495–527.

Kinder, Donald, and Lynn Sanders (1987) "Pluralistic Foundations of American Opinion on Race," paper at the annual meeting of the APSA, Chicago.

Kinder, Donald, Gordon Adams, and Paul Gronke (1989) "Economics and Politics in the 1984 American Presidential Election," *AJPS* 33, 2: 491–515.

King, Martin Luther, Jr. (1967) *Where Do We Go From Here: Chaos or Community?* (Beacon Press).

Kirp, David (1992) "Good Schools in Bad Times," *Los Angeles Times Magazine*, Jan. 5: 18–19, 35–37.

Kirp, David, and Ronald Bayer (1993) "Needles and Race," *Atlantic Monthly* 272 (July): 38–42.

Kirschenman, Joleen (1991) "Gender within Race in the Labor Market," paper at the Urban Poverty and Family Life Conference, U. of Chicago.

Kirschenman, Joleen, and Kathryn Neckerman (1991) "'We'd Love to Hire Them, But . . .': The Meaning of Race for Employers," in Christopher Jencks and Paul Peterson, eds., *The Urban Underclass* (Brookings Institution), 203–32.

Kjellstrand, Carl (1988) "Age, Sex, and Race Inequality in Renal Transplantation," *Archives of Internal Medicine* 148: 1305–9.

Kleck, Gary (1993) "The Incidence of Gun Violence among Young People," *Public Perspective* 4, 6: 3–6.

Kleppner, Paul (1982) *Who Voted? The Dynamics of Electoral Turnout, 1870–1940* (Praeger).

Klose, Kevin (1984) "A Tormented Black Rising Star, Dead by Her Own Hand," *Washington Post*, Aug. 5: C1, C2 .

Kluegel, James, and Eliot Smith (1983) "Affirmative Action Attitudes," *Social Forces* 61, 3: 797–824.

——— (1986) *Beliefs about Inequality* (Aldine de Gruyter).

Knight, Athelia (1987) "Environment Fosters Mediocrity; Doing Well Is Not 'Cool' at Inner-City School," *Washington Post*, Sept. 13: A1, A22.

Knight, Kathleen (1992) "In Their Own Words: Contributions of Natural Language Responses to Understanding Racial Prejudice," paper at the annual meeting of the APSA, Chicago.

Knobel, Dale (1986) *Paddy and the Republic: Ethnicity and Nationality in Antebellum America* (Wesleyan U. Press).

Knoke, David, and Richard Felson (1974) "Ethnic Stratification and Political Cleavage in the United States, 1952–68," *AJS* 80, 3: 630–42.

Koelewijn-Strattner, Gijsberta (1990) "Race, Gender, and the Scientific Professions" (U. of Maryland, Dept. of Sociology, M.A. thesis).

Kohn, Hans (1957) *American Nationalism* (Macmillan).

Kohn, Howard (1994) "Service with a Sneer," *NYT Magazine*, Nov. 6: 42–47, 58, 78–81.

Kolata, Gina (1989) "In Cities, Poor Families Are Dying of Crack," *NYT*, Aug. 11: A1, A13.

Kotlowitz, Alex (1991) *There Are No Children Here* (Doubleday).

Kozol, Jonathan (1991) *Savage Inequalities: Children in America's Schools* (Crown).

Kramnick, Isaac (1990) *Republicanism and Bourgeois Radicalism* (Cornell U. Press).

Krause, Paul (1992) *The Battle for Homestead, 1880–1892* (U. of Pittsburgh Press).

Kristol, Irving (1966) "The Negro Today Is Like the Immigrant Yesterday," *NYT Magazine*, Sept. 11: 50–51, 124–42.

Kunjufu, Jawanza (1986) *Motivating and Preparing Black Youth to Work* (African American Images).

Kurtz, Howard (1992) "Young Media Trio Behind Bush Ads," *Washington Post*, Feb. 9: A16.

Kuttner, Bob (1983) "The Declining Middle," *Atlantic Monthly* 252, July: 60–72.

LH Research (1993) "A Survey of Experiences, Perceptions, and Apprehensions about Guns among Young People in America," for Harvard School of Public Health (N. Y.: LH Research).

Labaton, Stephen (1994a) "Denny's Restaurants to Pay $54 Million in Race Bias Suits," *NYT*, May 25: A1, A18.

——— (1994b) "Denny's Gets a Bill for the Side Orders of Bigotry," *NYT*, May 29: E4.

LaBier, Douglas (1986) *Modern Madness: The Emotional Fallout of Success* (Addison-Wesley).

Ladd, Everett (1993) "Thinking About America," *Public Perspective* 4, 5: 19–34.

——— (1994) *The American Ideology* (Storrs, CT: Roper Center for Public Opinion Research).

Lafer, Gordon (1994) "Measuring the Jobs Gap" (Yale U., Dept. of Political Science).

Lamont, Michéle (1992) *Money, Morals, and Manners* (U. of Chicago Press).

——— (forthcoming) "National Identity and National Boundary Patterns in France and the United States" *French Historical Studies*, fall.

Landry, Bart (1987) *The New Black Middle Class* (U. of California Press).

Lane, Robert (1991) *The Market Experience* (Cambridge U. Press).

Lane, Roger (1979) *Violent Death in the City: Suicide, Accident, and Murder in 19th Century Philadelphia* (Harvard U. Press).

Langton, Kenneth, and M. Kent Jennings (1972) "Political Socialization and the High School Civics Curriculum in the United States," in Charles Bullock III and Harrell Rodgers, Jr., eds., *Black Political Attitudes* (Markham), 60–71.

Lardner, George Jr., and Margot Hornblower (1980) "Miami: Brutality Was Not Expected," *Washington Post*, May 25: A1, A16, A17.

Laseter, Robert (1991) "Black Men: Work and Family Life," paper at the Urban Poverty and Family Life Conference, U. of Chicago.

La Sorte, Michael (1985) *La Merica: Images of Italian Greenhorn Experience* (Temple U. Press).

Lawson, Bill (1992) "Uplifting the Race," in Bill Lawson, ed., *The Underclass Question* (Temple U. Press), 90–113.

Lazere, Edward, and Paul Leonard (1989) "The Crisis in Housing for the Poor" (Washington, D.C.: Center on Budget and Policy Priorities).

Lazere, Edward, et al. (1991) *A Place to Call Home: The Low Income Housing Crisis Continues* (Washington, D.C.: Center on Budget and Policy Priorities and Low Income Housing Information Service) .

Lears, T. J. Jackson (1985) "The Concept of Cultural Hegemony," *Am. Historical R.* 90, 3: 567–93.

Ledebur, Larry, and William Barnes (1992) *City Distress, Metropolitan Disparities, and Economic Growth* (Washington, D.C.: National League of Cities).

Lee, Jessica (1981) "Life at Cabrini Green," in Gannett News Service, *Equality: America's Unfinished Business* (Washington, D.C.: Gannett News Service), 4–5.

Lefton, Mark (1968) "Race, Expectations, and Anomia," *Social Forces* 46, 3: 347–52.

Leggon, Cheryl (1980) "Black Female Professionals," in La Frances Rodgers-Rose, ed., *The Black Woman* (Sage), 189–202.

Lemann, Nicholas (1991) *The Promised Land: The Great Black Migration and How It Changed America* (Knopf).

——— (1993) "Black Nationalism on Campus," *Atlantic Monthly* (Jan.): 31–47.

Leonard, Jonathan (1984) "Antidiscrimination or Reverse Discrimination: The Impact of Changing Demographics, Title VII, and Affirmative Action on Productivity," *J. of Human Resources* 19, 2: 145–74.

Leonard, Paul, and Edward Lazere (1992) *A Place to Call Home: The Low Income Housing Crisis In 44 Major Metropolitan Areas* (Washington, D.C.: Center on Budget and Policy Priorities).

Lerman, Robert (1986) "Do Welfare Programs Affect the Schooling and Work Patterns of Young Black Men?" in Richard Freeman and Harry Holzer, eds., *The Black Youth Employment Crisis* (U. of Chicago Press), 403–38.

Lerner, Melvin (1980) *Belief in a Just World* (Plenum Press).

Lerner, Melvin, and Sally Lerner, eds. (1981) *The Justice Motive in Social Behavior* (Plenum Press).

Lester, Julius (1981–82) "The Black Writer," *New England J. of Black Studies* 2: 82–85.

——— (1991) "Black and White Together," *Lingua Franca*, Feb.: 30–32.

Leung, Kwok, and Fritz Drasgow (1986) "Relation between Self-esteem and Delinquent Behavior in Three Ethnic Groups," *J. of Cross-Cultural Psychology* 17, 2: 151–67.

Levy, Frank (1987) *Dollars and Dreams: The Changing American Income Distribution* (Russell Sage Foundation).

Levy, Frank, and Richard Michel (1991) *The Economic Future of American Families* (Urban Institute Press).

Levy, Frank, and Richard Murnane (1992) "US Earnings Levels and Earnings Inequality," *J. of Economic Literature* 30, 3: 1333–81.

Levy, Sheldon (1972) "Polarization in Racial Attitudes," *Public Opinion Q.* 36, 2: 221–34.

Levy, Sydelle (1983) *Choices and Life Circumstances* (N. Y.: Manpower Demonstration Research Corporation).

Lewin, Tamar (1992) "Study Points to Increase in Tolerance of Ethnicity," *NYT*, Jan. 8: A12.

Lewis, Dan, and Kathryn Nakagawa (1994) *Race and Educational Reform in the American Metropolis* (SUNY Press).

Lewis, I. A., and William Schneider (1983) "Black Voting, Bloc Voting, and the Democrats," *Public Opinion* 6, 5: 12–15, 59.

—— (1985) "Hard Times: The Public on Poverty," *Public Opinion* 8, 3: 2–7, 59–60.

Lichter, Daniel, and David Eggebeen (1993) "Rich Kids, Poor Kids: Changing Income Inequality among American Children," *Social Forces* 71, 3: 761–80.

Lichter, Linda (1985) "Who Speaks for Black America?" *Public Opinion* 8, 4: 41–44, 58.

Lichter, Linda, and S. Robert Lichter (1989) *Howard Beach Youth: A Study of Racial and Ethnic Attitudes* (N. Y.: Am. Jewish Committee).

Lichter, S. Robert, and Linda Lichter (1988) *Television's Impact on Ethnic and Racial Images: A Study of Howard Beach Adolescents* (N. Y.: Am. Jewish Committee).

Lieberson, Stanley (1980) *A Piece of the Pie: Blacks and White Immigrants Since 1880* (U. of California Press).

Lieberson, Stanley, and Mary Waters (1988) *From Many Strands: Ethnic and Racial Groups in Contemporary America* (Russell Sage Foundation).

Lifton, Robert Jay (1973) *Home from the War: Vietnam Veterans, Neither Victims nor Executioners* (Simon and Schuster).

Lincoln, C. Eric, and Lawrence Mamiya (1990) *The Black Church in the African American Experience* (Duke U. Press).

Lipset, Seymour (1977) "Why No Socialism in the United States?" in Seweryn Bialer and Sophia Sluzar, eds., *Radicalism in the Contemporary Age*, v. 1: *Sources of Contemporary Radicalism* (Westview Press), 31–149.

Litwack, Leon (1991) "Hellhound on My Trail: Race Relations in the South from Reconstruction to the Civil Rights Movement," in Harry Knopke, Robert Norrell, and Ronald Rogers, eds., *Opening Doors: Perspectives on Race Relations in Contemporary America* (U. of Alabama Press), 3–25.

Locke, John (1980 [1690]) *Second Treatise of Government*, ed. C. B. MacPherson (Hackett).

Loewen, James (1988) *The Mississippi Chinese: Between Black and White* (Waveland Press).

Lofgren, Charles (1987) *The Plessy Case* (Oxford U. Press).

Logan, John, and Richard Alba (1993) "Locational Returns to Human Capital," *Demography* 30, 2: 243–68.

Longshore, Douglas (1988) "Racial Control and Intergroup Hostility," *Research in Race and Ethnic Relations* (JAI Press): 5: 47–73.

Lorenz, Gerda (1972) "Aspirations of Low-Income Blacks and Whites," *AJS* 78, 2: 371–98.

Los Angeles Times (1983) Poll no. 71: "National Survey," Sept. 18–22.

—— (1985) Poll no. 96: "The Poverty Poll," April 20–26.

—— (1991a) untitled, June 28–30.

—— (1991b) Poll no. 259: "Judge Thomas, Race Relations and Ronald Reagan," Sept. 21–25.

Loury, Glenn (1985) "The Moral Quandary of the Black Community," *Public Interest* 79: 9–22.

—— (1987) "Why Should We Care about Group Inequality?" *Social Philosophy and Policy* 5, 1: 249–71.

—— (1990) "Black Dignity and the Common Good," *First Things*, June–July: 12–19.

—— (1993) "Free at Last? A Personal Perspective on Race and Identity in America," in Gerald Early, ed., *Lure and Loathing: Essays on Race, Identity, and the Ambivalence of Assimilation* (Penguin Press), 1–12.

Lubenow, Gerald (1983) "'He Changed a Lot of Things,'" *Newsweek*, Aug. 29: 16.

Lubiano, Wahneema (1992) "Black Ladies, Welfare Queens, and State Minstrels," in Toni Morrison, ed., *Race-ing Justice, En-gendering Power* (Pantheon), 323–63.

Lucas, Lawrence (1988) "Lessons from Tawana Brawley's Case," *New York Amsterdam News*, Aug. 6: 17.

Lugones, Maria, and Elizabeth Spelman (1983) "Have We Got a Theory for You!: Feminist Theory, Cultural Imperialism, and the Demand for 'The Woman's Voice,'" *Women's Studies International Forum* 6, 6: 573–81.

Lundgren-Gaveras, Lena (1991) "Informal Network Support, Public Welfare Support and the Labor Force Activity of Urban Low-Income Single Mothers," paper at the Urban Poverty and Family Life Conference, U. of Chicago.

Luttrell, Wendy (1993) "'The Teachers, They All Had Their Pets': Concepts of Gender, Knowledge, and Power," *Signs* 18, 3: 505–46.

Lynch, Frederick (1989) *Invisible Victims: White Males and the Crisis of Affirmative Action* (Greenwood Press).

Lynd, Robert, and Helen Lynd (1930) *Middletown* (Harcourt, Brace, and Co.).

Lynn, Laurence (1990) "Opportunities for the Ordinary: Rethinking the Goals of Social Welfare," *Report* (Graduate School of Public Policy Studies, U. of Chicago), 13: 1–3, 8–10.

McAdoo, Harriette (1985) "Racial Attitude and Self-Concept of Young Black Children Over Time," in Harriette McAdoo and John McAdoo, eds., *Black Children* (Sage), 213–42.

——— (1988) "Transgenerational Patterns of Upward Mobility in African-American Families," in Harriette McAdoo, ed., *Black Families*, 2d. ed. (Sage), 148–68.

McCaffrey, Lawrence (1976) *The Irish Diaspora in America* (Indiana U. Press).

McCall, Nathan (1994) *Makes Me Wanna Holler: A Young Black Man in America* (Random House).

McClain, Leanita (1986) *A Foot in Each World*, ed. Clarence Page (Northwestern U. Press).

McClosky, Herbert, and Alida Brill (1983) *Dimensions of Tolerance: What Americans Believe about Civil Liberties* (Russell Sage Foundation).

McClosky, Herbert, and John Zaller (1984) *The American Ethos: Public Attitudes toward Capitalism and Democracy* (Harvard U. Press).

McConahay, John (1983) "Modern Racism and Modern Discrimination," *Personality and Social Psychology Bulletin* 9, 4: 551–58.

McConahay, John, and Betty Hardee (1989) "Race, Racial Attitudes and the Perception of Interpersonal Distance," paper at the annual meeting of the Am. Psychological Society, Alexandria, VA.

McCord, Colin, and Harold Freeman (1990) "Excess Mortality in Harlem," *New England J. of Medicine* 322, 3: 173–77.

McCord, William, et al. (1969) *Life Styles in the Black Ghetto* (Norton).

McDaniel, Paul, and Nicholas Babchuk (1960) "Negro Conceptions of White People in a Northeastern City," *Phylon* 21, 1: 7–19.

McFadden, Robert (1988) "Brawley Case: Public's Conflicting Views," *NYT*, Oct. 29: 1, 32, 33.

McFate, Katherine (1989) *Crime, Drugs and the Urban Poor* (Washington, D.C.: Joint Center for Political and Economic Studies).

McFate, Katherine, and Todd Turner (1994) *Community Programs That Serve Young Black Males* (Washington, D.C.: Joint Center for Political and Economic Studies).

McGee, Jim (1989) "Peace Corps Worker Alleges Rep. Savage Assaulted Her," *Washington Post*, July 19: A1, A8.

McGouldrick, Paul, and Michael Tannen (1977) "Did American Manufacturers Discriminate Against Immigrants Before 1914?" *J. of Economic History* 37, 3: 723–46.

McKay, Nellie (1992) "Remembering Anita Hill and Clarence Thomas," in Toni Morrison, ed., *Race-ing Justice, En-gendering Power* (Pantheon), 269–89.

McLanahan, Sara (1988) "Family Structure and Dependency: Early Transitions to Female Household Headship," *Demography* 25, 1: 1–16.

MacLean, Judy (1990) "Revealed! White Males Linked to S&L Debacle," *Washington Post*, Aug. 5: D4.

MacLeod, Jay (1987) *Ain't No Makin' It: Leveled Aspirations in a Low-Income Neighborhood* (Westview).

McLeod, Ramon (1988a) "Good Jobs Keep Receding Beyond Black Workers' Grasps," *San Francisco Chronicle*, Mar. 29: A1, A4.

––––– (1988b) "Different Views of Gains by Blacks," *San Francisco Chronicle*, Mar. 30: A1, A4.

McMillan, Terry (1987) "Two Mr. Wrongs Can Never Equal One Mr. Right," *NYT*, Oct. 15: C2.

McMillen, Neil (1989) *Dark Journey: Black Mississippians in the Age of Jim Crow* (U. of Illinois Press).

McWilliams, Wilson Carey (1990) "*Pudd'nhead Wilson* on Democratic Governance," in Susan Gillman and Forrest Robinson, eds., *Mark Twain's Pudd'nhead Wilson* (Duke U. Press), 177–89.

Madhubuti, Haki, ed. (1993) *Why L.A. Happened: Implications of the '92 Los Angeles Rebellion* (Third World Press).

Majors, Richard, and Janet Billson (1992) *Cool Pose* (Lexington Books).

Malebranche, David (1989) "No Labels, Please," *Vigil* (student newspaper at Princeton U.) 1, 1: 8.

Malveaux, Julianne (1979) "Black Women on White Campuses," *Essence*, Aug.: 78–79, 102–9, 130.

Malveaux, Julianne, and Phyllis Wallace (1987) "Minority Women in the Workplace," in Karen Koziara, Michael Moskow, and Lucretia Tanner, eds., *Working Women* (Washington, D.C.: Bureau of National Affairs), 265–98.

Mangione, Jerre (1942) *Monte Allegro: A Memoir of Italian American Life* (Harper & Row).

Mann, Arthur (1979) *The One and the Many: Reflections on the American Identity* (U. of Chicago Press).

Mansbridge, Jane (1992) "Feminist Identity" (Northwestern U., Center for Urban Affairs and Policy Research).

Marable, Manning (1982) "Reaganism, Racism, and Reaction," *Black Scholar* 13: 2–15.

––––– (1992) "Black America: Multicultural Democracy in the Age of Clarence Thomas, and David Duke" (Westfield, NJ: *Open Magazine* pamphlet series).

Marinucci, Carla and Walt Gibbs (1986) "Drug King Felix Mitchell: Good or Not, He Died Young," *San Francisco Examiner*, Aug. 31: A1, A10.

Marks, Nadine (1993) "Caregiving Across the Lifespan" (U. of Wisconsin, Center for Demography and Ecology).

Marriott, Michel (1992) "A Tough Job Made Harder as City Burns," *NYT*, May 2: 7.

Marsden, Peter, and Joseph Swingle (1994) "Conceptualizing and Measuring Culture in Surveys," *Poetics* 22: 269–89.

Marsh, Dave (1987) *Glory Days: Bruce Springsteen in the 1980s* (Pantheon).

Marshall, Nancy, and Rosalind Barnett (1991) "Race, Class and Multiple Role Strains among Women Employed in the Service Sector," *Women and Health* 17, 4: 1–19.

Martin, Ben (1991) "From Negro to Black to African American," *Political Science Q.* 106, 1: 83–107.

Martin, Hosea (1991) "A Few Kind Words for Affirmative Action," *Wall Street J.*, April 25: A15.

Martineau, William (1976) "Social Participation and a Sense of Powerlessness among Blacks," *Sociological Q.* 17, 1: 27–41.

Martz, Larry, Mark Starr, and Todd Barrett (1990) "A Murderous Hoax," *Newsweek*, Jan. 22: 16–21.

Marx, Gary (1964) "Negro Political Attitudes" (also titled "Anti-Semitism—Negro Oversample") (U. of California, Berkeley, Survey Research Center).

———— (1969) *Protest and Prejudice: A Study of Belief in the Black Community* (Harper Torchbooks).

———— (1990) "Reflections on Academic Success and Failure," in Bennett Berger, ed., *Authors of Their Own Lives* (U. of California Press), 260–84.

Massey, Douglas, and Nancy Denton (1987) "Trends in the Residential Segregation of Blacks, Hispanics, and Asians: 1970–1980," *ASR* 52, 6: 802–25.

———— (1988) "Suburbanization and Segregation in U.S. Metropolitan Areas," *AJS* 94, 3: 592–626.

———— (1993) *American Apartheid: Segregation and the Making of the Underclass* (Harvard U. Press).

Massey, Douglas, and Mitchell Eggers (1990) "The Ecology of Inequality: Minorities and the Concentration of Poverty, 1970–1980," *AJS* 95, 5: 1153–88 .

Massey, Grace, Mona Scott, and Sanford Dornbusch (1975) "Racism without Racists," *Black Scholar* 7, 3: 10–19.

Masters, Stanley, and Rebecca Maynard (1981) *The Impact of Supported Work on Long-term Recipients of AFDC Benefits* (N. Y.: Manpower Demonstration Research Corporation).

Mather, Cotton (1970 [1702]) *Magnalia Christi Americana*, ed. and abr. Raymond Cunningham (Frederick Ungar).

Matsueda, Ross, et al. (1992) "The Prestige of Criminal and Conventional Occupations," *ASR* 57, 6: 752–70.

Matthews, Donald, and James Prothro (1961) "The Negro Political Participation Study" (U. of North Carolina), March–June.

Matthews, Fred (1970) "White Community and 'Yellow Peril,' " in Leonard Dinnerstein and Frederic Jaher, eds., *The Aliens: A History of Ethnic Minorities in America* (Appleton-Century-Crofts), 268–84.

Mayberry, Katherine (1994) "White Feminists Who Study Black Writers," *Chronicle of Higher Education*, Oct. 12: A48.

Maynard, Rebecca (1980) *The Impact of Supported Work on Young School Dropouts* (N. Y.: Manpower Demonstration Research Corporation).

Mbiti, John (1969) *African Religions and Philosophy* (Praeger).

Mboya, Mzobanzi (1986) "Black Adolescents: A Descriptive Study of Their Self-Concepts and Academic Achievement," *Adolescence* 21, 83: 689–96.

Mead, Lawrence (1992) *The New Politics of Poverty* (Basic Books).

Media General/Associated Press (1988) "National Poll #21," June 22–July 3.

Medrich, Elliott, et al. (1982) *The Serious Business of Growing Up* (U. of California Press).

Meeker, Edward, and James Kau (1977) "Racial Discrimination and Occupational Attainment at the Turn of the Century," *Explorations in Economic History* 14, 3: 250–76.

Meier, August (1992) *A White Scholar and the Black Community, 1945–1965* (U. of Massachusetts Press).

Meier, Kenneth, Joseph Stewart, Jr., and Robert England (1989) *Race, Class, and*

Education: The Politics of Second-Generation Discrimination (U. of Wisconsin Press).

Meisenheimer, Joseph, III (1990) "Black College Graduates in the Labor Market, 1979 and 1989," *Monthly Labor R.* 113, 11: 13–21.

Menchik, Paul (1993) "Economic Status as a Determinant of Mortality among Black and White Older Men" *Population Studies* 47, 3: 427–36.

Mendelberg, Tali (1992) "The Politics of Racial Resentment," paper at the annual meeting of the MWPSA, Chicago.

Merelman, Richard (1991) *Partial Visions: Culture and Politics in Britain, Canada, and the United States* (U. of Wisconsin Press).

——— (1994) "Racial Conflict and Cultural Politics in the United States," *J. of Politics* 56, 1: 1–20.

Merritt, Deborah, and Barbara Reskin (1992) "The Double Minority: Empirical Evidence of a Double Standard in Law School Hiring of Minority Women," *Southern California Law R.* 65, 5: 2299–2360.

Merton, Robert (1938) "Social Structure and Anomie," *ASR* 3, 5: 672–82.

——— (1949) "Discrimination and the American Creed," in R. M. MacIver, ed., *Discrimination and National Welfare* (Harper & Brothers), 99–126.

——— (1972) "Insiders and Outsiders," *AJS* 78, 1: 9–47.

Metropolitan Chicago Information Center (MCIC) (1991–94) "Metro Surveys," Oct. of each year.

Mickelson, Roslyn (1990) "The Attitude-Achievement Paradox among Black Adolescents," *Sociology of Education* 63, 1: 44–61.

Mickelson, Roslyn, and Carol Ray (1994) "Fear of Falling from Grace: The Middle Class, Downward Mobility, and School Desegregation," *Research in Sociology of Education and Socialization* 10: 207–38.

Middleton, Russell (1963) "Alienation, Race, and Education" *ASR* 28, 6: 973–77.

Miller, Abraham, Louis Bolce, and Mark Halligan (1977) "The J-Curve Theory and the Black Urban Riots," *APSR* 71, 3: 964–82.

Miller, Arthur, et al. (1981) "Group Consciousness and Political Participation," *AJPS* 25, 3: 494–511.

Miller, Dale, and William Turnbull (1986) "Expectancies and Interpersonal Processes," *Annual R. of Psychology* 37: 233–56.

Miller, David (1992) "Distributive Justice: What the People Think," *Ethics* 102, 3: 555–93.

Miller, Eleanor (1986) *Street Woman* (Temple U. Press).

Miller, Norman (1981) "Changing Views about the Effects of School Desegregation," in Marilyn Brewer and Barry Collins, eds., *Scientific Inquiry and the Social Sciences* (Jossey-Bass).

Miller, Perry, and Thomas Johnson, eds. (1963) *The Puritans*, vol. 1 (Harper Torchbooks).

Miller, Randi (1990) "Beyond Contact Theory: The Impact of Community Affluence on Integration Efforts in Five Suburban High Schools," *Youth and Society* 22, 1: 12–34.

Milloy, Courtland (1983) "Voices of Experience Changed This Skeptic," *Washington Post*, Aug. 28: 1, 19.

——— (1990) "Bearing the Burden of Being the Black Mayor of the White Man's Plantation," *Washington Post*, Jan. 21: A16.

Mills, Carol, and Harvey Noyes (1984) "Patterns and Correlates of Initial and Subsequent Drug Use among Adolescents," *J. of Consulting and Clinical Psychology* 52, 2: 231–43.

Mills, Charles (1994) "Under Class Under Standings," *Ethics* 104, 4: 855–81.

Mincy, Ronald (1994) "The Underclass: Concept, Controversy, and Evidence," in

Sheldon Danziger, Gary Sandefur, and Daniel Weinberg, eds., *Confronting Poverty* (Harvard U. Press), 109–46.

Mincy, Ronald, ed. (1994) *Nurturing Young Black Males* (Urban Institute Press).

Minerbrook, Scott (1990) "Gender-Line Anxieties," *Emerge*, Jan.: 32–36.

Mirowsky, John, II, and Catherine Ross (1980) "Minority Status, Ethnic Culture, and Distress," *AJS* 86, 3: 479–95.

Mische, Ann (1993) "From 'Cultural Toolbox' to Cultural Projections: Strategies of Hope among Urban Youth in Transition," paper at the annual meeting of the ASA, Miami Beach.

Mishel, Lawrence, and Jared Bernstein (1992) "Declining Wages for High School *and* College Graduates" (Washington, D.C.: Economic Policy Institute).

Mitchell, Bert, and Virginia Flintall (1990) "The Status of the Black CPA: Twenty Year Update," *J. of Accountancy*, Aug.: 59–69.

Mitchell, Jacquelyn (1982) "Reflections of a Black Social Scientist," *Harvard Educational R.* 52, 1: 27–44.

—— (1983) "Visible, Vulnerable, and Viable: Emerging Perspectives of a Minority Professor," in James Cones III, John Noonan, and Denise Janha, eds., *Teaching Minority Students* (Jossey-Bass), 17–28.

Mocan, H. Naci, and Kudret Topyan (1993) "Illicit Drug Use and Health" (NBER).

Model, Suzanne (1993) "The Ethnic Niche and the Structure of Opportunity," in Michael Katz, ed., *The "Underclass" Debate* (Princeton U. Press), 161–93.

Monkkonen, Eric (1989) "Diverging Homicide Rates: England and the United States, 1850–1875," in Ted Gurr, ed., *Violence in America* (Sage), 1: 80–101.

Monroe, Kristen (1983) *Presidential Popularity and the Economy* (Praeger).

Monroe, Sylvester, and Peter Goldman (1988) *Brothers: Black and Poor* (William Morrow).

Moore, Deborah (1981) *At Home in America: Second Generation New York Jews* (Columbia U. Press).

Morawska, Eva (1982) "The Internal Status Hierarchy in the East European Immigrant Communities of Johnstown, PA 1890–1930's," *J. of Social History* 16, 1: 75–107.

Morgan, Dan (1993) "Pablo & Pretty Boy," *Washington Post*, Dec. 12: C1, C2.

Morgan, Edmund (1975) *American Slavery, American Freedom* (Norton).

Morganthau, Tom (1992) "It's Not Just New York . . .," *Newsweek*, Mar. 9: 25–29.

Morin, Richard (1990) "57 Percent of Poll Respondents Say the Mayor Should Resign," *Washington Post*, Jan. 21: A17.

—— (1991) "America's Middle-Class Meltdown," *Washington Post*, Dec. 1: C1, C2.

—— (1994) "From Colored to African American," *Washington Post*, Jan. 23: C5.

Morone, James (1990) *The Democratic Wish* (Basic Books).

Morris, Martina, et al. (1994) "Economic Inequality," *ASR* 59, 2: 205–19.

Morrison, Toni (1992) *Playing in the Dark* (Harvard U. Press).

Moses, Yolanda (1989) *Black Women in Academe* (Washington, D.C.: Assoc. of American Colleges).

Mosley, Myrtis (1980) "Black Women Administrators in Higher Education," *J. of Black Studies* 10, 3: 295–310.

Moss, Philip, and Chris Tilly (1991) "Raised Hurdles for Black Men," paper at the annual meeting of the Assoc. for Public Policy Analysis and Management, Bethesda, MD.

Murnane, Richard, John Willett, and Frank Levy (1991) "Skills, Skill Payments, and the Mismatch Hypothesis" (NBER).

Murphy, Kevin, and Finis Welch (1989) "Wage Premiums for College Graduates," *Educational Researcher*, May: 17–26.

Murphy, Raymond, and James Watson (1970) "The Structure of Discontent," in Nathan Cohen, ed., *The Los Angeles Riots* (Praeger): 140–257.

Murray, Charles (1986) "No, Welfare Isn't Really the Problem," *Public Interest* 84: 3–11.

"My God, This Is It. . . ." (1992) *Los Angeles Times*, May 11: 11–13.

"My Town, The Nation" (1992) *Public Perspective* 3, 5: 94–96.

Myers, Samuel, Jr. (1989) "How Voluntary Is Black Unemployment and Black Labor Force Withdrawal?" in Steven Shulman and William Darity Jr., eds., *The Question of Discrimination* (Wesleyan U. Press), 81–108.

——— (1992) "Crime, Entrepreneurship, and Labor Force Withdrawal," *Contemporary Policy Issues* 10, 2: 84–97.

Myrdal, Gunnar (1944) *An American Dilemma* (Harper & Brothers).

NBC News (1989a) "R.A.C.E.— Racial Attitudes and Consciousness Exam" (N. Y.: NBC News).

——— (1989b) "Social Issues Poll," Aug. 3–13.

Nackenoff, Carol (1994) *The Fictional Republic: Horatio Alger and American Political Discourse* (Oxford U. Press).

Nacoste, Rupert (1985) "Selection Procedure and Responses to Affirmative Action," *Law and Human Behavior* 9, 3: 225–42.

——— (1989) "Affirmative Action and Self-Evaluation," in Fletcher Blanchard and Faye Crosby, eds., *Affirmative Action in Perspective* (Springer-Verlag), 103–9.

——— (1994) "If Empowerment Is the Goal. . .: Affirmative Action and Social Interaction," *Basic and Applied Social Psychology* 15, 1–2: 87–112.

Naff, Katherine (1994) "Perceptions of Discrimination: Moving Beyond the Numbers of Representative Bureaucracy," paper at the annual meeting of the MWPSA, Chicago.

Naison, Mark (1992) "Outlaw Culture and Black Neighborhoods," *Reconstruction* 1, 4: 128–31.

Nasaw, David (1979) *Schooled to Order: A Social History of Public Schooling in the United States* (Oxford U. Press).

Nash, Gary (1982) *Red, White, and Black: The Peoples of Early America* (Prentice-Hall).

Nasir, Jamillah (1991) "The Search for the Corporate Brother," *Urban Profile* 3, 4: 24–26.

Nathan, Richard, and Paul Dommel (1987) "Needed—A Federal Safety Net for Communities," statement to U.S. Senate Committee on Governmental Affairs, Subcommittee on Intergovernmental Relations, June 25.

Nathan, Richard, and Charles Adams, Jr. (1989) "Four Perspectives on Urban Hardship," *Political Science Q.* 104, 3: 483–508.

National Black Child Development Institute (1989) *Who Will Care When Parents Can't?* (Washington, D.C.: National Black Child Development Institute).

National Center for Children in Poverty (1990) *Five Million Children: A Statistical Profile of Our Poorest Young Citizens* (Columbia U., School of Public Health).

National Center on Child Abuse Prevention Research (1994) *Current Trends in Child Abuse Reporting and Facilities* (Chicago: National Committee for Prevention of Child Abuse).

National Conference (1994) *Taking America's Pulse: The Full Report of the National Conference Survey on Inter-Group Relations*, by LH Research (N. Y.: National Conference of Christians and Jews).

National Opinion Research Center (1944) "Attitudes toward Negroes," May.
———— (1950) "Attitudes toward Jews and Communism," Nov.
———— (1963) "Survey Research Service Amalgam Survey," April–July.
———— (1968) "SRS Amalgam Survey," April.
National Survey of Black Americans, 1879–1980 (NSBA) (1980) James Jackson and Gerald Gurin, principal investigators (U. of Michigan, Institute for Social Research).
Natriello, Gary, and Sanford Dornbusch (1984) *Teacher Evaluative Standards and Student Effort* (Longman).
Naughton, Jim (1992) "Bull Market," *Washington Post Magazine*, Feb. 9: 10–15, 24–29.
Neather, Andrew (forthcoming) "Labor Republicanism, Race, and Popular Patriotism in the Era of Empire, 1890–1914," in John Bodnar, ed., *Bonds of Affection: Americans Define Their Patriotism* (Princeton U. Press).
Neckerman, Kathryn (1991) "What Getting Ahead Means to Employers and Disadvantaged Workers," paper at the Urban Poverty and Family Life Conference, U. of Chicago.
Neckerman, Kathryn, and Joleen Kirschenman (1991) "Hiring Strategies, Racial Bias, and Inner-City Workers," *Social Problems* 38, 4: 433–47.
Neidert, Lisa, and Reynolds Farley (1985) "Assimilation in the United States," *ASR* 50, 6: 840–50.
Neighbors, Harold (1986) "Socioeconomic Status and Psychologic Distress in Adult Blacks," *Am. J. of Epidemiology* 124, 5: 779–93.
Nelsen, Hart, Thomas Maldron, and Raytha Yokley (1975) "Black Religion's Promethean Motif: Orthodoxy and Militancy," *AJS* 81, 1: 139–46.
New Jersey Hospital Association (1993) *Boarder Babies and Children* (Princeton: New Jersey Hospital Assoc.).
New York City Board of Education (1994) "Reported Incidents—Comparison Report" (New York City Board of Education, Division of School Safety).
New York State Judicial Commission on Minorities (1992) *Report*, vol. 1: *Executive Summary*, in *Fordham Urban Law J.* 19, 2: 181–311.
New York State United Teachers (1991) *1991 Education Opinion Survey* (Delmar, NY: New York State United Teachers).
NYT (1987) "New York City Race Relations Survey," March 8–11.
———— (1991) "Metropolitan Area Poll," Nov. 2–12.
———— (1994), untitled, Feb. 15–17.
NYT/CBS News (1989) "Drug Survey," Sept. 6–8.
———— (1991a) "April Survey," April 1–3.
———— (1991b) "Clarence Thomas Panel," Sept. 3–Oct. 14.
———— (1992) untitled, May 6–8.
———— (1993a) untitled, Feb. 9–11.
———— (1993b) untitled, March 28–31.
———— (1994a) untitled, Sept. 8–11.
———— (1994b) untitled, Oct. 29–Nov. 1.
NYT/WCBS News (1985) "New York City Race Relations Survey," April 27–May 3.
———— (1988) "New York Survey," June 21–25.
NYT/WCBS-TV Channel 2 News (1993) New York City Poll, Oct. 20–24.
———— (1994) "New York City Poll," June 12–15.
NYT/WCBS TV News (1989) "New York City Survey," June 11–17.
———— (1990) "Race Relations—New York City," June 17–20.
Newman, Katherine (1988) *Falling From Grace: The Experience of Downward Mobility in the American Middle Class* (Free Press).

—— (1993) *Declining Fortunes: The Withering of the American Dream* (Basic Books).

Nie, Norman, et al. (1988) "Participation in America: Continuity and Change," paper at the annual meeting of the MWPSA, Chicago.

Nieli, Russell, ed. (1991) *Racial Preference and Racial Justice* (Washington, D.C.: Ethics and Public Policy Center).

Nixon, Regina (1985a) *Climbing the Corporate Ladder: Some Perceptions among Black Managers* (Washington, D.C.: National Urban League).

—— (1985b) *Black Managers in Corporate America: Alienation or Integration?* (Washington, D.C.: National Urban League).

—— (1985c) *Perceptions of Job Power among Black Managers in Corporate America* (Washington, D.C.: National Urban League).

Njeri, Itabari (1993) "Sushi and Grits: Ethnic Identity and Conflict in a Newly Multicultural America," in Gerald Early, ed., *Lure and Loathing: Essays on Race, Identity, and the Ambivalence of Assimilation* (Penguin Press), 13–40.

Nkomo, Stella, and Taylor Cox, Jr. (1990) "Factors Affecting the Upward Mobility of Black Managers in Private Sector Organizations," *R. of Black Political Economy* 18, 3: 39–57.

Noel, Donald (1964) "Group Identification among Negroes," *J. of Social Issues* 20, 2: 71–84.

Noel, Donald, and Alphonso Pinkney (1964) "Correlates of Prejudice," *AJS* 49, 6: 609–22.

Norris, Michele (1989) "6-Year Old's Md. Home Was a Modern-Day Opium Den," *Washington Post*, July 30: 1, 22, 23.

Norton, Anne (1986) *Alternative Americas: A Reading of Antebellum Political Culture* (U. of Chicago Press).

Novack, David (1987) "Forced Busing in South Boston: Class, Race, and Power," *J. of Urban Affairs* 9, 3: 277–92.

Office of Criminal Justice Plans and Analysis (1992) "Homicide Report" (Washington, D.C.: Office of Criminal Justice Plans and Analysis).

Ogbu, John (1974) *The Next Generation* (Academic Press).

—— (1978) *Minority Education and Caste* (Academic Press).

—— (1983) "Minority Status and Schooling in Plural Societies," *Comparative Education R.* 27, 2: 168–90.

—— (1988) "Diversity and Equity in Public Education," in Ron Haskins and Duncan MacRae, eds., *Policies for America's Public Schools* (Ablex), 127–70.

O'Hare, William (1983) *Wealth and Economic Status: A Perspective on Racial Inequality* (Washington, D.C.: Joint Center for Political Studies).

O'Hare, William, and Brenda Curry-White (1992) *The Rural Underclass* (Washington, D.C.: Population Reference Bureau).

Oliver, Melvin, and Mark Glick (1982) "An Analysis of the New Orthodoxy on Black Mobility," *Social Problems* 29, 5: 511–23.

Oliver, Melvin, and Thomas Shapiro (1989) "Race and Wealth," *R. of Black Political Economy* 17, 4: 5–25.

Oliver, William (1989) "Black Males and Social Problems: Prevention Through Afrocentric Socialization," *J. of Black Studies* 20, 1: 15–39.

Olsen, Marvin (1970) "Social and Political Participation of Blacks," *ASR* 35, 4: 682–97.

Olson, James, C. Peter Herman, and Mark Zanna, eds. (1986) *Relative Deprivation and Social Comparison* (Erlbaum).

Olzak, Susan (1992) *The Dynamics of Ethnic Competition and Conflict* (Stanford U. Press).

Olzak, Susan, and Suzanne Shanahan (1994) "Deprivation and Race Riots" (Stanford U., Dept. of Sociology).

Olzak, Susan, Suzanne Shanahan, and Elizabeth West (1994) "School Desegregation, Interracial Exposure, and Antibusing Activity in Contemporary Urban America," *AJS* 100, 1: 196–241.

Olzak, Susan, et al. (1994) "Poverty, Segregation, and Race Riots, 1960–1993" (Stanford U., Dept. of Sociology).

Omi, Michael, and Howard Winant (1986) *Racial Formation in the United States* (Routledge).

O'Neill, June (1990) "The Role of Human Capital in Earnings Differences Between Black and White Men," *J. of Economic Perspectives* 4, 4: 25–45.

"Opinion Roundup: Poverty in America" (1985) *Public Opinion* 8, 3: 21–40.

Orfield, Gary (1993) "The Growth of Segregation in American Schools" (Harvard U., Graduate School of Education).

Orlean, Susan (1993) "Shoot the Moon," *New Yorker*, March 22: 74–85.

Orren, Karen (1991) *Belated Feudalism: Labor, the Law, and Liberal Development in the United States* (Cambridge U. Press).

Orsi, Robert (1992) "The Religious Boundaries of an Inbetween People: Street *Feste* and the Problem of the Dark-Skinned Other in Italian Harlem, 1920–1990," *Am. Q.* 44, 3: 313–47.

Osofsky, Joy (1993) "Violence in the Lives of Young Children" (Louisiana State U. Medical Center, Depts. of Pediatrics and Psychiatry).

Osofsky, Joy, et al. (1993) "Chronic Community Violence," *Psychiatry* 56, 1: 36–45.

Osterman, Paul (1980) *Getting Started: The Youth Labor Market* (MIT Press).

Pacyga, Dominic (1991) *Polish Immigrants and Industrial Chicago* (Ohio State U. Press).

Page, Clarence (1986) "Introduction," in Leanita McClain, *A Foot in Each World* ed. Clarence Page (Northwestern U. Press).

Pagnini, Deanna, and S. Philip Morgan (1990) "Intermarriage and Social Distance among US Immigrants at the Turn of the Century," *AJS* 96, 2: 405–32.

Paige, Jeffery (1971) "Political Orientation and Riot Participation," *ASR* 36, 5: 810–20.

Pappas, Gregory, et al. (1993) "The Increasing Disparity in Mortality Between Socioeconomic Groups in the United States, 1960 and 1986," *New England J. of Medicine* 329, 2: 103–9.

Parent, T. Wayne (1984) "Individual Explanations for Structural Problems: Blacks and Economic Redistribution Policy," paper at the annual meeting of the MWPSA, Chicago.

——— (1985) "A Liberal Legacy: Blacks Blaming Themselves for Economic Failures," *J. of Black Studies* 16, 1: 3–20.

Parent, T. Wayne, and Paul Stekler (1985) "The Political Implications of Economic Stratification in the Black Community," *Western Political Q.* 38, 4: 521–38.

Parker, Seymour, and Robert Kleiner (1966) *Mental Illness in the Urban Negro Community* (Free Press).

Patterson, Orlando (1973) "The Moral Crisis of the Black American," *Public Interest* 23: 43–69.

——— (1989) "Toward a Study of Black America," *Dissent*, fall: 476–86.

Patterson, Orlando, and Rhonda Datcher (1992) Exchange, *Reconstruction* 1, 4: 64–77.

Paul, Rodman (1970) "The Origin of the Chinese Issue in California," in Leonard

Dinnerstein and Frederic Jaher, eds., *The Aliens: A History of Ethnic Minorities in America* (Appleton-Century-Crofts), 161–72.

Pear, Robert (1983) "U.S. Finds Black Economic Improvement Halted," *NYT*, Aug. 22: A22.

———— (1984) "Leading Black Republicans Assail Reagan Rights Aide," *NYT*, July 9: A10.

Pearson, Hugh (1994) *The Shadow of the Panther: Huey Newton and the Price of Black Power in America* (Addison-Wesley).

Pedder, Sophie (1991) "Social Isolation and the Labour Market: Black Americans in Chicago," paper at the Urban Poverty and Family Life Conference, U. of Chicago.

Pedraza, Silvia (1991) "Women and Migration," *Annual R. of Sociology* 17: 303–325.

People for the American Way (1989) *Democracy's Next Generation: American Youth Attitudes on Citizenship, Government and Politics* (Washington, D.C.: People for the American Way).

———— (1992) *Democracy's Next Generation II: A Study of American Youth on Race* (Washington, D.C.: People for the American Way).

Perlmann, Joel (1988) *Ethnic Differences: Schooling and Social Structure among the Irish, Italians, Jews, and Blacks in an American City, 1880–1935* (Cambridge U. Press).

Petersen, William (1987) "Politics and the Measurement of Ethnicity," in William Alonso and Paul Starr, eds., *The Politics of Numbers* (Russell Sage Foundation), 187–233.

Peterson, Bill (1988) "Flap Over Ex-Aide's Remarks Is New Blow to Chicago Mayor," *Washington Post*, May 10: A1.

Peterson, Jonathan (1992) "Times Get Harder for the Poor," *Los Angeles Times*, Mar. 16: A1, A14.

Petroni, Frank (1970) "'Uncle Toms': White Stereotypes in the Black Movement," *Human Organization* 29, 4: 260–68.

Pettigrew, Thomas (1964) *A Profile of the Negro American* (Van Nostrand).

Pettigrew, Thomas, and Joanne Martin (1987) "Shaping the Organizational Context for Black American Inclusion," *J. of Social Issues* 43, 1: 41–78.

Phillips, Kevin (1970) *The Emerging Republican Majority* (Anchor Books).

Pierce, Yolanda (1992) "Bring Rodney King Lessons Home to Princeton," *Daily Princetonian*, May 8: 9.

Piliavin, Irving, and Rosemary Gartner (1981) *The Impact of Supported Work on Ex-Offenders* (N. Y.: Manpower Demonstration Research Corporation).

Pinderhughes, Diane (1987) *Race and Ethnicity in Chicago Politics* (U. of Illinois Press).

Plotnick, Robert (1992) "The Effects of Attitudes on Teenage Premarital Pregnancy and Its Resolution," *ASR* 57, 6: 800–811.

Pocock, John (1975) *The Machiavellian Moment* (Princeton U. Press).

Poindexter, Paula, and Carolyn Stroman (1981) "Blacks and Television," *J. of Broadcasting* 25, 2: 103–22.

Polling Report (1994) 10, 18, Sept. 12.

Pooley, Eric (1991) "Kids with Guns," *New York* 24, 3 (Aug. 5): 20–29.

Popkin, Susan (1990) "Welfare: Views from the Bottom," *Social Problems* 37, 1: 601–16.

Popkin, Susan, James Rosenbaum, and Patricia Meaden (1993) "Labor Market Experiences of Low-Income Black Women in Middle-Class Suburbs," *J. of Policy Analysis and Management* 12, 3: 556–73.

Porter, James (1974) "Race, Socialization, and Mobility in Educational and Early Occupational Attainment," *ASR* 39, 3: 303–16.

Porter, Judith, and Robert Washington (1979) "Black Identity and Self-Esteem," *Annual R. of Sociology* 5: 53–74.

Portes, Alejandro, and Kenneth Wilson (1976) "Black-White Differences in Educational Attainment," *ASR* 41, 3: 414–31.

Portland Public Schools (1990) *African-American Baseline Essays* (Portland: Multnomah School District 1J).

Portney, Kent, Jeffrey Berry, and Ken Thomsom (1993) "Race, Neighborhoods, and Strong Democracy," paper at the Workshop on Race, Ethnicity, Representation, and Governance, Harvard U.

Potter, David (1954) *People of Plenty: Economic Abundance and the American Character* (U. of Chicago Press).

Powers, Daniel (1994) "Transitions into Idleness among White, Black, and Hispanic Youth," *Sociological Perspectives* 37, 2: 183–201.

Powledge, Fred (1991) "George Bush Is Whistling 'Dixie,'" *The Nation*, Oct. 14: 446–49.

Prager, Jeffrey (1982) "American Racial Identity as Collective Representation," *Ethnic and Racial Studies* 5, 1: 99–119.

"Predicting Behavior: Roles of Race and Class," (1987) *Washington Post*, Nov. 30: A9.

Press, Pat (1984) "Black Women, Alone," *Washington Post*, Mar. 18: C8.

Pressley v. *Etowah County Commission* (1992) 112 S. Ct. 820.

Pryor Brown, Lannie, Jack Powell, and Felton Earls (1989) "Stressful Life Events and Psychiatric Symptoms in Black Adolescent Females," *J. of Adolescent Research* 4, 2: 140–51.

"Public Opinion and Demographic Report," *Public Perspective*:
   (1993a) 4, 4: 82–104
   (1993b) 4, 5: 82–104
   (1993c) 4, 6: 82–104
   (1994a) 5, 2: 82–104
   (1994b) 5, 5: 73–96.

Puzo, Mario (1971) "Choosing a Dream: Italians in Hell's Kitchen," in Thomas Wheeler, ed., *The Immigrant Experience* (Penguin Books), 35–49.

Rabinovitz, Jonathan (1993) "Police Look for the Spark That Led to the Shootings," *NYT*, Dec. 10: B8.

Radzilowski, John (1994) "Re: German-Americans: Don't Call Us White," message to bulletin board h-ethnic@uicvm.uic.edu, July 20.

Rae, Douglas (1988) "Knowing Power," in Ian Shapiro and Grant Reeher, eds., *Power, Inequality, and Democratic Politics* (Westview Press), 17–49.

Rae, Douglas, et al. (1981) *Equalities* (Harvard U. Press).

Ramirez, Manuel, III, and Douglass Price-Williams (1976) "Achievement Motivation in Children of Three Ethnic Groups in the United States," *J. of Cross-Cultural Psychology* 7, 1: 49–60.

Ramist, Leonard, and Solomon Arbeiter (1984) *Profiles, College-Bound Seniors, 1982* (N. Y.: College Entrance Examination Board).

Range, Peter (1974) "Making it in Atlanta: Capital of Black-is-bountiful" *NYT Magazine*, April 7: 28–29, 68–78.

Ransford, H. Edward, and Jon Miller (1983) "Race, Sex and Feminist Outlooks," *ASR* 48, 1: 46–59.

Reagon, Bernice (1991) "'Nobody Knows the Trouble I See,'" *J. of Am. History* 78, 1: 111–19.

Redd, Marva (1989) "Alcoholism and Drug Addiction among Black Adults," in Reginald Jones, ed., *Black Adult Development and Aging* (Cobb & Henry), 351–74.

Reed, Adolph (1986) *The Jesse Jackson Phenomenon* (Yale U. Press).

Reed, Ishmael (1988) ". . . and the Maligning of the Male," *Life Magazine*, spring: 67.

Reed, Ishmael, et al. (1989) "Is Ethnicity Obsolete?" in Werner Sollors, ed., *The Invention of Ethnicity* (Oxford U. Press), 226–35.

Reed, Veronica (1991) "Civil Rights Legislation and the Housing Status of Black Americans," *R. of Black Political Economy* 19, 3–4: 29–42.

Reed, William (1989) "The S.O.B. Group," *Norfolk [VA] J. and Guide*, April 5: 8.

Reese, Laura, and Ronald Brown (1995) "The Effects of Religious Messages on Racial Identity and System Blame among African Americans," *J. of Politics* 57, 1: 24–43.

Reinhold, Robert (1992) "A Show of Attention Brings a Show of Wearied Shrugs," *NYT*, May 8: A1, A18.

Reischauer, Robert (1987) "The Size and Characteristics of the Underclass," paper at the annual meeting of the Assoc. for Public Policy Analysis and Management, Bethesda, MD.

Research and Forecasts (1983) *The Grolier Survey: What Parents Believe about Education* (New York: Research and Forecasts, Inc.).

The Research Bulletin (1991) "Disadvantaged Urban Eighth Graders" (Washington, D.C.: Hispanic Policy Development Project).

———— (1992) "High Expectations" (Washington, D.C.: Hispanic Policy Development Project).

Reuter, Peter, et al. (1988) *Drug Use and Drug Programs in the Washington Metropolitan Area* (Santa Monica: Rand Corporation).

Reuter, Peter, Robert MacCoun, and Patrick Murphy (1990) *Money From Crime: A Study of the Economics of Drug Dealing in Washington, D.C.* (Santa Monica: Rand Corporation).

Rice, Mitchell (1992) "Justifying State and Local Government Set-aside Programs Through Disparity Studies in the Post *Croson* Era," *Public Administration R.* 52, 5: 482–90.

Richters, John, and Pedro Martinez (1993) "The NIMH Community Violence Project: I. Children as Victims of and Witnesses to Violence," *Psychiatry* 56, 1: 7–21.

Ricketts, Erol, and Ronald Mincy (1990) "Growth of the Underclass, 1970–80," *J. of Human Resources* 25, 1: 137–45.

Riley, Norman (1986) "Attitudes of the Black Middle Class," *Crisis* 93, 10: 14–18, 31–32.

Ritter, Martha, and Sandra Danziger (1983) *After Supported Work: Post-Program Interviews with a Sample of AFDC Participants* (N. Y.: Manpower Demonstration Research Corporation).

Rivera, Edward (1982) *Family Installments: Memories of Growing Up Hispanic* (Morrow).

Robinson, Gene (1990) "Television Advertising and Its Impact on Black America," in Janet DeWart, ed., *State of Black America 1990* (N. Y.: National Urban League), 157–71.

Rodgers, Daniel (1978) *The Work Ethic in Industrial America, 1850–1920* (U. of Chicago Press).

Rodgers, John, and Joan Rodgers (1991) "Measuring the Intensity of Poverty among Subpopulations," *J. of Human Resources* 26, 2: 338–61.

Rodman, Hyman, Patricia Voydanoff, and Albert Lovejoy (1974) "The Range of Aspirations," *Social Problems* 22, 2: 184–98.

Rodriguez, Richard (1981) *Hunger of Memory* (Godine).

Roediger, David (1991) *The Wages of Whiteness* (Verso)

—— (1994) *Towards the Abolition of Whiteness* (Verso).

Rohrlich, Ted, and Rich Connell (1992) "Police Pullout, Riot's Outbreak Reconstructed," *Los Angeles Times,* May 5: A1, A19.

Rolark, Stanley, Claudette Bennett, and Roderick Harrison (1994) Tables on Multiracial Responses and on Interracial and Interethnic Couples and Children, presented at Workshop on Race and Ethnicity Classification, National Academy of Sciences, Committee on National Statistics, Feb.

Roper Organization (1986) "The American Dream Survey," for the *Wall Street J.,* Oct.

Rose, Harold, and Paula McClain (1990) *Race, Place, and Risk: Black Homicide in Urban America* (SUNY Press).

Rosen, Bernard (1969) "Race, Ethnicity, and the Achievement Syndrome," in Bernard Rosen, Harry Crockett Jr., and Clyde Nunn, eds., *Achievement in American Society* (Schenckman), 131–53.

Rosenbaum, James, et al. (1993) "Can the Kerner Commission's Housing Strategy Improve Employment, Education, and Social Integration for Low-Income Blacks," *North Carolina Law R.* 71, 5: 1519–56.

Rosenberg, Morris, and Roberta Simmons (1972) *Black and White Self-Esteem* (Washington, D.C.: ASA).

Rosenfeld, Michel (1991) *Affirmative Action and Justice* (Yale U. Press).

Rosenstone, Steven, and John Mark Hansen (1993) *Mobilization, Participation, and Democracy in America* (Macmillan).

Roskolenko, Harry (1971) "America, the Thief: A Jewish Search for Freedom," in Thomas Wheeler, ed., *The Immigrant Experience* (Penguin Books), 151–178.

"Round-table: Doubting Thomas" (1991) *Tikkun* 6, 5: 23–30.

"Round-table: Sexuality after Thomas/Hill" (1993) *Tikkun* 7, 1: 25–30, 96, cover.

Royster, Deirdre (1991) "Public Training—Help or Hindrance? An Exploration of Employers' Perceptions of the Publicly-Trained," paper at the Urban Poverty and Family Life Conference, U. of Chicago.

Rubin, Lillian (1994) *Families on the Fault Line* (HarperCollins).

Rubin, Zick, and Letitia Peplau (1973) "Belief in a Just World and Reactions to Another's Lot," *J. of Social Issues* 29, 4: 73–93.

—— (1975) "Who Believes in a Just World?" *J. of Social Issues,* 31, 3: 65–89.

Rucinski, Dianne (1993) "Rush to Judgment? Fast Reaction Polls in the Anita Hill-Clarence Thomas Controversy," *Public Opinion Q.* 57, 4: 575–92.

Ruggles, Patricia (1989) "Short and Long Term Poverty in the United States" (Washington, D.C.: Urban Institute).

Ruggles, Patricia, and Charles Stone (1992) "Income Distribution over the Business Cycle," *J. of Policy Analysis and Management* 11, 4: 709–15.

Runciman, Walter (1966) *Relative Deprivation and Social Justice* (U. of California).

Russell Reynolds Associates (1990) *Men, Women, and Leadership in the American Corporation* (N. Y.: Russell Reynolds Associates).

Rutten, Tim (1992) "A New Kind of Riot," *New York R. of Books,* June 11: 52–54.

Ryscavage, Paul, and Peter Henle (1990) "Earnings Inequality Accelerates in the 1980's," *Monthly Labor R.* 113, 12: 3–16.

Ryscavage, Paul, Gordon Green, and Edward Welniak (1992) "The Impact of Demographic, Social, and Economic Change on the Distribution of Income," *Studies in the Distribution of Income*, P60–183 (U.S. Bureau of the Census), 11–30.

St. George, Arthur, and Patrick McNamara (1984) "Religion, Race, and Psychological Well-Being," *J. for the Scientific Study of Religion* 23, 4: 351–63.

Sanders, James (1977) *The Education of an Urban Minority: Catholics in Chicago, 1833–1965* (Oxford U. Press).

Sandler, Bernice (1986) *The Campus Climate Revisited: Chilly for Women Faculty, Administrators, and Graduate Students* (Washington, D.C.: Assoc. of American Colleges).

Sandmeyer, Elmer (1939) *The Anti-Chinese Movement in California* (U. of Illinois Press).

Saxton, Alexander (1971) *The Indispensable Enemy: Labor and the Anti-Chinese Movement in California* (U. of California Press).

Schaefer, Richard (1984) *Racial and Ethnic Groups*, 2d ed. (Little, Brown).

Schein, Lawrence (1986) "Current Issues in Human-Resource Management," *Research Bulletin* (publication of The Conference Board), no. 190.

Scheinfeld, Daniel (1983) "Family Relationships and School Achievement among Boys of Lower-Income Urban Black Families," *Am. J. of Orthopsychiatry* 53, 1: 127–43.

Schermerhorn, R. A. (1956–57) "Power as a Primary Concept in the Study of Minorities," *Social Forces* 35, 1–4: 53–56.

Schlesinger, Arthur (1992) *The Disuniting of America* (Norton).

Schlozman, Kay, and Sidney Verba (1979) *Injury to Insult: Unemployment, Class, and Political Response* (Harvard U. Press).

Schmidt, William (1984) "Desegregation Worries a Black College," *NYT*, Oct. 14: E2.

—— (1987) "What's Wrong With City's Seal? Racism, to Some," *NYT*, Sept. 14: A16.

Schofield, Janet (1982) *Black and White in School* (Praeger).

Schooler, Carmi (1976) "Serfdom's Legacy: An Ethnic Continuum," *AJS* 81, 6: 1265–86.

Schumacher, Ernst (1989) *Small is Beautiful* (Harper & Row).

Schuman, Howard, and Shirley Hatchett (1974) *Black Racial Attitudes* (U. of Michigan, Institute for Social Research).

Schuman, Howard, Charlotte Steeh, and Lawrence Bobo (1988) *Racial Attitudes in America* (Harvard U. Press).

Scott, James (1985) *Weapons of the Weak* (Yale U. Press).

—— (1990) *Domination and the Arts of Resistance* (Yale U. Press).

Scott, Kesho (1991) *The Habit of Surviving: Black Women's Strategies for Life* (Rutgers U. Press).

Scully, Gerald (1974) "Discrimination: The Case of Baseball," in Roger Noll, ed., *Government and the Sports Business* (Brookings Institution).

Searles, Ruth, and J. Allen Williams Jr. (1962) "Negro College Students' Participation in Sit-ins," *Social Forces* 40, 3: 215–20.

Sears, David (1988) "Symbolic Racism," in Phyllis Katz and Dalmas Taylor, eds., *Eliminating Racism* (Plenum Press), 53–84.

Sears, David, and John McConahay (1973) *The Politics of Violence* (Houghton Mifflin).

Secret, Philip, James Johnson, and Audrey Forrest (1990) "The Impact of Religiosity on Political Participation and Membership in Voluntary Associations among Black and White Americans," *J. of Black Studies* 21, 1: 87–102.

Seltzer, Richard, and Robert Smith (1985) "Race and Ideology," *Phylon* 46, 2: 98–105.

Sewell, William, and Robert Hauser (1993) "A Review of the Wisconsin Longitudinal Study of Social and Psychological Factors in Aspirations and Achievements 1963–1993" (U. of Wisconsin, Center for Demography and Ecology).

Shakoor, Bambade and Deborah Chalmers (1991) "Co-victimization of African-American Children Who Witness Violence," *J. of the National Medical Assoc.* 83, 3: 233–38.

Shea, Christopher (1993) "A Cloud Over Symbols: Once-Honored College Mascots Like Indians and Minutemen Now Irk Many on Nation's Campuses," *Chronicle of Higher Education*, Nov. 10: A33, A35.

Shenon, Philip (1988) "Black F.B.I. Agent's Ordeal: Meanness That Never Let Up," *NYT*, Jan. 25: A1, A18.

——— (1990) "Black F.B.I. Agent Looks Back on Years of Harassment," *NYT*, Aug. 12: 18.

Shingles, Richard (1981) "Black Consciousness and Political Participation," *APSR* 75, 1: 76–91.

Shklar, Judith (1984) *Ordinary Vices* (Harvard U. Press).

——— (1991) *American Citizenship* (Harvard U. Press).

Short, James, Jr., Ramon Rivera, and Ray Tennyson (1965) "Perceived Opportunities, Gang Membership, and Delinquency," *ASR* 30, 1: 56–67.

Short, James, and Fred Strodtbeck (1965) *Group Process and Gang Delinquency* (U. of Chicago Press).

Shull, Steven (1993) *A Kinder, Gentler Racism? The Reagan-Bush Civil Rights Legacy* (M. E. Sharpe).

Sidanius, James, and Felicia Pratto (1993) "The Inevitability of Oppression and the Dynamics of Social Dominance," in Paul Sniderman, Philip Tetlock, and Edward Carmines, eds., *Prejudice, Politics, and the American Dilemma* (Stanford U. Press), 173–211.

Siegel, Paul (1965) "On the Cost of Being a Negro," *Sociological Inquiry* 35, 1: 41–57.

Sigelman, Lee, and Susan Welch (1991) *Black Americans' Views of Racial Inequality* (Cambridge U. Press).

Sigelman, Lee, et al. (1993) "Making Contact? Black-White Social Interaction in an Urban Setting," paper at the annual meeting of the APSA, Washington, D.C.

Simmons, Carole (1992) "The Facts of Life," *Urban Profile* 4, 1: 23.

Simon, Kate (1982) *Bronx Primitive* (Viking).

——— (1986) *A Wider World* (Harper & Row).

Simon, Rita, and Jean Landis (1989) "Women and Men's Attitudes about a Woman's Place and Role," *Public Opinion Q.* 53, 2: 265–76.

Sinopoli, Richard (1992) *The Foundations of American Citizenship* (Oxford U. Press).

Skolnick, Jerome (1989) "Gang Organization and Migration" (Sacramento: Ca. Dept. of Justice): 1–19.

Skolnick, Jerome, et al. (1990) "The Social Structure of Street Drug Dealing," *Am. J. of Police* 9, 1: 1–41.

Skrzycki, Cindy (1989) "Healing the Wounds of Success," *Washington Post*, July 23: H1, H4.

Smith, A. Wade (1985) "Social Class and Racial Cleavages on Major Social Indicators," *Research in Race and Ethnic Relations* (JAI Press), 4: 33–65.

Smith, C. Calvin (1990) "The Civil Rights Legacy of Ronald Reagan," *Western J. of Black Studies* 14, summer: 102–14.

Smith, Earl (1991a) "A Comparative Study of Occupational Stress from a Sample of

Black and White U.S. College and University Faculty," in *Research in Race and Ethnic Relations* (JAI Press), 145–63.

Smith, Earl (1991b) "African American Chemists in the American Chemical Society," *Workforce* (journal of the ACS), 1–6.

Smith, Earl, and Stephanie Witt (1990) "Black Faculty and Affirmative Action at Predominantly White Institutions," *Western J. of Black Studies* 14, 1: 9–16.

——— (1994) "The Experience of African American Women in the Professoriate: Doubly Disadvantaged or Benefiting from Greater Equality of Opportunity," *R. of Public Personnel Administration*.

Smith, Earl, and Monica Seff (1989) "Race, Position Segregation and Salary Equity in Professional Baseball," *J. of Sport and Social Issues* 13, 2: 92–110.

Smith, James (1975) "White Wealth and Black People," in James Smith, ed., *The Personal Distribution of Income and Wealth* (Columbia U. Press), 329–63.

Smith, James, and Finis Welch (1989) "Black Economic Progress after Myrdal," *J. of Economic Literature* 27, part 1, 2: 519–64.

Smith, Judith (1992) "Creating 'Everyman' After WWII," paper at the Am. Studies Assoc., Cosa Mesa, CA.

Smith, Robert (1988) "Sources of Urban Ethnic Politics," *Research in Race and Ethnic Relations* (JAI Press), 5: 159–91.

Smith, Robert, and Richard Seltzer (1992) *Race, Class, and Culture: A Study in Afro-American Mass Opinion* (SUNY Press).

Smith, Rogers (1988) "The 'American Creed' and American Identity," *Western Political Q.* 41, 2: 225–51.

——— (1993) "Beyond Tocqueville, Myrdal, and Hartz," *APSR* 87, 3: 549–66.

Smith, Shelley (1991) "Sources of Earnings Inequality in the Black and White Female Labor Forces," *Sociological Q.* 32, 1: 117–38.

Smith, Timothy (1966) "New Approaches to the History of Immigration in Twentieth-Century America," *Am. Historical R.* 71, 4: 1265–79.

Smith, Tom (1987a) "The Welfare State in Cross-national Perspective," *Public Opinion Q.* 51, 3: 404–21.

——— (1987b) "Public Opinion and the Welfare State: A Crossnational Perspective," paper at the annual meeting of the ASA, Chicago.

——— (1988) "Social Inequality in Cross-National Perspective" (U. of Chicago, National Opinion Research Center).

——— (1990) "Ethnic Images" (U. of Chicago, National Opinion Research Center).

Smith, Tom, and Glenn Dempsey (1983) "Ethnic Social Distance and Prejudice," *Public Opinion Q.* 47, 4: 584–600.

Smith, Warren (1961) *White Servitude in Colonial South Carolina* (U. of South Carolina Press).

Smolensky, Eugene, and Robert Plotnick (1993) "Inequality and Poverty in the United States: 1900 to 1990" (U. of Wisconsin, IRP).

Sniderman, Paul (1985) *Race and Inequality* (Chatham House).

Sniderman, Paul, Philip Tetlock, and Thomas Piazza (1991) "Race and Politics Survey" (U. of California, Berkeley, Survey Research Center), Feb. 1–Nov. 21.

Snyder, Melvin, Walter Stephan, and David Rosenfield (1978) "Attributional Egotism," in John Harvey, William Ickes, and Robert Kidd, eds., *New Directions in Attribution Research* (Erlbaum), 91–117.

Sobol, Marion (1979) "Factors Influencing Private Capital Accumulation on the 'Eve of Retirement'," *R. of Economics and Statistics* 61, 4: 585–93.

Sokoloff, Natalie (1992) *Black Women and White Women in the Professions* (Routledge).

Sollors, Werner (1986) *Beyond Ethnicity* (Oxford U. Press).

Soltow, Lee (1972) "A Century of Personal Wealth Accumulation," in Harold Vatter and Thomas Palm, eds., *The Economics of Black America* (Harcourt Brace Jovanovich), 80–84.

Sombart, Werner (1976 [1906]) *Why Is There No Socialism in the United States?* (M. E. Sharpe).

Sonenshein, Raphael (1993) *Politics in Black and White* (Princeton U. Press).

Sorensen, Elaine (1991) "Gender and Racial Pay Gaps in the 1980s" (Washington, D.C.: Urban Institute).

Spayd, Liz, and Joel Brenner (1993) "Area Blacks Have Worst Bank Access," *Washington Post*, June 7: A1, A8.

Spenner, Kenneth, and David Featherman (1978) "Achievement Ambitions," *Annual R. of Sociology* 4: 373–420.

Spickard, Paul (1989) *Mixed Blood: Intermarriage and Ethnic Identity in Twentieth-Century America* (U. of Wisconsin Press).

Spring, Joel (1972) *Education and the Rise of the Corporate State* (Beacon Press).

Stack, Carol, and John Cromartie (c. 1990) "The Journeys of Black Children" (U. of California, Berkeley, School of Education).

Stanfield, John, II, ed. (1993) *A History of Race Relations Research: First-Generation Reflections* (Sage).

Stanfield, John, II, and Rutledge Dennis, eds. (1993) *Race and Ethnicity in Research Methods* (Sage).

Staples, Brent (1994) *Parallel Time: Growing Up in Black and White* (Pantheon).

Staples, Robert (1979a) "The Myth of Black Macho," *Black Scholar* 10, 6–7: 24–32.

———— (1979b) "Black Feminism and the Cult of Masculinity," *Black Scholar* 10, 8–9: 63–67.

Steckel, Richard, and Jayanthi Krishnan (1992) "Wealth Mobility in America" (NBER).

Steele, Shelby (1990) *The Content of Our Character* (St. Martin's Press).

Steil, Janice (1983) "The Response to Injustice," *J. of Experimental Social Psychology* 19, 3: 239–53.

Stein, Howard (1975) "Ethnicity, Identity, and Ideology," *School R.* 83, 2: 273–300.

Steinberg, Laurence, Sanford Dornbusch, and B. Bradford Brown (1992) "Ethnic Differences in Adolescent Achievement," *Am. Psychologist* 47, 6: 723–29.

Stephenson, Stanley, Jr., (1976) "The Economics of Youth Job Search Behavior," *R. of Economics and Statistics* 58, 1: 104–111.

Stern, Alan, and Donald Searing (1976) "The Stratification Beliefs of English and American Adolescents," *British J. of Political Science* 6, part 2: 177–201.

Stevenson, Brenda (1993) "Take a Step toward Trust," *Perspectives* (Am. Historical Assoc. Newsletter), 31, 6: 14, 16–17.

Stevenson, Harold, Chuansheng Chen, and David Uttal (1990) "Beliefs and Achievement: A Study of Black, White, and Hispanic Children," *Child Development* 61, 2: 508–23.

Stevenson, Robert Louis (1895) *The Amateur Emigrant* (Stone and Kimball).

Stouffer, Samuel, et al. (1949) *The American Soldier: Adjustment during Army Life* (Princeton U. Press).

Straight, Susan (1994) "The Gun in the Closet," *Harper's Magazine*, July: 72–83.

Street, David (1969) *Race and Education in the City* (U. of Chicago, Community and Family Study Center).

Stricker, Lawrence (1982) "Dimensions of Social Stratification for Whites and Blacks," *Multivariate Behavioral Research* 17, 2: 139–67.

Strohmer, Arthur (1988) "Comprehensive Training," in Donna Thompson and

Nancy DiTomaso, eds., *Ensuring Minority Success in Corporate Management* (Plenum Press), 283–94.

Sullivan, Mercer (1989) *"Getting Paid:" Youth Crime and Work in the Inner City* (Cornell U. Press).

Sumner, William Graham (1914) *The Challenge of Facts and Other Essays* (Yale U. Press).

Survey Research Center, U. of California, Berkeley (1964) "Anti-Semitism in the United States," for Anti-Defamation League of B'Nai B'rith, Oct.

Swidler, Ann (1986) "Culture in Action," *ASR* 51, 2: 273–86.

Sykes, Charles (1992) *A Nation of Victims: The Decay of the American Character* (St. Martin's Press).

Szajowski, Zosa (1951) "The Attitude of American Jews to East European Jewish Immigration (1881–1893)," *Publications of the Am. Jewish Historical Society,* 40, part 3: 221–80.

Szekelyi, Maria, and Robert Tardos (1993) "Attitudes that Make a Difference: Expectancies and Economic Progress" (U. of Wisconsin, IRP).

Takaki, Ronald (1979) *Iron Cages: Race and Culture in 19th-Century America* (U. of Washington Press).

——— (1994) *From Different Shores: Perspectives on Race and Ethnicity in America,* 2d ed. (Oxford U. Press).

Tate, Katherine (1986) "Class, Consciousness, and Black Public Opinion," paper at the annual meeting of the APSA, Washington, D.C.

——— (1993) *From Protest to Politics: The New Black Voters in American Elections* (Harvard U. Press).

——— (1992) "Invisible Woman," *American Prospect* 8: 74–81.

Tate, Katherine, and Ronald Brown (1991) "The Black Church and Political Participation Revisited," paper at the annual meeting of the MWPSA, Chicago.

Taub, Richard (1991) "Differing Conceptions of Honor and Orientations Toward Work and Marriage among Low-Income African-Americans and Mexican-Americans," paper at the Urban Poverty and Family Life Conference, U. of Chicago.

Taxi and Limousine Commission, City Commission on Human Rights, and Mayor's Office of Operations (1988) "Results of Operation Passby" (N. Y.: Taxi and Limousine Commission).

Taylor, Bron (1991) *Affirmative Action at Work* (U. of Pittsburgh Press).

Taylor, D. Garth (1991) *1991 Metro Survey Report* (Metropolitan Chicago Information Center).

——— (1992a) *1992 Metro Survey Report* (Metropolitan Chicago Information Center).

——— (1992b) "When Worlds Collide: Culture Conflict and Reported Hate Crimes in Chicago" (Metro Chicago Information Center).

——— (1993) *1993 Metro Survey Report* (Metropolitan Chicago Information Center).

——— (1994) *1994 Metro Survey Report* (Metropolitan Chicago Information Center).

Taylor, John (1991) "Don't Blame Me!: The New Culture of Victimization," *New York,* June 3: 26–34.

Taylor, Kenneth (1992) "Hill, Thomas, and the Politics of Race," *Report from the Institute for Philosophy and Public Policy* 12, 1: 16–19.

Taylor, Robert (1986) "Receipt of Support from Family among Black Americans," *J. of Marriage and the Family* 48, 1: 67–77.

Taylor, Robert, and Linda Chatters (1989) "Family, Friend, and Church Support

Networks of Black Americans," in Reginald Jones, ed., *Black Adult Development and Aging* (Cobb and Henry), 245–72.

Taylor, Robert, et al. (1990) "Developments in Research on Black Families," *J. of Marriage and the Family* 52, 4: 993–1014.

Tentler, Leslie (1983) "Who Is the Church? Conflict in a Polish Immigrant Parish in Late Nineteenth-Century Detroit," *Comparative Studies in Society and History* 25, 2: 241–76.

Teres, Harvey (forthcoming) *Renewing the Left: Politics, Imagination, and the New York Intellectuals* (Oxford U. Press).

Terkel, Studs (1980) *American Dreams, Lost and Found* (Pantheon).

Terkildsen, Nayda (1993) "When White Voters Evaluate Black Candidates," *AJPS* 37, 4: 1032–53.

Terrell, Henry (1971) "Wealth Accumulation of Black and White Families," *J. of Finance* 26, 2: 363–77.

Terry, Don (1991) "Blacks See Old Hate Behind Duke's New Strength," *NYT*, Nov. 9: 8.

Testa, Mark (1991) "Male Joblessness, Nonmarital Parenthood, and Marriage," paper at the Urban Poverty and Family Life Conference, U. of Chicago.

"Thirty Years after 'I Have a Dream'" (1993) *The Polling Report* 9, 18 (Sept. 13): 2.

"This Time, the Downturn Is Dressed in Pinstripes" (1990) *Business Week*, Oct. 1: 130–31.

Thomas, David, and Clayton Alderfer (1989) "The Influence of Race on Career Dynamics," in Michael Arthur, Douglas Hall, and Barbara Lawrence, eds., *Handbook of Career Theory* (Cambridge U. Press), 133–58.

Thomas, Laurence (1981) "Sexism, Racism, and the Business World," *Business Horizons* 24, 4 (July/Aug.), 62–68.

Thomas, Stephen, and Sandra Quinn (1993) "The Burdens of Race and History on Black Americans' Attitudes Toward Needle Exchange Policy to Prevent HIV Disease," *J. of Public Health Policy* 14, 3: 320–47.

Thomas, Stephen, et al. (1994) "The Characteristics of Northern Black Churches with Community Health Outreach Programs," *Am. J. of Public Health* 84, 4: 575–79.

Thompson, Daniel (1986) *A Black Elite* (Greenwood Press).

Thornton, Michael, and Robert Taylor (1988) "Black American Perceptions of Black Africans," *Ethnic and Racial Studies* 11, 2: 139–50.

Thornton, Michael, et al. (1990) "Sociodemographic and Environmental Correlates of Racial Socialization by Black Parents," *Child Development* 61, 2: 401–9.

Thurow, Lester (1986) "New Punishment for the Middle Class: The Hidden Sting of the Trade Deficit," *NYT*, Jan. 19: sec. 3, 3.

Tienda, Marta, and Haya Stier (1991a) "Makin' a Livin': Color and Opportunity in the Inner City," paper at the Conference on Urban Poverty and Family Life, U. of Chicago.

——— (1991b) "Joblessness and Shiftlessness," in Christopher Jencks and Paul Peterson, eds., *The Urban Underclass* (Brookings Institution), 135–54.

Timberlake, James (1963) *Prohibition and the Progressive Movement, 1900–1920* (Harvard U. Press).

Tomaskovic-Devey, Donald (1993) *Gender and Racial Inequality at Work* (ILR Press).

Toner, Robin (1990) "Running for Senate, Ex-Head of Klan Trails in Polls but Shakes Louisiana," *NYT*, Oct. 1: A18.

Towers Perrin (1992) "Workforce 2000 Today: A Bottom-Line Concern" (New York: Towers Perrin).

Trescott, Jacqueline, and Dorothy Gilliam (1986) "The New Black Woman: Mold-Breakers in the Mainstream," *Washington Post*, Dec. 28: A1, A8, A9.

Truman, David (1951) *The Governmental Process* (Knopf).

Tucker, Charles (1980) "The Cycle, Dilemma, and Expectations of the Black Administrator," *J. of Black Studies* 10, 3: 311–21.

Tucker, M. Belinda, James Jackson, and Ronald Jennings (1979) "Occupational Expectations and Dropout Propensity in Urban Black High School Students," in A. Wade Boykin, Anderson Franklin, and J. Frank Yates, eds., *Research Directions of Black Psychologists* (Russell Sage Foundation), 277–93.

Turner, Castellano and William Darity (1973) "Fears of Genocide among Black Americans as Related to Age, Sex, and Region," *Am. J. of Public Health* 63, 12: 1029–34.

Turner, Castellano, and William Wilson (1976) "Dimensions of Racial Ideology," *J. of Social Issues* 32, 2: 139–52.

Turner, Garrett (1989) "Epitaphs," *Vigil* (student newspaper at Princeton University), spring: 5.

Turner, Margery, Michael Fix, and Raymond Struyk (1991a) *Opportunities Denied, Opportunities Diminished: Racial Discrimination in Hiring* (Washington, D.C.: Urban Institute).

Turner, Margery, Raymond Struyk, and John Yinger (1991b) *Housing Discrimination Study: Synthesis* (U.S. Dept. of Housing and Urban Development).

Turner, Roberta (1991) "Affirming Consciousness," in Joyce Everett, Sandra Chipungu, and Bogart Leashore, eds., *Child Welfare: An Africentric Perspective* (Rutgers U. Press), 36–57.

Tuttle, William, Jr. (1969) "Labor Conflict and Racial Violence: The Black Worker in Chicago, 1894–1919," *Labor History* 10, 3: 408–32.

Tyack, David (1974) *The One Best System: A History of American Urban Education* (Harvard U. Press).

Tyack, David, and Elisabeth Hansot (1982) *Managers of Virtue: Public School Leadership in America, 1820–1980* (Basic Books).

Ueda, Reed (1989) "False Modesty," *New Republic*, July 3: 16–17.

Ugwu-Ojo, Dympna (1992) "What Should I Tell My Innocent Black Children?" *Princeton Packet*, May 5: 12A, 13A.

Updegrave, Walter (1989) "Race and Money," *Money*, Dec.: 152–72.

U.S. Bureau of the Census (1970) *Poverty in the United States: 1969*, P60–76 (USGPO)

——— (1975) *Historical Statistics of the United States, Colonial Times to 1970* (USGPO).

——— (1977) *Characteristics of the Population Below the Poverty Level: 1975*, P60–106 (USGPO).

——— (1986) *Household Wealth and Asset Ownership: 1984*, P70–7 (USGPO).

——— (1989) *Money Income of Households, Families, and Persons in the United States: 1987*, P60–162 (USGPO).

——— (1991) "Census Report Says Male-Owned Minority Businesses Outpace Women-Owned Firms in Average Annual Receipts," *United States Dept. of Commerce News* (Bureau of the Census, Economics and Statistics Administration) Sept. 19.

——— (1993a) *Money Income of Households, Families, and Persons in the United States: 1992*, P60–184 (USGPO).

——— (1993b) *Statistical Abstract of the United States 1993* (USGPO).

——— (1993c) *Poverty in the United States: 1992*, P60–185 (USGPO).

——— (1994) *Household Wealth and Asset Ownership: 1991*, P70–34 (USGPO).

U.S. Congress (1989) House of Representatives, Select Committee on Children,

Youth, and Families, *Born Hooked: Confronting the Impact of Perinatal Substance Abuse*, Hearing, April 27 (USGPO).

—— (1990) Joint Economic Committee, Democratic Staff Study, "Falling Behind: The Growing Income Gap in America."

—— (1991) House of Representatives, Committee on Ways and Means, *1991 Green Book* (USGPO).

—— (1992) House of Representatives, Committee on Ways and Means, *1992 Green Book* (USGPO).

U.S. Dept. of Education (1990a) *The Civics Report Card*, by Lee Anderson et al. (Princeton: Educational Testing Service, National Assessment of Educational Progress).

—— (1990b) National Center for Education Statistics, *A Profile of the American Eighth Grader: NELS: '88 Student Descriptive Summary* (USGPO).

—— (1991a) National Center for Education Statistics, *Digest of Education Statistics, 1990* (USGPO).

—— (1991b) National Center for Education Statistics, *The Condition of Education, 1991*, vol. 1, *Elementary and Secondary Education* (USGPO).

—— (1992a) National Center for Education Statistics, *Characteristics of At-Risk Students in NELS: '88* (USGPO).

—— (1992b) National Center for Education Statistics, *A Profile of Parents of Eighth Graders* (USGPO).

—— (1993a) National Center for Education Statistics, *The Condition of Education, 1993* (USGPO).

—— (1993b) *America's High School Sophomores: A Ten Year Comparison* (USGPO).

—— (1994a) *Report in Brief: NAEP 1992 Trends in Academic Progress* (Office of Educational Research and Improvement).

—— (1994b) "Dropout Rates in the United States: 1993," by Marilyn McMillan, Phillip Kaufman, and Sumner Whitener (USGPO).

U.S. Dept. of Health and Human Services (1985) National Center for Health Statistics, *Vital Statistics of the United States, 1980*, vol. 2, *Mortality, Part A*.

—— (1988) National Institute of Drug Abuse, *National Household Survey on Drug Abuse: Main Findings 1985* (USGPO).

—— (1990a) National Institute of Drug Abuse, *National Household Survey on Drug Abuse: Main Findings 1988*.

—— (1990b) Office for Substance Abuse Prevention, *Alcohol, Tobacco, and Other Drugs May Harm the Unborn* (USGPO).

—— (1990c) "OIG Management Advisory Report: 'Boarder Babies,'" by Richard Kusserow.

—— (1991a) National Institute of Drug Abuse, *National Household Survey on Drug Abuse: Main Findings 1990*.

—— (1991b) National Institute on Drug Abuse, *Drug Use among American High School Seniors, College Students and Young Adults, 1975–1990, v. I: High School Seniors*, by Lloyd Johnston, Patrick O'Malley, and Jerald Bachman.

—— (1993a) National Institute of Drug Abuse, *National Household Survey on Drug Abuse: Population Estimates 1992* (USGPO).

—— (1993b) National Institute on Drug Abuse, *Drug Abuse among Racial/Ethnic Groups*, by Andrea Kopstein and Patrice Roth.

—— (1994a) National Center for Health Statistics, *Vital Statistics of the United States 1990*, vol. 2, *Mortality, Part A*.

—— (1994b) *Preliminary Estimates from the 1993 National Household Survey on Drug Abuse*.

U.S. Dept. of Health, Education, and Welfare (1963) National Center for Health Statistics, *Vital Statistics of the United States, 1960*, vol. 2, *Mortality, Part A*.

―――― (1974) National Center for Health Statistics, *Vital Statistics of the United States, 1970*, vol. 2, *Mortality, Part A*.

U.S. Dept. of Housing and Urban Development (1979) *Measuring Discrimination in US Housing Markets*, by Ronald Wienk et al.

U.S. Dept. of Justice (1988) Bureau of Justice Statistics, "Drug Use and Crime," by Christopher Innes.

―――― (1990) Bureau of Justice Statistics, "Drugs and Crime, 1989."

―――― (1993) Bureau of Justice Statistics, "Gun Acquisition and Possession in Selected Juvenile Samples," by Joseph Sheley and James Wright.

―――― (1994a) Bureau of Justice Statistics, *Criminal Victimization in the United States: 1973–92 Trends*.

―――― (1994b) Bureau of Justice Statistics, "Women in Prison," by Tracy Snell.

―――― (1994c) *Sourcebook of Criminal Justice Statistics—1993* (USGPO).

―――― (1994d) "Two Banks to Pay Damages Following Justice Probes into Lending Practices," Jan. 24.

U.S. Dept. of Labor (1970) Bureau of Labor Statistics, "Wage Expectations," in *Youth Unemployment and Minimum Wages*.

―――― (1990) Office of Federal Contract Compliance Programs, *Director's Report, Fiscal Year 1989*.

―――― (1991) *A Report on the Glass Ceiling Initiative*.

U.S. General Accounting Office (1994) "Equal Employment Opportunity: Displacement Rates, Unemployment Spells, and Reemployment Wages by Race."

U.S. v. Yonkers Board of Education (1985) 624 F. Supp. 1276, S.D. New York.

Valelly, Richard (forthcoming) "National Parties and Racial Disfranchisement," in Paul Peterson, ed., *Classifying by Race* (Princeton U. Press).

Valentine, Bettylou (1978) *Hustling and Other Hard Work: Life Styles in the Ghetto* (Free Press).

Van den Berge, Pierre (1967) *Race and Racism* (Wiley).

Vanderbilt, Cornelius (1972 [1931]) "How Al Capone Would Run This Country," in *America: An Illustrated Diary of Its Most Exciting Years, Gangsters and Gangbusters, Book 1* (Valencia, CA: American Family Enterprises), 10–15.

Vanneman, Reeve, and Lynn Cannon (1987) *The American Perception of Class* (Temple U. Press).

Vega, William, et al. (1993) "Prevalence and Magnitude of Perinatal Substance Exposures in California," *New England J. of Medicine* 329, 12: 850–54.

Verba, Sidney, and Gary Orren (1985) *Equality in America: The View From the Top* (Harvard U. Press).

Verba, Sidney, et al. (1993) "Race, Ethnicity, and Political Resources," *British J. of Political Science* 23, 4: 453–97.

Veroff, Joseph, Elizabeth Douvan, and Richard Kulka (1981) *The Inner American: A Self-Portrait from 1957 to 1976* (Basic Books).

Villemez, Wayne, and Candace Wiswell (1978) "The Impact of Diminishing Discrimination on the Internal Size Distribution of Black Income, 1954–74," *Social Forces* 56, 4: 1019–34.

Virtanen, Simo (1992) "The Impact of Perceived Group Conflict on White Opposition to Racial Policies," paper at the annual meeting of the APSA, Chicago.

Viscusi, W. Kip (1986) "Market Incentives for Criminal Behavior," in Richard Freeman and Harry Holzer, eds., *The Black Youth Employment Crisis* (U. of Chicago Press), 301–46.

Vroman, Wayne (1991) "Industrial Change and Black Men's Relative Earnings," *Research in Labor Economics* (JAI Press), 12: 213–44.

Wachter, Susan, and Isaac Megbolugbe (1992) "Racial and Ethnic Disparities in Homeownership," *Housing Policy Debate* 3, 2: 333–70.

Wacquant, Loic (1994a) "Advanced Marginality in the City" (Russell Sage Foundation).

——— (1994b) "Inside the Zone: The Social Art of the Hustler in the Contemporary Ghetto" (Russell Sage Foundation).

Walaszek, Adam (1988) " 'For in America Poles Work Like Cattle'—Polish Peasant Immigrants and Their Industrial Work in America, 1890–1891," in M. DeBouzy, ed., *In the Shadow of the Statue of Liberty* (Saint-Denis: Presses Universitaires de Vincennes).

——— (1989) "Was the Polish Worker Asleep? Immigrants, Unions, and Workers' Control in America, 1900–1922," *Polish Am. Studies* 46, 1: 74–96.

Waldinger, Roger, et al. (1990) *Ethnic Entrepreneurs: Immigrant Business in Industrial Societies* (Sage).

Waller, Altina (1984) "Community, Class, and Race in the Memphis Riot of 1866," *J. of Social History* 18, 2: 233–46.

Walton, Anthony (1989) "Willie Horton and Me," *NYT Magazine*, Aug. 20: 52, 77.

Ward, James (1991) "The *Croson* Decision and the Demise of Set-asides," paper at the annual meeting of the APSA, Washington, D.C.

Warden, Sharon (1994) "What's Happened to Youth Attitudes since Woodstock?" *Public Perspective* 5, 4: 19–24.

Warner, W. Lloyd, and Leo Srole (1945) *The Social Systems of American Ethnic Groups*, vol. 3 (Yale U. Press).

Washington Post (1992) "*Washington Post* Poll: Race Relations," Feb. 28–Mar. 3.

Wasserman, Ira (1989) "Prohibition and Ethnocultural Conflict: The Missouri Prohibition Referendum of 1918," *Social Science Q.* 70, 4: 886–901.

Waters, Mary (1990) *Ethnic Options: Choosing Identities in America* (U. of California Press).

——— (forthcoming) "Ethnic and Racial Identities of Second Generation Black Immigrants in New York City," *International Migration R.* 29.

Watson, John, and Leo Simpson (1978) "A Comparative Study of Owner-Manager Personal Values in Black and White Small Businesses," *Academy of Management J.* 21, 2: 313–19.

Weimann, Gabriel (1991) "The Influentials: Back to the Concept of Opinion Leaders?" *Public Opinion Q.* 55, 2: 267–79.

Weis, Lois, Eleanor Farrar, and Hugh Petrie (1989) *Dropouts From School* (SUNY Press).

Weiss, Bernard (1982) *American Education and the European Immigrant, 1840–1940* (U. of Illinois Press).

Weissbourd, Rick (1989) "Public Elementary Schools: A Ladder Out of Poverty?" (Harvard U., Kennedy School of Government).

Welch, Susan, and Michael Combs (1985) "Intra-racial Differences in Attitudes of Blacks," *Phylon* 46, 2: 91–97.

Welch, Susan and Lorn Foster (1987) "Class and Conservatism in the Black Community," *Am. Politics Q.* 15, 4: 445–70.

Welch, Susan, et al. (1994) "Justice for All: Still an American Dilemma," *Challenge* 5, 1: 19–37.

Wellman, David (1977) *Portraits of White Racism* (Cambridge U. Press).

——— (1993) "Honorary Homey's, Class Brothers, and White Negroes," paper at annual meeting of the ASA, Miami.

Welsh, Patrick (1988) "The Black Talent Trap," *Washington Post*, May 1: C1, C4.

Wenneker, Mark, and Arnold Epstein (1989) "Racial Inequalities in the Use of Procedures for Patients with Ischemic Heart Disease in Massachusetts," *J. of the Am. Medical Assoc.* 261, 2: 253–57.

West, Cornel (1988) *Prophetic Fragments* (William Eerdmans).

―――― (1992) "Equality and Identity," *Am. Prospect* 9: 119–122.

―――― (1993) *Race Matters* (Beacon Press).

Westie, Frank, and David Howard (1954) "Social Status Differentials and the Race Attitudes of Negroes," *ASR* 19, 5: 584–91.

White, Michael (1987) *American Neighborhoods and Residential Differentiation* (Russell Sage Foundation).

White, Michael, et al. (1994) "Ethnic Neighbors and Ethnic Myths: An Analysis of Segregation in 1910," in Susan Watkins, ed., *After Ellis Island* (Russell Sage Foundation), 175–208.

Wideman, John (1984) *Brothers and Keepers* (Penguin Books).

Wieseltier, Leon (1989) "Scar Tissue," *New Republic*, June 5: 18–20.

Wilcox, Clyde (1992) "Racial and Gender Consciousness among African-American Women," paper presented at the annual meeting of the APSA, Chicago.

Wilder, Laura Ingalls (1940) *The Long Winter* (Harper & Row).

Wilentz, Sean (1984) *Chants Democratic: New York City and the Rise of the American Working Class, 1788–1850* (Oxford U. Press).

Wiley, Ed, III (1991) "Sexism vs. Racism," *Black Issues in Higher Education* 8, 9: 1, 8–9.

Wilkerson, Isabel (1988) "Detroit Drug Empire Showed All the Traits of Big Business," *NYT*, Dec. 18: 1, 42.

―――― (1989a) "Memphis Blacks Charge Calendar Slurs Dr. King," *NYT*, Jan. 15: 16.

―――― (1989b) "Discordant Notes in Detroit: Music and Affirmative Action," *NYT*, March 5: 1, 30.

―――― (1990) "Middle-Class Blacks Try to Grip a Ladder While Lending a Hand," *NYT*, Nov. 26: A1, B7.

―――― (1992) "Riots Shook Affluent Blacks Trying to Balance 2 Worlds," *NYT*, May 10: 1, 20.

Wilkins, Roger (1982) *A Man's Life* (Simon and Schuster).

William T. Grant Foundation Commission on Work, Family, and Citizenship (1988) *The Forgotten Half: Non-College Youth in America* (Washington, D.C.: William T. Grant Foundation).

Williams, Brett (1992) "Poverty among African Americans in the Urban United States," *Human Organization* 51, 2: 164–74.

Williams, David, David Takeuchi, and Russell Adair (1992) "Socioeconomic Status and Psychiatric Disorder among Blacks and Whites," *Social Forces* 71, 1: 179–94.

Williams, John (1971) "Time and Tide: Roots of Black Awareness," in Thomas Wheeler, ed., *The Immigrant Experience* (Penguin), 133–50.

Williams, Juan (1990) "The Mind of Rayful Edmond," *Washington Post Magazine*, June 24: 16–21, 32–34.

Williams, Lena (1986) "Race Issues Key to Judicial Nominee," *NYT*, March 14: 36.

―――― (1993) "After Train Killings, A Rise of Black Anxiety," *NYT*, Dec. 13: B6.

Williams, Linda (1990) "White/Black Perceptions of the Electability of Black Political Candidates," *National Political Science R.*, vol. 2, *Black Electoral Politics* (Transaction), 45–64.

Williams, Patricia (1987) "Alchemical Notes: Reconstructing Ideals from Deconstructed Rights," *Harvard Civil Rights, Civil Liberties Law R.* 22, 2: 401–33.

Williams, Robin, Jr. (1964) *Strangers Next Door: Ethnic Relations in American Communities* (Prentice-Hall).

Williams, Terry (1989) *The Cocaine Kids* (Addison-Wesley).

Williams, Terry, and William Kornblum (1985) *Growing Up Poor* (Lexington Books).

Willis, Paul (1977) *Learning to Labour* (Saxon House).

Wilson, Amos (1990) *Black-on-Black Violence* (Afrikan World Infosystems).

——— (1991) *Understanding Black Adolescent Male Violence* (Afrikan World Infosystems).

Wilson, Franklin, Marta Tienda, and Lawrence Wu (1993) "Racial Equality in the Labor Market: Still An Elusive Goal?" (U. of Wisconsin, IRP).

Wilson, William (1980) *The Declining Significance of Race* (U. of Chicago Press).

——— (1987) *The Truly Disadvantaged* (U. of Chicago Press).

——— (1991) "Studying Inner-City Social Dislocations," *ASR* 56, 1: 1–14.

Winant, Howard (1994) *Racial Conditions* (U. of Minnesota Press).

Winger, John (1986) "Measuring Racial Discrimination with Fair Housing Audits," *Am. Economic R.* 76, 5: 881–93.

Wolf, Charlotte (1990) "Relative Advantage," *Symbolic Interaction* 13, 1: 37–61.

Wolf, Marion, and Aron Mosnaim, eds. (1990) *Posttraumatic Stress Disorder* (Am. Psychiatric Press).

Wolff, Edward (1993) "The Rich Get Increasingly Richer: Latest Data on Household Wealth during the 1980s" (Washington, D.C.: Economic Policy Institute).

Wolfgang, Marvin, and Franco Ferracuti (1967) *The Subculture of Violence* (Tavistock).

Wolfgang, Marvin, Terence Thornberry, and Robert Figlio (1987) *From Boy to Man* (U. of Chicago Press).

Wolfinger, Raymond, and Steven Rosenstone (1980) *Who Votes?* (Yale U. Press).

Woodward, C. Vann (1963) *Tom Watson: Agrarian Rebel* (Oxford U. Press).

——— (1991) *Reunion and Reaction: The Compromise of 1877 and the End of Reconstruction* (Oxford U. Press).

Woody, Bette (1992) *Black Women in the Workplace* (Greenwood Press).

Work, John (1980) "Management Blacks and the Internal Labor Market," *Human Resource Management* 19, 3: 27–31.

Wright, Eric, et al. (1982) "The American Class Structure," *ASR* 47, 6: 709–26.

Wright, James (1976) *The Dissent of the Governed: Alienation and Democracy in America* (Academic Press).

Wulczyn, Fred, and Robert Goerge (1992) "Foster Care in New York and Illinois," *Social Service R.* 66, 2: 276–94.

Wyllie, Irvin (1954) *The Self-Made Man in America* (Free Press).

Xu, Wu, and Ann Leffler (1992) "Gender and Race Effects on Occupational Prestige, Segregation, and Earnings," *Gender and Society* 6, 3: 376–92.

ya Salaam, Kalamu (1979) "Revolutionary Struggle/Revolutionary Love," *Black Scholar* 10, 8–9: 20–24.

Yankelovich Clancy Shulman (1992) "Rodney King Verdict and the Los Angeles Riots," for *Time* and Cable News Network, April 30.

Yarkin, Kerry, Jerri Town, and Barbara Wallston (1982) "Blacks and Women Must Try Harder," *Personality and Social Psychology Bulletin* 8, 1: 21–24.

Young, Michael (1958) *The Rise of the Meritocracy, 1870–2033* (Penguin Books).

Zajonc, Robert, and Philip Brickman (1969) "Expectancy and Feedback as Independent Factors in Task Performance," *J. of Personality and Social Psychology* 11, 2: 148–56.

Zaller, John (1992) *The Nature and Origins of Mass Opinion* (Cambridge U. Press).

Zangrando, Joanna, and Robert Zangrando (1970) "Black Protest: A Rejection of the American Dream," *J. of Black Studies* 1, 2: 141–59.

Zilber, Jeremy (1994) "Group Consciousness and Black Political Participation Revisited," paper at the annual meeting of the MWPSA, Chicago.

Zipp, John (1994) "Government Employment and Black-White Earnings Inequality, 1980–1990," *Social Problems* 41, 3: 363–82.

Zwerling, Craig, and Hilary Silver (1992) "Race and Job Dismissals in a Federal Bureaucracy," *ASR* 57, 5: 651–60.

INDEX

Abernathy, Ralph, 339n.13
Abotare, Akua, 105
absolute success, 16, 24–25, 28, 253
acquiescence, poor African Americans and, 181–83, 321nn. 41 and 45
affirmative action: African Americans' views on, 147; and middle class African Americans' beliefs about American dream, 98–102, 111, 291–92nn. 34, 35, 37, 40, 41, 42, 44, 46, 47, 48, 49, and 51; whites' views on, 144
African Americans, 39–51, 55–71
—affirmative action and, 147
—African Americans versus white Americans: causes of death among young men, 202, 203; and reasonable expectation of success, 285n.20; and socially undesirable behavior, 186–87; socioeconomic indicators, 42, 43–44, 45, 276–77nn. 30, 31, 37, 38, and 46
—African Americans' versus whites' beliefs about American dream, 4–6, 55–71; African Americans' quandary, 69–70; about association of success and virtue, 59–60, 65, 67, 288n.44; about effects of discrimination, xi, 57–59, 60–63, 215–16, 279n.12, 283nn. 7, 10, 285n.20, 299n.10, 331n.4; implications of, 65–71, 281nn. 35 and 38; about others' chances to achieve, 60–71, 279n.17, 280nn. 21, 23, 26, and 27, 281nn. 31 and 33; overall beliefs, 55–56, 278nn. 3 and 5; overview of, 4–6; about own chances to achieve, 56–60, 65–71, 278nn. 9 and 10, 279n.12; about reasonable expectation of success, 56–57, 58–59, 64, 278n.9; about success based on individual volition, 57, 64–65, 66-67, 278n.10, 287–88nn. 33 and 40; survey evaluation and, 70–71, 281–82n.41; whites' quandary, 68–70, 281n.38
—AIDS and, 106
—and Los Angeles riots (May 1992), 149
—middle class African Americans, 43–45; and black power movement, 138–39, 305n.82; collective involvement of, 129–

31, 299n.1; defined, 276n.16, 282n.3; disparities between poor African Americans and, 47–51; improving status of, 43–44, 276nn. 17 and 24; participation of, in Million Man March, xiii; perceptions of discrimination, 73–75, 215–16, 331–32nn. 4 and 5; social mobility among, 44–45; television watching by, 135–36, 304n.72, 305n.74
—middle class African Americans' beliefs about American dream, 91–153; affirmative action and, 98–102, 111, 291–92nn. 34, 35, 37, 40, 41, 42, 44, 46, 47, 48, 49, and 51; and African Americans' views of whites' competitive; success, 145–47, 309nn. 23 and 28; and Afrocentricity, 136–40, 305nn. 76, 78, and 82, 306nn. 86, 87, and 88; American dream as "acting white," 132–35, 303–4nn. 50, 53, 55, 63, 65, and 70; American dream as hollow promise, 135–36, 304nn. 71, 72, 305n.74; American dream as selfish individualism, 129, 301–3nn. 35, 36, 39, 40, 42, 44, 47, and 48; and beliefs about others' lives, 122–40; and beliefs about their own lives, 91–121; and commitment to poor African Americans, 124–25, 299n.1, 300nn. 15, 18, 20, 21, 22; competitive success and, 141–53; and the costs of success, 92–93; economic insecurity and, 93–98, 123, 289–91nn. 6, 8, 10, 13, 17, 18, 19, 22, 26, 27, 28, 29, 30, and 31, 299n.5, 299–300nn. 5 and 6; and felt responsibility for their race, xiii, 127–29, 301nn. 30, 31, 32, and 34; and the future of the American dream, 251–52, 339n.1; gender relations and, 108–12, 293nn. 73, 74, 75, 78, 81, 82, 83, 84, 85, and 86, 295–96nn. 88, 92, 93, 95, 97, 101, 105, and 107; individual achievement versus collective identity and, 147-51, 299n.1, 309–10nn. 29, 31, 32, 33, 35, and 38; and nostalgia for the past, 126, 301n.27; overview of, 91–92, 120–23, 141, 151–53, 310–11nn. 42, 43, 44, and 45; racism, racial discrimination, race manipulation and, 112–21,